C000170612

The Ultimate James Bond Fan Book: Fun, Facts, & Trivia About the James Bond Movies, © 2006, 2007, 2020 by Deborah Lipp. All rights reserved. No part of this book may be used or reproduced, stored in a retrieval system or transmitted in any form, or by any means, electronic, mechanical, photocopied, recorded or otherwise, without written permission of the publisher except in the case of brief quotations embodied in critical articles and reviews.

Published by Deborah Lipp
Jersey City, New Jersey 07302
www.DeborahLipp.com
Cover design by Jeffrey Marshall

SECOND EDITION
© 2020, Revised and with new materials
Interior illustrations by the author from her memorabilia collection.

First printing © 2006
Second printing with index © 2007

Library of Congress Control Number: 2020918018
Primary ISBN 978-1-7357410-0-0 Paperback
ISBN 978-1-7357410-1-7 e-book
Printed in the United States of America

THE ULTIMATE JAMES BOND FAN BOOK

ABOUT THE AUTHOR

Deborah Lipp is the author of nine books. As a pop culture writer, she's perhaps best known as the co-founder of *Basket of Kisses*, the premiere *Mad Men* blog. She is also a contributor to *Mad Men Carousel* by Matthew Zoller Seitz. A fan of James Bond since childhood, *The Ultimate James Bond Fan Book* is a labor of love.

Deborah lives in Jersey City, New Jersey, with her spouse, Melissa, and an assortment of cats. She enjoys old musicals, romantic comedies, puzzles of all kinds, fabulous restaurants, and winning at James Bond trivia.

THE ULTIMATE JAMES BOND FAN BOOK:

Fun, Facts, & Trivia

About the James Bond Movies

Deborah Lipp

This book is dedicated to the coolest Bond fan I know,
my beloved child Ursula
For a lifetime of loving movies together.

CONTENTS

ACKNOWLEDGMENTS

There are a lot of people without whom this book wouldn't be remotely possible. From Ian Fleming to Harry Saltzman, from the Broccoli family to Sean Connery, there are a whole lot of people who made my love of James Bond a thing so rich I simply had to write about it.

I am primarily indebted for this work, though, to the vast and fascinating community of Bond fans. Mostly through the Internet, I got to know the intelligence, wit, opinions, loves, and hates of a huge variety of people; teens and seniors, men and women, New Yorkers and Australians; each unique, each holding at least one opinion on Bond that no one else seems to share, They have also answered my surveys, read my essays, criticized and disagreed with me in ways that improved my understanding, and just in general have been great to hang out with. The fans I know best are on the message boards of Absolutely James Bond, CommanderBond.net, The Internet Movie Database, and the 007 discussion board of Cinescape (the last two no longer exist). If I may pull out a few names to thank, those names (or nicknames) are SiCo, Nick, UncleAgent, Dr. Blade, Joseph William Darlington (aka Leiter-CIA), Sheriff JW Pepper, Cranebridge, GlennME, Otis Adams, Ken Oerkvitz, Conman, Mike Cooper, Jordan Charter, Tom Hilton, Icebreaker, Bengray, Martini97, John Cox, Athena Stamos, Evan Willnow, and the inimitable and irreplaceable Bryce. Both David Worrall and Lee Pfeiffer were extraordinarily helpful and kind. Michael Newton was an invaluable correspondent. John Griswold read excerpts and offered suggestions right up to the last minute. Matt Sherman was helpful in so many ways, not least, he bent over backwards finding *Die Another Day* homages. Thanks, Matt.

At one time, there existed a website known first as Make Mine a 007, and later as Atomic Martinis. The site owner, known only as the Minister of Martinis, catalogued Bond's drinking habit in exquisite detail. Throughout 2005 and 2006, the M. of M. and I corresponded often, but he never provided a real name. A hard drive crashed wiped out a ton of old email, so when the website disappeared, I lost contact with him. Not only do I regret being unable to provide this as a resource, I regret that the Minister will remain unacknowledged for his hard work.

I must also thank my late father, Michael Lipp, for taking me to my first Bond film.

For the second edition, I must add thanks to Ian McKeachie, for endless discussion and insight, and again thank Matt Sherman, who came through with "fifty years of Bond" homages in *Skyfall*.

Cover artist Jeff Marshall is a legend among Bond fans; it was frankly intimidating to reach out for this project. But he is as gracious and generous as he is talented, and the collaboration was a joy.

I must acknowledge that *No Time to Die*'s release date was pushed out because of the coronavirus pandemic, giving me available time for this rewrite. Many people had pandemic projects, this was mine. That being the case, it is proper to remember the hundreds of thousands of souls lost to COVID-19, and wish them peace.

INTRODUCTION TO THE NEW EDITION

I n creating the new edition of **The Ultimate James Bond Fan Book** , I had to ask myself if I was updating or rewriting entirely. This book was originally written in coordination with the release of *Casino Royale*, meaning it included *Dr. No* through *Die Another Day*, and entirely precedes the Daniel Craig era of films. Any Bond fan knows, this isn't just "a few films are omitted" kind of change. The Craig movies rebooted and reconsidered the entire franchise. They are substantively different from the preceding films. How might I incorporate that?

In addition, media, social media, and the means by which fans interact with one another all dramatically changed. I wrote this book before Blu-ray, before podcasts, before Twitter, and at the very beginning of Facebook. So, sources of information and discussion have changed, and that impacts all of the numeric data (ratings and rankings).

So here's what we've got:

The Ultimate James Bond Fan Book is fully updated, but not entirely rewritten. Essays, including the original introduction, are intact. They have been re-read and checked for errors, but are fundamentally the same. Where appropriate, information addressing the most recent films has been appended. Numbers and facts in such essays (such as "there are twenty official Eon films") have been updated, but the content is otherwise the same. From time-to-time, there are notes—clearly indicated—that update information for the newer movies.

Many essays reference "younger fans." That was fifteen years ago. Those kids are in their thirties now, and "younger fans" today weren't reading yet back then. An attempt to rewrite all those references wouldn't make sense. They remain intact, in the context of the essays as and when they were written.

Where the text references people who were living in 2006 and have since passed, their deaths have been acknowledged.

All old survey data was regathered from scratch. (Only fan polls and rankings inclusive of *Spectre* have been used (as with the original edition, many such polls exclude *Never Say Never Again*, but I include it wherever available). In THE RATINGS AND RANKINGS, at the end of the book, I compare 2006 and 2020 results.

Ratings (on a scale of one-to-ten) were harder to find this time. Instead of trying to gather it from fans, I've used published sources: The IMDb, Rotten Tomatoes, and Metacritic.

Naturally, my own rankings and ratings have also been reconsidered and are brand new.

Wherever a chapter has a Top Five/Bottom Five list, worthy entries from Craig pictures are added as "and." For example:

1. **Tracy di Vicenzo,** *On Her Majesty's Secret Service*
2. **Elektra King,** *The World is Not Enough*
3. **Domino Derval,** *Thunderball*

4. Anya Amasova, *The Spy Who Loved Me*
5. Xenia Onatopp, *GoldenEye*
AND: Vesper Lynd, *Casino Royale*

Thus, my original essays about each top/bottom five remains. I haven't, for example, thrown out my write-up of Xenia to make room for Vesper, but a new write-up for Vesper (and all such "and" additions) is included.

Anything described as a "complete list" is complete as of summer 2020 (prior to the release of *No Time to Die* but including the preceding four Craig films). *No Time to Die* is included where possible, based on pre-release information. This includes the information in 007 AT THE OSCARS. Similarly, any sections that include statistics (and even numerical asides) have been fully updated. For example, all the stuff in the BOND GIRLS chapter on how many women have been allies or villains, and how many women Bond has slept with.

The entire chapter on the actors who have played Bond has been rewritten.

The entire RESOURCES section has been rewritten. Every link has been verified. Dormant sites—even really good ones—have been replaced with currently-active ones.

One chapter needed a new title, and YOU ONLY LIVE SIX TIMES is now YOU ONLY LIVE SEVEN TIMES.

A recipe for dirty martinis has been added.

Some change in the order of chapters was needed. This book includes two mini-chapters between each movie chapter, and so six new mini-chapters were needed. I placed these where they made sense, not at the end. For example, the chapter on tarot in *Live and Let Die* is placed immediately after the chapter on that movie. This meant that original mini-chapter order was slightly reconfigured.

Of course, corrections of typos and factual errors have been made to the original material, and new trivia has been added for older movies.

INTRODUCTION

"Bond, James Bond."

"Shaken, not stirred."

"License to kill."

Even if you've never seen a James Bond movie, you've heard of them and you surely know the familiar phrases; James Bond has touched your world.

Bond film franchise-co-founder Albert R. (Cubby) Broccoli once said that half the world's population has seen at least one James Bond movie. James Bond came in third on the American Film Institute's list of 50 Greatest Heroes. Bond movies have made almost $4,000,000,000. *Die Another Day* spent time on the top 100 highest grossing movies of all time (U.S.). It was the tenth highest-grossing movie of 2002, and the highest-grossing Bond movie of all time, earning over $400,000,000.

But those are just the numbers. If you're reading this book you're probably already a Bond fan, and to you (and to me), James Bond is personal. You don't just watch him for the thrills and the fun, you watch him because he means something to you, because in some way, those movies *get* to you.

This is a book about James Bond, but in a way, it's also about Bond fans. It talks about, thinks about, pours over, and enjoys the Bond movies in the way that fans do. It involves you, the reader, in a dialogue about Bond, allowing us to discuss 007 together.

What Is a Bond Fan?

A Bond fan, simply put, is anyone who loves James Bond. In these pages, we're mainly talking about the Bond movies, but many fans love the books as well—both the Ian Fleming originals and those written after his death by John Gardner, Raymond Benson, and others. Although just about anyone might see a Bond movie, a fan is someone who gets excited about it, who loses sleep in the days and weeks leading up to a new release, someone who can recall intricate movie details that elude most others.

Fans may love Bond but have no involvement beyond seeing the movies, or possibly reading the books. On the other hand, they may participate in Internet or social media groups, go to conventions, hold Bond-themed parties, make a point of drinking vodka martinis, collect memorabilia, write fan fiction, decorate their rec rooms with Bond movie posters, write a book, or read a book. In other words, a Bond fan ranges from someone with a particular feeling, to someone with a consuming hobby, and a whole lot of folks in between.

There is no "typical" Bond fan. The age range is broad, including older people who have been fans since reading **Casino Royale** in 1953, as well as teenagers who first discovered 007 as a video game character. Most Bond fans are male (about five-to-one, I'd wager), although I am, as a female fan, by no means an oddity. Bond fans exist all over the world; worldwide appeal is a big part of 007's success.

Nor is there any one taste that Bond fans share, not even for medium dry vodka martinis (shaken, not stirred). In my experience, it is extremely unusual for any group of fans to be so diverse in their preferences. For example, if you surveyed Trekkies/Trekkers about their favorite and least favorite *Star Trek* episodes, you would find an enormous uniformity to their lists ("The Trouble with Tribbles," anyone?). Fantasy fans will praise the same classics by Tolkein and LeGuinn. *Rocky Horror Picture Show* cultists all love the song "Sweet Transvestite," and most find that the "creation scene" drags.

Yet among Bond fans, no such agreement is readily found. If you survey a decent-sized group of Bond fans for their five favorite and least favorite films, you'll find almost every single film on both lists. One survey found twelve of twenty films appearing as number one for at least one respondent, and five out of twenty receiving at least one vote for both best and worst (first and twentieth). This is typical. The same is true for such Bond basics as actors, title songs, and villains.

Take George Lazenby, for example. Most people disdain his amateur acting in his one outing as James Bond, yet Lazenby has a loyal following among a significant minority of followers, and this is someone whom "everyone" hates.

Just about every Bond fan has a profound affection for his or her introduction to Bond. The majority of us, who first met Bond in the films, continue to think of the actor we first saw portray him as the real and definitive James Bond, and the movie we first saw almost always remains high in our esteem. So, while there are Bond fans of every age, and there are Bond fans of every taste, there is a tendency for tastes to be predicated in part on age (although I wouldn't bet on it!). There are Fleming purists, whose loyalty is to the original novels; further entries into the series are judged by their fidelity to Fleming's material. There are Connery purists, for whom Sean Connery's portrayal of Bond is more than definitive; to them, it is the only portrayal. Among these two, there are plenty of people who adore James Bond but have stopped watching the new movies, having no interest in Roger Moore or Pierce Brosnan (Timothy Dalton had a strong following among Fleming purists).

But while many fans have essentially frozen their love for 007 at what they consider an ideal moment in time, many more have entered the 21st century with their passion intact. Certainly Brosnan has had an enormous following among teens and twentysomethings, but older fans have found that even after forty years, nobody does it better than James Bond. When I saw *Die Another Day* on its release (November 22, 2002), the man sitting next to me appeared to be older than my own father, while on my other side sat my child—twelve years old at the time. A look around the sold-out theater revealed a similar range.

What Do Bond Fans Talk About?

Since I have said that **The Ultimate James Bond Fan Book** will talk about Bond the way that fans do, it just about demands that the question be answered: What do we talk about, and how?

First of all, Bond fans get personal. By this I mean both that Bond is linked to our personal lives, and that Bond fans "take it personally," as I mentioned above. We remember the first Bond movie we ever saw, our impressions, our reactions, and probably when and where The Event took place. For male fans, the first viewing is often recalled as an adolescent rite of passage, and is fraught with the mystery and excitement of the world of adulthood to come.

For many of us, regardless of gender, our first Bond movie and our first crush went hand-in-hand, and many of our hearts still skip a beat when we see the face—of Bond or a Bond girl—which first so moved us. Wonderful recollections are often shared among fans; online, in print, or in person.

We also take it personally in an emotional sense, loving the good stuff and getting angry at the flubs. Great Bond movies are dear to our hearts, bad Bond movies (inasmuch as such a thing exists) offend our sensibilities. You have to really love a subject to get hot under the collar when someone screws it up.

Bond fans are an opinionated bunch. Since we disagree about everything, we can really go at it—with passion, with joy, with vitriol, with indignation. Since we care so much about our subject matter we can wax poetic about both its virtues and its flaws, and defend it fiercely against criticism we feel is undeserved. The truth is, being a Bond fan is fun. There is as much agreement as disagreement, and the feeling of a shared passion is a truly enjoyable one.

But Bond fans love one thing above all else: *Lists*. We love lists: Best Girls. Worst Songs. Bond Films in Order of Preference. Bond Actors on a Scale of One to Ten. Number of Explosions. Number of Vodka Martinis. Favorite One-Liners.

All manner of lists. Lists of quantity, lists of favorites, bests, worsts, ranks, or ratings. When I meet a Bond fan, they invariably ask me a list, rank, or favorite-based question.

Here's a typical day on a Bond discussion board: Favorite Bond Decade, Rank All 20 Bond Films, Top Three Bond Movie Poster Art, Best "bad" Bond film, Top Ten Favorite Scenes, Worst Villain Death, Best Teaser (pre-titles sequence), Best Blofeld, Best Villain Death, Best Outfit, Worst Miniature Ever, and on and on.

The Bond Formula

One reason Bond fans love lists is that there are so many things to list; there are so many items in the Bond formula. Bond films have been derided for being predictable and many film critics don't get excited about new Bond films, citing "formulaic" film-making as the reason. But the Bond formula is quite intricate, with a high number of component parts. It cannot be summed up concisely. In fact, comparing the Bond formula to other movie formulas is like comparing the recipe for Boeuf Bourguignon with that of hamburger.

Let's look at the Bond formula compared to, say, a romantic comedy formula.

A romantic comedy must have a plot trajectory consisting of:
- Boy and Girl meet (though there are gay romantic comedies too).

- Obstacle of some kind keeps Boy and Girl apart. Obstacle is usually one or more of the following: Initial dislike, different backgrounds, family problems, one or both have a Big Secret that must be kept from the other, one or both is already in a relationship, general timing problems.
- At about mid-point of the film, couple generally makes a tentative step towards romance, may share a kiss (or more), but part from each other when the Obstacle appears or reappears.
- Often the Big Secret is revealed at just this point, keeping the couple apart for almost the remainder of the movie.
- The couple realize their love for one another only at the last moment.

A romantic comedy must contain the following components:

- An attractive couple.
- An obstacle.
- An evil rival, and/or bumbling oaf.
- Often, a secondary romance that either begins or resolves, and sheds light in some way on the main romance.
- Often, a comedic or musical interlude.

That's pretty much it. In general, this formula is rigidly adhered to. I adore romantic comedies, and can think of quite a lot of good and excellent ones that follow this formula to a T, including: *Four Weddings and a Funeral, Notting Hill, It Happened One Night, Moonstruck, Return to Me, You've Got Mail, Bridget Jones's Diary, Some Like It Hot,* and musical romantic comedies such as *Top Hat* and *Singin' in the Rain.*

The above is pretty simple, and some film critics will sneer at romantic comedies in much the same way they sneer at Bond films. Let's look at the Bond formula now.

The narrative will include:

- A pre-titles sequence that may or may not have much bearing on the main plot.
- An introduction of the villain's plot, often in a veiled or mysterious manner, such as an inexplicable murder.
- An introduction of Bond, often interrupted in the midst of gambling or a tryst, in which he is informed of his assignment.
- Bond begins his investigation by making his presence known to the villain, and there is an initial combat or chase of some kind.
- Bond meets the Bond girl, whom he must protect, work with, or free.
- A significant ally is killed (the "sacrificial lamb"), inflaming Bond's need for revenge.
- A confrontation with the villain reveals some portion of the plot, and makes the two direct enemies; they both drop their cover and reveal themselves as villain and agent.
- Some kind of chase ensues.

- Captured, or having broken into the villain's lair, Bond learns the remainder of the plot and the importance of stopping it.
- Bond defeats and kills the villain, destroying his headquarters or a significant portion of his operation/base.
- Bond remains in the vicinity of the villain's former lair, with the Bond girl, possibly while M is wondering where he is, and the end credits roll over their final embrace.

A Bond film must include the following components: (As with the romantic comedies, there are exceptions. For example, *Live and Let Die* lacked a Q scene)

- The gunbarrel opening
- A pre-titles sequence
- A title sequence involving the bodies or silhouettes of beautiful women, during which the title song is sung or played
- A soundtrack that will include use of the James Bond Theme and, usually, the title song in instrumental form
- A scene with M
- A scene with Moneypenny
- A scene with Q
- Exotic locations in more than one country (not counting England)
- At least one really cool car
- At least one chase scene, by car or otherwise (boat, ski, bobsled, bus...)
- Romantic encounters with at least two beautiful women, at least one of whom survives to the end credits
- Gadgets
- Gunplay
- Finely tailored clothing for Bond, often including a tuxedo
- Exotic drinks and/or a vodka martini and/or champagne
- Lavish set design, often of a larger-than-life nature
- A villain, often with an unusual appearance, with a nefarious and murderous plot, who is somewhat formal and often polite towards Bond
- A secondary villain, employed by the first, who has great strength and/or an unusual appearance, and whose role is primarily physical (he neither plots nor talks much)
- A villain's headquarters of a highly exotic or unusual nature, which does not survive the end credits.

Looking at the above, we notice two things. First, it's possible I left something out that you're wondering about. (To which I say, "oops.") Second, it is amazingly detailed and complex.

No wonder Bond fans love lists! The plot-points and components listed above could serve as topic headings for lists which could be pored over, analyzed, or discussed. Lists might be objective, or they might be subjective, and discuss best, worst, most outlandish, most exciting, or what have you. Making lists of facts can create an excuse to re-watch the movies and making lists of bests and worsts creates fertile discussion and argument. (You'll find plenty of facts, bests, and worsts in the pages that follow.) The formula feeds and excites the fan base, and yet is so complex that it is never dull.

Different fans will love and appreciate different parts of the Bond formula to a greater or lesser extent. There are fans focused on the musical scores. Not being a musician, I don't necessarily understand the nuances of their discussions. Other fans obsess over the cars, certainly a legitimate area of interest for a Bond fan, but again, cars are not my own passion. No two fans are alike, and this book will reflect *my* concerns, *my* favorites, and *my* interests.

A Bond Story

In April of 1965, when my mother was in labor with her third child (my sister), my dad went to collect his parents and bring them to the hospital for the blessed event. He went into the Deluxe Theater in Brooklyn, New York, and pulled them out of a re-release double feature of *Dr. No* and *From Russia with Love*. They were watching *Dr. No* when Dad walked in.

My first Bond flick was half of *Thunderball*. In the latter half of 1970 and the first part of 1971, my father was severely impaired by bronchial asthma, so much so that he had difficulty walking more than a few steps. We went to a lot of movies, since this was something he could do with his kids while sitting down. On one memorable occasion, we saw a triple-feature of *Thunderball, You Only Live Twice,* and *Goldfinger* at the Queen Anne Theater in Bogota, New Jersey. We came in partway through *Thunderball*, watched the next two, and then stayed to see the beginning of *Thunderball* again. The influence of this experience on my young mind cannot be understated—six hours in a dark theater left me in a state of Bond-brainwash worthy of *The Ipcress File*! I was blinking, bleary-eyed, and the whole world was James Bond. In addition, my perception of *Thunderball* was hopelessly skewed—I found it incomprehensible yet fascinating, and didn't understand the plot for another twenty years. All three movies were blurred together by the long session of movie-viewing. I had no understanding of plot or character, just pictures and feelings. As a child, my knowledge of Bond was shaped by this onslaught of imagery that was beyond my understanding—sexy, exotic, colorful, very adult, yet somehow accessible.

A short time after this experience, *Diamonds Are Forever* was released, and for the first time I saw a Bond film in current release. To tell you the truth, I think I was too young to know the difference between a re-release and a new movie, although *Diamonds Are Forever* stands out more in my mind because it wasn't blurred together with two other films! I know that my father was enthusiastic about Connery's return, and during the pre-titles sequence, he whispered to me that Bond was seeking Blofeld because he had killed Bond's wife—at the time, I thought this meant Kissy, the woman he "married" in *You Only Live Twice* (my father hated George Lazenby, and never took me to see *On Her Majesty's Secret Service*).

To a certain extent, *Diamonds Are Forever* got blended in my mind with the earlier Connery movies I had seen a few weeks or months before, but it also stood out. More than any other movie, if you say "James Bond" I'll think of *Diamonds Are Forever*. When Connery walks down the beach towards that soon-to-be topless sunbather and gives his name as "Bond, James Bond," he is in some way always talking to me.

To me, this is what it is to be a Bond fan—to possess that story, that image, that sense of participation, and to cherish it. Mine is *Diamonds Are Forever*, perhaps yours is *Dr. No,* or perhaps it is *Die Another Day*, or perhaps it is the opening line of **Casino Royale**. Whatever it is, we share something as special and as delicious as an ice cold vodka martini, shaken, not stirred.

On the Following Pages...

This book will consist of the things that fans love—personal stories, opinions, arguments, and lists, lists, lists. It is not a trivia book (although it includes trivia), an encyclopedia, or a social history—there are plenty of those, many quite good, many on my shelf at this very moment. Rather, it is, as the title says, a fan book, a book of involvement; intimate, quirky, and exciting, just as fandom is.

You'll find each movie, in chronological order, reviewed and discussed, with both factual and subjective information presented. Between movie sections will be various lists, and a few essays, of the sort that are the meat and potatoes (or caviar and toast) of a good Bond discussion. The book can be read straight through, or flipped through at random.

WARNING!

The discussions of the movies in this book reveal numerous plot points and surprises. I have assumed that the reader has seen all the movies being discussed, and have made no effort to avoid spoilers. If you haven't seen all the Bond films, consider that *On Her Majesty's Secret Service, Diamonds Are Forever, Live and Let Die, For Your Eyes Only, GoldenEye, The World is Not Enough*, and *Die Another Day* have the greatest impact when seen without too much prior knowledge.

What Is a Bond Movie?

This may seem like a silly question, but in fact, there are several possible answers. The official Bond movies, those made by Eon Productions, number twenty-five as of this writing; *Dr. No* through *No Time to Die* (2020). Only Eon has the use of the gun-barrel logo and the James Bond Theme.

Never Say Never Again is certainly a James Bond movie, but it is not an Eon film, and not part of the official series. The rights to the story of **Thunderball** were won by rival filmmaker Kevin McClory in a lawsuit. McClory was unsuccessful in his attempt to gain the right to make new Bond films, and so he remade *Thunderball* in 1983 as *Never Say Never Again*. The film has Sean Connery as James Bond, as well as the familiar Bond allies M, Q, Moneypenny, and Felix Leiter. However, many fans disavow it because it isn't part of producer Cubby Broccoli's film series.

The better-known of two earlier *Casino Royale* films (prior to 2006) was a 1967 parody of James Bond films. In this bizarre, disjointed, and barely plotted spoof, David Niven plays the "real" James Bond, a retired spy who doesn't drink, doesn't smoke, doesn't womanize, doesn't use gadgets, and utterly disdains his modern imitators who rely on any or all of the above. The madcap action has M killed early on, and a host of characters who take the name James Bond, including

Peter Sellers, Ursula Andress, and Woody Allen. Some Bond fans enjoy it, many hate it, and none take it seriously.

The first *Casino Royale* was a one hour live-action drama shown on the TV show *Climax!* in 1954. It is a fairly straight adaptation of Ian Fleming's first novel, given the constraints of format and time. The lead character was an American named Jimmy "Card Sense" Bond, and his British ally was Clarence Leiter. Peter Lorre played the villain Le Chiffre. It was a serviceable drama, taut if unremarkable.

But the question remains, at least for the purposes of this book, which of these are Bond films? I have decided to count those films which are intended as adventures of MI6 agent 007, James Bond. With that definition, there are twenty-six films; Eon's twenty-five plus *Never Say Never Again*. I'm omitting the '67 *Casino Royale* because it doesn't want to be a James Bond film, just a spoof. I'm leaving out the '54 *Casino Royale* because it is not a feature-length film, because it is so unlike anything we know as Bond, and also because it remains so obscure that it is of little interest to all but the most obsessed fans. It rarely appears on surveys about Bond movies, making it difficult to create the survey data discussed in the next section. The twenty-six films I settled on are the ones most fans occupy themselves discussing, and so they are the ones that best fit with the theme of this book. As of this writing, *No Time to Die* has not yet been released and is not, for the most part, discussed here, except where pre-release information is of interest.

What's With the Surveys?

One writer (that's me) can only present one viewpoint. In order to break free of that constraint, I use both discussion and surveys. In discussion, you'll find that wherever I express a controversial view, I attempt to fairly describe the opposing view.

For surveys, I have combined the data from a number of different sources: Questions and surveys posted on various James Bond Internet message boards (see RESOURCES) in 2020, official surveys run by the Internet Movie Database, and surveys from major U.S. networks, the BBC, and entertainment media. In addition, I've looked at Bond film rankings written by film critics and media pundits.

Each movie's chapter will open with a section that looks like this:

(Keep in mind that *Never Say Never Again* is often not on surveys and fan rankings.)

Survey Says!
　　Percent Favorite
　　Top Five Cumulative
　　Numeric Rating
　　Ranking
My Rating and Ranking

Percent Favorite: What percent of the time does this movie come out as number one? A low score doesn't mean people voted for the movie as bad, they might like it very much, but simply like another one better (there are certain movies that are often rated highly but rarely hit the #1 spot)..

Top Five Cumulative: Many times, people are polled for their Top Five Bond films. In this case, a score is derived as follows:

- Five points for first place
- Four points for second place or first place tie
- Three points for third place or three-way tie for first
- Two points for fourth place
- One point for fifth place

Movies are then given a total score, and are ranked in order of score, top to bottom. From the point of view of the person gathering data (me), this is much more cumbersome than a simple "Name Your Favorite" poll, but I think it is more accurate. It allows a movie that consistently hits second or third place to benefit. The top five of ranking (below) is included here.

Numeric Rating: This rating is on a scale of one to ten. Totals are averaged. This is the equivalent of a critic's number of stars.

Ranking: One thing that the message boards love to ask is for users to put all the Bond movies in order of preference, with the favorite at number one. The flaw is that this is probably the most changeable of all. My top five usually doesn't change, and I'll always give *From Russia with Love* a 10 out of 10, but on any given day, my preference for *Dr. No* over *Tomorrow Never Dies* is subject to change, and this inconsistency depending on mood is something that many fans report. Keep in mind too, that a "low" score on ranking isn't necessarily that meaningful. If you love Bond, then even around the level of #15, you're still going to really like the movie!

For each movie's ranking you'll see something like 8.75 (8th). The first number is an average and the second number is placement. In this case, it means that *Dr. No*'s average ranking was 8.75, and on the list of average rankings, it placed eighth.

Finally, I'll give you **My Rating and Ranking** for each movie. That allows you to see where I am on or off the beaten track. If, while reading my review of *Diamonds Are Forever*, you think "she's crazy," all you have to do is compare my ratings to the survey results to realize that most people agree with you!

To see all the lists in one place, see THE RATINGS AND RANKINGS at the end of the book.

And after all that, the purpose of this book is to expand upon the Bond experience, and to have fun. So let's get started!

DR. NO (1962)

Survey Says!
Percent Favorite: 1.5%
Top 5 Cumulative: 10/25
Numeric Rating: 8.2/10
Ranking: 8.8 (5th/26)
My Rating and Ranking
Rated: 9/10
Ranked: 8 out of 26

Summary

The first Bond movie pits our hero against the evil Dr. No, agent of SPEC-TRE, who plans to cause international strife by "toppling" U.S. missiles (knocking them off course). With the aid of CIA agent Felix Leiter, Bond reaches Dr. No's privately-owned island off of Jamaica; Crab Key. There he meets Honey Ryder, and they are captured by the villain before defeating and killing him.

James Bond: Sean Connery
Honey Ryder: Ursula Andress
Felix Leiter: Jack Lord
Dr. No: Joseph Wiseman
Professor Dent: Anthony Dawson
Miss Taro: Zena Marshall
Sylvia Trench: Eunice Gayson
M: Bernard Lee
Moneypenny: Lois Maxwell
Major Boothroyd: Peter Burton
Directed by Terence Young

Discussion

The first three quarters of an hour of *Dr. No* is a seminal movie experience—startling, bold, sexy, and alluring, forever changing the way movies are viewed. Title designer Maurice Binder slaps us in the face with his genius; first by giving us the gunbarrel shot that will become James Bond's signature for the rest of the 20th century and into the 21st. Then, the hyperkinetic dots tell us to hold onto our seats, then the dancing silhouettes superimpose a male figure over the first female figure—highly erotic while "showing" nothing. By the time the movie begins, we have experienced four distinct music shifts—first a strange, alien sound while Bond shoots into the gunbarrel, then the James Bond theme (over the dots), into the bongos (over the dancers) and then into the primitive singing style of Three Blind Mice. This gives us a sense of movement, of a movie that will take us to all sorts of places, where we'll find danger (the gunbarrel), sex (the dancers) and exotic locales.

Dr. No is less appreciated by younger fans. To them, the dots just say "sixties," and they miss the signature elements that were not yet part of the series—the pre-titles sequence, the title song, bigger action pieces, and gadgets. *Dr.No* has fairly cheap special effects, which look particularly bad to eyes raised on a slicker movie experience. Thus, while most teen and twentyish Bond fans love Connery's films, *Dr. No* tends to suffer in comparison with some of the others.

By modern standards, the action is relatively light. There are two car chases, both rather poorly done. There are two brief fistfights (choreographed by Bond legend Bob Simmons); one culminates in bad guy Mr. Jones taking cyanide. The second is resolved by all parties discovering they are on the same side, when Bond takes on Quarrel and Puss-Feller. Bond fights our title character during the big climax, but with the entire island blowing up around them, it becomes part of a sea of chaos, rather than a really good fight. Nothing big blows up until that final scene. Overall, *Dr. No* can be hard to swallow for younger, more adrenaline-addicted fans.

Bond's introduction is a classic of understatement. "Bond, James Bond" is said to be the best-known movie line ever spoken, and when fans are polled as to their favorite utterance of it, they usually turn to the very first time it was spoken. In an elegant casino, talking to a beautiful woman, the camera avoids Connery's face, cutting to him only as he introduces himself; cigarette dangling, insouciant with a hint of challenge, our first sight of James Bond is a piece of film history that has lost none of its impact over the decades.

Over the next several minutes, *Dr. No* establishes much of the formula that will sustain 007 for more than forty years. Leaving the casino, Bond has a warm, cuddly meeting with Moneypenny and receives a stiff reprimand from M, before returning to his apartment for a casual sexual encounter initiated by Sylvia Trench (the first "Bond girl"). In addition, Bond has been issued, and has drawn, his Walther PPK. This could function as a list of "Bond musts" (casino, girl, M, Moneypenny, Walther), but they were all new here, and presented with freshness and class.

When Bond arrives in Jamaica, we get another vital component of the series—exotic locations. Bond visits a Jamaican marina, bar, and nightclub, and meets native islander Quarrel, who becomes his ally. We also see a component that really should be considered vital—mystery. At once we see a dark stranger spying on Bond in the airport. Friend or foe? He turns out to be recurring ally Felix Leiter, here portrayed by Jack Lord. Many fans consider Lord's portrayal of the character definitive, although I find him rather flat. (Some would argue that a buttoned-down CIA agent is supposed to be flat.)

The premise of *Dr. No* is simple, straightforward and effective. It's a real espionage movie; not about saving the world, just about stopping one villain's finite scheme. The plot unfolds well, one revelation logically following another until Dr. No's lair is reached. Bond doesn't know what's going on except that two British agents (Strangways and his secretary) were murdered, he doesn't know who the villain is or what his motive might be. He finds out information the way a spy should; by investigating, asking questions, and poking his nose where it doesn't belong. His only gadget is his Geiger counter. One of my favorite scenes is him preparing his room to warn of break-in, by placing the hair and the talc. He moves silently, in that sensual style so often called "cat-like," and by just walking around, wins about half the hearts in the audience.

When the villainous Professor Dent gives his report to the still unseen Dr. No, another key ingredient of the Bond formula is revealed: Ken Adam's extraordinary set design. Certainly interiors are lush throughout, but the signature set of *Dr. No* is the one Adam designed when his budget ran out—the interrogation room. With hardly any money left to create this set, Adam devised a bare room, a too-small chair, and an enormous round skylight with bars casting an ominous cell-like shadow. It was a masterpiece. The set is jarring; completely unlike anything we've seen before in this movie, and in 1962, it was unlike anything we'd seen anywhere. Because this is our first sight of the evil doctor's headquarters, he is imbued with great menace; we know he is unique and powerful.

Finally, just past the forty-five minute point, we reach one of the most legendary scenes in the history of the movies. This is the moment when Ursula Andress, as Honey Ryder, rises like a goddess from the sea. Wearing a white bikini and a knife at her hip, she galvanized the adolescence of every youth who saw her.

In reading Fleming's fiction, I have had occasion to regret that he never wrote romances. It is often the case that his most interesting characters are his women, and Honeychile Ryder (changed to Honey for the movie) was one of his best.

Extraordinarily beautiful, powerful, athletic, and graceful; she fits no known stereotype of femininity. Honey is the Wild Child, she is innocent of the world and yet wounded by it, uneducated yet literate, fiercely combative yet delicately fearful. She grieves the guard that Bond kills, yet murders the man who raped her in an especially gruesome fashion. Bond, like everyone else, is attracted to her, yet he is also protective of her and treats her with considerable tenderness. I am always moved by his final rescue of her—while everyone is running away from the about-to-explode atomic reactor, Bond is running back into danger, because he will not leave without this vulnerable woman.

After Honey's introduction, the film takes a bit of a nosedive. The guard talking tough into a megaphone is corny and unpersuasive, the "dragon" is truly a joke, and Dr. No himself doesn't hold one's interest. In all fairness, he remains some people's favorite villain—the prototype of the impassive, polite, evil genius; the first one to wear the Nehru collar and coolly serve his enemy champagne while explaining how he will die. But to me, he doesn't live up to his press; the loyalty and terror he inspired, the interrogation, and the tarantula. Somehow, a Nehru jacket and a pair of shiny hands just don't fulfill all that promise. To some extent, Ken Adam again comes to the rescue, as Dr. No's living and dining rooms are eye-popping. But it all seems anti-climactic. The film picks up again at the very end, because really, an entire island blowing up is fairly visual. There are evil lackeys belly-flopping into the sea, explosions, and extraordinary sound effects. I love the way there are two different alarms going off, plus the television report of the moon launch continues throughout, creating an exciting cacophony.

Dr. No ends with another scene that will become part of the formula—Bond and the girl, at last in one another's arms, avoiding rescue so they can fool around uninterrupted (See THE "OH, JAMES" MOMENT).

The High Points

- "Bond, James Bond" uttered with panache, and for the very first time in film history.
- The introduction of Monty Norman's "James Bond Theme."
- Honey Ryder emerging from the sea, and her character generally.
- The final confrontation with Professor Dent (see QUOTABLE QUOTES).
- The Three Blind Mice committing the opening murders.
- The thrilling title sequence.
- One of the very best Moneypenny scenes.
- The entire M/Boothroyd scene, including the scolding and the gun exchange.

The Low Points

- The dragon.
- James Bond ordering Quarrel to "fetch my shoes" is an embarrassing moment of racism.
- The eroticizing of rape—Honey tells her story of being raped, and then is raped by No's guards (she had pants on when she was taken out of the room, and didn't have them when she was rescued), and then makes love to Bond. It is as if her victimization adds to her attractiveness. Ick.
- While the James Bond Theme is, in my opinion, the greatest single pop instrumental ever recorded, here it is played over and over and over as if, having come up with a masterpiece, Norman and composer John Barry had run out of ideas.
- Dr. No himself is anti-climactic. His artificial hands lend nothing important to the plot.

Quotable Quotes

M: "When do you sleep?"
Bond: "Never on the firm's time, sir."

Bond to Dent: "That's a Smith and Wesson, and you've had your six."

Bond (in regard to the corpse in the back of his car): "Sergeant, make sure he doesn't get away." This is the very first "death quip."

Bond (watching the hearse crash): "I think they were on their way to a funeral."

Facts and Figures

SEXUAL ENCOUNTERS

Three: Sylvia Trench, Miss Taro, and Honey Ryder (with Honey we assume post-credits sex; they seem to be at the getting-cuddly stage when Leiter appears).

BOND'S CAR

1962 Sunbeam Alpine (light blue)
(A few sources have this as a Sunbeam Tiger, which is an Alpine with a Ford Falcon engine. Most sources simply say it is an Alpine.)

DEATHS

<u>Eleven</u>, plus an unknown number, possibly zero, killed when Crab Key blew up:

- Strangways, Strangways's secretary, Mr. Jones, the 4 occupants of the hearse (the Three Blind Mice plus their driver), Professor Dent, the guard in the swamp, Quarrel, and Dr. No.

Bond Kills

- <u>Two</u> directly (Dent and the guard)
- <u>Five</u> indirectly (Dr. No and the hearse occupants), plus he can be considered responsible for any deaths caused by the destruction of Crab Key.

EXPLOSIONS

<u>Two</u>: The hearse, and Dr. No's headquarters at Crab Key.

BOND'S FOOD AND DRINKS

Vodka Martinis

- Two; one upon arriving at the hotel, one served by Dr. No.

Other Drinks

- Two indeterminate drinks; one at the Queen's Club, one at Puss-Feller's
- A vodka on ice at the hotel
- Dom Perignon 1955 with dinner at Dr. No's lair
- Red wine with dinner with Dr. No (we see the half-empty glass).

Food

- Bond and Honey are served coffee and breakfast, but the drugged coffee takes effect before either eats.
- We see only the aftermath of dinner with Dr. No, and we do not see what is served. We join the scene at dessert, where fruit and some sort of cakes are visible on the table. In a rather strange bit of set dressing, each plate has two or three round objects that appear to be very large grapes or black olives.

GAMBLING AND SPORTS

- Bond plays chemin-de-fer.
- Sylvia plays golf in Bond's apartment (presumably with his clubs).
- Bond plays solitaire while waiting for Dent.

Amaze Your Friends! (Best Trivia)

- The gunbarrel shot was invented by Maurice Binder, who really did aim the camera down a gunbarrel.
- The first person to appear in the movies as James Bond is not Sean Connery, but stuntman Bob Simmons, who appears in the gunbarrel before the movie begins.
- Peter Burton's character, Boothroyd, takes away Bond's Beretta and replaces it with a Walther PPK. In *The Spy Who Loved Me*, Anya Amasova greets Q (Desmond Llewelyn) as "Major Boothroyd." Which is to say Burton is playing Q, and will be replaced in the next picture by Llewelyn.

Most Interesting Goofs

One of the world's most unusual hobbyists is surely the 'goof' collector. Goofs are visible cameramen, boom-mics in the shot, continuity errors, and so forth. Bond films have more than their share. My goof listings are not meant to be at all comprehensive, merely entertaining. (For comprehensive goof lists, check some of the websites in the RESOURCES chapter, or the Internet Movie Database (www.imdb.com)).

The Atomic Power Issue: Two facts are established; first, that toppling is achieved with a radio signal, second, that Dr. No uses atomic energy to power his operation. It is unclear, then, why the reactor should be placed in the middle of the radio control room, since the two operations are entirely separate. In the end-film chaos, we don't much notice this, but there you are.

The Ripped T-Shirt: Bond is wearing a brown Nehru jacket for dinner, when the guards are instructed to "soften him up." We see the beginning of this beating, and the jacket is on. Then he wakes up in his cell, still wearing the jacket, which appears fairly neat and clean. When he takes off the jacket, the t-shirt beneath is ripped and dirty. Why? Did the guards take off the jacket at some later point in the beating, rip the undershirt, then put the jacket back on so Bond could rest comfortably? Or does the ripped shirt merely look earthy and exciting? I suspect the latter.

Leiter is Late: Bond and Leiter discuss that the moon launch is in 48 hours, and Bond tells Leiter to come back for him in twelve hours, and to bring the Marines. Bond is indeed on the island for 48 hours, and leaves during the moon launch. Only then do Leiter and the Marines arrive.

THE UNSUNG HEROES OF BOND

The success of the James Bond film franchise is a team effort. The average admirer of the series probably knows little about the people behind the scenes. They know of Connery, of course, and most know his successors as well. They know of Ian Fleming too, almost certainly. But of the behind-the-scenes team, only the hardcore fan is likely to hear. For what it's worth, I'd like to sing the praises of the hidden heroes of James Bond.

John Barry

WHO HE WAS

Oscar- and BAFTA-winning (see 007 AT THE OSCARS) composer of eleven James Bond films:

> *Dr. No*
> *From Russia with Love*
> *Goldfinger*
> *Thunderball*
> *You Only Live Twice*
> *On Her Majesty's Secret Service*
> *Diamonds Are Forever*
> *The Man with the Golden Gun*
> *Octopussy*
> *A View to a Kill*
> *The Living Daylights*

WHY HE'S IMPORTANT

Bond films don't just have a particular look and style, they also have a particular sound, and John Barry (1933–2011) is responsible for that sound. It is a sound enormously admired by Barry's peers in the film industry, as evidenced by his four Academy Awards. His influence extends far beyond Bond movies, to film composition in general.

Barry wove the "James Bond Theme" (written by Monty Norman) and original material into a complex and lush sound. Starting with Goldfinger he used each movie's theme song as part of his score, changing it in ways that surprised the listener and added to the movie's depth. The same melody would be adventurous, vampy, romantic, or tense, depending upon Barry's orchestration. He also used secondary themes (such as Mr. Kiss-Kiss, Bang-Bang in *Thunderball*) and wrote the 007 Theme, which was used in five Bond films.

If you're not attuned to music (as I sometimes am not) you may not realize how important a film score is to the overall impression a movie creates. Try watching *Never Say Never Again* sometime and hear for yourself how various scenes are ruined by that lousy score. If nothing else changed about *Never Say Never Again*, but a John Barry score was added (as has been tried by fans), it would be a much better film.

Barry is the most acknowledged and well-known of the "unsung" contributors to Bond's films. He made a cameo appearance in his last James Bond movie—look for the orchestra conductor in the final scene of *The Living Daylights*.

OTHER MUSICAL GREATS

Monty Norman (composer of the famous James Bond Theme), David Arnold (composer for every Bond move from *Tomorrow Never Dies* through *Quantum of Solace*, and other films, Emmy and many other award winner), Thomas Newman, composer for *Skyfall* and *Spectre*, 15-time Oscar nominee.

Ken Adam

WHO HE WAS

Production designer on seven Bond films:

> *Dr. No*
> *Goldfinger*
> *Thunderball*
> *You Only Live Twice*
> *Diamonds Are Forever*
> *The Spy Who Loved Me*
> *Moonraker*

In addition, subsequent Bond production designer Peter Lamont worked under Adam on seven films, including four Bond films, so that Adam's influence stays with the Bond crew to this day.

WHY HE'S IMPORTANT

The look created by Sir Kenneth Adam (1921–2016), Oscar and BAFTA winner, stepped just an inch outside of reality. His sense of space, shape, and line, as well as his use of design to create character, was nothing short of remarkable. It all started, really, with that amazing interrogation room in *Dr. No*—bare skylight, tiny chair, stark, cell-like shadows. Adam gave his all on Dr. No's control room, and then made low-budget a virtue by squeezing that one last set out of thin air.

Bond films, as designed by Adam, look like you are walking into a heightened world, someplace a little more alive, a little more exciting. The sets, the furniture, the colors, make the adventures and the technology believable. I think the look of these films was as important to Bond's early success as the adventures themselves. Few people have successfully imitated Adam—most who have tried ended up going over the top, and their designs look more like 60's go-go bars than exciting worlds of adventure. I firmly believe that the visual world of James Bond, as designed by Ken Adam, was essential in making these movies so memorable.

OTHER DESIGN GREATS

Syd Cain (worked with Ken Adam on *Dr. No*, Art Director on *From Russia with Love*, Production Designer on *On Her Majesty's Secret Service*), Peter Murton (Art Director on *Goldfinger* and *Thunderball*, as well as such classics as *Dr. Strangelove, The Ipcress File,* and *The Lion in Winter*), Peter Lamont (Production Designer on nine Bond films, worked on five others; Academy Award winner for Art Direction on *Titanic*), Dennis Gassner (Production Designer on *Quantum of Solace, Skyfall,* and *Spectre,* Academy Award winner for Art Direction on *Bugsy*).

Peter Hunt

WHO HE WAS

Editor of:

> *Dr. No*
> *From Russia with Love*
> *Goldfinger*

Supervising Editor of:

> *You Only Live Twice*

Director of:

> *On Her Majesty's Secret Service*

WHY HE'S IMPORTANT

Peter Hunt (1925–2002) created an innovative and startling new editing style that influenced everything from action movies to MTV. What was unusual about Hunt's technique was that he removed sections of the action. For example, you might see Bond pull his arm back to hit an opponent, and then see the opponent fall; Hunt realized it wasn't necessary to show every step of the process in order to convey what was happening, and the result was more intense and exciting than fight scenes (particularly) had ever been before. At first, people found these action scenes disturbing, although younger people, who are used to rapid cutting, might not see what the fuss is about.

Hunt also "under-cranked" film—making it run a bit faster than normal—in order to accentuate action; something he sometimes overused. *On Her Majesty's Secret Service* was his directorial debut, and here his hyperkinetic style went too far. Still, Hunt's influence and importance cannot be ignored, and his editing left such a mark that no other Bond editor has distinguished himself by comparison. It is only Hunt whom you will find discussed as an editor by Bond aficionados.

Bob Simmons

WHO HE WAS

Frequent Connery body double and stuntman on numerous Bond films, Bob Simmons was the man appearing in the gunbarrel in:

> *Dr. No*
> *From Russia with Love*
> *Goldfinger*

Stuntman on:

> *Dr. No*
> *From Russia with Love*
> *Thunderball*

Stunt Coordinator on:

> *Goldfinger*
> *You Only Live Twice*
> *Diamonds Are Forever*
> *Live and Let Die*
> *The Spy Who Loved Me*
> *Moonraker*
> *For Your Eyes Only*
> *Octopussy*
> *A View to a Kill*

WHY HE'S IMPORTANT

Bob Simmons (1933–1988), was one of the true innovators in the field of stunt work. He is one of the people responsible for transforming the role of a stuntman from 'guy who falls down,' to someone who choreographs and designs action. Simmons worked to push the envelope for what a stunt could do. His influence in coordinating stunts extends far beyond the Bond world to every film where stunts are needed.

One of the things that Bond films are famous for is the authenticity of their stunts. Sure, it isn't Sean Connery or Roger Moore or Pierce Brosnan doing them, but in almost every case, a live person, not an effect, has performed the stunt in question. That's an impression that cannot be faked, and the respect the audience gives the stunt is raised accordingly. That's a real (and record-setting) bungee jump at *GoldenEye*'s opening. As well, that's really Jake Lombard and B.J. Worth fighting off the back of an airplane while hanging on a net in *The Living Daylights*. You feel like you're seeing something spectacular because you are!

OTHER STUNT GREATS

Vic Armstrong, Willy Bogner (skiing), Joie Chitwood (driving), Simon Crane, Martin Grace, Richard Graydon, Rémy Julienne (driving), George Leech, Jake Lombard (aerial), Wayne Michaels, Rick Sylvester (aerial), B.J. Worth (aerial)

Maurice Binder

WHO HE WAS

Creator of the famous gunbarrel opening. Title Designer on:

> *Dr. No*
> *Thunderball*

You Only Live Twice
On Her Majesty's Secret Service
Diamonds Are Forever
Live and Let Die
The Man with the Golden Gun
The Spy Who Loved Me
For Your Eyes Only
Octopussy
A View to a Kill
The Living Daylights
Licence to Kill

WHY HE'S IMPORTANT

The look of the Bond films is vital, as discussed under Ken Adam. No one is more important to the signature imagery of James Bond than Maurice Binder (1925–1991). For the gunbarrel shot alone, Binder would be remembered forever. Fans, when discussing *Never Say Never Again*, often complain that a movie without a gunbarrel shot just doesn't feel like Bond, darn it!

But Binder created more than a single piece of extraordinary film. He created an entire language of Bond imagery, of dancing silhouettes and flowing water, light moving with the title song and suggestive placement of phallic weaponry. He experimented with overlays, filters, paint, and anything else he could get his hands on, without any of the computer technology his successor, Danny Kleinman, used so ably. In some ways, he could be said to have been making music videos before MTV.

To an immeasurable extent, when people think of James Bond movies, they think of the sensual and exciting videos created by Maurice Binder.

OTHER TITLE DESIGN GREATS

Robert Brownjohn (titles for *From Russia with Love* and *Goldfinger*). Daniel Kleinman (title designer for all the Brosnan Bond films as well as the 2006 *Casino Royale*; Kleinman brought Bond titles into the digital age and added animation to the famous gunbarrel shot).

Harry Saltzman and Albert R. (Cubby) Broccoli

WHO THEY WERE

Saltzman and Broccoli co-owned the production rights of the Bond films until 1975, when Saltzman sold his share of Eon Productions to United Artists. On the first four Bond films, Saltzman and Broccoli collaborated closely. Subsequently, they alternated who was in charge of the production of specific films.

Saltzman and Broccoli co-produced:

Dr. No
From Russia with Love
Goldfinger

You Only Live Twice (Broccoli served as the main producer)
On Her Majesty's Secret Service (Saltzman served as the main producer)
Diamonds Are Forever (Broccoli served as the main producer)
Live and Let Die (Saltzman served as the main producer)
The Man with the Golden Gun (Broccoli served as the main producer)

Saltzman and Broccoli "presented," and worked as uncredited producers on:

Thunderball

Cubby Broccoli served as sole producer on:

The Spy Who Loved Me
Moonraker
For Your Eyes Only
Octopussy
A View to a Kill

Cubby Broccoli co-produced (with stepson Michael Wilson):

The Living Daylights
Licence to Kill
GoldenEye

WHY THEY'RE IMPORTANT

When Albert R. (Cubby) Broccoli (1909–1996) and Harry Saltzman (1915–1994) began as independent producers, they created, with *Dr. No*, a low budget master-piece. In a book such as this, Saltzman and Broccoli's contribution needs hardly be explained. But it didn't have to be that way. Their surprise hit could have gone off in any number of directions, but they stood solidly by a vision that was uniquely theirs.

Saltzman and Broccoli brought something new into the world, inventing their own genre and transforming cultural consciousness the world over. *Dr. No*'s premiere changed the concept of the spy genre.

Moreover, Broccoli and Saltzman brought together a team that worked uniquely well together, and they nurtured that team through many movies. There is no gossip suggesting anything except that working on Bond films is a terrific experience for cast and crew, so much so that practically the only people who don't come back for more films are actors whose characters are killed off. And even that didn't stop such folks as Charles Gray or Joe Don Baker. Look at the long list of movies for the "heroes" listed above. The Bond "family" has long nurtured creativity and made the working environment exciting.

Each of the "unsung heroes" above is wonderful in his own right, but it was Saltzman and Broccoli, and then Broccoli and his family, who held them all together, and held them in combination, valuing a whole package of actors, musicians, stunt-men, designers, and so on, and treating them all with sufficient respect and decency to make them eager to stay a part of the group.

Cubby Broccoli was given the Thalberg Award in 1981 (see 007 AT THE OS-CARS). He passed away in 1996 (Saltzman had died two years earlier). By this time, his stepson, Michael Wilson, was already a vital part of the Bond team and co-producer. Wilson and Broccoli's daughter Barbara continue to helm the Bond pictures. *Tomorrow Never Dies* (1997) was dedicated to Cubby Broccoli's memory.

BOND GIRLS

Many would argue that I, as a feminist, should not be using the phrase "Bond girls." After all, we're talking about adult women. I would argue that the phrase has acquired its own unique meaning, and as such, should be left intact. It doesn't mean merely a girl or woman who is in a Bond picture. Women such as Judi Dench's M, or Jacoba Brink (*For Your Eyes Only*), or Moneypenny, are not indicated by the phrase "Bond girl." If we change "Bond girl" to "Bond woman," we either lose the unique identifier for a certain kind of Bond woman, or we are in the awkward position of saying that Moneypenny et al aren't "Bond women." I prefer to use "Bond woman" to mean any woman in a Bond movie, and "Bond girl" to mean a female lead, a seductress, or a woman cast primarily for sex appeal.

Before we talk about the best and worst Bond girls, let's look at the various kinds of women who fill the Bond girl shoes (or bikinis).

Sexually Aggressive Women

The first Bond film introduces Sylvia Trench, a very forward woman. She knows what she wants, and seeks it aggressively, inviting herself into Bond's life and then showing up at his apartment and dressing in his pajamas. In a man, pursuing a woman is considered perfectly normal. In a woman, even in the 21st century, the act of hot pursuit is still sometimes called 'slutty'. In fact, in a message board discussion about sexual attraction and seduction in the Bond films, I suggested that many women might find the young Connery attractive enough to be forward with him, and one response said such a woman was a "raging whore." I suppose I had no reason to be shocked, but I was. The most shocking part was how I was being accused of anti-feminism, for believing it was okay for women to be sexual aggressors. Feminism, to me, empowers women to make choices, without being punished for those choices. Sylvia Trench was making a choice. In 1962 she must have been shocking indeed. If a woman can be called a "whore" in 2003 for coming on to James Bond, what must people have thought forty-one years earlier? Yet Sylvia is portrayed in an entirely positive light. She is elegant, sophisticated, and beautiful. Bond enjoys her company and, in fact, she is back for the next movie. In no way is she punished or degraded for making the first move or enjoying her sex life. Most other movies wouldn't catch up with this enlightened attitude for another twenty years!

"I know what I want" sexuality is more common than not among Bond girls; both the good and evil enjoy themselves, and enjoy Bond. They are unashamed of their choices, and they are delightfully indiscreet. This raised horrified eyebrows in the sixties, and as the above conversation shows, still does so today. But I say, good for them! Just as Bond lives a life that men can dream of living (but probably wouldn't actually choose), Bond girls have a boldness that real women can appreciate and envy.

Types of Bond Girls

There are different types of Bond girls. We can start by dividing them into the broad categories of "good girls" and "bad girls." Let's leave bad girls, fun as they are, for later.

Dr. No introduces the basic prototypes for good Bond girls. First, in Sylvia Trench, we meet a secondary woman with whom Bond has a romantic encounter, generally before the main action starts. We'll see this in seventeen of the Bond films.

The Pre-action Encounters

Sylvia Trench: *Dr. No*
Sylvia Trench: *From Russia with Love*
Bonita (pre-titles): *Goldfinger*
Dink (masseuse): *Goldfinger*
Patricia Fearing: *Thunderball*
Ling: *You Only Live Twice*
Miss Caruso: *Live and Let Die*:
"Log Cabin Girl": *The Spy Who Loved Me*
Bianca (Caribbean agent): *Octopussy*
Patricia Fearing: *Never Say Never Again*
Kimberly Jones (woman in sub): *A View to a Kill*
Linda (bored woman on yacht): *The Living Daylights*:
Caroline (the psychologist/psychiatrist): *GoldenEye*
Prof. Inga Bergstrom: *Tomorrow Never Dies*
Dr. Molly Warmflash: *The World is Not Enough*
Bond's lover (in Turkey): *Skyfall*
Estrella (Mexico City): *Spectre*

The second Bond good girl appearing in *Dr. No* is of the sort most people think of when they hear "Bond girl"—the type defined by Honey Ryder. She is "the" Bond girl, the one he embraces at the film's end. In this case, she is a woman he happens to meet in the course of his adventure. Because she is peripheral to the action, present only to be beautiful, exciting, and perhaps rescued, this type of woman is seen less nowadays. In the modern films, most Bond girls will be allies, or equals, or will have skills vital to Bond's success. Honey establishes herself as an equal person to Bond by pointing out he knows far less about nature and animals than she, but this gives her no advantage (in the book, Honeychile's rapport with animals allows her to free herself and help Bond).

Good Bond Girls

Note: This includes all movies through *Spectre*

Type	Total
Primary characters peripheral to the action	7
Secondary characters peripheral to the action	20
Girls in need of rescue from the villain	12
Allies/agents	21
Bad girls who become good after encountering Bond	5

Notes: The "Primary characters peripheral to the action" may have important skills (such as Natalya's computer skills) but they are caught up in the action rather than an essential part of it; the Honey Ryder model. In the "Secondary characters" Sylvia Trench was counted only once. Finally, the "Girls in need of rescue", are women who are encountered in this situation, such as Andrea Anders or Lupe Lamora. It doesn't include women who are, at some point in the action, briefly imprisoned by the villain, such as Tracy or Mary Goodnight.

BOND'S EQUAL

Ultimately, a changing world gave women stronger roles in the Bond films. It seems that the publicity for every Bond film of the last thirty-five years and more has included the female lead explaining that she was different from those other Bond girls (starting with Honor Blackman, I believe). I think a sea change can be fairly pinned to 1977. It is *The Spy Who Loved Me* which can legitimately claim to have the first "new" Bond girl. Although the first female agents/allies appeared in *Thunderball*, Mademoiselle LaPorte's brief appearance, merely standing next to Bond in the pre-titles, was unremarkable, and Paula Caplan did little until she was murdered.. Aki, in *You Only Live Twice*, was smart and able, but she bought the farm at the halfway point and was replaced by Kissy, who did little more than defend her virginity and run for help. In *The Spy Who Loved Me*, Anya Amasova was an agent in more than name; she was tough, competent, and survived to the final credits. Bond treated her with the respect a renowned Soviet agent deserved. A dozen years later, Pam Bouvier in *Licence to Kill* was strident about deserving equal treatment, practically yelling at Bond. Eleven years after *that*, Michelle Yeoh told the media that her *Tomorrow Never Dies* character represented a new kind of Bond woman—you had to wonder where she'd been all these years!

The Agents/Allies

Mademoiselle LaPorte (France): *Thunderball*
Paula Caplan (MI6): *Thunderball*
Aki (Japan): *You Only Live Twice*
Kissy Suzuki (Japan): *You Only Live Twice*
Miss Caruso (Italy): *Live and Let Die*
Mary Goodnight (MI6): *The Man with the Golden Gun*
Anya Amasova/Agent XXX (USSR): *The Spy Who Loved Me*
Dr. Holly Goodhead (CIA): *Moonraker*
Manuela (Brazil): *Moonraker*
Bianca (unnamed Caribbean nation; Cuba is hinted at): *Octopussy*
Nicole/Agent 326 (MI6): *Never Say Never Again*
Kimberly Jones (MI6): *A View to a Kill*

Pam Bouvier (CIA): *Licence to Kill*
Wai Lin (China): *Tomorrow Never Dies*
Dr. Molly Warmflash (MI6): *The World is Not Enough*
Giacinta "Jinx" Johnson (NSA): *Die Another Day*
Vesper Lynd: *Casino Royale**
Camille Montes: *Quantum of Solace*
Strawberry Fields: *Quantum of Solace*
Eve Moneypenny: *Skyfall***

*Vesper is an asterisk here, because she betrays Bond, but is also an ally.

**Eve is a field agent in* Skyfall. *By the end of the movie, and into* Spectre, *she takes the traditional role of Moneypenny and no longer "counts" as a Bond girl.*

Bond girls are most often strong women these days; one rarely sees anyone as vulnerable as Honey anymore. I think this is a mistake. There has always been, and should always be, a great variety of women in the Bond films. There is nothing wrong with being someone other than a secret agent, or having abilities other than kicking ass. One of my favorite characters is Kara Milovy of *The Living Daylights*. A concert cellist, she is certainly more than competent in her own field, but she is also somewhat naive, somewhat sheltered, and utterly inexperienced in Bond's world of adventure. I don't think this makes her less of an adult, less of a "modern woman," or less than equal to Bond. I like the contrast of having Bond matched with someone from a different walk of life and a different temperament. I love Anya, Wai Lin, and Jinx, but I hope they aren't the only kind of Bond girl we'll get in the 21st century.

HEAVENLY CHOIRS SINGING

Bond's sexual prowess functions on a symbolic as well as an erotic level. He seduces women, not merely to his bed, but to his side—the side of good. In *Thunderball*, Fiona Volpe mocked this when she said, "But of course, I forgot your ego, Mr. Bond. James Bond, who only has to make love to a woman and she starts to hear heavenly choirs singing. She repents, and immediately returns to the side of right and virtue. But not this one." Poor Fiona discovered too late that evil women seduced by Bond have only two choices; had she chosen differently she might have survived to the final reel.

In all, Bond has met thirteen women who were the villain's girlfriend, or worked for him, or were sponsored by him. He slept with twelve of the thirteen (Bibi Dahl was too young for him). Bond's success rate with these women isn't all that impressive; six of them were killed by the villain.

Rescue Me!

Jill Masterson: *Goldfinger* (killed)
Domino Derval: *Thunderball*
Solitaire: *Live and Let Die*
Andrea Anders: *The Man with the Golden Gun* (killed)
Corinne Dufour: *Moonraker* (killed)
Bibi Dahl: *For Your Eyes Only*
Domino Petachi: *Never Say Never Again*

Kara Milovy: *The Living Daylights*
Lupe Lamora: *Licence to Kill*
Paris Carver: *Tomorrow Never Dies* (killed)
Solange: *Casino Royale* (killed)
Severine: *Skyfall* (killed)
Lucia Sciarra: *Spectre*

Despite Fiona's mockery, bad girls who repent and return to the side of right and virtue have a considerably better survival rate. Of the five, only May Day doesn't survive, heroically sacrificing herself. Three of the remaining four end up in Bond's arms as the end credits roll.

Bad Girls Who Turn Good

Pussy Galore: *Goldfinger*
Tiffany Case: *Diamonds Are Forever*
Octopussy: *Octopussy*
Magda: *Octopussy*
May Day: *A View to a Kill*

WHEN THEY'RE BAD, THEY'RE VERY, VERY BAD

Villains are often more fun than heroes. Darth Vader is doubtless more popular than that wimpy Luke fellow. Frankenstein's monster earns more sympathy than Dr. Frankenstein himself. Alan Rickman's deliciously evil Sheriff of Nottingham was the best part of *Robin Hood: Prince of Thieves*. Villains have pizzazz; they have sex appeal. When those appealing villains also happen to be beautiful, seductive, often highly-sexed women, how much more thrilling!

Bond bad girls debuted with Bond himself, in *Dr. No*, which featured two. The photographer portrayed by Marguerite LeWars, a former Miss Jamaica, was beautiful, ill-tempered, and scratched Quarrel's face with a broken flashbulb. However, it was Miss Taro who fits the mold we have come to know. She's a double-agent, working as a secretary in the British Foreign Service office while spying for Dr. No. She's beautiful and seductive, sleeping with Bond in order to keep him at her apartment so that he can be murdered by Professor Dent. Atypically, Bond lets her live.

It is in the fourth movie, *Thunderball,* that the icon of the bad girl really blooms. Fiona Volpe, with her sarcastic disdain of heavenly choirs, is a force with which to be reckoned. Her interplay with Bond is witty and sparkling; their potent chemistry is only enhanced by the fact that, from the beginning, they know they are adversaries. Bond recognizes Fiona's SPECTRE ring, but doesn't know he is, himself, recognized. In turn, Fiona doesn't realize Bond knows she is an enemy. Each toys with the other with an equal mixture of pleasure and enmity. Their sex scene ("Do you like wild things Mr. Bond, James Bond?" "Wild! You should be locked up in a cage.") is among the most erotic of the series.

One senses, with Miss Taro, that she is reluctant to sleep with Bond, that she does so only because she sees no alternative. But with wild girls like Fiona, Helga Brandt *(You Only Live Twice)* and Fatima Blush *(Never Say Never Again)*, we have no doubt that both the sexual experience and the evil are relished. Several of these women make a fetish out of loving the man they will kill—Helga even dresses up for the occasion. Xenia Onatopp *(GoldenEye)*, the most perverse of the lot, achieves orgasm when killing. Of all of them, only Rosie Carver, *Live and Let Die*'s turncoat CIA agent, believes the sex is meaningful—and she is quickly proven wrong. Bond's bad girls are thrill-seekers, their lives of crime are lives of excitement. We may cheer when they meet their much-deserved ends, but in the meantime, we enjoy them thoroughly. Often, they outshine their virtuous sisters, and figure heavily among fans' favorites.

The Bad Girls

Photographer: *Dr. No*
Miss Taro: *Dr. No*
Bonita: *Goldfinger*
Fiona Volpe: *Thunderball*
Helga Brandt: *You Only Live Twice*
Bambi: *Diamonds Are Forever*
Thumper: *Diamonds Are Forever*
Rosie Carver: *Live and Let Die*
Log Cabin Girl: *The Spy Who Loved Me*
Naomi: *The Spy Who Loved Me*
Fatima Blush: *Never Say Never Again*
Xenia Onatopp: *GoldenEye*
Elektra King: *The World is Not Enough*
Miranda Frost: *Die Another Day*

Figure 1 :*Interior spread in the* Thunderball *program book, showing the magnificent women of* Thunderball. *(For the story behind that book, see Figure 6)*

Sex! Sex! Sex!

How often does Bond have sex anyway? There are a few ambiguous situations, as well as a few near-misses. In *Diamonds Are Forever*, poor Plenty O'Toole, stripped to her panties and ready to enjoy her evening with James, was thrown into the pool by Tiffany's gang before anything further could occur.

Bond definitely has sex with at least sixty-two women, and perhaps as many as sixty-seven, in twenty-five movies. For a per-movie average, add one—Sylvia Trench is his paramour in both *Dr. No* and *From Russia with Love*, so she's counted once as a woman but twice as sex-in-a-movie. Since all sex occurs off-camera anyway, I see no reason to exclude sex that happened before the movie began (Bonita in *Goldfinger*, "Log Cabin Girl" in *The Spy Who Loved Me*) or happens after the movie ends (Honey Ryder in *Dr. No*, Kissy in *You Only Live Twice*).

Did They or Didn't They?

There are five ambiguous situations, in which we are never one-hundred percent certain of Bond's status with particular women.

Dink: *Goldfinger*—Might Bond simply be slapping a pretty woman on the bottom, one who, as a hotel employee, is unwilling to spurn him? Heck no! Bond treats Dink with an easy familiarity that implies they know each other, at least physically, rather well. He doesn't flirt so much as assume, indicating, to me, that they are already lovers.

Did They or Didn't They? Yes.

Mademoiselle LaPorte: *Thunderball*—The French agent in the *Thunderball* pre-titles sequence is a model of reserve. Beautiful, yes—but intimate? Perhaps not. In the same movie, Bond is a gentleman with his MI6 ally Paula Caplan, and they have separate rooms. If anything, she is even more beautiful than the French agent, and hangs around in a bikini rather than a conservative coat and scarf. Clearly, Bond is maintaining some control over his urges for this adventure. The physical distance maintained when he and LaPorte stand near one another, and his "Later, perhaps" when she seems to flirt, both imply that nothing unprofessional has happened between them.

Did They or Didn't They? No.

Ling: *You Only Live Twice*—Bond is in bed with Ling, and entirely relaxed, appearing satiated, as we join him in Hong Kong during the pre-titles sequence. Yet he tells Moneypenny that they were interrupted before anything happened. Oh, puh-leeze! Why anyone should believe a white lie he tells Moneypenny over the evidence of our own eyes is beyond me!

Did They or Didn't They? Yes.

Bianca: *Octopussy*—The Caribbean agent in the pre-titles would at first glance seem a beautiful but professional alliance in the manner of Mademoiselle LaPorte. But at second look, there is an intimacy of touch when Bianca puts Bond's identification on his coat, and the fake moustache on his lip. Her "James, please be careful," is spoken like a lover, not a colleague, and when they part he gives her a delicate kiss on the cheek.

Did They or Didn't They? Yes.

Eve: *Skyfall*—We cut away from Eve and Bond as she is rather intimately shaving him in his hotel room. Next they are in the casino. He compliments her appearance, and she compliments his. Then, when he encounters Severine, she sounds just a little jealous. Back at MI6, they act like nothing happened. To me it's obvious that they want to put the past behind them in order to keep their jobs, and it all seems very much like the back story that Sean Connery and Lois Maxwell created for *their* Bond and Moneypenny.

Did They or Didn't They? Yes.

This brings our total to sixty-six, for a per-movie average of 2.6.

The Appetites of Actors

Sean Connery as Bond usually slept with three or four women per picture, although he shares the record for fewest—only one in *Diamonds Are Forever* (remember that Plenty landed in the pool). Connery averaged 3.3 partners per film.

George Lazenby enjoyed the company of three women in his one film.

Roger Moore averaged 2.9 partners per movie, surprising those of us who think of him as randier than Connery.

Timothy Dalton had two partners in each of his two movies.

Pierce Brosnan averaged 2.5 over four films.

Daniel Craig: Craig slept with only one woman in each of his first two movies, and three each in his next two, averaging two per movie.

Best and Worst: Girls We Love, Girls We'd Rather Do Without

The problem with choosing a favorite, or least favorite Bond girl, is that there are so many standards by which to judge. Is the "best" Bond girl the most beautiful, the best portrayal by the actress, the one with the most interesting character, or the best dialogue, or the best chemistry with her costar? Someone might choose a favorite based on any or all of these, or might list different characters for each possible standard. Some cannot narrow their favorites list to fewer than a half-dozen, which, given that just under eighty women could fairly be considered to have been Bond girls, is not so large a number.

Among fans, there are some clear favorites, although often there are surprises as well. As with the Bond films, even unpopular Bond girls have their backers.

Top Five / Bottom Five

Fan Favorites ("Best")
1. Tracy di Vicenzo, *On Her Majesty's Secret Service*
2. Elektra King, *The World is Not Enough*
3. Domino Derval, *Thunderball*
4. Anya Amasova, *The Spy Who Loved Me*
5. Xenia Onatopp, *GoldenEye*
AND: Vesper Lynd, *Casino Royale*

Fan Least Favorites ("Worst")
1. Stacey Sutton, *A View to a Kill*
2. Dr. Christmas Jones, *The World is Not Enough*
3. May Day, *A View to a Kill*
4. Bibi Dahl, *For Your Eyes Only*
5. Rosie Carver, *Live and Let Die*

The Girls We Love

The following women usually hit the top five in "Best Bond girl" surveys, more or less in the order presented. Such surveys are far more variable and impressionistic than those for best film, as mentioned above. So, it was impossible to garner real statistics. Nonetheless, after reading these surveys for a few years, certain results are predictable. Any top five surveys will usually include at least three of the five above, and a top ten will probably have all of them. These aren't my personal five favorites, which I'll mention as they arise.

Contessa Teresa (Tracy) di Vicenzo

No Bond girl is more popular among fans than Tracy; the only woman to whom Bond ever proposed marriage. In *On Her Majesty's Secret Service*, Tracy married Bond and died mere hours later. She is one of the few points of continuity in the Bond series, having been explicitly mentioned in three subsequent movies: In conversation with Anya in *The Spy Who Loved Me*, when Bond visits her grave in *For Your Eyes Only*, and when Felix tells Della that Bond was once married in *Licence to Kill*.

When the Bond producers decided to film *On Her Majesty's Secret Service*, they knew they'd need a really special actress if the fans were to accept her as a worthy Mrs. Bond. Diana Rigg, cat-suited, high-kicking star of television's *The Avengers*, was an ideal choice. She was elegant, she was tough, and she was already the heartthrob of millions.

This is the part where I'm supposed to wax poetic about the wonders of Diana Rigg. Unfortunately, I have never understood her appeal. The coolly dignified, somewhat distant portrayals she excels at have never been my cup of tea; my favorite actresses have more warmth. Dame Diana Rigg is a competent actress, and her love scenes with Lazenby have conviction and charm. Certainly many of the beauty queens and models hired as Bond girls for their looks could not have done such a fine job, although the role is well within the reach of any reasonably skilled actress.

Yet we never really get to know Tracy, and in watching her, I never feel swept away, as the audience should with a romance.

Diana Rigg, as Mrs. Peel, was the ideal woman for millions in *The Avengers*, and as Tracy, for Bond in *On Her Majesty's Secret Service*. While she remains the ideal woman for many, many Bond fans to this day, she leaves this fan behind.

Elektra King

The duplicitous apparent victim portrayed by Sophie Marceau in *The World is Not Enough* proves again that hiring a real actress can make a strong impression on the audience. It also proves how strongly the fans respond when Bond lets his guard down and allows his feelings to show. From the beginning, Bond is captivated by Elektra, reading about her kidnapping ordeal and watching a video of her vulnerable, tear-streaked face. In the novels, we learned that Bond had a soft spot for a "bird with a wing down;" a woman in need of rescue. In the movies this has often proved out as well. Tracy, whom he met when he stopped her suicide attempt, is surely the woman most in need of rescue in the Bond films, and is also the woman he marries. In Elektra, it appears Bond is reminded of Tracy. Many fans believe that when Elektra asks, "Tell me, have you ever lost a loved one, Mr. Bond?" and Bond doesn't answer, this is meant as a reference to Tracy's death. Certainly the audience is reminded of her when they ski together, and Elektra wears an outfit pointedly similar to one worn by Tracy in *On Her Majesty's Secret Service*. As happened with Tracy in the earlier film, Bond and Elektra are caught in an avalanche. Elektra's claustrophobic panic attack when this happens allows Bond to protect her, to hold her, and surely, to care about her.

Not numbering *The World is Not Enough* among my favorite Bond films, I cannot include Elektra King among my personal favorite Bond girls either. The weaknesses of the film drag her down a bit. But I can certainly admire Marceau's performance, her complexity, and her beauty. Pierce Brosnan has some of his finest scenes with her. When Elektra says "You wouldn't kill me. You'd miss me," she pushes Bond into his most cold-blooded assassination since Professor Dent's in *Dr. No*. And when he answers "I never miss" he replaces the death quip with a worthy follow-up to "That's a Smith and Wesson, and you've had your six." Elektra King is a fan favorite not just because she is a beautiful woman, but because she serves as both a true love interest and a worthy adversary.

Dominique (Domino) Derval

Domino is perhaps not as interesting as some other fan favorites; she usually makes the cut for "most beautiful," or "most desirable" on fan surveys, and appears a bit less often as "best" or "favorite."

In the novel **Thunderball**, Domino Vitali is one of Fleming's finest characters. I'd call her the best of the literary Bond girls. She is playful and childlike, yet womanly and assertive. The character's name was changed when French beauty queen Claudine Auger was cast in the role. She played Domino almost as a lost child, soft and lovely. But not entirely soft—this is the woman who says "What sharp little eyes you have," and it is she, not Bond, who kills the villain. Still, it is hard to argue that her great popularity among fans is due more to these traits than to how she looks in a bathing suit. In fact, she looks fantastic in several beautifully-designed suits, and she wears little else.

Figure 2: An even better spread from the Thunderball *program, featuring one of Domino's stellar bathing suits.*

Anya Amasova (Agent XXX)

Long before Vin Diesel came along, the spy world had a more attractive XXX in the form of *The Spy Who Loved Me's* Anya Amasova. Barbara Bach is a woman of such beauty and captivating screen presence that it took me four or five viewings of *The Spy Who Loved Me* to realize that she really can't act worth a damn! She exudes such loveliness that she still looks good wearing the stupidest accessory ever forced upon a Bond girl—a crocheted cap that looks more like a tea cozy than something a glamourous woman would wear.

Indeed, Anya is one of my favorite Bond girls, despite her thespian weaknesses, and *The Spy Who Loved Me* one of my favorite movies. Agent XXX embodies the title to which so many Bond actresses try to lay claim—the "new and different kind of Bond girl." She wasn't the first female spy Bond encountered—Aki and Kissy were agents of the Japanese Secret Service ten years earlier—but she was the first one presented as Bond's equal, in this case, his Soviet counterpart. In the next movie, *Moonraker*, Bond reacts to Dr. Holly Goodhead with a chauvinistic surprise, not quite believing that a woman can be a scientist. Yet here Bond knows all about Major Amasova, including what she drinks, and never doubts her competence. The only nod to sexism in *The Spy Who Loved Me* is not on Bond's behalf but on Eon's. Anya is introduced in a love scene with Sergei Barsov. When the call comes for Agent XXX, we are meant to be surprised that it is she, and not her lover, who answers. (Such clever scenes always fall victim to a movie's promotion, and no one is ever surprised by them.) Anya doesn't take her place in a more modern age of spy movies by announcing it, but simply by being who she says she is—a competent and dangerous agent who is also a woman.

Throughout the movie, Bond and XXX compete with one another, playing a game of espionage one-upmanship. They enjoy this game, and so, eventually, they come to enjoy each other. Their chemistry is plausible because it develops in a context we (the audience) can appreciate.

Anya Amasova, with her huge, soulful eyes, her unwillingness to take guff from 007, her fierce loyalty to her slain lover, and her remarkable way of filling out an evening gown, is truly one of Bond's greatest co-stars.

Xenia Zaragevna Onatopp

Few villains, male or female, manage over-the-top with any real style. Most Bond villains, modeling themselves after Dr. No, the original, keep a cool and formal exterior. Excess can become ridiculous, as when Christopher Walken, playing *A View to a Kill*'s Max Zorin, giggles after failing to kill Bond. Giggling has never impressed me as very villainous.

Bond bad girls tend to be as cool as the bad boys. Fiona Volpe was dignified, always on top of the situation. Elektra King was at first tragic; when she later transformed into a villain, she held a hard edge, and when she slipped into traditional villainous dramatics, "Pretty thing. Did you have her, too?" she loses control of her performance.

But there is one villainess who turns over-the-top into high art, and makes you regret her inevitable demise. *GoldenEye*'s Xenia Onatopp is as delightful as she is maniacal, as exciting as she is evil. Famke Janssen really lets herself go in the part; she isn't afraid of overacting, but she doesn't play her character like a cliché. I love little touches of the portrayal, like the cigar-smoking, and how she scowls with anger when she loses at chemin-de-fer. It is so like a villain to stay cool, perhaps to threaten Bond, but to maintain a demeanor that suggests that only inferiors lose their temper. Xenia isn't about the cool demeanor, or world conquest, or being a loyal member of the Janus Group. She's in it for the sensation, for the thrill. She hates Bond, but when she realizes he's going to ram the train, her eyes light with excitement and pleasure; she is aroused by the danger, and aroused by the man who dares it.

As mentioned before, her extreme portrayal is marked by an extreme character trait—one that wouldn't have existed in a Bond movie before the 1990s. Xenia achieves orgasm when killing (apparently, only when killing, although that is hard to judge). In action movies, we quickly become inured to violence and death. It is hard to grasp the true tragedy of murder when it is depicted in spectacular cinematic fashion. When Xenia pants with excitement while slaughtering the computer technicians of Severnaya, we are horrified. This is different, this isn't just a random death in a Bond film. This is pleasure of the most evil sort. *GoldenEye* is exceptionally good at reminding us that death is terribly costly; when Natalya grieves for her friends in the aftermath of the slaughter, we are moved, and it is one of the few occasions in Bond movie history where a main character is given time to mourn. Both the movie and the character drive home the idea that murder is not merely a cinematic game, and yet allow the audience to enjoy the visceral thrill of watching extravagant evil. Xenia embodies the very concept that killing is fun, that it is sexy;

that for her it is sex. By stating this disturbing concept outright, by relishing and then destroying it, *GoldenEye* gives us one of the movies' most memorable characters.

Xenia is both a fan favorite and a personal favorite of mine. She tends to come out as number one on "bad girl" surveys among younger fans, but she is also popular among fans like me, who were around in the Connery era. She is a little lower on general Bond girl surveys, where bad and good characters are mixed, but she remains near the top.

Vesper Lynd

"I'm complicated," she says, and perhaps this is why Vesper shot to the top of most fans' list of favorite Bond co-stars. Vesper starts out as an ally, but not exactly a friendly one. Her "skewering" of Bond in their fabulous and memorable first meeting, in the dining car of the train to the Casino Royale in Montenegro, immediately makes her special. As portrayed by Eva Green, Vesper is certainly beautiful, but her primary appeal is verbal—she engages in repartee with Bond in a way normally reserved for Moneypenny. She "sizes him up" and takes him to task. So many women have fallen into James's willing arms, it's absolutely delightful to see a woman spar with him.

There is a lovely piece of foreshadowing as they prepare to go to the poker game. They're getting dressed, and Vesper is putting on her makeup. Her bare, vulnerable face shows us the vulnerability and bareness we will soon meet in earnest; in a way, it foretells the shower scene.

Yep, the shower scene. Traumatized and terrified—and not without reason—Vesper sits in the shower, fully clothed, trying to feel that the blood will wash away. Bond, seeing how shattered she is, joins her there. Together, fully clothed, soaking wet, they sit beneath the shower stream, and he holds her until she stops shivering, kissing her fingers. It is one of the finest scenes in any Bond movie, a masterful scene in *any* movie of any kind. It is romantic, tender, and compassionate. Later, Bond will say to Vesper that he has no armor because of her; here, she is the one without armor. It is also a 180 degree flip of what we know of her. We've seen her be prickly, smartass, and cool, but now we begin to see the complexity.

As Bond gets to know her, he knows she is a woman with a secret. He thinks the secret is her lover—the mysterious Algerian who gave her the necklace she wears. But we learn it is much darker than that—for the sake of that Algerian, she is the traitor who sells Bond out and then, hating herself for what she has done, and truly in love with Bond, she drowns herself.

As Blofeld says in *Spectre*, Vesper Lynd was "the one." For the Daniel Craig movies, she serves the function that Tracy served from *Diamonds Are Forever* all the way through *Die Another Day*; remembered, referenced, the dark cloud in Bond's heart.

More Girls We Love

As I've said before, it's hard to get Bond fans to agree. A top five list of favorite women leaves off many fan favorites. The following women tend to do well in "best Bond girl" surveys, and each of them is someone's number one. They're presented in chronological order, by movie.

37

Honey Ryder

Ursula Andress's iconic portrayal has lost a bit of cachet over the years. Younger fans may still adore Connery, but they connect to the girls on more of a gut level, and they prefer the ones that are part of their own era. Nonetheless, for an entire generation of men, Honey Ryder's exquisite, athletic body in a white bikini pretty much defined the possibilities of sex. And even for younger fans, there is no denying the primeval appeal of Honey's emergence from the sea, of her overwhelming beauty and the sense of power that emanates from her. I don't think a modern Bond girl would cling to 007's arm in fear as Honey does, yet no one would mistake her for meek.

Pussy Galore

Another knockout blonde, but of an entirely different sort, Pussy is the first Bond girl to meet 007 face to face, fight him, and then love him. Honor Blackman is also the first time a real star (of television's *The Avengers*) was cast as a Bond girl; Andress was cast in *Dr. No* based on a photograph, and Daniela Bianchi was a beauty queen. But for *Goldfinger*'s pivotal Pussy, the Bond producers wanted someone with more skill. She remains an unforgettable part of one of the most popular movies, of any sort, ever made.

Ian Fleming wrote Pussy as a lesbian gangster (not pilot) in **Goldfinger**. For the movie, director Guy Hamilton struggled to satisfy U.S. censors, while retaining enough innuendo to satisfy those in the know. Some say Pussy "converted" for James, but a single affair with an attractive man doesn't necessarily indicate a change in orientation. Some say Pussy changed sides because of Bond's sexual prowess (a charge answered by Fiona Volpe, who says—as quoted earlier—"James Bond, who only has to make love to a woman and she starts to hear heavenly choirs singing. She repents, and immediately returns to the side of right and virtue. But not this one"). But it is also possible that, given the opportunity that intimacy afforded, Bond was able to persuade Pussy that Goldfinger planned mass murder.

Fiona Volpe

Fiona is the prototype that allowed Xenia to exist. Dynamic, gorgeous, and utterly in command, she is the epitome of what a Bond villainess should be. Virtually all of the dialogue between Bond and Fiona is quotable, it crackles with a Howard Hawks kind of wit. Even before they sleep together, their encounters while driving, and when Fiona is in the bath, are edged with a smart sexuality. And when they finally do sleep together, the sex is some of the hottest seen in a Bond film. She runs a strong second on "bad girl" polls, and is a favorite of mine.

Aki

One of two Japanese agents romanced by Bond in *You Only Live Twice*, Aki is never given a last name. This is better than Kissy gets; the latter woman is never named at all—"Kissy" appears only in the credits. Kissy is the "Bond girl of record" in *You Only Live Twice*, the woman who ends up in Bond's arms at the end of the film, because Aki has been killed before the mission is completed. Yet Kissy makes less of an impression, and is not, in my opinion, nearly the beauty that Aki is.

For the record, Aki is the second female agent in the main body of a Bond film, and the first really important one (Paula Caplan is largely pushed aside in *Thunderball*). She gives Bond a run for his money—literally, as he chases her through the subway, not knowing he is being led into an embarrassing trap that will bring him to the underground offices of Tiger Tanaka. She delivers a sweet double entendre ("I think I shall enjoy very much working under you") and is one of the few Bond girls to have enough sense of self to have confidence about her relationship with James. It is a real pleasure when she calls Helga Brandt a "horrible girl" whom Bond wouldn't touch (even though she is only right about the "horrible" half of this).

Bond genuinely enjoys her presence. His happy cry of "Aki!" when they are reunited is full of affection, and he gives her a sweet look when he is told he must marry. He is angry at her murder; one of the more gruesome and tragic in the series.

Aki is rarely found on a favorites list, but she is on mine. I think this Bond girl, portrayed by Akiko Wakabayashi, deserves more credit than she gets.

Solitaire

Live and Let Die's psychic virgin is very popular among fans, although for the life of me I can't say why. Oh, I'll be fair. She's beautiful, she's exotic, and Jane Seymour is a fine actress. But the role is woefully underwritten. She is treated badly by Bond, and she has some of the worst costumes I've ever seen. Even Anya Amasova's head-cozy can't compare to Solitaire's draperies and plastered-on eye makeup. But she has a following. Go figure.

Naomi

Probably no Bond actress has made such a huge impact with so little screen-time as Caroline Munro in *The Spy Who Loved Me*. As Stromberg's pilot, she does little more than smile engagingly, wear a dynamite bikini, and flirt with Bond from afar in their battle to the death (which, of course, she loses). She never so much as kisses 007, yet many fans remember her fondly as a favorite Bond girl.

Melina Havelock and Countess Lisl Von Schlaf

For Your Eyes Only is an interesting film for Bond girls, having two fairly popular ones, neither of whom fit any standard Bond girl mold. (It also has one of the most hated Bond girls, as we'll see shortly.)

Carole Bouquet, playing Melina, was another gorgeous model-turned-actress, but she wasn't cast for her body. Her beauty is in her lovely eyes and stunning head of hair. Her figure is slender, not the buxom bikini-filling sort most Bond movies favor. In fact, the closest Melina gets to a bathing suit is a bikini bottom paired with a modest white blouse. Her revenge-driven character is hard, even stern, and often unsmiling. Unfortunately, this minimizes the chemistry between her and Bond, and their "darling" moment at the end feels tacked on. Still, Melina's striking appearance and emotional complexity win favor with many fans.

The Countess Lisl is the opposite—she is a character with very little back story, but loads of warmth. Also not a bathing beauty, she is more mature (twenty-nine when *For Your Eyes Only* was released, compared with Carole Bouquet's twenty-four and Lynn-Holly Johnson's twenty-three) with depth and experience in her eyes. It is this, I think, which gives her such wonderful chemistry with Bond; they feel like equals, even friends. Her death feels like a real loss, both to Bond and to us—I cannot help gasping whenever I see it.

Lisl also played an important role in Bond history. The actress who played her was Cassandra Harris, late wife of Pierce Brosnan. It was through Harris that Brosnan first met the Broccolis and landed on the list of potential future Bond actors.

Fatima Blush

Nearly as outrageous as Xenia Onatopp is the villainess from *Never Say Never Again*. Fatima Blush, played by Barbara Carrera, is gleeful, over-sexed, manic, and murderous. She also water skis. She wants to murder as much as possible, and have as much sex as possible, and if they coincide, so be it. The thing that always floors me about Fatima is her wardrobe. Balloon pants, strategically sliced barely-there blouses, capes, sequins—she is a freak show of '80s fashion excess, and she makes it look good. Fatima's ultimate demise is gruesomely funny, she is incinerated, leaving only a pair of high heels behind. Only *GoldenEye*'s Boris Grishenko has a funnier and more poetic death.

Natalya Fyodorovna Simonova

Speaking of *GoldenEye*, Bond's co-star in that film is very popular, especially among younger fans. Izabella Scorupco portrays a computer programmer inadvertently left alive by Xenia at Severnaya. She is more resourceful than the typical victim, however, and struggles to survive and help Bond throughout the film, in a way that is immensely sympathetic. She struggles even to reach Bond emotionally, demanding "How can you be so cold?" in one of Bond's rare scenes of personal revelation.

Natalya spends the first half of the film in a very dowdy outfit; realistic for a computer tech in a remote location, but disappointing to many viewers. She compensates by getting scantily glamorous in bikini and sarong when she accompanies Bond to the tropics.

Miranda Frost

It seems the way to achieve popularity in a Bond film is as a villainess, as most make a decent showing in "best" surveys, and few appear in "worst" surveys. Audiences seems to love the icy unapproachable beauty, the woman who is both seductive and coolly removed. No Bond girl is icier than the aptly named Miranda Frost; blonde, aloof, and at home in Gustav Graves's ice palace.

The two women of *Die Another Day* play off one another like chess pieces, with Halle Berry's Jinx, the black queen, and Rosamund Pike's Miranda, the white queen. Berry has said in interviews that the opposites thing worked so well that they kept emphasizing it, with Jinx becoming warmer and more streetwise, while Miranda became cooler and more posh.

Miranda's dialogue is certainly part of her appeal. From her cool reserve when she tells M that Bond is a "blunt instrument" to the moment of revelation when she says "It really is death for breakfast," Miranda's sharp tongue issues considerably more interesting bon mots than Jinx (see below). Pike must also be given credit for holding her own against such a seasoned cast. A mere twenty-three years old when *Die Another Day* was released, and in her first movie role, Pike was polished and effective in a cast that included two Oscar winners.

Solange

In her brief screentime in *Casino Royale*, Caterina Murino as Solange managed sexy, funny, playful, and melancholy. On horseback in a bikini, she made one of the most breathtaking entrances of any Bond character. Being a good actress helped, and being stunningly beautiful helped. Her death, when it came too soon, had real impact.

The Girls We Hate

It's not all sweetness and light in the world of Bond girls. There are, shall we put it gently, some casting mishaps from time to time; women who can't convince us they are the characters they are meant to portray. These are women who shriek; women whose appearance is so out of place, so ill-suited to a Bond movie, that we are baffled. "What were they thinking?" is the question you'll hear among fans.

Stacey Sutton

One of the common points that unites nearly all Bond fans is our hatred of *A View to a Kill*'s Stacey Sutton, played by Tanya Roberts in a Razzie-nominated "performance." To compile a list of worst Bond girls, one must either ask for the worst three, or ask for "worst other than Stacey," otherwise she'll "win" in an overwhelming sweep.

No one has ever shrieked more repetitively and unpleasantly than this character. The last time we watched *A View to a Kill*, my kid and I started playing "Shriek Along With Stacey" at about the halfway point, and our neighbors could probably hear us through the walls, yelling "JAMES! JAMES!" every time Stacey did.

Tanya Roberts simply does everything wrong. She is meant to be a geologist, and the daughter of a wealthy and educated man, yet her delivery swings from cool indifference, to helpless girl, to streetwise slang, without the professionalism or intelligence her role demands. She whines, she whimpers, and she can't act.

Stacey behaves foolishly throughout. Probably her most offensive behavior is screaming "James! Don't leave me!" in the burning elevator shaft. This when Bond is leaving in order to effect a rescue! Clearly, she would prefer they die together, rather than be left briefly alone so that Bond can save her.

Every now and then, someone will mention that Tanya Roberts is very pretty. Most of us are too busy covering our ears when another piercing "JAMES!" is released to notice.

Dr. Christmas Jones

As with Stacey, there is from time to time a fan who will defend Christmas Jones on the basis of the beauty of Denise Richards, the actress who played the part in *The World is Not Enough*. There is no doubt that one's babe factor increases hugely among a segment of male fans when one has a hot lesbian scene, as Richards did in *Wild Things*. Nonetheless, the great majority of fans deplore both her performance in *The World is Not Enough*, and the casting.

When *The World is Not Enough* was released, Ms. Richards was 28 years old, so let's say she was 27 during production. I'd guess 26 is the minimum age one could possibly be when possessing a Ph.D. in nuclear physics, and this particular physicist also speaks fluent Russian and has a position of authority in decommissioning a plant. On the face of it, it's ridiculous, and that's before we add that this young physicist is a babe in an itty-bitty outfit of tight t-shirt and shorts which displays her navel piercing. Somehow I, and just about every fan out there, thinks 'NOT!'

Denise Richards's Christmas Jones doesn't look, dress, act, or speak like a scientist. She is an ornament in a role which requires far more. She is also nearly twenty years younger than Pierce Brosnan, which is a tad discomfiting. The whole thing screams of a production decision to stick a hot babe in the film for the youth audience—self-conscious and self-defeating.

May Day

Grace Jones gave us a character in *A View to a Kill* who straddles two Bond types—the Bond girl and the henchman. As a Bond girl, she is a disaster; as a latter-day Jaws, she has real style. If they had simply kept her a villain, the character would have worked marvelously, but because she and Bond have a (stomach-turning) sex scene, she is often counted (and rejected) as a Bond girl.

May Day is a freakish woman, and she is played by an actress/singer who made her mark in the 80's by being freakish, and more than a little androgynous. As I said, this works for a villain, and is fabulous for a performance artist—while we are watching her kill, frighten horses, and leap off the Eiffel Tower, we can appreciate her presence. But then, after they have met and scowled at one another (she scowls, he smirks), Bond slips into May Day's bed to avoid being caught sneaking around Zorin's mansion. Now, this may be a clever way, on 007's part, to create a plausible excuse, but as a seduction technique, I find it offensive. If I were May Day and entered my room to find a man I disliked naked in my bed, I'd show him the door in short order. Does May Day, tougher and meaner than me by far, do so? No! She gets into bed with Bond in one of the grand *What are they thinking?* moments of Bond history.

Bibi Dahl

Shall we start with the name? There are obscene Bond girl names (Pussy Galore, Holly Goodhead), and ordinary Bond girl names (Kara Milovy, Anya Amasova), and then there are dumb Bond girl names. The name Bibi Dahl (Baby Doll) is one of the dumb ones. (The other really dumb name is Jenny Flex—most people don't even realize it's a play on "genuflect" when they first hear it.)

Oh, let's skip the name, and move right to the character. Lynn-Holly Johnson's acting abilities are pretty limited, and her shrill, irritating character certainly gives her no chance to show she can do better.

What the heck is she there for anyway? She doesn't drive *For Your Eyes Only*'s plot in any meaningful way. She isn't a love interest, she isn't even all that pretty. She is an annoying child, the Wesley Crusher of Bond films (as Trekkers would say). Rumor has it that she was cast for her skating ability—Cubby Broccoli was impressed by her in *Ice Castles* (her first movie after leaving pro skating to act). If that's the case, then the role suffers from poor directing, because we see very little skating in the film.

Rosie Carver

The other Bond girl from *Live and Let Die* comes in for a lot of fan wrath. She is part of a series of early 70's Bond girls, (from *Diamonds Are Forever, Live and Let Die,* and *The Man with the Golden Gun*) who act, at least some of the time, like idiots or pawns. Bond's first liaison with an African-American woman was meant to break down a barrier, but the character played by Gloria Hendry was by turns so stupid, so superstitious, and so foolish, that she did little except irritate the audience. Her wide-eyed terror at a voodoo sign, and her inability to function even minimally as a CIA agent are bad enough, but when revealed as a traitor, her expectation that Bond will treat her gently because they have made love is unfathomable.

Rosie's scenes were written so that her affair with Bond could be removed from the film without harming the continuity of the story. In 1973, the Bond producers still had reason to fear that there were theaters in the U.S. that would be unwilling to show the movie without editing out something so shocking. As it turned out, most fans are happy that Gloria Hendry's role can be easily forgotten, for reasons having nothing whatsoever to do with race.

The Girls We Both Love And Hate

This last group of Bond girls are those who prove the adage "it takes all kinds to make a world." All of the following characters appear on various fan "best" and "worst" lists (although not the same fans). Beloved by some, they are despised by others, often because fans view the characters through different lenses, or judge by different standards.

Tiffany Case

It's possible that the reason fans are of two minds about *Diamonds Are Forever*'s Tiffany is that she is very nearly two different women. She is introduced as a smooth, self-sufficient diamond smuggler who takes no guff from Bond ("I don't dress for the hired help"). It's really a terrific entrance, sexy, amusing, and a bit startling. Bond is impressed, and so are we.

When Tiffany, played by Jill St. John, decides to show Bond her softer side, it is for her own reasons, when she determines it is in her best interest. In fact, there is a certain amorality about Tiffany that is delightful, she changes sides freely to save her hide, all the while smiling sweetly as if to say "Can you blame me?"

Where most fans lose her is in the final act. She screws up switching the villain's data tape for a music tape, prompting Bond to call her a "stupid twit" when he realizes she's undone his effort and put the data back into the computer. Then she cannot handle the retort of a machine gun and falls into the water. An awful lot of fans agree with Bond's assessment, and call Tiffany a bimbo, an idiot, and worse. I feel the poor woman gets a bad rap. The switch was vague—Bond gave Tiffany a tape without telling her he'd already switched tapes. She risked her neck to switch them thinking that was the right thing to do.

Some fans, like me, feel her early performance is so strong that they forgive her later failures. Others can't stand her. Many complain about Jill St. John's acting, but I think her naturalism is very refreshing compared to the amateurish stiffness ("Look at me, I'm acting!") that Bond girls sometimes evidence (Talisa Soto, anyone?).

Mary Goodnight

Poor Mary! Locked in a car trunk, stuffed in a closet, and forced to wear a baby-doll nightie—how can fans love someone with such an utter lack of dignity? Well, most don't—she's rather widely hated. But if you're played by the delicious Britt Ekland, many fans will forgive you. And many do see Goodnight as a good Bond girl suffering under a bad script. *The Man with the Golden Gun* is despised by many people, and some fans consider it the worst Bond film—yet Christopher Lee's Scaramanga is considered a great villain. Why then shouldn't Ekland get a break? Well, some fans think she should, but many pair her with Tiffany Case in the bimbo category.

Paris Carver

Great character, bad actress. Fans disagree on *Tomorrow Never Dies*'s Paris because they judge by different standards. There is no doubt that Teri Hatcher completely failed to deliver her dialogue in a persuasive manner. Yet the idea of a woman from Bond's past, still in love with him yet married to another man, has a romantic appeal. Too bad the casting department blew it.

Tatiana (Tanya) Romanova and Kara Milovy

I group these two women together because in movies twenty-four years apart, they are similar characters who garner similar fan reaction.

Tatiana is the Russian clerk in *From Russia with Love* who is manipulated by SPECTRE. She believes she is serving her country when she pretends to have fallen in love with Bond from afar. Eventually, she really does fall in love with him.

Kara, in *The Living Daylights*, is a Czechoslovakian cellist who is also manipulated by the villain. She believes she is posing as a KGB sniper to lend credibility to her lover's defection. Instead she is a pawn in a complex scheme meant to leave her dead.

Both women are beautiful and appealing. The acting in both roles, by Daniela Bianchi and Maryam d'Abo, is rather good. Both are portrayed with a sort of feminine delicacy, a sweetness, an innocence of the dangerous world they have unwittingly entered. And this is precisely the problem. A lot of fans, especially younger ones, are turned off by these "wimpy" women. They are more accustomed to strong, action-oriented heroines, especially in Bond movies. Neither Tanya nor Kara has the least capacity to kick ass, and Bond needs, in both cases, to guide, help, and scold each of them. For some fans, this is realistic and endearing. For others, it is an irritation.

Kara is one of my personal favorite characters, and Tatiana is the favorite of a good friend of mine, who more or less worships her, although this hasn't interfered with his life, as far as I know.

Dr. Holly Goodhead

I struggle to understand Holly Goodhead's appeal. Is it her wooden acting, her lack of chemistry with James Bond, or her general bitchiness that some fans find so attractive? I'll never know. Many fans feel as I do about the CIA operative played by Lois Chiles in *Moonraker*, but others adore her, finding her sexy and entertaining. Her hideous final line, "Take me around the world one more time" is thought clever and naughty by some. Not me.

Colonel Wai Lin

Michelle Yeoh was already famous for her martial arts films when *Tomorrow Never Dies* was made, although she had yet to achieve the wider acclaim and attention she found in *Crouching Tiger, Hidden Dragon*. Nonetheless, many fans complain that her role in the movie is "too equal" with Bond's; she even has a solo fight scene. With fans, you can't win sometimes! They complain that my beloved Kara is too weak, and then that Wai Lin is too strong. Some fans find her unattractive, and many complain that she and Bond have no chemistry together, and their "Oh James" moment is tacked on and merely obligatory. With this last complaint, I agree. Wai Lin and Bond come to respect and, eventually, enjoy one another over the course of the film, but there is no evidence of heat between them until suddenly we see them snuggling up. The other complaints I find unimpressive. Yeoh's fighting skills are awesome and deserve the extra screen time they're given. She is an expressive actress who conveys great depth through her eyes. I enjoy her presence.

Giacinta (Jinx) Johnson

If fans complained about Yeoh's fight scene, you should have seen them go at Halle Berry's shared billing in the *Die Another Day* advertising! Berry was cast as Jinx (pre-release information had her character's last name as Jordan) before she won her Best Actress Oscar for *Monster's Ball*, but MGM would have been crazy not to take advantage of her acclaim. Fans, on the other hand, want a Bond movie's advertising to feature...Bond. So Jinx was controversial even before *Die Another Day* was released.

It's no surprise that the controversy continued when the movie opened. On the one hand, Halle Berry is a woman of extraordinary beauty, and her *Dr. No* homage, emerging from the sea in a bikini with a knife belt, is entirely worthy of the Ursula Andress original. Her character was fresh and cheerful. She didn't compete with Bond, or snap at him, she just went about her business and always seemed glad to see him; the first female agent since XXX to have no defensiveness about being both female and an agent, Berry has terrific screen presence, and a natural grace that is more than physical.

On the other hand, much of the character's dialogue was disappointingly cliché, or downright awful. As one fan put it, "It would be great, just once, to see a fight between two women in which one doesn't call the other 'Bitch.'" The "Yo' momma" and "you're a big boy" remarks were equally trite and unnecessary. Miranda Frost had much the better dialogue of the two. According to action aficionados, Berry was also unconvincing in action scenes, and when holding/firing a gun. I confess I am not enough an expert on gunplay to see much flaw.

People tend to react most strongly to the movie they've just seen, so in the weeks following *Die Another Day*'s release, Jinx appeared on several "worst" lists and a few "best" lists. (In subsequent years, fan opinion has dropped, and I no longer find her on "best" lists).

The Complete List

For those of you with a passion for completeness, here is a comprehensive list of Bond girls and actresses by movie. All characters listed had dialogue and/or a sexual encounter (consummated or not) with Bond.

Dr. No (Sexual encounters: 3)

> **Sylvia Trench** (Eunice Gayson)
> **Photographer** (Marguerite LeWars, a.k.a. Margaret LeWars)
> **Honey Ryder** (Ursula Andress)
> **Miss Taro** (Zena Marshall)

From Russia with Love (Sexual encounters: 4)

> **Sylvia Trench** (Eunice Gayson)
> **Tatiana (Tanya) Romanova** (Daniela Bianchi)
> **Vida the Gypsy girl** (Aliza Gur)
> **Zora the Gypsy girl** (Martine Beswick)

Goldfinger (Sexual encounters: 3)

> **Bonita,** the dancer from the pre-titles sequence (Nadja Regin)
> **Dink** (Margaret Nolan)
> **Jill Masterson** (Shirley Eaton)
> **Tilly Masterson** (Tania Mallet)
> **Mei-Lei** (Mai Ling)
> **Pussy Galore** (Honor Blackman)

Thunderball (Sexual encounters: 3)

> **Mademoiselle LaPorte,** the French agent (Mitsouko)
> **Patricia Fearing** (Molly Peters)
> **Fiona Volpe** (Luciana Paluzzi)
> **Dominique (Domino) Derval** (Claudine Auger)
> **Paula Caplan** (Martine Beswick)

You Only Live Twice (Sexual encounters: 4)

> **Ling** (Tsai Chin)
> **Aki** (Akiko Wakabayashi)
> **Kissy** (Mie Hama)
> **Helga Brandt** (Karin Dor)

On Her Majesty's Secret Service (Sexual encounters: 3)

> **Contessa Teresa (Tracy) di Vicenzo** (Diana Rigg)

Ruby Bartlett (Angela Scoular)
Nancy, the German girl (Catherine Von Schell)

Diamonds Are Forever (Sexual encounters: 1)

Marie, the topless girl in the pre-titles sequence (Denise Perrier)
Tiffany Case (Jill St. John)
Plenty O'Toole (Lana Wood)
*Bambi (Lola Larson)
Thumper (Trina Parks)

* Many sources wrongly list Bambi as Donna Garrett. Garrett was originally signed to play the role but was replaced. The *Diamonds Are Forever* DVD has footage of both women as Bambi, and it is clear that the actress in the movie is Larson.

Live and Let Die (Sexual encounters: 3)

Miss Caruso, the Italian agent (Madeline Smith)
Rosie Carver (Gloria Hendry)
Solitaire (Jane Seymour)

The Man with the Golden Gun (Sexual encounters: 2)

Saida, the belly dancer (Carmen Sautoy)
Chu Mee (Francoise Therry)
Andrea Anders (Maud Adams)
Mary Goodnight (Britt Ekland)

The Spy Who Loved Me (Sexual encounters: 3)

Log Cabin Girl (Sue Vanner)
Felicca, the woman at Fekkish's home (Olga Bisera)
Anya Amasova, Agent XXX (Barbara Bach)
*Egyptian treasure (Dawn Rodriques)
Naomi (Caroline Munro)
Hotel Receptionist (Valerie Leon)

* Four women are listed as "Arab beauty" in *The Spy Who Loved Me*'s end credits. Ms. Rodrigues is the one who offered a rose, and herself, to Bond, causing him to reply "When one is in Egypt, one should delve deeply into its treasures." Hence I list her as "Egyptian treasure."

Moonraker (Sexual encounters: 3)

Private Jet Hostess (Leila Shenna)
Corinne Dufour (Corinne Clery)
Dr. Holly Goodhead (Lois Chiles)
Manuela (Emily Bolton)

For Your Eyes Only (Sexual encounters: 2)

Melina Havelock (Carol Bouquet)
Countess Lisl Von Schlaf (Cassandra Harris)
Bibi Dahl (Lynn-Holly Johnson)

Octopussy (Sexual encounters: 3)

Miss Penelope Smallbone (Michaela Clavell)
Bianca, the Caribbean agent (Tina Hudson)

Magda (Kristina Wayborn)
Octopussy (Maud Adams)

Never Say Never Again (Sexual encounters: 4)

Patricia Fearing (Prunella Gee)
Domino Petachi (Kim Basinger)
Fatima Blush (Barbara Carrera)
Fishing Boat Woman (Valerie Leon)
Nicole, Agent 326 (Saskia Cohen Tanugi)

A View to a Kill (Sexual encounters: 4)

Kimberly Jones, the iceberg/submarine captain (Mary Stavin)
Jenny Flex (Alison Doody)
May Day (Grace Jones)
Stacey Sutton (Tanya Roberts)
Pola Ivanova (Fiona Fullerton)

The Living Daylights (Sexual encounters: 2)

Linda, the bored woman on a yacht (Kell Tyler)
Kara Milovy (Maryam d'Abo)

Licence to Kill (Sexual encounters: 2)

Lupe Lamora (Talisa Soto)
Pam Bouvier (Carey Lowell)
Della Churchill Leiter (Priscilla Barnes)

GoldenEye (Sexual encounters: 2)

Caroline, the psychologist/psychiatrist (Serena Gordon)
Xenia Zaragevna Onatopp (Famke Janssen)
Natalya Fyodorovna Simonova (Izabella Scorupco)

Tomorrow Never Dies (Sexual encounters: 3)

Prof. Inga Bergstrom (Cecile Thomsen)
Paris Carver (Teri Hatcher)
Colonel Wai Lin (Michelle Yeoh)

The World is Not Enough (Sexual encounters: 3)

Dr. Molly Warmflash (Serena Scott Thomas)
Elektra King (Sophie Marceau)
Dr. Christmas Jones (Denise Richards)

Die Another Day (Sexual encounters: 2)

Peaceful Fountains of Desire (Rachel Grant)
Giacinta (Jinx) Johnson (Halle Berry)
Miranda Frost (Rosamund Pike)

Casino Royale (Sexual encounters: 1)

Vesper Lynd (Eva Green)
Solange (Caterina Murino)

Quantum of Solace (Sexual encounters: 1)

Camille Montes (Olga Kurylenko)
Strawberry Fields (Gemma Arterton)

Skyfall (Sexual encounters: 3)

"Bond's lover" (Tonia Sotiropoulou)

Eve Moneypenny (Naomie Harris)

Severine (Bérénice Lim Marlohe)

Spectre (Sexual encounters: 3)

Estrella (Stephanie Sigman)

Lucia Sciarra (Monica Bellucci)

Madeline Swann (Léa Seydoux)

No Time to Die (Sexual encounters: unknown)

Paloma (Ana de Armas)

Madeline Swann (Léa Seydoux)

Nomi (Lashana Lynch)

FROM RUSSIA WITH LOVE (1963)

Survey Says!

Percent Favorite 14%
Top 5 Cumulative: 2/25
Numeric Rating: 8.5/10
Ranking: 5.8 (2nd/25)

My Rating and Ranking

Rated: 10/10
Ranked: 1 out of 25

Summary

SPECTRE returns, and we "meet" Blofeld (his arms and cat, anyway). In a plot conceived by chessmaster Kronsteen, Bond and Russian cipher clerk Romanova are brought together to steal the Lektor decoder. Romanova believes she is working for Mother Russia by posing as a woman ready to defect for the love of an agent whose photograph she has seen. Bond cooperates with her to get the Lektor, but both are being manipulated by SPECTRE, which plans to kill them, steal the device, and create a sex scandal. Bond defeats the murderous Grant, but is nearly defeated by Klebb, until Romanova shoots her, choosing love over country.

James Bond: Sean Connery
Tatiana "Tanya" Romanova: Daniela Bianchi
Rosa Klebb (SPECTRE #3): Lotte Lenya
Donald "Red" Grant: Robert Shaw
Ernst Stavro Blofeld: Anthony Dawson, voice of Eric Pohlmann
Kronsteen (SPECTRE #5): Vladek Shaybal
Kerim Bey: Pedro Armendariz
Morzeny: Walter Gotell
M: Bernard Lee
Moneypenny: Lois Maxwell
Q: Desmond Llewelyn
Directed by Terence Young

Discussion

From Russia with Love is the greatest Bond film for three reasons: villainy, sex, and adventure. These vital components are all at perfect pitch. Add to this magnificent locations and a superb cast, and you have a Bond movie that will probably never be topped.

In terms of villainy, we first meet the ice-cold Robert Shaw, playing Donald Grant; forty years later he's still one of Bond's most threatening foes. An ordinary man on the surface, he is as deadly and dangerous as the bizarre and apparently superhuman villains who will come later, such as Oddjob and Jaws. The scene on SPECTRE Island, of Grant leaping to attention, and Rosa Klebb punching him swiftly with brass knuckles, is chilling and memorable—who among us didn't wince? This is a man of steel, and we already know he has been training to kill 007.

Figure 3: Replica of the photo of Tanya that Moneypenny gives to Bond. A gift to the author from David Zaritsky (see Resources*).*

The Bond formula, which will finally gel with *Goldfinger*, adds two vital components in *From Russia with Love*: The pre-titles sequence and Desmond Llewelyn as Q.

For the first time, we see a pre-titles sequence in a James Bond movie; the mini-drama, part of the plot or not, that has opened Bond films ever since. In this first one, Grant is a silent stalker. He remains silent through most of the rest of the movie, shadowing Bond, appearing wherever Bond appears, and committing seven separate murders. When he finally opens his mouth to speak, we have no idea what to expect but we are primed to listen, which is part of what makes his seven minutes of dialogue so riveting.

Rosa Klebb herself, portrayed by the great Lotte Lenya, is creepy, frightening, ugly, cruel, and bizarre. The small, "toadlike" female villain was a favorite of Fleming's, and will reappear in *On Her Majesty's Secret Service* in the form of Irma Bunt. But Klebb is better; scarier, weirder, and by virtue of the chronology of films, more original.

The bad guy contingent is filled out by the chilling first appearance of the unseen Blofeld and his white cat, the evil chessmaster Kronsteen, and Morzeny, the oddly cheerful head of SPECTRE island operations (he is played by Walter Gotell, who will later become a Bond regular as General Gogol). There has never been a more villainous Bond film.

For sex, we have a very racy plot for its day, one that is still titillating all these years later. We join Bond in a somewhat weak scene with Sylvia Trench; it is interesting primarily in that it is the only romantic liaison in 007 history that continues for more than one film. (As of this writing—although Léa Seydoux is back for *No Time to Die*, we do not yet know if the romantic aspect of her relationship with Bond resumes in that film. From the previews, it appears that it does, so Sylvia will probably lose her "only" status)

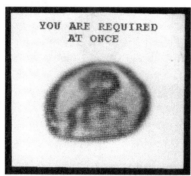

Figure 4: Replica of the note found by Kronsteen at the bottom of his drinking glass.

The entire plot drives on sex—Tatiana says she will betray her country if Bond will sleep with her, believing that her country has ordered her to do this. Both SPECTRE and MI6 send off agents to have sex with the enemy in the name of country or cause. In the novel, Bond refers to himself rather glumly as a "pimp for England." As if that wasn't sufficient, SPECTRE's real goal is two-fold—steal the Lektor, and create a scandal. To that end, the bridal suite tryst between James and Tanya is secretly filmed, adding voyeurism to the sexual stew.

In Tanya, we have a rare instance of a woman falling for Bond for a reason. At first she is indifferent to Bond, merely following orders. By the next morning, her feelings are entirely changed, and she begs for Bond's constant lovemaking. The suggestion is that she was won by Bond's sexual prowess and...ahem...equipment (see BOND'S BEST GADGET). This is heady stuff.

Finally, take a look at the meeting between Rosa Klebb and Tatiana, their frank discussion of sex, and Klebb's roving hands. In the novel, Klebb's pass at Tanya was far more vulgar and humiliating; 1963-era censorship required more subtlety, and the movie actually benefits from this, as the original scene was grotesque. As played in the movie, Klebb's treatment of Tanya is the slimy manipulation by a superior of a helpless underling, whereas in the book, it was more of a freak show.

Let's not forget adventure. Bond travels to exotic locations (primarily Turkey, but also Venice), and rides the famed Orient Express. The location footage is gritty and real, not just the exotic beauty of minarets and mosques, but the side streets, the catacombs, the little apartment where Tanya meets Rosa Klebb—these aren't from a travel brochure, and they impart the odor of authenticity.

The adventure builds slowly, bringing more tension than action in the first half, but with never a dull moment. All of the fight scenes in *From Russia with Love* are way above average. Consider: The gypsy camp fight, a mass of chaos in which we can nonetheless follow everything that's happening (always a challenge in large-scale battles, one that is not always successfully met); the ground-breaking fight between Bond and Grant on the Orient Express, a justly- famous scene that uses dim lighting, smoke (the remains of the exploded tear- gas canister), sound effects, and Peter Hunt's innovative editing style to create heart-stopping combat between a powerful hero and an equally powerful killer; the *North by Northwest* homage—a helicopter chase that ends with a real bang—and the final battle with Rosa Klebb, her poisoned shoe (fatal in 12 seconds) and general deadliness made even more strange by the maid's uniform and wig. These action sequences are all excellent. The gypsy fight is amusing, with Bond staying relatively unengaged. It forms a strong contrast with his hand-to-hand fight to the death with Grant; one is large, one intimate, one is fun, the other deadly serious. The other two scenes also form an interesting pair of opposites; Bond against a machine much larger than himself, and Bond against a woman much smaller than himself. In the first of each pair, there is lots of room; the entire gypsy camp and the hills across which Bond runs, in the second, there is confinement; the small train compartments and the hotel room.

From Russia with Love is also a movie that values actors. For many years, the Bond films were cast based on looks, or oddities—anything but talent. It's only in the Brosnan era that they got back to giving important secondary roles to talented people, returning to the values of the earliest Bond films. Shaw and Lenya were top talent and Pedro Armendariz had a fine reputation.

Daniela Bianchi is wonderful despite her inexperience. She is beautiful and sexy, both innocent and worldly, and she unmistakably enjoys herself. And, O that neck ribbon! What is it about that accessory that makes a woman so desirable? Is it gift wrap, telling you that if you untie the bow, the package is yours? Is it both collar and leash, and the woman a willing slave? Is it a dividing line, between mind and body, human and animal; between the tense flirtation above its line, and the naked and willing body below?

From Russia with Love emphasizes the animalistic nature of fear and sex. The Siamese fighting fish and the rats—both terrific scenes—serve to illustrate the human behavior in the film; nothing overdone or arty, just a natural comparison by placing fearsome animals in the right places—in other words, good writing.

The High Points

- The location footage, especially Istanbul.
- The ensemble cast, notably Armendariz, Shaw, Lenya, and Bianchi, as well as regulars Connery, Bernard Lee, and Lois Maxwell.
- The introduction of Desmond Llewelyn to the series.
- Bond's warm friendship with Kerim Bey.
- The amused attitude towards espionage in Turkey; Bulgars following Kerim Bey's son, Kerim spying from below on the Russians, "very friendly."
- The fight on the Orient Express between Bond and Grant—still often cited as one of the finest hand-to-hand combats in movie history!
- The delightful and innovative titles by Robert Brownjohn.

- The lush John Barry score. Many wonderful musical touches including the blending of the title song with the James Bond Theme, the introduction of the 007 Theme, the emulation in the score of train sounds during the Orient Express sequence, the musical punctuation used perfectly in the pre-titles sequence, and much more.
- The highly erotic first meeting of Bond and Tatiana; she slipping naked into his bed, that exquisite black ribbon about her neck and nothing else, while they demurely shake hands and engage in sensual repartee.
- A consistent plot that holds together and makes sense.

The Low Points

- The gypsy girl fight is a tad gratuitous, and a bit prejudicial about gypsies. (All of it comes straight out of the novel.)
- Tanya is a little too dumb and innocent. For example, hearing the porter say that Kerim Bey has been in a terrible accident, she asks if they're still going to dinner.
- Some of the back projection is just terrible, and Bond's hand waving good-bye as "The End" appears is particularly bad.
- • Matt Munro's merely adequate vocals on the equally adequate lyrics for the title song.

Quotable Quotes

(Following the explosion in Kerim's office):
Kerim: "The girl left in hysterics."
Bond: "Find your technique too violent?"

Bond (looking at Tatiana's legs): "From this angle, things are shaping up nicely."

Tanya: "Careful! Guns upset me."
Bond: "I'm a bit...uh...upset myself."

Tanya: "I think my mouth is too big."
Bond: "No, it's the right size. For me, that is."

Krilencu escapes from his apartment through Anita Ekberg's mouth (see AMAZE YOUR FRIENDS!) and is shot by Kerim Bey.
Bond: "She should have kept her mouth shut."

Bond: "Red wine with fish, well, that should have told me something."
Grant: "You may know the right wines (but) you're the one on your knees."

Grant: "The first one won't kill you, nor the second. Not even the third—not 'til you crawl over here and kiss my foot!"

Bond (death quip for Klebb): "She's had her kicks."

Facts and Figures

SEXUAL ENCOUNTERS

<u>Four</u>: Sylvia Trench, Tatiana, and Vida and Zora (the gypsy girls).

BOND'S CAR

A dark green vintage Bentley (Bond's personal car in the novels). This is seen parked while Bond picnics with Sylvia Trench.

DEATHS

<u>Approximately twenty-six</u>:

- The seven killed by Grant, in order: The Bond-substitute in the pre-titles sequence, the Bulgarian spy following Bond from the airport, the man about to kill Bond during the gypsy battle, the Bulgarian spy in the Mosque of St. Sophia, Kerim Bey and Benz (the man with Kerim), and Captain Nash, whom he then impersonates.
- Kronsteen, Krilencu, Grant, Klebb, two men in the helicopter.
- There are twelve men in the boat chase; four per boat, at least four die, including Morzeny.
- During the gypsy camp battle, we see Bond shoot five successfully, and fire six more times. We see four others fall from gunfire (not counting the one Grant kills), and a great deal of gunfire that we don't see hit its target. We don't know how many of the fallen die or are wounded, but if we count all visible hits as deaths, the total is nine.

Bond Kills

- <u>Six</u> directly (Grant and five at the gypsy camp)
- <u>Six</u> indirectly (four in the boat chase, two in the helicopter—he wounds one of the men in the helicopter, who drops a grenade)

EXPLOSIONS

<u>Five</u>: Two really good ones—the helicopter goes up with a satisfying BOOM, and Morzeny's boat, already on fire, goes up when the fire reaches the ammunition. A so-so display when the helicopter drops a grenade on the flower truck. Two off-screen explosions (we see rubble and hear noise), first at Kerim Bey's office, second at the Russian embassy.

BOND'S FOOD AND DRINKS

Vodka Martinis

One, approximately. There is a martini shaker visible when Bond is with Sylvia. We don't know how many martinis either has had, or if they were vodka martinis.

Other Drinks

- A bottle of champagne is chilling in the river when Bond is with Sylvia. We'll never know if they had a chance to drink it.

- Raki at the gypsy camp.
- Blanc de Blanc champagne with dinner on the Orient Express.
- Champagne with breakfast in Venice. According to the Minister of Martinis, "At Bond's hotel room in Venice, he and Tatiana are eating breakfast outside. There are two bottles on the table, appearing to be champagne and vermouth (possibly Cinzano). Bond and Tatiana have glasses of orange juice, so it is possible they're having mimosas."

Food

- The contents of Bond and Sylvia's picnic basket cannot be seen.
- Green figs, yogurt, and black coffee ordered at the hotel in Istanbul.
- Grilled sole on the Orient Express.
- Breakfast at the hotel in Venice contains at least bread and orange juice, the rest of the table is obscured.

GAMBLING AND SPORTS

Bond doesn't participate in any. He rests with Sylvia while another couple goes by in a boat, and the man poling the boat says, "Great sport this punting." Sylvia responds "I may even give up golf for it."

Amaze Your Friends!

- Sylvia Trench was intended as a recurring character. At the beginning of each movie, she was to be interrupted during a tryst with Bond when he is called away to that film's mission. The actress, Eunice Gayson, was a friend of director Terence Young's. When Young did not return for *Goldfinger*, Sylvia was written out.
- Two of the women in this movie will appear in later Bond films, as different characters. Nadja Regin, who plays Kerim Bey's girlfriend (the one who left in hysterics), will be back in *Goldfinger* as Bonita. Martine Beswick, who plays Zora, one of the wrestling gypsies, will appear in *Thunderball* as Paula Caplan.
- When Tanya sneaks into Bond's bed, she really is nude, but it isn't Daniela Bianchi. They used a body double.
- The movie poster that hides Krilencu's escape route is for *Call Me Bwana*, starring Anita Ekberg. This was an inside joke; the movie was produced by Saltzman and Broccoli. In the novel, the movie was *Niagara* and Krilencu crawled through Marilyn Monroe's mouth.

Most Interesting Goofs

The Agent of Choice: Kronsteen tells Blofeld that the person MI6 will "almost certainly use in a mission of this sort will be their agent James Bond." Almost certainly? The operation is designed so that Bond is specifically requested!

The Flooded Bridal Suite: Bond starts his bath, hears a noise, goes to investigate, finds Tanya in his bed, speaks with her, and kisses her. Fade to black. The bath is still running.

ALLIES

Despite his stern proclamation in *Licence to Kill* that "I work better alone,"James Bond has generally had one or more significant allies on each of his adventures. These allies can be...

- The staff of MI6
- Allies who are also Bond girls
- Other allies, usually male, who appear for one or a few films.

MI6 will be covered later, and Bond girls have already been discussed, so let's focus on the last category.

Ian Fleming was fond of father figures, and his books featured several allies that were older than Bond, whom he respected, admired, and sometimes loved. In addition to M, the one-shot allies who fit this mold were Kerim Bey (*From Russia with Love*—known as Darko Kerim in the novel), Marc Ange Draco (*On Her Majesty's Secret Service*), and Tiger Tanaka (*You Only Live Twice*). These men were affable, expansive, and strong. All were natural leaders—Kerim was the head of Section T (Turkey), Draco was head of the Union Corse (a Sicilian criminal organization), and Tiger was the head of the Japanese Secret Service. In this manner, all served as counterparts to M in their own realm. Columbo (*For Your Eyes Only*) might have been such a father figure with a different cast, but, although Topol did a wonderful job in the role, he is eight years younger than Roger Moore!

(In the Craig era, René Mathis fits the father figure mold.)

The amiable father isn't the only ally "type." There are comrades such as Felix Leiter, who provide support in the field. Sometimes such a comrade is incredibly bland, and really does nothing except provide that support—John Terry's portrayal of Felix in *The Living Daylights* was so neutral that many fans forget Felix even appeared in that film. Other times, an ally can function as a foil, a straight man, or a contrast to 007. An ally can also provide local "color," and a native point of view. Some allies function as comic relief, although mostly such characters are unpopular with the fans.

The Felix Factor

Ian Fleming introduced Felix Leiter in the very first James Bond novel, **Casino Royale**. Bond's CIA liaison was described as a lanky, blond Texan with a hawk-like face. Leiter is tough on the inside but the exterior is casually sarcastic and extremely loquacious. Fleming used Felix to describe all manner of details to Bond and the reader, and it was from him that we learned the rules of blackjack, the history of Saratoga Springs, the reasoning behind extra large olives used by hotel bars, and a great deal more. Infinitely friendly, Felix was cheerful in rattling off long lists of things he disliked, mostly various rules, regulations, and customs in the U.S. that baffled Ian Fleming. Felix lost an arm and a leg, and suffered damage to his face, in **Live and Let Die** , the second Bond novel—the same attack wouldn't occur in the movies until *Licence to Kill*. Bond noted with pleasure and relief that Felix was not embittered by his loss; he remained a basically good-humored person, and wasn't averse to joking about the effects his hook hand had on the ladies.

Not only did he appear in the first novel, Felix also showed up in the first movie; *Dr. No*. There was no part for him in either the book or movie of *From Russia with Love*. The story goes that when *Goldfinger* was in preproduction, Jack Lord was contacted to reprise his role as Felix. Eon considered Lord's salary demands unreasonably high, and figured that having the same actor return to the role wasn't that important. Instead, the device used in *Dr. No* became standard, and in movie after movie, a mysterious stranger hanging around Bond, who may be an ally or a foe, turns out to be Felix. In each of Felix's films, from *Goldfinger* through *The Living Daylights* (*Licence to Kill* is the exception), a different actor portrays Felix, and each time we are left to wonder who this stranger is, until Bond greets him as his old buddy. From 1962 through 2006, Leiter appeared in eight films, and was portrayed by seven different actors.

Fans regularly bemoaned Felix's absence from the Brosnan films (he never worked with Pierce Brosnan's Bond on a case), and wished he would return. Their wish was granted with the release of 2006's *Casino Royale*, in which is he is portrayed by Emmy- and Golden Globe-winner Jeffrey Wright. His injuries in *Licence to Kill* would preclude him from active field agent status in the CIA, but the "reboot" (See Casino Royale) erased that problem.

With Brosnan, Eon seemed bent on replacing Leiter with a new U.S. contact. The first such attempt was Jack Wade, played by Joe Don Baker in *GoldenEye* and *Tomorrow Never Dies*. I found Wade to be a delightful character. Both Wade and Zukovsky prove you can have a comic quality without being a fool. Wade's laid back, good ol' boy attitude struck some fans as very un-CIA, but I relished it. Here's a guy who can do his job, and do it well ("Yo, Marines!" had a laudatory effect), without being another humorless CIA stereotype. He was somewhat more clownish in his second appearance, and turned some fans off, but many, including me, would have welcomed his return.

It seems that Jack Wade had been phased out by *The World is Not Enough*, and in *Die Another Day*, Bond was teamed with the National Security Agency rather than the CIA. Numerous fans have pointed out that this is a gaffe—the NSA is the intelligence branch that specializes in codes and cryptology, and doesn't use field agents. Meanwhile, Michael Madsen, playing Damien Falco of the NSA, seemed positioned to be Bond's new U.S. ally. He wasn't popular with the fans, though, and his sour, "I don't like you" demeanor suggests an American cop movie with bickering partners, rather than a James Bond adventure.

Here's a highly subjective rundown of the Felix Leiter portrayals:

JACK LORD, *Dr. No*

The "Book him, Danno" style that Lord brings to the part has a classic spy feel, but not much personality. Lord's approach is "I'm gruff, I'm tough, I'm an American agent." It definitely has appeal, but it certainly isn't the Felix that Ian Fleming wrote about, the guy who would give a ten minute lecture on the perfect martini. That Felix was a real friend as well as an ally, and had none of Lord's grim formality.

CEC LINDER, *Goldfinger*

Remarkably, Jack Lord is a year older than Cec Linder, yet Felix in *Goldfinger* has, to all appearances, moved from hotshot man of action to crusty old guy in ill-fitting suit. Cec Linder seems less a CIA agent than the sort of middle- aged police chief of a mid-sized city seen on so much network television. He is the least competent Felix, completely incapable of providing any support for Bond for most of the picture. He fails to be alarmed at Bond's disappearance, or respond to his signal (although M is equally guilty, it is Felix who is in the field). He makes himself painfully, almost childishly obvious to Auric Goldfinger when spying on him, making the CIA itself seem amateurish. On the bright side, he at least manages to make smarmy jokes about Bond's drinking and womanizing; over and over, in case we didn't get it the first time.

RIK VAN NUTTER, *Thunderball*

Often cited as the worst Felix, Van Nutter is the actor who most resembles Fleming's descriptions of the lanky blond Texan. Fans who love the Fleming novels love this about Van Nutter. His acting is terribly stiff and his voicing amateurish; on the other hand, he is given very little to do, and there is very little in the part to be screwed up by poor performance.

NORMAN BURTON, *Diamonds Are Forever*

Director Guy Hamilton's idea was that, since the plot of *Diamonds Are Forever,* and Bond himself, were more comical and wild than in the past, Felix should be more button-down and proper, more of a straight man. To that end, Norman Burton was cast. There is nothing wrong with Burton's performance, which is ably delivered, with a light touch and a good sense of comic timing. The problem is the character himself; some fans simply don't want Felix Leiter to be that guy. Personally, I enjoy him, but he's not the American counterpart to Bond that most fans consider the ideal Felix.

DAVID HEDISON, *Live and Let Die*

Hedison's first portrayal of Felix isn't much of a departure from Burton's in the previous film. In his first three appearances, Felix Leiter was just a field agent, a man sent to do his job. In *Diamonds Are Forever, Live and Let Die* and *The Living Daylights*, he appears to have gotten a promotion, and is leading a field team. In *Live and Let Die*, it is Leiter's team, in the form of Charlie and, especially, Harold Strutter, who fill the shoes of the mysterious and threatening stranger who fools the audience into thinking him a villain.

Hedison, like Burton, is fairly proper, and takes the damage Bond does with somewhat more seriousness, and is a bit comic in his reaction to Bond's mayhem. However he is also younger, taller, and a touch more tough. His physicality is a better match for Bond, and he is a charming screen presence. If Van Nutter looks most like Fleming's Felix, than Hedison speaks most like him, with a hint of laughter always just below the surface.

BERNIE CASEY, *Never Say Never Again*

In a movie with so much wrong, everything right about *Never Say Never Again* can be summed up with one word: Casting. Bernie Casey not only does a fine job as Felix Leiter, but is an inspired choice. Some people raised their eyebrows at placing an African-American in the role, but besides coloring, Casey is far more the literary Leiter than Cec Linder or Norman Burton. This is very much Fleming's character, an equal to Bond and a pal, joking with him, enjoying the challenge of working together, and functioning as an appropriate second. Casey has a laid back quality that adds fun (but not clowning) to the proceedings.

JOHN TERRY, *The Living Daylights*

As bland as Van Nutter, it's hard to tell if Terry can act, because the role is so invisible. What he can't do is hold the screen with Timothy Dalton. It's as if they are in two different movies, and Terry simply disappears. However, I do like the way Leiter brings Bond in—sending the two women to invite him to a party!

DAVID HEDISON, *Licence to Kill*

Probably the single best Felix Leiter movie scene is when Hedison and Timothy Dalton parachute into Felix's wedding. What a lovely acknowledgment of twenty-seven years of friendship. Choosing James as his best man, and establishing a friendship between James and Della, creates a new and welcome view of the relationship between these two men of action. Choosing to bring back an actor who had already played the role really cemented the feeling of a friendship that was long-standing and real.

The entire role is soured for many, though, by Felix's last scene. Here he is, in the hospital, his new wife raped and murdered, his leg and hand chewed off, and yet he laughs on the phone with Bond and suggests a fishing trip. It seems distasteful. *Licence to Kill* director John Glen often had a heavy hand with humor and didn't know how to hold it back, which probably explains this disturbing scene. On the other hand, maybe Felix was on a lot of medication!

David Hedison passed away in 2019 at the age of 92.

JEFFREY WRIGHT, *Casino Royale* and *Quantum of Solace*

For the first time in the Bond franchise, Leiter is played by the same actor in consecutive movies. Jeffrey Wright creates a unique character for Leiter, imbuing him with a great deal of personality despite limited screen time (especially in *Quantum of Solace*). Gruff, thoughtful, friendly but self-contained, this is not Fleming's Leiter, or anyone's Leiter but Wright's, and he works as an ally; someone Bond can trust. He shows up at the right moment, staking Bond in *Casino Royale*, and refusing to betray him in *Quantum of Solace*, while still primarily loyal to the CIA.

Leiter is mentioned but not seen in *Spectre*, and returns, played by Wright, in *No Time to Die*.

MI6 and the CIA Working Together

Felix Leiter (see above)
Johnny, *Goldfinger*
Charlie, *Live and Let Die*
Harold Strutter, *Live and Let Die*
Dr. Holly Goodhead, *Moonraker*
Chuck Lee, *A View to a Kill*
Pam Bouvier, *Licence to Kill*
Jack Wade, *GoldenEye* and *Tomorrow Never Dies*

Top Five/Bottom Five

Best

1. **Kerim Bey**, *From Russia with Love*
2. **Felix Leiter** (David Hedison), *Live and Let Die* and *Licence to Kill*
3. **Milos Columbo**, *For Your Eyes Only*
4. **Tiger Tanaka**, *You Only Live Twice*
5. **Valentin Zukovsky**, *GoldenEye* and *The World is Not Enough*
AND: **René Mathis**, *Casino Royale* and *Quantum of Solace*

Worst

1. **Sheriff J.W. Pepper**, *The Man with the Golden Gun*
2. **Nigel Small-Fawcett**, *Never Say Never Again*
3. **Jaws**, *Moonraker*
4. **Quarrel**, *Dr. No*
5. **Felix Leiter** (Cec Linder), *Goldfinger*

The Best Allies

Kerim Bey

Kerim greets Bond as "my friend" the moment they first meet, and from there until his tragic death, the warmth, friendship, and loyalty are utterly real. Kerim is a man who lives fully. A former circus strongman with a seemingly unlimited supply of sons, he approaches life with great zest. He loves beautiful women, his gypsy friends, drinking, and espionage. Life without any of these things would bore him. He may seem cuddly, but Kerim is fierce, too, and kills Krilencu as much for honor as because he knows he must. There is no doubt that Bond loved this man, and grieves his passage. So do we. Kerim is a constant favorite among Bond fans, and even the younger fans, with strong affection for allies of Brosnan's Bond, often cite him as their favorite.

Felix Leiter (David Hedison)

You've already read a full discussion of the many faces of Felix. Suffice it to say that one of the joys of this CIA agent is the consistency (and inconsistency) he brought to the series. Sooner or later, Felix would return. Perhaps this is a large part of why the one actor to play Felix twice is such a fan favorite.

Milos Columbo

Few don't love the character played by Topol in *For Your Eyes Only*. He has such effusive charm that, when introduced as the bad guy by Kristatos, who is posing as an ally, we are perplexed. This is a villain? It seems ridiculous, and it is the first indication that perhaps Kristatos isn't whom he purports to be. Columbo wins us as he wins Bond, by trusting him so completely that he hands him his gun back after capturing him, all the while munching pistachios. Another of Fleming's warm, affable leaders, you may see him as derivative or as thematic. Certainly this type of man was important to Fleming, and even villains, such as Goldfinger or Hugo Drax, form, in the novels, their dark counterpart.

The characters of Columbo and Kristatos, their good/bad switch, and the key scene of Columbo handing Bond his gun, all originate in the Ian Fleming short story "Risico." In the story, Colombo is based in Italy, not Greece.

Tiger Tanaka

Tiger is an interesting character. Another warm, friendly man greatly amused by Bond, he also is one up on Bond for most of *You Only Live Twice*. He is M's Japanese counterpart, yet he is also a man of action. His approach to espionage is more youthful and more involved than that of MI6's leader. The casting emphasizes this—Tetsuro Tamba is only eight years older than Connery, whereas Bernard Lee is twenty-two years older. This casting takes the role of the father figure and places it in the hands of an equal. Tiger, with his magnificent estate populated by beautiful women, his down-the-rabbit-hole subway headquarters, and his excellent taste in food and drink, is a man Bond can aspire to be. He takes Bond under his wing, teaching him the Japanese way and training him as a ninja. Both his interesting role and his full-bodied laugh earn him high marks among Bond fans.

Valentin Zukovsky

We're still grieving, and still hoping that the gunshot wound in *The World is Not Enough* didn't prove fatal. The delightful Robbie Coltraine gave an entirely original performance in two Bond films. An ex-KGB man, Valentin Zukovsky has acquired wealth in post-Soviet Russia through legitimate and illegitimate means. He is a powerful man both physically and personally; a force with which to be reckoned. In *GoldenEye*, Zukovsky hates Bond, who wins him over by appealing to his self-interest first, and by trying to demonstrate that in Janus, they have a common enemy.

By Zukovsky's second appearance, he is less dark as a character, and has some respect for Bond. Still, their alliance is again based on mutual self-interest, creating an enjoyable tension. We do not expect him to save Bond's life, and the scene in which he does is very well done.

Coltraine's character is a strong fan favorite. He is different, not an agent, not a button-down bureaucrat, not based on any familiar Bond character type. He is amusing, but not foolish, menacing, but not evil. Robbie Coltraine commands the screen with a strong presence, and faces Pierce Brosnan man-to-man, eye-to-eye.

René Mathis

Mathis is a musing, thoughtful presence, the father-figure ally that Bond loves best. He helps Bond immeasurably—getting rid of the Montenegro Chief of Police, getting Bond to Bolivia—and advocates for Vesper when Bond needs to hear it. His speech about forgiveness may be overblown, but few deaths in the Bond films are as touching as his.

The Worst Allies

In general, Bond fans are never happy with clowns, who turn Bond away from action-with-comedy, into comedy-with-action. Every Bond fan loves to laugh, but few of us want to see our beloved MI6 agent made party to idiocy.

Sheriff J.W. Pepper

This guy is the worst of the worst. He is loud, stupid, and out of place. He was bad enough in *Live and Let Die*, where he played a stereotypical redneck sheriff who encounters Bond when a speedboat chase disrupts his turf, but as an ally in *The Man with the Golden Gun*, he is unforgiveable.

The whole good ol' boy thing had a certain popularity in the 1970s, but viewed today, it simply isn't funny. Clifton James sputters, spits, and leaves his mouth hanging open like a cow engrossed with her cud. Apparently, all this enchanted the audience for *Live and Let Die* so much that Eon devised an excuse for him to appear in the next movie as well. Few things are as irritating as a highly contrived reunion—Pepper just happens to be in Bangkok when Bond is there—and to reunite with a character who was irritating to start with is nearly unbearable. Sheriff Pepper thinks he is an ally, but helps not at all and embarrasses himself and the audience by being overbearing, bigoted, and loud.

Nigel Small-Fawcett

Here you may begin to note a pattern—your author doesn't like comic fools. And among all comic fools, I might single out Rowan Atkinson for particular disfavor. In general, *Never Say Never Again* is a movie elevated by its cast—the return of Sean Connery, Klaus Maria Brandauer as Largo—but this particular choice gives me the shivers.

Jaws

I've got a great idea: Let's take one of the scariest, best henchmen that Bond has ever faced, and make him a cute guy who turns good for the love of a strange-looking woman! Yeah, that's the ticket! Or not.

Richard Kiel's character Jaws is a fan favorite, often cited on "Best Villain" or "Best Henchman" lists, but usually with the caveat: Jaws in *The Spy Who Loved*

Me. His popularity wanes in his *Moonraker* outing, where he is more Wile E. Coyote than Bond villain. His appearance bodes ill right from the pre-titles sequence, when he flaps his arms in order to avoid crash-landing (without a parachute). Subsequently, he meets Dolly, the strange young woman with braces and a Tyrolean get-up, who wins his heart. Sure, I'm glad the guy lives happily ever after, but why did he have to ruin the mystique of an excellent character first?

Quarrel

It's not John Kitzmiller's fault that Quarrel is such an awful character. The novel **Live and Let Die** (Fleming's second), which introduced him, affords Quarrel dignity and talent. When he reappears in **Dr. No**, he makes a serious error, one that endangers 007, but he does so at a point in the story when no one believes there is a real threat. Then along come the movies, and it is as if all the racism in Fleming's novel is condensed into this one hapless character. Quarrel is superstitious, a drunk, and a coward, and Bond treats him as a servant instead of an ally. All of this is a shame, because in his first moments on-screen, suspicious and uncooperative, the character seems formidable. Unfortunately, this proves not to be the case.

In the movie *Live and Let Die*, the character is redeemed in the form of Quarrel, Jr., a competent native agent who is very much the Quarrel envisioned by Fleming.

Felix Leiter (Cec Linder)

As described above, fans tend to cite Cec Linder or Rik Van Nutter as the worst Felix. Van Nutter is the lesser acting talent, but Linder's dialogue and behavior are atrocious, and he gets the uncoveted trophy.

The Complete List

Female allies listed under Bond Girls are not repeated here.

Dr. No

> **Felix Leiter**, CIA agent (Jack Lord)
> **Quarrel**, local fisherman (John Kitzmiller)
> **Plydell-Smith**, Principal Secretary (Louis Blaazer)

From Russia with Love

> **Kerim Bey**, Head of Station T (Pedro Armendariz)
> **Kerim's chauffeur** and son (Neville Jason)

Goldfinger

> **Felix Leiter**, CIA agent (Cec Linder)
> **Johnny**, CIA agent (Peter Cranwell)

Thunderball

> **Felix Leiter**, CIA agent (Rik Van Nutter)
> **Pinder**, Head of Bahama Station (Earl Cameron)

You Only Live Twice

> **Tiger Tanaka**, Head of Japanese Secret Service (Tetsuro Tamba)
> **Dikko Henderson**, Head of Tokyo Station (Charles Gray)

On Her Majesty's Secret Service

> **Marc Ange Draco**, Head of Union Corse (Gabriele Ferzetti)
> **Sir Hillary Bray**, Basilisk of Royal College of Arms (George Baker)
> **Campbell**, Secret Service Agent, Switzerland (Bernard Horsfall)

Diamonds Are Forever

> **Felix Leiter**, CIA agent (Norman Burton)
> **Willard Whyte**, rich guy (Jimmy Dean)

Live and Let Die

> **Felix Leiter**, CIA Agent (David Hedison)
> **Charlie**, CIA agent/cab driver (Joie Chitwood)
> **Harold Strutter**, CIA agent (Ron Satton)
> **Quarrel, Jr.**, fisherman agent (Roy Stewart)

The Man with the Golden Gun

> **Lt. Hip**, Secret Service agent, Hong Kong (Soon-Taik Oh)
> **Colthorpe**, Ballistics expert, Q Branch (James Cossins)
> **Sheriff J.W. Pepper**, obnoxious acquaintance (Clifton James)

The Spy Who Loved Me

> **Admiral Hargreaves**, Royal Navy Admiral (Robert Brown)
> **Sheik Hosein**, friend of Bond (Edward de Souza)
> **Captain Benson**, liaison at Polaris Submarine Base (George Baker)
> **Captain Carter**, U.S.S. Wayne (Shane Rimmer)
> **Commander Talbot**, H.M.S. Ranger (Bryan Marshall)

Moonraker

> **Jaws**, bad guy who changes sides (Richard Kiel)

For Your Eyes Only

> **Milos Columbo**, Greek smuggler (Topol)
> **Ferrara**, Secret Service agent, Northern Italy (John Moreno)
> **Jacoba Brink**, skating instructor (Jill Bennett)

Octopussy

> **Jim Fanning**, MI6 art expert (Douglas Wilmer)
> **Sadruddin**, Head of Station I (Albert Moses)
> **Vijay**, agent of Station I (Vijay Armitraj)

Never Say Never Again

> **Felix Leiter**, CIA agent (Bernie Casey)
> **Nigel Small-Fawcett**, Nassau embassy officer (Rowan Atkinson)

A View to a Kill

> **Sir Godfrey Tibbett**, MI6 horse expert (Patrick Macnee)
> **Achille Aubergine**, French detective (Jean Rougerie)
> **Chuck Lee**, CIA agent (David Yip)

The Living Daylights

> **Felix Leiter**, CIA agent (John Terry)
> **Saunders**, Head of Section V (Thomas Wheatley)
> **Rosika Miklos**, operative at Trans-Siberian pipeline (Julie T. Wallace)
> **General Pushkin**, Head of KGB (John Rhys-Davies)
> **Kamram Shah**, Mujahadeen leader (Art Malik)

Licence to Kill

> **Felix Leiter**, DEA agent (David Hedison) (No explanation is given for Felix's transfer from Intelligence to Drug Enforcement.)
> **Sharkey**, fisherman in Key West (Frank McRae)

GoldenEye

> **Jack Wade**, CIA agent (Joe Don Baker)
> **Valentin Zukovsky**, Russian crime boss (Robbie Coltraine)
> **Dimitri Mishkin**, Russian Defense Minister (Tcheky Karyo)

Tomorrow Never Dies

> **Jack Wade**, CIA agent (Joe Don Baker)
> **Dr. Dave Greenwalt**, USAF expert on GPS (Colin Stinton)

The World is Not Enough

> **Sir Robert King**, oil tycoon (David Calder)
> **Valentin Zukovsky**, Russian crime boss (Robbie Coltraine)

Die Another Day

> **Falco**, Head of NSA (Michael Madsen)
> **Mr. Chang**, Chinese agent (Ho Yi)
> **Raoul**, Cuban sleeper agent (Emilio Echevarria)

Casino Royale

> **Felix Leiter**, CIA agent (Jeffery Wright)
> **René Mathis**, French agent, (Giancarlo Giannini)

Quantum of Solace

> **Felix Leiter**, CIA agent (Jeffery Wright)
> **René Mathis**, retired French agent, (Giancarlo Giannini)

Skyfall

> **Kincade**, groundskeeper (Albert Finney)

Spectre

> None: Bond works entirely with his MI6 allies and Madeline.

BOND'S BEST GADGET

A book about James Bond is indelicate almost by definition, being concerned with lust, weaponry, sex, death, and excitement. Here, however, we are intrepidly crossing the boundaries of good taste to talk about 007's most famous, and least described, gadget: His masculine equipment. Oh, my.

As difficult as it is to talk about, it's also a difficult topic to avoid. James Bond represents a masculine ideal, and he surrounds himself with the very best of the accouterments of masculine identity, including a powerful gun and a fast sports car—both stereotypical phallic symbols. It makes sense that, if Bond is the man who every man wishes to be, and if Bond has everything that every man wishes to have, he simply must have the one thing that men long for even if they already possess it (doubting they possess it in sufficient magnitude)—a very large penis.

It is common wisdom in our post-Freudian world that ostentatious weaponry and cars are a form of compensation for a man's inadequacies, or perceived inadequacies, in this very area. Certainly you've heard that a big (gun, car, knife, walking stick) means a small (be brave) package. It should be noted that both Bond's original Beretta and his Walther PPK are rather small guns, designed in part for concealment. In the early posters that show Connery with a very large gun, he is holding a Walther air pistol, not the PPK. Ian Fleming was no stranger to the theory, and wrote, in **The Man with the Golden Gun** , "It is a Freudian thesis...that the pistol, whether in the hands of an amateur or of a professional gunman, has significance for the owner as a symbol of virility—an extension of the male organ."

Even James Bond jokes about this, when, in *Goldfinger*, Bonita asks him why he always carries a gun. "I have a slight inferiority complex," he quips. All the more reason for the films to emphasize that Bond has neither an inferiority complex, nor reason to have one. Starting with *From Russia with Love*, numerous remarks are made in the Bond movies that specifically refer to Bond's size and/or potency.

There is another explanation for this. Especially in the pre-**Hite Report** years, Bond's extraordinary success with women was credited to the magic down below. Nobody did it better because nobody was better-equipped. I think of this as purely a male myth—men think, or thought then, that the physical attribute accorded aptitude in bed. There is a certain ridiculousness to the whole thing, in that Bond cannot possibly be bedding women based on his personal assets, because women don't see those assets until after they have joined him in bed! Nonetheless, the myth persists.

Sizeable References

Here then, a collection of references to Bond's size, virility, potency, and use of aphrodisiacs. I hope you enjoy reading them as much as I enjoyed collecting them.

From Russia with Love

> **Tanya:** "Careful! Guns upset me."
> **Bond:** "I'm a bit, uh, upset myself."

Tanya: "I think my mouth is too big."
Bond: "No, it's the right size. For me, that is."

Goldfinger

Bonita (referring to Bond's gun): "Why do you always wear that thing?"
Bond: "I have a slight inferiority complex."

Bond (on the phone with Felix, while in bed with Jill): "Something big's come up."

Bond: "What would it take to for you to see things my way?"
Pussy: "A lot more than you've got."
Bond: "How do you know?"

In *Goldfinger*, one could add the laser pointed at the part of Bond he would most miss. Bond's manhood is also threatened by the villain in *Live and Let Die*, *The Spy Who Loved Me*, and *Never Say Never Again*. (And see below for *Casino Royale*.)

Thunderball

Bond: "Have some of my conch chowder."
Domino: "You've been reading the wrong books, Mr. Bond."
Bond: "About conch chowder?"
Domino: "Being an aphrodisiac."
Bond: "Well, it just so happens that I like conch chowder."

Later, Bond is at Largo's home and is invited to stay for lunch.
Domino: "Come along, Mr. Bond, the conch chowder smells delicious."

You Only Live Twice

Bond (pushing away a plate of oysters after Kissy has rejected him): "Well, I won't be needing these."

On Her Majesty's Secret Service

Ruby writes her room number in lipstick on Bond's bare thigh.
Irma Bunt: "Is there anything the matter, Sir Hilary?"
Bond: "Just a slight stiffness coming on. In the shoulder."
The next morning...
Irma Bunt: "Good morning, Sir Hilary. Your stiffness of last night, it is all gone?"
Bond: "For the time being, I think."

Q (at Bond's wedding): "Don't forget, if there's anything you ever need..."
Bond: "Thank you, Q, but this time, I've got the gadgets, and I know how to use them."

Diamonds Are Forever

> **Bond** (interrupted with Plenty): "I'm afraid you've caught me with more than my hands up."

> (Bond is naked.)
> **Tiffany:** "I'm very impressed! There's a lot more to you than I had expected."

Live and Let Die

> **Miss Caruso:** "One more time again? Ma non e possible amore!"

> **Solitaire:** "Is there time before we leave for Lesson #3?"
> **Bond:** "Absolutely. There's no sense in going off half-cocked."

Is this a reference to making love three times? Bond has delineated Lessons #1 and #2 as non-sexual, but given his response, and given the earlier scene with Miss Caruso, it seems likely.

For Your Eyes Only

> Lisl has oysters, but these seem more a luxury item than an aphrodisiac in this context.

Never Say Never Again

> **Nurse:** "Mr. Bond, I need a urine sample. If you could fill this beaker for me."
> **Bond:** "From here?"

> **Bond:** "You're marvelously well-equipped."
> **Fatima:** "Thank you, James." (a glance at his body) "So are you."

> **Fatima Blush** (pointing gun): "Guess where you get the first one?"

Octopussy

> In the final scene, *Octopussy* kisses James while he is in traction. As they kiss, his leg, in a cast, rises suggestively. Cut to an exterior shot and *Octopussy* exclaims "James!" in the surprised tone of a woman who has just discovered something big.

A View to a Kill

> **Bond:** "I'm an early riser myself."

GoldenEye

> **Caroline:** "You are just trying to show of the size of your...your..."
> **Bond:** "Engine?"
> **Caroline:** "Ego."

> **Bond:** "It seems we share the same passions. Three, anyway."
> **Xenia:** "I count two: Motoring, and baccarat." (Bond loses the hand.)
> **Xenia:** "I hope the third is where your real talent lies."
> **Bond:** "One rises to meet a challenge."

The World is Not Enough

> **Elektra** (sitting in Bond's lap while he is in torture chair): "You know what happens when a man is strangled?"

Die Another Day

> **Bond:** "Oh, I'm just here for the birds." (He indicates his binoculars.) "Ornithologist."
> **Jinx:** "Ornithologist, huh?" (She glances down) "Wow. Now there's a mouthful."

> **Verity:** "I see you handle your weapon well."
> **Bond:** "I have been known to keep my tip up."

Casino Royale

The entire torture sequence is an explicit conversation about Bond's "manhood," physical and metaphorical. Relevant quotes from the scene are:

> **Le Chiffre:** "Wow, you've taken good care of your body. You know, I never understood all these elaborate tortures. It's the simplest thing to cause more pain than a man can possibly endure. And of course, it's not only the immediate agony, but the knowledge that if you do not yield soon enough, there will be little left to identify you as a man."
> ...
> **James Bond:** "I've got a little itch, down there. Would you mind?"
> ...
> **James Bond:** "Now the whole world's gonna know that you died scratching my balls!"
> ...
> **Le Chiffre:** "I think I will feed you what you seem not to value."

GOLDFINGER (1964)

Survey Says!

> Percent Favorite: 12%
> Top 5 Cumulative: 4/25
> Numeric Rating: 8.7/10
> Ranking: 7.5 (4th/25)

My Rating and Ranking

> Rated: 9/10
> Ranked: 7 out of 25

Summary

Bond is investigating a gold smuggling scheme by Auric Goldfinger when he discovers the villain's real scheme: Operation Grand Slam. Goldfinger intends to break into Fort Knox and detonate an atomic bomb, thereby contaminating the United States' gold supply. Bond must persuade Goldfinger's pilot, Pussy Galore, to change sides and save the lives of everyone in Knoxville, as well as the U.S. economy.

> **James Bond:** Sean Connery
> **Pussy Galore:** Honor Blackman
> **Jill Masterson:** Shirley Eaton
> **Tilly Masterson:** Tania Mallet
> **Felix Leiter:** Cec Linder
> **Auric Goldfinger:** Gert Frobe
> **Oddjob:** Harold Sakata
> **M:** Bernard Lee
> **Moneypenny:** Lois Maxwell
> **Q:** Desmond Llewelyn
> **Directed by** Guy Hamilton

Discussion

Goldfinger is the single most popular James Bond film. More than fifty years later, it remains a phenomenon in and of itself. It is the favorite by far among the general public, is consistently in the top five among fans, and among younger, Brosnan-era fans, is the only Connery movie that has lost none of its cachet and is not considered dated. I have heard it said that, if a person has seen only one Bond movie, that movie is likely to be *Goldfinger* (or, after 2006, *Casino Royale*). The things that are recognizably Bondish to people who aren't fans are often things from *Goldfinger*: the Aston Martin DB5 with the ejector seat, the name "Pussy Galore," and of course, the golden girl.

The third James Bond movie adds the final components to what will become the Bond formula: Desmond Llewelyn in *From Russia with Love* was not playing a character, he was simply a device by which the attache case was explained. It was

Guy Hamilton who instructed Llewelyn to be surly with Bond, and who added the line "I never joke about my work," thus creating one of the most beloved characters in movie history. *Goldfinger* also introduces a title song to the formula, making a star of Shirley Bassey and opening the door for many movies—especially but not exclusively Eon's—to use a title song to throw a hit on the charts.

Although *Goldfinger* doesn't introduce the pre-titles sequence, it sets the standard for the teaser as a mini-movie. In it, Bond carries out a mission that has nothing to do with the main plot of the movie. It is not only a wonderful little tale, but in four and a half minutes gives us humor, style, sex, and violence, all in an elegant dinner jacket.

Goldfinger is beloved because, simply put, it is a terrific movie. It appears on Roger Ebert's 100 Great Movies list, and on the American Film Institute's list of 100 Most Thrilling American Films (despite being British). Goldfinger himself is one of AFI's 50 Greatest Villains of All Time (he placed at #49). This doesn't make it beyond reproach. Fleming purists deplore *Goldfinger* for introducing elaborate gadgetry to the Bond films, the success of which meant that 007 largely parted ways from the simple, streamlined espionage of the novels and the first two films. Others complain that Bond spends most of the movie helpless, acted upon by others. And I have already had my say about Cec Linder as Felix Leiter.

As with *From Russia with Love*, we see in the third Bond outing the importance of great villains. In large part, *Goldfinger* is great because Auric Goldfinger, and his companion Oddjob, are great. The villain who utters the single most popular one-liner in Bond history ("No, Mr. Bond, I expect you to die!") is masterful. Gert Frobe gives his character menace, intelligence, a driving will, a hint of madness that grows through the course of the movie, and a pleasingly sick enjoyment of the challenge afforded him by James Bond. Underneath this overpowering figure is a frustrated lech, a man who must pay a woman to "be seen with him," and who enjoys painting her gold (in the novel, enjoying the company of gold-painted women was Goldfinger's particular fetish), and who makes a failed and embarrassing pass at a woman with whom Bond succeeds.

And then there's Oddjob, one of Fleming's great creations. Silent, huge, sadistic, and just plain strange, Oddjob is a man Bond knows he cannot beat. He is bigger, stronger, and immovable.

Ian Fleming was so good at giving his villains little oddities that made them unpleasant. The clothing worn by both Goldfinger and Oddjob comes straight out of the novel, including the fact that Oddjob's hat is too small for his head. These small details add up to a large impression, and *Goldfinger* has unforgettable bad guys.

Visually, it is a remarkable film. The credit can be shared among many for that. The use of locations in Europe is excellent, although Kentucky looks pretty sleazy. Switzerland is particularly lovely, and one shot stands out as most memorable; Goldfinger stops at a roadside stand/scenic view for a snack; the camera pans back and we see that, further up the mountain, 007 has a view of Goldfinger; pan again, and we see that Tilly has an equally long view of Bond. A very nice piece of camera work, and a lovely view.

The set design is amazing. Ken Adam returns after a one-picture absence with the apparent goal of popping the eyes out of several million faces, and he succeeds marvelously. Much has been said about the Fort Knox set, certainly magnificent, but there is also Goldfinger's "rumpus room," with its revolving pool table, moving floor, and mechanical horse. Hood's conventions never looked so good. The costume design is wonderful. In the 2002 movie *Catch Me If You Can*, Leonardo DiCaprio's character is so enamored of *Goldfinger* that he not only buys an Aston Martin DB5, he has a tailor make him an exact duplicate of James Bond's gray three-piece suit. Pussy Galore in her purple blouse or her gold vest is equally fetching, but the best "costume," and most iconic image, from *Goldfinger* is surely Shirley Eaton's 24-carat full body makeup. Yowza!

Speaking of the DB5, well, what is there to say? It changed the Bond films forever, for good or ill, making Bond not merely a spy, but the owner of a dazzling array of gadgetry (Sorry, Q, I mean the temporary owner, of course) which often grabs the spotlight and pushes 007 himself into a secondary role. Purists complain and filmgoers applaud, but no one can deny that these gadgets, used properly, are buckets of fun.

What of the story? *Goldfinger* is the last movie until *Licence to Kill* in which 007 screws up, consistently and repeatedly. He begins by antagonizing Goldfinger, a man he is supposed to observe. In the novel, he is actually hired (privately, between missions) to uncover and foil Goldfinger's card-cheating scheme, and it is only a coincidence that the man is his next assignment. Ian Fleming even addressed the problem of coincidence, in perhaps his most famous quote, when he has Goldfinger say, "'Mr Bond, they have a saying in Chicago: 'Once is happenstance. Twice is coincidence. The third time it's enemy action.'"

Coincidence in a story can be a sign of lazy writing, but perhaps it is preferable to Bond foiling Goldfinger out of sheer cussedness, with too little regard for consequences. Next Bond gets captured, messes up his escape by falling for the old mirror trick, escapes and gets captured again, this time by foolishly standing overlong out in the open. He very nearly blows the whole hero routine by being unable to find an Off switch. In *Goldfinger*, Bond is acted upon more than he acts. Some fans like this, considering it humanizing—he's not a superhero, after all—others do not.

Bond is stupid at times, but he is darn clever at other times. Who doesn't grin with pleasure at his escape from the cell in Goldfinger's basement, or at his foiling Mei-Li's attempt to spy on him in the bathroom of the plane?

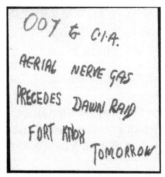

Figure 5: Replica of the note Bond drops in Mr. Solo's pocket (to no avail, alas)

Goldfinger's scheme is amazing—grandiose, hugely evil, and with the glint of possibility that, 'hey, it could work.' He says it has taken fifteen years of planning; a little remark I enjoy, as some of these elaborate plots seem pulled from the villain's hat. The stupidities of any Bond film—why doesn't he take the gold out of the car before crushing Mr. Solo?—are absorbed in Goldfinger's madness and the size of the gestures he chooses to make. This is key, I think. It's not that there mustn't be plot holes—even Hitchcock was riddled with them—but that they must be given breathing room. If the audience can accept the scale and shape of a film, the glitches will fall into place and be acceptable. *Goldfinger* the movie knows this.

Few films have ever sounded as good as *Goldfinger*, which has a great title song, and one of John Barry's best scores. The use of the title song as a musical motif set a standard for future movies, and there are lots of little flourishes that set character and place, such as the vamp for Pussy's Flying Circus and a bit of local music at the Kentucky horse farm.

The women in *Goldfinger* are mostly fantastic. Shirley Eaton as Jill Masterson makes a huge impact with almost no screen time. Even before she is made into the golden girl, she exudes an inviting sensuality that translates into chemistry with Sean Connery, both sweet and hot.

Tania Mallet as Jill's sister, Tilly, is less of a success. In Fleming's novel, there were two kinds of lesbians: Those cold to Bond, and those who were waiting for him to unlock their latent heterosexuality. This archaic view made Fleming depict Tilly with a great deal of hostility, as she was of the former type. The movie character retains the negative qualities, although her sexual orientation has been written out. She enters rudely, honking her horn in a way that everyone with a driver's license recognizes as offensive. Her lame-brained attempts to kill Goldfinger get her killed and Bond captured. Her death saddens Bond, but I suspect most of the audience is relieved.

Things brighten up considerably after Bond's capture. We meet Pussy Galore, a dream indeed. She is smart, sharp-tongued, wry, and beautiful. Her spurning of Goldfinger's advances bespeaks her excellent taste. Her lesbianism isn't entirely written out, just left to a few hints that could pass the censors of the day. Certainly I could pick up the hints even at a young age, and I have always thought she had a bit of a thing going with Champagne Leader. I do love the erotic quality she brings to being the boss of a group of beautiful, perky pilots.

There is a nice note of continuity: When Bond is on Goldfinger's plane, he asks if his attaché case is aboard. Mei-Lei says "Black attaché case damaged during inspection. So sorry." This is the attaché from *From Russia with Love*, which emits teargas when opened the wrong way.

The High Points
- The magnificent opening teaser sequence; removing the wet suit to reveal the dinner jacket, waiting in the bar for the heroin plant to blow up, seeing an assassin reflected in Bonita's eye, and their "shocking" fight to the death.
- A great villain (Goldfinger) and great henchman (Oddjob).
- The Aston Martin DB5 and its ejector seat.
- Jill Masterson becoming the golden girl.
- Pussy Galore and her Flying Circus.

- The entire "hood's convention" scene.
- The scene of the car being crushed.
- The thrilling Fort Knox sequence, including the shocking sight of soldiers falling dead, the entry into the fortress, the shoot-out, and the gripping final combat with Oddjob.

The Low Points

- Cec Linder as a clumsy, foolish, obnoxious Felix Leiter.
- Tilly Masterson, the Bond girl who couldn't shoot straight.
- The suggestion that Bond is forcing himself on Pussy sexually, and that she becomes excited and willing. Ugh.
- The subsequent suggestion that Pussy has decided to change sides only because Bond has made love to her—a bit smarmy, no?
- Bond screws up his assignment in Miami by allowing himself to be recognized by Goldfinger. He screws up further by not realizing he is recognized, and acting during the golf game as if Goldfinger doesn't know him.
- The unattractive Kentucky locations.

Quotable Quotes

Bond (electrocutes bad guy): "Shocking. Positively shocking."

Bond: "Do you expect me to talk?"
Goldfinger: "No, Mr. Bond, I expect you to die!"

Bond: "Ejector seat? You're joking!"
Q: "I never joke about my work, 007."

Bond: "Auric Goldfinger? Sounds like a French nail varnish."

Bond: "My dear girl, there are some things that just aren't done, such as drinking Dom Perignon '53 above a temperature of 38 degrees Fahrenheit. That's as bad as listening to the Beatles without earmuffs."

Pussy Galore: "You like close shaves, don't you?"

Goldfinger (about Mr. Solo): "Unfortunately, he has a pressing engagement."

Bond (about Oddjob): "Oh, he blew a fuse."

Bond (last line): Oh, no you don't! This is no time to be rescued."

Facts and Figures

SEXUAL ENCOUNTERS

<u>Four</u>: Bonita, Dink, Jill Masterson, and Pussy Galore.

BOND'S CAR

1964 Aston Martin DB5 (silver) (see A FEW OPTIONAL EXTRAS).

DEATHS

Approximately forty-eight:

- Jill Masterson, Tilly Masterson, twelve gangsters in the rumpus room, Mr. Solo, Mr. Kisch, an unknown number during the Fort Knox combat (as a guess, thirty), Oddjob, Goldfinger.

Bond Kills:

- Two directly: Oddjob and Goldfinger.

EXPLOSIONS

Four: The heroin plant in the pre-titles sequence is huge. One of the cars chasing Bond at Auric Enterprises is exceptionally satisfying, because it continues to explode as it falls downhill. The Fort Knox explosion is so-so, a mere prequel to the action. The plane crashing at the very end is nice.

BOND'S FOOD AND DRINKS

Vodka Martinis

One, on the plane to Baltimore (he asks for a martini, shaken not stirred—he fails to ask for a vodka martini (see SHAKEN? STIRRED?)

Other Drinks

- An unknown drink with a straw is beside Bond while he gets a massage from Dink. Perhaps a rum and Coke.
- There are five cans of what appears to be beer in the refrigerator at the Fountainbleu.
- Dom Perignon '53 with Jill.
- At dinner with M and Smithers, two glasses of cognac (we see Bond refill the snifter), described as "30-year-old Fins indifferently blended...with an overdose of Bon Bois."
- We see wine glasses besides the brandy snifters at the same dinner. Since the plates have been cleared away, these are after-dinner drinks, more likely to be port wine than table wine.
- Brandy after dinner on the plane to Baltimore.
- A mint julep on Goldfinger's stud farm, ordered "Sour mash, but not too sweet."

Food

- Dinner in the hotel with Jill consists of a salmon platter with stuffed tomatoes and salad, what appears to be an appetizer tray, and a fruit bowl.
- There appears to be a package of ground meat in the refrigerator at the hotel.

- We do not see dinner with M and Smithers, we join the scene over after-dinner drinks and cigars; we do see a fruit bowl and a platter with breadsticks on the sideboard.
- Dinner on the plane to Baltimore; the plate cannot be made out, but a coffee cup and brandy for after dinner are seen.

GAMBLING AND SPORTS

- Gin rummy between Goldfinger and Simmons at the Fountainbleu.
- Golf between Goldfinger and Bond.
- Seeing Tilly's gun case, Bond asks if she's in Switzerland for the hunting season. She replies that the case is for her ice skates. "Lovely sport!" Bond says.

Amaze Your Friends!

- When scouting locations in Kentucky, Guy Hamilton saw Kentucky Fried Chicken and thought it a stroke of luck to find this bit of local color. He was embarrassed afterwards to learn it was a national chain.
- Gert Frobe spoke very little English. His voice was dubbed by actor Michael Collins.
- During the title sequence, scenes from the movie are shown inside the golden girl silhouette. If you look closely, you'll see the helicopter chase from *From Russia with Love* mixed in with the *Goldfinger* scenes.

Most Interesting Goofs

Skin Asphyxiation: Medically, there is no such thing as skin asphyxiation, although in 1964, people believed there was. The dangers that are posed to the human body by being covered with paint (overheating, toxins) are not alleviated by a small bare patch at the base of the spine.

Carry That Weight: If you crush a car, with a lot of heavy gold, and a human body, into the shape of a large cube, you have changed the size, but not the weight. The crushed cube dropped into the back of Oddjob's pickup truck weighed the same as a Lincoln Continental with a passenger and luggage. Had the truck been able to handle the weight at all, we would at least have seen it sink.

That's Some Blowout: Bond refers to the damage to Tilly's car as a "double blowout." Well, yes, two tires are gone, but the metal between them is also shredded!

007 AT THE OSCARS

Bond movies are far more popular with moviegoers than with film critics. No James Bond movie has ever received an Academy Award nomination in any of the six major categories—Best Picture, Best Director, Best Actor, Best Actress, Best Supporting Actor, or Best Supporting Actress.

However, the Bond films haven't been completely forgotten during Oscar season, or by Oscar recipients. Not only have there been nominations and wins for Bond, but Academy Award winners populate the Bond films.

Awards and Nominations

Following are the Bond films that have been nominated for, or won, an Academy Award (Oscar). The Academy Awards are held the year after the movie is released. Hence, 1964 movies are recipients of the 1965 Oscar.

Result	Year	Movie	Category	Nominee(s)
Won	1965	*Goldfinger*	Best Effects, Sound Effects	Norman Wanstall
Won	1966	*Thunderball*	Best Effects, Special Visual Effects	John Stears
Nominated	1972	*Diamonds Are Forever*	Best Sound	Gordon K. McCallum, John W. Mitchell, Al Overton
Nominated	1974	*Live and Let Die*	Best Music, Song	Paul McCartney, Linda McCartney For the song "Live and Let Die"
Nominated	1978	*The Spy Who Loved Me*	Best Art Drection, Set Decoration	Ken Adam, Peter Lamont, Hugh Sciafe
Nominated	1978	*The Spy Who Loved Me*	Best Music, Original Score	Marvin Hamlisch
Nominated	1978	*The Spy Who Loved Me*	Best Music, Song	Marvin Hamlisch (music), Carole Bayer Sager (lyrics)
Nominated	1980	*Moonraker*	Best Effects, Visual Effects	Derek Meddings, Paul Wilson, John Evans

Result	Year	Movie	Category	Nominee(s)
Nomi-nated	1982	*For Your Eyes Only*	Best Mu-sic, Song	Bill Conti (music), Mick Leeson (lyrics) For the song "For Your Eyes Only"
Won	2013	*Skyfall*	Best Mu-sic, Song	Adele, Paul Epworth, for the song "Skyfall"
Won	2013	*Skyfall*	Best Sound Ediiting (tied with Paul N.J. Ottosson for *Zero Dark Thirty*)	Per Halberg, Karen Baker Landers
Nomi-nated	2013	*Skyfall*	Best Cine-matog-raphy	Roger Deakins
Nomi-nated	2013	*Skyfall*	Best Mu-sic, Origi-nal Score	Thomas Newman
Nomi-nated	2013	*Skyfall*	Best Sound Mix-ing	Scott Millan, Greg P. Russell, Stuart Wilson
Won	2016	*Spectre*	Best Mu-sic, Song	Sam Smith, Jimmy Napes, for the song "Writing's on the Wall"

In addition to the above, Albert R. (Cubby) Broccoli was given the Irving G. Thalberg Memorial Award in 1981. The Thalberg is an honorary award given to "creative pro-ducers whose bodies of work reflect a consistently high quality of motion picture production." The award is not given every year. As a producer, almost half of Broc-coli's lifetime of work was on the Bond films—including all of his work in the ten years prior to receiving the award. Despite the general snub of Bond by the Oscars, this is a deep acknowledgment of the value of producing those films.

Oscar Winners in the Bond Films

Following is an alphabetic list of Oscar winners who have appeared in, or worked be-hind the scenes on, Bond films. Only a handful of actors have received Oscars prior to appearing in a Bond film: Halle Berry, Christopher Walken, Javier Bardem, Chris-toph Waltz, and Rami Malek. Berry received her Academy Award during production of *Die Another Day*. Judi Dench received her Oscar after she began playing M, but she was technically hired as an Oscar-winner for her post-1998 appearances.

Freddie Young, the renowned cinematographer, had won two Oscars by the time he worked on *You Only Live Twice*.

Sam Mendes, director of *Skyfall* and *Spectre*, was the first Oscar-winning director to work on a Bond film.

It's possible that there are omissions on this list. Cast and crew on each film can easily number over a hundred people, and for twenty-six films, that's a lot of names! It has been difficult to be perfectly thorough, and so I apologize if anyone who has been improperly left out.

Name	Bond Film(s)	Award(s)	Film(s)	Year(s)
Ken Adam	*Dr. No, Goldfinger, Thunderball, You Only Live Twice, Diamonds Are Forever, The Spy Who Loved Me, Moonraker*	Best Art Direction, Set Decoration	*Barry Lyndon* *The Madness of King George*	1975 1994
Javier Bardem	*Skyfall*	Best Supporting Actor	*No Country for Old Men*	2009
John Barry	Eon films (not *Never Say Never Again*): *Dr. No* through *Diamonds Are Forever, The Man with the Golden Gun, Octopussy* through *The Living Daylights*	Best Original Score (all four)	*Born Free* *The Lion in Winter* *Out of Africa* *Dances With Wolves*	1967 1969 1986 1991
Kim Basinger	*Never Say Never Again*	Best Supporting Actress	*L.A.Confidential*	1997
Halle Berry	*Die Another Day*	Best Actress	*Monster's Ball*	2001
Sean Connery	*Dr. No* through *You Only Live Twice, Diamonds Are Forever, Never Say Never Again*	Best Supporting Actor	*The Untouchables*	1987
Bill Conti	*For Your Eyes Only*	Best Original Score	*The Right Stuff*	1984

Name	Bond Film(s)	Award(s)	Film(s)	Year(s)
Roger Deakins	*Skyfall*	Best Cinematography	*Blade Runner 2049* *1917*	2018 2020
Benicio Del Toro	*Licence to Kill*	Best Supporting Actor	*Traffic*	2000
Judi Dench	*GoldenEye* through *Skyfall*	Best Supporting Actress	*Shakespeare in Love*	1998
Dennis Gassner	*Quantum of Solace, Skyfall, Spectre*	Best Art Direction, Set Decoration	*Bugsy*	1992
Paul Haggis	*Casino Royale*	Best Picture, Best Original Screenplay	*Crash*	2006
Lindy Hemming	*GoldenEye* through *Casino Royale*	Best Costume Design	*Topsy-Turvy*	2000
Jordan Klein	*Thunderball, Live and Let Die, Never Say Never Again*	**Technical Achievement Award	*For his pioneering efforts in the development and application of underwater camera housings for motion pictures.*	2002
Peter Lamont	*Thunderball, On Her Majesty's Secret Service* through *GoldenEye (except Never Say Never Again), The World is Not Enough, Die Another Day, Casino Royale*	Best Art Direction, Set Decoration	*Titanic*	1997
Rami Malek	*No Time to Die*	Best Actor	*Bohemian Rhapsody*	2019
Derek Meddings	*Live and Let Die, The Man with the Golden Gun, The Spy Who Loved Me,*	*Special Achievement Award for Visual Effects	*Superman*	1978

Name	Bond Film(s)	Award(s)	Film(s)	Year(s)
	Moonraker, For Your Eyes Only, GoldenEye			
Sam Mendes	*Skyfall, Spectre*	Best Director	*American Beauty*	2000
Chris Munro	*Tomorrow Never Dies, The World is Not Enough, Die Another Day*	Best Sound	*Black Hawk Down*	2001
John Richardson	*Moonraker, Octopussy, A View to a Kill, The Living Daylights, Licence to Kill, Tomorrow Never Dies, The World is Not Enough, Die Another Day*	Best Effects, Visual Effects	*Aliens*	1987
Christopher Walken	*A View to a Kill*	Best Supporting Actor	*The Deer Hunter*	1978
Christoph Waltz	*Spectre, No Time to Die*	Best Supporting Actor	*Inglourious Basterds* *Django Unchained*	2010 2013
Freddie (Frederick A.) Young	*You Only Live Twice*	Best Cinematography, Color (two times) Best Cinematography	*Lawrence of Arabia* *Doctor Zhivago* *Ryan's Daughter*	1963 1966 1971

* *The Special Achievement Award is given for an achievement which makes an exceptional contribution to the motion picture for which it was created, but for which there is no annual award category.*

** *Technical Achievement Awards are not given for specific films, but for "those accomplishments that contribute to the progress of the industry."*

THINGS THAT GO BOOM

O ne evening, my kid and I sat down to watch a Bond DVD. Ursula, then eleven years old, turned to me with a big grin and said, "One of the great things about James Bond movies is that you can always be sure there will be things that go 'boom.'"

What it is about explosions? Movies are full of them, more so in the past fifteen or twenty years. Why are they such crowd pleasers?

I think they provide a gut-level feeling of release. It's like shouting or breaking dishes; we want that satisfying level of noise and that blaze of light and things flying about. We want to feel that something has happened; something big, something that breaks the tension. It breaks all sorts of tension, doesn't it? The tension in the movie, yes, but it also releases some of the built-up tension from just being alive.

Counting the Booms

When I began tracking the explosions in Bond films, it never occurred to me that the process was so subjective. I mean, it's counting—what could be more objective than that? But it turns out that there are so many variables that a solid number is hard to come by. If an explosion causes a domino effect, for example, if it hits the ever-handy munitions storage, do the subsequent explosions count separately? So that if one big boom causes a series of six little ones, is it one, or seven, or two (one plus the series)? Does it have to have a boom to be an explosion? What about a wall of flame—fire and destruction, but no telltale sound effect? Or what about the boom but not the flame, as in an avalanche? Does a grenade attack count as one series, or one per grenade? These niggling little questions have taken more of my attention than I ever thought possible, and left me wondering if the whole thing was worth it. In the end, of course, it was all fun, but I think you'll find my figures fall short of gospel. Be so advised.

Have Bond Movies Become More Explosive?

There is no question that the constant boom, bang, flash of action movies is a modern affair; the most explosive Bond movies were made in the 1980's or later (with the exception of *The Spy Who Loved Me*, the only highly combustible of the seventies movies). Pierce Brosnan is the only Bond star for whom the number of explosions has always been in the double digits (see chart). While earlier Bond movies consistently sought, and generally achieved, impressive pyrotechnics, it is only since the 1990's that explosions have been a beginning-to-end affair. Many fans complain, with some justification, that modern action movies are overwhelming, adrenalin-based events that leave one exhausted rather than exhilarated. A movie like *On Her Majesty's Secret Service* has only two explosions, but one of them is absolutely amazing and cathartic. For better or worse, the sixties are over, and in 1999 we were treated to a total of nineteen explosions in *The World is Not Enough*. Ironically, the last of these is something of a fizzle.

Fifty+ Years of Explosions	
Dr. No	2
From Russia with Love	5
Goldfinger	4
Thunderball	3
You Only Live Twice	6
On Her Majesty's Secret Service	2
Diamonds Are Forever	6
Live and Let Die	2
The Man with the Golden Gun	1
The Spy Who Loved Me	11
Moonraker	6
For Your Eyes Only	5
Octopussy	2
Never Say Never Again	5
A View to a Kill	6
The Living Daylights	12
Licence to Kill	7
GoldenEye	14
Tomorrow Never Dies	10
The World is Not Enough	19
Die Another Day	19
Casino Royale	3
Quantum of Solace	3
Skyfall	10
Spectre	7
Total	**170**

Bond fans would be happier with less boom and more spying, and are increasingly annoyed that modern filmmaking takes Bond away from his espionage roots. *Die Another Day* in particular received much fan wrath in that regard (even though its boom-count is identical to *The World is Not Enough*), with the explosive break-up of the Antonov jet the subject of sneering.

That said, when done right, when a little restraint is used earlier in the movie, and in balance with spying, sex, and style, fans can certainly be guaranteed that things will go boom, and will actually enhance the experience.

Top Ten Explosions in Bond Films

Following are great, satisfying, loud, impressive booms. But I can't quite put them in quality order. Whichever one I'm watching at the moment is best. Whichever one I saw most recently is the one that gave me goosebumps. So, here they are, in chronological order.

Goldfinger: The Heroin Processing Plant

Oh, sure, we saw him break in and plant the explosives. But the casual glance at his watch, followed by that huge boom, was surprising and delightful, and remains a highlight of a great pre-titles sequence.

Thunderball: The Disco Volante

When Largo's yacht crashes and explodes in the climax, debris flies everywhere.

Windows broke as far as twenty miles away, according to special effects designer John Stears. *Thunderball* received an Academy Award for special effects.

On Her Majesty's Secret Service: Piz Gloria

There is little that could overstate the impression created by blowing up the top of an Alp.

For Your Eyes Only: Kristatos's Warehouse

Not as memorable as blowing up an Alp, but in the context of the film, quite a blast. The explosion is aided by the fact that it tops an excellent battle scene that is long on shadows and darkness. Then, just before dawn, the warehouse (another heroin site) blows up in a spectacular display.

Octopussy: The Hangar

This happens in the pre-titles sequence; Bond has planted a bomb in the hangar, but he has been caught and the bomb disabled. Now he's being chased by a heat-seeking missile in the Acrostar. He flies back through the hangar, and the missile accomplishes his mission for him. We're treated to the flying trick, then the camera backs away so we get a long shot of the explosive result.

Never Say Never Again: Fatima Blush

Leaving only her shoes. Not as big or showy as a heroin plant, but with an exceptionally cool result.

Licence to Kill: the First Tanker

The finale of *Licence to Kill* has a terrific series of explosions; four tankers, a flaming car, and Sanchez going up in a big FOOM! of fire. Choosing a favorite depends upon if you like sheer explosive force, or dramatic/emotional impact. Surely the emotional winner is Sanchez, but by then, we've been subject to a long series of explosions, and the effect is starting to wear down. I'm going for the first one, which is huge, impressive on any scale, and is our first clear understanding that chasing around in gasoline tankers poses a few logistical problems.

GoldenEye: Severnaya

This is probably the one where a certain segment of fans start getting grumpy about how 'Bond has turned into *Die Hard*' or a movie of the week or something. It's not just that *GoldenEye* is twice as explosive as the previous film, but that the booms come so fast, one right on top of another, as if there is no other way to excite an audience.

Nonetheless, I think this one is magnificent. Ourumov and Onatopp commit a horrific act of mass murder, and when we think it's over, we are met with Natalya dealing with a tragic and frightening aftermath. Then, when we think that's over, the whole thing blows up, and my goodness does it blow!

Tomorrow Never Dies: The Arms Bazaar

Unlike the previous explosion, you know this one is coming. You see the missile being launched, you watch its trajectory, and you watch Bond's desperate race to escape and to prevent a nuclear meltdown that will "make Chernobyl look like picnic." What is wonderful about this one is the filming; the framing of the huge explosion behind Bond as he flies away.

The World is Not Enough: Vauxhall

Our first sight of the exterior of MI6—at the real MI6 building, at Vauxhall. Few explosions have such a startling impact on Bond's world. This isn't a satisfying end to the villain's schemes and/or life, but an ugly beginning to a difficult adventure. Positively shocking!

THUNDERBALL (1965)

Survey Says!

> Percent Favorite: 3%
> Top 5 Cumulative: 7/25 (tied)
> Numeric Rating: 7.4/10
> Ranking: 9.6 (8th/25)

My Rating and Ranking

> Rated: 9/10
> Ranked: 12 out of 25

Summary

SPECTRE is back, with a plan to steal two atomic bombs by replacing a NATO observer with a surgically-altered duplicate. They demand a ransom of $100 million worth of flawless diamonds. Bond encounters the NATO pilot's body while recuperating from pre-title injuries, and requests assignment to Nassau, where the pilot's sister, Domino, is living. In Nassau, Bond teams up with Felix Leiter, and seduces Domino. He encounters SPECTRE agents Fiona Volpe, an assassin, and Emilio Largo, owner of the Disco Volante. Bond finds the bombs and with the help of U.S. military frogmen, defeats Largo's men. While Bond and Largo are engaged in hand-to-hand combat, Domino kills Largo.

> **James Bond:** Sean Connery
> **Dominique "Domino" Derval:** Claudine Auger
> **Fiona Volpe: (SPECTRE #3):** Luciana Paluzzi
> **Emilio Largo (SPECTRE #2):** Adolfo Celi
> **Ernst Stavro Blofeld:** Anthony Dawson, voice of Eric Pohlmann
> **Felix Leiter:** Rik Van Nutter
> **Patricia Fearing:** Molly Peters
> **Paula Caplan:** Martine Beswick
> **M:** Bernard Lee
> **Moneypenny:** Lois Maxwell
> **Q:** Desmond Llewelyn
> **Directed by** Terence Young

Discussion

Thunderball is a wonderful Bond movie, and an elegant one. However, it has two fatal flaws that prevent it from being the greatest Bond movie of all: A reliance on coincidence, and a lackluster half-hour's worth of underwater action. I say this, knowing full well that there is a sizeable minority of fans who believe *Thunderball* is the greatest Bond movie. Placing seventh on the "Top Five Cumulative" is no small potatoes, and *Thunderball* is much beloved. Many fans, though, bemoan the plodding pace of the underwater scenes, and I will never deviate from my position that, when the director turns the camera away from a climactic fight scene to show beautiful octopuses and eels, you know you've got a real snorer on your hands. The filming of these scenes is simply too detailed. Look at Largo's men retrieving the bombs and camouflaging the plane—where are Peter Hunt's rapid cuts when they're needed? Peter Hunt was indeed the supervising editor, and his signature style is in evidence in the final fight between Largo and Bond on the Disco Volante, but rapid cutting wasn't used in the scenes in question.

The second problem, coincidence, is troubling in terms of the intelligence of the story, but doesn't interfere with moment-by-moment enjoyment. Bond just happens to be in Shrublands at the same time as Count Lippe and the late Major Derval's remains. Bond films, unlike many action-adventures, are usually refreshingly free of "just happens" plot devices. It is a shame this one remained in the script.

But why focus on the negative? *Thunderball* is still nearly everything a Bond movie should be. The plot is fantastic. The audacious theft of a Vulcan aircraft with two atomic bombs aboard is a joy to watch. The meticulous planning, from the plastic surgery and voice lessons that turn Angelo Palazzi into Francois Derval, to the underwater landing lights, to the carefully-devised demand for uncut diamonds, all provide moment after moment for the audience to quietly whisper "Wow!" The cool hand of SPECTRE never supplied more chill, beginning with our first view of their headquarters at the International Brotherhood for the Assistance of Stateless Persons, the meeting, the very permanent dismissal of a traitorous member, and Largo's nonchalant reaction to it—it all adds up to a team of villains both powerful and fascinating to watch.

From the SPECTRE meeting we segue into Bond's visit to Shrublands.In the novel **Thunderball**, this was a comedic look at health faddism, and was probably the funniest thing Ian Fleming ever wrote. The humor angle was played when *Thunderball* was remade as *Never Say Never Again*. In this earlier movie, the spa visit is played fairly straight, and it is interesting to see the apparently indestructible James Bond being treated for injuries we saw him incur. In fact, this is the last time we see Bond actually injured until *The World is Not Enough* (he is faking an injury at the end of *Octopussy*). Some fans find the spa scenes dull, but I like the unusual setting, the odd source of danger (those traction machines always did look scary, didn't they?), and the seduction of Patricia Fearing. There is distaste looking back at the seduction, during which Bond blackmails Patricia into sex. But that was the era when movies assumed a woman might say "No, no, no" with her lips, and "Yes, yes, yes" with her eyes. Patricia smiles and laughs when she says, "You don't mean...!" There is no doubt, upon review, that she is an entirely willing partner who doth protest too much.

The scene of the meeting of "Every double-0 man in Europe" is nicely paralleled to the SPECTRE meeting, and its tantalizing glimpse at the workings of MI6 keeps fan tongues wagging to this day. Ken Adam's set design deserves much of the credit for making the interior of MI6 so enticing.

The dialogue in *Thunderball* is crisp and rapid-fire, reminiscent of *His Girl Friday* more than James Bond. Fiona Volpe and Domino Derval are two of the finest Bond girls to ever grace the screen. Fiona, the model for all villainous vixens to come, is luxuriously sexual, a sharp-tongued wildcat who is happy to make love to a man and just as happy to then kill him. Domino is a wounded innocent, a lost soul, awaiting her next tragedy with downcast eyes. Claudine Auger is no actress, and her final shift into toughness is unconvincing, but she paints a lovely picture, and she holds the screen, winning Bond's and the viewer's heart. *Thunderball* is lavish with its casting of beautiful women; in addition to Fiona and Domino, we are offered two female agents (Mademoiselle LaPorte and Paula Caplan) and a gorgeous physical therapist (Patricia Fearing) with a weakness for mink gloves.

Connery gives one of his very best performances (his own personal favorite). He toys with Largo while playing the fool, he flirts with Domino and then feels for her. The only weak spots in the cast are Rik Van Nutter as Felix and Adolfo Celi as Largo. Unlike Van Nutter, Celi is a good enough actor, but his character was unformed. He had strength and toughness, but was an unimpressive villain to follow Goldfinger. It was as if Eon thought that the eyepatch gave sufficient character. On the other hand, Largo gets off some good lines ("Vargas doesn't drink, doesn't smoke, doesn't make love. What do you do, Vargas?") and he is the first villain with a shark pool. That shark pool is a neat trick, very scary—too bad feeding people to sharks became a Bond cliché.

Thunderball is one of the most beautiful of the Bond films. The Nassau locations are dazzling. The cinematography is gorgeous, with lush colors and hot locations, especially during the extended and wonderful Junkanoo sequence. Domino is almost always seen dressed in black and/or white—during Junkanoo she appears in a red gown that accentuates the danger and excitement of the scene. The festival was filmed on location with local participants wearing their own costumes (albeit off-season; see below), and the sense of naturalism makes a big difference. Compare this scene to the similar one in *Moonraker* (at Carnival in Rio), which was filmed in the studio, and you'll see the strength of location footage.

The floating and gyrating women in *Thunderball*'s title sequence is truly Maurice Binder's signature piece. Remember that Binder's *Dr. No* titles were quite different from the style that typifies his work, and that Robert Brownjohn did the titles for the next two films. It is for work like *Thunderball* that Binder became famous; nude women moving seductively—swimming, dancing, leaping—through a colored backdrop while scenes suggestive of the plot appear in the background.

Thunderball also has an excellent pre-titles sequence. It is not the perfect mini-movie of *Goldfinger*'s pre-titles, but it is a fine self-contained tale that features the very famous Bell Textron jet pack. It is hard to explain now how that device amazed and impressed 1965 audiences.

Sadly, the movie falls apart right when it should come together. The mass underwater combat could have been a thrilling climax if the problem of slow underwater movement and masked faces had been overcome. The sometimes gruesome battle (harpoons passing through an arm, entering an eye) could have been much more exciting. One point of interest is that Bond moves through the combat almost exactly as he does in the gypsy camp battle in *From Russia with Love*. Not part of either group, he causes mayhem that turns the tide, yet stands apart.

After this slowdown, the film overcompensates with a too-fast battle aboard the Disco Volante, the film speed cranking higher and higher until we expect the voices to come out in squeaks. Peter Hunt innovated a rapid editing technique and then didn't know when to call it quits; the same problem is in evidence in *On Her Majesty's Secret Service*, his directorial debut.

Figure 6: Cover to the program book for Thunderball, circa 1965. A blind date brought this as a gift; we never dated again, but his long-ago thoughtfulness is still appreciated. Worn and aged, it is far from collectible condition, but I treasure it.

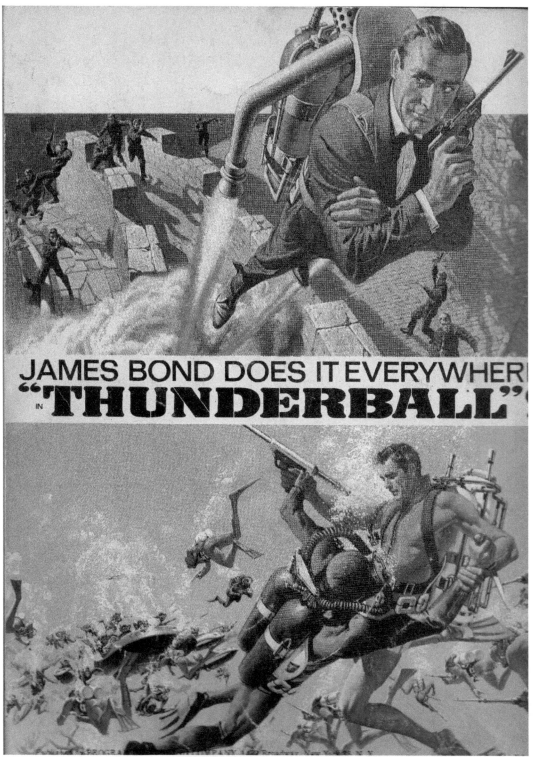

Figure 7: Back cover of the Thunderball program book

The High Points

- Sparkling dialogue, excellent screenplay.
- The return of SPECTRE and the unseen Blofeld.
- Two great, frankly sexy Bond girls: Domino and Fiona, and three more for good measure.
- Four (count 'em) gorgeous designer bathing suits for Domino.
- A fascinating and exciting plot, involving stolen identity, stolen bombs, and the blackmail of NATO.
- Gorgeous Nassau locations, and terrific "local color" during the Junkanoo.
- A swimming pool full of "the notorious Golden Grotto sharks."
- Wonderful title sequence.
- Great John Barry score.

The Low Points

- Drawn-out underwater sequences, especially the final combat, in which movement is slow and it is hard to tell who is who.
- Hyper-cranked final combat between Largo and Bond.
- An uninteresting main villain.
- Rik Van Nutter's wooden performance as Felix Leiter.

Quotable Quotes

Bond to Patricia (under his breath): "See you later, irrigator."

Domino: "What sharp little eyes you have."
Bond (to himself): "Wait 'til you get to my teeth."

Bond (as Fiona drives over 90 miles an hour): "Fly here often?"

Fiona: "Some men don't like to be driven."
Bond: "No, some men don't like being taken for a ride."

Bond: "That gun...looks more fitting for a woman."
Largo: "Do you know much about guns, Mr. Bond?"
Bond: "No. I know a little about women."

Fiona to Bond: "But of course, I forgot your ego, Mr. Bond. James Bond, who only has to make love to a woman and she starts to hear heavenly choirs singing. She repents, and immediately returns to the side of right and virtue. But not this one."

Bond (about Fiona): "Mind if my friend sits this one out? She's just dead."

Bond (removes a poisonous spine from Domino's foot with his teeth): "That's the first time I've tasted women. They're rather good."

Bond harpoons Vargas: "I think he got the point."

Domino harpoons Largo: "I'm glad I killed him."
Bond: *"You're* glad?"

Facts and Figures

SEXUAL ENCOUNTERS

<u>Three</u>: Patricia Fearing, Fiona Volpe, and Domino Derval.

BOND'S CAR

The Aston Martin DB5

DEATHS

<u>Thirty-two</u>:

- Colonel Jacques Botier, SPECTRE #9, Count Lippe, Francois Derval, Angelo Palazzi, the three men on the Vulcan with Palazzi, the thug sent to spy on Bond; who is dispatched in the shark pool, Paula Caplan, Fiona Volpe, Vargas, Largo.
- In the final underwater battle, nineteen, counted as follows: Serious wounds by harpoon are counted as deaths; removing masks or oxygen are not counted—the divers swim towards the surface; knocking someone on the head or knocking him over is not counted, floating bodies are not counted—we probably saw the same men wounded earlier.

Bond Kills

- <u>Seven</u> directly: Botier, Vargas, four in the final underwater battle, Largo.
- <u>One</u> indirectly: He places Fiona in the line of her own man's fire.

EXPLOSIONS

<u>Three</u>: Lippe's car, a rather impressive one when the Disco Volante "cocoon" blows, and the mother of them all when the rest of the yacht goes up. John Stears, who won an Academy Award for *Thunderball*'s special effects, recalls that blowing up the Disco Volante broke windows twenty miles away!

BOND'S FOOD AND DRINKS

Vodka Martinis

<u>One</u>, when Bond is in the hotel with Felix, after kicking out Largo's spy. He pours himself the ingredients, but no shaker is in evidence.

Other Drinks

- A bottle of red wine poolside with Domino. We see the wine in glasses and we see a bottle in an ice bucket. Chilled red wine is normally a faux pas, but it might be acceptable in a very hot climate like Nassau. I wondered about conch (fish) soup with red wine. According to the Minister of Martinis "Bahamian conch chowder is actually a tomato-based soup (like Manhattan clam chowder) so red wine is... an acceptable accompaniment."

- Dom Perignon 1955 ordered at the casino.
- Rum Collins with Largo at Palmyra.
- A unidentified champagne with Domino at the Junkanoo.

Food

- On the phone, Moneypenny says that while at Shrublands, Bond is on a diet of "yogurt and lemon juice."
- Conch chowder with Domino poolside.
- Beluga caviar with Domino at the casino.
- Bond lunches at Palmyra, which we do not see. Domino remarks that they are having conch chowder, but this may be sarcasm.

GAMBLING AND SPORTS

- Chemin-de-fer; Bond defeats Largo.
- Target shooting at Palmyra.

Amaze Your Friends!

- In the pre-titles sequence, the Aston Martin shoots water out the back, a feature not found in *Goldfinger*. The car is parked while this happens. That is because there was no room for both the engine and the water!
- Luciana Paluzzi (Fiona Volpe) originally auditioned for the part of Domino.
- *Thunderball* was intended to be the first Bond movie, but plans were changed because of the Kevin McClory lawsuit. As a result of that lawsuit, McClory owned the rights to *Thunderball* and is credited as the film's producer; it is the only Eon Productions Bond film not produced by Harry Saltzman, Cubby Broccoli, or a member of the Broccoli family.
- This is the first Bond movie in which Sean Connery, rather than stuntman Bob Simmons, appears in the gunbarrel. It is also the first gunbarrel sequence in which the dot zooms into the pre-titles sequence, instead of going white.
- When Bond leaves Shrublands, Patricia tells him "anytime, anyplace," and Bond responds "Another time, another place." This is an in-joke referring to the movie *Another Time, Another Place* starring Sean Connery.

Most Interesting Goofs

What a Time for a Party: Junkanoo is normally held the day after Christmas, December 26. *Thunderball* takes place in May (dates for delivery of the ransom are given).

A few of the more noticeable editing errors include

- When Felix lets Bond into the water to look for the Vulcan, he is wearing shorts, then long pants, then shorts again.

- During the final combat, a shot of an American diver being killed is used twice.
- Bond is wearing a blue mask, has the mask ripped off, and steals a black mask from one of Largo's men. Immediately, the mask is blue again.

VILLAINS

There are basically two kinds of bad guys in a Bond movie; the brains and the brawn, otherwise known as villains and henchmen. Villains are the guys (or gals) with a master plan, a scheme (see HE'S QUITE MAD, YOU KNOW for details). The henchmen, on the other hand, are the muscle, the killers and fighters; the front and rear guard. Either literally or figuratively, they are mute. A third sort of villain is a secondary employee of the mastermind. He might be a techno-henchman, like Ricky Jay's character Henry Gupta in *Tomorrow Never Dies*; brains rather than brawn, but not the brains behind the operation. He is secondary to the operation, but may have a significant scene or two in the movie—like Professor Dent in *Dr. No*.

Because there are so many, and because their roles differ so much, henchmen and villains are covered in separate sections, with secondary villains like Dent and Gupta placed with henchmen. Here, we're concerned with the brains of the outfit. In a few cases, a secondary villain is given; one who is so important to the plot he or she functions almost as a partner to the main villain.

The Villain Type

Bond is often faced with enemies who, like M, and like many of his allies, are a kind of father figure. They are older men, and in a perverted way, they often advise him. They tell him the way of the world, the "true wisdom" of their villainy. Dr. No hoped that Bond would change sides and become his protégé. Some of these villains compete with Bond, both father-to-son, and man-to-man. Several competed for the same women, usually a deadly game for the woman.

Although many consider Blofeld the true model for villainy, (e.g. the model that was copied for Dr. Evil), it was the first Bond film villain, Dr. No, who set the form. It was Dr. No who first wore the Nehru jacket, who spoke politely and reasonably about villainy, who called his enemy "Mr. Bond" and served him champagne. After that, the dye was cast. Blofeld in three movies, Hugo Drax, and Elliot Carver all buttoned straight up to the chin, and villains such as Kananga and Stromberg had outfits that suggested the Nehru look even when it wasn't duplicated exactly.

Most Bond villains may be of a type, but in general, that type is successful. Even those in fairly bad movies, such as Scaramanga in *The Man with the Golden Gun*, have a high quality of menace and charisma, and are worthy adversaries for the world's greatest secret agent. Fleming was a master at sketching a repulsive yet fascinating character, and those drawn directly from his novels are a significant part of the Bond mystique.

Fleming established a type of female villain as well. He had no interest in femmes fatale, such characters as Fiona Volpe and Helga Brandt were entirely cinematic creations. Fleming's villainess was short, squat, and ugly. In **From Russia with Love**, Rosa Klebb is a Russian lesbian, whereas in **On Her Majesty's Secret Service**, Irma Bunt is heterosexual; she is Blofeld's German lover. Otherwise, the two women are nearly identical both in appearance and in personality. They are hard, formal, compulsively orderly, and they relish violence.

Playing Against Type

Some villains have been maniacal rather than cool, although surprisingly, this is hard to pull off. Christopher Walken, normally a great actor, made mania seem silly in *A View to a Kill*, and many fans look upon Jonathan Pryce's performance in *Tomorrow Never Dies* with equal distaste.

A few villains have broken the mold entirely, with mixed results. Since "the mold" was created by Ian Fleming, you'll find these characters in the later films, which depart partly or entirely from Fleming's source material. Many Bond movies of the 60's and '70's stray from Fleming's plots and situations while keeping his characters—examples include *You Only Live Twice*, *Live and Let Die*, and *The Man with the Golden Gun*. Eventually, though, the source material ran out. Fleming's short story "From a View to a Kill" had no strong villain, the character of Max Zorin, as well as the entire plot of *A View to a Kill*, were created for the film from whole cloth.

In addition to maniacal villains, these later creations include a former ally (Alec Trevelyan, *GoldenEye*) an apparent victim (Elektra King, *The World is Not Enough*), and an enemy in the nearly impenetrable disguise of a benefactor (Gustav Graves, *Die Another Day*).

Groups of Bad Guys

The Bond movies have, for the most part, carefully avoided real criminal or political organizations. By sticking with entirely fictional baddies, two goals are achieved: No one is insulted, and the movies do not become dated. Were Bond fighting SMERSH and the Russians, as he did in most of the books, the end of the Cold War would have been a problem. But serious evil on the part of Russians has always been depicted as untoward and unauthorized. Competition is okay (as in *For Your Eyes Only*, in which the goal is merely acquisition of an item), but murder and mayhem are not ascribed to any real government or group.

When governments have been wholly corrupt, in *Live and Let Die* and *Licence to Kill*, the films gave us a fictional country to be governed. The Mafia has been depicted in isolated cases, but never as the main villainous entity. In fact, the Sicilian crime organization Union Corse was Bond's ally in *On Her Majesty's Secret Service*.

Fictional, enemy crime organizations have been depicted in *Live and Let Die* (Mr. Big's gang) and *GoldenEye* (The Janus Group), and fictional corporations have frequently been fronts for criminal activities. They include...

• Auric Enterprises (*Goldfinger*)
• Osato Chemical & Engineering Co. (*You Only Live Twice*)
• Hai Fat Enterprises (*The Man with the Golden Gun*)
• Drax Industries (*Moonraker*)
• Zorin Industries (*A View to a Kill*)
• Carver Media Group (*Tomorrow Never Dies*)
• King Oil (*The World is Not Enough*)

• Greene Planet (*Quantum of Solace*)

But all of this is beside the point. In most fans' minds, there is only one criminal organization in the Bond world: SPECTRE, the Special Executor for Counter-Intelligence, Terrorism, Revenge, and Extortion, plagued Bond and the world at large for six of his first seven movies (Auric Goldfinger was an independent operator, financed by the Chinese government, and not connected to SPECTRE). Actually, it is unclear if SPECTRE existed after *You Only Live Twice*.

Ernst Stavro Blofeld (see below), the head of SPECTRE, was the villain in the next two movies, but the numbered agents and the name of the organization did not appear. It is possible, even likely, that SPECTRE was destroyed in the massive battle at the end of *You Only Live Twice*, and that Blofeld, alone, regrouped and reestablished himself, without his organization. Maybe that's why he needs to tinker with science in *On Her Majesty's Secret Service*, and steal Willard Whyte's company in *Diamonds Are Forever*.

Be that as it may, SPECTRE remains the only effective multi-film criminal organization, the only one that gave Bond real trouble, the only one that fans consistently remember. With its numbered agents, its ruthless discipline, and its murder-training facility, SPECTRE gave us the right kind of chills and thrills. They recruited from everywhere, including the Tong and the KGB, and had agents all over the world. It was as fascinating as MI6 and functioned as that agency's evil counterpart. It's a shame that Eon Productions is no longer interested in keeping a villain alive, because it was the continual re-arising of SPECTRE and Blofeld that made such an impact.

If you are only into the movies and have never read an Ian Fleming book, I recommend reading **Thunderball** if you are really interested in SPECTRE. This is the book that first introduced them, and it establishes their rules and structure in the kind of fascinating detail that a movie just can't get into.

The Craig Movies

In the first four Craig movies, we find exceptions to some of the above: First, a new criminal organization: Quantum, is introduced. In *Spectre*, this organization is subsumed into SPECTRE, but it appears to have originally been intended to replace the older organization, not be a part of it.

In *Spectre*, we spend time, for the first time, with a corrupt government organization working with the villain. C, head of joint security, is secretly working with SPECTRE, even while manipulating heads of state all over the world.

Ernst Stavro Blofeld

As Felix Leiter is to allies, Blofeld is to enemies. He was established with both significant continuity and significant lack of continuity. By this I mean, Bond got a recurring enemy, someone he always sought, but who continued to elude him. This gave the early films a consistent thread and a renewed tension that really worked. On the other hand, Blofeld was played by a different actor in most appearances—the only repeat being the voice and body roles in the two films when his face was unseen. He is immensely popular among fans, but the question, as with Felix, is which "he" we are talking about. Blofeld was nominated for AFI's 50 Greatest Villains of All Time; but didn't make the final cut.

THE UNSEEN BLOFELD, From Russia with Love and Thunderball

In a rather brilliant cinematic trick, the evil mastermind behind all of Bond's film woes (to that point); the dark force that even Rosa Klebb feared, was introduced as a voice and a pair of hands petting a cat. The sinister quality of this cannot be over-stated. Whatever, whoever it is that we cannot see is terrifying, powerful, cold, and deadly. The cat adds a strange effeminacy to the image, not merely an animal but a pedigreed, pampered, exotic animal in a diamond collar. It sits in Blofeld's lap being petted—soft, sensual, and apparently relaxed. The contrast is perfect. Unsurprisingly, "the unseen Blofeld" is the most popular Blofeld portrayal among fans, and among the most popular of any Bond villain.

Blofeld was played in these two movies by Anthony Dawson, who played Professor Dent in *Dr. No.* He was voiced by Eric Pohlmann, although many sources incorrectly cite Joseph Wiseman (Dr. No) as the voice in *Thunderball*.

DONALD PLEASENCE, You Only Live Twice

Eventually it had to happen. You can't play the invisible villain thing forever, or it becomes comedic. Eon Productions used SPECTRE more than Fleming did, tying them into *Dr. No* and *From Russia with Love*. Fleming (with Kevin McClory) introduced Blofeld in **Thunderball,** so that by the time Bond met him in person, he had only been behind the scenes once.

Eon's insertion of Blofeld into earlier films was a great idea, but by 1964 they were at the point of filming the novels where Blofeld actually appears. The original plan was to make *On Her Majesty's Secret Service* the fifth Bond film, followed by *You Only Live Twice*. In the novels, Blofeld kills Bond's wife in **On Her Majesty's Secret Service** (the movie follows the book quite closely) and then seeks (and gets) revenge in **You Only Live Twice.** Had the original order been kept, the movie *You Only Live Twice* would have been quite different. However, the severe weather conditions in the Alps gave Eon a fairly small window of opportunity for filming *On Her Majesty's Secret Service*, and scheduling requirements pushed it back.

The upshot is that the fifth film, *You Only Live Twice*, was adapted only in the loosest sense from the novel that shares its name, and Blofeld was seen in it for the first time.

It was a smart move to start with Blofeld unseen. In *You Only Live Twice*, his entire presentation is at first reflective of *From Russia with Love*. We see the cat, the feet and hands, and hear a voice. We see henchmen standing before him, afraid, and we see one of them die. Once again, Blofeld kills, but by merely pushing a button. Once again, he is removed, apart from the mayhem he creates.

Finally the moment comes, when Ernst Stavro Blofeld turns his chair to face James Bond. What a thrill that must have been in 1967! And what a letdown. At that moment, I think that no one could have matched the power and mystique of the unseen. Yet Pleasence was certainly not the man to try. His Blofeld is not popular among fans, and is sometimes cited among the worst of Bond villains, although I think this is an overstatement—a product of longing for what might have been, rather than an actual assessment of the portrayal. He is certainly a weak Blofeld small, toadish, and creepy—a villain in the Bond style, to be sure, but not the mastermind, the figure of terror and awe, that we had come to expect.

TELLY SAVALAS, On Her Majesty's Secret Service

Some fans like this performance. Some fans number it among their favorites. They believe that Blofeld should be tough, and Savalas is tough. They believe that Pleasence was a mistake, and Savalas is his diametric opposite. I, however, despise the performance, and cannot write a convincing case in its favor.

The casting of Telly Savalas baffles me. Other than the fact that Pleasence was also bald, he had nothing in common with any previous conception of SPECTRE's head. Savalas was known for thuggish, psychotic, or sadistic roles, and perhaps Eon wanted a more fearsome quality to Blofeld. But Blofeld is also brilliant, aloof, and, of course, European. Savalas is none of these things. He portrays Blofeld as a macho hood. For such an actor to portray a scientist with a soothing voice that makes the delicate ladies of the clinic trust him is beyond laughable. The ludicrousness of an American gangster type playing this role, and the fact that Blofeld's accent has suddenly become American, seems to have been noticed by no one—no one except the audience.

Savalas briefly holds the white cat and then shoves it roughly aside—obviously, this is not an actor who can convincingly pet a cat. He looks like he wants to throw a punch, not push a button and let his piranha fish do the dirty work. In essence, this Blofeld has nothing to do with the Blofeld from three previous movies. Not to mention he has one of the oddest and most irritating mannerisms I have ever seen on-screen—smoking while holding his cigarette straight up in a fist. No wonder he switched to lollipops!

CHARLES GRAY, Diamonds Are Forever

Blofeld needs to be large and imposing, unlike Donald Pleasence. He needs, unlike Telly Savalas, to portray an effete sort of snobbery, a bit of prissiness, consistent with a villain who pets a cat and doesn't dirty his hands by performing the killings he orders. He needs a commanding voice, since we were introduced to him as a voice alone, and a distinctive personal style. Charles Gray would seem the perfect choice.

Gray's portrayal of Blofeld is widely hated by fans. They call him effeminate and ridiculous, and they gasp in horror at his transvestite escape. I'll allow that this last bit was played too much for laughs, but machismo was not called for. Blofeld, in four prior movies, never punched anyone, he sneered and corrected more than he yelled, he hid behind a desk and a glass barrier. Gray played the mannered man of evil to the hilt, the cigarette holder, the "pussy," and the plummy accent. In my opinion, he was a fine choice and an excellent Blofeld. But that dress...fans will never forgive it, nor the hideous makeup job, and he is forever condemned as the wrong man for the part.

JOHN HOLLIS, *For Your Eyes Only*

Credited merely as "Man in Wheelchair," Eon decided to finish Blofeld off well and truly. When *The Spy Who Loved Me* was in production, Blofeld was the villain of record, and Kevin McClory threatened another lawsuit, claiming he owned SPECTRE and Blofeld. Eon decided they'd had enough. They didn't need Blofeld or his organization to make successful Bond films, and that was the end of that. Fans, though, weren't satisfied. If you watch *Diamonds Are Forever*, it is pretty obvious that Blofeld was killed—left helpless in a crushed and battered "bath-o-sub" on an exploding oil rig. But we didn't see him die (purposely, since Eon hoped to bring him back). There was a sense of dissatisfaction over the ambiguous end for the man responsible for widowing James Bond (people rarely mention that it was actually Irma Bunt who pulled the trigger).

So, for his film directing debut, John Glen killed off Blofeld in the pre-titles sequence, giving him no name, but making sure the bald head and white cat left the audience without doubt.

Unfortunately, this final moment of satisfaction was played as a joke—a joke on the fans, if you ask me! Blofeld squawks like a chicken, begging for his life, and inexplicably offering to buy Bond a delicatessen—one of the stupidest, unfunniest lines ever delivered in a Bond film. By the time Bond finishes him off, we no longer regret the character's departure from the series.

MAX VON SYDOW, *Never Say Never Again*

At last, the right actor for the part! Von Sydow is everything that Blofeld should always have been. At 6'3" he is long and lanky, matching the physique of the arms and legs we saw in *From Russia with Love* and *Thunderball*. He is an actor of great dignity, and subtle but pervasive menace. He played similarly deadly men in such spy movies as *The Quiller Memorandum* and *Three Days of the Condor*.

Alas, the right actor, the right role, and the wrong movie. Von Sydow is not only in a rather bad Bond film, but he is woefully underused, with barely any screen time, and none of it all that memorable. The part is little more than a tease, a tantalizing hint of the Blofeld-who-might-have-been.

CHRISTOPH WALTZ, *Spectre*

Waltz was introduced as a tease to the world, listed as Oberhauser in the credits and promotional materials. Fans quickly identified the name Oberhauser from Bond's childhood: The film *Spectre* follows the short story "Octopussy" in describing Hannes Oberhauser as a climbing instructor who became a surrogate father to Bond—Franz, though, is a cinematic invention. From there, the rumor mill had Waltz as Blofeld long before the film was released.

At which point, fan reaction was...confused. Waltz was an Academy Award winner (see 007 AT THE OSCARS) for playing a Nazi in *Inglourious Basterds*, so you want to give him the benefit of the doubt—he sure can do evil. But he didn't seem very much like Blofeld. But wait and see, right?

Unfortunately, the movie brought fans' worst fears to life. This maniacal giggler wasn't Blofeld, he was an angry child. The entire plot reduced an evil mastermind to a petty and personal revenge scheme. Oddly, the iconic cat was present but never touched.

One excellent grace note was giving Blofeld injuries, late in the film, that exactly replicated the facial disfigurement Donald Pleasence had in *You Only Live Twice*.

Top Five/Bottom Five

Once again, this comes from a combination of major media surveys, small fan-based surveys, and personal bias.

Best
1. **Ernst Stavro Blofeld,** *From Russia with Love* and *Thunderball*
2. **Auric Goldfinger,** *Goldfinger*
3. **Alec Trevelyan,** *GoldenEye*
4. **Francisco Scaramanga,** *The Man with the Golden Gun*
5. **Maximillian Largo,** *Never Say Never Again*
 AND: Le Chiffre, *Casino Royale*

Worst
1. **"Man in Wheelchair,"** a.k.a. **Ernst Stavro Blofeld,** *For Your Eyes Only*
2. **General Georgi Koskov** and **General Brad Whitaker,** *The Living Daylights*
3. **Dr. Kananga/Mr. Big,** *Live and Let Die*
4. **Ernst Stavro Blofeld** and **Irma Bunt,** *On Her Majesty's Secret Service*
5. **Karl Stromberg,** *The Spy Who Loved Me*
 AND: Dominic Greene, *Quantum of Solace*

The Best Villains

The Unseen Blofeld

As discussed above, there is perhaps nothing we can see on-screen as scary and impressive as that which remains unseen. When Blofeld's hand, ring, and cat appeared in *From Russia with Love*, we understood that Bond was fighting something larger than himself, more mysterious than the Cold War, and more dangerous than simple espionage. Blofeld and SPECTRE represented a poison seeping through the underpinnings of the world we knew, they created a need for a hero of Bond's magnitude, and they balanced Bond's heroism with equal and opposite weight. Bond wasn't too good to be true in a world in which someone as sinister as Blofeld could exist.

Auric Goldfinger

Here is a man of madness, style, intelligence, and weight. Here is a man with a truly masterful scheme. Here is a man with an outrageously bad fashion sense. The film's Goldfinger is every inch the character Ian Fleming created, including the clothing (except that Fleming's Goldfinger was short, only five feet tall). It is Goldfinger who gave us the most famous line ever spoken by a Bond villain ("No, Mr. Bond, I expect you to die"), the line we want every villain, in some way or another, to speak.

From a villainous point of view, Goldfinger just has everything right about him. He is usually a step or three ahead of Bond, but he is a couple of steps behind Pussy Galore. The old fool loses two women to Bond, and it is so appealing to have an absolute genius at crime be such a flop with the ladies.

The uncredited Michael Collins deserves recognition here. Gert Frobe is great, but so is the man who dubbed his dialogue.

Alec Trevelyan

Sean Bean's traitorous agent is a huge favorite among younger fans, and he was an excellent villain to introduce the modern Bond era. In the six years between *Licence to Kill* and *GoldenEye*, the Berlin Wall fell and the Cold War ended. The Bond films had never been particularly about the Cold War—SPECTRE was apolitical, as were the various corporate villains—but there was a perception that Bond was old hat—cue Agent 006. His character defines post-Cold War anxiety, questions about the validity of espionage, and the meaning of Bond himself. By betraying Bond and England, he defines Bond's role. By existing as a product of post-War British-Soviet relations, and building his criminality in post-Soviet Russia, Alec Trevelyan is a character who sketches the changes of an era; the changes of James Bond.

The portrayal is superb, with just the right combination of charm and sneering. Alec insinuates, he mocks, and he shows himself to be the anti-Bond, the dark side of James. The reductive game he plays on Bond, turning his character traits into cheap psychology, is potent because it seems to come from the inside—from Bond as much as from his enemy.

Alec Trevelyan was the right idea at the right time, and the right actor had the role.

Francisco Scaramanga

It is a credit to Christopher Lee's gravitas and charisma that Scaramanga is considered by so many fans to be among the greatest of Bond's enemies. Lee overcame a movie that many number among the worst. The very same fans will put Scaramanga in their Top Five, and *The Man with the Golden Gun* in their Bottom Five. Go figure.

The Man with the Golden Gun is a schizophrenic movie, a bizarre combination of excellence and nonsense. Lee's portrayal stands firmly on the side of excellence. He plays the title character with a smooth confidence, a sort of arrogance about the rightness of his amorality. His conviction that he is right is a little flawed, in that he doesn't show the craziness underneath. For some fans, he is simply too sympathetic where he should be distasteful. However, I'd cite the scene of erotic domination, where he caresses Andrea Anders with his gun, as an example of repugnant behavior. He creates exactly what a successful villain must, an attraction-repulsion reaction in the audience, who cannot but pity Andrea at the same time they are fascinated.

The literary Scaramanga was a tough-talking Italian-American gangster, and gangster slang was not one of Fleming's skills—I always wince when I read his dialogue for these characters, which always says to me that Ian Fleming never met a real gangster in his life. By changing the character to a suave British counterpart to Bond, Eon made the right decision.

Maximillian Largo

In almost every way, *Thunderball* is an immeasurably better movie than its remake, *Never Say Never Again*. But the latter's villain, Maximillian Largo, is a distinct improvement over *Thunderball*'s Emilio Largo. Adolfo Celi's character was lackluster; he had strength and menace, but little personality. Klaus Maria Brandauer, on the other hand, shows us how it ought to be done!

Brandauer's Largo is at once larger than life and utterly believable. His villainy has a playful quality, but he isn't played for laughs. He is simply relaxed about being crazy, and he knows he holds the reins.

The movie's best scene is Largo's display of sadism and madness, confronting Domino with a priceless treasure and then casually letting it drop. "You're insane!" she cries. He tilts his head to the side, as if listening to the voices, and says "Yah." It's as if he's saying, *What difference does it make? I may be insane, but I'm in charge here.* He then proceeds to sell her into slavery. The entire sequence is held together by Brandauer's electric presence, and he brings the rest of the movie to its knees.

Like Scaramanga, Max Largo is trapped in a movie far beneath him, but his superb villain should not be forgotten on that account.

Le Chiffre

Just as Vesper Lynd immediately shot to the top of fans' "Bond girl" lists, Le Chiffre forced fans to reorder their lists of favorite villains to include him, the moment *Casino Royale* was released.

Le Chiffre fits the mold of the great Bond villains; brilliant, calculating, and strangely deformed. The constant use of an inhaler as well as the bleeding eye give him an aura of strangeness, almost otherworldliness. He seems to know this, and use it to intimidate people, as we see with the poker game on his yacht.

Mads Mikkelsen's performance in *Casino Royale* is extremely controlled. Continually, we see a man on the edge, a man often driven by anger and fear, but he never completely lets go. It is unusual for a Bond villain to spend so much of the time aware that he is in trouble—when confronted by Obanno, when he loses at poker, when Bond refuses to succumb to torture, and finally, when killed by Mr. White. Most villains, by contrast, seem to have the upper hand until the very end. It gives Mikkelsen a wider range of emotions to portray, and he does so brilliantly.

More Great Villains

Rosa Klebb

It was hard to leave *From Russia with Love*'s Colonel Klebb out of the top five. She's supremely evil, really, really scary, and warped my childhood in unknowable ways. I am still scared of sensible shoes. The whole package is a creation of almost demonic brilliance—how did Fleming do it? Her tiny size, the formal scowl, the creepy insinuation, and the absolute commitment to violence. A woman with a poison knife in her shoe and brass knuckles in her pocket, and a certain nonchalance about using either. Like most of the great Bond villains, she loses the object of her desire to 007.

Elliot Carver

Fans hate this guy! They think his *Tomorrow Never Dies* scheme is stupid and they think Jonathan Pryce's acting is over the top. But I have to disagree. I like the way the manipulation of the media is utterly modern, yet classically evil. I like the crazed glint in Carver's eye, the way he struts his megalomania like a point of honor, and the threat behind even his mildest remark. I like the possessive power he wields over poor, tragic Paris. Pryce is famed as a star of the London and New York stage, and his performance is, at times, too theatric, but I think it works.

Franz Sanchez

You have to give credit to a guy who has funnier lines than Bond at every turn. Sanchez, in *Licence to Kill*, is too prosaic for many fans, he's nothing but a drug lord after all. But he's a drug lord with style, a wicked sense of humor, and he's given a really full-bodied portrayal by Robert Davi. He has presence. Sanchez is one of those guys who doesn't believe for a moment that he's the bad guy. After all, he rewards loyalty, punishes disloyalty, and treats his guests well. If he is tough, well, it's a tough business. Sanchez believes he is a law unto himself, and that he adheres to that law.

General Orlov

Like Jonathan Pryce, Steven Berkoff is a stage actor who gives a highly theatrical performance. In *Octopussy*, he chews the scenery in the name of Mother Russia, playing a fanatic who will stop at nothing, and who lets it all hang out. In the thirteenth Bond movie, 007 was finally up against a villain representing the Soviet Union. Even then, his political motivations were frowned upon by the powers that be (including familiar face General Gogol, making his fourth Bond appearance). Orlov cuts a dashing figure of crazed idealism, twisting and shouting his villainy in a truly memorable way.

The Worst Villains

"Man in Wheelchair," a.k.a. Ernst Stavro Blofeld

It shouldn't matter, right? It's just the unconnected pre-titles sequence of *For Your Eyes Only*, an otherwise pretty good movie. But it does. It galls. One of the greatest villains in movie history, a titan, brought to the level of self-parody in what we know beyond doubt is his final appearance. Damn.

(Note: *Knew* beyond doubt, until *Spectre*.)

General Georgi Koskov and General Brad Whitaker

I am perhaps cheating by grouping two together, as they are quite unlike each other except for their collaboration in *The Living Daylights*. Neither is all that bad, yet they conspire, not merely to smuggle diamonds and bring down General Pushkin, but to weaken the center of an otherwise excellent Bond film. They are a confused mess, two sloppily-drawn villains where one strong one was needed. Koskov is laid back, casual, and greedy. He is not so much evil as selfish and lazy, he conspires merely to have a better life. Whitaker has more interest, something could definitely have been done with his military fetish, but he is shoved into the background. Because the script is clumsy in deciding who is the villain and what the scheme is, we end up with two half-villains that neither frighten nor impress.

Dr. Kananga / Mr. Big

You'd think a respected actor in two roles could do at least one of them right. Yaphet Kotto is terrific in one of my all time favorite (non-Bond) movies, *Alien*. But in *Live and Let Die*, he has no naturalism or presence as either Mr. Big or Dr. Kananga. Mr. Big is little more than a stereotype, a jive-talking visitor from a blaxploitation flick with such heavy makeup that he appears to be gray with some disease. Kananga, on the other hand, is an attempt at a black Dr. No, smooth and brilliant. Instead, he is a jolly teddy bear of a villain, emanating no power, and demonstrating no menace. When he suffers the most ignoble death of any Bond villain, he represents another children's toy—balloon instead of teddy bear. It is bad to look a fool in life, but far worse to look a fool in death, and no one has ever died dumber than poor old Kananga.

Ernst Stavro Blofeld and Irma Bunt

Sometimes it's hard to be the author. Throughout this text, I am making every effort to temper my personal opinion with that of other Bond fans, using surveys and conversation to present, if not a balanced view, at least a broad one. But what am I to do with Savalas's performance in *On Her Majesty's Secret Service*? His Blofeld has a strong minority following, being in the top five for perhaps ten percent or more of Bond fans. Yet when I see him on-screen, I want to throw things at said screen!

Okay, so to be fair, I have added Irma Bunt to the mix, no one's favorite as far as I can tell, thereby decreasing the popularity of the overall Villain Package.

I have already written about Savalas. Irma Bunt is a fake Rosa Klebb, with a ski outfit and less interesting shoes. The implication that the two are a couple has an upsetting quality I'd rather not analyze.

Karl Stromberg

Unless you're a hardcore Bond fan, you might not even recognize the name. When you ask people about *The Spy Who Loved Me*, they'll say "Jaws," because Jaws was memorable, one of the great film henchmen of all time. But who the heck is Stromberg?

The lackluster villain played by Curt Jurgens was a last-minute substitute for Blofeld, when Eon and MGM decided to forego another battle with Kevin McClory. He has all the earmarks of a wannabe. He does nothing wrong, and nothing right, and is simply there to convey the plot by his mere presence, rather than to really drive it with any force. I remember Stromberg only because I watch the movies often enough to write about them—you have probably forgotten.

Dominic Greene

There are many Bond villain types. Prior to Dominc Greene in *Quantum of Solace*, "whiny" was not one of them. Greene is a petulant loser, and it's pretty clear that Camille sleeping with him to get information is the only way *anyone* sleeps with him—he reeks of "incel." He's a nasty little piece of business, with "little" being the operative word. Here's a villain who, when confronted "mano á mano" with Bond, shrieks like a banshee and slices his own foot open with an axe. Then gives Bond all the information he asks for. Then drinks motor oil. Dominc Greene just can't cut it.

The Mixed Bags

These last three are villains about whom the audience is very divided, with good and bad qualities. Here are some two-sided arguments for you to chew on.

Dr. Julius No

Why is Dr. No praised? Because he is the first cinematic Bond villain, the pace- setter, the mold. Who knows what manner of thugs and gangsters and crooks and creeps might have populated the Bond world had not Dr. No been chosen to lead the pack? Dr. No is praised because of the idea of Dr. No.

Why, then, condemn him? In a word, dullness. The man is stiff, flat, too restrained by half. Fleming's fascination with "mixed races" made a Chinese German interesting to the author, but the rest of us don't share that strange prejudicial obsession. The lack of hands, like Largo's eyepatch, simply cannot compensate for the lack of personality. Like Blofeld in *You Only Live Twice*, he cannot live up to the terrific prelude to his appearance.

Hugo Drax

Darn shame about Drax. The man has half the best lines ever spoken by a Bond villain. His wit is endlessly entertaining. But the acting! Have you ever watched *Moonraker* and wondered if Michael Lonsdale is even capable of moving his lips? I think it is entirely possible that all that great dialogue was spoken by a ventriloquist's dummy. Of course, this has never been proven.

Max Zorin

Ah, Mr. Walken, we had such high hopes. Many fans love Max Zorin in *A View to a Kill*, in part because they love Christopher Walken, and in part because he has a handful of amazingly good moments. The scene where he gleefully starts shooting down his own men in the mine is stunning, shocking, and 100% pure villainy. But for the most part, Zorin is too jolly and too slight. Most importantly, he is unworthy of the caliber of the actor playing him. Christopher Walken has given us many of cinema's creepiest characters, and we had every right to expect one in Max Zorin. Another opportunity lost.

The Complete List

If your favorite villain isn't listed here, check under Henchmen. Not every villain is here; these are the masterminds, the planners, and those who give orders to henchmen and lesser villains.

Dr. No

> **Dr. No** (Joseph Wiseman)

From Russia with Love

> **Ernst Stavro Blofeld, a.k.a. SPECTRE #1** (Anthony Dawson, voice of Eric Pohlmann)

> **Rosa Klebb, a.k.a. SPECTRE #3** (Lotte Lenya)

Goldfinger

> **Auric Goldfinger** (Gert Frobe)

Thunderball

> **Ernst Stavro Blofeld, a.k.a. SPECTRE #1** (Anthony Dawson, voice of Eric Pohlmann)

> **Emilio Largo, a.k.a. SPECTRE#2** (Adolfo Celi)

You Only Live Twice

> **Ernst Stavro Blofeld, a.k.a. SPECTRE #1** (Donald Pleasence)

On Her Majesty's Secret Service

> **Ernst Stavro Blofeld** (Telly Savalas)

> **Irma Bunt** (Ilsa Steppat)

Diamonds Are Forever

> **Ernst Stavro Blofeld** (Charles Gray)

Live and Let Die

> **Dr. Kananga/Mr. Big** (Yaphet Kotto)

The Man with the Golden Gun

> **Francisco Scaramanga** (Christopher Lee)

The Spy Who Loved Me

> **Karl Stromberg** (Curt Jurgens)

Moonraker

> **Hugo Drax** (Michael Lonsdale)

For Your Eyes Only

> **"Man in Wheelchair," a.k.a. Ernst Stavro Blofeld** (John Hollis)

> **Aris Kristatos** (Julian Glover)

Octopussy

> **Kamal Khan** (Louis Jordan)

> **General Orlov** (Steven Berkoff)

Never Say Never Again

> **Maximillian Largo** (Klaus Maria Brandauer)

> **Ernst Stavro Blofeld** (Max von Sydow)

A View to a Kill

> **Max Zorin** (Christopher Walken)

The Living Daylights

> **General Georgi Koskov** (Jeroen Krabbe)

> **Brad Whitaker** (Joe Don Baker)

Licence to Kill

> **Franz Sanchez** (Robert Davi)

GoldenEye

> **Alec Trevelyan, Agent 006** (Sean Bean)

Tomorrow Never Dies

> **Elliot Carver** (Jonathan Pryce)

The World is Not Enough

> **Elektra King** (Sophie Marceau)

> **Victor Zokas, a.k.a. Renard** (Robert Carlyle)

Die Another Day

Sir Gustav Graves (Toby Stephens)

Colonel Tan-Gun Moon (Will Yun Lee)

Casino Royale

Le Chiffre (Mads Mikkelsen)

Mr. White (Jesper Christensen)

Quantum of Solace

Dominc Greene (Mathieu Amalric)

Mr. White (Jesper Christensen)

Skyfall

Raoul Silva (Javier Bardem)

Spectre

Ernst Stavro Blofeld (a.k.a Franz Oberhauser) (Christoph Waltz)

No Time to Die

Ernst Stavro Blofeld (a.k.a Franz Oberhauser) (Christoph Waltz)

Safin (Rami Malek)

HE'S QUITE MAD, YOU KNOW

Bond says this to Pussy Galore about Goldfinger, after hearing his scheme. It is a sentiment repeated often in the Bond movies, and Elliot Carver, in *Tomorrow Never Dies*, had the definitive answer for it when he said "The distance between insanity and genius is measured only by success." Good enough—if any of Bond's enemies could succeed, they'd be impressive indeed. Even Bond admires the audacity and creative genius behind Goldfinger's plan. But could they succeed? Insane, sure, but plausible?

If we are to discuss these mad (mad!) schemes, there are a few questions to ask:

- Can it possibly succeed? (*Feasibility*)
- Is the goal worthwhile? (*Function*)
- Is it creative, new, different? (*Flair*)
- Is it an interesting or entertaining plan to watch? (*Fun*)
- Is it ridiculously complex? (*Follow*)

Based on these questions, every scheme can be rated on the **F Scale**. Each F (Function, Feasibility, Fun, Flair, and Following It) can be given a score from 1 (bad) to 5 (way cool), for a score of 5–25. "Fun" doesn't mean how fun the whole movie is, just the specifics of the scheme's unfolding. This seems like a more fun and diverting rating for schemes than Top Five/Bottom Five, so let's give it a go!

Dr. No

Scheme: Topple American missiles in order to increase international tensions, furthering SPECTRE's goal of world domination.

Feasibility: Dr. No has already successfully toppled several missiles. **5/5**: Very feasible.

Function: Although the scheme has definite value in harrying the enemy, ultimately it cannot work. Unlike the similar scheme in *You Only Live Twice*, toppling doesn't happen on a grand enough scale to cause major international tensions quickly enough. Inevitably, an agent will investigate, as both Bond and Leiter do, before an East vs. West showdown occurs. **3/5**: Mildly functional.

Flair: I don't think anyone had heard of toppling before *Dr. No*; it is flat but original. **3/5**: Somewhat creative.

Fun: Not only is the scheme not fun, it isn't meant to be. The fun is in watching Bond investigate Dr. No while avoiding the various attempts on his life. **1/5:** Not fun.

Following it: Simple and direct. **5/5:** Easy to follow.

Total Score: 17

From Russia with Love

Scheme: Manipulate an MI6 agent and a KGB clerk to steal a Lektor and be- come lovers, then kill both, thereby creating a sex scandal that will embarrass both organizations, having also acquired the Lektor.

Feasibility: If Red Grant had shot James Bond right away, it would have worked. **5/5:** Very feasible.

Function: Even Bond acknowledges its potential. The tangible goal of getting the Lektor is agreed upon as important by all three organizations (MI6, KGB, and SPECTRE). The sex scandal would have been a coup de grace. **5/5:** Very functional.

Flair: Wildly creative. **5/5:** Mucho flair.

Fun: Anything with a sex scandal, secret filming, and breaking into the Russian embassy is inherently fun. **5/5:** Buckets o' fun.

Following it: Kronsteen made it complicated on purpose. Those damn chess masters are like that! **3/5:** A little dicey.

Total Score: 23

Goldfinger

Scheme: Break into Fort Knox by sweeping the entire area with nerve gas, then det- onate an atomic bomb inside, thereby irradiating the entire U.S. gold supply, caus- ing chaos in the West and making Goldfinger a very rich man.

Feasibility: It has a mad sort of genius, doesn't it? The intricacy seems to beg for a flaw or a change of heart, which is after all what happens, but other than that, it's a goer. **4/5:** Feasible.

Function: I have a certain distaste for schemes that depend on predicting future human behavior. Sure, Goldfinger's gold will probably increase in value many times, as he predicts, but so will everyone else's. On the other hand, gold values may collapse and the world economy may become dependent on a new standard. Who knows? Still, it would probably work. **4/5:** Functional.

Flair: Imaginative and unpredictable. **5/5:** Fantastic!

Fun: Almost beyond measure. This is a scheme that involves pilots, gangsters, the inside of Fort Knox, and an atomic bomb! How cool is that? **5/5:** Fun! Fun! Fun!

Following it: Goldfinger explains everything to Bond very clearly. **5/5:** Easy to follow.

Total Score: 23

Thunderball

Scheme: Replace a NATO officer with a SPECTRE agent in order to steal a plane with two atomic weapons on board. Demand $100 million for the return of the weapons.

Feasibility: Rather brilliant, actually. Hiding the bombs underwater is what makes it work. **5/5:** Very feasible.

Function: $100 million in diamonds is hard to argue with. **5/5:** Very functional.

Flair: Utterly new. **5/5:** True creative flair.

Fun: Fewer frogmen would've been more fun. Still, we have the identity switch to keep us entertained. **4/5:** Darn fun.

Following it: Pretty simple actually—steal something, get something for it. **5/5:** Easy to follow.

Total Score: 24

You Only Live Twice

Scheme: Kidnap U.S. and Soviet astronauts and their vessels in order to increase international tensions and cause a war between the two, furthering SPECTRE's goal of world domination and receiving a payoff from the Chinese.

Feasibility: If you could really devise a vessel that could swallow other vessels, and you could hide an operation the size of NASA, build the vessel, house all the equipment, and finance all of it (even though you didn't get the diamonds you were counting on from your last big operation), I still don't think you could launch the vessel repeatedly without detection. **1/5:** Not bloody likely.

Function: Supposing it succeeded, then war seems the likely outcome, however, payment from your secret partners might be more difficult to arrange. **3/5:** Mildly functional.

Flair: As soon as you see a spaceship being swallowed by another spaceship, you know it's something really different. **5/5:** Space flair!

Fun: Oh, sure. *You Only Live Twice* is all about fun. **5/5:** More fun than a day at the circus.

Following it: No brainer. **5/5:** Easy to follow.

Total Score: 19

On Her Majesty's Secret Service

Scheme: Secretly brainwash a group of women by ostensibly treating their allergies, so that they become "Angels of Death," able to infect the world's food supply (plant and animal) with an infertility virus. Demand, as ransom, amnesty for all past crimes and the title of Comte de Bleauchamp.

Feasibility: This is more plausible than most brainwashing schemes, in that the women aren't being asked to go against their own sense of right and wrong, along the lines of *The Manchurian Candidate* or *The Ipcress File*. The science and the smuggling both seem straightforward. **5/5:** Very feasible.

Function: The triviality of Blofeld's goal makes it easy to achieve, but he hasn't even factored in any money to finance the operation! **4/5:** Functional.

Flair: Lots of movies in the 60's were using the brainwashing motif, but the viral infertility was new. **3/5:** Some flair.

Fun: Never more subjective than in this controversial movie! The scheme involves genealogy, ditzy women with weird dietary restrictions, and hypnosis. Only the women are visually interesting. **3/5:** Mildly fun.

Following it: I had to read the book to discover that the reason the clinic was populated entirely by ditzy women was because they were thought to be the best hypnotic subjects. **4/5:** Fairly easy to follow.

Total Score: 19

Diamonds Are Forever

Scheme: Kidnap a reclusive millionaire and use his resources to build and launch a satellite. Smuggle diamonds from South Africa to a laboratory in the U.S. Use the diamonds to power a giant laser, attach it to the satellite (before launching), and hold the world for ransom with the superweapon thus created.

Feasibility: None. Kidnapping Willard Whyte must have been quite a trick, and the science is shaky at best. **1/5:** Not feasible.

Function: Ransom plots are among the more functional, and blowing up cities is a reasonably strong incentive. **5/5:** Very functional.

Flair: Maybe too creative. **4/5:** Overkill flair.

Fun: Lots of fun! Each step of the plot is surprising and designed for maximum entertainment. **5/5:** Hoo-boy!

Following it: The many links in the smuggling chain are complex enough without trying to figure out why all the smugglers are being killed, and where the satellite comes in. **2/5:** Not impossible, but...!

Total Score: 17

Live and Let Die

Scheme: Flood the U.S. market with free heroin, thereby breaking the back of the Mafia and doubling the number of addicts. Then, with a monopoly in place, charge very high prices and get rich.

Feasibility: Oh, sure, the Mafia's going to just roll over and die. I believe that. **1/5:** Not feasible.

Function: Doubling the price of heroin will cause addicts to dilute the drug, killing off many of the new customers Kananga has created. Making back an enormous investment seems unlikely. **1/5:** Not functional.

Flair: Corner the market on drugs? Yawn. **1/5:** Same ol' same ol'.

Fun: The plot is an afterthought, we are exposed to very little of it. **1/5** Not fun.

Following it: If you haven't fallen asleep by that point, easy. **5/5:** Easy to follow.

Total Score: 9

The Man with the Golden Gun

Scheme: Steal a solar energy concentrator and sell it to the highest bidder.

Feasibility: Stealing works. Selling works. **5/5:** Very feasible.

Function: Clearly, if he sells the Solex, he will succeed in making a lot of money. **5/5:** Very functional.

Flair: Scaramanga as a character is very creative, but not his scheme. **1/5:** So what?

Fun: The movie breaks down whenever it goes near the Solex. The scheme is entirely disconnected from the Man with the Golden Gun himself; it doesn't require the world's greatest assassin, a damsel in distress, or any of the established plot. The movie might well have been better with a scheme more natural to Scaramanga. **1/5:** Not fun.

Following it: The connection between Scaramanga, Hai Fat, and the Solex might give momentary pause. **4/5:** Fairly easy to follow.

Total Score:16

The Spy Who Loved Me

Scheme: Kidnap U.S. and Soviet submarines with missiles aboard. Shoot a Soviet missile at New York and a U.S. missile at Moscow, destroying both cities and leading to war, thereby decimating the Earth's population and paving the way for Stromberg to create an underwater society.

Feasibility: He can certainly start a war, but whether that war will destroy the world's population isn't certain. **3/5:** Mildly feasible.

Function: Inasmuch as he hates humanity and wants them dead, it is functional, but forcing the population to live underwater seems an off-chance. For example, they might head underground, or into space. Or, there might be plenty of livable land remaining. There is no plan at all for an undersea society, just Stromberg's imagining that there would be one. **2/5:** Barely functional.

Flair: *You Only Live Twice* in a boat, with an ecological twist tacked on. **2/5:** Not much flair.

Fun: The fun of this movie has nothing to do with Stromberg's scheme. Atlantis is beautiful, but the submarine stuff is a replay of *You Only Live Twice* and therefore uninteresting. **1/5:** Not fun.

Following it: Easy, especially since we are merely reviewing the plot of a previous movie. **5/5:** Easy to follow.

Total Score: 13

Moonraker

Scheme: Create a deadly poison using a rare Amazonian orchid extract. Create a secret space station, and populate it with "perfect human specimens." Kill off human life on Earth by releasing the poison, using specially-manufactured glass globes. Repopulate the Earth with the new Master Race, who will be ruled by the space-based dynasty of Hugo Drax, benevolent god-like dictator.

Feasibility: The science is all fiction, especially "cloaking" a space station. Too many people involved, too many witnesses. **3/5:** Mildly feasible.

Function: There is a mad beauty to this, the ultimate end product of villainous megalomania. It is too bad the actual scheme was given short shrift by the script, because it is really something! **5/5:** Very functional.

Flair: A creative take on the whole world domination bag. **5/5:** Very neat.

Fun: Not playtime fun, but fascinating, disturbing, and bizarre. **5/5:** For variant definitions of fun.

Following it: The only flaw is the way it is pulled out of a hat at the end. Many crazy plot holes surround it, but the scheme itself is fine. **4/5:** Fairly easy to follow.

Total Score: 22

For Your Eyes Only

Scheme: Find the sunken ATAC and sell to the KGB. Convince Bond that you're on his side and that your enemy is his enemy.

> **Feasibility:** Stealing the ATAC is plausible, convincing Bond that Columbo is a bad guy is not. **3/5:** Mildly feasible.

> **Function:** The goal is money, and money is always functional. **5/5:** Very functional.

> **Flair:** The ATAC is reminiscent of the Lektor, but the basic plot of opposite sides racing to recover the same object hasn't been done in a Bond film before. **3/5:** Fairly creative.

> **Fun:** The plot is purposely pared down, like *Dr. No*, the scheme here is not the point. **1/5:** No fun.

> **Following it:** The red herring of Columbo as a bad guy, the involvement of Lisl, and the several locations can be mildly confusing, but overall the plot is understandable. **4/5:** Fairly easy to follow.

> Total Score: 16

Octopussy

Scheme: Steal the treasures of Czarist Russia and replace them with forgeries. Give the jewels to Prince Kamal Khan in exchange for the use of the Octopussy Circus as a means of smuggling a nuclear weapon into West Germany. Detonate the weapon so that it appears to be a nuclear accident. This will cause the West to immediately disarm to prevent future accidents, at which point, the Soviet Union will invade and take over.

> **Feasibility:** The scheme involves duping an international jewel thief as well as the Kremlin, in addition to smuggling a nuclear bomb across the Berlin Wall. **2/5:** Not very feasible.

> **Function:** The primary goal—Soviet takeover of the West—depends upon speculation. Orlov assumes the West will disarm based upon psychosocial factors, which are always iffy. He also assumes that Brezhnev, after stating categorically that the U.S.S.R. will not wage war on the West, will change his mind once disarmament occurs. **1/5:** You're kidding me.

Flair: You'd think someone would have done "Mad Russian General" by now, but the idea was new to the Bond world. Add in a circus, Faberge eggs and Sotheby's, and you can see that someone's creative juices were really flowing. **5/5:** Full of flair.

Fun: The enormous complexities have a great deal of visual and dramatic appeal, but because the plot is confusing, there is no satisfying "click" of seeing it come together. **3/5:** Somewhat fun.

Following it: Quantum physics is less complicated. **1/5:** Byzantine.

Total Score: 12

Never Say Never Again

Scheme: Remake of *Thunderball*: Seduce and corrupt a NATO officer in order to steal a plane with two atomic weapons on board. Demand 25% of every nation's annual oil expenditures as ransom for the return of the weapons.

Feasibility: As M said about the corneal implant, "Oh, do come along!" Jack Petachi's bomb theft has less of a build-up than Angelo Palazzi's, and Largo's acquisition of the bombs is completely glossed over. A means for delivering the ransom is never specified. **3/5:** Could be more feasible with a little effort.

Function: Huge sums of money are a lovely gift and fit with every decor. **5/5:** Very functional.

Flair: Let's get real; it's a remake. **1/5:** No flair.

Fun: The "Tears of Allah" map is an old adventure movie trick, and drug addiction is less interesting than an identity switch, so the "improvements" of the remake aren't. **2/5:** Some leftover fun.

Following it: Pretty simple actually—steal something, get something for it. **5/5:** Easy to follow.

Total Score: 16

A View to a Kill

Scheme: Stockpile silicon chips. Cause a massive earthquake in Silicon Valley by flooding both the Hayward and San Andreas faults, and blowing up the "key geological lock" that keeps the two faults separate, thereby destroying the source of all existing microchips. Sell your chips at an enormous profit.

Feasibility: Earthquakes are unpredictable animals. The idea that causing a quake would create known, quantifiable results seems iffy. **2/5:** Not very feasible.

Function: The chip shortage will surely be short-term. The likelihood of garnering sufficient profit before prices even out isn't that great. **2/5:** Not very functional.

Flair: This is a virtual *Goldfinger* remake, with destroyed chips replacing irradiated gold. **1/5:** Where's the flair?

Fun: Flooding the fault is probably the most fun this movie offers; which isn't saying much. **3/5:** A tad o' fun.

Following it: Mocking its stupidity may cause inattention, and there are numerous red herrings (i.e. the racehorse scheme, the pulse-resistant chips). Otherwise, no problem. **4/5:** Fairly easy to follow.

Total Score: 12

The Living Daylights

Scheme: Arrange with American partner to sell illegal arms to the Soviet Union. Use payment from U.S.S.R. to finance heroin trade with the Mujahadeen, without providing arms to Soviets. When KGB head Pushkin suspects, establish evidence of Smiert Spionam program and fake a defection in order to persuade MI6 to assassinate him.

Feasibility: Playing on international tensions, and the existing air of secrecy, keeps everyone blind to the plot—MI6 believes both the defection and the assassination program; Koskov's status allows him to behave irregularly in the name of "State secrets." **5/5:** Very feasible.

Function: Koskov is already using the plot to live far more luxuriously than he otherwise might have. **5/5:** Very functional.

Flair: Finding a way to bring in Smiert Spionam from the Fleming novels was a great idea, but an arms-heroin deal was not. **2/5:** Momentary flair.

Fun: Unfolding the first part of the plot is great fun: Establishing Smiert Spionam, the defection and "recapture" of Koskov, and the involvement of Pushkin are all top-notch. In the plot's denouement, though, when we discover that it's just dirty tricks on people who are already playing dirty tricks, there is a great letdown. That's it? **3/5:** Halfway to fun.

Following it: Waitaminnit...who gave money to whom for what? **2/5:** Hard to follow.

Total Score: 17

Licence to Kill

Scheme: Sell cocaine in huge quantities at huge profits, and kill anyone who gets in the way.

Feasibility: It's been done. **5/5:** Very feasible.

Function: What have I told you about money? **5/5:** Very functional.

Flair: Sanchez is a great character who deserved a script that played to his grandiosity. **1/5:** No flair.

Fun: Some of the window dressing of this particular arrangement, particularly the phone-in religious "donations" and the gasoline dilution, are fun, but the actual selling of cocaine is old hat. **2/5:** I've had better times.

Following it: Piece o' white powdery cake. **5/5:** Easy to follow.

Total Score: 18

GoldenEye

Scheme: Steal control of a device that creates an electromagnetic (EM) pulse, destroying all electronic devices in the area where it detonates. Hack into Bank of England computers and transfer billions into your account just before detonating the device over London, wiping out all record of the transaction and causing massive financial and social chaos by destroying the financial and legal records of most of the U.K.

Feasibility: Given the existence of a GoldenEye device, the rest of it is a fantastic plan. **5/5:** Very feasible.

Function: With revenge as a primary motivator, the plan is incredibly functional. However, Trevelyan may be underestimating the financial chaos—the money transfer may have no value. **4/5:** Quite functional.

Flair: The electronic transfer idea has been used in several films, notably *Sneakers*, which also used a version of the revenge against society concept. A secret satellite is nothing new. The rogue 00 agent is a great idea that might have been used much sooner. The real flair comes in understanding how devastating such a pulse would be, as 006 outlines. People underestimate the real cost of blowing up bombs because they've seen too many movies. **3/5:** Flair in some areas.

Fun: *GoldenEye* has many diversions; we are misled about who the villain is, and his scheme. Because a device is stolen early on, it creates curiosity about how and why the device will be used. **4/5:** Good fun.

Following it: Could have been complex in the wrong hands, but the script keeps it very clear. **5/5:** Easy to follow.

Total Score: 21

Tomorrow Never Dies

Scheme: Use a Global Positioning System controller to send a British submarine off-course into Chinese waters, creating an international incident. Using stealth technology and murder, increase international tensions and cause war between China and Britain. Gain exclusive broadcasting rights in China for the next one hundred years.

Feasibility: It seems quite plausible, yet I wonder if British submarines wouldn't have an external way of checking position besides GPS. **4/5:** Feasible.

Function: Some fans think that broadcasting rights aren't much of a goal, but I think Carver makes a persuasive case. **4/5:** Functional.

Flair: The submarine/warfare portion of the script is a rewrite of *The Spy Who Loved Me*. The use of a media-based scheme is quite creative. **3/5:** Halfway to flair.

Fun: When the media is spinning headlines and the world powers are posturing, there is a definite electricity. But all the submarine action is dark and gloomy. **3/5:** Poorly-lit fun.

Following it: If you've heard of the Philippine War, very easy. **4/5:** Mostly quite easy to follow.

Total Score: 18

The World is Not Enough

Scheme: Two schemes: First, murder your father and persuade M to investigate, for revenge on both. Second, steal plutonium and detonate on a hijacked submarine; contaminating competing oil pipelines so that you own the only viable one.

Feasibility: Killing Dad is easy. Dragging M out of her office should not have been. Stealing the plutonium is easy. Hijacking the sub should not have been. **3/5:** Mildly feasible.

Function: Revenge as a motive cannot be questioned. Oil pipelines have indisputable value.**5/5:** Highly functional.

Flair: M's personal involvement is a bit soap-operatic. Kidnap victim with Stockholm Syndrome works. Radioactive contamination has been used too often in Bond films. Oil pipelines haven't. **3/5:** A bit of flair.

Fun: The poor little rich girl portion of the scheme played well, but everything having to do with the pipeline and the submarine was dark and ugly. **3/5:** A little dab of fun.

Following it: On the convoluted side. **2/5:** Not easy to follow.

Total Score: 16

Die Another Day

Scheme: Genetically alter your appearance. Use stolen diamonds to establish yourself as a diamond miner and philanthropist. Launch a satellite, ostensibly an energy source, that will destroy the minefield in the demilitarized zone between North and South Korea, clearing the way for the North to invade the South, bringing about a unified Korea under Northern rule. Proceed to invade Japan.

Feasibility: Establishing an identity worthy of knighthood takes longer than indicated. The weapon and the genetic engineering are science fiction. If the weapon existed, it could certainly turn the tide of a war. **2/5:** Just barely feasible.

Function: Giving the villain a psychological motivation based on his relationship to his father supercedes the practical concerns of function. Graves is willing to destroy anything and anyone to prove himself. **5/5:** Highly functional.

Flair: The satellite is too similar to *Diamonds Are Forever*. The rest of the plot is extremely creative. **4/5:** A good bit of flair.

Fun: Watching the plot unfold took us to sets and locations the likes of which we haven't seen since the 1970's. **5/5:** A roller-coaster.

Following it: Harder to write up than to understand. **5/5:** Easy to follow.

Total Score: 21

Casino Royale

Scheme: Receive huge sums as the "banker to the world's terrorists" and agree to invest it conservatively. Short-sell stock in an airline as it is about to launch a major new design. Blow up the design and make a fortune. When that scheme fails, win the money back in a high-stakes poker game.

> **Feasibility:** Playing the market is risky, and doing so with the money of known murderers isn't as smart as Le Chiffre otherwise appears to be. The rest of it—the poker game—is desperation, not a real scheme. **3/5:** Not anyone's best idea.

> **Function:** Huge profits are impossible to argue with, although surely he was already well-paid? **4/5:** Almost but not quite indisputable.

> **Flair:** The scheme is an excuse for the poker game. **2/5:** Not so much with the flair.

> **Fun:** The globetrotting, as well as the airport chase, were enormously fun. Watching Le Chiffre melt down when it all went to hell was fun in the 'Wow, look at the crazy guy' sense of the word. **5/5:** Scary fun.

> **Following it:** M helped us out if we didn't know what "short-selling" was. **5/5:** Easy to follow.

Total Score: 19

Quantum of Solace

Scheme: Hire a geologist to find underground water in Bolivia, dam it (causing a drought) and then kill the geologist so as not to be discovered. Finance and support a military coupe to take over Bolivia, in exchange for ownership of the land where you have dammed underground water. Charge the new military leader exorbitant rates for the only available water in his country.

> **Feasibility:** The plot depends on an enormous and resource-rich organization. If we assume that Quantum can lay down the financial groundwork, and invest the time, it can all work. **4/5:** Feasible within reason.

> **Function:** Cornering the market on a vital natural resource has always worked in the past. **5/5:** Totally functional.

Flair: It's an interesting twist, for sure—Bond villains don't normally focus on ecological issues. It's also very close to some real-life corporate misfeasance, so it's hard to call it really original. **3/5:** Some but not all of the flair.

Fun: These are horrible people doing horrible things. **1/5:** I did not have fun.

Following it: The misdirection to oil didn't make it too complex. **5/5:** Easy to follow.

Total Score: 18

Skyfall

Scheme: Blow up MI6 main headquarters by hacking into their utility systems and causing a gas explosion, forcing them into emergency underground headquarters. Allow yourself to be captured knowing you will be held in the underground HQ. Encrypt your computer in such a way that, when decrypted, programs will trigger that will free you from captivity. Do this exactly when M will be testifying before a Parlimentary committee so that you can break in, disguised as police, and murder her (or kidnap and then murder her).

Feasibility: I can't even with this plot. **1/5:** Who are we kidding, here?

Function: As we've said before, deranged revenge plots are their own reward. **5/5:** Functional for the revenge-crazed loon within us all.

Flair: Super-hacking is not very original, including the kind of *deux ex machina* hacking that stretches plausibility to the limit. On the other hand, Silva and his personal scheme are wholly original. **3/5:** Half the flair.

Fun: Oh, this is full of fun, and unfolds with such bizarre intelligence that it takes some doing to remember that none of it can work. **5/5:** Super-duper fun.

Following it: Wasn't sure I could even write it up. **1/5:** Hard to follow.

Total Score: 15

Spectre

Scheme: Two schemes: First, engineer terrorist attacks all over the globe, motivating world powers to unite their security forces under a single umbrella organization, which you secretly run, thereby providing yourself with the ability to spy on every government in the world. Second, make James Bond miserable because you have hated him since boyhood.

Feasibility: Once again, we have a plot based on the assumption that we know how people (and governments) will behave in response to a provocation. It's unclear to me why an international intelligence service would seem the best way to combat terror, and C is not exactly a charismatic voice. As to the second plot, if you have the spy technology to follow someone all over the world, you can surely make him miserable. **3/5:** Fifty-fifty feasible.

Function: Revenge functionality cannot be questioned. Spying on all world governments and knowing what they know certainly makes international crime easier to commit. **5/5:** Completely functional.

Flair: We had a super-hacker in the previous movie. **2/5:** Not really flairy.

Fun: The terrorism/world domination plot is the least interesting part of the movie, and the 'torment my boyhood pal' is the most annoying. **1/5:** Not fun.

Following it: Transparent. **5/5:** Wish it wasn't this easy to follow.

Total Score: 15

The Winners:

First Place	*Thunderball* (24)
Second Place (Tie)	*From Russia with Love, Goldfinger* (23)
Third Place	*Moonraker* (22)

YOU ONLY LIVE TWICE (1967)

Survey Says!

> Percent Favorite: 2%
> Top 5 Cumulative: 15/25 (tied)
> Numeric Rating: 6.7/10
> Ranking: 13 (14th/25)

My Rating and Ranking

> Rated: 8/10
> Ranked: 11 out of 25

Summary

U.S. and Soviet rockets are being attacked in space, and each side accuses the other. The U.K. suspects that the attacking launches are coming from Japan, and sends Bond to investigate, first faking his death so that he may work unimpeded. Once in Japan, Bond teams with the head of the Japanese Secret Service and two of his female agents, eventually "becoming" Japanese himself. Together they uncover SPECTRE's secret base in a hollowed-out volcano, where rockets are being launched that "swallow" and kidnap the U.S. and Soviet rockets. SPECTRE has teamed with China to cause war between the two major powers, but Bond and a team of ninjas save the day.

> **James Bond:** Sean Connery
> **Tiger Tanaka:** Tetsuro Tamba
> **Aki:** Akiko Wakabayashi
> **Kissy:** Mie Hama
> **Ernst Stavro Blofeld:** Donald Pleasence
> **Helga Brandt (SPECTRE #11):** Karin Dor
> **Mr. Osato:** Teru Shimada
> **Dikko Henderson:** Charles Gray
> **M:** Bernard Lee
> **Moneypenny:** Lois Maxwell
> **Q:** Desmond Llewelyn
> **Directed by** Lewis Gilbert

Discussion

You Only Live Twice is the first (but sadly, not last) Bond movie that doesn't care about the story. It is an assemblage of pieces—some excellent, some not—strung loosely together in the hopes that it would appear to be a coherent story. It is the *Independence Day* of Bond movies, designed for the immediate thrill, not for bearing up under even the most cursory examination. *You Only Live Twice* is great fun, one of the most watchable of Bond films, and therefore a source of delight to fans. It is also a source of great aggravation, as it proved to the producers that nothing what-ever needs to make sense if it looks good, and fans often wish the producers had never learned that lesson.

The problems all come down to scenes that seem like really cool ideas, that the producers just had to get in there, while their relation to the plot was an after-thought.

"Let's open the movie by killing Bond!" What a cool idea! A producer begins to salivate at the thought—how clever, how new! But it makes no sense, and as a re-sult, I am forced to subject you, the reader, to my *You Only Live Twice* pre-titles se-quence rant.

If you want your enemies to believe you're dead, there are two ways to do it (other than by dying). 1) Just plant stories in the media and have a funeral. 2) If you think that won't trick them, stage a public death with lots of witnesses.

But of course, *You Only Live Twice* opts for the third method: Kill him pri-vately, in a sexually intimate situation, in a way that is doubtless upsetting, but fools no one because only the participants see it. Oh good idea! Unless, that is, someone involved in the staged killing was an enemy agent?

Bond says that he and Ling have had "some good times" and Moneypenny implies she is an MI6 operative. Is she a mole who really intends to kill him? Do the gunmen not know they're shooting blanks?

If Ling believes she has set Bond up for murder, all of the staging is for the benefit of one SPECTRE (or other enemy) operative. If so, Helga should not have known about Bond's death because she read it in the papers (and isn't it adorable that in those days even SPECTRE agents believed what they read in the papers?), but because an operative reported it. Even if Ling was a non-SPECTRE enemy, we know that SPECTRE has spies in the KGB and elsewhere.

So Ling is a cipher, and probably because of poor scripting, not because of any real mystery. Let's move on. Some people kill him, in the privacy of this boudoir, and suddenly, we hear police sirens! Who called the cops? Well, since they knew who Bond was, they must have been agents, but how did they get there so fast? Okay, it was pre-planned, but if they're faking being ordinary cops, why show up so much sooner than cops could have?

Of course, they also "knew" he was "dead" without examining the body or even checking for a pulse, but never mind. Blood on a mattress is considered con-clusive proof of death by most coroners. Yep.

How about the funeral? I am thinking that MI6 has access to plenty of corpses, and could have buried one of them, instead of risking drowning Bond, not to mention risking getting caught at the deception by sending divers down! Clearly plenty of people knew by then that Bond was alive, because they had to prepare his "body." So other than theatrics, why bury Bond instead of a corpse or a sack of rice?

Phew. I suppose I had to get that out of my system. On to the rest of the movie.

(*Note:* I wrote all of the above years before I wrote VOYEURISM IN YOU ONLY LIVE TWICE, a very different take on the same material. I hope you enjoy both perspec-tives.)

Another cool-yet-senseless scene is when the car is picked up with a big magnet and dropped into the water. This is producer-drool again. Wow, they think, How great it'll look. And of course it does. Until you think it through. Aki wants the car chasing them to get "the usual reception." Usual? You mean cars are regularly picked up by a helicopter and dropped into the water? What does the citizenry think of this? Why haven't the bad guys figured it out yet? What does it look like on the evening news? Do Japanese citizens just shrug and say, "Ah, my, another car in the water. Nice to know the Secret Service is at work"?

You Only Live Twice has all these lovely flourishes, so bold, glorious, and ridiculous, that it is no wonder that it is the prototype for Bond parodies, for Dr. Evil and for Saturday Night Live.

But let's not put the movie down too much. The location shooting is fantastic, and for its day, it was very respectful of Japanese culture. *You Only Live Twice* used ninjas several years before martial arts movies had reached the U.K. or the U.S., and was probably rather daring in using real martial artists where possible, rather than European stuntmen. Just so, it used real sumo wrestling (because the wrestlers thought it inappropriate to fake for the camera, so a real match was filmed, giving us a very authentic scene), and real Japanese wedding and funeral rites. The overall result is a profound sense of place; we know that Bond is in Japan, the movie is suffused with a sense of the Japanese. In 1967, Japanese culture was not familiar in the West. Few Americans knew about ninjas, or that sake is served warm. It all looked terribly exotic and it was well done. *You Only Live Twice* looks deeper than the clichés. Sure, you see geishas and sumo wrestling, but you also look at a Japanese fishing village and get a Ken Adam-eye view of high-tech Japanese industry (also unheard of in those days). Compare this to *Octopussy*, which travels all the way to India just to show us a bunch of grade school clichés, white women in saris and a fakir on a bed of nails!

You Only Live Twice has some of Bond's finest action sequences. The Little Nellie scene is perhaps the most famous—very exciting both in concept and in execution—the aerial photography is great. But the hand-to-hand fights should not be forgotten. The fight between Bond and the Japanese agent in Osato's office is wild, knocking apart furniture, really grabbing the audience by the throat. Later, there is the terrific running fight on the Kobi docks, the camera backing further and further away until a crane shot shows us the whole thing, giving it a sense of choreography, a panoramic adventure rather than the intimacy of hand-to-hand combat. A smart decision, as we'd already had a great hand-to-hand scene, this shot adds to the sweeping look of the film. Finally, there is the large-scale combat in the volcano, with ninjas descending on ropes, rockets, grenades, and I swear I saw a kitchen sink! It is a wonderful battle, culminating in a dandy explosion that rocks you to your foundations.

The women in this movie are an odd bunch. Aki is a beauty, and charming besides. Kissy is an afterthought—so much so that she is never named. In the novel, she is Kissy Suzuki, and many fans have taken to calling the movie character by that name. But she is credited only as "Kissy," and no one ever speaks her name in the course of the film.

The third woman is Helga Brandt, rather a strange bird. She seems to be an imitation of Fiona Volpe, and at first glance, one can barely tell them apart, although to me Luciana Paluzzi is the more beautiful. But Helga has some qualities that might raise even Fiona's lovely eyebrows. Fiona enjoys sex and she enjoys violence. But Helga fetishizes violence, she wants to combine the two. Helga dresses up for the occasion of torturing Bond (who she thinks is merely an industrial spy), and makes love to him as a prelude to a bizarre murder attempt. Fiona is wild and evil, but Helga is genuinely perverse. She also has one of the best, sickest, most cinematic deaths of any Bond villain—eaten by Blofeld's piranha after a demonstration of their deadly power on a hunk of meat—what a way to go!

The movie is a visual and auditory feast, featuring one of John Barry's loveliest scores, and some of Ken Adam's most audacious production design. This is, of course, the movie with the hollowed-out volcano, but it is also the movie with the sky-lit operating theater, a Hong Kong boudoir with a Murphy bed, and Mr. Osato's private office, with its exotic art and built-in bar/closet. There's also Dikko's "odd mix" of Japanese and Victorian, a set Adam very much wanted to convey the personality of an Englishman living in Asia.

The title song has one of the most haunting melodies of any Bond song, used well throughout the movie. The song also has an interesting lyric, but Nancy Sinatra's weak, strained vocals detract from its charm.

The High Points

- Japanese locations and settings (sumo wrestling match, fishing village, ninja school).
- The Little Nellie sequence.
- The set design, especially the hollowed-out volcano lair.
- The very cool opening sequence of a rocket swallowing another rocket.
- Helga's death-by-fish.
- Aki, the first female agent paired with Bond.
- Aki's death-by-thread, very creative.
- Tiger Tanaka, a great ally, and his private subway office.
- Blowing up the mountain!
- Wonderful soundtrack.

The Low Points

- The ill-conceived fake death.
- Connery's lackluster, by-the-numbers performance.
- Helga's very fake, very dumb-looking parachute jump.
- Donald Pleasence as Blofeld.
- A movie that prioritizes exciting scenes over coherence.
- The second rocket-swallow, a dull repeat of the first.

Quotable Quotes

Tiger Tanaka: "My friend, now you take your first civilized bath."
Bond (looking at the bikini-clad women): "Really? Well, I like the plumbing."

Helga: "Mr. Osato likes a healthy chest."

Aki: "I think I will enjoy very much serving under you."

Aki (about Helga): "He wouldn't touch that horrible girl. You wouldn't, would you?"
Bond: "Oh, heaven forbid!"

Bond (undressing Helga): "Oh, the things I do for England."

Blofeld. "It won't be the nicotine that kills you, Mr. Bond."

Facts and Figures

SEXUAL ENCOUNTERS

<u>Four</u>: Ling, Aki, Helga Brandt, and Kissy.

BOND'S CAR

None. Aki drives a 1967 Toyota 2000 custom convertible (white)

DEATHS

<u>Approximately one hundred three</u>:

- The U.S. astronaut who was space-walking, Henderson, four gunmen in the car that was dropped by the helicopter (presumed dead), Helga Brandt, Aki, Mr. Osato.
- In the climactic volcano-based combat, a body count is hard to determine. There are roughly one hundred SPECTRE people in the base, estimated by the number of various crews in various different uniforms, their movements, their locations, and so on. When Blofeld blows up the base, we see ninjas and Japanese agents escape, but no SPECTRE agents, however, it is unreasonable to assume that they were all killed. About fifteen ninjas are killed by crater guns, but it is dark and the shooting continues while we watch Blofeld talk about it. Four ninjas die while entering the crater on ropes. In the subsequent battle, counting anyone who falls as a death (wounded survivors cancel out those who die off-screen), twenty-seven bad guys and seven good guys. At a guess, another thirty when the volcano blows. Plus, the eleven individuals killed by Bond (below).

Bond Kills

- <u>Fifteen</u> directly: The man who killed Henderson (perhaps), the guard at Osato, one at the Kobi docks, four in Little Nellie (assuming only one per helicopter), the assassin who killed Aki, the fake ninja during combat training, the technician killed with the cigarette, and five in the volcano-base combat. (So, ten individuals directly plus five directly in the final battle.)
- <u>One</u> indirectly: Hans is tossed into the piranha pool; Bond doesn't know what's in the pool.

EXPLOSIONS

<u>Six</u>: The four helicopters that chase Little Nellie, one of which could be counted as two—the helicopter taken out by a flame thrower explodes once when the flame thrower hits it, and a second time when it crashes. Helga's plane is a nice one, but ruined by her very fake parachute escape. The mother of them all: The volcano base (somewhat ruined by obvious stock footage of a volcano exploding). There are numerous small explosions during the volcano-base combat, but they are subsumed by the larger one.

BOND'S FOOD AND DRINKS

Vodka Martinis

- One, served "stirred, not shaken" by Dikko Henderson, but made with Russian vodka.

Other Drinks

- Siamese vodka after the fight in Osato's office.
- Japanese sake with Tiger Tanaka, served at 98.4 degrees Fahrenheit.
- Dom Perignon '59 with Helga Brandt and Mr. Osato.
- Unknown drinks with Tiger Tanaka at his home.
- Sake during the fake wedding. (I had long thought this was a tea ceremony, but the Minister of Martinis determined it was sake.)
- Unknown drinks with Kissy at her home (with the oysters).

Food

- Bond pushes oysters aside when he realizes that Kissy will not sleep with him.

GAMBLING AND SPORTS

- Sumo wrestling.

Amaze Your Friends!

- During the climax in the volcano base, you'll see that Blofeld is holding the cat and, when he fires his pistol, the cat leaps out of his arms and runs away. During rehearsals, they never fired the gun, and when the scene was filmed, the sound of the gunshot terrified the cat. The cat, a "professional," was so traumatized that it refused to ever work again. Eon was obliged to offer a financial settlement to its owner.
- Aerial photographer Johnny Jordan was severely injured while filming the Little Nellie scene. His leg was caught by the blade of a helicopter below him, and ultimately he had to have it amputated. Jordan continued to work as an aerial photographer, and designed the innovative rig used in *On Her Majesty's Secret Service* that allowed a 360 degree range for filming the various scenes in the Alps. He was killed in another aerial accident during the filming of *Catch-22*.
- The shot of the submarine rising up under the raft was impossible to film—every time the sub came up, its waves pushed the raft aside. It was finally

filmed backwards—the raft was on top of a sub, which descended into the water. Then the film was reversed.

• The year before *You Only Live Twice*, Mie Hama and Akiko Wakabayashi co-starred in another spy film, the parody *What's Up, Tiger Lily?* This movie was written and directed by, and featured, Woody Allen, who played "Jimmy Bond" (a.k.a. Dr. Noah) in *Casino Royale* (1967).

Most Interesting Goofs

Omniscient cameras: The view-screen in Aki's car shows the helicopter dropping the car into the water. Who is photographing it? In order to get that shot, there would have to be a second helicopter filming the first. Likewise, Blofeld's view-screen shows his ship about to swallow another rocket. There is no third ship in space that could get that shot, especially since we see it from two distinct points of view.

Tropical Russia: The shot of the Soviet space launch clearly shows palm trees in the foreground—not something normally found in the Soviet Union. What actually happened is that the footage for the two launches was accidentally switched—we are seeing the Cape Kennedy footage for the Russian launch, and the Russian footage for the U.S. launch.

Disappearing/Reappearing Clothing: Kissy dives into the water (in the cave) barefoot and comes out with shoes on. Similarly, we see Bond wearing a fisherman's shirt that, when wet, shows bare skin underneath. Later, he strips off that shirt and there is a ninja catsuit underneath.

U.S./Soviet Cooperation: The entire time that Blofeld's technicians are watching the U.S. rocket launch on their omniscient camera, we see "CCCP" in huge letters on the rocket's side. (CCCP is the Russian version of USSR.)

CODE WORDS

One of the coolest moments in a spy movie is when the code words are exchanged. They appear in fewer than half of the Bond films.

Here's a complete list:

Dr. No

Strangways's assistant gives the following code to headquarters: W6N calling G7W.

From Russia with Love

Agent 1: Can I borrow a match?
Agent 2: I use a lighter.
Agent 1: Better still.
Agent 2: Until they go wrong.

You Only Live Twice

"I love you."

This is delivered to Bond without a counter-sign. The first time, Bond says it to Aki, and she responds, "I have a car nearby." The second time, Bond asks Tiger, "How do you feel about me?" and Tiger responds with the code.

Live and Let Die

When Bond arrives at Kennedy airport, he is given a baggage check of 545-BBB. This matches the license plate of a waiting taxi, and serves as a code that the taxi is driven by a CIA agent.

For Your Eyes Only

Ferrara: The snow this year is better at Innsbrook.
Bond: But not at St. Moritz.

Octopussy

Vijay plays the Bond theme.

Bond: Charming tune, do you take English money?
Vijay: Only gold sovereigns.

A View to a Kill

Lee: Looking for something special?
Bond: Yes, soft shell crabs.
Lee: I might have some in the back.

GoldenEye

> **Bond:** In London, April's a spring month.
> **Wade:** Whereas in St. Petersburg, we're freezing our butts off. (Somehow, Bond doesn't regard this as correct.)

Die Another Day

The Delectado cigar is a code word, and apparently so is the Volado tobacco. How much of the entire exchange is coded is not clear.

> **Bond:** I'm here to pick up some Delectados. (No recognition from the man at the desk.) Universal Exports. Check with your boss.
> After having been taken to see Raoul...

> **Raoul:** I come to think the Delectados would never be smoked. They are particularly hazardous to one's health. Do you know why, Mr...?
> **Bond:** Bond.
> **Raoul:** Mr. Bond. Do you know why?
> **Bond:** It's the addition of the Volado tobacco. Slow burning—it never goes out.

Casino Royale

- Bond thinks that ELLIPSIS is a code word, but this is misdirection, as he eventually learns it's a keypad code.

VOYEURISM IN YOU ONLY LIVE TWICE

This originally appeared as an article in the now-defunct HMSS.com online magazine. It has been fully edited and revised.

You Only Live Twice is often regarded as a silly film. It has long seemed to me to be delightful but fundamentally incoherent. However, upon seeing it in an old theater palace, I got introspective, and began to see there was more to it.

You Only Live Twice is, at its core, about the voyeurism of spying. It has an obvious, consistent, repeated motif of cameras, film, and media, and is concerned with perception. Within the course of the movie, every major character is seen filming, being filmed, or both, and every major scene has visible recording equipment of some kind, or talks about the media in some way.

This motif is connected to the plot element addressed in the title: Bond is "killed" because his enemies plague him. M says, "Well now that you're dead, perhaps some of your old friends will pay a little less attention to you for a while. Give you more elbow room."

A real spy needs elbow room, and he needs secrecy, but Bond has neither. He is that bizarre oxymoron, a "famous spy."

In the novel **Diamonds Are Forever** , Bond, posing as Peter Franks, has the following conversation with Tiffany Case:

> *"Got a passport?"*
> *"Well, I have," admitted Bond. "But it's in my real name."*
> *"Oh." She was suspicious again. "And what might that be?"*
> *"James Bond."*
> *She snorted. "Why not choose Joe Doe?"*

By the time of the 1971 film of that novel, Tiffany Case is horrified that "Peter Franks" has killed the famous James Bond.

Between the two extremes falls *You Only Live Twice*. Bond is a famous spy, but his fame is perceived accurately as a problem, and MI6 attempts to solve it by faking Bond's death. The fake death, though, is the opening volley in a curious game of who's watching whom, and all of it is reflected in images of the media: film, newspapers, recordings, and photography.

Certainly one of the subjects of this cinematic conversation about voyeurism is the audience: Much of the adventure and much of the display is played directly to the fourth wall. Time and again, when we ask "Who is watching that?" the answer is: Us. Time and again, when we ask, "Who is filming that?" the answer is, "The filmmakers, for the audience's benefit." On the one hand, it's sloppy filmmaking, but on the other, it's a sophisticated understanding of voyeurism as a two-handed game. A spy is a voyeur, but the watcher requires the watched. A voyeur must either have an unwilling victim, or a willing exhibitionist. Alfred Hitchcock—long understood to be an influence on the Bond films—realized that a film audience is also a voyeur, and the film itself is an exhibitionist. Hitchcock's film *Rear Window* directly addresses that subject. Hitchcock also knew that perfect logic didn't matter in filmmaking, he coined the term "icebox scene" to refer to a question or inconsistency that strikes you after you've gone home and start pulling cold chicken out of the *icebox*. If the film works while you're watching it, it works.

My attempt here is to take the movie *You Only Live Twice* very seriously, and to explore its motif of voyeurism through the audience and through the media. I know full well that the filmmakers didn't necessarily intend all or, perhaps, any of these incidents to seem thematic. The beauty of art is that it often surpasses the artist's intentions. Once you look at it, voyeurism in *You Only Live Twice* is virtually another character. Sequence by sequence, scene by scene, it makes its presence known.

A close analysis finds three interwoven motifs: Voyeurism as evidenced by surveillance, surveillance equipment, and omnipresent media; the necessity of observing reality, and the interplay of fakery and fake spying with reality (all being observed); and the presence of real secrecy and real spying, which is not observed. That last is subtle, but it is present, and it underlies and supports all the artificiality.

First, remember that the gunbarrel shot itself is a voyeuristic and impossible view. In every movie, we are reminded that we observe a spy in his work from an angle that we cannot possibly observe. And right here, we know that this shot is something Maurice Binder came up with because it was cool-looking, and didn't have any self-important meaning attached to it, yet it sets the tone, doesn't it?

The moment that *You Only Live Twice* opens, we are introduced to surveillance equipment before we are introduced to any characters. We start by seeing the NASA Jupiter 16 shot, and immediately we see an array of monitors as well as a radar dish. From here, we go to the meeting of the USSR, USA, and UK delegates, all of whom talk about "tracking stations."

So, before we've even gotten to Bond, we have governments talking about the act of spying, and how they all know, observe, and record one another's secrets, and we see the equipment by which this is accomplished.

The next scene is Bond's "death." This scene has, for a very long time, driven me crazy. If we allow it to wash over us, it's exciting, visually gripping, sexy, bizarre, compelling: It's just a great piece of film. But, at the "icebox," it's a tangled web of confusion. Is Ling an enemy or not?

If she's an enemy, then the "killers" (shooting blanks) are MI6, and they are putting on a show for Ling's benefit, allowing a double-agent to go free (at least temporarily) in order to fake Bond's death. But Moneypenny's later mention of Ling didn't indicate a plot against her.

If she's *not* an enemy, then who is the show for? If no one sees that Bond is dead but agents and allies in on the charade, why play dead at all? The story could simply have been planted.

The obvious answer is that the audience, the fourth wall, is the whole point of this bit of play acting. The charade is *about* charade, the point is that a spy is putting on a show for an audience.

After the titles, this show continues. We start with Bond's burial at sea, and immediately we are presented with our twin themes of surveillance and media: A man with binoculars observes the burial at sea, while we see that next to him is a newspaper, the Standard, with a massive headline "British Naval Commander Murdered."

Again, why does Bond actually have to be in the body bag? The film treats us to a second look at the binoculars, and a second look at the headline. Observation is the point, and underneath all the fakery, there has to be something real. Just as with Bond's fake death, Bond's fake burial requires the presence of a real spy. His real body had to be "killed" and "buried."

Now begins the presence of real secrecy. In Jungian psychology, water and bodies of water represent the unconscious mind and secrecy. The "depths" of our psyches are invisible to us, they are "beneath the surface," in "murky waters." We will notice that true secrecy in *You Only Live Twice* is always signaled by being underwater or underground, and nothing underwater is filmed. Blofeld's base is effectively hidden, because it is both underground *and* underwater; the fake lake camouflage is effective until Bond actually touches it.

The scuba divers retrieve Bond when he's out of sight and underwater. This is a real secret; the observer on the shore doesn't see it, and for a while Bond is truly believed to be dead.

Now Bond meets with M, and M talks about "elbow room." Here they have created a new secret, but immediately return to the subject of voyeurism:

> Bond: *"Any reconnaissance?"*
> M: *"Every inch photographed. Nothing."*

Bond also burns the piece of paper with the address at which he's to make contact with Henderson.

Note that both the secret and the voyeurism in this scene are useless: Photography turned up nothing, and Henderson's address is compromised and Henderson killed.

At the end of this scene, Bond leaves underwater. His departure is truly secret—his enemies don't know he's in Japan.

In Japan, Bond meets Aki watching a sporting event—a public spectacle with a large audience.

He meets Henderson, chases Henderson's assassin, breaks into a safe, and again encounters Aki. She drives him into Tokyo, and Bond turns and observes camera/recording equipment in the back of the car. This is a strange moment, with the movie lingering over the equipment, just as it lingered over the newspaper headline.

A few minutes later, Bond chases Aki to Tanaka. Tanaka's office has video monitors that show Bond everything we've just seen: The chase and the "rabbit hole." In addition, Tanaka already knows that Bond is "dead." Tanaka's underground stronghold is absolutely safe (remember, underground things are *really* secret) and is something like a center of voyeurism, where he can observe everything around him and have it played back. There's definitely a fetishistic, almost homoerotic component to this: The "I love you" password exchange, the cozy chair Bond lands in, and Tanaka luxuriating in comfort while watching others. It's not a major element of the story, but it's there, and it matters because, after all, voyeurism *is* a fetish.

Naturally, then, the first thing that Bond requests of Tanaka relates to photography: He asks him to enlarge a negative. Soon, they are looking at the photograph of the Ning-Po, observing it so closely that they enlarge a microdot of information. The movie seems to be telling us that film and photography can and must be observed at a minute level.

The next day, Bond arrives to see Osato, giving a pseudonym. Osato's assistant spies on Bond from a camera; the video is at his desk. Bond observes the camera observing him, a beautiful reflection of voyeurism. Osato then uses an X-ray, at *his* desk, to take a different kind of picture, finding Bond's gun as he does so. The image that Osato captures is shown to us repeatedly.

Osato instructs his henchmen to kill Bond, but Aki helps Bond escape. Now the video equipment in her car, that Bond lingered over, is brought into play. We see Tiger's face in the car via video phone when Aki asks for the "usual reception." Via an impossible video, we see the helicopter dropping the car, then the pool in the water which the car leaves in its wake, and then Tiger again.

Again remember, this is a major sequence in the movie, shown entirely via video.

Next, we learn that the photograph of the Ning-Po was analyzed and a specific coastline discerned, reinforcing the idea that the medium is effective for spying.

The next major sequence is Little Nellie, and we can see a camera on Bond's helmet throughout the scene.

Next is the Russian space shot—more radar and monitors. The space module is captured by Blofeld, and the Americans say "Moscow radio's already saying that we did it,"—this is, again, knowledge gained from media. Then we see video in the Pentagon, and video communication from NASA. The Americans say:

"Forget Japan."

"I agree."

"We've re-photographed every square inch."

They are relying on the fake spying of media, but the real secret is underground and underwater, and cannot be photographed.

At last we get our first look in Blofeld's base, and as soon as we see Osato and Helga Brandt, we see a bunch of video monitors, even before we see Blofeld's cat and know who the villain is.

Now comes a crucial scene in regard to media and spying and secrecy.

Osato and Brandt are called into Blofeld's apartment. (They are shown walking past a large bank of video screens.) Blofeld shows a *picture* of Bond's gun, taken in Osato's office, and Osato acknowledges it's a Walther PPK. When Blofeld says that Mr. Fisher was actually James Bond, Osato says, "But Bond is dead," and Brandt adds, "It was in all the newspapers."

Bond created a fake death, directly addressing the voyeurism of his world. That death fooled Osato and Brandt *so well* that even photographic evidence that he is alive didn't convince them of it. The media worked to blind them to real spying, blinding them to their *own* voyeurism. They, and we, are such consumers of media exhibitionism, that we cannot see real evidence. Blofeld, though, who lives underground and beneath a lake, and whose face is never seen (so far) can perceive the truth beyond the media show.

Tiger, too, is concerned with true spying; he has ninjas. When Bond questions what ninjas are, Tiger says "The art of concealment and surprise, Bond-san."

Soon, though, Bond tells Tiger he sounds "like a commercial," indicating he's corrupted by media. Sure enough, the ninja camp (neither underground nor underwater) is infiltrated.

By contrast, Blofeld has a cave in the water with poison gas, which Bond says is "to keep visitors away." Here we are again: Underground, underwater, and concealed. Voyeurism is both the business and the enemy of the spy.

Our video experience is hardly over. We see more video monitors at NASA for the third, launch, then Houston calls Washington on video monitors, and then there's more video at NASA, and then we're back to a bank of monitors in the volcano lair.

Blofeld may reject the media, but he's a part of all this voyeurism and replication of imagery. He spots Bond's mistake with his air conditioner via monitor, and Tiger's invading ninjas are also spotted that way.

Finally, Blofeld addresses the issue directly: "The firing power inside my crater is enough to annihilate a small army. You can watch it all on TV. It's the last program you're likely to see."

Then there's the famous, and ridiculous, moment of watching the SPECTRE rocket almost swallow the American rocket on the monitors: What could possibly film it? What third ship is in space with a camera? There are even multiple camera angles. But the point is *our* voyeurism and our absorption in media and experiences filtered through media.

Back at the U.S. monitors, there's all this stock footage of war on the US monitors—where would they get that? I mean, why would they see pictures of the planes taking off?

I haven't examined every Bond movie for this motif, but I doubt there's any that's as media-saturated until we reach *Spectre*. In *Spectre,* the whole point is the surveillance, and it's discussed as text throughout, so that every look at a camera or newspaper circles back to the explicit point of the plot. By contrast, *You Only Live Twice*, that big, silly beast, keeps the theme as subtext, and lets you discover it, or not. It's possible to see it dozens of time and never notice the them, but I believe this movie is truly grappling with the notions of observation, media, voyeurism, exhibitionism, and concealment. It adds up to a rich visual experience in a movie not often examined for richness.

ON HER MAJESTY'S SECRET SERVICE (1969)

Survey Says!

> Percent Favorite: 17%
> Top 5 Cumulative: 1/25
> Numeric Rating: 6.93/10
> Ranking: 5.6 (1st/25)

My Rating and Ranking

> Rated: 4/10
> Ranked:23 out of 25

Summary

Bond meets, rescues, and makes love to the beautiful but melancholy Tracy. Her father, Marc Ange Draco, tries to bribe Bond into marrying her. Money doesn't persuade Bond, but Draco has information on Blofeld's whereabouts. With this information, Bond finds Blofeld's Piz Gloria "allergy clinic," where he is brainwashing innocent women to spread plant and animal infertility. Bond is found out and escapes. In an interlude, Tracy finds him and helps him, and Bond proposes marriage. After Blofeld is defeated, Bond and Tracy marry, but mere hours after the wedding Blofeld and the evil Irma Bunt shoot and murder Bond's new bride.

> **James Bond:** George Lazenby
> **Marc Ange Draco:** Gabriele Ferzetti
> **Contessa Teresa (Tracy) di Vicenzo:** Diana Rigg
> **Ernst Stavro Blofeld:** Telly Savalas
> **Irma Bunt:** Ilsa Steppat
> **Ruby Bartlett:** Angela Scoular
> **M:** Bernard Lee
> **Moneypenny:** Lois Maxwell
> **Q:** Desmond Llewelyn
> **Directed by** Peter Hunt

Discussion

On Her Majesty's Secret Service is a movie that justifies the High Points/Low Points feature of these chapters, because there are so many of each within it. So much is wrong with the movie, and quite a lot, but not enough, is extraordinarily right. In disliking *On Her Majesty's Secret Service*, I stand in rather a strange place. This movie tends to be a favorite among hardcore fans, and is disliked by more casual Bond admirers (although its cachet has risen over the years). In the main, I'm pretty hardcore, but I cannot rewrite my great distaste for *On Her Majesty's Secret Service* to suit the party line. Still, in part because of the insistence of friends, I have seen enough of *On Her Majesty's Secret Service* to appreciate its merits. Believe it or not, my rating of four is an upgrade—the first time I saw the movie I gave it a two!

On the bright side, *On Her Majesty's Secret Service* is a tour de force of stunning photography. Aerial photographer Johnny Jordan, who lost a leg filming *You Only Live Twice*, devised a special rig that hung from a helicopter for *On Her Majesty's Secret Service*. This allowed him panoramic views that had never before been filmed. Not to be outdone in innovation, stunt skier Willy Bogner, Jr. had developed a hand-held camera and two-way skis so that he could capture the motion and excitement of skiing in a new way. Bogner, a champion German skier and former Olympic athlete, had directed a documentary called *Skifascination*, which led to his being hired by the Bond team. He went so far as to ski backwards in front of the skiers so that he could film them from new and exciting angles. All of the Alpine photography is breathtaking, and the snow action is superb, culminating in a two-mile long avalanche which has the devastating realism that only the real thing provides. (Inserts and supplemental footage had to be added, of course.) Second unit director John Glen had no way of knowing how much of an avalanche the explosives would create. It turned out to be bigger and scarier than he had ever imagined, and it shows!

Figure 8: Autographed picture of George Lazenby as 007. Won by the author in a James Bond trivia competition.

Peter Hunt was committed to a "back to basics" Bond film, and the movie has very few gimmicks. In fact, the Q scene itself is a mockery of the whole gadget concept, which is an enjoyable bit of humor, although in retrospect, one wants Q to get more of his due. The stripped-down approach is laudatory; to me, the end of a ruler and ripped-out pockets are cooler than a gadget whipped up by Q Branch. Also praiseworthy is Hunt's devotion to his source material. He has said he carried the novel *On Her Majesty's Secret Service* with him throughout filming.

However, I believe Hunt misunderstood the whole concept of working from the novel. On the one hand, his dedication to the original plot gives us the biggest gaffe in Bond history; Blofeld, who met Bond in the previous movie, here doesn't recognize him. Of course, the novel **On Her Majesty's Secret Service** preceded the novel **You Only Live Twice**, but being true to one's source shouldn't mean ignoring the movies entirely!

On the other hand, Hunt mangles the novel's sequence just where it needs to be respected. In the novel, Bond meets Tracy at the casino, and sleeps with her. Then, knowing she may be suicidal, he follows her to the beach, where he watches her surreptitiously. At the beach, Draco's men arrive and a fight ensues before they succeed in bringing Bond and Tracy to their boss. All of this makes narrative sense. First meet her and make love to her, then save her. Only after Bond is involved with Tracy is Tracy's father interested in Bond as a son- in-law.

In the movie, Bond sees a stranger on the beach and, for reasons that have never been clear to me, assumes she is committing suicide. He is attacked violently immediately upon saving Tracy. This isn't a "come with me" kind of attack—one of the men seems ready to assassinate Bond. (How else do you explain being made to lie down and having a gun pointed at your head?) After this, Bond meets Tracy, but then is again attacked by one of Draco's men. After the second attack, Bond and Tracy sleep together. Finally, Draco's men succeed in kidnapping Bond.

None of the movie version makes sense. Bond saves a woman he cannot know needs saving. Draco seeks after Bond (in his violent fashion) before Bond knows Tracy. Draco's men are murderously violent, in utter opposition to their purpose. It's just a mish-mash of senseless violence, made even more senseless by the flow (or lack thereof) of the opening scene. Bond chases Tracy into the water because he (telepathically) knows that she intends to die. The moment he touches her, she faints. Why? Then Bond and Tracy are attacked.

One man puts a knife to Tracy's throat and begins to kidnap her, but when she struggles, he drops her and joins the fight against Bond. Peter Hunt was focused entirely on making the fight exciting, but he completely forgot that the audience also likes to know what's going on. Add to that his speeded-up style of filming and the entire sequence resembles nothing so much as a cartoon.

Most of the fight scenes have this hyperkinetic style, with huge movement at insane speeds. It is as if one is watching the Saturday Night Live version of the Keystone Cops doing James Bond. My eyeballs jiggle.

My feelings about Telly Savalas have already been amply covered under VILLAINS, and Diana Rigg is discussed under BOND GIRLS. Rigg is, of course, the most popular Bond girl among fans (or was until Vesper Lynd came along). I am not a member of her cult, but she is competent, professional, attractive, and entirely persuasive. She looks very fetching in her fur hat.

Although I don't doubt that Bond could fall in love with this woman, the romance is developed childishly. When a film resorts to vignettes shown from a distance, you know the screenwriter failed to come up with a way to write it up close, with dialogue. One such vignette actually shows them petting a puppy together! Can Agent 007 fall in love that way? I think not.

One tactical error of this film is dropping SPECTRE. The movies had established Blofeld as a man of great menace in part by showing him as the head of a complex organization of numbered, obedient agents. The henchmen in *On Her Majesty's Secret Service* are merely thugs. Fans will argue that this is as in the novel, but the movie established a different sort of precedent. Without SPECTRE behind him, Blofeld is just one more nasty villain.

On Her Majesty's Secret Service has some outstanding and justifiably famous action. The bobsled chase is one of the highlights of the film. The ski chases are also brilliant, and the avalanche is a tour de force of cinematography. Since nowadays filmmakers would almost certainly use CGI, this piece of real film is a treasure. The foot chase through the Christmas Eve crowd is marvelous as well, a very old-fashioned bit of suspense.

However, the chases go on forever—although each was exciting on its own, a ski chase, a foot chase, a car chase, and then a second ski chase start to look like a joke. As well, there is virtually no action for the longest time—two early fights with Draco's men and then over an hour without action. Then, from about the hour and twenty-five minute mark, the movie is action packed, virtually breathless, which creates a lopsided feel. Of course, most action movies tend to lay in the heavy artillery towards the end, but at two hours and twenty minutes long, balance is crucial.

Peter Hunt tried several interesting things with camera angles, however there is an ill-conceived artsy moment when Bond is knocked unconscious and then awakens staring at a Christmas angel. The blurry, emerging angel seems to imply that it *Means Something*, but of course it doesn't.

You may have noticed by now that I have completely omitted the most singular and notable part of *On Her Majesty's Secret Service*—that it stars George Lazenby as James Bond. It's not that I forgot; I was saving it. It has been my observation that whenever a Bond fan criticizes *On Her Majesty's Secret Service*, the response is that he or she is just failing to look past Lazenby's performance (or something like that). So, before getting into a discussion of the way in which *On Her Majesty's Secret Service* introduces a new Bond, and how that Bond performs, I wanted to take the time to establish that Lazenby isn't the only thing wrong with the movie. In fact, he sometimes performs adequately, although I think anyone who rates him higher than that is grasping at straws.

On Her Majesty's Secret Service opens with an homage to prior Bond films in the title sequence. Later, we are treated to another round of reminiscing as Bond packs his desk. These references seem forced and embarrassed to me. They scream "We know you'd rather have Connery! Really! We know!" Besides which, it was unlikely for Bond to have any of the particular souvenirs used.

Physically, Lazenby is very credible. He fights with terrific vigor, and he looks menacing and strong. His constant tendency to pose and grin like a mannequin works against him, however when he remembers to act, he does well facially. The nuance shown when he argues with M is wonderful. M pulls him off the Blofeld operation, and Bond's face goes through these complex permutations of frustration, anger, and obedience. Then he opens his mouth.

Lazenby has said in interviews that he was making a constant effort to control what was then a very broad Aussie accent—I guess he had nothing left over to give to this performance. His voice is dreadful, he barks most of his lines. If the nuance in his face during his M scenes had been anywhere present in his speaking, there might have been something wonderful there. His delivery of one-liners is horrendous, there's a quality of broadcasting each joke, so that even the amusing ones sound bad, *and the bad ones...!*

Unfortunately, the movie chose to pay too much attention to Lazenby's best asset—his physicality. He not only looked like a mannequin, he was generally treated like one. The audience was constantly reminded that this was a model, not an actor, by his many foppish costume changes. Bond in a ruffled tux. Bond in a bright orange golf ensemble. Bond in a kilt. Bond in an ascot. Bond in a bright blue ski ensemble. He looks the fool and it detracts from the audience's great admiration for the character of 007.

But the odd-looking glossiness of *On Her Majesty's Secret Service* isn't confined to Lazenby. 1969 was a difficult year for movies that valued class, traditionalism, and fashion. A Bond film of that era wouldn't and couldn't acknowledge the world that was changing around it; it couldn't remove Bond's tie and give him a beard. At the same time, the movies hadn't yet figured out how to dress Bond, or, for that matter, the entire film, in a timeless style that wouldn't look dated ten minutes after release. Later, Roger Moore will suffer under safari suits, but first we have to ruffle poor George. Everything in this film, including the purple wallpaper, screams 1969, and most of what aims for glamour ends up as fleeting fashion. Colors seem over-saturated, and the costumes on Blofeld's "Angels of Death" are especially overdone.

I'm not saying movies of 1969 of necessity look weird. Some of the great movies of that year were period pieces (*Butch Cassidy and the Sundance Kid, Anne of a Thousand Days*), which conveniently bypassed the fashions of the year. But *Midnight Cowboy* and *Easy Rider* succeeded with a naturalistic look that was present in its era but not ridiculous. Hitchcock's *Topaz* had rich colors without looking over-painted. *On Her Majesty's Secret Service* simply looked like a fashion magazine.

Moneypenny, on the other hand, looks fantastic. Peter Hunt decided to give her a glamorous new look, and succeeded marvelously. With her stylish fitted suit and her posh new up-do, she never looked lovelier. The wedding also looks lovely, and the scene is nicely done. It was a fine opportunity for in-jokes and references, done with some panache.

Speaking of the Angels of Death, their appearance is an oddity which, to me, stops the film. The first time I saw *On Her Majesty's Secret Service*, I thought, "How come only women have allergies?" One friend of mine has explained to me, painstakingly, that this is because it's a Bond movie. But every time a movie forces you to offer yourself that sort of explanation, it damages the suspension of disbelief that is so much a part of enjoyment. In fact, Fleming offered an explanation in the novel—Blofeld believed that young women of sheltered backgrounds were the most susceptible subjects for hypnosis. A single line of dialogue to this effect would have made the "harem" seem less of a smutty joke.

Overall, *On Her Majesty's Secret Service* doesn't work for me. I have come to enjoy its finer points, but I will never be able to appreciate Lazenby's clumsiness, Savalas's miscasting, or the hyperactive editing that makes the fights look comic. The movie is worthwhile primarily for its exciting snow sequences, and you can always use your fast-forward button to get there sooner.

The High Points
- Thrilling ski chases and bobsled chase.
- Breathtaking avalanche.
- One of the finest John Barry scores.
- Moneypenny looking glamorous and polished.
- The marriage proposal scene.
- Lovely wedding scene, with several amusing conversations.
- Diana Rigg as Tracy.
- The skating rink foot chase.
- The lack of reliance on gadgetry.

The Low Points
- Lazenby's performance.
- Telly Savalas unable to persuasively pet a cat!
- Senseless pre-credits sequence with hyperkinetic but meaningless action.
- The one and only time that a Bond film breaks the fourth wall.
- The worst one-liner in Bond history ("He had a lot of guts"—yuck!)
- The very corny love montage.
- A too-long movie with repetitive chase sequences.
- The loud, attention-grabbing costumes.
- Angela Scoular's obnoxious turn as Ruby.
- Bond's use of the same dialogue on two different women is sleazy.

Quotable Quotes
Bond (to camera): "This never happened to the other fellow."

Draco: "I was not sure you would accept a formal invitation."
Bond: "There's always something formal about the point of a pistol."

Bond: "Moneypenny, what would I do without you?"
Moneypenny: "My problem is, you never do anything with me."

Bond: "I love you. I know I'll never find another girl like you. Will you marry me?"
Tracy: "You mean it?"
Bond: "I mean it." (They kiss) "Mr. and Mrs. James Bond."

Draco (after punching Tracy): "Spare the rod, spoil the child, eh?"

Facts and Figures

SEXUAL ENCOUNTERS

<u>Three</u>: Tracy, Ruby, and Nancy.

BOND'S CAR

> 1969 Aston Martin DBS (dark green) (widely reported as gray or black, an Aston Martin collector assures me it is green)

DEATHS

<u>Seventeen</u>:

- Campbell, two of Blofeld's men in the first ski chase, one in the snow chopper, two of Blofeld's men in the avalanche.
- In the raid on Piz Gloria, Tracy kills one, Bond kills three, Draco's men kill seven. None of Draco's men are killed or wounded.

Bond Kills

- <u>Four</u> directly: One skier whom he strangles with a ski, and three in the Piz Gloria raid.
- <u>One</u> indirectly: He whacks a skier with a ski, and the skier falls over the cliff.

EXPLOSIONS

<u>Two (or three)</u>: Irma's Mercedes in the stock car race, Piz Gloria itself (an impressive one), and the third, if you count it as an explosion, is the avalanche. Personally, I don't think it counts, but it is dazzling.

BOND'S FOOD AND DRINKS

Vodka Martinis

<u>Two</u>: One, "shaken, not stirred" with Draco. Again, it is not called a vodka martini. Bond asks Tracy to "keep my martini cool" in Switzerland, but we don't see him drink one.

Other Drinks

- Dom Perignon '57 at the casino.
- When Bond is packing up his office, he toasts the portrait of the Queen and drinks something from a silver flask.
- Champagne at Draco's birthday party.
- Malt whiskey and branch water before dinner at Piz Gloria.
- Two glasses of red wine with dinner at Piz Gloria.
- At the skating rink, Bond orders and drinks a beer from a stand while trying to blend in with the crowd.
- Bond sends a St. Bernard for brandy ("Five-star Hennessey of course!") but we never see it.

Food

- Caviar for two which he intends to share with Tracy ("Royal Beluga, north of the Caspian.")
- Café complait for two with orange juice for breakfast the next morning (but Tracy is already gone).
- Irma tells Bond she ordered him "Steak Piz Gloria" for dinner. We see a plate with steak, green beans, and what appears to be some sort of French fries.

GAMBLING AND SPORTS

- Chemin-de-fer at the casino.
- Bond sets out to play golf but is abducted by Draco's men before he leaves the hotel.
- Portuguese bullfighting at Draco's birthday party (a different sport than Spanish bullfighting, in which the bull is wrestled but not killed).
- Horseback riding with Tracy.
- Curling.
- Skiing.
- Bobsled.

Amaze Your Friends!

- Director Peter Hunt has a cameo: He is one of the pedestrians seen in the reflection in the "Universal Exports" sign in the movie's opening shot.
- Telly Savalas and Dani (aka Sally) Sheridan, who played "The American Girl," met and began an affair while working on this movie. The relationship lasted for many years. They had one son, Nicholas Savalas. Sheridan is the mother of *Desperate Housewives* star Nicollette Sheridan.
- The line "Never mind that, go and get the brandy" was an ad lib when the St. Bernard surprised Lazenby by rolling over and playing.
- "We Have All the Time in the World" was the last song recorded by Louis Armstrong before his death.

Most Interesting Goofs

Bond who? *On Her Majesty's Secret Service* has the biggest and most obvious goof in franchise history: Bond and Blofeld met in *You Only Live Twice*, but a mere one movie later, Blofeld doesn't recognize his nemesis. Maybe the kilt threw him off.

Upsy-Daisy: During the chase at the stock car races, one of the regular race cars flips over. Rather than film the inside of an upside-down car, a piece of film was turned over. You can see, behind the driver, that the bleachers (which have writing on them) are also upside-down.

CHEMIN-DE-FER

If you've ever watched a Bond movie and wondered, 'What is that game and what does it all mean?' then this section is for you. Following is a simple description of the game of chemin-de-fer, played by James Bond in five official movies. The game is the driving force behind the plot of the novel **Casino Royale**, and it is played in both 1954 and 1967 filmed versions of that story. (For the 2006 version starring Daniel Craig, the game is Texas Hold'em poker.)

Chemin-de-fer is a variation of baccarat. The rules of card play are the same, but the betting is somewhat different. As in most casino games, card play itself is fairly simple, and betting is most of the game and its complexity.

The Cards

The object of the game is to come the closest to, or reach, nine points, in two or three cards.

- Only the last digit of a number counts; if two cards add up to sixteen, the score is six, if seventeen, the score is seven, and so on.
- Picture cards and tens are worth zero.
- Aces are worth one. All other cards are face value.
- Several decks of cards (at least three) are shuffled and placed in an object called a "shoe," from which cards are dealt.
- The dealer gives two face-down cards to his opponent, and two to himself.
- If these two cards add up to eight or nine, that is a "natural." The cards are turned face up and the game is over; the player with the natural is the winner, but a natural nine beats a natural eight. (Ties are re-dealt, but there has never been a tie in a Bond film.)
- If the opponent doesn't have a natural, he may stand or ask for a card. Normally, you always draw on zero through four, and always stand on six or seven. With a five, you "have the option," and the odds are nearly even.
- The drawn card, if any, is dealt face up.
- Now the dealer makes the same decision, stand or draw. The dealer has a very slight advantage, in that he knows what the other player has done.
- Cards are now revealed and the player closest to nine has won.

The Betting

The evening's play begins with an auction; high bidder wins the bank and be- comes the dealer.

- The amount by which the banker (dealer) has won is the amount of the bank. Betting cannot exceed this amount.
- Betting begins from the dealer's right and proceeds around the table. Each person can bet any portion of the total bank.
- To bet the entire bank, or the entire remaining bank, you say "Banco."

Example: The bank is won at $1,000. First player bids $100. "Banco" by the next player is a bet for $900.

- If the bank is not yet met after all seated have had a chance to bet, bystanders around the table can also bet.
- If the bank is still not met, the house can cover the difference, or play can proceed for the partial amount.
- The banker is playing against everyone else. Since only two hands are dealt, whoever has bet the highest plays against the banker.
- If the banker loses, he passes the bank to his right.
- If the banker wins, the amount of the bank increases by his winnings. That is, if the $1,000 bank in the example above was met, the banker's winnings are $1,000 and the bank for the next hand is $2,000. This means that, as play continues with the same banker, stakes and risk increase.
- However, the banker can always pass the shoe at the end of any hand.

Major Differences from Baccarat

There are several differences, but these two will let you know quickly if you are watching a game of baccarat or chemin-de-fer. In *GoldenEye*, Xenia Onatopp says that she and Bond both enjoy playing baccarat, but they are playing chemin-de-fer. This may not be an error, as the full name of the latter game is actually baccarat chemin-de-fer.

1. Baccarat is played with three hands rather than two: The banker deals to his right, his left, and himself. Players can bet on one or both of the opposing hands.
2. In baccarat, the shoe doesn't automatically pass when the banker loses. The banker can continue until his entire bank is gone.

Chemin-de-Fer in the Bond Films

Now that you can follow what's going on, it's fun to revisit those previously baffling casino scenes.

BOND VS. SYLVIA TRENCH, Dr. No

Three hands are played.

1. When we enter the casino, Bond has the shoe. Bond turns over a natural: Jack and nine (total 9). Sylvia has a Queen and a three (total 3)—she doesn't have the opportunity to draw because of Bond's natural. Bond wins.
2. Sylvia asks for a card, but before she gets it, Bond turns over another natural: King and nine (9). Bond wins.
3. Sylvia gets a natural eight (we don't see the cards). She thinks her luck has changed. Bond gets a natural nine (again, unseen), which beats her. Bond wins.

BOND VS. EMILIO LARGO, *Thunderball*

Three hands are played.

1. Bond enters the casino and sees Largo has the shoe. Bond goes Banco.
2. Bond gets a King and a Queen (zero), asks for a card and draws an eight. Largo doesn't show his cards, he has lost. Bond wins.
3. Bond takes the shoe. Bond gets a seven. Largo gets a six. (We don't see any of the cards close up.) Bond wins.
4. Largo turns over a King and an eight—a natural 8. He thinks he has won. Bond shows a natural 9 (but not to the audience). Bond wins.

BOND AND TRACY, *On Her Majesty's Secret Service*

1. For the first hand, neither Bond nor Tracy are yet playing. We see a natural 8 (King and eight) beat a zero (King and ten).
2. Bond goes Banco upon arriving, and wins with a natural 9 (Jack and nine).
3. Time has passed, and Bond has the shoe. His opponent has zero (two Queens) and draws a nine. Bond had a Queen and four. We can assume he drew a card, but we do not see it. Bond loses.
4. The shoe has passed. Betting at the table is complete and the bank isn't covered. The croupier calls for bets. Tracy comes from the back of the crowd and says Banco. The banker has a Queen and King, and draws a nine (9). Tracy has a Queen and five, and draws a five (zero). Tracy loses.

BOND VS. "BUNKY," *For Your Eyes Only*

Two hands. Bond's opponent is a man known only as "Bunky," who is being goaded by Countess Lisl.

1. Bond has the shoe. Bunky has a five and a three, a natural 8. Bond has a Queen and five (5), but the shoe does not pass, and everyone acts as if Bond has won.
2. Bunky asks for a card. We don't see any of his cards.
3. Bond has a Queen and five (5), is advised by Kristatos to stand, and draws a four (9). Bond wins.

For Your Eyes Only is the only Bond movie in which there is a serious error in the play of chemin-de-fer. It appears to be a filming error, as Bond has the same Queen-and-five hand both times. Apparently, Bond was meant to win with a natural 9 the first hand (the only way he could have beaten a natural 8) but somewhere in the course of editing, he was shown with the same hand both times.

BOND VS. XENIA, *GoldenEye*

Xenia is already playing when Bond enters.

1. Xenia gets two Kings (or a King and a Jack?) and a seven. (Note that this is 007.) The croupier announces "Madam wins."
2. Upon entering, Bond goes Banco. Xenia has an Ace and a seven (8). Bond has a five and a two (7). The croupier announces "Madam wins."

3. Xenia doubles the bet. Bond asks for a card. Xenia shows a Jack and a five (5). She deals Bond a six, and stands with her 5. Bond shows a King and a Queen (6). (Note that this is 006.) The croupier announces "Madam loses."

DON'T LET HIM GET AWAY!

O ne thing you can be sure of in a Bond film is a chase sequence. These movies have had them all, the thrilling ones, the amusing ones, the utterly bizarre ones. Bond has had foot chases, motorcycle chases, and of course, car chases with and without gadgetry.

The Top Ten Best Chases

1. *Goldfinger*: The original gadget car chase, with Bond in the first, the original, and still the best, Aston Martin DB5. The scene that made "ejector seat" a household phrase.

2. *On Her Majesty's Secret Service*: The first ski chase remains one of the most outstanding chase sequences ever committed to film. When you view it as a continuous chase—skis to foot chase (at the skating rink) to car chase (including the stock car race sequence) it is even better. If the romantic evening was just a pause, and you tack the second ski chase and the avalanche onto it, then, by golly, you've really got something.

3. *The Spy Who Loved Me*: Bond in the Lotus Esprit along the treacherous cliffs of Sardinia, escaping first the motorcycle, then Naomi in the helicopter, who flirts enticingly as she tries to kill him. The chase ends with the Lotus driving off a pier and converting to Wet Nellie.

4. *Diamonds Are Forever*: Terrific chase through the streets of Las Vegas, pursued by numerous cops through the crowded streets of the strip. Towards the end, we are treated to a lovely crane shot of a parking lot full of wrecks, very amusing without being dumb. The scene is marred only by the right/left wheel blooper, the rest of it is loads of fun.

5. *From Russia with Love*: Bond vs. helicopter in an homage to *North by Northwest*. I was scared, weren't you?

6. *The Living Daylights*: The first gadget-car chase in ten years had lots up its sleeve, was very entertaining, and culminated in the cello ride (see below).

7. *Live and Let Die*: Playing bumper cars on the FDR Drive. For a New Yorker like me, nothing ever looked so real. Bond has to deal with a dead driver behind the wheel, but when does he use the brakes anyway?

8. *GoldenEye*: Ferrari vs. Aston Martin, a purely fun chase, with nothing at stake, Bond and Xenia are merely entertaining themselves. And us. Terrific!

9. *Live and Let Die*: The speedboat chase is thrilling, but it goes on and on and on...!

10. *Die Another Day*: The loaded Aston Martin vs. the loaded Jaguar. If anything, this scene is too much—too exciting, too many explosions, and filmed in too dizzying a fashion.
    AND: *Casino Royale:* No discussion of James Bond chases could be complete without updating it for this stunning freerunning scene. It has *everything*—a construction site, equipment, height, then the embassy. The chase stops for a mid-air fight, then continues, then ends explosively. The chase

also serves as a character sketch for Bond, epitomized by Mollaka elegantly leaping through a window and Bond following by crashing through the wall.

The Ten Most Unusual Chases

1. *Moonraker*: The "Bondola" that drives out of the canals and into the streets of Venice was bad enough, but Bond is being chased by a hearse-gondola! The stupid reaction shots include, but are not confined to, a double-taking pigeon. And for no reason at all, the bad guys simply leave once Bond goes ashore. Bond's gondolier hat is pretty bad too.
2. *Diamonds Are Forever*: Moon-buggies are very practical. Fast, too. Who knew?
3. *Live and Let Die*: It turns out that double-decker buses are really convertibles. Another surprise.
4. *On Her Majesty's Secret Service*: A bobsled chase was not the usual Bond sort of thing. Two bobsleds chasing each other are certainly exciting. Bond hanging onto the back of Blofeld's bobsled is amazing.
5. *Licence to Kill*: Tanker trucks can do wheelies!
6. *GoldenEye*: Bond steals a Russian tank to save Natalya. This is fun, particularly when you learn that, unlike in the *Licence to Kill* tanker chase, the tanks here were not tricked out or modified in any way. They really did that stunt driving.
7. *Tomorrow Never Dies*: 007 doesn't need to be in the front seat of the car, he just needs to drive it.
8. *A View to a Kill*: Bond steals a fire engine from the scene of a fire. This is not only an unusual chase because of the vehicle, but because Bond behaves so badly, endangering the lives of those who may still be trapped in, or fighting, the fire.
9. *Tomorrow Never Dies*: 007 and Wai Lin, handcuffed together, on a motorcycle being chased by a helicopter through the streets of Saigon. Unusual yes, and also absolutely thrilling.
10. *The Living Daylights*: Downhill sledding on a cello case, using the cello to steer.

The Ten Worst Chases

1. *Moonraker:* See the "Bondola" entry under Most Unusual.
2. *Dr. No:* Bond vs. Hearse—has anything ever looked more fake?
3. *For Your Eyes Only:* The cross-country ski chase, in which a biathalon contender cannot shoot Bond even when he's standing still, and wearing a bright blue jacket visible for yards and yards against a white background.
4. *Octopussy:* The "hunt" sequence, in which Bond is chased by Kamal Khan on an elephant. Presumably, director John Glen thought of this as an homage to *The Most Dangerous Game*, but it's really "The Least Dangerous Game," and is made a mockery of when Bond tells a tiger to "Sit!" and then delivers a Tarzan yell.
5. *The Man with the Golden Gun:* Other than one awesome stunt—the Spiral Jump—which is ruined by a silly sound effect, this is a very weak chase. The stunt driving is good of course, but we're used to that. In exchange for it,

we're forced to endure the return of J.W. Pepper, an offensive confrontation with the Hong Kong police, Goodnight "in the boot," and Scaramanga's very silly car plane.

6. *Diamonds Are Forever:* The moon-buggy chase: See MOST UNUSUAL.

7. *A View to a Kill:* The car chase in Paris is nothing but a series of clichés and deja vu (the wedding as in *Live and Let Die*, stealing the car as in a thousand movies, etc.). Add to that the extremely poor stunt doubling; never has it been more obvious that Moore was nowhere near!

8. *Octopussy:* Replace the usual chase clichés with India clichés and tennis jokes, and you've got *Octopussy*'s golf cart chase sequence.

9. *Die Another Day:* With the right driver, a race car can outrun a beam of light.

10. *You Only Live Twice:* The car chase that ends in a splash. Bond isn't even driving and the silliness of the "drop in the ocean" detracts.

DIAMONDS ARE FOREVER (1971)

Survey Says!

> Percent Favorite: 1%
> Top 5 Cumulative: 14/25
> Numeric Rating: 6.37/10
> Ranking: 17.55 (22nd/25)

My Rating and Ranking

> Rated: 8/10
> Ranked: 6 out of 25

Summary

James Bond is called in to infiltrate a diamond smuggling chain of enormous proportions. Links in the chain, which extend from South Africa to Nevada, with stops in Holland and Los Angeles, are being murdered, and Her Majesty's government wants to uncover the operation before it is completely shut down. With smuggler Tiffany Case, Bond discovers that Blofeld is behind the operation, masquerading as reclusive billionaire Willard Whyte. Blofeld is using the diamonds to create a powerful orbiting laser weapon with which he will hold the world ransom. With the help of Felix Leiter, Bond frees Whyte, stops Blofeld, and gets the girl. The diamonds, however, remain in orbit.

> **James Bond:** Sean Connery
> **Tiffany Case:** Jill St. John
> **Ernst Stavro Blofeld:** Charles Gray
> **Mr. Wint:** Bruce Glover
> **Mr. Kidd:** Putter Smith
> **Felix Leiter:** Norman Burton
> **Willard Whyte:** Jimmy Dean
> **Plenty O'Toole:** Lana Wood
> **Bambi:** Lola Larson
> **Thumper:** Trina Parks
> **M:** Bernard Lee
> **Moneypenny:** Lois Maxwell
> **Q:** Desmond Llewelyn
> **Directed by** Guy Hamilton

Discussion

Diamonds Are Forever puts me in the odd position of having to defend myself. I am not alone among Bond fans in loving this film, but boy, it sure feels that way sometimes! The charges come down to: It is too campy, the plot makes no sense, and Tiffany is a bimbo. There are also complaints that the plot is confusing and/or senseless. I have defended Charles Gray in the Villains section. I shall try to answer the other charges, explain the plot, and talk about why I love this film.

In the Introduction, I point out that *Diamonds Are Forever* was the first individual Bond movie I saw. It was definitive for me—people complain that Sean Connery was old and overweight in this film, but to me, he looks exactly right, exactly as I always remember him. Though I realize this is entirely subjective, aren't we all subjective when it comes to Bond?

That said, I think there are plenty of objective reasons to love *Diamonds Are Forever*.

Diamonds Are Forever has, in its favor, a marvelous sense of pacing. Consider the pre-titles sequence. Setting aside the culmination of this scene—the strange and unsatisfying mud bath battle—consider the way it is entered. We open with a peaceful, beautifully-appointed Japanese room. The room is suddenly disrupted with a crash of violence. CUT and we are in a Cairo casino, with a quiet and exotic scene again broken up. CUT and we are on an exotic beach with a beautiful woman, and "Bond, James Bond." These are wonderful cuts and wonderful approaches to scenes, and this style will be reflected throughout the movie. While we are being taught about diamond smuggling in an amusing and intelligent fashion, we are watching Messrs. Wint and Kidd commit a series of murders that we do not understand. Only gradually does it unfold that each victim is a link in the smuggling chain, and that the chain is being shut down.

Keep in mind that "silly" Bond movies are often criticized for their lack of espionage. *Diamonds Are Forever* is replete with real spying—Bond must follow a trail of murder back to the top of its chain, and he must impersonate one of the intended victims in order to do so. He must smuggle diamonds with the skill and ingenuity of a real smuggler, and he must anger his smuggler employers enough to get their attention, but not so much as to get killed. 007 fulfills his mission with flare and panache, tossing off some of the franchise's best witticisms in the process.

Let's pause for an explanation of the plot, which often confuses people, in part because the screenplay itself loses the thread in a couple of spots. For this, it really helps to have read the book.

The core of the scheme is a diamond smuggling chain. This chain is extremely careful and circuitous. Most links in the chain don't know who their contact is. Or they know the person they receive from but not the person to whom they deliver. Tiffany knows the "little old lady" in Holland, but hasn't met Peter Franks before. The chain has double-blinds along the way, people who watch each link to prevent theft or disobedience. We know from Tiffany that she doesn't know who she will deliver to, or how, until she arrives at the next spot.

So, the dentist receives diamonds from miners, and sells to the helicopter pilot. The pilot delivers to Mrs. Whistler (the little old lady), who delivers to Tiffany. Tiffany hires different smugglers to get the diamonds into the U.S., this time she has hired Peter Franks. She and Franks sit separately on the airplane so that if either is arrested, the entire operation isn't blown, and they are both watched on the plane. Upon arrival in Los Angeles, they are to await instruction. In this case, instruction arrives in the form of Morton Slumber's men, who will deliver to Shady Tree, who will (presumably) deliver to Bert Saxby.

At the top of the chain, the diamonds are being used by Blofeld to build a satellite laser. When enough diamonds have been acquired to complete the laser, every link in the chain will be murdered (by Wint and Kidd) in order to "bury" (sorry) the evidence. The exception seems to be Morton Slumber, who is a part of Blofeld's murder operation, not primarily his smuggling operation.

Bond disrupts the operation by switching the real diamonds for fakes (Leiter pulls the actual switch). This stops Wint and Kidd from killing him, because he cannot die until he makes his delivery. His goal is to get the attention of the head of the operation, initially so he can report back to MI6, but of course, as things do with 007, things change.

On close examination, there are some flaws in this plotting. There was originally no plan to use a body to transport the diamonds—that was an idea born of necessity when the body of "James Bond" (Peter Franks) suddenly needed disposing of. Despite this, a hearse arrives to take the diamonds as if it had been planned all along. While Slumber appears to be a part of the murder operation, Shady Tree is not; he is himself murdered. So, why does he know that Bond is in the cremation box? Still, these are small flaws in an otherwise tightly-plotted scheme.

Figure 9: Replica of the Shady Tree and the Acorns brochure found by Bond; note that future star Valerie Perrine is one of the Acorns (on the left)

Visually, *Diamonds Are Forever* is among the greats. Ken Adam outdoes himself; every interior is exquisite. The laboratory setting in the desert is outrageous, Whyte/Blofeld's penthouse apartment is amazing, the Slumber Funeral Home is a riot of color and light, Bond and Tiffany's suite at the Whyte House, with an aquarium in the waterbed, is beyond words. The exterior elevator on the Whyte House was exotic and eye-popping at the time, although many chic buildings now have them. The brief visit to Circus Circus leant the best location footage that Las Vegas had available to the film. Tiffany's outrageous costumes, and the Palm Springs home used as Willard Whyte's summer house, add the final touches, making this Bond movie a masterpiece of design.

Until the end, the action in *Diamonds Are Forever* is fantastic. People remember the very unmemorable battle at the off-shore oil drilling location. They remember it, of course, because this is where the movie utterly falls apart, and it is exactly where a Bond movie must succeed—the big blow-out at the end. The filming here is sloppy; explosions were set off during what should have been a rehearsal, and so the crew scrambled to get as much footage as they could, but some of the best shots were permanently lost (once you've blown up your location, there's no going back).

But let's look at the action prior to that. The fight with Peter Franks in the glass elevator remains one of the best fist-fights in the series, and indeed is sometimes mentioned among the best fist-fights in any movie. The movie features two large chases—the dumb moon buggy one, and the outstanding car chase through the streets of Las Vegas (see DON'T LET HIM GET AWAY!). "Mountain climbing" up the outside of the hotel is a great scene, opening as it does with Bond's ride on the top of the elevator, pausing, of course, to smell his lapel flower. Then there is the momentary claustrophobia of the elevator closing Bond into a very tight space, followed by the opposite, as he must swing out over the top of the city; all very elegantly accomplished. *Diamonds Are Forever* also features Bond's scariest close-call—the cremation (see YOU LIKE CLOSE SHAVES, DON'T YOU?)

Two action sequences are particularly bad; the mud bath and the battering "bath-o-sub." Both come in for frequent fan ire, but I think the movie has enough good action to hold up its head.

For some reason, this is the sexual ambiguity Bond. Wint and Kidd are lovers, Bambi and Thumper have an undisclosed relationship, but are certainly erotically violent, and Blofeld dresses in drag. In 1971, this was a relatively untouched topic and added a thrill-chill to the proceedings. The idea of lover/killers was comic and scary at the same time. From the opening murders we know that Wint and Kidd are a force to be reckoned with; they quickly and brutally dispatch three smugglers (the dentist, the helicopter pilot, and Mrs. Whistler). The comical elements of their relationship have a distinct chill; we do not dismiss them because they are campy—they remain dangerous.

Diamonds Are Forever spends a lot of time introducing fear with a naughty-plus-nice edge. The sugary sweetness of Wint and Kidd adds to their creepiness and threat. To me, we expect a killer to be angry, vicious, malevolent, and we expect sweet people to be, well, sweet. It's the combination of gentility and evil that is truly scary—think Hannibal Lecter. The same juxtaposition, differently placed, is used to good effect with Bambi and Thumper—a couple of ugly guys beating up Bond wouldn't have been as thrilling, would it? Neither would a couple of women in bathing suits just hanging around. It's the combination that creates the impact.

If you weren't alive in 1971, allow me to assure you that audiences went wild for Bambi and Thumper. Nothing like them had ever been seen before and the fight was a huge crowd-pleaser. I remember being blown away by it. I look at it now more critically and see how weak the fight really was—too stagy, nothing like a real fight, Bond waiting for them to strike their blows, and no reason at all for Bond to win in the end. Nonetheless, there's a lot of raw power in the scene, and it looks great.

Many fans think Tiffany Case is a bimbo. I beg to differ. Tiffany is smart, tough, and self-sufficient. She does a few stupid things, and can't handle a machine gun—but hey, neither can I. And that cassette switch was hardly her fault! Meanwhile, she stays on top of every situation, saves her own behind by playing both sides to her own advantage, doesn't sleep with Bond until she's sure it's a good idea to do so, and comes out clean in the end despite being a career criminal. She is pretty much a heterosexual Pussy Galore. Her outfits are outrageous and gorgeous—not at all "bimbo" for 1971.

Because Connery plays Bond fairly straight, bemused and witty but not tongue-in-cheek, he allows the camp element of *Diamonds Are Forever* to work. Connery is the sane center that allows everything around him to go crazy. I find this a distinct contrast to Roger Moore's humor. Moore mugged and acted silly, he deprived his movies of that center and so the camp was too much. Connery's smoothness here is exactly what makes the zanier plot points work.

In the end, *Diamonds Are Forever* does collapse. The final combat is pathetic, the science fiction goes too far, and Blofeld's undignified and unsatisfying end as a battered ram is no way to go. The coda, however, redeems the film. The last fight with Wint and Kidd, and Tiffany's sly closing line, bring a satisfying conclusion to a movie that had strayed off-course for a while.

The High Points

- The return of Sean Connery to longing audiences.
- The interesting and clever unfolding of the smuggling chain.
- The fight in the elevator between Peter Franks and James Bond.
- The dynamic entrance of Tiffany Case, (almost) wearing "a nice little nothing," and a series of wigs.
- Very witty dialogue and one-liners.
- Charles Gray's effete but masterful performance as Blofeld.
- Wint and Kidd as murderous lovers, coolly and campily slaying the competition.
- Bambi and Thumper taking Bond for a merry ride.
- The Mustang chase around the Vegas strip.
- The cremation scene.
- Some of Ken Adam's best set design.
- A sensual John Barry score. Note that Wint and Kidd have their own theme music.
- Great editing by Bert Bates and John Holmes; a constant flow of movement and plot revelations. Look at the Circus Circus sequence, and see how easy it is to follow the complex moves of Tiffany through the huge crowd, and the CIA following her.
- A villain based on the mysterious and elusive Howard Hughes, leading to...
- The surprise return of Blofeld.
- Wint and Kidd's postscript battle on the ocean liner, and Kidd going up in flames.

The Low Points

- Blofeld in drag.
- Wint and Kidd "killing" Bond by putting him in a construction site—how cheesy!

- Tiffany getting ditzy in the final reel.
- Blofeld's "death by mud bath" and that entire fight scene.
- Unsatisfying and lackluster final battle on the oil rig.
- Blofeld's second "death," in his bath-o-sub.
- The moon buggy chase.
- Bond's short pink tie: Maybe his very worst fashion faux pas.

Quotable Quotes

Bond to Tiffany: "That's a nice little nothing you're almost wearing. I approve."

Bond to Tiffany (when asked what hair color he prefers): "Oh, providing the colors and cuffs match..." (shrug)

(Leiter examines Franks's corpse and cannot find the diamonds.)
Bond: "Alimentary, dear Leiter."

Wint (upon putting Bond in the cremation oven): "Very moving."
Kidd: "Heartwarming, Mr. Wint."
Wint: "A glowing tribute, Mr. Kidd."

Plenty: "Hi, I'm Plenty."
Bond: "But of course you are."
Plenty: "Plenty O'Toole."
Bond: "Named after your father, perhaps?"

Bond (to Tiffany, after escaping the desert laboratory): "If you see a mad professor in a mini-bus, just smile."

Tiffany: "Darling, why are we suddenly staying in the bridal suite at the Whyte House?"
Bond: "In order to form a more perfect union, sweetheart."

Bond: "Relax, darling, I'm on top of the situation."

Blofeld: "Right idea, Mr. Bond."
Bond: "But wrong pussy."

Bond: "Give me five minutes to get up there and five minutes to find Whyte."
Felix: "Are you sure you know what you're doing?"
Bond: "Ask me again in ten minutes time."

Bond (to rat): "One of us smells like a tart's handkerchief."

Bond: "I was just out walking my rat and I seem to have lost my way."

Bond (after throwing Mr. Wint overboard): "Well, he certainly left with his tails between his legs."

Facts and Figures

SEXUAL ENCOUNTERS

<u>One</u>: Tiffany Case (this is the only monogamous Bond movie prior to the Daniel Craig films).

BOND'S CAR

1971 Mustang Mach 1 (red)

DEATHS

<u>Approximately one hundred forty-seven</u>:

- The guy in the mud bath, a guard at the mud bath, the dentist, the helicopter pilot, Mrs. Whistler, the guard killed by Peter Franks (reported by Q on the phone, not seen on-screen), Peter Franks, Shady Tree, Plenty O'Toole, the duplicate Blofeld, Bert Saxby, Mr. Kidd, and Mr. Wint.
- From Blofeld's satellite, three men standing next to the missile that blows up at SAC, everyone on the Russian submarine (estimated at 116 based on news reports of the submarine crew of the Kursk), two at the Chinese missile base During oil rig battle, at least five of Blofeld's men, two helicopters blow up for approximately eight more.

Bond kills:

- <u>Six</u> directly: Two at the mud bath, Peter Franks, the duplicate Blofeld, Mr. Kidd, Mr. Wint.

EXPLOSIONS

<u>Six</u> (Five plus a group of several): The helicopter in South Africa is a good one, the two mushroom clouds, at SAC and from the submarine, are obvious stock footage, the Chinese base, a series of several at the oil rig, which include some nice fireworks, and Wint's bomb (attached to Wint).

BOND'S FOOD AND DRINKS

Vodka Martinis

<u>One</u>: The fixings are visible in his room at the Tropicana, although we never see him order or drink one.

Other Drinks

- Solera sherry with Sir Donald, (from an 1851 vintage)
- Scotch whiskey at Tiffany's apartment, from which she gets a fingerprint
- Unknown liquor on a tray in the background when Bond and Tiffany are in the aquarium waterbed at the Whyte House
- Mouton Rothschild '55 served by Wint on the ocean liner (which is a claret)

Food

- Dinner on the ocean liner consists of oysters andaluce, shashlik (shish ka-bob), tidbits, prime rib au jus, salade utopia, and a fake la bombe surprise.

GAMBLING AND SPORTS

- Blackjack and roulette at the casino in Cairo.
- Slots and blackjack in the background in Las Vegas.
- Q tricks the slot machines.
- Bond plays craps (Plenty "helps").
- Tiffany plays blackjack and then water balloons at Circus Circus.

Amaze Your Friends!

- Bruce Glover (Mr. Wint) is the father of Crispin Glover, best known as George McFly in *Back to the Future*.
- The character of Willard Whyte is based on reclusive billionaire Howard Hughes, who spent the late sixties and most of the seventies (he died in 1976) isolated in various penthouse suites, including that of the Desert Inn in Las Vegas, which he owned. Hughes was a long-standing friend of Cubby Broccoli's, and his permission was crucial in getting the Las Vegas location footage filmed.
- Jill St. John, at the time of filming, was promoting her own line of wigs, hence her hair color changes in her first scene.
- Sammy Davis, Jr. had a cameo in the film that was deleted. He is visible in the entertainment brochure that Bond is looking at while bathing, on the page opposite that featuring "Shady Tree and his Acorns."

Most Interesting Goofs

The Most Famous Goof in Bond History: The Mustang goes into the alley on its right wheels, and comes out on its left wheels. When the goof was discovered, shots of the car switching sides were inserted. However, had there been room in the alley for the car to switch sides, there would have been room to go through on four wheels.

Follow That Cat! Tiffany, who doesn't know anything about her contact except "a voice on the phone," should find nothing suspicious about Blofeld's white cat, and has no reason to follow him.

I Smell a Rat: Rats are not native to Las Vegas. Roof rats (the kind Bond was "just out walking) were first found there in 1990.

Must Have Had a Blow-Dryer: Bond battles Bambi and Thumper in the pool, gets out, and within five minutes is completely dry.

"MANO A MANO, FACE TO FACE"

What is more Bondian than a fistfight? In a good one you can feel every blow, cringing as you see them coming, and your heart pounds with adrenal action. In a bad one, you cringe for a different reason, sinking lower into your seat, embarrassed that someone is passing this off as a fight.

By the way, the chapter title is a quote from Scaramanga in *The Man with the Golden Gun*, when he suggests to Bond that they have an old-fashioned duel.

Top Five

1. From Russia with Love: James Bond vs. Red Grant on the Orient Express

Simply one of the finest fights in movie history, this one has it all. At its heart are two incredibly powerful men; two actors, well-matched physically, doing most of their own stunt work. The editing, justifiably famous, adds a speed and brutality not seen before in movie fistfights. A broken window brings the sound of the train in from outside, while broken lights bathe the room in an eerie darkness, made even more macabre by the remains of teargas floating in the air. Watching this one over and over will never diminish its impact.

2. Diamonds Are Forever: James Bond vs. Peter Franks in a teensy weensy elevator

Bond's fight with Grant was the purest form of a fight—two people facing off. But some fights add other components. Some, for example, add an outside threat, something that can intrude on the fight and kill either or both combatants. A dramatic example of an outside threat is the fight between Necros and Bond off the back of the airplane; while the fight is going on, each is also endangered by the possibility of falling.

The fight between Bond and Franks (played by Joe Robinson) has a more down-to-earth threat, but a significant one nonetheless. During the intense action, either or both could be crushed by being in the wrong spot as the elevator rises to the next floor.

The fight is all about confinement and space. Two large men in an elevator not much bigger than a phone booth. Glass breaks, the entire thing is moving, and every time either one of them swings, he hits a wall. A classic!

3. Die Another Day: James Bond vs. Zao at the Los Organos Clinic

While the Blades swordfight (see below) got all the media attention and fan buzz, this gem has gone virtually unmentioned. From the moment Bond wakes Zao by squeezing his IV bag (Yow! That's gotta hurt!), we know he is a man on the edge, and that this fight will stop at nothing. And we're right—later in the fight, Bond will attempt to strangle Zao with the medical tubing still attached to his body.

The use of space here is fantastic, as the combatants maneuver around the crowded hospital room, using quite a range of medical equipment, and banging into and breaking it; setting a fire while they're at it. My favorite moment is when the magnetic resonance machine first grabs both men's weapons, and then Bond turns it off to neatly catch his gun.

Part of the pleasure is our first glimpse of the freakishly half-transformed Zao, shirtless and obviously very, very fit.

4. Goldfinger: James Bond vs. Oddjob inside Fort Knox

Unlike in the previous fights, the opponents here are anything but equal. Bond has already seen that Oddjob is virtually unbeatable—he is immensely strong, impervious to pain, and has no regard for human life. Add to that a killer hat, and you have a perhaps impossibly dominant foe.

This brings up a third kind of fight, one that is a distraction from a more important task. Bond must stop the atomic bomb, but Oddjob is in his way. The entire time they battle, we are aware of that ticking timer and what it means.

Bond fights Oddjob while he fights the clock, and he uses his resourcefulness, his wits, and his courage in the face of impossible odds to win the day.

5. GoldenEye: James Bond vs. Alec Trevelyan on the satellite dish

This is another great Brosnan fight scene. It is very raw, and Bond's most human, most personal combat. Whereas most of the greatest fights exist in a confined space, the showdown between 007 and 006 ranges all over the satellite dish; across a catwalk, in a gear room, and finally dangling from the top of the transmitter.

This is a match between equals. Alec is meant to be Bond's exact counterpart, their style and demeanor are at first nearly identical, until Alec is revealed to be a brute and a villain.

AND: *Casino Royale: James Bond vs. Fisher in a bathroom*

The black and white pre-titles sequence is masterful. This fight, seen in snippets as Bond and Dryden calmly talk, is brutal. Dryden says, "Made you *feel* it, did he?" and we agree. It's raw, rough, and introduces a new Bond and a new style of Bond movie quickly and unforgettably.

Honorable Mention

The James Bond movies wouldn't be much of a series if there were only five great fights! Here are some more fantastic fights, in chronological order.

Goldfinger: James Bond vs. Capungo

From the reflection in Bonita's eye, to the struggle for the gun, to the "shocking" ending, this is a perfect fight in a perfect pre-titles sequence.

You Only Live Twice: James Bond vs. an anonymous assassin in Osato's offices

One gets the impression that Bond is about to fight a sumo wrestler. The guy is, in a word, huge. He need merely stand up to appear threatening. He looms.

The beauty here, as in many great fights, is in the use of space. The offices are magnificent, and they are magnificently destroyed. The couch, the statue, everything that isn't nailed down—all fated to become so much rubble.

On Her Majesty's Secret Service: James Bond vs. SPECTRE agent in a bell room

Probably Bond's loudest fight, it was inspired when director Peter Hunt saw a room full of bells while scouting locations. The bizarre playing of an array of bells throughout the short but powerful fight is what makes this one a stand-out.

Octopussy: James Bond vs. three assassins in Octopussy's bedroom

One of Roger Moore's few really strong fight scenes.

The Living Daylights: Necros vs. the safe house kitchen staff

This one has, literally, everything and the kitchen sink. All the goodies you expect in a kitchen fight; knives, boiling water, lots of convenient set dressing. It's a vicious, deadly, high-stakes battle coupled with the enjoyable addition of a kind of revelation; "Aha! Even M's household staff is trained for combat."

Licence to Kill: James Bond and a cigarette lighter vs. Franz Sanchez

A bit too brief to stand among the very best, it is nonetheless an excellent culmination to a destructive and emotional enmity. What is impressive is, in part, how battered both men are by the end.

GoldenEye: James Bond vs. an anonymous assassin on the Manticore

In an homage to the pre-titles sequence fight in *Goldfinger*, Bond sees an assassin approaching in a reflection in polished brass while he spies on the yacht Manticore. This fight is very short, but absolutely perfect. When Bond uses the towel to wipe his brow when it's all over, we know we are in the territory of real cool.

Tomorrow Never Dies: Wai Lin vs. everyone else at her HQ in Saigon

I cannot bring myself to include a fight that doesn't star James Bond among the top five, but in terms of quality, this one stands among the greats. Michelle Yeoh at the time of filming had not yet won acclaim for *Crouching Tiger, Hidden Dragon*, but was already famous in Asia as an action star, and in this scene, she struts her martial arts stuff to perfection.

Die Another Day: James Bond vs. Gustav Graves at Blades

This great, great fight fails to make the top five on a technicality: It is not a fist-fight (although a few punches are thrown). Filmed in a very 21st century style that uses too few medium shots for my taste (the camera doesn't back up and let us see everything at once), it is nonetheless everything a fight should be. As the "friendly" match proceeds, a veneer of civility is stripped away, and the level of violence increases. This is an edge-of-your-seat battle; intense and destructive. It has a terrific amount of movement at a wonderful location, one that Fleming fans have longed to see.

Skyfall: James Bond vs. Patrice silhouetted against Shanghai

This is an excellent fight, but earns its place more for the beauty of the cinematography than for anything particularly notable about the action. As the two men face off in shadow, a brilliant lightshow of neon dazzles behind them. Stunning.

Bottom Five

1. The Man with the Golden Gun: James Bond vs. the sumo wrestlers at Hai Fat's estate

The absolute worst fight in Bond history features 007 defeating an opponent by grabbing his cheeks and giving him a big ol' wedgie. Thank heavens Nick Nack arrived to knock Bond unconscious before the "action" could continue.

2. Diamonds Are Forever: James Bond vs. Ernst Stavro Blofeld and a bunch of mud.

Does anyone know what's going on in this one? Why is a guy in a mud bath fully clothed and carrying a gun? Why does pouring mud on that same guy kill him? Why does going into the mud kill the fake Blofeld? Why are we watching this instead of a real fight?

3. Moonraker: James Bond and Holly Goodhead vs. Jaws atop the cable cars

You know what's wrong with fighting on top of cable cars? You fight verrrrrrry slooooooowly. Very slowly. You step carefully around the supporting cables, and move carefully away from or towards your opponent. This scene reminds me of a Looney Tune in which Bugs Bunny and Elmer Fudd have a slo-mo chase.

4. The Man with the Golden Gun: James Bond and two teenage girls vs. an entire karate school

It's a sad, sad thing for one movie to have two fight scenes in the bottom five, but *The Man with the Golden Gun* earns that "honor." Everything about this fight is dumb. The lead-in fight (Bond vs. the karate students) is dumb. The presence of cute teens in school uniforms is dumb. That the girls take over the fight, pushing Bond behind them, is dumb. That Bond stands and watches and doesn't participate is dumb. That one girl defeats one opponent by using a watermelon is dumb. And that Lt. Hip leaves Bond behind is extraordinarily dumb.

5. A View to a Kill: James Bond, Stacey Sutton, and Grandpa's ashes vs. some assassins

Compared to the other fights on this list, this one isn't really that bad. On the other hand, Stacey Sutton is in it, the gun isn't really loaded, a bad guy gets conked with an urn full of ashes, and Bond is over 200 years old. All of which count strongly against it.

THE BIG BATTLES

J ames Bond is most famous for his lone wolf activities. He is one man, inserted in an enemy situation, emerging victorious. In between, he kicks some ass. But Bond isn't always in a *mano a mano* situation. There are times in Bond films that an all-out battle, a mini-war, takes place. Bunch o' bad guys vs. bunch o' good guys, and the good guys, Bond among them, always win.

In Bond history, there have been twelve such battles. It is interesting to note that the last one was in *The Living Daylights* in 1987. Pierce Brosnan's Bond always operated alone or with individual allies (Wade, Zukovsky); he was never part of a large team.

It's hard to make a large-scale battle work. All fights have to be exciting, to be sure, but these group combats have the additional burden of being potentially hard to follow. The director has to make sure that the audience can figure out who is doing what to whom. If it's all chaos, the mind goes numb and the viewer stops caring. On the other hand, a well-done battle is a grand thing; the viewer enjoys the sense of scale, sees a flow of action, and finds the excitement grows as each step builds on the one before.

The Best

Top Five/Bottom Five hardly seems applicable to a category in which the total is only twelve, so let's just see the best and worst battles Bond has to offer.

1. Goldfinger: The raid on Fort Knox

A classic, of course. It works in part because of the set-up; the sight of all those soldiers falling over, apparently dead; of Felix laying equally "dead" in his car, makes the battle terribly exciting once it begins. In addition, we have Goldfinger cleverly transforming himself into a general and killing his own man, and we have the juxtaposition of what's going on inside and outside that vault. All this while the timer is ticking!

2. The Living Daylights: The Afghan airbase raid

There's an awful lot of movement in this one, but director John Glen, whose work I don't always admire, here makes it all clear. Despite the many different things happening at once, you can follow everything perfectly. There are Russians with high-tech equipment, there's Koskov and Necros operating separately from them, there are the Mujahadeen on horseback, there's Bond, and there's Kara, going off on horseback on her own, all amid planes, people- movers, Jeeps, and a shower that falls over.

3. From Russia with Love: Battle in the gypsy camp

The beauty here is how Bond moves in and around the action, but holds himself apart. He is the good parallel to Red Grant, who is also apart from, but participating in, the action. Neither engages with the main flow of combat, but both have significant kills by the time it's all over.

The Worst

1. Thunderball: The underwater battle

This one is rather famously bad, simply because without it, *Thunderball* would be among the very best of Bond films. It drags interminably, is impossible to follow, and the camera wanders about like a distracted child longing for something interesting to look at.

Figure 10: Center spread of the underwater battle from the Thunderball *program*

2. Diamonds Are Forever: The oil rig attack

The main problem here is that it is shot far too much in distance shots, and this was an unintentional error. Nonetheless, one never feels truly a part of this battle, and what we do see up close is disconnected and ugly.

3. Moonraker: The space battle

One hardly needs say anything at all here. Has anything ever been this goofy?

The Complete List

1. *From Russia with Love*: Battle in the Gypsy camp
2. *Goldfinger*: Raid on Fort Knox
3. *Thunderball*: The underwater battle

4. *You Only Live Twice*: The ninjas vs. Blofeld's men
5. *On Her Majesty's Secret Service*: The raid on Piz Gloria
6. *Diamonds Are Forever*: The oil rig attack
7. *The Spy Who Loved Me*: U.S. submarine crew vs. Stromberg's men inside the tanker
8. *Moonraker*: The space battle
9. *For Your Eyes Only*: Columbo's raid on Kristatos's warehouse
10. *Octopussy*: Circus performers raid Kamal Khan's castle
11. *Never Say Never Again*: Shootout at the Tears of Allah
12. *The Living Daylights*: The Afghan airbase raid

LIVE AND LET DIE (1973)

Survey Says!

> Percent Favorite: 1.5%
> Top 5 Cumulative: 17/25
> Numeric Rating: 6.3/10
> Ranking: 12.3 (13th/25)

My Rating and Ranking

> Rated: 2/10
> Ranked: 24 out of 25

Summary

Three MI6 agents are killed while investigating Dr. Kananga, Prime Minister of the island nation of San Monique. When Bond investigates, he is temporarily ensnared by the Harlem-based gang of "Mr. Big." Arriving on San Monique, he seduces Solitaire, Kananga's virgin tarot reader, and escapes with her. Bond discovers that Mr. Big and Kananga are one and the same. He plans to grow and process poppy in San Monique as Kananga, and distribute the heroin in the U.S. as Mr. Big. With the help of Felix Leiter, Bond destroys the poppy fields and kills Kananga, but not his mysterious associate Baron Samedi.

> **James Bond:** Roger Moore
> **Solitaire:** Jane Seymour
> **Kananga/Mr. Big:** Yaphet Kotto
> **Baron Samedi:** Geoffrey Holder
> **Tee Hee:** Julius Harris
> **Felix Leiter:** David Hedison
> **Rosie Carver:** Gloria Hendry
> **M:** Bernard Lee
> **Moneypenny:** Lois Maxwell
> **Directed by** Guy Hamilton

Discussion

In all the back and forth about *Live and Let Die*, the controversy over whether or not it's racist (on which I will certainly weigh in), the arguments and counter-arguments, the one factor that will override all others is this: *Live and Let Die* is a bad movie. In a good movie, like *Dr. No*, we will take some racism with a grain of salt, we will find it unfortunate and unpleasant, but it is a small part of an otherwise fine Bond film. But in *Live and Let Die*, pretty much the whole discussion is about racism, because there's not much else to it. By most standards, and with the exception of a few good moments (which all Bond movies have), *Live and Let Die* is not a good movie.

Live and Let Die opens flat, with a murder mystery that features no sign at all of our hero. The murders themselves are stylishly done, but the cries of "Where's Bond?" are still heard among fans. From the pre-titles sequence, we move into a fairly lifeless title sequence that seems uninterested in showing much of any- thing except a black woman staring straight ahead, as if to say "this is blaxploitation and nothing else."

We are introduced to a new James Bond with M's first and only visit to Bond's flat, where 007 is trysting with an Italian agent. Moore does a good job on his first outing, holding himself more in check than he later will, and seeming to take the job a little bit seriously. However, the introductory scene is ill-conceived, with Bond fussing in the kitchen, Moneypenny acting to assist Bond's philandering, and Q written out entirely. Q's absence has upset more fans than Bond's from the pre-titles sequence, although, until the Craig movies, it made a nice little trivia ques- tion (*What was the only Bond movie in which Q does not appear?* With *Casino Roy- ale* and *Quantum of Solace*, the number reaches three.). Add to all this the dizzying black dot decor, and you have a definite mess.

Jane Seymour as Solitaire is badly used; she's a sexy, talented woman, but has little opportunity to shine in this. Her wardrobe usually drapes her from chin to ankle, her modest demeanor and innocence make her more an object to be pro- tected than desired. Yet, does Bond protect her? He tricks her into making love, and although she enjoys the physical experience, she is anguished by it. Bond doesn't care, he abuses her trust, telling her he'll protect and care for her when he is really using her as bait. Overall, it is a mean sort of trickery, with none of the regard that Connery's Bond had for the women with whom he was paired. Connery may have called Tiffany Case a stupid twit, but he didn't lie to her, manipulate her, or place her in harm's way. Besides which, Connery didn't need any trickery to persuade a woman to share his bed!

The other woman in *Live and Let Die* is far worse. Rosie Carver is beyond doubt the stupidest woman to share an adventure with Bond. She does everything wrong, is fearful, superstitious, vain, and naive. Yet, Bond's treatment of her is still terribly unpleasant. His remark that he would rather kill her after making love than before is beyond callous, it is abusive. I am thankful that no Bond script has ever again sunk so low.

As a villain, Yaphet Kotto is surprisingly dull. Surprising because he is a good actor, respectable in that Bond-fan favorite *The Thomas Crown Affair* (the original, that is), and delightful in *Alien* (a personal favorite). But in *Live and Let Die*, Kotto is not threatening, not interesting, and his secret identity holds no surprises for any but the most inattentive of audience members. His scheme is both banal and un- workable (see HE'S QUITE MAD, YOU KNOW for a run-down).

Now it's time to address the issue of racism. I think *Live and Let Die* is terri- bly, offensively, racist, but since many fans disagree with me, I want to address their points fairly. First, let me explain why I think it's racist, because this is unclear to some folks. Stereotypes are one thing, but what really bothers me is the dual-edged sword that all heroic men and good-hearted women are white, and that all blacks are part of a vast conspiracy of villainy. Bond travels 1500 miles, from Harlem to New Orleans, yet every black face he sees, and every place in a black neighborhood he goes, is part of this web of communication and crime. This cannot help but paint a picture of Good Whites vs. Bad Blacks. In *Live and Let Die*, there are only two good black characters. One of them, Strutter, mocks Bond for being a "white face in Harlem," essentially supporting the idea that all blacks hang together as a group which is threatening and dangerous to whites. Quarrel, Jr. is the son of a past ally, a character who was himself a racist stereotype. His small role, however, is a positive and refreshing portrayal.

The racism is exacerbated by tying the plot into Voodoo. Prejudice against Voodoo hasn't changed much in the years since. It is still all too easy to take the religious practices of so many black Haitians and New Orleanians, and treat it as nonsensical and primitive superstition; threatening, bizarre, and ultimately stupid. The Voodoo subplot has much the same anxiety as the Harlem-wide network; white people wondering "What are those blacks doing behind our backs, and will it hurt us?"

One of the arguments I have heard is that the movie needs to be seen in the context of its time. I assure the reader too young to remember that people in 1973, especially black people, found the movie racist. (I am a little too young to remember the social context, but I have spoken to plenty of Bond fans older than me.) A related argument has to do with the fact that blaxploitation movies were in their heyday, and it makes sense for Bond to ride the crest of that wave, just as Bond would later ride the space movie craze in *Moonraker*. However, the very essence of blaxploitation is that it is about black heroes. These heroes fight black villains, in their own neighborhoods, using their own slang, and wearing their own styles. It celebrated African-Americans by creating a unique oeuvre for them. But *Live and Let Die* has a white hero, and that white hero wanders lost through the black world like an alien. Black characters had been shown up and humiliated by whites for decades, it is what blaxploitation was reacting to. Bond may have dressed up like blaxploitation for *Live and Let Die*, but he exploited, rather than "blaxploited."

Another argument that doesn't work for me is the one that goes, 'it isn't really racist, even though it seems to be. If you watch closely, you'll see that it isn't.' It is true that Eon wanted very much to avoid making a racist movie. Essentially, they had a very racist source novel, and hoped that by filming it as blaxploitation, and taking care to avoid certain egregious offenses, they could get a good movie out of the deal. The character of J.W. Pepper was introduced into *Live and Let Die* in part to have a negative white character, so that no one could say that all the white people in *Live and Let Die* were smart, good, and able. Another careful step was to make sure that Bond didn't murder the first African-American woman he slept with; it was Kananga who killed her (remotely) so that a delicate and explosive situation could be avoided.

My basic answer to this, though, is that if a movie seems racist, and it has to be closely examined to erase that impression, then it is racist. If you paint a canvas blue and then make a few green dots on it, it is disingenuous to argue when someone accuses you of painting a solid blue canvas. An effort here, an effort there—it is very nice to know that Eon was well-intentioned, but they failed nonetheless. The fact that Eon was capable of stereotyping Southerners in a way popular at the time, especially, doesn't prove they weren't stereotyping!

Figure 11: Autographed picture of Geoffrey Holder (Baron Samedi) received by the author at a Bond Fan Weekend (see Resources).

Finally, some say that Bond movies cannot be racist, because their villains are invariably cartoonish. The larger-than-life characters stand apart from race. I think this argument ignores how very good a movie like *You Only Live Twice* can be about showing us another culture, and treating it with respect. I specifically choose *You Only Live Twice* because it is even older than *Live and Let Die*, and so belies the "those were the times" argument as well.

Once again, I can point out that movies like *Dr. No* or *From Russia with Love* might have prejudicial aspects, but they are also such rollicking fine films that we can forgive their errors. *Live and Let Die* is merely imitative of other, better Bond films. It takes the island setting and Quarrel from *Dr. No* (yes, it is true that both original novels were set in Jamaica and featured Quarrel, and that **Live and Let Die** was actually the earlier novel. It is also true that Eon has always taken whatever liberties it needs with its source material, so that's hardly an excuse), the shark pool from *Thunderball*, and the train fight from *From Russia with Love*. It borrows blaxploitation and a stupid Southern sheriff from popular movies of the day. It has little flourish or originality of its own, and these are precisely what we seek in Bond movies.

The title song of *Live and Let Die* is fantastic, but its melody is used in an odd and jarring way during the movie. The soundtrack never really works; George Martin didn't seem to know how to turn the great song into a workable accent to the film.

The gadgets in *Live and Let Die* are another weakness. The magnet watch is a stupid device, and the saw blade at the end comes from nowhere. The death of Kananga is poorly done, and humiliating to boot. No other Bond villain has been treated so foolishly, although I can't say he deserved better.

Live and Let Die isn't all bad. Some of the action is exceptionally well done. I love the driverless car chase on the FDR Drive (for you non-New Yorkers, that's the highway along the East River that takes you to the United Nations). The speedboat chase is also quite exciting, even with the presence of the slobbering Sheriff J.W. Pepper.

The use of tarot cards adds an interesting element; the whole psychic phenomenon bit could have been played up more to good effect. Geoffrey Holder is a pleasure, and holds the screen every time he appears. (He also choreographed all the dancing and the Voodoo ceremonies.) The final Voodoo ceremony is terrific to watch, a long scene carried without dialogue, mostly by dance, it is very effective.

The highlight of the movie is the crocodile farm scene. This is really scary; the crocs are real, and threatening as hell. Tee Hee is a modern day Captain Hook, showing Bond/Peter Pan the source of his "problem" so that we have no chance of underestimating the danger.

David Hedison is the best Felix Leiter, and he carries his scenes well, retaining much of the exasperation and humor the character had in *Diamonds Are Forever*.

The High Points
- A great, great title song.
- The deadly walk across living crocodile "stepping stones."
- Geoffrey Holder as Baron Samedi, including the last shot.
- Deadly bumper cars in New York City with a dead man at the wheel.
- David Hedison as Felix Leiter.
- The speedboat chase.
- The double-decker bus chase.
- Kananga fooling the CIA with a tape recorder.
- The New Orleans funeral scenes.

The Low Points
- Rosie Carver's eye-rolling, shrieking presence.
- Kananga's ridiculous death-by-inflation.
- A lackluster plot involving poppy fields.
- Bond tricking Solitaire into sleeping with him.
- No Q!
- J.W. Pepper, especially when he shoves his tongue forward into his lower lip.
- George Martin's ear-piercing score.
- Overall, the racism, and the rip-off of blaxploitation themes.
- Solitaire's ridiculous costumes. One gets the impression that psychic powers are derived primarily from sequins.
- The train car scene that imitates *From Russia with Love* but has nothing to add.
- Pursuits that seem pointless; most of the chases are mere set pieces with little narrative attached.

Quotable Quotes
Miss Caruso (as Bond uses his watch to unzip her): "Such a delicate touch."
Bond: "Sheer magnetism, darling."

Bond: "A genuine Felix lighter. Illuminating!"

Rosie: "I'm going to be completely useless to you."
Bond: "I'm sure we'll be able to lick you into shape."

Bond: "It's just a hat, darling, belonging to a small-headed man of indigent means who lost a fight with a chicken."

Bond: "My name is..."
Mr. Big: "Names is for tombstones, baby!"

Bond: "I once had a nasty turn in a booth."

Bond (to Tee Hee): "Butterhook."

Bond (when Kananga dies): "He always did have an inflated opinion of himself."

Bond (when Tee Hee dies): "Just being disarming, darling."

Facts and Figures

SEXUAL ENCOUNTERS

Three: Miss Caruso, Rosie Carver, and Solitaire.

BOND'S CAR

None. Bond arrives in New York by plane, uses taxis, boats, a train, a hang-glider, and a bus, but has no car.

DEATHS

Eleven:

- Dawes, Hamilton, Baines (the three pre-titles victims), Charlie, Rosie Carver, Strutter, the guy who stole Billy Bob's boat, the priest in the goatskin at the Voodoo ceremony, a man in white, with a sword, at the Voodoo ceremony, Kananga, Tee Hee.

Bond kills:

- Four directly: Two at the Voodoo ceremony, Kananga, and Tee Hee.

EXPLOSIONS

Two: One of the Bayou speedboats, and a huge explosion (actually, a series of six) when Kananga's poppy fields go up.

BOND'S FOOD AND DRINKS

Vodka Martinis

None.

Other Drinks

- Bond orders bourbon and water, no ice, at the Fillet of Soul in New York, but doesn't have a chance to drink.
- Bond orders Bollinger at the hotel in San Monique.
- Bond and Rosie have champagne on their picnic.
- At the Royal Orleans hotel, champagne is brought to Bond and Felix.
- Bond orders bourbon no ice, again at the Fillet of Soul in New Orleans, but Felix changes the order to two Sazeracs.
- Kananga shares champagne with Bond and Solitaire shortly before his ignoble death.

- While playing gin rummy with Solitaire, two wine glasses are on the table. They appear to be white wine glasses (smaller than red wine glasses) but a slight red tint at the bottom of the glasses hints that they had contained red.

Food

- None, but for the first and only time, we see Bond's kitchen. In it, Bond makes espresso with an elaborate setup.

GAMBLING AND SPORTS

- Bond hang glides (but as transportation, not sport).
- Bond and Solitaire play gin rummy on the train.

Amaze Your Friends!

- The address of the "Oh Cult Voodoo" shop is 33 East 65th Street.
- The Olympia Band, which performed during the two New Orleans funerals, was real, and performed at funerals much as seen on-screen, except without the murder.
- While scouting locations, the filmmakers came across a sign that said "Trespassers Will Be Eaten" and stopped to investigate. They had found the crocodile farm owned by Ross Kananga. The script was rewritten, removing a different escape and replacing it with the one from the crocodile farm. Yaphet Kotto's character was named in honor of Ross Kananga, who also performed the stunt of walking across the crocodile's backs. The sign that appears in the movie is not the same sign as Kananga's (it is nicer looking), but the phrase is the same.
- Geoffrey Holder encountered someone dressed and performing as the Haitian folklore figure of Baron Samedi when he was a teenager, and developed the character based on that experience. Since Samedi is the God of Life and Death, he cannot die, and so Holder suggested the ending, in which Samedi returned from apparent death, to screenwriter Tom Mankiewicz.

Most Interesting Goofs

Death Takes a Holiday: Three cards from Solitaire's deck are burned, then Baron Samedi draws the Death card from the remaining deck. Later, Felix shows Bond three burned cards, and Death is one of them. (There is only one of each card in a tarot deck.)

James Bond is More Famous Than We Realized: The Fergus Hall tarot deck used by Solitaire is the same one created to market as a movie tie-in. In other words, it has the "007" motif on the back. This is very clear, for example, when Solitaire has Bond turn over a card for himself, that turns out to be The Fool.

THE TAROT IN LIVE AND LET DIE

This originally appeared as an article in the now-defunct HMSS.com online magazine. It has been fully edited and revised.

In *Live and Let Die*, Solitaire is a tarot reader of extraordinary psychic skill. As I am both a Bond fan and a tarot reader, I set out to explore the details of the cards used in the movie.

The Fergus Hall Tarot

Very little has been published on the subject of the tarot deck used in *Live and Let Die*. Research in both Bond and tarot sources turned up tantalizing tidbits, but few solid facts.

Eon Productions commissioned Scottish artist Fergus Hall to create a unique tarot deck for use in *Live and Let Die*. It appears that Hall was unable to complete work in time for the film, which created two interesting discrepancies. First, not all of the tarot cards seen in the film are by Hall, and second, the cards released for sale are different in some significant ways from the cards that appear in the film. We'll get to that in a little bit.

The deck was first released in 1973 under the name James Bond 007 Tarot. The box it came in was yellow and had a Roger Moore film tie-in illustration on the cover. The back of the cards was blue, with a repeated "007" motif. In 1974, the deck was released by U.S. Games Systems under the name Tarot of the Witches, with a conventional card back known as "tarotee." The box cover was purple and shows the High Priestess card. At around this time, U.S. Games also released the same deck under the name The Devil's Tarot. It is currently available as Tarot of the Witches with the tarotee back. Because of the profusion of names, and because an entirely different deck known as The Witches' Tarot is popular, most tarot collectors call this deck the Fergus Hall Tarot.

Some Quick Tarot Facts

To understand the history of this deck, it's helpful to know a little about the tarot. A tarot deck has 78 cards, consisting of 22 *major arcana*, and 56 *minor arcana*. The major arcana ("majors" or "trumps") are each uniquely illustrated. The minor arcana ("minors") are the origins of modern playing cards. There are four suits, each running ace through ten, with four "court" cards: Page, Knight, Queen, and King. In modern playing cards, the Knight was dropped, and Jack is another name for Page.

The suits are cups (which correspond to hearts), pentacles, discs, coins, or plates (diamonds), swords (spades), and wands, rods, or batons (clubs).

Until 1909, only the "majors" and court cards were fully illustrated. Like playing cards, numbered tarot cards merely had the right number of pips in the appropriate suit. Then came Arthur Edward Waite and Pamela Coleman Smith. Waite and Smith were occultists, members of the renowned magical lodge known as the Golden Dawn. Together they designed and published the first tarot deck which illustrated all 78 cards. This deck, known as Rider-Waite or Waite-Smith (Rider was the publisher), became the world's most popular and influential tarot. It appears in *Live and Let Die*, as we shall see.

Discrepancies

Two tarot decks appear in *Live and Let Die*: Fergus Hall and Waite-Smith. Both decks appear with the same back, a *red* 007 pattern. The pattern is the same as the published version, but as far as I have been able to determine, no deck was ever published with a red 007 back; it is only in the movie.

The movie shows cards in the suit "wands." This suit is "batons" in published form.

The movie shows two fully illustrated minors: the Six of Swords and Six of Wands. The published deck has numbered pips for the minors, and these illustrations do not appear.

The Meaning

Tarot cards have generally agreed-upon meanings, but how those meanings are interpreted is very much up to the individual reader. Some readers are far more "by the book," while others rely more heavily upon intuition. Even a by the book reader must interpret, since each card has several possible meanings.

In addition to memorizing meanings and being intuitive, many readers interpret the illustrations. The profusion of tarot decks available today (U.S. Games Systems alone has 184 in their current catalog) is because of the impact illustration has.

Fergus Hall illustrated each suit with different colored backgrounds, and varied the background color for the majors. Color is an important way to derive meaning from a picture. The Waite-Smith deck varies the background less, but uses other colors, such as garments, symbolically.

The plot of *Live and Let Die* has Solitaire as a psychic of profound power—until Bond takes it away, that is. For her, the cards are merely a conduit. Nonetheless, the meanings she ascribes to the cards are roughly accurate; the Six of Swords *is* a card of travel, and the Tower does indeed bring destruction.

Card Appearances: The Details

Following is every card that appears in *Live and Let Die*, and everything I've been able to figure out about it.

1. *A Man Comes*

Tarot cards first appear at the 12:29 point on my Special Edition DVD (the scene title is "Road Rage"). After the titles, we are introduced to Roger Moore as our new James Bond, when M and Moneypenny arrive in his flat. The next scene shows Solitaire reading cards as Bond flies to New York.

She lays down the following Fergus Hall cards, speaking with each card:

- Knight of Wands ("A man comes")
- Six of Swords ("He travels quickly")
- Knight of Swords ("He has purpose")
- (As we see an exterior shot of Bond's flight, she says "He comes over water, he travels with others.")
- Six of Wands ("He will oppose")
- The Tower ("He brings violence and destruction")

2. *Fillet of Soul*

At about 23:51, Bond meets Solitaire for the first time, at the beginning of the scene titled "It's in the Cards." This is when Bond has a "nasty turn in a booth" and finds himself in Mr. Big's custody. She is again using the red-backed Fergus Hall deck. We don't actually see card faces until 25:06, they are:

- The Moon
- The High Priestess
- The Queen of Cups

Solitaire has Bond turn over a card and we see

- The Fool (she says "You have found yourself.")

After Mr. Big enters and leaves, she has Bond pick a card for his future, and we see

- The Lovers

All the cards in this scene are identical to the published version, except for the color of the backs.

3. *Breakfast's Up*

At 38:30, in the "Morning Fishing" scene, Bond finds a tarot card with his breakfast while waiting for Rosie Carver to get out of the shower. It is the Fergus Hall Queen of Cups, the same card he'd seen Solitaire turn over in the back room of the Fillet of Soul.

At exactly 39:00 in the same scene, Bond goes into town and enters a store with a huge tarot display in the window. This is our first glimpse of the Waite-Smith tarot. The large poster is the High Priestess, and this is surrounded by the Ace of Swords and all the Sword court (Page, Knight, Queen, King) on the left, and the Ace of Wands and all the Wand court on the right. All of the cards in the window display are Waite-Smith cards.

4. He Comes Again

At 41:45, the scene "Future Teller" opens with Solitaire at a desk, a great many cards spread out before her. The scene is juxtaposed with images of Bond hang-gliding. We see only one card clearly, and glimpse a bit of another. They are again from the Fergus Hall deck and are:

- The Lovers
- The Chariot (this card can be identified only by the numeral VII)

5. It Must Have Been the Girl's Death

At 46:00, Kananga confronts Solitaire, who is in her truly insane crown-and-cloak get-up. For most of this scene ("Where is Bond Now?"), we cannot see any cards. There are six cards laid out face up in front of Solitaire, but they are barely visible. The cards are definitely Fergus Hall. The best shot of the cards is at 47:09.

On our right (Solitaire's left):

- The High Priestess
- The Moon
- The Queen of Cups

On our left:

- I am almost certain the top card is Judgment, but I cannot make out the other three.

Blasphemous Bond

At 49:05, Bond lays out the Chariot, the Fool, and the High Priestess. Solitaire calls it blasphemy (the DVD scene is called "Blasphemous Bond"). Then Bond fans his stacked deck, and Solitaire picks the Lovers. All of these are Fergus Hall.

By the way, Bond created a tarot deck of one card. That must mean he bought 78 decks. Quite an expenditure

The Waite-Smith Reading

In the final tarot reading of the film, Solitaire has lost her virginity and her power, and Kananga tests her. The reading is huge, she lays out card after card, using most of the deck, and here we see the Waite-Smith tarot in use for the first time. Significantly, many of the cards used have not been seen before in the film.

The scene begins at 1:10:54 in "Unmasked Man and Plan," and continues into "Solitaire/Death Card." Bond is back in Big's hands, and will soon learn the truth of Big's dual identity.

As the scene opens, Strength and Justice are visible on the table among fourteen cards. Later, I make out the Hanged Man, the World, Temperance, and the Wheel of Fortune. None of these were ever shown from the Fergus Hall deck, suggesting they had not yet been created.

Solitaire turns over a fifteenth card in response to Kananga's question, we don't see it.

When Baron Samedi enters, he picks up the High Priestess card from the reading and burns it. This card had previously been associated with Solitaire (albeit in a different form). He then turns over the Death card, and the camera zooms in.

Interestingly, these Waite-Smith cards have the red 007 back of the Fergus Hall cards. Strange that the filmmakers were willing to substitute radically different pictures on the fronts, but seemed to feel that a different back could not be tolerated.

The cards make an encore appearance at 1:39:58. Here Felix shows Bond three burned cards; Death, the High Priestess, and the Moon. They are all Waite-Smith cards with the red 007 back. This is definitely a goof, since Samedi burned only one card in the earlier scene. !

Conclusion

Fergus Hall was unable to fulfill his commission, but his unusual illustrations were used anyway. He seems to have worked on the specific cards needed for the film, perhaps in order of the scenes (he may have been given the script to work with) and ran out of time. Working from a script, in order, explains why it is in the last scene that other cards must be substituted.

When it was time to publish a tie-in deck, Hall may have lost interest, or may have had other commissions. Regardless, he discarded his two illustrated sixes and instead created pip cards for the 40 numeric minors.

I'd have to consider the use of the 007 back a "goof," even though it was clearly done on purpose. Seeing Bond's number on Solitaire's cards is certainly a bizarre way to break the fourth wall!

The tarot cards that appear in *Live and Let Die* are absolutely unique. Nothing identical to them was ever published, making them the rarest of collectibles.

TITLE SONGS

It started with "Goldfinger". Shirley Bassey belted out a bold, brassy, remarkable title song that changed everything. Oh, sure, Matt Munro had sung "From Russia with Love," but over the end credits, not over the titles. Besides, a sweet- voiced crooner delivering a pretty but bland love song was not about to make movie music history! No, it was Shirley who turned the tide, busting her vocal chords on Newley and Bricusse's lyric while she busted the charts. From then on, a Bond film had to have a great (at least in theory) title song, and the rest of the movie industry sat up and took notice—movies sell songs, and songs sell movies.

I have spent, in the course of researching this book, considerable time looking at favorite song surveys, from BBC's Top of the Pops to Bond fan-sites and beyond. After pouring over pages and pages of results, I have come to the conclusion that they're nearly useless. Possibly I have lost some credibility by this point, since I have already gone on at some length about how fans have such varied opinions, but really, this is different. With the Bond films, there are advocates and detractors for each, it is true, but there are certain broad areas of agreement. Without looking at the results of a survey—any survey, from any source—I can be confident that *Goldfinger* will place high, and *A View to a Kill* will place low. But with a song survey, I cannot even be certain of more than one (if that) of the top five. In fact, of all the songs, there is general consensus on only about five, top or bottom, and of course, there's disagreement on those.

Musical tastes always vary. Just look at how many records sell massive numbers of copies while they are also widely hated. Movies, television, literature, and games, all have greater continuity of taste and aesthetic common ground than music. Every time you look for something on the radio in an unfamiliar area, you are faced with the knowledge that someone actually likes that stuff. You and I probably have different definitions of "that stuff," but the experience, the bafflement, is shared. In part, taste in music is shaped by your age and where you are from—two factors that strongly influence the music you grew up with. When I was in high school, different "crowds" listened to different bands, and I imagine that is still true today.

So, in order to do any kind of fair survey, you would have to factor for age, location, and lifestyle—far more than your lone author can manage, and something none of the surveys I've seen have attempted. Therefore, to a certain extent, I'm winging it. What follows, when talking about the tastes of fans other than myself, is entirely informal. It comes from numerous uncontrolled surveys, as well as many, many conversations with fans over a period of years. Please don't put money on any of it.

What is a Bond Song?

Your first thought may be that there is one song per movie, with (almost always) the movie title being the same as the song title. Not quite. The first Bond movie, *Dr. No*, didn't have a title song at all as we think of them now, causing fans who write surveys to retrofit one of the four *Dr. No* songs into the category. *From Russia with Love* had an instrumental version of the title song played over the main titles, the sung version plays during the end credits. And "From Russia with Love" isn't the only song unique to a Bond movie's end credits. Movies such as *Licence to Kill* and *Tomorrow Never Dies* have additional songs, which expands the number of songs one might include on the list.

Then there are the incidental songs, songs which are played during the course of the movie. Some are background songs that receive a lot of attention—such as *Dr. No*'s "Jump Up, Jamaica"—and some are barely noticeable—like *Licence to Kill*'s "Dirty Love." When fans, in their passion for lists, compile a list of Bond songs, they have to make individual decisions about each. The one incidental song that everybody seems to include is "We Have All the Time in the World" from *On Her Majesty's Secret Service*. The song serves far more than an incidental purpose in the movie, it is the love theme for the relationship that is the core of the story. Unlike any other Bond song, it is sung during a montage in the middle of the movie, and its title is the film's last line. This unique importance, combined with the fame of the lead singer, and the fact that the title song, "On Her Majesty's Secret Service," is an instrumental, give "We Have All the Time in the World" more significance in fans' minds than any other non-title Bond song.

So where do I slice? Do I include every song on every soundtrack? What about remixes? What about cover versions? Since this is a book about Bond movies, I have chosen only to discuss those songs that occur during the course of a Bond movie. This prevents you from having to run out and buy a soundtrack CD in order to know what I'm talking about—every song I'm discussing can be heard by viewing a video or DVD.

Trivia Bonus

Five Bond "title" songs don't share the name of their movie:

- *The Spy Who Loved Me*: "Nobody Does It Better,"
- *Octopussy*: "All Time High."
- *Casino Royale* "You Know My Name"
- *Quantum of Solace*: "Another Way to Die"
- *Spectre*: "Writing's on the Wall"

The Almost, Sort of, Bond Song

"Mr. Kiss-Kiss, Bang-Bang" is in an odd sort of limbo. The original thought was that the movie title "*Thunderball*" just wouldn't work for a song. Leslie Bricusse (co-lyricists on "Goldfinger") penned the lyrics for a John Barry piece to be sung during *Thunderball*'s title sequence, and Dionne Warwick recorded it. As an added touch, the dance club where Fiona Volpe is shot was renamed from the Jump Jump Club to the Kiss Kiss Club, and that scene is one of the several times in the course of *Thunderball* that the instrumental version of "Mr. Kiss-Kiss, Bang-Bang" can be heard. At the last minute, though, the producers wanted a song called "Thunderball," and Don Black and John Barry obliged them. The sung version of "Mr. Kiss-Kiss, Bang-Bang" was removed from the movie, although it appears on the soundtrack. It is certainly a Bond song, but it cannot be heard in a Bond movie.

Top Five/Bottom Five

Best

1. "The James Bond Theme:" Monty Norman Orchestra, *Dr. No*
2. "Live and Let Die:" Paul McCartney and Wings, *Live and Let Die*
3. "A View to a Kill:" Duran Duran, *A View to a Kill*
4. "Nobody Does It Better:" Carly Simon, *The Spy Who Loved Me*
5. "Goldfinger:" Shirley Bassey, *Goldfinger*

Worst

1. "Man with the Golden Gun, The:" Lulu, *The Man with the Golden Gun*
2. "Never Say Never Again:" Lani Hall, *Never Say Never Again*
3. "The Experience of Love:" Eric Serra, *GoldenEye*
4. "Licence to Kill:" Gladys Knight, *Licence to Kill*
5. "Make It Last All Night:" Bill Conti and Rage, *For Your Eyes Only*

The Best Songs

There are far more than five great Bond songs—they tend to be of very high quality. The ones I've chosen are the ones that get the widest agreement from fans and listeners.

The James Bond Theme

If I could walk through life with a soundtrack, like a movie character, this would be it. Monty Norman's instrumental paean to cool is, in my opinion, the single greatest pop recording of the 20th Century. It is so passionately beloved by Bond fans that surveys of best songs cannot be conducted unless it is removed from contention. It is equally beloved by musicians, and has been covered, sampled, and remixed untold dozens of times. It is instantly recognizable, exciting, and ever so much fun.

Live and Let Die

Just about everybody seems to like this one, although it couldn't get near the top five on the BBC Top of the Pops survey. Oddly, enough, I wasn't crazy about it when it first came out. The combination of the Wings sound with a Bond song didn't seem right—so much of Bond was in the midst of an awkward transition in the 70s, from his sound to his wardrobe. Wings recorded the first young, hip Bond song, which was odd not just for Bond fans, who remembered what Bond had said about the Beatles in *Goldfinger*, but for McCartney fans as well. In retrospect, "Live and Let Die" has earned its place among the greats, describing the life of 007 in a new, yet authentic, way.

A View to a Kill

In the 80s, when Duran Duran had about five hits on the radio simultaneously, I wanted to wipe them off the face of the Earth. They had a ubiquitous, hit-friendly sound that seemed intent on drowning out the more quirky, individual, and to me exciting, New Wave artists. But with perspective comes appreciation. This is a powerhouse of a song, and surely the best part of a rather dismal movie. It is alive, sexy, and has an undecipherable pseudo-mystical lyric that is always interesting. It is also the only Bond song to date to have hit number one on the U.S. charts (see below).

Nobody Does It Better (*The Spy Who Loved Me*)

After breaking down the barrier between rock artists and James Bond with "Live and Let Die," the franchise stumbled badly with their next song, "Man with the Golden Gun, The." With Roger Moore's third Bond movie, it was time to get it right, and get it right they did! Following the first modern rock theme, by Paul McCartney, Carly Simon gave us the first modern love theme. The sly, sexy lyric, sung by a woman smitten with Bond, was tamed by a soft, discreet vocal that made it all sound so romantic to talk about 'doing it.' Maybe "Nobody Does It Better" set a bad precedent, since Rita Coolidge's song is so imitative of it, but we can't blame Carly for that.

Goldfinger

I hesitated to include this in the Top Five, because it has lost a lot of ground with the fans. It is loud, it is brassy, and it is obnoxious. But hell, I love it. It's a classic. That bold, overpowering sound is what made the whole idea of "Bond song" happen. Shirley Bassey sings her heart out, pouring conviction onto every note. When the song ends, your head is kind of ringing, isn't it? Fabulous! I picture the song as sung by Jill Masterson, the girl who knows firsthand the dangers of Goldfinger's "Midas touch."

Honorable Mention

There are so many great songs that don't make a top five, including my personal favorite. Just to round out the list, here are some more greats.

GoldenEye

This is my favorite Bond song, and no matter how often I listen to my Bond compilation CD, it is "GoldenEye" that is guaranteed to make my heart race. Indeed, it is only this one and the Bond theme itself that I will replay once or twice before moving on to the next track. "GoldenEye" is an absolutely remarkable piece of music. Tina Turner is Shirley Bassey with restraint, she can belt out every note that Bassey can, with at least as much skill, but she has a better ear for when to pull back and let it build. The lyric is haunting, compelling, mysterious, visual. It seems to be spoken from the villain's point of view, hinting at a lifelong vendetta—the song stalks you. It is delivered with a wallop. A perfect song.

Surrender (*Tomorrow Never Dies*)

Among Bond fans, this is the lesser-known song (not being a title piece) that is most often mentioned as a favorite. Few singers have the flawless strength of k.d. lang. She probably has the most perfect living voice on sheer technical merit. She can do standards, rock, country, jazz —anything, really. Sometimes her choice of material strikes me as shaky, but with "Surrender," she's on the money. If you don't know the song, make sure to listen straight through the end credits of *Tomorrow Never Dies*; you're in for a treat.

On Her Majesty's Secret Service

John Barry knows his way around an instrumental that tells a story. This one tells us that James Bond is a man of adventure, that we are here to be thrilled and we will be. It is a dynamic piece, and one that could have served as another Bond theme.

The World is Not Enough

This gets mixed reviews among fans, and it is unfortunate that the band Garbage gave themselves a name so easy to mock. The rich alto vocals draw you in to a compelling song. "The World is Not Enough" is all about *mise en scene*—it brings you into an era, an idea, a moment. The song, another that seems to be sung by the villain, evokes a world of glamour and desire.

The Worst Songs

Only a small handful of Bond songs are genuinely bad. Some are bland, and some are misplaced and don't belong in a Bond film. A few are painfully trapped in their time or genre. There are several fairly good songs that just don't measure up to the high standards set by the Bond masterpieces.

For example, "All Time High" is an example of a tremendously bland Bond song. It is neither bad nor good; a mild bit of neutral ground fed to us like the radio version of boiled rice. "All Time High" is vilified by people who hate this sort of music, the mind-numbing emptiness of a soulless song that pretends to have soul. On its own, it doesn't deserve to be hated, merely ignored or mildly enjoyed. But to stand it beside such class acts as "Nobody Does It Better" or "Moonraker" is to show it in a very poor light indeed.

"Living Daylights, The" is a non-Bond Bond song. It is a good song, and its lyrics have a distinct insight into James Bond's character. "Comes the morning and the headlights fade in rain" is evocative of the exhaustion Bond felt in the novels, and "The living's in the way we die" sounds like a good match for "the world is not enough" as a James Bond motto. But musically, it doesn't work. If you heard it on the radio, it wouldn't stand out as a Bond song, and in the film, it doesn't seem to move the title sequence (which is bland anyway) along. Here is a song that would be very good if it didn't need to be a movie song as well as just a song.

As to prisoner of genre, I direct your attention to "Make It Last All Night," discussed below.

The Man with the Golden Gun

This is truly the worst of the worst, as most fans will agree. Yes, even the notoriously disagreeable Bond fans can stand together and declare that "Who will he bang?" is a nauseating lyric. The entire song is nothing but a phallic joke, except that it's not funny. Lulu was not a belting sort of singer, but she says that was how John Barry insisted she deliver the song, and the unnatural quality of her voice is grating—you can tell it's forced. Lulu substitutes shouting for conviction.

Never Say Never Again

You might remember the chorus, a catchy repetition of the title that sounds more sixties than eighties. But tell me, can you remember one single note or word from the rest of the song? Yeah, I thought not. Maybe all that "never" translated into "nothing" somewhere in the songwriting process, because this one is a complete zero.

The Experience of Love (*GoldenEye*)

Why should a movie with such a great title song close with a different song in the first place? And having chosen to do so, why a song with a bland, uninspired lyric that has no connection to anything else in the movie? And why add insult to injury by singing in that whiny, I'm-holding-my-nose heartfelt seventies New Age Guy voice?

I have no idea.

Licence to Kill

If Gladys Knight weren't singing the title song, she wouldn't rank so low, but a title song is more important than an end credits song. "Licence to Kill" isn't worse than, say, "If You Asked Me To," but sitting up in front like that, it needs to be much better. Knight is a fine singer, but the vocals seem to be on auto-pilot.

The lyrics is where this one really falls apart. In an attempt to have the title make sense for the smokey singing style, the words assign a license to kill to a jealous lover, who presumably will be using it to kill off the competition. Not a pretty thought. Knight has said in interviews that, as a non-violent person, singing these lyrics made her uncomfortable. Perhaps this discomfort is what holds her voice back and gives the song a sense of insincerity.

Make It Last All Night (*For Your Eyes Only*)

Bill Conti, Academy Award winner (see 007 AT THE OSCARS) ought to be ashamed of himself. I toy with the idea that the utter badness of this song is meant as wry commentary on the villain—not unlike Minnie Driver's ear-drum-damaging version of "Stand By Your Man" in *GoldenEye*. But, if Conti thought this sleazoid dance-by-the-pool number had any quality at all, he should stand in the corner.

The Chart Toppers

It seems the U.K. likes Bond songs more than the U.S. does, but both charts have seen their share of 007-based hits. Here's the rundown, in chart order.

U.S. Charting Songs

#1	"A View to a Kill"
#2	"Live and Let Die"
#2	"Nobody Does It Better" (*The Spy Who Loved Me*)
#4	"For Your Eyes Only"
#8	"Goldfinger"

#8 "Thunderball"
#8 "Die Another Day"
#8 "Skyfall"
#36 "All Time High" (*Octopussy*)
#71 "Writing's on the Wall" (*Spectre*)
#79 "You Know My Name" (*Casino Royale*)
#81 "Another Way to Die" (*Quantum of Solace*)
#139 "Moonraker"

U.K. Charting Songs

#1 "Writing's on the Wall" (*Spectre*)
#2 "A View to a Kill"
#2 "Skyfall"
#3 "Die Another Day"
#5 "The Living Daylights" "
#6 "Licence to Kill"
#7 "Nobody Does It Better" (*The Spy Who Loved Me*)
#7 "You Know My Name" (*Casino Royale*)
#8 "For Your Eyes Only"
#9 "Live and Let Die"
#9 "Another Way to Die" (*Quantum of Solace*)
#10 "GoldenEye"
#11 "You Only Live Twice"
#11 "The World is Not Enough"
#12 "Tomorrow Never Dies"
#13 "James Bond Theme" (released with *Dr. No*)
#13 "From Russia with Love" "
#21 "Goldfinger"
#35 "Thunderball"
#38 "Diamonds Are Forever"
#39 "From Russia with Love instrumental"

("We Have All the Time in the World" reached #1 in the U.K. in 1995 following a rerelease after it was used in a commercial. It did not chart in 1969 on original release.)

The Complete List
Dr. No

"**James Bond Theme**," Monty Norman Orchestra: During the titles and throughout.
"**Three Blind Mice**," Byron Lee Band: During the titles.
"**Jump Up, Jamaica**," Byron Lee Band: Played by the Byron Lee Band in Puss-Feller's club.
"**Underneath The Mango Tree**," Byron Lee Band: Heard on Miss Taro's record player, sung by Honey on the beach, sung by Bond back to her.

From Russia with Love

Instrumental **"From Russia with Love,"** John Barry Orchestra: During the titles.

"From Russia with Love," Matt Munro: On the radio while Bond and Sylvia picnic, and during the end credits.

Goldfinger

"Goldfinger," Shirley Bassey: During the titles.

Thunderball

"Thunderball," Tom Jones: During the titles.

You Only Live Twice

"You Only Live Twice," Nancy Sinatra: During the titles.

On Her Majesty's Secret Service

"On Her Majesty's Secret Service," John Barry & His Orchestra: During the titles and throughout.

"We Have All the Time in the World," Louis Armstrong: During the montage of Bond and Tracy falling in love.

"Do You Know How Christmas Trees Are Grown," Nina: At the skating rink while Bond is fleeing Irma Bunt and her men.

Diamonds Are Forever

"Diamonds Are Forever," Shirley Bassey: During the titles.

Live and Let Die

"Live and Let Die," Paul McCartney and Wings: During the titles.

The Man with the Golden Gun

"Man with the Golden Gun, The," Lulu: During the titles.

The Spy Who Loved Me

"Nobody Does It Better," Carly Simon: During the titles.

Moonraker

"Moonraker," Shirley Bassey: During the titles.

For Your Eyes Only

"For Your Eyes Only," Sheena Easton: During the titles.

"Make It Last All Night," Bill Conti and Rage: At Gonzalez's pool, it is the disco song that some people are dancing to.

Octopussy

"All Time High," Rita Coolidge: During the titles.

Never Say Never Again

"Never Say Never Again," Lani Hall: During the titles.

A View to a Kill

"A View to a Kill," Duran Duran: During the titles.

The Living Daylights

"**The Living Daylights**," a-ha: During the titles.

"**Where Has Everybody Gone**," The Pretenders: On Necros's headphones whenever he is listening to music.

"**If There Was a Man**," The Pretenders: During the end credits.

Licence to Kill

"**Licence to Kill**," Gladys Knight: During the titles.

"**Dirty Love**," Tim Feehan: In the Barrelhead Bar, it's the song the woman on stage is dancing to.

"**If You Asked Me To**," Patti LaBell: During the end credits.

GoldenEye

"**GoldenEye**," Tina Turner: During the titles.

"**The Experience of Love**," Eric Serra: During the end credits.

Tomorrow Never Dies

"**Tomorrow Never Dies**," Sheryl Crow: During the titles.

"**Surrender**," k. d. lang: During the end credits.

The World is Not Enough

"**The World is Not Enough**," Garbage: During the titles.

Die Another Day

"**Die Another Day**," Madonna: During the titles.

Casino Royale

"**You Know My Name**," Chris Cornell: During the titles.

Quantum of Solace

"**Another Way to Die**." Jack White and Alicia Keys: During the titles.

Skyfall

"**Skyfall**," Adele: During the titles.

Spectre

"**Writing's on the Wall**," Sam Smith: During the titles.

No Time to Die

"**No Time to Die**," Billie Eilish

THE MAN WITH THE GOLDEN GUN (1974)

Survey Says!

Percent Favorite: 0%
Top 5 Cumulative: 24/25
Numeric Rating: 5.17/10
Ranking: 16.4 (20th/25)

My Rating and Ranking

Rated: 6/10
Ranked: 20 out of 25

Summary

Bond's search for Dr. Gibson, inventor of the "Solex Agitator" is halted when a golden bullet engraved with "007" is received by MI6. Since the bullet appears to be from Francisco Scaramanga, "The Man with the Golden Gun," Bond decides to go after Scaramanga, finding him in Hong Kong. When Scaramanga kills Gibson and steals the Solex, the two investigations merge. Bond meets Andrea Anders, lover of Scaramanga, who sent the bullet in hopes Bond would rescue her. Unfortunately, Scaramanga kills Andrea and kidnaps Bond's assistant, Mary Goodnight. Bond tracks Scaramanga to his private island, killing him, finding the Solex, and rescuing Goodnight.

James Bond: Roger Moore
Mary Goodnight: Britt Ekland
Francisco Scaramanga: Christopher Lee
Nick Nack: Herve Villechaize
Andrea Anders: Maud Adams
Lt. Hip: Soon-Taik Oh (a.k.a. Soon-Tek Oh)
M: Bernard Lee
Q: Desmond Llewelyn
Moneypenny: Lois Maxwell
Directed by Guy Hamilton

Discussion

Most fans reject *The Man with the Golden Gun* forcefully, and with good reason. It appears on many "worst" lists, and lands at the bottom of most fans' rankings, although, like all Bond films, it has its supporters. It is plagued by infantile humor, ill-conceived set pieces, and a lack of regard for the rudiments of plot. Yet, the movie has some fine qualities and sterling assets that may surprise you. *The Man with the Golden Gun*-that-might-have-been is worth looking at and appreciating.

Imagine *The Man with the Golden Gun* as a movie suffering from Multiple Personality Disorder. The dominant personality is the movie so detested by fans, which we will discuss shortly. But there is another personality, one often ignored, but present in almost equal measure. This other *The Man with the Golden Gun* is a serious espionage movie. Bond has no outrageous gadgets, in fact, few gadgets at all. It takes its villain seriously, and its secondary heroine is tragic and lost. Here is that movie:

Bond's life is threatened by a mysterious assassin, Scaramanga. His only lead is that Scaramanga is believed to have killed 002, Bill Fairbanks, five years earlier. 007 travels to Beirut to investigate that murder, and finds the bullet that killed Fairbanks. Q Branch uses forensics to determine the likely manufacturer of the custom bullet. Bond travels to Macau and confronts the bullet-maker, who gives him another lead. Bond witnesses a neat exchange at a casino and follows Andrea Anders. Confronting her in her hotel, he learns he can find Scaramanga at a night-club that evening. Outside the nightclub, he witnesses Scaramanga assassinate another man entirely, and realizes he is not Scaramanga's target.

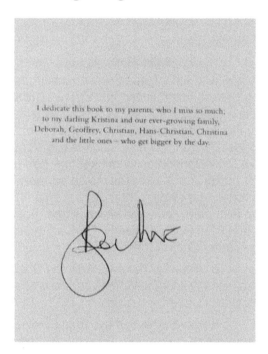

Figure 12: Roger Moore's memor: cover and autograph. I stood on line for over an hour to meet Sir Roger, gain this autograph, and give as a gift a copy of the first edition of the very book you're reading now.

Now Bond teams up with Lt. Hip and learns of Hip's mission, to retrieve the "Solex Agitator." Returning to his hotel, he finds Andrea Anders waiting for him, and one part of the mystery is uncovered—she has summoned Bond to her with a fake threat. He agrees to meet her the next day at a kick-boxing stadium, where she will give him the Solex, but she is dead when he arrives, and he at last meets Scaramanga. While leaving the stadium with the Solex, Bond's assistant, Mary Goodnight, is captured by Scaramanga. Now Bond must rescue Mary from Scaramanga's private island, and retrieve the Solex.

If you read the above, you find a clean, intelligent script in the making. It has a fine narrative thread of espionage; Bond investigates one lead to find the next, step by step. Nothing is handed him, and his own resources, not gadgetry, must pull him through. The movie doesn't rely on big explosions, having only one. It has exotic locations and a host of interesting characters. Andrea is a terrific idea, the villain's mistress who reaches out to his rival for rescue. A world famous killer-for-hire who has murdered a double-0 in the past, Scaramanga is a worthy enemy. All of this juicy, wonderful material is visible in the final product, even though it has been beaten into submission by a sophomoric revisioning. Oh, the movie that could have been!

The relationship between Scaramanga and Andrea Anders is complex and creepy. It has sadistic overtones that seem decidedly non-consensual. Andrea seems little more than a sex slave, imprisoned by her knowledge of Scaramanga's ability to kill her. When she towels him off, or when she submits to being stroked by his golden gun, her eyes and posture convey tremendous sorrow; she doesn't want to be there. For his part, Scaramanga seems hardly to care what she wants, as long as he can use her.

There are yet more pluses to the film. Roger Moore gives a good performance, with a cool cruelty in some scenes worthy of the era of *From Russia with Love*. He seems focused and strong. The set design is magnificent—the sunken Queen Elizabeth set is one of my very favorites in the Bond series, and it is a fine parallel to Scaramanga's funhouse—both MI6 and the villain are in crooked, crazy worlds. The funhouse set itself is excellent, and the concept—of a killer who uses it as a Most Dangerous Game setting—has real possibilities. Britt Ekland is gorgeous, and for the first half of the movie performs well. By the time she is Scaramanga's prisoner, she evinces little more than a fine body and a blank stare, but prior to that she is human, sexy, and sharp-witted. She rejects Bond admirably, and then returns to him ("I'm weak") sweetly. Too bad the character was dumbed down for the ending—rather like Tiffany Case.

By the way, *The Man with the Golden Gun* also has one of my very favorite Moneypenny scenes. When Bond says "Fairbanks" and Moneypenny answers "Alaska," I smile every time.

However, this is a two-faced movie, and we must now, alas, turn our attention to the negative side. This is, tragically, the Bond movie that confuses smutty with sexy, and the Bond movie as obsessed with the human rear end as a class of preschoolers. Saida grabs Bond's hands and puts them on her ass, Bond grabs a sumo wrestler's cheeks and then gives him a wedgie, an entire nightclub is devoted to "bottoms," and finally, Goodnight pushes a button with her bottom in extreme closeup. The smut also includes the third nipple jokes—and two closeups!— and a kick in the crotch. None of this is remotely funny, and none of it belongs in a Bond film.

Certainly the very worst part of the movie is the presence of Sheriff J.W. Pepper. I know some fans like him, but my God, at least in *Live and Let Die* he had a reason for being there. Now, in addition to sitting through scenes with this buffoon, we must swallow the outrageous coincidence of him encountering Bond a second time! You know those companies that are editing videos to remove "offensive" material? Sometimes I want to remove J.W. Pepper in just that way.

The Man with the Golden Gun also has some senseless set pieces, meaningless action for the sake of action, with no regard for how it fits in with the movie. Ask yourself this: Who was beating Bond up in Beirut and why? Does everyone who visits Saida's dressing room get a beating? That can't be good for business. Or, are they leftover baddies from a previous adventure? Certainly, they never reappear in this adventure, nor are they ever mentioned.

What about the karate school? I actually like the idea of Hai Fat having Bond killed elsewhere. Keeping his home sacrosanct is a good justification for the eternal "why not just shoot him?" question. But once at school, no one acts as if the goal is to kill Bond; it all seems so much entertainment. When this idiocy devolves even further, into high-kicking schoolgirls, it's hard to keep watching.

Then there's Bond, posing as Scaramanga, explaining in detail who James Bond is to Hai Fat. Nice discretion, James!

Nick Nack is problematic. He is a good character, but he cannot be seen as a threat, and when Bond finally fights him, it is humiliating to watch. Director Guy Hamilton found the idea of an assistant who honed the killer's edge very interesting. Unfortunately, the rest of us had already seen *A Shot in the Dark* (1964), in which the same idea was used as slapstick comedy.

The music in *The Man with the Golden Gun* is as schizophrenic as the rest, with one of the worst title songs in the series, and one of the best scores.

The use of the title melody as a honky-tonk tune in the funhouse is terrific, and Nick Nack's theme is a nice touch. Then again, it's John Barry who had the bright idea (not) to use a slide whistle during the Spiral Jump. (He later regretted it.)

The Man with the Golden Gun also opens badly. It suffers from a pre-titles sequence that generates far too much sympathy for the villain, and never features James Bond, except in effigy. The title sequence is as lackluster as possible, with no memorable images of any kind.

In the end, I must rate *The Man with the Golden Gun* almost as poorly as most fans do, even while mourning the excellent parts of it that got buried under the offal.

High Points

- Exquisite locations: Macau, Bangkok, Phuket.
- The magnificent set of the crooked headquarters on the sunken Queen Elizabeth.
- Bond meets Lazar.
- Christopher Lee: a masterful actor playing a strong villain.
- Intricate and lovely John Barry score.
- Wonderful Moneypenny interaction, moving from wit to flirtation to anger in one short scene.
- Fine interchange with M, including the sly nod towards Bond's "unauthorized" activity.
- Andrea's tragic death.
- The Spiral Jump stunt.

Low Points

- The return of Sheriff Pepper.
- Saida: The least attractive Bond girl in the series.
- A title song that is an offense to the ears.
- The karate school fight.
- The schoolgirl fight.
- The sumo wrestler fight.
- A "topical" plot that dates the movie.
- All of the dialogue and visuals about Scaramanga's third nipple.
- Goodnight's stupidity in the final reel.
- The close-up on Goodnight's button-pushing bottom.
- A lackluster and unmemorable title sequence.
- Scaramanga and Nick Nack's unfortunate similarity to Clouseau and Cato.
- The slide whistle marring the Spiral Jump stunt.

Quotable Quotes

Bond: "Who would pay a million dollars to have me killed?"
M: "Jealous husbands, outraged chefs, humiliated tailors; the list is endless."

Bond to Lazar: "I'm now aiming precisely at your groin, so speak or forever hold your piece."

Bond (about Hai Fat): "He must have found me titillating."

Goodnight: "Oh, darling, I'm tempted, but killing a few hours as one of your passing fancies isn't quite my scene."
(Later)
Goodnight: "My hard to get act didn't last very long, did it?"
Bond: "I was trained to expect the unexpected, but they never prepared me for anything like you in a nightie!"
(They kiss)
Goodnight: "James, I thought this would never happen."
Bond: "What made you change your mind?"
Goodnight: "I'm weak."

Goodnight: "I always wanted to take a slow boat from China."

Nick Nack: "I may be small, but I never forget!"

Facts and Figures

SEXUAL ENCOUNTERS

<u>Two</u>: Andrea Anders and Mary Goodnight.

BOND'S CAR

1975 AMC Hornet (red): This is the car Bond takes from the dealership and uses to perform the Spiral jump.

DEATHS

<u>Six</u>:

- Rodney, Gibson, the first combatant at Hai Fat's karate school, Hai Fat, Scaramanga, and Kra

Bond kills:

- <u>One</u>, directly: Scaramanga.

EXPLOSIONS

<u>One</u>: The enormous series of explosions that destroy Scaramanga's island.

BOND'S FOOD AND DRINKS

Vodka Martinis

- None.

Other Drinks

- Bond has red wine while at the belly-dance establishment in Beirut.
- Bond brings champagne to Andrea's room.
- Bond and Goodnight are served Phuyuck '74 (sparkling white wine) with dinner.
- Nick Nack serves Bond Dom Perignon '64 when he arrives at the island.
- A red wine in silver goblets is served by Nick Nack at lunch; Bond remarks that it is "slightly reminiscent of a '34 Mouton."

Food

- Nick Nack serves an elaborate luncheon; the main course appears to be meat or chicken on a bed of saffron rice. There is a salad at each place; Scaramanga's appears to have fish in it, and Bond's appears to have grapes. Scaramanga comments on the mushroom side dish.

GAMBLING AND SPORTS

- Gambling at the casino in Macau (Bond observes, doesn't gamble)
- Kick-boxing

Amaze Your Friends!

- This is the only Bond movie in which Bond kills just once.
- The identification number on the Solex Agitator is H/220.

- Phuket (pronounced poo-ket), Thailand, is the home of Khow-Ping- Kan in the Phang Nga Bay. Khow-Ping-Kan was Scaramanga's island in the film. After *The Man with the Golden Gun* was released, it was re-christened "James Bond Island," and is now a major tourist attraction.
- Mary Goodnight was a recurring character in the Ian Fleming novels. She was James Bond's secretary after Loeila Ponsonby left to get married. As in the movie, she was reassigned to foreign duty and **The Man with the Golden Gun** mission was a reunion for them. Also as in the movie, they were never intimate when working together in London, and became so only on this mission.
- Christopher Lee and Britt Ekland co-starred in the cult horror classic *The Wicker Man (1973)*. That movie also featured Diane Cilento—ex-wife of Sean Connery.
- Ekland has an additional Bond connection—she was married to Peter Sellers, star of the 1967 version of *Casino Royale*.

Most Interesting Goofs

Color Blind: Goodnight tells Bond she's in a brown car with a black roof. Bond immediately spots the car, even though the roof is brown.

Solitary Strip: When Andrea goes to Bond's hotel room, she strips, and there's an insert shot of her robe dropping to the floor. It is clear that she is alone in the shot although we know she is standing next to Bond.

Absolute Zero, Give or Take: The energy processing plant has the amusing sign "Absolute Zero Must Be Maintained to Prevent Prompt Criticality" (I must find an excuse to use "prompt criticality" in a sentence). "Prompt criticality" is apparently what happened when Goodnight knocked Kra into the vat. However, the whole thing is nonsense. Absolute zero is a theoretical temperature. Whatever temperature very close to absolute zero actually existed in the vat, it could not be maintained in an open-air vat; the air temperature would warm it.

YOU ONLY LIVE SEVEN TIMES

In five pretitle sequences, James Bond appeared, however briefly, to be dead. In a sixth movie, 007 actually was dead, momentarily. So, our favorite agent is now on his seventh life.

From Russia with Love

The movie opens with Bond being stalked through a dark garden, where he is eventually garroted by Donald Grant (Robert Shaw). Only after he is dead is his mask removed and we discover he is not Bond at all.

Thunderball

The dot from the gunbarrel zooms in on the initials "JB." As the camera pulls back, we see they are on a coffin. Then the camera pulls back further and we see that Bond is attending the funeral, not the guest of honor.

You Only Live Twice

This is the most vivid of Bond's deaths.

After establishing the plot—the space capsule disappearing, the angry meeting between diplomats—we join Bond in Hong Kong, where he is in bed with the beautiful Ling. Ling gets out of bed and suddenly pushes a button: The bed folds into the wall, and soldiers burst into the room, spraying the wall/bed with machine gun fire. The police arrive, and declare that Bond "died on the job" as the camera zooms into his supine form in a pool of blood.

After the titles, we attend a funeral at sea, and see Bond's obituary in a newspaper. A body is returned to sea, and then divers retrieve it and bring it aboard a submarine. Cutting the wrappings open, they reveal Bond's "body" inside, complete with breathing apparatus. Bond sits up and asks, "Permission to come aboard, sir?"

The Man with the Golden Gun

We see Scaramanga in his funhouse, stalking a victim (Rodney), and suddenly we come upon James Bond, only to realize that it is a mannequin, not our hero. After Rodney is dispatched, Scaramanga turns and shoots the fingers off of the Bond mannequin. Since we are already almost certain this isn't the real Bond, this is the least deceptive of his deaths.

Die Another Day

In the pre-titles sequence, Bond is captured, and during the titles, we see some of his imprisonment ordeal. Then Bond is released and taken to a shipboard medical facility, where he is told that he has been deactivated from the Secret Service. Contemplating his escape, Bond remembers the mind control exercises he perfected during captivity. Using this skill, Bond stops his own heartbeat long enough for the medical staff to believe he has died, and rush in to save him, at which point he revives and effects his escape.

Skyfall

As the pre-titles sequence ends, Eve has accidentally shot Bond, and he falls from the top of the train into the water (presumably the Sea of Marmara, since he is in Istanbul). Immediately after the titles, we see M composing Bond's obituary. From here we immediately go to Bond with a beautiful woman, clearly alive. Later in the movie, Silva asks Bond what his hobby is, and he says "Resurrection." Truer words were never spoken.

DEFORMITIES AND DIFFERENCES

W hat's up with Dr. No's hands, anyway? Ian Fleming was fascinated by the odd, the deformed, and the different, and the characters in his novels often had something odd about their appearance. These oddities were in three basic categories: In most cases, they were sinister, and tainted the villain with an air of evil he could not hide; sometimes they were exotic, and made women stand apart from the crowd, often attracting Bond to them; occasionally they were heroic, and denoted great risk-taking in Bond's allies, who had received their deforming injuries in the line of duty.

Fleming's writing was also distinctly racist. It is impossible to read his work without noting the disparaging remarks about quite a number of ethnic groups. Fleming's basic approach was to characterize a person by ethnicity— both Bond and M, in the novels, believed that they could know a person by knowing his or her background. People of mixed race were especially suspect, because their nature was "confused." This was said of Bond's wife Tracy; her psychological problems were attributed to being half English and half Sicilian.

In the novel **Diamonds Are Forever** , Bond referred to the prospect of marrying Tiffany Case as a "mixed marriage," the mix being an Englishman and an American. It hardly needs adding that Fleming had a particular distaste for homosexuality.

Over the years, the Bond films have distanced themselves from this offensive quality. The racism is still visible in *Dr. No*, but is mostly dropped afterwards. Sexism is obviously present, but faded with the times, the Bond films not lagging noticeably behind other films of their era. Homosexuality was sinister in both *From Russia with Love* and *Goldfinger*, and perhaps, an object of ridicule in *Diamonds Are Forever*, but again, not more so than in other films made in 1963, 1964, or 1971.

Today, we can see an array of differences as adding color to the Bond film palette, without bearing any prejudice. In compiling a list of oddities and differences, I am including things that Fleming considered suspect (such as homosexuality), without sharing his view. (Being queer, I celebrate appearances Fleming probably found disturbing.) I hope you will find this list interesting and entertaining, without attributing any prejudice to its author.

Here, then, in chronological order...

The Sinister

Dr. No

- The good (bad) doctor has no hands. In the book, he had claws. It is unclear what his artificial hands are made of in the movie—either metal or highly polished, painted wood. He is also of mixed race—the son of "a German missionary and a Chinese girl of good family."

- The mixed race issue affects many of Dr. No's henchmen, who are that offensive coinage, "Chigroes" (Fleming's word for "Chinese Negroes"). The movie never explained that certain characters in Dr. No's employ were of mixed race, but Jamaican actress Marguerite LeWars, who played the photographer, has said that she and several others had their eyes taped to look Chinese.

From Russia with Love

- Rosa Klebb's lesbianism is more overt in the novel than the film, but her creepy pass at the lovely Tatiana still serves as motivation for Tanya to later choose Bond over Mother Russia.

Goldfinger

- Oddjob is a mute (in the book, this is the result of a cleft palette).
- Pussy Galore is described as a lesbian in the novel; in fact, Tilly Masterson falls in love with her. In the movie, Pussy's sexuality is somewhat veiled, but still apparent. In keeping with Fleming's mistrust of homosexuality, Pussy's moment of transition from villain to ally occurs hand-in-hand with her transition from lesbian to happy heterosexual. She is double-listed under THE EXOTIC.

Thunderball

- Emilio Largo, in the film, has one eye. (In the book, he is quite handsome.)
- Count Lippe has a tattoo. Tattoos have a long history, in films and in society, of being marks of the sinister. Think, for example, of Robert Mitchum's foreboding "LOVE/HATE" tattoos in the classic *Night of the Hunter*.

You Only Live Twice

- Blofeld is here revealed to have a disfigured face (he's bald, too).

On Her Majesty's Secret Service

- Other than surgically-removed earlobes, none.

Diamonds Are Forever

This movie specializes in sexual ambiguity:
- Blofeld cross-dresses (but his face is looking much nicer, and he has a lovely head of hair.)
- Wint and Kidd are same-sex lovers.
- Bambi and Thumper—are they or aren't they?

Live and Let Die

- Tee Hee has a prosthetic arm (he lost the arm to a crocodile).
- Whisper may have something wrong with his throat, or he may just be soft spoken.

The Man with the Golden Gun

- Scaramanga has a third nipple.
- Nick Nack is a dwarf.

The Spy Who Loved Me

- Stromberg has webbed hands. One knows this only by reading promotional material or trivia about the movie—it is rarely visible. Supposedly, it explains his affinity for the sea.
- Jaws is both a giant and has metal teeth. His gigantism becomes an issue in the next film.

Moonraker

- Jaws appears for the second time.

For Your Eyes Only

- The "Man in Wheelchair" in the pre-titles teaser is, well, in a wheelchair. If we assume (as we are meant to) that this is Blofeld, then we can also assume that he is disabled as a result of the injuries incurred at the climax of *Diamonds Are Forever*, although director John Glen actually had the injuries from *On Her Majesty's Secret Service* in mind.

Octopussy

None.

Never Say Never Again

None, except inasmuch as Fatima Blush's insatiable sexual appetite could be considered a perversity. Others have mentioned this in regard to Xenia Onatopp (*GoldenEye*), but I can't really bring myself to count it.

A View to a Kill

- Max Zorin is a product of genetic engineering, and albino.

The Living Daylights

None.

Licence to Kill

None.

GoldenEye

- Alec Trevelyan is heavily scarred, as a result of the explosion at the Arkangel Chemical Weapons Facility. This is an exceptionally sinister deformity, as it was acquired in the process of Alec switching from hero to villain.

Tomorrow Never Dies

- Stamper is unable to feel pain. Because scenes explaining this ended up on the cutting room floor, the concept was revived for the next movie's villain.

The World is Not Enough

- Renard has a bullet-hole scar on his forehead, and is unable to feel.
- Elektra King has a deformed ear. Like Alec, she acquired this deformity in changing sides (choosing to align with Renard against her father), and she also revealed it when revealing herself as the villain.
- Bull has gold teeth reminiscent of Jaws's steel ones. (The actor, Goldie, is famed for these teeth.)

Die Another Day

- Zao has a face scarred (diamond-studded) by Bond.

Casino Royale

- Le Chiffre bleeds from his left eye, and also uses an inhaler.
- Mollaka has a scarred face: This is suggested to be a product of his villainy (he's a bombmaker, and perhaps this is from an accident while making bombs)
- Gettler wears eyepatch glasses.

Quantum of Solace

- Elvis acquires a neckbrace during the course of the movie (after Fields causes him to fall down a flight of stairs)..

Skyfall

- Silva's face has been damaged by swallowing cyanide. This deformity is part of what turned him from hero to villain.

Spectre

- In the final scene, Blofeld acquires the disfigurement familiar from *You Only Live Twice*.

No Time to Die

- Blofeld returns, with a face still disfigured.
- Safin appears to have facial disfigurement as well..

The Exotic

There are few of these, so I won't list the "none" movies. Most in this category, for obvious reasons, aren't physical—they don't mar the beauty of the exotic woman.

Dr. No

- In the novel, Honeychile Ryder had a broken nose that gave her face an odd appearance and made her self-conscious. Bond came to be fond of the unique look it gave her.

Goldfinger

- Pussy Galore's lesbianism presents a stereotypical "challenge" to Bond. Of course, he rises to the occasion.

Thunderball

- Again, novel only. Domino has one leg an inch shorter than the other, and walks with a limp.

On Her Majesty's Secret Service

- Tracy's mixed ethnic background, as well as her suicidal tendencies, give a slight whiff of the exotic.

Live and Let Die

- Solitaire's psychic talent, given that it is hereditary and tied to a physical condition (virginity) could fit the bill.

Octopussy

- Magda (and presumably Octopussy herself) has a tattoo.

The World is Not Enough

- Dr. Christmas Jones has a navel piercing.

Quantum of Solace

- Camille's back has been burned in a fire. This is revealed to be part of her motivation for pursuing Medrano.

The Heroic

From Russia with Love

- Bond himself, we learn, has a rather ugly scar at the base of his spine, re-marked upon by both Sylvia and Tanya, but never explained. The novels give him a facial scar, as well as a scar inflicted by SMERSH in **Casino Royale**, which is removed by plastic surgery. The remnants of plastic surgery are visible on his hand.

You Only Live Twice

- Dikko Henderson has a wooden leg; apparently a duty-related injury.

Licence to Kill

- Felix Leiter, ally in so many films, is gobbled by a shark; losing a leg and part of an arm. In the novels, this injury occurred in **Live and Let Die**.

GoldenEye

- Valentin Zukovsky uses a cane to walk; he was shot in the knee by Bond. The cane itself is significant in *The World is Not Enough*.
- Jack Wade has a tattoo.

Tomorrow Never Dies

- Jack Wade returns.

The World is Not Enough

- Zukovsky returns.

It is obvious that deformity is far more sinister than it is exotic or heroic.

THE SPY WHO LOVED ME (1977)

Survey Says!

>Percent Favorite: 7%
>Top 5 Cumulative: 7/25 (tied)
>Numeric Rating: 6.83/10
>Ranking: 9 (6th/25)

My Rating and Ranking

>Rated: 10/10
>Ranked: 5 out of 25

Summary

When a British and Soviet submarine disappear, MI6 and the KGB discover that someone has developed a submarine tracking system. They send their best agents to Cairo, where it is being offered to the highest bidder. Bond and KGB Agent XXX (Anya Amasova) compete for the microfilm, but the evil Stromberg has sent Jaws to retrieve it and kill anyone who has seen it. Soon Bond and XXX team up to discover Stromberg's plan, and end up on a U.S. submarine that is also captured by the villain. Bond escapes and frees the submarine crews; together they subvert Stromberg's plans for creating World War III. Bond then rescues Anya from Stromberg's lair, just as the U.S. military destroys it.

>**James Bond:** Roger Moore
>**Anya Amasova, Agent XXX:** Barbara Bach
>**Karl Stromberg:** Curt Jurgens
>**Jaws:** Richard Kiel
>**Naomi:** Caroline Munro
>**General Gogol:** Walter Gotell
>**M:** Bernard Lee
>**Moneypenny:** Lois Maxwell
>**Q:** Desmond Llewelyn
>**Directed by** Lewis Gilbert

Discussion

Famed film critic Pauline Kael called *The Spy Who Loved Me* the best of the Moore Bond movies, and I agree. It is his most fully-realized film, the closest to flawless, the only one with no really embarrassing moments. It has some of the silliness, the nod-and-wink jokiness, that is typical of a Moore movie, but at no time does the humor overwhelm the film. *The Spy Who Loved Me* is a Bond movie, not a comedy, and it is an exciting, sexy, fun, thrilling, scary, and yes, funny Bond movie at that.

The Spy Who Loved Me brings together excellent set pieces and a strong cast. It is a very well-rounded film: It works visually, as an adventure, and as spectacle; it's funny, exciting, and doesn't insult the intelligence.

The movie opens with one of the most thrilling of all Bond stunts (see THE MEGA-STUNTS). In fact, *The Spy Who Loved Me* boasts the greatest of the mega-stunts, mind-blowers that function as signature pieces for the films they are in. The parachute ski jump isn't just a great stunt, it is also beautifully placed in the film. After establishing the need for Bond, we move to a cabin in Austria, where we find him in the expected embrace. Following a witty bit of dialogue with a lovely blonde, a thrilling ski chase begins. The wit and the chase lead into the extraordinary stunt; we are already on an adventure. Compare this to the Spiral Jump stunt in *The Man with the Golden Gun*—the car chase itself has begun to peter out, and the dialogue is with the infinitely irritating J.W. Pepper. The stunt, when it comes, cannot compensate for the scene's flaws, and then there's the sound effect! In *The Spy Who Loved Me*, the chase that leads up to the stunt could easily stand on its own, enhanced as it is by Willy Bogner's incredible ski stuntwork and filming. When the peak of excitement is reached, the music stops, letting the moment of flight stand alone, in silence, giving the audience a true sense of awe. We are stunned as much by the beauty of nature as by the thrill of the jump; it is the combination of the two, without music trying to tell us what to feel, that lets us feel so much.

From this great pre-titles sequence we move into one of the finest Bond songs ever, played during one of the finest title sequences. This was Maurice Binder's first really interesting innovation since *Thunderball*, using his signature dancing silhouettes with Bond himself, and unmistakably conveying the central romance of the film while lacing the entirety with the provocative sight of women vaulting over giant pistols.

I am not the first Bond author to point out that every Bond girl says that she's different from her predecessors, every Bond girl claims to be a 'new kind' of Bond girl (or Bond woman). As far back as *Goldfinger*, Honor Blackman felt honor-bound to point out that she wasn't really a "Bond girl" because she wasn't a bimbo. As if Ursula Andress was! (Blackman continued to say this until her death in 2020.) This 'new kind' of Bond girl is almost a joke. In the documentary *Bond Girls Are Forever*, it seems half of the women interviewed make this claim—one could make a drinking game of it. If you watch the 'making of' documentaries on the Blu-rays/DVDs, you could play the same game. I'll say to my kid, "Here's where she says that there's never been a Bond girl like her before." And she will.

The Spy Who Loved Me is probably the only Bond movie that can lay fair claim to that 'new woman' crown. There is, to my mind, a clear distinction between pre-Anya and post-Anya Bond girls. Seeing it in the 70s, it was clear I was seeing something new and different. Anya Amasova is tough, sexy, beautiful (and how!), smart, emotional, and cool. She's the only "Bond's equal" woman who truly is his equal, until Wai Lin comes along twenty years later. Interestingly, there is no self-consciousness to the feminism of *The Spy Who Loved Me*, XXX is known to Bond as his counterpart, and there is no conversation, either surprised or disparaging, about her femininity. The competition is between two spies; it is never a war of the sexes. Oh, for *Moonraker* to have taken a similar tact!

The core of the movie is the relationship between Anya and Bond, and it's terrific throughout; from their one-upmanship to their distrust to their eventual passion, and most especially the intense moment when she discovers he killed her lover—Moore's acting in that scene was commendable. In fact, Bach's acting, often shaky, was spot on in that scene as well, and many fans cite it as a favorite scene from the series as a whole. I like how Anya and Bond function both as human beings and as symbols for their organizations; this is especially clear when M and Gogol are whispering their "well done"s to their respective agents, mirroring between the two leaders the competition happening between the field agents, and between the countries.

Then there's Jaws; a uniquely terrifying character. He embodied a lot of comic relief yet still managed to scare the beejeezus out of me. What a terrible shame that his scariness was drained out of him in the following movie. Jaws is to Moore what Oddjob was to Connery, an unbeatable adversary, both formidable and comic, who, despite his humorous qualities, must be overcome in earnest.

The Spy Who Loved Me has outstanding locations; moreover, it shows magnificent use of those locations. There are times when a great location is just used as a 'drive-thru,' it isn't really a part of the movie. For example, Bilbao, Spain, in *The World is Not Enough*—blink and you'll miss it. But the locations are intrinsic to the events in *The Spy Who Loved Me*, and that makes them all the more enjoyable.

Figure 13: Richard Kiel's autobiography: cover and autograph. I met Kiel (Jaws) at a Chiller Theater event (see Resources).

Consider the scene at the pyramids; a perfect blend of action with location. Using the nighttime show as a backdrop, with the voice-over, music, and spotlight becoming part of the *mis en scene* is perfection, and the light/dark contrast, almost noirish in its drama, is expertly done. With scenes such as this, we are involved in location footage, not merely watching it pass by. Just so, Austria becomes the setting for an extraordinary ski adventure (even though the jump itself was filmed in Canada), and Sardinia is used for its winding roads and lovely beach.

Location movies should really delve into their settings. Just as *You Only Live Twice* gave us more of Japan than sumo wrestling, so *The Spy Who Loved Me* gives us more of Egypt than the pyramids. The various ruins (three different sites) are exquisite, the ride across the desert on camel (and straight into a Ken Adam-designed sheik's tent), and the boat trip, give a sense of the range of this vast country. I love the scene at Max Kalba's nightclub, and the whirling dervish dancers.

Marvin Hamlisch's score has been much criticized, and there are certainly sequences that are far too "pop" (a drum machine appears to be in evidence), and simply sound dated. There are long sections, though, that are lovely, and "Nobody Does It Better"'s melody is integrated very nicely.

As a villain, Stromberg is simply not memorable. Jurgens is a strong actor and he brings a certain weightiness to his scenes, but he disappears from the mind when off-screen. This is the fault of the script, not the man. The entire conception of Stromberg as a creature of the sea is lost somewhere; I have zoomed in to confirm for myself that yes, he has webbed hands—this after wondering for years if it was just a strange rumor. It simply isn't apparent, and the whole obsession with life underwater gets too little play to communicate to the audience. I do love the confrontation at the end, when Bond, thinking his plan is extortion, asks him "How much?" Stromberg as much as says I'm not Blofeld and this isn't SPECTRE. I find that very entertaining!

Ken Adam comes through again. I find Stromberg's Atlantis headquarters one of the most creative and attractive sets in the series. It combines Adam's love of curves and moving furnishings with a unique sense of being its own little city, and the lovely ability to submerge and re-emerge from the sea. The windows are reminiscent of Dr. No's lair, but more realistic. *The Spy Who Loved Me* achieves a terrific blending of exteriors with interiors; Atlantis in its oceanic context, Hussein's tent in the desert, the makeshift headquarters in a ruin. The wild sets look like they belong exactly where they are.

The large-scale combat is a mixed bag. It is neither on my Best nor Worst list (see THE BIG BATTLES), falling somewhere in between. It is muddled and hard to follow in parts, but has some terrific flourishes. It is nice to see some "ordinary" people behave heroically, particularly the British submarine captain, and the young British sailor who sacrificed himself trying to break into the control room. Bond's ride atop the security camera was a clever and creative touch.

My sentiment is to give the movie a "10" and move on, but it does have some flaws; flaws which bring with them some strong detractors among Bond fans. Since a vocal minority deplore the movie, the problems deserve discussion.

Most fans complain about the silliness, which is a little odd, given how much stronger *The Spy Who Loved Me* is than its two Roger Moore predecessors. Maybe the objection is that a good silly movie establishes the potential success of silliness, and prevents Eon from seeing the need for more seriousness. This is the movie where Moore starts smirking, using a knowing grin as a weapon. I wouldn't have blamed Anya for slapping his silly, smiling face on at least a couple of occasions. In a film where he has two strong, serious scenes (the aforementioned confrontation with Anya, and their first meeting at the bar), such nonsense is especially unwelcome.

Fans, including me, also object to the excess of in-jokes. *Lawrence of Arabia*, anyone? This sort of thing is too cute for the more ardent fans, al-though they tend to play well in the theater.

I would say that *The Spy Who Loved Me* is the beginning of truly formulaic Bond movies. The plot, and its unfolding, is essentially a remake of *You Only Live Twice*, using water instead of space. The real story is the relationship, so this doesn't detract from the film's progress, but plot recycling sets a bad precedent.

Also formulaic is the use of certain scenes, which at about this point have become as standard to the series as the interplay between Bond and Moneypenny, or Q saying "Right, now pay attention." They are: A villain using sharks to dispose of both enemies and accomplices. A car chase interrupted by a big truck going the wrong way. A fight in a train berth with a woman conked out or otherwise out of the way.

As mentioned under *The Man with the Golden Gun*, I have no objection *per se* to villains failing to kill Bond simply and quickly when they have the chance. However, such behavior must be justified, however thinly. In *The Spy Who Loved Me*, it is done quite poorly: Stromberg tells Jaws to let Bond and Anya reach shore and then kill them, after the movie has already established that he likes to kill people on or while leaving Atlantis.

Overall, we have in *The Spy Who Loved Me* a great Bond movie, certainly Roger Moore's greatest, with few enough flaws. The goofiness never stops the story, and we all have a lot of fun.

High Points

- Great pre-titles sequence with great ski jump parachute stunt.
- Magnificent title song.
- Wonderful title sequence.
- Bond's first post-feminist alliance is not strident or preachy; the equality is a given and is done very well. The relationship is both competitive and sexy.
- Barbara Bach is beautiful, and her deep eyes are hypnotic. Eventually you may realize that she can't act, but those eyes will probably make you forget.
- Jaws!
- Gorgeous Egyptian locations.
- Wonderful use of camera angles and framing; look at Bond framed in an alley with a minaret behind him, or Sandor's eyes peering through a peephole. Creative and lovely.
- Gogol and M competing via their agents.
- Anya and Bond's confrontation over Sergei; "When the mission is over, I will kill you."
- Naomi flirting with Bond from the helicopter while trying to kill him.

Low Points

- Musical in-jokes.
- The entire Q lab scene, especially the use of slow motion.
- Stromberg's ludicrous pink tie.
- The fight with Sandor on the roof of Fekkesh's home; fake and stunty.
- Moore smirking.
- Barbara Bach's unflattering costumes, especially the hideous knit cap.
- Moneypenny is barely in the movie at all!

Quotable Quotes

Bond: "Q, have I ever let you down?"
Q: "Frequently!"

M: "Tell him to pull out immediately!"

Log Cabin Girl: "Oh, James, I cannot find the words."
Bond: "Well, let me enlarge your vocabulary."

Log Cabin Girl: "But, James, I need you!"
Bond: "So does England."

Anya: "Where is Fekkesh?"
Bond: "With the Pharoahs."

Bond (looking at Naomi...and her boat): "What a handsome craft, such lovely lines."

Bond (after the mattress truck explodes): "All those feathers and he still can't fly."

Anya (rams Jaws with van): "Shaken, not stirred."

Frederick Gray: "Bond, What are you doing?"
Bond (last line): "Keeping the British end up, sir."

Facts and Figures

SEXUAL ENCOUNTERS

Three: Log Cabin Girl, Egyptian treasure, Anya

BOND'S CAR

1977 Lotus Esprit S1 (white)

DEATHS

Approximately two hundred seventy:

- Sergei Barsov, Felicca, Aziz Fekkesh, Sandor, Max Kalba, Motorcycle rider (with jet sidecar), three men in the car with Jaws (Jaws emerges from the shack alone), Naomi, five divers who come after the Lotus.
- On the Liparus, two guards when Bond escapes, two guards when he frees the submarine crews, twenty-three of Stromberg's men during the battle, Captain Talbot, sixteen good guys (British and American, I didn't see any Russian).
- Stromberg's crew on both submarines (approximately 200).
- On Atlantis, Stromberg and an estimate of ten additional—these were not seen but earlier we saw a small maintenance crew, and it's reasonable to assume some death when the structure was torpedoed.

Bond kills:

- Fourteen directly (Sergei Barsov, Sandor, three of the divers, Naomi, four guards on the Liparus, at least three during the subsequent battle on the Liparus, Stromberg).
- Four indirectly (motorcycle rider, three in the car with Jaws).

EXPLOSIONS

Eleven: The mattress truck, Jaws's car in Sardinia (a small explosion after it lands in the shack), Naomi's helicopter, a series of several during the battle (as ever, groups of several are counted as one), the grenade that fails to open the control room, then the rigged bomb that succeeds, two nuclear mushrooms when the Soviet and British subs are destroyed, another series finishing up the battle, the torpedo from the U.S. sub that gets the Liparus and its wonderful, rolling series of follow-up explosions, another series to take out the Atlantis.

BOND'S FOOD AND DRINKS

Vodka Martinis

One, ordered for him by Anya in Kalba's club (the Mojaba). Bond says he is getting another but does not.

Other Drinks

- White wine is visible in the background in the Austrian cabin.
- Bond offers Anya champagne on the train, but the bottle is broken in the fight, and they don't drink.
- Bond and Anya finally have champagne together in Sardinia, where the open bottle is visible in the background.
- Bond and Anya share Dom Perignon '52 in Stromberg's escape pod, which Anya opens in dramatic fashion.

Food

- Anya thanks Bond for a delicious meal on the train, but we do not see them eat or know what they had.

- Hussein offers Bond sheep's eyes and dates, probably sarcastically. Bond doesn't eat.

GAMBLING AND SPORTS

None.

Amaze Your Friends!

- This is the first Bond film produced by Cubby Broccoli alone, following the breakup of his partnership with Harry Saltzman.
- When Ian Fleming sold the rights to his James Bond novels to Broccoli and Saltzman, he sold the rights to the title of **The Spy Who Loved Me** only—the contents could not be used. He considered the novel so out of character for James Bond that he didn't want it filmed. **The Spy Who Loved Me** tells a story in three parts: A young woman, Vivienne Michel, looks back on her life in part one, in the second part, she manages a cheap motel, when one night two gangsters arrive, intending to kill her and burn down the hotel. In the final third, James Bond arrives by happenstance, saving Vivienne and killing the gangsters.
- In order to accommodate the set for the interior of the Liparus, housing three submarines, the world's largest soundstage ("The 007 Stage") was built on Pinewood studios.
- The underwater footage of "Wet Nellie" was filmed in the Bahamas.
- Although the closing of the film says "James Bond Will Return in For Your Eyes Only," the next film was *Moonraker*.
- This movie has a total of fourteen actors and actresses who have appeared, or will appear, in other Bond films as other characters—the most of any Bond movie (see ENCORE! ENCORE!).
- Admiral Hargreaves notes that Bond served on the Royal Ark.

Most Interesting Goofs

Bottom's Up! When the Lotus goes off the dock and into the water, we briefly see its underside, which is open, as is normal for the car. In the water, the underside is enclosed, as would be expected for a submersible.

Over...and Out? Log Cabin Girl radios the skiers to tell them Bond is on the way, and says "Over and out." The skiers then respond. "Over and out" means she's done, and they are not to respond. If she was done speaking and awaiting a response, she should have said "Over."

Goof or Not? Anya Amasova expresses shock when the Lotus goes off the dock, gasping and throwing up her arms. Later, she says she saw the blue- prints for the submarine-car two years ago. Many fans consider this a goof, and it is often cited on goof lists (for those who collect such things). However, it seems plausible to be initially shocked when your car enters the water. Also, Anya may have seen interior blueprints but not known what model car it would go into. Overall, it is hard to count this as a full-out error, and I mention it only because of the fervor it causes among fans.

HENCHMEN

Villains are important to a Bond movie, and no one would say otherwise, but it is rare that Bond and the villain really spend any quality time. The major interactions between Bond and the brains behind the scheme will usually occur in the second half of the film. In the meantime, there are others causing trouble for Bond—the henchmen. Goldfinger is nothing without Oddjob, and Stromberg is nearly forgotten without Jaws. These henchmen plague, follow, and threaten Bond, and are essential for the all-important fight scenes.

Rarely does a main villain get his hands dirty (Alec Trevelyan excepted); for a real punch-'em-up, you need a henchman.

Henchmen Types

Strong and Silent

The prototypical Bond henchman is physically imposing and largely silent. When he (or she) speaks, it is softly and slowly. His role is to frighten and to fight.

Examples: Red Grant, Oddjob, Jaws, Gobinda.

Among these strong and silent henchmen is a large subgroup of blond musclemen. It started in *From Russia with Love* with Red Grant, but it continued into the Brosnan era. To date, there have been six such henchmen.

The Aryan Supermen
Donald "Red" Grant: *From Russia with Love*
Hans: *You Only Live Twice*
Peter Franks: *Diamonds Are Forever*
Eric Kriegler: *For Your Eyes Only*
Necros: *The Living Daylights*
Stamper: *Tomorrow Never Dies*

Femmes Fatale

These women combine murderous intent with irresistible powers of seduction. They are desirable and dangerous in equal parts. By the way, I would categorize May Day as "strong and silent," not as a femme fatale. Her primary qualities are strength and violence, and she doesn't seduce Bond so much as end up in bed with him by happenstance.

Examples: Fiona Volpe, Helga Brandt, Xenia Onatopp

Smart and Slimy

Although the villain is the master planner, he sometimes needs more than musclemen to implement his plan—he needs specific technical experts. Smart and slimy henchmen are more common in the post-computer era of Brosnan and Craig, but even Goldfinger had scientists helping him with the complexities of having an atomic bomb around.

Examples: Truman-Lodge, Boris Grishenko, Vladimir Popov

Accomplices

These are people whose aims run parallel to that of the villain; who ally with him as a convenience.

Examples: Colonel Heller, General Ourumov

Miscellaneous

Some of the uncategorizable people working for the villain are just generic muscle and chair-fillers, while some have unusual roles—like the photographer in *Dr. No*. Both the photographer and Professor Dent, in that movie, seem to be fearful—are they villains, or simply controlled by someone too powerful to resist? Surely both behave in an evil manner, but one wonders about Dr. No's recruitment methods.

Examples: The photographer in *Dr. No*, Shady Tree, Baron Samedi, Nick Nack

Top Five/Bottom Five

My first move will be to eliminate from contention all the femmes fatale. They contended under BOND GIRLS and it seems unfair to let them win or lose in two categories. They are included on the complete list below, just because it is "complete," but for discussion, see the BOND GIRLS chapter.

Most surveys concentrate on the main villains, or mix the two groups together. I have derived some information from surveys, and the rest from fan discussion and the cobwebs of my own mind.

Best
1. Jaws, *The Spy Who Loved Me*
2. Donald "Red" Grant, *From Russia with Love*
3. Oddjob, *Goldfinger*
4. Baron Samedi, *Live and Let Die*
5. Dr. Kaufman, *Tomorrow Never Dies*

Worst
1. Jaws, *Moonraker*
2. Mr. Kil, *Die Another Day*
3. Bull, *The World is Not Enough*
4. Dr. Carl Mortner, *A View to a Kill*
5. Eric Kriegler, *For Your Eyes Only*
AND: Elvis, *Quantum of Solace*

The Best Henchmen

It's a good thing I decided to eliminate femmes fatale. Otherwise, how could I narrow to just five with Xenia Onatopp and Fiona Volpe in contention?

Jaws, The Spy Who Loved Me

Few villains have ever created such a stir. Jaws is as famous a bad guy as Darth Vader or Norman Bates (Jaws was nominated for the AFI 50 Greatest Villains list, but didn't make the final cut. Both Bates and Vader were in the Top 50, along with Goldfinger). And rightly so. The moment we first see Richard Kiel in the role, we cannot help but be intimidated by his looming presence. Then he smiles.

At 7'2", Kiel's career consisted mostly of heavies and monsters, but in real life, he was a gentle guy (he died in 2014). I think we should give him more credit as an actor, for creating a sense of sadism and menace. True, the prosthetic teeth did a lot of the work for him, but Kiel brought power to his portrayal.

Jaws had comedic qualities in *The Spy Who Loved Me*, but he wasn't a clown. He had one of the best "jump scenes" in the franchise, scaring the bejeezus out of Anya and the audience when he appeared in the train compartment closet. His vampiric killings and attempted killings were horrifying, so that his jokier side functioned as needed relief. Jaws has superhuman qualities, but no more so than Oddjob, who is also impossibly strong and apparently unbeatable. He works in the Bond tradition, as a nearly unbeatable henchman who nonetheless fails to stop 007.

Jaws is one of only three (possibly four) undefeated major henchmen; the others are Baron Samedi, who survived, and May Day, who changed sides. Hinx is our potential fourth. It is not 100% clear, at the end of *Spectre*, if Hinx has survived. (Minor underlings and control room operators may have survived various adventures, and the minor character Professor Kutze survived *Thunderball* by switching sides.)

Donald "Red" Grant, From Russia with Love

Without strange deformities, bizarre attributes, or superhuman qualities, Robert Shaw's Red Grant holds the screen and freezes the blood. He is the coldest of cold-blooded killers, the angriest, and the most confident. Only Grant ever suggested that James Bond should kiss his foot.

People often talk about Scaramanga as Bond's counterpart, but Grant is Bond's shadow. He follows Bond, anticipating his moves, and killing on his behalf before their final showdown. The most committed assassin of all, Grant, in the novel **From Russia with Love** , had gone over to SMERSH because the British wouldn't let him kill for his country, and all he wanted to do was kill.

This is suggested in the movie when Morzeny refers to his psychological profile.

Oddjob, *Goldfinger*

Oddjob was the first really weird henchman, the first to make us say, "What the...?" Like Jaws, he has a comical quality, but he is ultimately too deadly to laugh at. Harold Sakata's gleeful devotion to Goldfinger and to killing are amazing—even Kisch thinks he's crazy to evince such loyalty.

I think Oddjob is a major part of what made *Goldfinger* the phenomenon it was and is. Surely Auric Goldfinger is among the greatest of villains, but without his deadly sidekick, he would not be as strong or as memorable.

Baron Samedi, *Live and Let Die*

Let me say first that this is my kid's very favorite henchman. Only Baron Samedi survives and remains evil (although Jaws would qualify if he hadn't returned). Only Samedi remains a mysterious and laughing threat, and only *Live and Let Die* ends with such a threat, hovering over the traditional "Oh James" embrace.

In addition, Samedi is the only Bond henchman with mystical overtones; it is never clear how much of his magic is fakery, or what his connection is to the real Baron Samedi—the Voodoo god of the graveyard.

Geoffrey Holder, possessor of a deep, resonant voice, dancer, choreographer, 6'6" tall, and highly theatrical, brought qualities to the character that were utterly unique. He was dynamic, unpredictable, and captivating, and remains one of the few bright spots in a fairly dismal Bond film.

Years ago, I worked in the Manhattan neighborhood where Mr. Holder (who passed away in 2014) resided, and we happened to use the same bank. I was surprised to discover that his deep voice is entirely unaffected. Geoffrey Holder said good morning and cashed a check in the same melodic tones in which he laughs at James Bond.

Dr. Kaufman, *Tomorrow Never Dies*

A minor henchman with only one scene, Vincent Schiavelli's Dr. Kaufman steals the movie, and has most of the best dialogue in the entire screenplay. He is everything a henchman should be; deadly, creepy, memorable, and a real challenge to 007. Like many of the greats, Kaufman has humorous overtones, but that doesn't make him laughable. He is more than dangerous, he is responsible for a death that really wounded Bond, which makes him an important foe indeed. I have often heard fans comment that they were sorry Kaufman was killed in *Tomorrow Never Dies*, they would have welcomed a return engagement.

It doesn't hurt that Kaufman was portrayed by one of the great modern character actors. Schiavelli has had roles in such classics as *One Flew Over the Cuckoo's Nest*, *Fast Times at Ridgemont High*, *Amadeus*, and *Ghost*. He passed away in 2005.

The Worst Henchmen

When looking at the lists of Best and Worst henchmen, the striking thing is that henchmen have gotten worse with time. None of Connery's opponents appear in the "Worst" listing, and two of Brosnan's are there. Brosnan's only "Best" henchman is a minor character with a single scene. (Among main villains, Brosnan's opponents appeared on neither the Best nor the Worst list—I guess Brosnan movies are more driven by the hero.) It seems that Eon lost touch with how to create a character that is both fanciful and threatening; many of the most recent henchmen have simply been ordinary, and might have been found in any action/crime film.

Jaws, Moonraker

From the sublime to the ridiculous. When fans praise Jaws, I have almost always seen them say "Jaws in *The Spy Who Loved Me*" is a favorite. Hardly anyone wants to claim that Jaws in *Moonraker* is a quality bad guy. Jaws's first appearance was as a menacing, looming killer with strength of a nearly superhuman level and some comedic qualities. His second appearance was as a clown with some villainous qualities; a pseudo-funny parody of a henchman, with strength that rivals that of a Marvel Comics character.

Jaws in *Moonraker* is the worst henchman because he falls from such a height, both literally and figuratively. Figuratively, he is a mockery of one of the great film characters—Jaws in his first incarnation—and so he incurs the wrath of fans who may have wanted him back after seeing *The Spy Who Loved Me*, but in retrospect wish that Eon had left well enough alone. Literally, Jaws does fall from an enormous height in the pre-titles sequence, and when we see him land, without a parachute, on a circus tent, and survive, we know the movie is in big trouble.

Mr. Kil, Die Another Day

"Now there's a name to die for." Time was when a henchman was more than a construct around which to deliver a flaccid one-liner. Mr. Kil is of a modern breed of henchmen who simply stand around and don't do much of anything but look imposing. He has one scene in which he slavers with sadistic glee, but it only lasts a moment and it's not enough to compensate for the dumb name and the lack of presence. He is nearly identical in role and style to Gabor in *The World is Not Enough*.

Bull, The World is Not Enough

Casting a music star in a movie is always a risk. You could get a terrific performance, like Ice Cube in *Three Kings*, or you could end up with a load of Bull.

Why is this guy around anyway? He is ugly but not interesting, poses no threat, and runs away like a dog. He is a poseur, standing around acting as if he's the real thing, and withdrawing when the going gets not-really-that- tough.

Dr. Carl Mortner, *A View to a Kill*

Of course, the mad Nazi doctor is a cliché, but it's a cliché with potential. *A View to a Kill*'s script squandered that potential in the creation of Dr. Mortner. He is confined entirely by the boundaries of his cliché; the monocle, the demeanor, even the casting of Willoughby Gray. He lacks any sort of edge, any sort of difference. He is simply a stock character. I'd say he brings the movie down, but this particular movie couldn't go any lower.

Eric Kriegler, *For Your Eyes Only*

The Aryan super-henchman is a Bond stock character (see list, THE ARYAN SUPERMEN). All icy-blond, all hard-as-nails buff, all cold-hearted killers. As with Dr. Mortner, we have to recognize the need to rise beyond the stock nature of such a character, and imbue it with personality. His only affect is a scowl that is so constant that it loses whatever threat he possesses. The only personality John Wyman gives his character is that he is repulsed by a girl who is, let's face it, repulsive. Most damning of all, he isn't scary. I rest my case.

Elvis, *Quantum of Solace*

The great henchmen have distinction—Oddjob's silence and his hate, Jaws's teeth. Some are physically imposing, some are brilliant (Ricky Jay as Henry Gupta in *Tomorrow Never Dies*), some are funny (Dr. Kaufman in the same movie).

Elvis has an ugly toupee. No, seriously, that's it. He has ugly bangs, and he is injured by a cute young woman with an office job.

The Complete List

Here are all the henchmen and henchwomen who aren't listed in the VILLAINS section. For sake of completeness, all secondary villains are included and the leading henchman character or characters are <u>underlined</u>. You'll find some female characters listed here who are also listed under BOND GIRLS.

Okay, I admit, this isn't *all* the henchmen. There are myriads of minor and non-speaking villainous roles in a Bond movie, and you don't want to wade through a list of, e.g. all the technicians in the *You Only Live Twice* volcano lair.

Dr. No

<u>**Prof. R.J. Dent**</u> (Anthony Dawson)

<u>**Miss Taro**</u> (Zena Marshall)

Photographer (Marguerite LeWars, a.k.a. Margaret LeWars)

Mr. Jones (Reginald Carter)

From Russia with Love

<u>**Donald "Red" Grant**</u> (Robert Shaw)

Kronsteen (Vladek Sheybal)

Morzeny (Walter Gotell)

Krilencu (Fred Haggerty)

Goldfinger

<u>Oddjob</u> (Harold Sakata)

Kisch (Michael Mellinger)

Capungo (Alf Joint)

Mr. Ling (Burt Kwouk)

Thunderball

<u>Fiona Volpe</u> (Luciana Paluzzi)

<u>Vargas</u> (Philip Locke)

Angelo Palazzi (Paul Stassano)

Count Lippe (Guy Doleman)

Jacques Botier/Bouvoir (Bob Simmons/Rose Alba)

Quist (Bill Cummings)

Professor Ladislav Kutze (George Pravda)

You Only Live Twice

<u>Helga Brandt, SPECTRE #11</u> (Karin Dor)

<u>Mr. Osato</u> (Teru Shimada)

Hans (Ronald Rich)

SPECTRE #3 (Burt Kwouk)

On Her Majesty's Secret Service

Grunther (Yuri Borienko)

Diamonds Are Forever

<u>Mr. Wint</u> (Bruce Glover)

<u>Mr. Kidd</u> (Putter Smith)

Bert Saxby (Bruce Cabot)

Bambi (Lola Larson)

Thumper (Trina Parks)

Shady Tree (Leonard Barr)

Professor Metz (Joseph Fürst)

Peter Franks (Joe Robinson)

Morton Slumber (David Bauer)

Live and Let Die

<u>Tee Hee</u> (Julius Harris)

<u>Baron Samedi</u> (Geoffrey Holder)

<u>Rosie Carver</u> (Gloria Hendry)

Whisper (Earl Jolly Brown)

      Cab Driver (Arnold Williams)

The Man with the Golden Gun

      <u>**Nick Nack**</u> (Herve Villechaize)

      Hai Fat (Richard Loo)

      Chula (Chan Yiu Lam)

      Kra (Sonny Caldinez)

The Spy Who Loved Me

      <u>**Jaws**</u> (Richard Kiel)

      Naomi (Caroline Munro)

      Sandor (Milton Reid)

Moonraker

      <u>**Jaws**</u> (Richard Kiel)

      Chang (Toshiro Suga)

For Your Eyes Only

      <u>**Emile Leopold Locque**</u> (Michael Gothard)

      <u>**Eric Kriegler**</u> (John Wyman)

      Hector Gonzales (Stefan Kalipha)

      Claus (Charles Dance)

Octopussy

      <u>**Gobinda**</u> (Kabir Bedi)

      Knife-Throwing Twins (David and Anthony Meyer)

      Thug with Yo-yo (William Derrick)

Never Say Never Again

      <u>**Fatima Blush**</u> (Barbara Carrera)

      Lippe (Pat Roach)

      Dr. Kovac (Milow Kirek)

A View to a Kill

      <u>**May Day**</u> (Grace Jones)

      Bob Conley (Manning Redwood)

      <u>**Dr. Carl Mortner, a.k.a. Hans Glau**</u> (Willoughby Gray)

      Scarpine (Patrick Bachau)

The Living Daylights

      <u>**Necros**</u> (Andreas Wisniewski)

      00 Imposter (Carl Rigg)

Licence to Kill

      <u>**Dario**</u> (Benicio Del Toro)

Milton <u>Krest</u> (Anthony Zerbe)

Ed Killifer (Everett McGill)

Truman-Lodge (Anthony Starke)

Professor Joe Butcher (Wayne Newton)

Col. Heller (Don Stroud)

GoldenEye

<u>Boris Grishenko</u> (Alan Cummings)

<u>Xenia Onatopp</u> (Famke Janssen)

General Arkady Grigorovich Ourumov (Gottfried John)

Tomorrow Never Dies

<u>Stamper</u> (Götz Otto)

<u>Dr. Kaufman</u> (Vincent Schiavelli)

<u>Henry Gupta</u> (Ricky Jay)

The World is Not Enough

Cigar Girl (Maria Grazia Cucinotta)

Gabor (John Seru)

Mr. Bullion, a.k.a. Bull (Goldie)

Sasha Davidov (Ulrich Thomsen)

Die Another Day

<u>Zao</u> (Rick Yune)

<u>Miranda Frost</u> (Rosamund Pike)

Vladimir ("Vlad") Popov (Michael Gorevoy)

Mr. Kil (Lawrence Makoare)

Dr. Alvarez (Simón Andreu)

Scorpion Girl (Tymarah)

Casino Royale

<u>Alex Dimitrios</u> (Simon Abkarian)

Kratt (Clemens Schik)

<u>Carlos</u> (Claudio Santamaria)

Steven Obanno (Isaach De Bankole)

Valenka (Ivana Milicevic)

Mollaka (Sébastien Foucan)

Adolph Gettler (Richard Sammel)

Quantum of Solace

<u>Elvis</u> (Anatole Taubman)

<u>General Medrano</u> (Joaquin Cosio)

Craig Mitchell (Glenn Foster)

Mr. Slate (Neil Jackson)

Chief of Police (Fernando Guillén Cuervo)

Yusef Kabira (Simon Kassianides)

Skyfall

Severine (Bérénice Lim Marlohe)

Patrice (Ola Rapace)

Spectre

Hinx (Dave Bautista)

C (Andrew Scott)

Marco Sciarra: (Alessandro Cremona)

Blofeld's Right Hand Man (Gediminas Adomaitis)

Guerra (Benito Sagredo)

No Time to Die

Primo (Dali Bensallah)

THE MEGA-STUNTS

Mega-stunts are stunts performed primarily by people, not by machines. Things like the jet pack in *Thunderball*, Little Nellie (the autogyro in *You Only Live Twice*) or the Acrostar (the mini-jet in *Octopussy*) delight the audience and serve the same dramatic function as a stunt, but are essentially showing off a piece of technology. To me, a great stunt is something amazing done by one or more individuals, with or without the aid of technology. The "Spiral Jump" car-flip in *The Man with the Golden Gun*, for example, is not a cool car, it's something really cool done with a car. To me, that's a stunt.

The following amazing stunts are the greatest in the Bond films. My search for top stunts gave me seven impressive results. I see no reason to knock the list down to a Top Five. Here they are, in order of preference.

The Top Seven

1. The Spy Who Loved Me: The Asgard Jump

The mother of all stunts, performed by Rick Sylvester. Bond leaves a cabin in Austria and is attacked by KGB agents. He shoots an agent while skiing backwards, turns, and skis right off a cliff. Then, releasing his skis, he opens a Union Jack parachute. The stunt, still considered by many film buffs to be the greatest real (not CG-enhanced) stunt ever performed on-screen, was done off the Asgard Peak in Baffin Island, Canada. In actuality, it combines stunt skiing done in Austria by Willy Bogner with the famed leap by Rick Sylvester. Superb!

2. GoldenEye: The Dam Jump

Performed by Wayne Michaels. To break into a chemical weapons facility located at the base of a dam, Bond bungee jumps 700 feet (220 meters), then fires a piton into the top of the structure below so that he can pull himself the rest of the way down. This breathtaking, beautiful stunt opens the film, and it set a world record for bungee jumping from a fixed object. It is filmed cleanly and directly, allowing the audience to appreciate its natural glory. The only 007 stunt to match the sheer perfection of the Asgard Jump, the Dam Jump was done at the Dam of Lake Verzasca, Locarno, Ticino, Switzerland.

In a Sky Movies survey, this stunt was voted the greatest movie stunt of all time. The top ten list featured four Bond films, including the stunts listed here as #1, 2, and 5. (The fourth Bond sequence that made the list was the boat chase in *The World is Not Enough*'s pre-titles sequence.)

3. The Living Daylights: The Cargo Net Fight

Performed by Jake Lombard and B.J. Worth. Bond and Necros are hanging onto a cargo net filled with bags of heroin; the net dangles out the back of a Hercules jet whose cargo door Kara Milovy has inadvertently opened. The two men fight in mid-air while holding onto the net. The net is sliced open and the bags fly out, hitting the men and buffeting them in the wind while they continue to fight. Meanwhile, the bomb that Bond had intended to defuse ticks away.

This one has all the thrills and danger one could possibly ask for. It is far longer than most stunt pieces, it changes throughout (full net, empty net, rope breaking, jet in danger, bomb ticking...) and the action is gripping. Simply a great fight and great stuntwork!

4. *Moonraker: The Parachute Wrestle*

Performed by B.J. Worth and Jake Lombard. Bond is left in a crashing airplane without a parachute. Wrestling with the pilot for his parachute, he is pushed out of the plane by Jaws. He then fights the pilot, mid-air and in freefall, and gets his 'chute from him. This stunt is a masterpiece of film and stunt innovation. The hidden parachute was designed in order to accomplish it. Next, a helmet-anchored widescreen camera was invented; previously, widescreen cameras weighed too much and would have snapped an aerialist's neck. Finally, the photographer used a rope to slow the opening of the parachute so that his neck would be hit with less force.

Careful direction was crucial: Only a few seconds (usually three) could be filmed during each jump before the stuntmen had to open their parachutes. John Glen had to keep careful track of exactly where the fight left off and should begin again with the next leap. In all, a total of eighty-eight jumps were made to complete the scene. The entire mid-air fight is breathtaking.

By the way, this was Jake Lombard's first film stunt-role. He doubled for James Bond—an auspicious beginning!

But this is a great stunt marred by a bad joke. The awe-inspiring aerial work is given a Wile E. Coyote coda when Jaws, realizing he is going to hit the ground without a parachute, flaps his arms and lands on a circus tent. Jaws is completely unnecessary to the entire scene—he shows up without explanation on the plane, and has nothing to do with the main trajectory of action. Darn shame.

5. *The Man with the Golden Gun: The AMC Spiral Jump*

Coordinated by W. Jay Milligan, Jr. and performed by Lauren "Bumps" Willard. Bond is chasing Scaramanga, who has tricked him by taking a different road. Bond must cross a river to regain Scaramanga's trail, but the bridge is out. He drives his car (an AMC Hornet Hatchback "borrowed" from a dealership) so that it leaps across the gap in the bridge, rolls over 360 degrees, and lands on the other side, where he can continue pursuit. The roll was computer-calculated by Raymond McHenry, factoring weight, angle of ascent and descent, balance, speed, and so on. The steering and seat were moved to the center of the car, and unnecessary weight was removed from the car to make it lighter.

Unfortunately, the effect of the stunt was spoiled by the placement of a slide whistle on the soundtrack, making it seem a joke instead of an adventure. Even John Barry today admits it was a mistake.

6. *Licence to Kill: Waterskiing Without Skis*

Performed by David Reinhardt. Bond, escaping the Wavekrest, battles underwater with Krest's divers. With his air supply cut, he escapes by harpooning the base of the seaplane that had rendezvoused with Krest. As the seaplane begins to take off, Bond waterskis, without skis, behind the plane, and then pulls himself aboard, where he throws the pilot and co-pilot out and takes over. The aerial stuntwork is again performed by Lombard and Worth, with Lombard doubling Dalton. It's an excellent stunt with a good series of changes—underwater, on the water, in the air. On the whole, though, it simply fails to stand out the way its fellows on this list do.

7. *A View to a Kill: The Eiffel Tower Leap*

Performed by B.J. Worth. After May Day kills Bond's Paris contact, he chases her up the Eiffel Tower. To effect her escape, she leaps off the tower and parachutes to safety. The stunt is wonderful, but it is brief, whereas the chase up the Eiffel Tower is long, slow, and awkward.

Honorable Mentions

- *Licence to Kill*: Bond is lowered from a plane and hooks the tail of Sanchez's plane: Dangerous for the stuntman, and very exciting for the audience.
- *Tomorrow Never Dies*: The motorcycle leap: From a rooftop, over the rotating blades of a helicopter, to the next rooftop. In order to get a real motorcycle in the shot, no safety net could be used.
- *On Her Majesty's Secret Service*: All of the stunt skiing and bobsledding is terrific, but skiing on one ski at 60 mph is especially notable.
- *Diamonds Are Forever*: The two-wheel driving stunt would have been a classic if not for the big blooper—going in the alley on the right wheels and coming out on left. Oh, well.
- *For Your Eyes Only*: The rock-climb, and fall, outside of St. Cyril's in Meteora, Greece. Stuntman Rick Sylvester explains that it is very hard for a climber to make himself fall, when so much of his training is about not falling.
- *Live and Let Die*: The speedboat jump actually set a world record at the time, yet it is little-discussed now. Overall, I think the speedboat chase was so extended, with so many thrills, that the singular stunt failed to stand apart, but it should not be overlooked.
- *Octopussy*: Bond hangs by his fingers onto the outside of a small plane. Surely a spectacular stunt, it suffers from implausibility; I clearly remember sitting in a movie theater in 1983 saying "No way!"
- *The World is Not Enough:* The boat chase in the pre-titles sequence is a fan favorite, and is sometimes cited as a great stunt sequence. It is an exciting chase, with excellent stunt-work, but there is no singular "mega-stunt" in it.
- AND*: Casino Royale*: The Aston Martin DBS roll. Realizing that Vesper has been kidnapped by Le Chiffre, Bond races after them at high speed, and suddenly sees Vesper tied up in the middle of the road. Veering, he rolls the Aston Martin seven times. This stunt set a world record for most assisted cannon rolls. "Assisted" because the car simply would not roll—it was too

stable. In addition to using an 18 inch ramp, the car was "fitted with a gas cannon that used pressurised nitrogen to punch a metal ram out of the bottom of the car and flip it onto its roof."

The Future of Stunts?

The "stunts" in *Die Another Day* do not bode well for the future of the honorable and impressive stunt history outlined above. Sure, CGI (computer-generated imagery) has been used in Bond films for quite a while. But the 21st century brings us an entire stunt sequence that doesn't really exist.

Bond is hanging from the edge of an ice cliff—a distinctly phony ice cliff. He fashions a para-surfboard from the hood and brake parachute of Graves's race car. From here follows what is essentially a cartoon. Bond is para-surfing among icebergs, but there is no Bond, no water, and no ice. The sequence is remarkably cheesy-looking, and could not persuade even an unsophisticated viewer of its veracity. Bond looks like an avatar in a video game. The icebergs are especially bad, they don't even look as good as CGI— they look like ice cubes filmed in a bathtub.

But let's not get lost in how unattractive it is. Here's a case where it really is the principal of the thing. Bond films are famous for the reality of their stunts. We know deep down that the actor playing James Bond isn't doing those stunts, but we also know that someone is. The quality of realism-in-fantasy is part of what makes the Bond films unique in the action genre. The famous *The Spy Who Loved Me* jump is breathtaking in part because it is unmistakably real. The cargo net fight in *The Living Daylights* is astonishing because you know that somehow, there are actually two guys who hung off that plane! There is nothing involving about Yosemite Sam falling off a cliff, because the audience knows it didn't happen.

Film analysts have been asking for forty years what makes Bond different from other spies, and Bond movies different from others of their genre. The commitment to authentic stunt-work is one such distinction, and to watch *Die Another Day* is to know that Eon Productions is willing to abandon that commitment. It makes me sad. It makes most fans very angry. Seeing *Die Another Day* made me wonder if this MEGA-STUNTS chapter was final and complete, never to be added to. I sincerely hope not!

It was a relief to hear that *Casino Royale* had a renewed commitment to authenticity. As a coda to this chapter, the Craig movies turned out to provide real stunts, and real action, and a star who did as much of his own stunts as possible.

MOONRAKER (1979)

Survey Says!

> Percent Favorite: 3%
> Top 5 Cumulative: 13/25
> Numeric Rating: 6.33/10
> Ranking: 15.7 (16th/21)

My Rating and Ranking

> Rated: 5/10
> Ranked: 22 out of 25

Summary

When the Moonraker spacecraft is hijacked, Bond investigates its manufacturer, Hugo Drax. From his California shuttle facilities, Bond travels to Drax's glassworks in Venice and then to a Drax subsidiary in Rio de Janeiro. Each time, he meets up with Dr. Holly Goodhead, an astrophysicist and CIA agent. With the help of Jaws, Drax captures Bond and Dr. Goodhead at his launch site in the Amazon, but our heroes elude execution and follow Drax into space, where, with the aid of NASA, they foil Drax's plan to destroy human life and repopulate the earth.

> **James Bond:** Roger Moore
> **Dr. Holly Goodhead:** Lois Chiles
> **Hugo Drax:** Michael Lonsdale
> **Jaws:** Richard Kiel
> **Corinne Dufour:** Corinne Clery
> **General Gogol:** Walter Gotell
> **M:** Bernard Lee
> **Moneypenny:** Lois Maxwell
> **Q:** Desmond Llewelyn
> **Directed by** Lewis Gilbert

Discussion

Moonraker is a movie gone out of control. Its bloated budget and locations in seven countries were a monster; a hydra with too many arms for director Lewis Gilbert to keep track of.

On first examination, *Moonraker* is an easy movie to disregard. It is cartoony, comedic, and senseless. Although all Bond movies require a certain leap of faith where plot is concerned, the audience wants to be met halfway. *Moonraker* throws bits and pieces of potential plot in the air, and lets them fall willy-nilly. Like *The Man with the Golden Gun*, the movie is much-despised by fans, although *Moonraker* has more of a following than the earlier film. If *The Man with the Golden Gun* has Multiple Personality Disorder, then *Moonraker* is truly schizophrenic, it is shattered into a zillion disparate pieces without a single guiding personality holding it all together. *Moonraker* has some incredibly stupid set pieces, and several outstanding ones, but none of them join together to form a movie.

The things that fans hate most about *Moonraker*, and I'm with the majority on this, is that it's a cartoon. Jaws, who was nearly superhuman in *The Spy Who Loved Me*, has apparently been bitten by a radioactive spider in the interim, because he now appears immortal, able to survive: A fall from an airplane without a parachute, crashing into a mountain from on top of a cable car, and falling from a space station, among other things. He responds to most of these not with menace, but with a goofy confusion that is meant to be an audience pleaser, but elicits primarily groans. Finally, Jaws falls in love with a woman who is herself a cartoon character, done up in strangely clichéd Tyrolean garb, Dolly looks like nothing so much as Bugs Bunny in drag (but with great cleavage). While Jaws is busy playing Wile E. Coyote, James Bond is occupied humiliating himself by riding a "Bondola," accompanied by the wearing of a funny hat. Many people refer to *Moonraker* as "the double-taking pigeon movie" and arguably, that one wildly ill-conceived moment epitomizes the film. Other cartoon moments include Jaws flapping his arms when he sees he is crashing without a 'chute, the use of circus music to emphasize the "humor" of the situation, Jaws's inability to touch things without breaking them (parachute, boat steering wheel), the entire gondola sequence, including the gondola-hearse, and the flimsy fight between Bond and the not-very-scary big snake.

Although Hugo Drax has a master plan worth noticing (see HE'S QUITE MAD, YOU KNOW), his behavior as the plan unfolds is beyond senseless, outstripping even Bond for behaving in a way that is designed merely to generate the next set piece. Bond's initial meeting with Drax is bizarre. First, Drax assumes that a "secret" agent has been sent as an official envoy of the British government. Then, having established this cover—the outraged industrialist whom the British must appease—he immediately blows that cover by trying to murder Bond.

A few other senseless moments that might give pause...

- Why does MI6 decide to focus its investigation on the Moonraker's manufacturer? Would such an investigation have turned up anything if Drax hadn't immediately tried to kill Bond?
- Why does Drax's "humble pilot" share luxurious quarters on his estate? Why does she know where the safe is?
- Who is Drax on the phone with when he discovers Jaws is "available"? The Henchman Employment Service? Do they deliver?
- Since Jaws was not yet employed during the pre-titles sequence, why was he on that plane?
- When Drax decides to kill Bond during the pheasant shoot, why does he first hand Bond a rifle?
- When Bond kills Drax's sniper, why does Drax merely shrug with disappointment, and make no further attempt on Bond's life? His killer dogs were right there.
- Since when can NASA launch a shuttle on a moment's notice? If they are launching a shuttle to investigate a large, unknown object

in space, why is that shuttle occupied by an army of laser-armed astronauts?

Drax himself is another post-Blofeld wannabe, a graduate of the Dr. No Dress-for-Villainous-Success Program. His plans for world domination are better thought-out than Stromberg's, and he has some of the wittiest lines of any villain in the series (see QUOTABLE QUOTES). But for all his intelligence, Hugo Drax doesn't move his lips. I never get over this. I watch Michael Lonsdale's performance over and over, waiting for evidence that he is really a mannequin, zooming in to look for telltale seams in the jaw. He appears convincingly human, and perhaps is practicing ventriloquism, but it makes for a very flat performance.

For Bond girls this time out, we have one entirely lacking warmth, and one entirely lacking spine.

Dr. Goodhead's hostile approach is unattractive and senseless. Particularly at the point where he knows she is CIA, and she knows he is MI6, there is no reason for her to deceive him; these are supposed to be friendly organizations. The only reason for their chilly competition is as an attempt to imitate *The Spy Who Loved Me*, but here it is unjustified and not at all sexy. Oh, yes, some fans find Lois Chiles very sexy indeed, but there is no chemistry with Moore, and her demeanor ranges from aloof to prickly.

Corinne Dufour is lovely, sad, and pathetic. Her love scene with Bond is so strange, and Bond uses her at least as badly as he used Solitaire in *Live and Let Die*. He flat out tells her that he has come to her for information, not for love, and then she sleeps with him anyway, and acts surprised that he is spying. He does nothing to protect her from being killed as a result of his spying, and apparently never even realizes that she is gone.

In sum, then, *Moonraker* is a movie with a lousy plot, a flagrant disregard for common sense and good taste in almost every scene, and unappealing characters. Yet it can be immensely enjoyable to watch, because of its outstanding cinematography and several outrageously good set pieces.

The pre-titles parachute stunt is mind-blowing (see THE MEGA-STUNTS). The pre-titles sequence exemplifies the entire movie—very exciting, wonderfully filmed, absolutely senseless (why is Jaws on the plane? Why crash the plane instead of just pushing Bond out?), and marred by sophomoric humor. Despite its flaws, it is infinitely watchable and never fails to bring a sense of awe.

The movie also boasts a terrific boat chase on the Amazon River—better than the boat chase in *From Russia with Love*, and as good as the one in *The World is Not Enough*—and a fine fight scene which should be remembered by those who think *Die Another Day* is Bond's first time with a sword. There is also the very exciting centrifuge sequence; which includes a rare use of flashback in a Bond film (see FLASHBACK).

Two excellent scenes deserve particular note for their filming and pacing. First is the death of Corinne Dufour, chased by dogs through the woods. Ruthless and scary, but juxtaposed with a lovely woman in this floaty white dress, and all this gorgeous dappled sunlight around her, it is a marvel of contrast. Later comes Manuela at Carnival in Rio, as Jaws approaches her down the narrow alley. It is especially interesting how this scene parallels the sequence in the woods, a dark woman trapped by an approaching killer (with sharp teeth!), so that you feel certain what will happen next, and so that her rescue is a complete surprise.

From the space launch to the end, even fans of the movie agree it's a waste of time. The musical emergence of the space station seems like an homage to *2001: A Space Odyssey*, but with none of the grandeur. The laser gun battle is silly beyond my ability to describe. The 'Oh, James' moment is gruesome. The combination of four feet dangling mid-air, and Q's exceptionally graphic double entendre, simply goes too far for my taste in Bond films.

High Points

- The parachute fight stunt.
- Corinne's final run in the woods.
- The centrifuge scene.
- Jaws nearly killing Manuela during Carnival.
- The Amazon boat chase and gorgeous Amazon locations.
- The fight in the glass museum.
- Drax's speech on the space station, in which we learn the true scope of his evil scheme.

Low Points

- Lackluster title sequence.
- Jaws's transformation into a cartoon character.
- Jaws's romance with a cartoon character.
- Stiff performances by Michael Lonsdale and Lois Chiles.
- Bond's callous disregard for Corinne Dufour.
- Dr. Goodhead's irritating hostility towards Bond.
- Slow, laborious fight on top of the cable cars.
- Silly wrestling match with a big snake.
- Senseless plot that meanders every which way.
- "Attempting re-entry."
- The first major use of product placement in a Bond film was over-obvious and disruptive.

Quotable Quotes

Bond (after being shown the darts for his watch): "Very novel, Q. We could get them in the stores for Christmas."

Drax: "Look after Mr. Bond. See that some harm comes to him."

Bond: "A woman?"
Dr. Goodhead: "Your powers of observation do you credit, Mr. Bond."

Bond (after trying Dr. Goodhead's flame-throwing perfume): "Trifle overpowering, your scent."

Bond (after Chang lands in a piano): "Play it again, Sam."

Drax:"Mr. Bond, you defy all my attempts to plan an amusing death for you."

Drax: "James Bond. You appear with the tedious inevitability of an unloved season."

Drax: "At least I shall have the pleasure of putting you out of my misery."

Bond: "Take a giant step for mankind."

Q: "I think he's attempting re-entry, sir."

Facts and Figures

SEXUAL ENCOUNTERS

<u>Three</u>: Corinne Dufour, Dr. Goodhead, Manuela

BOND'S CAR

None.

DEATHS

<u>Approximately one hundred forty-one</u>:
- Crew of the plane that was carrying the hijacked Moonraker shuttle (apparently four), the sharpshooter in the tree, Corinne, Drako the gondolier, the knife-thrower who killed Drako, Chang, two scientists killed by the poison gas, six on the Amazon (3 in each of 2 boats), Hugo Drax.
- Twenty-three in the battle outside the space station.
- An unknown number when the space station blows up; approximately one hundred.

Bond Kills:
- <u>Ten</u> directly (sharpshooter, knife-thrower, Chang, six on the Amazon, Drax).
- <u>Two</u> indirectly (the scientists were an accident; Bond didn't know the gas was deadly).

EXPLOSIONS

<u>Six</u>: The 747 in the pre-titles sequence, a small one when Q's dummy is blown up by the bolos, the cable car into the 7-Up stand generated plenty of rubble, but no sparks, flame or light, both boats on the Amazon, the second one being really nifty, and the space station was quite huge.

BOND'S FOOD AND DRINKS

Vodka Martinis

<u>One</u>, mixed for Bond by Manuela when they meet in his suite.

Other Drinks

- Champagne on the plane in the pre-titles sequence; we see the bottle and half- empty glasses.
- Bollinger champagne with Holly Goodhead in her hotel room, the champagne may or may not have been '69, depending upon if she was expecting him. We do not see him drink.

Food

- Drax offers Bond tea and cucumber sandwiches; Bond refuses.

GAMBLING AND SPORTS

- Pheasant shooting

Amaze Your Friends!

- According to Richard Kiel, the producers had wanted to cast a giant as Jaws's girlfriend, but Kiel objected. He won the argument when he pointed out that his own wife was 5'2" (the same size as Blanche Ravalec, the actress who played Dolly).
- *Moonraker*'s budget was greater than all previous Bond films combined.
- Hugo Drax's estate, which was brought, stone-by-stone, from France and rebuilt in California, actually exists and was filmed in France, at Vaux-Le-Vicomte, Melun.
- Following in the footsteps of *The Spy Who Loved Me*, *Moonraker* contains three musical references: The lock on the Venice laboratory plays the alien signal music from *Close Encounters of the Third Kind* (and we hear it three times), the theme music from *The Magnificent Seven* is played when Bond rides on horseback to the Brazilian MI6 base, and the Romeo and Juliet theme was used as Jaws's and Dolly's love theme.
- Bernard Lee's last appearance as M.

Most Interesting Goofs

Weightlessness is Soooo Tricky: There are numerous errors during the weightless sequence, including long hair that falls attractively onto women's shoulders, and a blanket that lays carefully in place.

Poison Pen: The gadget pen with which Bond stabs the python is Holly Goodhead's. How did Bond end up with it?

KILLER OR CLOWN?

Whenever a review of a James Bond movie is written, by me or by anyone else, the question is asked, however indirectly—Is 007 a killer or a clown? In other words, are Bond movies spy movies, or comedies?

As a general rule, the geekier the fan ("geeky" being a compliment, of course), the more likely he or she is to favor a more serious Bond. The hardcore, convention-attending, website-posting types tend to favor the more espionage-driven movies, and you'll have noticed by now that I share that bias. The movie-going public that simply enjoys 007 without any particular commitment is far more likely to appreciate comedic flourishes whether or not they make sense, and to care little for the dignity of their favorite MI6 agent. Like all general rules about Bond, there are plenty of exceptions, and it's also true that those of us who favor espionage enjoy the comedic side of Bond (in context) and those who enjoy a humorous Bond still want some action and adventure in the mix.

But Bond movies aren't really comedies. They certainly wink at the spy genre, and have since *Dr. No*, but they are also a straight-ahead part of that genre. No one goes to see a parody of a movie that is, itself, a parody. Characters like Derek Flint and Austin Powers work as spoofs of James Bond precisely because Bond is, to some extent, serious. The controversy is more accurately about how far Bond's comedy can go, and still be Bond.

Every Bond fan loves to laugh, but most of us love our hero too much to want him to be a clown. I'd also argue that the humor simply doesn't work when Bond is clownish.

The Bond formula works well because of its unique combination of danger, sex, humor, and toys. If the danger isn't dangerous, the humor is heavy-handed because it exists without contrast, it is merely silly. The key is balance.

There's a terrifying fight, the audience holds its collective breath. Bond wins, the audience exhales. Bond then says, "Shocking, positively shocking." The audience laughs. If Bond had just said it, it wouldn't have been funny. If the fight scene wasn't exciting, the audience wouldn't have needed the laugh. Laughs for their own sake are comedy, laughs in the context of adventure are comic relief.

Connery was brilliant because he functioned as a wry straight man in contrast to outlandish villains. In Connery's era, Bond functioned as our grounding—he kept us in the picture—a superhuman us, but a legitimate fantasy projection. Bond films were funny, but Bond himself was not a joke. Bond was a sane center and comedy swirled around him. He kept the core of the film going.

With the worst Moore vehicles, Moore allowed Bond himself to be an object of humor, a silly little man with a cute little eyebrow. The humor was so outlandish that the movies weren't action-comedies anymore, just comedies. In *Live and Let Die*, Moore is the butt of racial jokes ("like following a cue ball"). In *The Man with the Golden Gun*, Moore is the object of smutty jokes (the nipple). In *Moonraker*, everything is a joke. When a villain flaps his arms to keep from crashing, you've lost any sense that such a villain is dangerous, so what does the adventure matter?

On the opposite extreme, *Licence to Kill* was a movie most fans found too serious. When director John Glen found that Timothy Dalton's portrayal gave him a serious Bond, he decided to play to that seriousness. This was his mistake. A serious Bond can exist successfully in the context of a playful movie; Connery did so before Dalton, and Brosnan would do so afterwards. Dalton himself did very well in *The Living Daylights*, a movie with both gritty and light-hearted elements, held together by the smoldering and dramatic spy at its center. But just as Moore sometimes failed to provide contrast to his silly surroundings, Dalton had no contrast to his dark surroundings in *Licence to Kill*. The movie's funniest moments—the Professor Joe Butcher sequence—are played without Bond, and so 007 is positively grim.

Some fans consider the absolute nadir of Bond's portrayal the moment when Roger Moore donned a clown suit in *Octopussy*. Other than the fact that it serves as an ironic commentary on his career as Bond, the moment is not bad at all. In fact, it typifies how to get the humor right. At the movie's dramatic climax, with a nuclear bomb ticking away, the fate of the world in balance, and Bond struggling mightily, the clown suit serves to highlight the tension, it says, look, *this* is funny, and *that* isn't. Oddly enough, in that particular scene, we knew Bond wasn't clowning around.

THE SACRIFICIAL LAMBS

A t some point in almost every James Bond film, a character's death impels Bond towards further anger at the villain, and drives his need for revenge. Fans usually call this character the sacrificial lamb. The lamb may be an ally, a lover, or both. The important part is that this person's death has meaning for Bond, and makes defeating the villain more personal; this is the point where 007 gets angry.

Here is a list of sacrificial lambs by movie, with explanation where needed.

Dr. No—Quarrel

Here the concept and meaning of the lamb is established, as Bond tells Dr. No that revenge for Quarrel's death is a priority for him.

From Russia with Love—Kerim Bey

Goldfinger—Jill Masterson

One could argue that both Jill and Tilly are lambs, but it is Jill's death that makes 007 really hate Goldfinger. Bond liked Jill and was somewhat annoyed by Tilly, so it is Jill's death that meant more to him.

Thunderball—Paula Caplan

You Only Live Twice—Dikko Henderson and Aki

Dikko, an agent-ally with whom Bond has just had a warm meeting, is a classic sacrificial lamb. However, Aki's death is certainly meaningful to James as well. In terms of story structure, the answer lies in the simple fact that Eon wanted a total of three women in the story, and so Aki was written to be eliminated. Thus, the story has two separate deaths of interesting characters who can be thought of as lambs.

On Her Majesty's Secret Service—Campbell, the Swiss agent

Campbell is the blond man whose body is so brutally displayed by Blofeld. Some fans think of Tracy as a lamb, but her death doesn't move the plot; rather, it serves as the denouement.

Diamonds Are Forever—Plenty O'Toole

Live and Let Die—Harold Strutter

Certainly there are plenty of agent deaths in *Live and Let Die*, the pre-titles sequence has three, including Baines, whom Bond "rather liked." Both Charlie and Strutter are CIA agents who help Bond. However, Bond had barely seen or spoken to Charlie before his death. Strutter seems placed in the story specifically to be a lamb. He tails Bond and fools us into thinking he's a bad guy, just as Felix normally would. The reason he isn't Felix seems to be solely to make him expendable.

The Man with the Golden Gun—Andrea Anders

The Spy Who Loved Me—Felicca

Felicca is a weak lamb, as Bond has barely met her. On the other hand, he has kissed her.

Moonraker—Corinne Dufour

It's hard to see Corinne in this light because we don't see her death affect Bond—on the other hand, it's a very affecting death for the audience.

For Your Eyes Only—Countess Lisl

Octopussy—Vijay

Never Say Never Again—Nicole (Agent 326)

A View to a Kill—Sir Godfrey Tibbett and Chuck Lee

As with *You Only Live Twice*, this is a distinct case of two sacrificial lambs at separate points in the narrative. As with Strutter in *Live and Let Die*, Chuck Lee appears at a point in the story where we would normally expect to see Felix. This is a big clue that he won't live to see the credits roll.

The Living Daylights — Saunders

Licence to Kill—Della Leiter

GoldenEye—None

Some fans argue that Russian Defense Minister Mishkin is the lamb in this film, but he is a weak choice, being neither an ally nor a friend. No, *GoldenEye* plays a bait-and-switch game. We are led to believe the sacrificial lamb is agent 006. This is reinforced in Bond's meeting with M, when Bond recognizes Ourumov. M warns him not to make the mission personal, which serves as both an oblique reference to his last film, and also echoes the scene in *Goldfinger* following Jill Masterson's death, where a different M warns a different Bond of the very same thing.

Tomorrow Never Dies—Paris Carver

The World is Not Enough—Sir Robert King

Although no other lamb was killed so early in the film, Bond's impassioned, desperate, and futile race to save him drives the rest of the movie.

Die Another Day—James Bond

In a movie that promised to be different from the rest, the Bond formula is played out in a way we haven't seen before. Captured at the end of the pre-titles sequence, Bond is imprisoned for fourteen months, and this is the sacrifice that drives the rest of the movie forward. The subtext of Bond-as-sacrifice is reinforced when 007 stops his own heart, thereby momentarily "dying," as a lamb must. None of the good guys die on-screen in *Die Another Day*.

Casino Royale—Solange and Vesper Lynd

Solange is a classic sacrificial lamb and needs no explanation. Vesper, like Tracy, doesn't die until the end. However, we don't hear the James Bond Theme until the end. The whole idea of this reboot is that James Bond isn't the 007 we know until this movie makes him so.

Quantum of Solace—Vesper Lynd, Strawberry Fields, and René Mathis

Vesper's death drives Bond for the entire movie. In fact, *Quantum of Solace* cannot be viewed fairly without that context. Fields *should* have been the sacrificial lamb, but her death seems not to affect Bond. But the in-movie death of Mathis a classic sacrificial lamb scene—and beautifully done at that.

Here's a movie that fans complain is too dark, and here's the evidence: Three sacrificial lambs is pretty extreme, and the only such extreme on this list.

Skyfall—Severine

Spectre—Mr. White

You could argue that M is the lamb here, since her video in the beginning brings her death front and center. But it is White's early death that compels the story forward from that point on, and sends Bond to Madeline.

FOR YOUR EYES ONLY (1981)

Survey Says!

> Percent Favorite: 5.5%
> Top 5 Cumulative: 12/25
> Numeric Rating: 64.3/10
> Ranking: 11.3 (10th/25)

My Rating and Ranking

> Rated: 7/10
> Ranked: 16 out of 25

Summary

The "ATAC" (Automatic Targeting Attack Communicator) is lost, and the British and Soviets race to retrieve it. British researchers Timothy and Iona Havelock are murdered by Soviet agents while seeking the ATAC, bringing Bond onto the case and sending the Havelocks' daughter Melina on a quest for revenge. Bond reluctantly teams up with Melina in a search that places him between rival smugglers Kristatos and Columbo. Bond and KGB head General Gogol reach the ATAC at the same time, and Bond destroys it rather than allowing it to fall into Soviet hands.

> **James Bond:** Roger Moore
> **Melina Havelock:** Carole Bouquet
> **Aris Kristatos:** Julian Glover
> **Milos Columbo:** Topol
> **Emile Leopold Locque:** Michael Gothard
> **Countess Lisl Von Schlaf:** Cassandra Harris
> **Bibi Dahl:** Lynn-Holly Johnson
> **Eric Kriegler:** John Wyman
> **Claus:** Charles Dance
> **Jacoba Brink:** Jill Bennett
> **Ferrara:** John Moreno
> **Chief of Staff Bill Tanner:** John Villiers
> **General Gogol:** Walter Gotell
> **Moneypenny:** Lois Maxwell
> **Q:** Desmond Llewelyn
> **Directed by** John Glen

Discussion

For Your Eyes Only is a fairly good Bond film, but overrated. Fans of Roger Moore point to it as "proof" that a Moore film can be tough, down-to- earth, and espionage-driven. But while *For Your Eyes Only* has some laudable qualities in that regard, it is also filled with silliness that is poorly balanced with the forward drive of the plot. The humor is often at odds with the serious side; it feels shoe-horned in, rather than integrated. By this I mean that the lilies joke at the end of the fight with the motorcyclists fits the scene and the situation, it makes sense and it brings a smile. The zamboni fight, on the other hand, comes out of nowhere and is just random silliness.

For Your Eyes Only is weakest in those parts where it is driven by its set pieces instead of narrative. Overall, the movie has a good narrative with which it stays in touch (as opposed to, say, *Moonraker*), but from time to time the flow is broken by nonsensical scenes. Thus you have Q in disguise, both out of character and in the wrong job. Likewise, there is the otherwise inexplicable presence of Bibi Dahl, and the several meaningless scenes with her in them. Bibi serves no real function in the film, as discussed under BOND GIRLS, the part was written for Lynn-Holly Johnson after Cubby Broccoli saw and liked *Ice Castles*.

The pared-down plot is a bonus, and proves that a Bond film can stand on a scheme that doesn't involve a threat to life as we know it or world peace. The race to find a strategically important device is reminiscent of *From Russia with Love*, and is one of this film's strengths. The script does an excellent job of weaving together the plots of two Ian Fleming short stories: From "For Your Eyes Only" we get the Havelock's daughter seeking revenge for her parents' death and interfering with Bond's mission, and from "Risico" we get the rival smugglers, with 007 initially on the wrong side, and Columbo using Lisl to get closer to Bond.

None of the action sequences are really terrific, although there are several exciting parts. Director John Glen had been a second unit director on *On Her Majesty's Secret Service*, *The Spy Who Loved Me*, and *Moonraker*, and was responsible for some of those movies' most exciting sequences, including the Asgard Jump and the mid-air parachute fight. Yet here, in the big chair, he disappoints. The action is often good, but never amazing. Probably the best action sequence is the Citroen CV2 car chase. It is humorous but not dumb, uses the Corfu location beautifully, and has some fine stunt driving. This chase introduced Rémy Julienne's driving team to the Bond films; Julienne and his family worked on a total of six consecutive Eon films (*For Your Eyes Only* through *GoldenEye*).

The ski chase doesn't succeed as well. The chase itself is full of the excitement provided by Willy Bogner's superb ski photography and some wonderful ski stunts, such as a mid-air spin, some wonderful leaps, and an extended chase down a bob run, with Kriegler on a motorcycle, behind Bond on skis, behind a bob team. But the chase is marred by the failure of the film to persuade us that Bond can successfully escape these guys. Eric Kriegler, Olympic-level shooting expert, cannot hit a bright blue Bond etched against a white background! He hits Bond's gun and his ski pole with astonishing accuracy, and then misses Bond himself by two feet or more. A better-designed chase would have created more convincing obstacles to the villain's success, and a more persuasive ending than Kriegler, with a clear shot and a perfect opportunity, simply throwing his gun away.

The hockey/zamboni fight is equally a mixed bag. The idea of hockey players suddenly attacking has a definite...quality. Anyone who has heard of the Jason movies knows that hockey masks are scary-looking. Those guys are threatening! But to end it on a zamboni is nonsense. Not only that, but again, John Glen fails us, using a crazy cut at the end to try to hide the fact that Bond really can't defeat a hockey team with a zamboni.

The keelhaul scene, while exciting, doesn't measure up to Fleming's original and is a bit of a disappointment. It's probably the best scene in the novel **Live and Let Die**; but is less successful on-screen. The problem is that it requires some exposition. In the book, Mr. Big gives a very chilling explanation of this as an experiment; he is timing how long it will take for Bond and Solitaire to be eaten. Without knowing this, it is just one more nasty thing that a villain does to Bond, we don't understand that it is particularly gruesome and painful. It's a good scene, made better by Julian Glover's sadistic smile of pleasure throughout, but I am often left wishing for more after seeing it.

The characters and espionage are for the most part top-knotch. Kristatos, Columbo, and Ferrara were all convincing, as were Melina and Countess Lisl. I liked the underworld intrigue between the Kristatos and Columbo—the first time I saw *For Your Eyes Only*, I really didn't know who the bad guy was. Topol, most famous for his starring role as Tevye in *Fiddler on the Roof*, is a wonderful actor, and has great presence—he's reminiscent of Kerim Bey as an ally. His shtick with the pistachio nuts—the actor's own idea—was amusing without being obtrusive. Glover was icy in just the right way.

Cassandra Harris as Countess Lisl seemed like a real person rather than a Bond girl, she and Bond seemed to connect as people. It is perhaps this that makes her so memorable, despite her limited screen time. Unfortunately, Lisl's death, although excitingly filmed and very touching, has a serious logical hole. At this point in the film, Kristatos is still trying to persuade Bond that he is the good guy and Columbo is the bad guy. Why, then, kill off Columbo's girlfriend? Surely that diverts suspicion away from him. Nonetheless, it is a well-done scene and Roger Moore, for once, gives the lady her due; we sense the feeling within him when he loses her.

Although Carol Bouquet has, by contrast, little chemistry with Bond, I like the idea of Melina Havelock, with her deadly intentions forcing her way into Bond's plans. Other than the tacked-on romance (and I just hated her use of the title in the final scene), the character is well-written and well-played.

About Bibi Dahl, the less said, the better.

John Villiers gives a prissy and unpleasant performance as the Chief of Staff, reminiscent of Edward Fox's strident M in *Never Say Never Again*. However, it is refreshing to see that for once, Bond wasn't expected to kill his target. When Tanner calls him to task for allowing Gonzales to be killed, it is reminiscent of *Goldfinger*'s M scene. Minister of Defence Freddy Gray is good in the scene as well.

Locations are gorgeous and well-integrated into the story. Using an Olympic site in Italy was a great idea, and the film is enhanced by shots of the ski jumps. This again reminds one of *Goldfinger*, when the camera pauses to admire a high-diver. Our tour of Greece is naturalistic and full of visual delights.

The worst parts of *For Your Eyes Only* are the beginning, the middle, and the end. In the beginning, we have that awful pre-titles sequence. It begins auspiciously, with Bond visiting Tracy's grave, a touching and worthwhile opening. But the action portion, although well-intentioned, was very badly done and remarkably implausible. The "Man in Wheelchair" (Blofeld) was an embarrassment, cackling like an old lady and then begging for his life. He bears no relation to the master genius who plagued Bond for five movies.

In the middle, we have the parrot problem. Bond and Melina have escaped from Kristatos but have lost his trail. With all of the resources of MI6 at his disposal, and with 007's own great skill as a secret agent, how can Kristatos be found? Why, by talking parrot, of course! This in the movie that claims to be "back to basics."

At the end, there are Janet Brown and John Wells doing a broad, comedic imitation of the Thatchers at home. Of course, they are joined by the parrot, just to put all the bad jokes together on-screen. The whole thing is such an embarrassment, that if there was one scene (and only one) I could erase from Bond history, I would probably choose this one (although the "stainless steel delicatessen" would be a contender). It's a shame that Glen's attempt at a harder edged Bond was partly spoiled by his own propensity for silly jokes.

For Your Eyes Only has a lovely title song, with a haunting melody, and an innovative Maurice Binder title sequence. Unfortunately, we are without John Barry this time around, and Bill Conti's score ranges from unremarkable to really bad (I hate the pop scoring of the ski chase). Conti is a renowned film composer, and he later wrote a marvelous score for another Bond actor—the music in *The Thomas Crown Affair* remake, starring Pierce Brosnan, is excellent. But in *For Your Eyes Only* he is disappointing at best.

As I said, *For Your Eyes Only* is a very good film. My ranking of #16 isn't as low as it seems, after all, I can't put them all in my top ten! I just wish that John Glen had followed through on his promise of a harder-edged Bond without needing to resort to parrots and mimics.

High Points

- The pared-down plot.
- Magnificent use of locations in Corfu, Greece, Meteora, Greece, and Cortina, Italy
- The witty "detente" denouement with General Gogol.
- Melina's quest for revenge.
- Gonzales collapsing in the pool.
- Cassandra Harris as Countess Lisl.
- Bond visits Tracy's grave.
- Excellent ski photography by Willy Bogner.
- Fun, entertaining car chase.
- Topol's fun-loving, expansive portrayal of Columbo.
- The bait-and-switch villains.
- The death of Locque.
- Sheena Easton singing the title song during the title sequence.

Low Points

- John Hollis as a simpering, cackling Blofeld, and his very unsatisfying demise.
- Bibi Dahl.

- Max the parrot.
- The zamboni.
- Kreigler's inability to hit a large stationary target.
- Bill Conti's score.
- The horrible disco dancing and music at Gonzales's pool.
- The Thatcher imitators.

Quotable Quotes

Priest: "They're sending a helicopter to pick you up. Some sort of emergency."
Bond: "It usually is. Thank you."

"Man in Wheelchair:" "Mr. Bond! We can do a deal! I'll buy you a delicatessen. In stainless steel! Please!"

Bond to Melina (during car chase): "I love a drive in the country, don't you?"

Bond: "The Chinese have a saying; Before setting out on revenge, you first dig two graves."
Melina: "I don't expect you to understand, you're English. But I'm half Greek. And Greek women, like Elektra, always avenge their loved ones."

Bond (to Bibi): "You get your clothes on and I'll buy you an ice cream."

Kristatos: "The odds favor standing pat."
Bond: "If you play the odds."

Lisl: "Me nightie's slipping."
Bond: "So's your accent."

Bond (after Locque's death): "He had no head for heights."

Bond to Gogol: "That's detente comrade. You don't have it. I don't have it."

Facts and Figures

SEXUAL ENCOUNTERS

<u>Two</u>: Melina and Lisl.

BOND'S CARS

1981 Lotus Esprit Turbo (white with red stripe) (this car self-destructs)
Citroen 2CV (yellow) (this is Melina's car, featured in the chase through the olive groves),
1981 Lotus Esprit Turbo (copper)

DEATHS

Approximately fifty-six:

- On the St. Georges, an estimate of twenty.
- Blofeld's pilot, Blofeld, Mr. and Mrs. Havelock, Hector Gonzales, one of Gonzales's guards, the guy who smashed the Lotus's window, motorcyclist, Luigi Ferrara, Lisl, Claus, Locque, deep-sea diver who gets blown up, mini-sub pilot (with glasses), three of Melina's crew (killed off-screen, reported by Kristatos), Kristatos's man who becomes shark food, Karageorge, Kriegler, Kristatos.
- At the warehouse raid, ten plus approximately five when the warehouse explodes.

Bond Kills:

- Eight directly (Blofeld, the motorcyclist, one in the warehouse raid, Locque, the diver, the mini-sub pilot, Karageorge, Kriegler).
- Three indirectly (the Lotus explosion was set by Bond, Claus, the shark food guy was knocked into the water by Bond).

EXPLOSIONS

Five: The St. Georges, the Lotus (a real audience-pleaser), a grenade at the warehouse, the entire warehouse, which is terrific, made more exciting by the fact that you are led to believe that the previous, smaller explosion was 'it,' the deep-sea diver who gets a bomb stuck to his back.

BOND'S FOOD AND DRINKS

Vodka Martinis

None.

Other Drinks

- Glüwein (a mulled wine) at Cortina ice rink with Kristatos.
- At the casino restaurant, Bond orders ouzo as an apértif.
- At the same meal, Bond and Kristatos discuss their wine order: Kristatos suggests "A white Robola wine from Kefalonía, my home-place?" Bond replies, "Well, if you'll forgive me, I find that a little too scented for my palate. I prefer the Theotaki aspro." (A white wine produced in Corfu.)
- Bond and Lisl share a bottle of champagne.
- On his yacht, Columbo pours drinks from a decanter. It appears to be whiskey, although the Minister of Martinis suggests it might be Metaxa, a Greek brandy. After some discussion, they toast and drink.

Food

- Prawns, salad, and Bordetto at the casino with Kristatos
- Oysters with Lisl.

GAMBLING AND SPORTS

- Bond watches Bibi ice skate.

- Bond watches Kriegler compete in the biathalon (cross-country skiing and target shooting).
- Ski jumping (we watch jumps, then Bond and Claus fight on the ramp).
- Skiing (Bond and Bibi ski downhill, then Bond skis to escape Kriegler).
- Team bobsledding (Bond skis behind the bobsledders).
- Ice hockey (Bond is not on skates when attacked at the rink by the skaters).
- Bond deals chemin-de-fer in the casino; Kristatos says he will stay and play chemin-de-fer ("chemmy") while Bond leaves with Lisl.
- Melina plays roulette in the casino.
- Bibi trains on a trampoline.

Amaze Your Friends!

- Cassandra Harris and Pierce Brosnan were newlyweds at the time *For Your Eyes Only* was filmed. It was when then-unknown Pierce visited his wife on-set that he first caught Cubby Broccoli's eye as a potential Bond. Harris died of cancer in 1991 and never saw her husband play Bond.
- *For Your Eyes Only* is the directorial debut of John Glen, who would go on to direct five consecutive Bond films, more than any other director.
- This is the only Bond movie without M. Bernard Lee died as filming began. Rather than scramble to replace him hurriedly, and out of respect, M is "on leave" in *For Your Eyes Only*.
- The scene with Q and Bond in a confession booth was originally intended to be M and Bond, as seen in an August 12, 1980 draft of the script (thanks to HMSSWebLog for this tidbit).
- Bill Tanner is not addressed by name in the film, he is merely called "Chief of Staff," although he is credited as Tanner. The character of Bill Tanner, Chief of Staff, who appeared in several of the Fleming novels, would reappear in *GoldenEye* and *The World is Not Enough*, played (far more warmly) by Michael Kitchen. Rory Kinnear took over the role in *Quantum of Solace* through *No Time to Die*.
- Tracy's gravestone reads
  Teresa Bond 1943–1969
  Beloved wife of James Bond
  We have all the
  time in the World
- One of the "pool girls" at Gonzales's poolside is played by an actress known as Tula (real name: Caroline Cossey). After the film was released, it was revealed that Tula was transgender (assigned male at birth). Rumor today has it that a "Bond girl" was "really a man." The rumor is false, or at least exaggerated. Tula was an extra, not a Bond girl, and she wasn't "really" a man, she was really a woman who was formerly known as a man. Now you know.
- Minor henchman Charles Dance, who played Claus, was once considered for the role of James Bond.
- Max Vesterhalt, who has a non-speaking role (sitting next to Bond in the casino), was originally cast as another love interest for Bond. According to Vesterhalt, director John Glen preferred filming action to love scenes, and rewrote the role.

Most Interesting Goofs

Misplay: Bond's cards are wrong in the chemin-de-fer game; his second hand is seen twice in error. See CHEMIN-DE-FER.

Olive season: Olives are harvested in Madrid in December and January, when it is too cold to lounge by the pool in bikinis, as shown at Gonzales's home.

Three poles: One of Bond's ski poles is shot by Kriegler. He uses the second to kill the motorcyclist. After that, he has one ski pole.

HER MAJESTY'S SECRET SERVICE

MI6, a.k.a. the Secret Intelligence Service, SIS, Her Majesty's Secret Service.

What is MI6?

The British Secret Service is roughly equivalent to the American CIA, just as MI5 is roughly equivalent to the FBI—MI6 handles foreign concerns, and MI5 handles concerns domestic to the UK (meaning that MI6 should not have been investigating Gustav Graves, a British citizen operating on British soil, in *Die Another Day*).

MI6 is James Bond's home away from home, his employer for over fifty years now. Bond's "secrecy" varies widely, sometimes he's the most famous "secret" agent in the world, as when Hugo Drax says "your reputation precedes you." Really? That's not very secret. Of course, even Tiffany Case, a petty diamond smuggler, had heard of the famous James Bond! But on those occasions when he is undercover, he works for Universal Exports, Ltd., (see UNIVERSAL EXPORTS. LTD.).if only to have a business card to hand out when pretending to be looking for sharks (*Licence to Kill*).

The Head of MI6

M. Just M. No names, just initials, we're secret.

The original head of the real MI6, Sir Mansfield Cummings, was known by his initial, C. Later heads of the organization kept the initial as a title in his honor. Using real life as a model, Ian Fleming named his character Admiral Sir Miles Messervey, and gave him the initial M. (It is also said that Fleming called his mother M, but Freud was unavailable for comment.) Subsequent heads will then call themselves M, as we've seen with the character played by Dame Judi Dench; called Barbara Mawdsley in the novelizations of the films, but unnamed on-screen. In *Skyfall*, a prop names her Olivia Mansfield. This *might* have been visible on-screen (although it was not) and therefore can be treated as canon, overruling the novelization.

In *Skyfall*, Ralph Fiennes character is introduced as Gareth Mallory, so we don't know if M is retained as a title, or if it remains an initial.

Playing the Part

Bernard Lee

Lee gave us a gruff, businesslike M who was perhaps a little shy. Ian Fleming wrote of a Victorian M, with prudish attitudes towards sex and self-indulgence, one with stiff, unchanging, and rather dull tastes. In the novels, Bond worshiped M, but disdained his choice of food, wine, and entertainment. Bernard Lee very much played to the literary conception of M.

Lee's M was sometimes astonished by 007 (as in the conversation about brandy in *Goldfinger*) and sometimes embarrassed by him (listening to the tape in *From Russia with Love*), but he was also entirely confident in his best agent (utterly supporting his change of assignment in *Thunderball*). He was like a father to Bond, reigning him in, scolding him, raising his eyebrows at him, but very proud indeed.

Bernard Lee underplayed the role beautifully, delivering his best lines in a mutter, under his breath, as though he can scarce believe he actually has to say them.

BEST SCENE

Oh, there's a lot to choose from. Lee played M for eleven films, and he was always good. When we meet him in *Dr. No*, he wants to know when 007 sleeps. In *Goldfinger*, he is angry at Bond's screw-up, then later bemused.

But my favorite Bernard Lee scene is in *Diamonds Are Forever*, primarily because he goes through so much. He is obviously quite pleased with himself to be able to correct Bond; "There is no year for sherry, 007," and then disgruntled when he is proven wrong. He then shoots off two of his best lines, "Refreshing to hear there's one subject you're not an expert on" (in regard to diamonds), and then, when Bond asks if MI6 has gathered certain intelligence "We do function in your absence, Commander." Way to go, M!

Robert Brown

Having been introduced to the world of Eon Productions in *The Spy Who Loved Me* (see ENCORE! ENCORE!), Brown returned to fill the late Bernard Lee's shoes in *Octopussy*, and stayed for four films. Brown's M was somehow less likeable, a bit of a martinet. He performed the role well, but without real distinction, and none of his scenes have the snap of his predecessor's.

BEST SCENE

The pre-titles sequence of *The Living Daylights* shows us an M in his naval uniform, behind a desk on an aircraft. His little speech about the training exercise, plus the amusing incongruity of a desk in such a setting, and his ruffled feathers when his papers are blown about, is all very sharp stuff.

Edward Fox

Never Say Never Again gave us a replacement M who disdains the double-0 section; in some ways presaging *GoldenEye*, where the concept was better executed. This M is an angry man, a tin dictator, and self-absorbed to boot. The fact that he ignores an attempt on Bond's life is inexcusable to me.

BEST SCENE

Telling Bond "do come along" when Bond comes up with the false eye idea.

Judi Dench

After a six-year hiatus between Bond films, a very significant six years historically, it was time to rethink the Bond franchise, and one of the things that needed rethinking was the role of M. With the Cold War over, the world was focused less on espionage, and the idea of putting a "bean counter" in the soundproof office was apt. Stella Rimmington was currently the first female head of MI5, inspiring the idea that a woman could be the head of MI6 in Bond's world (although Rimmington had retired by the time *GoldenEye* was released).

Dame Judi Dench was a great choice, a dignified, powerful actress with a steely voice who, by the time of *GoldenEye*, had already been nominated for twelve BAFTA (British Academy of Film and Television Arts) awards, of which she won six. She has since received thirteen more BAFTA nominations, four of which were winners. She probably first gained widespread U.S. attention in *GoldenEye*, and has since been nominated for four Academy Awards and brought home one Oscar.

Dame Judi created an M who is tough and intelligent. She is far more verbal than her predecessors, and snaps out some of the best dialogue of the series. From calling Bond a misogynist dinosaur, to telling an Admiral he thinks with his balls, it's great to have the medium of film to eavesdrop on what she says, because if she was talking straight to you, you'd be too busy ducking for cover.

THE STRANGE CONTROVERSY OF JUDI DENCH'S M(S)

There is a very credible theory that Judi Dench in the Brosnan movies and Judi Dench in the Craig movies are two different characters, both played by the same actor (see "I HAVEN'T SEEN YOU IN SIX MONTHS!") For the sake of my own sanity, I am here treating "Judi Dench's M" as a single character. However, since the series was rebooted, we can understand M as the same person and still understand her relationship with the two Bonds she played opposite quite differently.

While the Brosnan-Dench relationship was often a struggle of wills, the Craig-Dench relationship was that of a mentor with her protégé. When Craig's Bond jokes in *Quantum of Solace* that she thinks she's his mother, we understood how two-way that feeling was, justifying the end of *Skyfall*.

BEST SCENE

I always enjoy watching Dame Judi, especially in a Bond movie. She never had a bad scene for Eon, although I didn't relish seeing her "vulnerable" side as a kidnap victim in *The World is Not Enough*. Still, there's lots to choose from, from the aforementioned *Tomorrow Never Dies* scene ("What's your man doing?" "His job!") to a later scene in the same movie when she tells 007 to "pump" a former girlfriend. Good heavens, Bernard Lee would never have said that! Still, I have to go with her first on-screen meeting with Bond, a rapid-fire lobby of dialogue that I find riveting no matter how often I hear the opening "You don't like me, Bond." The scene establishes the character, the relationship, and the challenges each will face; challenges not unlike the themes of the movie as a whole.

Ralph Fiennes

Gareth Mallory is the first person we see *become* M. We meet him as the Chairman of the Intelligence and Security Committee, overseeing MI6 and serving as a liaison between MI6 and Parliament, he assumes the job of M following the death of his predecessor.

A former Lieutenant Colonel in the SAS (Special Air Service), Mallory served in Northern Ireland, where he was captured and held hostage, belying Bond's initial impression of him as a desk jockey.

Mallory is the roughest and earthiest M we have experienced, the one who tells Bond not to "cock it up," the one who lets the idea of what "C stands for" hang tantalizingly in the air before saying "careless." He is not uncomfortable with action, was wounded in *Skyfall* without losing a step, and understands the nitty-gritty of the job. His people are fiercely loyal, even if he does forget their birthdays.

BEST SCENE

Fiennes has been solid and enjoyable in his two (thus far) movies. The final scene of *Skyfall*, where the two men gently, and without words, acknowledge all that has come before, with Bond calling Mallory "M" for the first time, may never be topped.

Who is the Best M?

This is one of those perennial fan questions, since Bond fans just love to rate, assess, and rank, but I almost hate to include it here. Edward Fox is easy to dismiss, and Robert Brown almost as easy, but Dench and Lee are both powerhouses, and I am reluctant to rate one above the other. Fan voices divide mostly along age lines, with older fans and traditionalists favoring Lee, and younger fans favoring Dench. To put it another way, if your favorite Bond is Connery, your favorite M is probably Lee, and if you prefer Brosnan, you probably prefer Dench.

In the end, both fan surveys and my vote go to Bernard Lee, who gave us Ian Fleming's formal, resourceful, matter-of-fact father figure.

And now, of course, Fiennes has to be factored in. But I'll still vote for Bernard Lee.

Who Else Works There?

M has a secretary named Moneypenny (see below), a Chief of Staff named Bill Tanner, and, for three movies (*Tomorrow Never Dies*, *The World is Not Enough*, and *Die Another Day*) a Deputy Chief of Staff named Charles Robinson. In *Casino Royale*, she has an assistant named Villiers.

There are additional members of the clerical staff, for example, the people seen taking notes in the background of the 00 meeting in *Thunderball* (more on that shortly).

Q Branch (called Q Division in *The World is Not Enough*) is the Special Ordinance Section. It is headed by the Quartermaster, known as Q, and is populated by a variety of technicians and people who get trapped in couches and telephone booths. Q also consults with a number of experts, such as Colthorpe, the ballistics expert seen in *The Man with the Golden Gun*.

Specialists are employed by MI6 as a whole as well:

- Jim Fanning, antiquities expert, *Octopussy*,
- Sir Godfrey Tibbett, horse trainer, *A View to a Kill*.

In *Dr. No* we also saw a fairly large staff of radio operators who kept in communication with the foreign "stations"(see below). Not having visited that part of the offices since the first movie, we don't know how operations and staffing there have changed with technological advances.

In *Casino Royale*, we see the "hot room," with doctors and technicians on-call attempting to save 007 in the field.

Moneypenny

M's secretary has always been Miss Moneypenny. Until *Skyfall*, she had never been given a first name, in either the films or the novels; although Bond has called her "Penny" (in *You Only Live Twice*). This appeared to be a nickname based on the surname. In *Skyfall,* the character of "Eve" is introduced, and only revealed to be Eve Moneypenny at the end of the film. Here, we learn she is a field agent who gave up working in the field, preferring the office, and went to work for M. This backstory is, of course, a product of the 21st century, and not a part of the character's biography as previously known.

Eon toyed with replacing the character, which is why Miss Penelope Smallbone was introduced in *Octopussy*. Giving Moneypenny an assistant was like giving Q an assistant in *The World is Not Enough*; a way of preparing the audience for the original actor's eventual retirement (of course, no one anticipated Desmond Llewelyn's tragic death; John Cleese was meant to stay in the assistant's shoes indefinitely). Miss Smallbone was meant to stay on as Moneypenny's assistant, and then be the sole secretary after Lois Maxwell retired, but for whatever reason, she only appeared once. Probably, audiences didn't want anyone but Moneypenny in that office, and so they got their wish.

Moneypenny did not appear in *Casino Royale* or *Quantum of Solace*, but was reintroduced in *Skyfall* and has been in each movie since.

Playing the Part

Moneypenny seems to exist in the same Eternal Now as James Bond. While both M and Q age and depart, Moneypenny remains approximately the same age as 007, and remains his match. After Lois Maxwell's tenure, it seems to have become part of the franchise for each Bond actor to have "his" Moneypenny actress, at least so far. Caroline Bliss matched only with Timothy Dalton, and Samantha Bond felt it was appropriate to depart the series when Pierce Brosnan did (and said so even before it was announced that the character of Moneypenny would not appear in Daniel

Craig's first James Bond film). There is a certain advantage to this; it creates a sort of permanent tension between the non-couple couple, and allows each pair to have its own chemistry. For that reason, instead of simply looking at Moneypenny actresses, we'll explore acting couples.

Lois Maxwell and Sean Connery

Lois Maxwell has said that she and Connery decided to give their characters a back story to make them more interesting. The story they came up with was that Bond and Moneypenny had once had a weekend fling, had feelings for each other, and realized that one or both would lose their careers if they continued, so they agreed it would end with the weekend. This subtext permeates their relationship; sometimes Bond hotly pursues his "Penny," and sometimes she seeks more attention than she gets. There is mutual attraction, and mutual pulling back, and it is often very sexy indeed.

Sometimes Moneypenny longs for Bond (*Goldfinger*, *Diamonds Are Forever*) and sometimes it is Bond who seems to be the desirous one (*Dr. No*) but they always retain a knowing quality towards each other. In this relationship, Moneypenny says she wants a ring, a gift, a proposal, and Bond says he wants sex, loyalty, or trust, but both know they have exactly what they really want, and they are equals.

BEST SCENE

I think the establishing scene between these two remains their best. In *Dr. No*, they are cuddly and warm; very much like people with a mutual relationship hovering on the brink of something. Moneypenny looks very fetching in her black sheath, and Bond, humming to her while he half-dances with her, is far more intimate than we might expect. *Dr. No* is also the movie that introduces Bond's famous hat toss.

Lois Maxwell and George Lazenby

Bond is courtly towards Moneypenny, flirting broadly while still distinctly indicating that she is of a prior generation (he is twelve years her junior). Director Peter Hunt makes Lois Maxwell as glamorous and attractive as possible, and indeed she looks stunning, but not enough to mask the rather jarring shift in the Bond/Moneypenny relationship.

BEST SCENE

Who didn't mist up a bit when Bond tossed Moneypenny his hat at the wedding? A perfect moment.

Lois Maxwell and Roger Moore

In this version, Moneypenny and Bond have a pairing that has warmth, affection, and a lot of back-and-forth. They lack the sensuality of the Maxwell/Connery version, but make up for it with humor and a real sense of connection. There are times when I feel this relationship can be a bit too short-tempered on Moneypenny's part, and too dismissive on Bond's part. But there are other times when she is entirely supportive of him, and he entirely appreciative of her.

Unfortunately, although they are the same age (both born in 1927), in many of their movies, Maxwell looked considerably older than Moore. By *Octopussy*, this had straightened out, and for their last two movies together, they looked like two middle-aged people who had been flirting for many years (which is what they were). In earlier movies, though, Moore's preternatural youth made the relationship sometimes appear as unbalanced as that with Lazenby, with an older woman chasing a more attractive and (apparently) younger man.

BEST SCENE

For some of the best interplay between any Bond and Moneypenny, look to an unexpected source: *The Man with the Golden Gun*. It is witty, well-written, and in a single scene, the pair play out most of the permutations of their relation- ship. Consider:

- Bond enters with "Fairbanks," and Moneypenny immediately responds "Alaska," a quick show of wit and repartee that always makes me smile.
- Bond asks about Bill Fairbanks, and Moneypenny becomes wistful and sad ("Oh, poor Bill, I miss him"); a brief turn of sentiment, nicely done.
- This segues into a typical Bond/Moneypenny flirtation ("Moneypenny, you're better than a computer"/"In all sorts of ways"), delivered again with wit and a sense of play.
- As Bond is departing, he has another question and says "Just one moment darling." Here we see the stereotypical fawning Moneypenny, when called "darling," her entire demeanor changes in an instant; she fairly melts.
- But when it turns out that he has another official question, she becomes snippy and angry.

I love this scene for the many changes and turns outlined above, it is everything that Bond and Moneypenny are to each other in a nutshell. If Moneypenny weren't wearing the ugliest, busiest blouse ever designed, it would be absolute perfection.

Pamela Salem and Sean Connery

Poor Pamela Salem, hired for *Never Say Never Again* essentially to imitate Lois Maxwell! She never stood a chance of distinguishing herself in the role; had only one scene, and in it, was made a fool by Bond's teasing ("eliminate all free radicals" indeed!).

Caroline Bliss and Timothy Dalton

Although I'm an unabashed fan of Dalton, I must say that Caroline Bliss was the worst part of the Dalton movies, and I was delighted to see her go. Bliss loaded herself up with the big glasses and bun in her hair that Maxwell had wisely avoided. A pretty woman, she did and said everything imaginable to make herself a geek. Because of her awkwardness, her mooniness, and her tastelessness, we side with Bond when he avoids her advances. An unpleasant relationship.

BEST SCENE

I liked when Moneypenny was reviewing the photographic files of female KGB assassins in *The Living Daylights*. Although this launches into the hideous Barry Manilow conversation, while she is doing her job and showing us exactly why M values her, she is fine.

Samantha Bond and Pierce Brosnan

This is a brand new take on the Moneypenny/Bond relationship. Here Moneypenny is desired by Bond, and perpetually puts him off, hovering on insulting him while still engaging his attention ("As far as I know, James, you've never had me.") Of course she desires James, and makes her engagement ring jokes, but this Moneypenny, with a social life and an attitude, has significant power in the relationship. The flirting is mostly one-sided, with Bond doing the offering and Moneypenny doing the saying no, but Bond flirts in a way that may or may not be serious, and Moneypenny says no in a way that begs him to ask again. For my money, this is the best Moneypenny/Bond relationship since Connery's departure.

BEST SCENE

I am tempted to cite *GoldenEye*, as I did for Judi Dench, it is a witty and charming scene, and the "sexual harassment" repartee is excellent. However, I must vote for the surprise ending of *Die Another Day*, one of the best uses of virtual reality I've ever seen!

Naomie Harris and Daniel Craig

It seems to me that this is the explicit relationship that was implicit between Connery and Maxwell—basically, what happens in Macau stays in Macau.

It's tricky to pinpoint when this becomes "Bond and Moneypenny." In *Skyfall*, Naomie Harris is introduced as another field agent—Eve, although her name isn't given—and the movie's apparent "Bond girl." Only at the very end does she hang her coat on the famous coatrack (there are no hats on it, but there is space for them), and introduce herself. Bond calls her "Miss Moneypenny" or "Moneypenny" from then on.

So, is it at that moment that we should start thinking of her as Moneypenny, whereas before she was Eve, a Bond girl? Or is she herself throughout? Obviously, this is an insane question.

BEST SCENE

Since that *is* insane, the obvious best scene is when Eve shaves Bond. Sexy, enticing, intimate, I love everything about it, and of course, as filmed by Roger Deakins, it looks gorgeous.

Agents

Besides the staff above, there are the field agents. The elite among field agents are the double-0's, licensed to kill, but there appear to be many more agents than these. Some field agents are assigned to foreign stations and some are not. Miranda Frost, for example, was a field agent who professed great distaste for double-0's, and worked out of the London headquarters. Of course, she also slept with and betrayed a double-0, but that's another story.

00 Agents

How many double-0 agents are there, and who are they? We are never quite certain of this. In *Thunderball*, at a meeting of what Moneypenny says is "every double-0 man in Europe," we see nine chairs, and Bond sits in the seventh. This seems to indicate that they sit in code-number order, otherwise, it is a rather odd seat to save for a latecomer. *Thunderball* was a long time ago, and you'd think the staff might have increased. But we have never heard of any 00 agent with a double-digit number in the movies, although Ian Fleming wrote about a 0011 in **Moonraker**.

Nine seems to be the right figure. In **Moonraker**, Fleming indicates that the 00 prefix is added to whatever number you already had—Bond was number 7 before he became 007. Hence, the double-0 agents weren't in any kind of order. But the films treat it differently. The seating in *Thunderball* hints that there are nine licenses to kill, and that they were assigned in some kind of sequence. This is borne out by the fact that when 00s are replaced, old numbers are reassigned (at least in the cases of 002 and 009—see below).

If there are indeed nine 00 agents at any given time, we have met or heard of only seven. Neither 001 nor 005 has ever been seen or mentioned in a James Bond movie. Of the remainder:

- **002** The first 002 was Bill Fairbanks, killed in Beirut by Francisco Scaramanga (*The Man with the Golden Gun*). A later 002 was killed in the Gibraltar training exercises by one of Koskov's assassins (*The Living Daylights*).
- **003** Killed in Siberia; the microchip he was carrying was retrieved by Bond from his body (*A View to a Kill*).
- **004** Killed in the Gibraltar training exercises by one of Koskov's assassins (*The Living Daylights*).
- **006** Alec Trevelyan, killed by Bond after becoming the criminal Janus (*GoldenEye*).
- **007** Commander James Bond.
- **008** Never seen on screen, but mentioned in two movies. M threatens to replace Bond with 008 in *Goldfinger*. Later, Bond tells Goldfinger that if he is killed, 008 will be sent to replace him. In *The Living Daylights*, M again threatens to replace Bond with the more obedient 008.
- **009** The first 009 was killed in full clown regalia (how embarrassing!) by Mischka and Grischka, the knife-throwing circus performers (*Octopussy*). A later 009 managed to shoot the terrorist Renard in the head, but did not kill him (*The World is Not Enough*). In *Spectre*, Bond's DB10 is meant for 009, and his taste in music is not to Bond's liking.

The Foreign Stations

The naming of foreign offices by MI6 is remarkably inconsistent. Usually they have a single initial, but not always. Usually the single letter is the initial of the country in which the station is located, but not always. In one case, Station VH (see below), there is no rhyme or reason at all behind the initials that I have been able to discover. The letters "VH" stand for no city, country, or geographic region in Brazil, in English, Spanish, or Portuguese. One of my Brazilian friends suggests it may be slang for "very hot".

Figure 14: The inside front cover of the Thunderball *program, showing the meeting of "every 00 man in Europe."*

Just to further confuse the issue, the foreign stations in the films are not consistent with the foreign stations in the novels. In the books **Live and Let Die** and **Dr. No**, Bond's Jamaican contact is via Station C (Caribbean), but as you'll see below, packing beachwear for Station C in the films will yield less satisfactory results.

So, here are the foreign stations mentioned in the films, in chronological order:

- Station T (Turkey): Headed by Kerim Bey until his death. *From Russia with Love*
- Station Y (Yugoslavia): Captain Nash was affiliated with it until his death. *From Russia with Love*
- Station C (Canada): Mentioned by M, no agents mentioned. *Thunderball*
- Station VH (Rio de Janeiro): Manuela worked there. *Moonraker*
- Station I (India): Headed by Sadruddin. *Octopussy*
- Station V (Vienna): Headed by Saunders until his death. *The Living Daylights*
- Station H (Hong Kong): Formerly headed by M when Silva was an agent (1986–1997). *Skyfall*.

MI6 AROUND THE WORLD

O n occasion, MI6 has set up offices in field locations.

Thunderball

Where? In Nassau.

Who? Q, setting up a field office.

You Only Live Twice

Where? On a submarine that was, at least temporarily, off Japan.

Who? M and Moneypenny and various aides.

Where? In Japan, in Tiger's headquarters.

Who? Q, setting up a field office to assemble Little Nellie

Diamonds Are Forever

Where? At the Customs Office en route to Holland via hovercraft.

Who? Moneypenny.

The Man with the Golden Gun

Where? Inside the sunken Queen Elizabeth, in the waters between Hong Kong and Macau (between the Chinese and the American fleet).

Who? M and Moneypenny and various aides.

The Spy Who Loved Me

Where? Inside an Egyptian pyramid.

Who? Full offices; M, Moneypenny, and Q Branch.

Where? Sardinia.

Who? Q, delivering the car.

Moonraker

Where? In a monastery somewhere near Rio de Janeiro

Who? Full offices; M, Moneypenny, and Q Branch.

For Your Eyes Only
Where? A Greek church.

Who? Q, conveying information—no gadgets or lab.

Octopussy
Where? India, in a building that seems like an old palace.

Who? Q Branch.

The Living Daylights
Where? An airplane over Gibraltar.

Who? M, complete with desk.

Licence to Kill
Where? Hemingway House, Key West, Florida

Who? M and staff

Tomorrow Never Dies
Where? An airport in Germany.

Who? Q, delivering the car and gadgets.

The World is Not Enough
Where? In a Scottish castle after MI6 offices are destroyed.

Who? Full offices; M, Moneypenny, and Q Branch.

Die Another Day
Where? A ship in the waters off of Hong Kong (the same one as in *The Man with the Golden Gun*? If so, it has been straightened out).

Who? M and medical staff.

Where? An abandoned London Underground station.

Who? M, without her office, and Q, with a full lab.

Casino Royale
Where? Dimitrios's home in the Bahamas.

Who? M, Villiers, and a doctor with a portable kit.

Skyfall

Where? Emergency offices underground in London after MI6 offices are destroyed.

Who? Full offices; M, Tanner, and Q Branch.

Spectre

Where? A safe house in London at "Hildebrand."

Who? M with Moneypenny and Q (only M goes in).

OCTOPUSSY (1983)

Survey Says!

> Percent Favorite: 0%
> Top 5 Cumulative: 15/25 (tied)
> Numeric Rating: 5.67/10
> Ranking: 13.5 (16th/25)

My Rating and Ranking

> Rated: 7/10
> Ranked: 15 out of 25

Summary

Bond is investigating the death of 009, and following the trail of a forged Faberge egg. The complex plot involves a conspiracy between exiled prince Kamal Khan and renegade Soviet General Orlov. In exchange for the crown jewels of Russia, Khan will use Octopussy's circus to smuggle a nuclear bomb into West Germany. Bond finds an ally in Octopussy herself, who owes him a debt of gratitude, and with her help, he defuses the bomb at the final moment.

> **James Bond:** Roger Moore
> **Octopussy:** Maud Adams
> **Kamal Khan:** Louis Jordan
> **General Orlov:** Steven Berkoff
> **Magda:** Kristina Wayborn
> **Gobinda:** Kabir Bedi
> **Vijay:** Vijay Armritraj
> **General Gogol:** Walter Gotell
> **M:** Robert Brown
> **Moneypenny:** Lois Maxwell
> **Q:** Desmond Llewelyn
> **Directed by** John Glen

Discussion

Here we have a nice, mid-level Bond movie, neither a startling work of genius nor an embarrassment to the genre. *Octopussy* is a good deal of fun, although it is also a disappointment on a number of levels. *Octopussy* has the veneer of a real espionage movie, but is, at heart, a collection of set pieces and illogic. It has more spectacle than action, although much of the spectacle is surely a pleasure. The movie boasts a fairly terrific cast of interesting characters, and a certain freshness of approach.

The plot should be disposed of quickly, because as my kid says, "Who cares about plot in a James Bond movie?" *Octopussy*'s plot is a labyrinthine tangle of cross-purposes, switches, and who-knows-what. Interpretations of certain actions (why does Orlov crush the egg?) have been in active dispute among fans for twenty years.

As a spy movie, *Octopussy* fails simply because screamingly obvious clues are overlooked. I dunno, if I found a spy who had been killed by a throwing knife while dressed in a clown suit, I'd immediately wonder about the presence of a circus in the vicinity, especially one that had knife-throwers. I find it absolutely astonishing that M can hand Bond a photograph of 009's body in full clown regalia, and they can both agree they have no clues beyond the Faberge egg. Isn't this the kind of movie moment where you want to scold the folks on-screen?

But heck, that's just the plot, which you probably can't follow anyway, so it's no big deal. *Octopussy* excels at the set piece, at disconnected scenes that don't form a terrific narrative, but stand on their own as thoroughly enjoyable. It's fitting, then, that the movie has a stand-alone pre-titles sequence sequence, in the fashion of *Goldfinger*. It is very nicely done, using the Acrostar—the world's smallest airplane—and a mini-adventure involving a Cuban air base, a horse show, and a beautiful woman. The stunt flying is great, and the sequence ends with a satisfying boom.

Figure 15: Another Chiller Theater acquisition—Maud Adams's autograph on my Octopussy *DVD.*

The use of the circus is terrific. I love the knife-throwing twins, the visual spectacle, the acrobats, and of course, Francisco the Fearless. Some fans find the raid on Kamal Khan's stronghold implausible and silly, but I find it clever and immensely entertaining. There's a wonderful "Aha" moment, when we realize, "Hey, they have acrobats; I bet that will help." Trains and trailers fit in well with the circus theme. I liked Bond hiding in a sea of trailers, and the run across the top of the train cars is very exciting. Unfortunately, it cannot help but remind the audience that a more popular and respected James Bond, Sean Connery, did the same thing four years earlier, in the 1979 movie *The First Great Train Robbery* (released in the U.S. under the name *The Great Train Robbery*). In fact, that Michael Crichton movie topped *Octopussy* in that Connery did much of the train stunt work himself.

The movie offers some really interesting characters. You would think that Mad Soviet General would have been a cliché by the thirteenth entry in a spy series, but in fact, it's untouched ground. Bond's early years were spent battling SPECTRE; real Cold War issues were not addressed. Orlov is a new kind of Bond villain, wonderfully overacted by Steven Berkoff, with a certain fascinating way of twisting his body in his mania. He is the sort of villain who believes he is really the good guy, but in the meantime, he's as crazy as a bag of rats.

Orlov is attention-grabbing and has compelling motivation, but he is an accomplice; the real villain, the one who doesn't buy it until the final reel, is Kamal Khan. Louis Jordan is perhaps unpersuasive as an Afghan prince, but he gives a richly mannered performance as a spoiled brat who will sacrifice anyone for wealth and power. Few moments of villainy are as funny and depraved as Khan ordering the loyal Gobinda onto the roof of the plane to get Bond. Gobinda himself is a fine henchman in the Oddjob/Jaws mold—largely silent and silently large.

Next we have Octopussy, the smart smuggler with the dumb nickname. Maud Adams clearly grew as an actress in the nine years since she'd played Andrea Anders in *The Man with the Golden Gun*. She brings strength and self-possession to the role, and a genuine chemistry with Roger Moore. For once, we see a plausible seduction, one with a passionate basis beyond the simple fact that every woman must sleep with James Bond. Like Countess Lisl, Octopussy comes across as equal to Bond, and a good match for him; and their scenes have real warmth.

Rounding out the cast are Vijay, an amiable ally, and Magda, a cipher; beautiful and ambiguous. On the one hand, she is willing to keep photographic souvenirs of the men she coldly sleeps with, presumably knowing they are doomed; on the other hand, she is equally cold about watching such a man escape and doing nothing. She changes sides in the end, but out of loyalty to Octopussy, rather than any obvious goodness of spirit.

At MI6 we have Robert Brown newly occupying the role of M; a serviceable enough performance (but no match for the late Bernard Lee's mastery), and Jim Fanning, a nicely sketched art expert played by Douglas Wilmer. A good cast is a crucial component of any movie, and almost everyone this time out is on the ball.

Two scenes are notable for well-developed tension. The "Den of Thieves" scene is nice; I like the one-eyed villain, and the yo-yo saw blade. The oeuvre probably constitutes a cliché, but a well-delivered one. The other tense scene is the opening of the film (post-titles)—the chase of a clown through a dark and mysterious woods. Unfortunately, once we learn that this clown was a double-0 agent, we are less impressed. His fearful reactions, his inability to stay unheard, and the frequent looking back over his shoulder in terror, might make for an interesting scene but are lousy behavior for a spy.

But Bond's spying is weak as well, from his initial failure to connect Octopussy's circus to 009's death (he catches on when he finds a handbill) to his botched interrogation of Orlov. His dressing as a clown has been mocked by fans many times, not merely because of the statement about Bond that it makes, but because doing the face makeup takes at least thirty minutes—believe me, I've done it.

Despite *Octopussy*'s many good points, it is clear that the silliness in evidence in Moore's previous outings (the clownishness, if you will) has not gone away. Probably the most outlandish behavior occurs during the hunt sequence, a rather dumb set piece to begin with, made worse by Bond telling a tiger to "Sit!" and then committing the Tarzan yell sin. The Tarzan yell offends fans not because it's a dumb joke (of which we enjoy plenty) but because it's self-referential. It says "Hey, this is just a movie" as surely as breaking the fourth wall does. *Octopussy* is also the movie in which 007 recognizes his own theme song (played by Vijay), which is as good as saying, "Don't absorb yourself in this movie, it isn't real." Well, we know it isn't real, but absorption in a fantasy world is part of the point. In a movie with this sort of foolery, outrageous stunts like hanging onto the outside of a plane lose all hint of credibility.

The attitude towards Indian culture in *Octopussy* strikes me as insulting, wallowing in clichés with no appreciation for the richness of the country. Ask anyone in the West what they know of India and they'll say "bed of nails, snake charmers, fire walkers." Those old saws about Indian culture have no foreignness to them—they don't transcend what you already know. Bond's far-flung locations need to show us something beyond the common knowledge. There's no India in *Octopussy* that you can't find in a Bugs Bunny cartoon.

The street scenes in *Octopussy* were done in the studio, and it shows. This isn't what a real Indian street looks like. I cannot help again comparing this to a Sean Connery movie, the classic *The Man Who Would Be King*, in which a few short scenes on the streets of India weave a cultural tapestry that lasts in the imagination. Most of the location footage of India in *Octopussy* is scenery, or the inside of luxurious buildings. Director John Glen's commitment to commonplace notions of India was so intense that he added footage of the Taj Mahal, in Agra, to a scene taking place about four hundred miles away in Udaipur.

Compare *Octopussy*'s locations to *For Your Eyes Only*'s. In the latter, there's a real Greek market with local people, while Bond and Melina sample local food; one gets a sense of place. If *Octopussy*'s style of "exoticism" had been used in *For Your Eyes Only*, we'd see location footage of the Parthenon, and studio shots of some Greeks smashing glasses and a gymnasium.

This kind of careless sketch is demeaning to the culture so dismissed. India is an ancient and complex place, here reduced to an unimaginative travel brochure. Bond stays in a Western-style hotel, and most of the beautiful women in saris are white. Compare this to *From Russia with Love*; in Istanbul Bond stays in a room that is clearly Turkish, and orders a Turkish breakfast.

Octopussy has some nice set design, with perhaps fewer interesting sets than the average Ken Adam affair, but two memorable ones: The Soviet meeting room at the Kremlin, with all the glitz of an Adam set, including moving furniture and animated wall maps, and Octopussy's bedroom, featuring the best bed ever slept in by a human being (with the possible exception of the *Diamonds Are Forever* aquarium waterbed). Fittingly, the Soviet meeting scene and Bond's love scene with Octopussy are both top-notch.

The title sequence is neither great nor poor, and is accompanied by a decent song, if not a memorable or meaningful one. At one point, I called "All Time High" "very mediocre." Yes, I know that's oxymoronic, but it's apt, don't you think?

High Points

- Mad General Orlov, as portrayed by Steven Berkoff.
- Fun self-contained pre-titles sequence.
- Strong visual appeal in the luxurious palaces of Octopussy and Khan, and in the circus.
- Mischka and Grischka, the evil knife-throwing twins.
- The auction at Sotheby's.
- Strong female lead with a good romantic connection to Bond and a hot seduction scene.
- Exciting fight with the yo-yo guy in Octopussy's bedroom.
- Acrobatic break-in to the Monsoon Palace.
- Vijay Armritraj and his ever-ready smile.
- Magda's clever escape from Bond's room, and Bond cleverly allowing her to steal the egg.
- Exciting train sequence.

Low Points

- Bond using a gadget to ogle an MI6 employee's cleavage.
- The Tarzan yell.
- "Sit!"
- Double-taking camel.
- Studio footage instead of good location work in India.
- Almost no action without some sort of gimmick present.
- Cliché-ridden, silly chase sequence through streets of Delhi.
- Incomprehensible plot with large, gaping holes.
- Bond's clown makeup.

Quotable Quotes

Bond: "Toro? Sounds like a load of bull."

Bond: "Vijay, we have company."
Vijay: "No problem, this is a company car."

(Q's climbing rope falls over)
Bond: "Having trouble keeping it up, Q?"

Magda: "I need refilling."

Kamal Khan: "Mr. Bond is indeed a very rare breed. Soon to be made extinct."

Kamal Khan: "You have a nasty habit of surviving."
Bond: "You know what they say about the fittest."

Facts and Figures

SEXUAL ENCOUNTERS

Three: Bianca (implied), Magda, and Octopussy.

BOND'S CAR

None. He steals an Alfa Romeo GTV to reach Octopussy's circus.

DEATHS

Approximately forty:
- During the pre-titles sequence, in the hangar that blows up, approximately twenty.
- 009, the two men on hooks whose bodies Bond hides with, Vijay, three assassins who attack Octopussy (yo-yo, one-eye, and another), three of Orlov's guard, Mischka and Grischka, Orlov, four of Kamal Khan's men during the raid, Gobinda, Khan.

Bond Kills:
- Nine directly (One of the assassins, Orlov's three guards, four at Kamal Khan's, Gobinda).
- Two indirectly (Bond knocked one assassin into the octopus tank, Khan died when his plane crashed).

EXPLOSIONS

Two: The airplane hangar in the pre-titles sequence, and Kamal Khan's plane at the very end.

BOND'S FOOD AND DRINKS

Vodka Martinis

One, served by Octopussy when she first meets Bond. The drink is never mentioned by name, but all the ingredients are present and she shakes, not stirs.

Other Drinks
- Champagne in an ice bucket awaits Bond when he arrives in his hotel room in Delhi.
- Bond and Magda drink champagne when they meet at the hotel (when his picture is taken).

- Bond and Magda drink champagne in bed together; they finish an entire bottle.
- Kamal Khan serves champagne with dinner when Bond is held prisoner.
- The German couple who give Bond a ride part-way to the circus offer Bond a beer (he declines).

Food

- At dinner with Kamal Khan, soufflé and stuffed sheep's head on saffron rice; a fruit bowl is on the table.
- In Octopussy's bedroom, another fruit bowl is visible; the saw blade yo-yo slices a pineapple.
- The German couple who give Bond a ride offer him wurst and strudel, again he declines.

GAMBLING AND SPORTS

- Bond plays backgammon against Kamal Khan.

  Note that this scene is a replica of the golf scene in *Goldfinger*. Bond catches the villain cheating a wealthy man (as Bond catches Goldfinger cheating at gin rummy). Bond challenges the villain in a "friendly" match, and then offers the villain a particularly valuable prize, something connected to his villainy, as a stake (in *Goldfinger* a gold bar, in *Octopussy*, the Faberge egg). Once Bond defeats the villain at the game, their enmity is clear and they no longer pretend to be cordial. This same scene will be played out again in *Die Another Day*, this time with fencing and a diamond as the stake.

- Kamal Khan uses a traditional Indian hunt to pursue Bond.
- Vijay mentions that Khan is quite a sportsman, and that he plays polo, cricket, and tennis.
- Vijay, played by a real life tennis star, also mentions that he is a tennis pro at Khan's club. Vijay then uses his tennis racket during the chase scene, and the crowd watching the chase emulates a tennis audience.

Amaze Your Friends!

- This is the first film to feature Robert Brown in the role of M. He will play the role a total of four times.
- Stuntman Martin Grace broke his pelvis while hanging off the outside of the moving train. After extensive hospitalization and rehabilitation, he was back for the next film.
- Maud Adams has a nude scene in the film, although without DVD or Blu-Ray technology, it is hard to spot. When Bond first arrives at Octopussy's floating palace, he spies a woman coming out of the pool; she is fully nude, seen only from the rear. Another woman wraps her in a towel, she walks a few paces away, and someone takes her towel and helps her into her octopus robe. While putting on the robe, she turns to the side, and some frontal nudity is visible.
- "All Time High" was the first Bond "title" song in which the title is never used. (The title song "On Her Majesty's Secret Service" is an instrumental,

but the title is used as its name.) Daniel Craig title songs have changed the tradition somewhat: Of his five movies, only two title songs —"Skyfall" and "No Time to Die"—use the film title. ("Another Way to Die" uses the word "solace" but not the entire film title.)

- Closing credits indicate that James Bond Will Return in From a View to a Kill. "From a View to a Kill" is the name of the original Ian Fleming short story, but as we all know, that title was shortened prior to the movie's release.

Most Interesting Goofs

Operation Trove: Perhaps this is a plot hole and not a goof, but what was 009's mission? Bond is assigned to "pick up" Operation Trove following his colleague's death, but in fact, everything that Bond does follows up on new information discovered after his death.

Not So Sharp: Towards the end of Bond's fight with Gobinda on the top of the train, just before they pass under an overpass, Gobinda swings at Bond and hits the top of the train, and his "sword" bends nearly 90 degrees from the impact.

Safety First: When Gobinda falls off the top of the plane at the end of the film, his jacket falls open and the stuntman's parachute is clearly visible.

THE "OH, JAMES" MOMENT

The closing scene of a Bond movie tends to follow a rather specific pattern. The scene is our cue that evil is vanquished and all is right with the world.

In a way, it's like comfort food; the familiar pattern of the final scene lets us know that it's okay for the movie to end.

The pattern is:

- Bond and the girl are on or near water
- Bond eschews rescue to remain with the girl
- M and Q catch Bond in *flagrante delicto*
- The girl says "Oh, James" (giving the scene, and this section, their name), or there is a double entendre, or both.

When movies deviate broadly from this pattern, we do *not* know that all is right with the world. *On Her Majesty's Secret Service* ends in purposeful violation of the norm, giving us a tragic Bond with his dead wife in his arms, rather than a successful Bond with a responsive lover. The murderous Blofeld and Irma Bunt speed away uncaptured, giving us the most dour of Bond endings. In *Live and Let Die*, Bond happily gets the girl, but the mysterious Baron Samedi remains alive, giving us a chill as the credits roll. *Live and Let Die* also gives us a death quip rather than a double entendre.

Here, ladies and gentlemen, for the first time anywhere, is your master guide to the Oh, James Moment.

(Daniel Craig movies have ended with considerably more darkness and less formula, but are included in the chart anyway.)

Movie	On or Near Water	Eschew Rescue	Caught by M/Q	"Oh, James" or double entendre
Dr. No	Boat	✓	Felix	✗
From Russia with Love	Gondola	✗	✗	A joke about the reel of film.
Goldfinger	Near the ocean or a bay	✓	✗	"This is no time to be rescued!"
Thunderball	Raft	Rescued	✗	✗
You Only Live Twice	Raft	✗	M and Moneypenny on the sub	✗
On Her Majesty's Secret Service	Water is visible from the car	✗	✗	✗

Movie	On or Near Water	Eschew Rescue	Caught by M/ Q	"Oh, James" or double entendre
Diamonds Are For-ever	Ocean liner	x	x	"Oh, James"
Live and Let Die	x	x	x	death quip
The Man with the Golden Gun	Boat (junk)	x	M	both
The Spy Who Loved Me	Boat (escape pod)	x	✓	double entendre
Moonraker	x	x	✓	double entendre
For Your Eyes Only	Boat/Swim	x	✓	"For your eyes only, darling."
Octopussy	Boat	x	x	"Oh, James"
Never Say Never Again	By the pool	x	x	Bond winks.
A View to a Kill	Shower	Bond is "missing"	Q	both
The Living Daylights	x	x	x	"Oh, James"
Licence to Kill	Swimming pool	x	x	"Why don't you ask me?"
GoldenEye	x	x	Jack Wade	double entendre
Tomorrow Never Dies	Makeshift raft	x	✓	double entendre
The World is Not Enough	x	Bond is "missing"	✓	double entendre
Die Another Day	On a cliff by the water	x	x	Series of double entendres open the scene. *
Casino Royale	✓	x	x	x
Quantum of Solace	x	x	x	x
Skyfall	x	x	x	Eve introduces herself as Moneypenny
Spectre	x	Bond leaves MI6	He takes his car from Q	x

* Although Jinx does not say "Oh, James," Moneypenny says it in the previous scene.

HE AIN'T BOND, HE'S SUPERMAN!

The guy's a dead shot with any kind of gun or rifle, and is expert in knife fights as well. He can throw a wicked punch and win in hand-to-hand combat even against four opponents. He's a tireless lover. He drives with the steel and speed of a NASCAR professional, and (when played by Pierce Brosnan) runs like the wind. But that's not all...

Bond Can Drive...

- Any car, very fast, in any conditions (many times)
- Motorcycles (Never Say Never Again, Tomorrow Never Dies)
- Tanker trucks (*Licence to Kill*)
- Fire trucks (*A View to a Kill*)
- Buses (*Live and Let Die*)
- Russian tanks (*GoldenEye*)
- Boats and speedboats (many times)
- Snowmobiles (*A View to a Kill*)
- Moon buggies (*Diamonds Are Forever*)
- Jet skis (*The Spy Who Loved Me*)
- Small airplanes (many times)
- Military jets (*The Living Daylights, Die Another Day*)
- Helicopters (*Spectre*)
- Hovercraft (*Die Another Day*)
- Construction Equipment (*Casino Royale, Skyfall*)

Bond Can Speak...

- German (*Octopussy, Tomorrow Never Dies*)
- Russian (*Never Say Never Again* {implied} and *The World is Not Enough*)
- Arabic (*The Spy Who Loved Me*)
- Very little Afghan (he can say "beautiful" but needs a translator for conversation (*The Living Daylights*)
- Enough French to play chemin-de-fer and speak to casino staff (many times)
- At least some Japanese (*You Only Live Twice*)
- Spanish (*Die Another Day Quantum of Solace*)
- A bit of Italian (*Moonraker, For Your Eyes Only, Spectre*)
- A very small amount of Greek (he says "please" instead of "thank you") (*For Your Eyes Only*)
- Beginner's Danish (*Tomorrow Never Dies*)

Bond Knows All About...

- Wines and brandies (many times)
- Vodka (many times)
- Lepidoptera (*On Her Majesty's Secret Service*)
- Caviar (*On Her Majesty's Secret Service*)
- Reading technical blueprints (*The Spy Who Loved Me*)
- The chemical formulas of plants (*Moonraker*)
- Orchids (*Moonraker*)
- Gas mixtures for deep-sea diving (*For Your Eyes Only*)
- Disarming nuclear weapons (*The Spy Who Loved Me, Octopussy*)
- Horse steroids (*A View to a Kill*)

Not Only That, But He Can...

- Ski (downhill and cross-country) (many times)
- Drive a bobsled (*On Her Majesty's Secret Service*)
- Hang-glide (*Live and Let Die, Moonraker*)
- Para-sail (*Die Another Day*)
- Surf (*Die Another Day*)
- Snowboard (*A View to a Kill*)
- Ride a horse (many times), including steeplechase (*A View to a Kill*)
- Ride a bicycle (*Never Say Never Again*)
- Perform CPR (*Die Another Day, Casino Royale*)
- Water-ski (*Licence to Kill*)
- Golf (*Goldfinger*)
- Play chemin-de-fer and baccarat (many times)
- Slow his own heartbeat through meditation (*Die Another Day*)
- Fence (*Moonraker, Die Another Day*)
- Play poker (*Casino Royale*)
- Hack a computer (*Casino Royale, Quantum of Solace*)
- Play backgammon (*Octopussy*)
- Make espresso (*Live and Let Die*)
- Tango (*Never Say Never Again*)
- Make quiche (*A View to a Kill*)
- Sky dive, with or without a parachute (many times)
- Scuba dive (many times)
- Deep-sea dive (*For Your Eyes Only*)
- High dive (*Diamonds Are Forever*)
- Bungee jump (*GoldenEye*)
- Mountain-climb (*For Your Eyes Only*)
- Rappel (many times)

But Even Superman Had Kryptonite.

- He doesn't know a lot about gold (*Goldfinger*) or diamonds (*Diamonds Are Forever*).

- He bleeds when shot (*Thunderball, Skyfall*).
- ...and loses consciousness when drugged (many times).
- He can be captured (briefly many times, for 14 months in *Die Another Day*)
- If he falls from a sufficient height, he can be injured (*The World is Not Enough*).
- His liver is "not too good" (*Die Another Day*)

Bond Can't...

- Hack a computer (*GoldenEye*)
- Disarm a nuclear weapon (*Goldfinger, The World is Not Enough*)
- Read an Asian keyboard (*Tomorrow Never Dies*)
- Pilot a space shuttle (*Moonraker*)

NEVER SAY NEVER AGAIN (1983)

Survey Says!

> Percent Favorite: 0%
> Top 5 Cumulative: 25/25
> Numeric Rating: 6.57/10
> Ranking: 19.9 (24th/25)

My Rating and Ranking

> Rated: 5/10
> Ranked: 21 out of 25

Summary

By corrupting Captain Jack Petachi and giving him a corneal implant to replicate the President's eye print, SPECTRE steals two nuclear warheads. SPECTRE then demands a ransom equal to twenty-five percent of the world's annual oil purchases for their return. Bond first encounters Captain Petachi and Fatima Blush at the Shrublands health facility, and then finds Maximillian Largo in Nassau. Bond and Felix Leiter spy on Largo's yacht underwater, and Bond is caught. He seduces Largo's girlfriend Domino Petachi, and gets a message to MI6 before being imprisoned in North Africa. From there, he escapes, frees Domino, and teams up with Leiter again to get the remaining warhead and save the world. It is Domino, though, who kills Largo, avenging her brother Jack's death.

> **James Bond:** Sean Connery
> **Domino Petachi:** Kim Basinger
> **Maximillian Largo:** Klaus Maria Brandauer
> **Fatima Blush:** Barbara Carrera
> **Ernst Stavro Blofeld:** Max von Sydow
> **Felix Leiter:** Bernie Casey
> **Nigel Small-Fawcett:** Rowan Atkinson
> **M:** Edward Fox
> **Moneypenny:** Pamela Salem
> **Q ("Algernon"):** Alec McCowen
> **Directed by** Irvin Kershner

Discussion

Never Say Never Again is the black sheep of the Bond series. It is not a part of the Eon franchise (which is why, for example, *Die Another Day* was promoted as "Bond 20" when it was the 21st Bond film). Rather, *Never Say Never Again* is the result of Kevin McClory's lawsuit against Ian Fleming for rights to the novel **Thunderball**. In addition to producing *Thunderball*, McClory won the right to do a remake provided he waited ten years. (He also sought the right to film original stories with James

Bond and the other characters from *Thunderball*, but did not succeed.) Despite his legal victory, McClory found it hard to secure the money to compete head-on with the world's most successful movie franchise, but once he had Sean Connery aboard, things fell into place.

At least financially. Making a good movie turned out to be a trickier proposition. The one thing that *Never Say Never Again* did unquestionably right is assemble an outstanding cast. In addition to Connery, Klaus Maria Brandauer makes a great, great Bond villain, while Bernie Casey as Felix and Max von Sydow as Blofeld each give one of the finest portrayals in their respective, much- portrayed roles. Kim Basinger is controversial, with some fans despising her and others praising her. I tend to think she's overrated as an actress, and found her Oscar-winning performance in *L.A. Confidential* unimpressive, but here I think she does fine with rather weak material.

Oddly, *Never Say Never Again* claims to be a refilming of the novel **Thunderball**, rather than a remake of the movie *Thunderball*, yet much in the newer movie is taken from the earlier film, and doesn't appear in Fleming's novel at all. The novel had no femme fatale working for SPECTRE (no women in SPECTRE at all), it had no female assistant to Bond—killed by the femme fatale or anyone else—and none of the novels had Q as a gadget master to the extent he was portrayed in the movies. Blofeld's cat, seen in *Never Say Never Again*, is an innovation of the Eon films, and was first seen in *From Russia with Love*. *Never Say Never Again* often seems more interested in mocking the Eon franchise than in being its own film. It even has its own version of the jet pack—the XT-7B—despite having no pre-titles sequence.

Certainly Bond's constant, instant sexual conquests strike one as parody—the paunchy, late-middle-aged Connery merely needs to look at a woman for her to be overcome by desire. I enjoy Bond's sexual magnetism immensely. I enjoy the seductions that have enough reality to them that I, sitting in the audience, am seduced as well, whether that reality is based on smoldering good looks, mutual understanding, gratitude, or simple randiness. But in *Never Say Never Again*, there is no reality of any kind, only the viewer's prior knowledge that Bond is irresistible to women.

Connery's sex appeal is at a lifelong nadir in 1983—he'd get sexy again later, but at this point he looks like hell. Yet he doesn't need to even try with the women in this movie, except for the somewhat creepy massage he gives Domino. The other three (Patricia Fearing, Fatima Blush, and the fishing boat lady) simply throw themselves at him the moment they lay eyes on him, as does the spa clerk for whom he cannot schedule another sex scene. It's dreadful to watch, more so because Connery phoned in the performance; he goes through the motions lifelessly most of the time, and his lisp is entirely out of control.

MI6 is mocked in a way that Bond fans will naturally tend to dislike, being fond of 007's home office. Edward Fox as M is shrill and unpleasant, a martinet who belies his supposed security service position by ignoring an attempt on an agent's life. Sending Bond to Shrublands is very amusing, but M and Q both bitching about budget cuts just isn't as funny as the script hopes. It certainly brings a smile when the delightful Algernon fantasizes about life in the CIA, but the whole complaint smacks of McClory's bitterness towards Eon rather than anything that actually belongs in the film. Note, though, that the Q scene squeezes in a joke that the Eon films will use years later in *Tomorrow Never Dies*—Bond asking about something that turns out to be perfectly ordinary. In *Never Say Never Again* it's Q's nasal inhaler, in *Tomorrow Never Dies* it's his lunch.

Fatima Blush also seems to be a parody, and sometimes a ridiculous one at that, as idiotic in her way as Nigel Small-Fawcett in his. At other times, I must admit to relishing her gleeful and insane sense of sex, death, and fashion. She's never boring, that's for sure. I can watch *Never Say Never Again* twice in a row and hate Fatima's zaniness the first time, and find her the best thing in the film the second time. Sometimes, it's better to just go with it.

Considering Fatima, we have to wonder about her sexual/drug enslavement of Jack Petachi. Again—creepy imprisonment or parody of a villainess? Seeing Jack crumble at the feet of Fatima Blush in a nurse's uniform while she baby-talks him is either a depiction of evil and depravity, or a very bad joke. I think it veers towards the serious here; certainly Domino is meant as a serious, believable character, so to see her connection to this broken and corrupted man is to feel sympathy for her loss and her plight.

Unfortunately, the character of Domino is rather empty. Despite fan sneering, I am among those who like Basinger's performance; she is warm and emotional, and she looks great in a leotard. However, her character, one of Fleming's most complex, is here reduced to a cliché. Domino Petachi is at first utterly in love with Max Largo, and has no idea that the man is a lunatic, despite his cheerful remarks about cutting her throat. Only Bond awakens her to Largo's villainy. This is all rather unconvincing, without much script to back it, making the character more an ornament to the script than a real person. There is also something very wrong with her liking Bond after a rather violating first encounter. One wonders, if she likes Largo, and also likes being massaged by someone who has deceived her about the situation of that massage, if she is attracted to men who violate or abuse her.

The very best part of *Never Say Never Again* is Klaus Maria Brandauer. Every time he's on-screen, the movie crackles with electric energy. The two standout scenes are his—the Domination video game, and the penultimate confrontation between Largo and Domino, which culminates in him offering her for sale to the highest bidder. We never doubt either his madness or his charisma; here is a man who could definitely hold the world at ransom, and could also successfully promote a children's charity, a man who could adore a young woman and then threaten to cut her throat. Brandauer is playing Ian Fleming's Largo, the handsome man with more vitality and energy than any of his underlings, the ladies' man with the expansive laugh who is nonetheless very, very dangerous.

Despite the delights of its cast, *Never Say Never Again* fails to come together as a film. It has little real action beyond one rather cool motorcycle chase, the filming often looks washed out and pale, the sets seem cheap, and the special effects are appalling. The scene where Bond and Domino leap off a cliff on horseback is transparently fake, and a poorly-done fall is meant as a substitute for a real fight. Perhaps nothing is as offensively bad in *Never Say Never Again* as its musical score, a series of cheesy disco sounds and been-there-done-that orchestrations.

Maybe the strangest thing about the film is the way it kind of forgets about its plot. Millions of lives are at stake, but there is no tension; Bond simply moves from place to place until he arrives at the bomb. This is exacerbated by the fact that the plot is barely elucidated, as if the viewer is expected to already know it from *Thunderball*. We see Jack switch the dummy warheads for real ones, but we never see how their targeting is changed, or how Largo gets them and hides them. Blofeld never specifies the terms of his ransom, only the amount. We have no idea why Bond has gone to the Bahamas—Largo is not a suspect. Recall that Largo is only obliquely linked to Jack (the matchbook) and that M forcefully dismisses Bond's eye transplant theory. In *Thunderball*, M pays attention to what Bond saw at Shrublands, and Bond knows that the pilot's sister is in Nassau. In *Never Say Never Again*, M rejects what Bond saw, and Bond doesn't find out about Domino until he arrives. Therefore, in the latter movie, there is no reason for Bond to be having fun in the sun—he just stumbles upon a suspect. There is no spying, no evidence, no discovery, no knowledge—the audience knows Largo is the villain, and apparently that's all it takes. Largo is never actually linked to the bombs until he admits to having them.

The changes in the plot are mostly weak. The one major improvement is that Jack Petachi is specifically being controlled in part by the threat to his sister. In the novel, SPECTRE doesn't even know that the NATO observer and Largo's girlfriend are related—a ridiculous oversight justified by their different last names (see AMAZE YOUR FRIENDS!). In this movie, the connection is unclear; is Largo ignorant, or manipulating the relationship? I think if you're going to have a brother and sister in the movie, having the relationship be coincidental or unclear is a mistake.

Rowan Atkinson is simply a disaster.

The High Points
- Klaus Maria Brandauer's bold and inspired performance as Maximillian Largo.
- Generally fine cast with excellent performances by Bernie Casey, Max von Sydow, Barbara Carrera, and Alec McCowen.
- Fatima Blush's shoes left behind when the rest of her departs.
- Nice waterskiing sequence.
- Motorcycle chase, especially Bond's wipe-out and recovery.
- The Domination video contest.
- Domino's dance workouts, and her impressive agility.
- Largo selling Domino into slavery.
- Tying the brother-sister relationship into the main plot.
- Fatima Blush's insane fashion sense.

The Low Points
- Sean Connery's lackluster, lisping performance—a heartbreaker for those of us who'd waited a dozen years for it.
- One of the worst scores in film history.
- A generally cheap look, with flimsy-looking set design and washed-out cinematography.
- Edward Fox's strident, old-womanish M.
- A barely sketched-in plot that requires the viewer to know *Thunderball* quite well in order to figure out what's going on, while leaving out major parts of SPECTRE's plan.

- Minimal action beyond a comedic fight, a close call with a shark, and the motorcycle chase.
- The ill-conceived presence of a fumbling and foolish Rowan Atkinson, single-handedly humiliating the very idea of Foreign Service.
- Unattractive and uninteresting titles; not a problem in most movies, but a shame in a Bond film.
- A slimy attitude towards sexuality that includes beautiful women throwing themselves at an elderly Bond at first sight, and Bond giving an illicit massage to Domino that borders on violation.
- A tango scene that makes me want to give up dance out of sheer embarrassment.

Quotable Quotes

Bond (in reference to war games): "Correction, sir, I lost both legs. I did not die."

Bond: "It can never be the same playing with blanks."

Bond: "Free radicals, sir?"
M: "Yeah, they're toxins that destroy the body and the brain, caused by eating too much red meat and white bread, and too many dry martinis."
Bond: "Then I shall cut out the white bread, sir."

Doctor (to Bond): "Your body's got enough scar tissue for an entire regiment."

Fatima: "How reckless of me! I made you all wet."
Bond: "Yes, but my martini's still dry."

Bond (to Fishing Boat Woman): "You did say you'd catch me later."

Domino: "You're crazy!"
Largo (thoughtfully): "Yah. Maybe. I'm crazy."

Bond: "Commander Pederson, are you equipped with the new XT-7Bs?"
Pederson: "That's top secret! How do you know about them?"
Bond: "From a Russian translation of one of your service manuals. Sorry about that."

(Last lines)
Nigel Small-Fawcett: "M says without you in the service he fears for the security of the civilized world!"
Bond: "Never again."
Domino: "Never?"
Bond: (winks)

Facts and Figures

SEXUAL ENCOUNTERS

<u>Four</u>: Patricia Fearing, Fatima Blush, Fishing Boat Woman, and Domino Petachi.

BOND'S CAR

Bond's personal vintage black Bentley is seen briefly at Shrublands.

DEATHS

<u>Approximately eighteen</u>:

Lippe, Jack Petachi, Nicole, Fatima Blush, Maximillian Largo.

At Palmyra, Bond's prison guard and three apparent deaths when Palmyra is bombed from the sea.

During the Tears of Allah raid, nine visible.

Bond Kills

- <u>Three</u> directly: Lippe, Fatima Blush, the prison guard.

EXPLOSIONS

<u>Five</u>: Jack Petachi's car, Bond's hotel room, a terrific slow approach and satisfying finale that takes out Fatima Blush, three in a series when Palmyra is attacked, and a whole barrage when the Tears of Allah is attacked.

BOND'S FOOD AND DRINKS

Vodka Martinis

<u>Three</u>; one that remains dry at the outdoor bar where Bond meets Fatima Blush, and one on the Flying Saucer with Max Largo (even though it's early in the morning—when Bond drank with Emilio Largo, he made note of whether it was afternoon yet). While Bond spies on Domino through a telescope, Nicole is stirring vodka martinis (a bottle of vodka is visible)—count as one since we don't see him drink.

Other Drinks

- Bond smuggles a bottle of vodka into his room at Shrublands (see also FOOD).
- In bed with Patricia Fearing, Bond drinks red wine while Patricia sleeps.
- Bond has a glass of champagne and an ice bucket by the bed while he makes love to Fishing Boat Woman.
- At the casino/arcade charity event, Domino orders "a double Bloody Mary with plenty of Worcestershire sauce" and Bond has vodka on the rocks (with lemon).
- In the final scene, Domino gives Bond a tropical drink and Bond, aghast, replies, "I always have a martini at five." The movie ends before we know whether he drinks the tropical drink or gets his traditional martini.

Food

- Beluga caviar, quail's eggs, and Strasbourg foie gras smuggled into Shrublands.
- Patricia Fearing offers Bond a "treat" of Lentil Delight, dandelion salad, and goat's cheese—he counters by showing her his smuggled spread.
- At his villa, Bond eats an apple just before he discovers Nicole's body.

GAMBLING AND SPORTS

- Fatima water-skis.
- Bond and Fatima scuba dive.
- Fishing Boat Woman fishes alone, and then with Bond.
- At the casino, roulette, arcade games (Galaxians is visible), and "Domination."

Amaze Your Friends!

- The character of Domino has changed her name quite a lot over the years. In the novel **Thunderball**, she began life as Domino Petacchi and changed her name to Domino Vitali. When a French actress was cast for *Thunderball*, her character was given the French surname of Derval. In *Never Say Never Again* she receives her fourth last name, Petachi, apparently adapted from her original name in the novel. Similarly, Domino's brother goes through three names, he is Giuseppe Petacchi in the novel, Francois Derval in *Thunderball*, and Jack Petachi in *Never Say Never Again*.
- The title designer, Micheline Roquebrune-Connery, is Sean Connery's wife.
- Connery's wife also supposedly came up with the title of the film, in response to Connery saying he would never play James Bond again.
- Valerie Leon had speaking roles in two Bond films: Fishing Boat Woman in *Never Say Never Again*, and Hotel Receptionist in *The Spy Who Loved Me*, but did not have a name in either.

Most Interesting Goofs

Is that shaken or stirred? At the outdoor bar in Nassau, Bond is given a vodka martini—we can see that the liquid is colorless. As the scene ends, a close-up reveals that the drink is now yellowish; it appears that Bond has a regular (gin) martini.

That's some stunt skiing! Fatima Blush is doing stunt skiing on one ski while Bond watches. When she skis up the ramp and into his arms, she suddenly has two skis.

Quick change artist: Although Fatima loves to change clothes often, this trick is beyond even her skills. As she approaches her hotel, she sees Bond arrive with Fishing Boat Woman, although she thought she had killed him. Quickly, she races to his room to plant a bomb while he checks at the desk for messages. She is wearing two different outfits when she sees him arrive and when she plants the bomb.

SHAKEN? STIRRED?

W hy does James Bond always ask for a martini "shaken, not stirred"? This is a simple explanation, meant for those who don't wish to be liquor connoisseurs.

A martini is made with gin and vermouth. Gin can be "bruised" by shaking, which is to say, shaking ruins the taste. (I'd say, shaking makes it taste worse, since I can't stand the stuff.)

However, James Bond doesn't drink regular martinis, he drinks vodka martinis. Vodka tastes best when very cold, and the best way to get it to the proper temperature is to shake it up with the ice.

Bartenders, though, are inclined not to shake martinis, because they are accustomed to martinis made with gin. I've tried this; if you order a vodka martini and don't specify that it should be shaken, it probably won't be properly cold when it arrives. You'd think bartenders would know to shake, just from watching Bond movies, but they often don't.

What is amusing is that in several Bond films (*Goldfinger* and *On Her Majesty's Secret Service*, for example), Bond gets a "martini, shaken, not stirred." If vodka martini isn't specified, then what you get is an improperly made gin martini. It is as if sometimes the screenwriters know the format but not the meaning.

The whole "shaken not stirred" thing may have originated with the Vesper—the drink invented by Bond in the novel **Casino Royale** (and the movie as well). Since this drink has *both* gin and vodka, one could legitimately not know whether to treat it like gin (stir it) or vodka (shake it up).

Well, now you know.

How to Make a Medium Dry Vodka Martini

4 parts vodka

1 part dry vermouth

- Shake in a martini shaker with lots of ice.
- Serve with a twist of lime, a twist of lemon, or an olive.

Note: In the novels, Bond usually preferred a medium dry martini with a twist of lime. In the movies, "very dry" is usually specified, and the twist, be it lemon or lime, or the olive, is not discussed. "Dryness" refers to the proportion of vodka to vermouth. Four-to-one is medium dry, five-to-one is dry. Some people love *very* dry vodka martinis made by swirling a bit of vermouth in a cold martini glass, just enough to wet the glass, dumping the vermouth, and then adding the ice cold vodka.

Dirty Martinis

Spectre introduced the "dirty" vodka martini to the world of 007. A dirty martini can be made with gin or vodka, as follows:

4 or 5 parts gin or vodka

1 part dry vermouth

1 part olive brine (use the liquid from a jar of olives)

- Shake a vodka martini, stir a gin martini .
- Serve with a 2-4 olives on a toothpick.

What Kind of Vodka?

In the novels, Bond preferred Russian vodka but didn't name a brand. He indicated this preference in the film *You Only Live Twice*. The movie brand of choice was Smirnoff from *Dr. No* through *The World is Not Enough* (except for *Never Say Never Again*, in which he drank Absolut). In 2002, prior to the release of *Die Another Day*, it was announced with no small fanfare that Bond's vodka endorsement was now with Finlandia, The brand is visible at the bar in the ice palace scene.

In July of 2006, it was announced that Smirnoff had renewed its relationship with the Bond films. Smirnoff appeared in *Casino Royale* and *Quantum of Solace*. Bond drank Grey Goose at the Golden Dragon Casino in *Skyfall* (this was not a paid promotional arrangement).

Again with a big promotional splash, Bond changed vodka brands for *Spectre,* and now drinks Belvedere.

Stolichnaya has also appeared in several Bond movies; *You Only Live Twice, A View to a Kill, The Living Daylights,* and *Licence to Kill*.

Your author generally drinks Ketel One or Belvedere.

ALL THE ROMANTIC VACATION SPOTS

Along with gadgets, women, and fast cars, the Bond films are defined by their locations. Bond travels to numerous exotic lands, giving the audience a glimpse of someplace they've never been. A great location provides an insider feel; this isn't the stuff you see in travel brochures, this is what it's like to really be there. Our eyes are opened to beauty, both natural and man-made.

What Makes a Good Location?

A good location...

- Is beautiful, or at least visually interesting
- Feels authentic
- Conveys a sense of what is unique about the place, showing something of the people, food, landscape, or culture.

A bad location...

- Is ugly
- Looks no different from the studio, or is supplemented heavily by studio footage
- Shows us only what we already know about the location; i.e. only the most famous landmarks or best-known aspects of the culture (the clichés)
- Is not identifiable as itself; is seen only briefly, or with few exterior shots (this is not so much bad as wasted).

Bond will sometimes go to unattractive locations; Bratislava in *The Living Daylights*, for example, was purposely gray and gloomy, the contrast created with later, lovelier places served to comment on the whole idea of defection.

The title of this section is from *The World is Not Enough*, when Bond comments on the various war-torn spots that Renard had been spotted; Iran, Iraq, Bosnia, Afghanistan, Cambodia. We know that Bond will sometimes be needed in such places; not every villain hangs out in Nassau, but an unattractive location can still inform the viewer, creating a strong impression and showing us something that adds to the experience of the film.

How Much Does Bond Travel?

On average, James Bond visits slightly over four different countries per film, including England. (Originally I had planned on excluding England from my calculations, but in three movies, *You Only Live Twice*, *The Spy Who Loved Me*, and *Licence to Kill*, he is never seen in his home country).

The least traveling done by Bond has been in *Dr. No*, in which he visited only two countries. The most traveling done in a Bond movie is six countries; visited in *The Living Daylights*, *The World is Not Enough*, *Die Another Day*, and *Quantum of*

Solace. In *Moonraker*, Bond visits five countries plus outer space. *Moonraker* is also notable for the most countries used as filming locations: In addition to the locations traveled to in the film, the crew visited France for filming Drax's estate, as well as using French studio space rather than Pinewood in England, and his Amazon headquarters were actually a Mayan ruin in Guatemala.

Top Ten / Bottom Ten

With a total of sixty-one unique locations (depending on how you count) in twenty-five movies, I didn't think Top Five/Bottom Five would adequately cover the subject. So, without further ado:

Best

1. Japan, *You Only Live Twice*
2. Phuket, Thailand, *The Man with the Golden Gun*
3. Swiss Alps, Switzerland, *On Her Majesty's Secret Service*
4. Istanbul, Turkey, *From Russia with Love*
5. Jamaica, *Dr. No*
6. Egypt, *The Spy Who Loved Me*
7. Nassau, Bahamas, *Thunderball*
8. Vienna, Austria, *The Living Daylights*
9. Corfu, Greece, *For Your Eyes Only*
10. TIE: "Vietnam," *Tomorrow Never Dies* and "Cuba," *Die Another Day*

Worst

1. Baku, Azerbaijan, *The World is Not Enough*
2. New York City, U.S., *Live and Let Die*
3. North Korea, *Die Another Day*
4. India, *Octopussy*
5. San Francisco, U.S., *A View to a Kill*
6. Outer space, *Moonraker*
7. TIE: Isthmus, *Licence to Kill* and San Monique, *Live and Let Die*
8. Florida, U.S., *Licence to Kill*
9. Rio de Janeiro, Brazil, *Moonraker*
10. Bilbao, Spain, *The World is Not Enough*

The Best Locations

Japan, You Only Live Twice

In every way, *You Only Live Twice* exemplifies the perfect use of a location shoot. It is suffused in local color and authenticity. It gives the user an unmistakable feeling of actually being in Japan. It looks at another culture with respect and interest. It is varied, and it is beautiful. From a city street to a private garden, from a busy loading dock to a remote fishing village, we are taken to a Japan much richer than that available on a tour bus.

Phuket, Thailand, The Man with the Golden Gun

Probably the single most exotic and amazing place ever in a Bond film, Scaramanga's island became a major tourist attraction because of its great beauty in this film, and is now known as James Bond Island.

Swiss Alps, Switzerland, On Her Majesty's Secret Service

The natural setting is, of course, breathtaking. But filming it is a challenge. *On Her Majesty's Secret Service* gave us never-before-seen panoramic views from helicopters and from on the ski slope, and even showed us a real avalanche. Piz Gloria itself is astonishing; who could believe such a location is real, and wasn't placed there just for Eon Productions? Yet you can visit it today. As if all that wasn't enough, there is the wonderful footage of a skating rink at Christmastime.

Istanbul, Turkey, From Russia with Love

From the opening sounds of a call to prayer as we see a minaret, through the underground catacombs with utterly inauthentic but very convincing rats, we know we have traveled. As a cherry on the sundae, we get an actual tour guide at St. Sophia. All this and a boat trip on the Bosporus.

Jamaica, Dr. No

As with *You Only Live Twice*, we get a real range at this location; a nightclub, a marina, a secluded beach, and all of it is breathtakingly beautiful; sun-drenched, with a heat you can feel, and at Dr. No's island, a sense of the untamed. Honey Ryder's emergence from the sea just adds to the natural beauty.

Egypt, The Spy Who Loved Me

Another movie where we see the tourist stuff (the presentation at the pyramids) and much more as well. The camel ride through the desert, the dervishes at the night club, and the magnificent ruins that fall on Jaws's head all give us a real sense of place. Egypt has a baked, sun-in-your-eyes shimmer to it in *The Spy Who Loved Me*, and it looks gorgeous.

Nassau, Bahamas, Thunderball

Nassau is probably not "exotic," in that it is fairly accessible to the average tourist. On the other hand, it is as beautiful a place as Bond has ever visited. The beaches have a purity of color, the water is exquisite, and everything you see makes you want to pack your bags and take the next flight out. And be sure to time your trip to coincide with Junkanoo!

Vienna, Austria, The Living Daylights

In *The Living Daylights* we have a location that is both beautiful and witty. *The Third Man* homage is a lovely touch, and not only did director John Glen work on that classic film, but so did veteran Bond director Guy Hamilton, making the movie a part of Bond history. *The Living Daylights* touches on the highlights of Vienna; waltzing, the Prater Wheel and the opera, but the film's use of this city stays above cliché by making them all sparkle with romance and magic.

Corfu, Greece, For Your Eyes Only

Another very real-looking place, with a glimpse not only of its beauty, but of life as it is lived there. The stroll through the marketplace has a joy to it that gives a nice pause in the film's pacing. The lovely ruins, town, and water, all make Corfu an important part of *For Your Eyes Only*'s appeal.

Vietnam, Tomorrow Never Dies and Cuba, Die Another Day

These are both excellent locations. Vietnam looks very gritty and interesting, and the rooftop chase is really rooted in place. Cuba looks dazzling, and the salsa beat on the soundtrack, as well as Bond's surprising purchase of a Cuban shirt, add to the local feeling. Unfortunately, both of these tie for last on our list, because neither is where it says it is. "Vietnam" is really Bangkok, and sunny Cuba is really cloudy Cadiz, Spain, with digital correction to improve the weather.

The Worst Locations

Baku, Azerbaijan, The World is Not Enough

Have you ever seen anything so ugly? The relentless gloom of the oil fields, the film saturated with a brownish tint that makes you wonder if they forgot to clean the camera lens—and this in a movie where Bond makes a sarcastic remark about traveling to unpleasant places! Maybe Baku in real life looks much nicer; everything in *The World is Not Enough* is too dark and too muddy, so I'll give it the benefit of the doubt.

New York City, U.S., Live and Let Die

Make no mistake, I am a New Yorker and I love my city. All the more reason to be offended that one of the greatest and most interesting cities in the world is reduced to an ugly ride on the FDR Drive, and some downtrodden street scenes designed to make a great place look like a hellhole. For shame, Eon!

North Korea, Die Another Day

Just as Cadiz was digitally made to look sunny, the North Korean footage was digitally made darker and gloomier, and frankly, they overdid it. It's almost hard to follow the action in the pre-titles sequence because the scenery is so shadowy and bland.

India, Octopussy

Isn't it amazing how one of the most lively and brightly-colored countries on Earth looks just like a Pinewood studio set? *Octopussy*'s India is the exact opposite of great locations like Japan in *You Only Live Twice*—there is absolutely nothing in the movie that you wouldn't see flipping through a travel brochure while seated comfortably in New Jersey.

San Francisco, U.S., A View to a Kill

Few U.S. cities are as visually interesting as San Francisco, but you'd never know it from watching *A View to a Kill*. This is a city that has been wonderfully filmed in so many movies; its streets were famously used in movies as divergent as *Bullitt and What's Up Doc?* But here we see nothing of the City by the Bay beyond the Golden Gate Bridge, which, again, is brochure material.

Outer Space, Moonraker

I don't think I need to justify this choice.

Isthmus, Licence to Kill and San Monique, Live and Let Die

On principal, I object to fictional locations when Bond films are famous for their real ones. For the record, Isthmus was shot in Mexico, and San Monique was a redressing of Jamaica (where the novel **Live and Let Die** was set).

Bahamas, Licence to Kill

A flat, uninspired place reflects this film's low budget. It is hard to believe the gorgeous locations of *Thunderball* are in the same islands as those briefly visited in *Licence to Kill*. The pre-titles sequence chase, through a scrubby, dusty area, looks like that park they always used on the original Star Trek series. Later, Bond meets Pam Bouvier at the Barrelhead Bar in Bimini; a sleazy, violent, thoroughly unpleasant place with the single worst "exotic dancer" I have ever seen.

Close runner-up is the Florida Keys in the same movie. All we see, beyond the causeway, is a drab warehouse, a suburban neighborhood that could be anywhere, and an airport exactly as flat and bland as every other airport.

Rio de Janeiro, Brazil, Moonraker

Another studio substitute. The filming of Carnival compares very poorly indeed with Junkanoo in *Thunderball*, and is replete with product placement, including Marlboro cigarettes.

Bilbao, Spain, The World is Not Enough

This one is the real thing, but why bother? Bond leaps out a window and walks away from Bilbao so quickly you hardly know you've been anywhere. There was no reason to shoot this on location at all.

Gosh, It Seems Like Bond Has Been Everywhere!

But he hasn't!

Here's a list of locations, by region, that Bond has never visited:

North America

- Canada
- Alaska, Hawaii, and numerous mainland U.S. locations of interest. (Bond has visited the U.S. often, so I hardly think it's a priority. Still, San Antonio, Texas, and Washington, D.C. are just two of the fascinating cities still waiting for 007 to stop by.)

The Caribbean

- Anyplace except Cuba (twice), Haiti, and the Bahamas.
- Choice locations include Puerto Rico, Grenada and Trinidad and Tobago.

Central America

- Anyplace—Bond has never visited this region, although Guatemala was dressed as the Amazon in *Moonraker*.
- Interesting choices include Panama, Belize, and El Salvador.

South America

- Bond has visited just three of this continent's thirteen nations—Argentina, Bolivia, and Brazil.
- Possibilities include Venezuela, Suriname, and Colombia.

Scandinavia

Only Iceland has been visited, leaving...

- Sweden
- Finland

- Norway (it appears this changes with *No Time to Die*)
- Denmark

Western Europe (Countries)

- Ireland
- Wales
- Belgium
- Luxembourg
- Andorra
- Liechtenstein
- Malta
- San Marino
- Vatican City

Western Europe (Cities and Regions)

- Madrid, Spain
- Toledo, Spain
- Florence, Italy
- Sicily
- Corsica

Central Europe

- Poland
- Hungary
- Romania
- Bulgaria
- Slovenia
- Bosnia-Herzegovina
- Serbia
- Kosovo
- Albania
- Macedonia
- The Baltic States (Lithuania, Latvia, Estonia)

Eastern Europe

- Ukraine
- Belarus
- Moldova

The Caucasus

- Georgia

- Armenia

Central Asia

- Kyrgyzstan
- Tajikistan
- Turkmenistan
- Uzbekistan

Northwest and Western Asia and the Middle East

- Cyprus
- Syria
- Jordan
- Israel
- Saudi Arabia
- Kuwait
- Yemen
- Oman
- The Gulf States (U.A.R., Qatar, Bahrain)
- Iran
- Iraq

Southern Asia

- Pakistan (in a deleted scene from *Casino Royale*, we learn that the fight sequence in the pre-titles sequence takes place in Lahore, meaning the anonymous bathroom is actually in Pakistan, but since this didn't make the final cut, it's fair to say Bond hasn't been there)
- Nepal
- Sri Lanka
- Bhutan
- Myanmar
- Bangladesh

Southeast Asia and Islands

- Laos
- Cambodia
- Indonesia
- Malaysia
- East Timor
- Brunei
- Singapore
- Philippines

The Rest of Asia

- Mongolia
- Taiwan
- Indian Ocean Islands (Comoros, Sri Lanka, Mauritius, Seychelles, Maldives)

Africa

- Of the 49 nations that comprise Africa, Bond has visited only two; Egypt and Morocco
- Interesting choices include South Africa, Kenya, and Ethiopia.

Oceania

Bond has never visited this continent, which includes...

- Australia
- Fiji
- New Zealand, and numerous additional island countries.

Antarctica

Not too hospitable, but there's always...

- Greenland

The Complete List

Keep in mind that this is a list of places James Bond has visited in the movies. It is not a list of filming locations. Thus, we have Cuba listed under *Die Another Day*, not Cadiz, Spain. This also includes locations that were created entirely in the studio, such as the unnamed Caribbean country in the *Goldfinger* pre-titles sequence.

It is also not a list of places seen in the movies. You'll find that South Africa is not listed under *Diamonds Are Forever*—that's because 007 himself never went there.

Dr. No

    England

    Jamaica

From Russia with Love

    England

    Turkey

    Yugoslavia

    Italy

Goldfinger

    unnamed Caribbean country (pre-titles sequence)

England

Switzerland

United States (Kentucky)

Thunderball

France

England

Bahamas

You Only Live Twice

Hong Kong

Gibraltar (burial at sea)

Japan

On Her Majesty's Secret Service

England

Portugal

Switzerland

Diamonds Are Forever

Japan

Cairo, Egypt

England

Netherlands

United States

Live and Let Die

England

United States (New York, New Orleans)

San Monique

The Man with the Golden Gun

England

Hong Kong

Beirut, Lebanon

Macau

Thailand

The Spy Who Loved Me

Austria

Scotland

Egypt

Italy

Moonraker

    England

    Italy

    U.S. (California)

    Brazil

    Argentina (Iguaca Falls are on the border of Argentina and Brazil)

    Outer space

For Your Eyes Only

    England

    Greece

    Italy

Octopussy

    Cuba (presumably)

    England

    India

    Germany

Never Say Never Again

    Bahamas

    England

    France

    Monaco

    Unnamed North African country (where Palmyra is)

A View to a Kill

    Russia (pre-titles sequence)

    England

    France

    United States (San Francisco)

The Living Daylights

    Gibraltar

    England

    Czechoslovakia (present-day Slovakia)

    Tangier, Morocco

    Vienna, Austria

    Afghanistan (filmed in Morocco)

Licence to Kill

    United States

> Bahamas
>
> Isthmus

GoldenEye

> Russia
>
> England
>
> France
>
> Monaco
>
> Cuba

Tomorrow Never Dies

> Russia, or near the Russian border (arms bazaar)
>
> England
>
> Germany
>
> Vietnam
>
> China (China Sea)

The World is Not Enough

> Spain
>
> England
>
> Scotland
>
> Azerbaijan
>
> Kazakhstan
>
> Turkey

Die Another Day

> North Korea
>
> Hong Kong
>
> Cuba
>
> England
>
> Iceland
>
> South Korea

Casino Royale

> Prague, Czech Republic
>
> Bahamas
>
> Madagascar
>
> Montenegro
>
> Italy (Como and Venice)

Quantum of Solace

> Italy (Siena and Talamone)

England

Port Au Prince, Haiti

Austria

 Bolivia

Kazan, Russia

Skyfall

Turkey

England

China

Macau

Scotland

Spectre

Mexico City, Mexico

England

Rome, Italy

Austria

Morocco

No Time to Die (note that this is pre-release information, other than Jamaica and England, we don't know where Bond will be, as opposed to a filming location that might be dressed as some other location, or a location visited only by other characters.)

Jamaica

England

Norway

Italy

Faroe Islands

Scotland

A VIEW TO A KILL (1985)

Survey Says!
Percent Favorite: 1.5%
Top 5 Cumulative: 20/25
Numeric Rating: 4.7/10
Ranking: 18 (23rd/25)
My Rating and Ranking
Rated: 2/10
Ranked: 25 out of 25

Summary

M16 discovers that new silicon chip technology is being leaked to the KGB, and sends Bond to investigate Max Zorin, whose purchase of the chip manufacturing company coincides with the leak. Bond first discovers that Zorin is tampering with race horses, and is the product of Nazi experimentation. He also discovers that Stacey Sutton has been given five million dollars by Zorin for an unknown reason. Bond follows Sutton to San Francisco, where he learns that Zorin is tampering with his oil fields in order to cause a massive double-fault earthquake that will flood all of Silicon Valley. With the help of Sutton and Zorin's girlfriend May Day, Bond stops the earthquake, defeats Zorin, and showers with Stacey.

James Bond: Roger Moore
Max Zorin: Christopher Walken
Stacey Sutton: Tanya Roberts
May Day: Grace Jones
Sir Godfrey Tibbett: Patrick Macnee
Pola Ivanova: Fiona Fullerton
General Gogol: Walter Gotell
M: Robert Brown
Moneypenny: Lois Maxwell
Q: Desmond Llewelyn
Directed by John Glen

Discussion

A View to a Kill is among the most hated of all Bond films. Nonetheless, it has its fans, more ardent, perhaps, in the face of opposition. Bond fans are iconoclasts, I think, and defend their favorites even more fervently when those films are not widely loved. Just look at me and *Diamonds Are Forever*! In the case of *A View to a Kill*, I hold with the majority, and the film lands at the very bottom of my personal ranking. Still, in writing up the movie, I'll try to remember those of you who love it.

There are numerous problems that can be addressed when reviewing the film: A disjointed plot, an almost astonishingly irritating female lead, a complete lack of real espionage, and very poor special effects all come to mind. But the worst part of this movie is clearly Roger Moore himself, a problem that, for me, cannot be alleviated by repeat viewings or a forgiving attitude.

What blows the ballgame for me is whatever the heck is going on with Moore's face. It is my understanding that he had a face lift or some sort of plastic surgery between *Octopussy* and *A View to a Kill*—for one thing, a mole has clearly been removed. But more than that, he seems to be wearing a baffling excess of makeup, making him appear at times to be one of Malcolm McDowell's gang from *A Clockwork Orange*. His dark-rimmed, wide-eyed stare, combined with an almost perpetual smirk, make his performance, his very presence, an annoyance. In *A View to a Kill*, James Bond smirks at everyone; at Stacey when he tells her, oh so disarmingly, "I'm English;" at May Day when he awkwardly tries to seduce her, and again when he—unbelievably—succeeds; at Scarpine when discussing horses, and at Zorin whenever the mood takes him. When Bond isn't smirking, he is scolding; not just in the role-playing he enjoys a bit too much with Tibbett, but towards Stacey (who can blame him?) and, at the end, towards May Day. In no other movie does Bond spend so much time saying "Hurry up!" "Hold on!" "Come on!"

Finally, Moore is at this time so old and so out of shape that the movie doesn't even pretend to cover for the constant use of stunt doubles. There are virtually no medium shots at all; Bond is doubled so much that all the movie can give us is close-ups of Moore and long shots of doubles. *A View to a Kill* has a jarring moment of the absolute worst stunt-doubling in the series. During the Paris car chase, when the roof of the car is sliced off, a head pops up that is so dissimilar to Bond that my kid immediately noticed when they were only nine years old! The back projection when Moore is on-screen is surprisingly shoddy; it's the eighties but looks like the sixties. This is the point where the problem with the movie's star segues into the problem with special effects. With Roger Moore absent from so much of the film, perhaps the feeling that it all looks fake is understandable. The biggest disappointment in this regard is surely the climax on top of the Golden Gate Bridge. The background for all the close and middle shots is a flat gray. Admittedly, this is a fair representation of San Francisco's typical foggy sky, but the sum effect is of a movie with too little budget to create good insert shots.

Speaking of disappointments, how bad is the performance by the only Oscar-winner ever cast in a twentieth-century Bond movie? (see 007 AT THE OSCARS) Here, I'll get some argument, as there are plenty of folks who really admire Christopher Walken's portrayal of Max Zorin. To me, his jerky body movements and unexpected, frequent giggles never add up to a convincing villain or a convincing psychotic. (One of my pet peeves about the script is that Bond keeps telling people that Zorin is psychotic, but we never see any really loony behavior until the very end, nor any evidence that Bond has a clue what it means to say someone is "psychotic." Frankly, Zorin's level of business success is more than unlikely with true psychosis.) Walken has a couple of good scenes; I very much like his wrestling match with May Day, and his sudden decision to open fire on his own men in the Main Strike mine—now that's psychotic!

Tanya Roberts has been adequately covered in the BOND GIRLS section. The character is poorly written as well as poorly played. From moment to moment, she is a bubblehead, a scientist, a rich girl raised with a silver spoon in her mouth, and someone who speaks quite roughly. Uppercrust scientists may say "shit," but usually refrain from "you betcha."

A View to a Kill is weak on "girls." May Day is a terrific henchman; an 80s Oddjob. She's bizarre, scary, and flamboyant. But she isn't sexy by any conventional definition, or appealing. If you think of her as a villain rather than as a Bond girl, she becomes an asset to the movie rather than another thing to complain about.

The only enjoyable Bond girl in this movie is Pola Ivanova, and she's delightful. First of all, Fiona Fullerton is great-looking; a little fuller-figured than the average Bond girl, which is refreshing; she's cuddly and coy, and looks lovely in a hot tub. The role was originally written with Anya Amasova in mind, but Barbara Bach declined. I do like to imagine it's Anya in that scene, as we see their relationship hasn't changed a bit.

MI6 doesn't do well as an organization this time out. For the second movie in a row, we open with the murder of a double-0 agent (*The Living Daylights* will get the hat trick). As in *Moonraker*, M simply hands the plot to Bond, who need investigate nothing, merely go after the nearest industrialist, and as in *Moonraker*, the Minister of Defence has no clue that wealthy industrialists are practically a breeding ground for villainy. Q apparently invented the Aibo toy dog years ahead of its time and used it for sexual voyeurism. How charming. Moneypenny is reduced to doing an Eliza Doolittle imitation, and while I love *My Fair Lady*, the joke went on too long, and was too out of place, to qualify as funny.

Speaking of out of place jokes, we are more or less obligated to discuss the Infamous Beach Boys Moment. Overall, I like the pre-titles sequence; the photography is pretty gorgeous, the locket is mysterious, and I've always liked the iceberg submarine. The use of "California Girls," though, is just wrong. The problem is not humor, but heavy-handedness, including how very long it goes on. When Bond starts using the ski from the snowmobile to surf, it's clever and funny. When the Beach Boys start up, it's like some drunken wag at a party shouting at you, "See, he's surfing! Get it? Get it?"

I found the Paris and San Francisco locations terribly disappointing. As with India in *Octopussy*, John Glen gave us only famous tourist attractions (Eiffel Tower, Golden Gate Bridge) and avoided any hint of real behind-the- scenes, what-it's-really-like filming. Likewise, the chase in each city was dissatisfying. The car chase in Paris was ludicrous, and recycled chase jokes from previous films (wedding, stolen car). In San Francisco, we're treated to the sight of Bond stealing a fire engine from the scene of a still-burning fire, endangering who knows how many firefighters and civilians? Not nice, James! And why, for that matter, does he climb outside the fire truck? It seems merely an imitation of scenes from *For Your Eyes Only* and *Octopussy*, it makes no sense on its own.

I promise I will soon give some time to *A View to a Kill*'s good parts, but first I am afraid I must rant about one of my most hated of all scenes in a Bond movie—the steeplechase scene. If needed, follow down the page until you see the "End Rant" notice.

The scene fails on three levels: It's badly directed, badly acted, and badly conceived.

In terms of directing, there's a clumsy, plodding, step-by-step scene structure. (a) Zorin makes jump. (b) Jump is made more dangerous. (c) Close- up reaction shot of Moore. (d) Distant shot of stunt rider making the jump. (e) Thug fails to make jump, falls. This a–e sequence is repeated three times, in a series of near-identical shots. By the third time through, the impact was a thud instead of a thrill.

As for acting, Moore's reaction shot is the same each time—surprise and horror. Why is he still surprised the second and third times? Where is any hint of the hero who knows he can do it, or is at least determined to try? Add to that a group of thugs who are so cartoon-mafia that they are in no way convincing as "exercise boys" (rather homoerotic, that). They look like fools—poor casting and minimal acting! Walken also comes off poorly, with his broadcast of the injection, lifting the cane and using his whole arm to push the little button ("Hey audience! I'm giving the injection now!"), although this could have been a directorial, not acting, decision.

That leaves the concept. We all know that "Why not just shoot him?" can never really be answered. We suspend disbelief because we enjoy the movies. But suspension of disbelief is a two-way street. I expect the director and screenwriter to meet me halfway. This sequence is one of the clumsiest, most far-fetched, and least-effective murder attempts on record—up there with the hunt in *Moonraker* or the karate school in *The Man with the Golden Gun*.

Why has Zorin chosen to murder Bond via a dangerous horse chase? I see two possible explanations; to make it look like an accident, or to toy with Bond— make it "sporting." But part-way through the chase (before Bond escapes the track) Zorin's thugs attack Bond on horseback, so the "sport" and the "accident" are both spoiled. Finally, they simply pull a gun on Bond, which they could have done before the race.

Making matters worse, Zorin's own men take up the rear, guaranteeing that they will be caught by the jumps that are meant for Bond. While we know Zorin doesn't value his men's lives, it doesn't take a nuclear physicist to figure out if he kills his own men, he'll have no available muscle to take care of Bond. Why doesn't he just put the jumps back? In sum, Zorin acts like an idiot, not only failing to kill Bond, but failing to properly execute his own attempt to do so.

End Rant

As promised, it's time to discuss *A View to a Kill*'s better side. In addition to May Day as a villain and Pola Ivanova as a bubble bath additive, there are a few very likeable qualities to *A View to a Kill*. The movie opens well, with an exciting and mysterious teaser sequence. *A View to a Kill* has Maurice Binder's last really good title sequence. The laser bullets and glow effect may seem cheesy today, but the body paint still looks very cool, the color scheme is bold and startling, and it is a real effort from Binder, not just the same ol' thing. We're treated to a title song that has improved with age while we watch painted women get remarkably intimate with their guns.

The sets were very good, especially the Great Stables of Chantilly, which Zorin owns in the film (see AMAZE YOUR FRIENDS!). A fire was not something we'd seen in a Bond film before, and I found it exciting and different. The flooding of the mine was equally exciting, and a good contrast (y'know, fire and water; not unlike the fire and ice of *Die Another Day* a mere seventeen years later). Patrick Macnee was a welcome presence.

It has often been said that *A View to a Kill* is a remake of *Goldfinger*. A villain stockpiles something precious (Zorin even draws an analogy between silicon chips and gold) and then plans on destroying the world's supply of it so that he holds a monopoly. The villain is European but his plan takes him to America. Once there, he holds a meeting, inviting criminal leaders to buy in. When one refuses, he is surreptitiously killed. Bond must defuse a bomb in order foil the villain's plan, and then defeat the villain in a fight involving flying (airplane/blimp).

We don't expect Bond films to be entirely original anymore, we like the formula, and we expect a certain amount of repetition along with the new elements. However, in *A View to a Kill*, the new elements don't add up to much. There is interest in many of the bits and pieces of *A View to a Kill*—a concentration camp surgeon, a KGB agent gone independent; a computer-chip conspiracy, and a geologic disaster. But the bits aren't put together properly; they're a crazy quilt without a primary narrative thrust. The whole, in this case, is actually less than the sum of its parts.

High Points

- Enjoyable title sequence and great song.
- Pola Ivanova.
- May Day and Zorin wrestling.
- Bond's clever escape from drowning by breathing tire air.
- Death in a car wash—I always knew they were scary!
- The charming Sir Godfrey Tibbett.
- Zorin opening fire on the workers at Main Strike.
- A good teaser sequence (minus a certain poorly-placed song).
- The hat-toss switch with Moneypenny.
- The stables in Chantilly, France.

Low Points

- Roger Moore's ghoulish eye makeup (or whatever it is).
- Bond's attitude—either smirking or scolding.
- The sex scene between Bond and May Day.
- Spying on the shower with a surveillance doggy.
- Need I say?—the steeplechase scene.
- Tanya Roberts. Tanya Roberts. Tanya Roberts.
- "California Girls."
- Poor back-projection, and excessive use of stunt doubles.
- Bond's miraculous ability to look at a vial and comprehend the entire steroid injection subplot, thereby eliminating the need for any actual spying.
- Mortner blowing himself up with some dynamite that the Acme Company had apparently failed to ship to Wile E. Coyote.

Quotable Quotes

Bond, referring to Aubergine: "There's a fly in his soup."

Pola Ivanova: "The bubbles tickle my...Tchaikovsky!"

Bond, after defeating the thugs at the chip-packaging plant: "Don't worry, it's all wrapped up."

Zorin: "You slept well?"
Bond: "A little restless but I got off eventually."

Zorin, after killing the Taiwanese tycoon: "Anyone else want to drop out?"

Bond: "Drat! Dropped the soap."
Stacey: "I'll get it."
Bond: "That's not the soap."

Q (via radio): "007 alive."
M: "Where is he? What's he doing?"
Q (last line): "Just cleaning up a few details."

Facts and Figures

SEXUAL ENCOUNTERS

Four: Kimberly Jones, May Day, Pola Ivanova, and Stacey Sutton.

BOND'S CAR

None. He steals a 1985 blue Renault II taxi in Paris, and Tibbett drives a Rolls Royce Silver Ghost.

DEATHS

Approximately 47–67:

- 003, two Russians in helicopter, Aubergine, Tibbett, the Russian spy at the pumping station, Chuck Lee, Taiwanese tycoon, Howe, Jeff the night guard at City Hall, May Day, Zorin, Scarpine, Dr. Mortner
- In the Main Strike Mine, Bob Conley, Jenny Flex, Pan Ho, approximately thirty workers; perhaps as many as fifty.

Bond Kills:

- Three, all indirect. Bond shoots a flare into the helicopter that crashes, and Zorin falls while fighting Bond.

EXPLOSIONS

Six: The snowmobile, the helicopter, a small explosion during the fire, an impressive one when the mine is flooded, the bomb that takes May Day, and an anti-climactic one when the blimp blows.

BOND'S FOOD AND DRINKS

Vodka Martinis

None.

Other Drinks

- Vodka with Kimberly Jones.
- Bollinger '75 and then Lafite Rothschild '59 with Achille Aubergine at the Eiffel Tower.
- What appears to be several glasses of champagne during Zorin's party.
- Two bottles of red wine shared with Stacey over quiche.
- Champagne is visible nearby while Bond and Stacey are in the shower.

Food

- Beluga caviar with Kimberly Jones.
- Quiche de Cabinet (an omelet) with Stacey.

GAMBLING AND SPORTS

- Horse race
- Steeplechase

Amaze Your Friends!

- *A View to a Kill* is the only Bond movie in which Bond doesn't kill anyone directly.
- The restaurant where Bond and Achilles Aubergine eat is Restaurant Jules Verne on the second level of the Eiffel Tower.
- Tanya Roberts was nominated for a Razzie Award for Worst Actress for her role in this film. She lost to Linda Blair for *Night Patrol*.
- The Rolls Royce driven by Sir Godfrey Tibbett was Cubby Broccoli's personal car. Understandably, he insisted they use a different Rolls for sinking in the lake.
- Zorin's estate is in Chantilly, France. It is known as Chateau Condé and the Great Stables of Chantilly. The story that Zorin tells is true, the duke he mentions was Louis-Henri, the Duke of Bourbon, who commissioned the stables in the 18th Century, hoping to be reincarnated as a horse there.

Most Interesting Goofs

Gogol's Super Speed: Gogol reprimands Zorin for attempting to kill Bond mere minutes after it happens. How on Earth did Gogol learn about it at all, let alone fast enough to arrive from Russia?

Grandad Was a Lightweight: There's no ash in the urn containing grandad's ashes, nor is there any ash on the floor after the urn is broken.

Dripless Hot Tub: When Bond gets out of the hot tub, his feet are dry, there is no drip at all. This isn't a major goof; it's the sort of thing you see in movies all the time, I just wish I had a hot tub like that!

Front Wheel Drive? How does a rear-wheel drive car continue to maneuver without any rear?

Funny Filing System: Stacey and Bond go to City Hall to look up Zorin's records, which should be under Z (I used to be a secretary, I'm quite sure of this). They find the Main Strike maps under M—why were they looking there?

Processing Plant: Maybe this isn't a goof, but I can't figure out why Zorin has his microchip processing works at his stables.

HEROIN-FLAVORED BANANAS

The pre-titles teaser segment has been a Bond film tradition since *From Russia with Love*. Some teasers are integral to the plot (*Licence to Kill*), some stand entirely alone (*Goldfinger*), and some function as their own adventure, while setting up plot points that will be important later (*Tomorrow Never Dies*). Whatever the scenario (the basics of which are outlined below), the pre-titles sequence functions as a mini-movie, sneaking you into Bond's world (usually) for a taste (a tease, actually) of what will come. Since *Thunderball*, the gunbarrel motif has accentuated that feeling, as the barrel becomes a peephole through which we spy on the pre-titles sequence adventure. As we outline the teaser types below, some multi-scene teasers will appear in more than one category; we may, for instance, see Bond on an adventure *and* peek behind the villain's door.

Pre-titles Trivia

- Only two Bond movies lack a pre-titles sequence: *Dr. No* and *Never Say Never Again*.
- James Bond does not appear in three pre-titles sequences: *From Russia with Love*, *Live and Let Die*, and *The Man with the Golden Gun*. In two of these, we briefly believe that 007 is present because of an imitator in *From Russia with Love*, and an effigy in *The Man with the Golden Gun*; making *Live and Let Die*'s the only James Bond pre-titles sequence with no James Bond!

Peeking in the Villain's Keyhole

The first James Bond pre-titles sequence brought us, not into Bond's world, but into SPECTRE's. The point here is to outline exactly how dangerous the threat is which Bond will face in the movie proper. The *From Russia with Love* teaser is truly a tease, tricking us into thinking it is Bond's adventure we are seeing.

There are five pre-titles sequences that tease us with villainy. We see behind the villain's closed doors in:

- *From Russia with Love*
- *Live and Let Die* (the Voodoo rite especially qualifies)
- *The Man with the Golden Gun*
- *Licence to Kill* (in which we see Sanchez sadistically maim Lupe's lover)
- *Die Another Day* (in the "anger management" scene)

We Join Our Hero...

This most typifies the James Bond pre-titles sequence. It's probably what most fans think of when they consider the form, and rightly so, since nineteen of the twenty-three pre-titles sequences can be described this way. In a "Join Our Hero" pre-titles sequence, 007 is carrying out, or finishing up, a prior assignment, or having an unexpected adventure. This adventure may stand completely apart from the post-titles action, as in *Octopussy*, or it may lead directly to the main adventure, as in *Die Another Day*, where the assignment to assassinate Colonel Moon led to 007's quest for Moon after being released from prison (remember that this quest was no longer his job). Often, the pre-titles sequence adventure stands essentially alone, but will ultimately be seen to connect to the main adventure. For example, in *Thunderball*, Bond incurs an injury which will leave him at Shrublands when the main movie begins, and in *Tomorrow Never Dies*, we see Henry Gupta acquire the GPS controller which will figure heavily in Carver's scheme.

Only in *Quantum of Solace* does the main movie begin immediately where the pre-titles sequence left off—it's a pre-titles sequence but not really a teaser; it might as easily have happened after the titles.

Carrying Out an Assignment

These are complete adventures; we see Bond begin and end the mission (not always successfully), and we have a fairly clear idea what Bond is doing and why.

- *Goldfinger*
- *Thunderball*
- *Octopussy*
- *The Living Daylights*
- *GoldenEye*
- *Tomorrow Never Dies*
- *The World is Not Enough*
- *Die Another Day*
- *Casino Royale*
- *Skyfall*
- *Spectre*

Finishing Up an Assignment

Bond is coming home from an assignment, or we meet him mid-adventure and aren't clued in to exactly what's going on.

- *The Spy Who Loved Me*
- *A View to a Kill* (we know a little about this one, but there are all sorts of loose ends)
- *Quantum of Solace* (this is a continuation of the end of *Casino Royale*, so we don't see the beginning, but we are expected to know what it was).

Random Acts of Violence and Senseless Action

Bond is attacked by a prior villain seeking revenge, or is involved in a private fight on his own time. (*Spectre* could be on this list, as the assignment is not official, but it *is* an assignment, albeit by the late M and not the current one.)

- *On Her Majesty's Secret Service* (private fight)
- *Diamonds Are Forever* (Bond's search for Blofeld is a private vendetta)
- *Moonraker* (villain seeks revenge)
- *For Your Eyes Only* (villain seeks revenge)
- *Licence to Kill* (Bond shares Felix's fight on his own time).

Only 007 Can Save Us Now!

In these three pre-titles sequences, we first see a villainous act or a threat to the world. MI6 agrees to assign James Bond, who must be found. We then cut to our hero.

- *You Only Live Twice*
- *The Spy Who Loved Me*
- *Moonraker*

Teaser Women

In six teaser sequences, Bond is found in the midst of an assignation with a woman we never see again. In one case, Bond meets the woman as the pre-titles sequence adventure winds down. Some of these women turn out to be traitorous. In one case, *You Only Live Twice*, we are never sure if the woman was evil or not—because of some loose scripting, we'll never know if Ling was trying to kill Bond, or was simply an agent helping to fake his death.

The following breakdown doesn't count women with whom Bond has a platonic or strictly professional relationship. It also doesn't count women who return for the main movie.

Traitorous Women

- *Goldfinger*: Bonita
- *You Only Live Twice*: Ling (?)
- *The Spy Who Loved Me*: Log Cabin Girl
- *Moonraker*: Stewardess

Good Women

- *Octopussy*: Bianca (we do not see any intimacy in the pre-titles sequence, but see BOND GIRLS)
- *A View To a Kill*: Kimberly Jones
- *The Living Daylights*: Linda
- *Spectre*: Estrella

No Women at All

Only a handful of pre-titles sequences lack even the brief appearance of a beautiful woman. They are:

- *From Russia with Love*
- *For Your Eyes Only* (however, it is the grave of a beautiful and beloved woman that 007 visits)
- *GoldenEye*
- *Die Another Day*
- *Casino Royale*
- *Quantum of Solace* (M appears, but Judi Dench's M is never sexualized)

Top Five/Bottom Five

As usual, I have relied heavily on fan surveys as well as my own pig-headed opinions. This is the rare category in which I have allowed ties, as I'll explain below.

Best Teasers

1. *Goldfinger*
2. *The Spy Who Loved Me*
3. *The Living Daylights*
4. *GoldenEye*
5. TIE: *Licence to Kill* and *The World is Not Enough*
AND: *Casino Royale/Spectre*

Worst Teasers

1. *The Man with the Golden Gun*
2. *Diamonds Are Forever*
3. *For Your Eyes Only*
4. *On Her Majesty's Secret Service*
5. TIE: *Thunderball* and *Live and Let Die*
AND: *Quantum of Solace*

The Best Pre-titles Sequences

Goldfinger

We see Bond swimming to an oil refinery in a wet suit, with a fake bird on his head for camouflage. Coming out of the water, Bond dispatches a guard, breaks into the refinery and sets explosives.

Then, 007 strips away the wet suit to reveal a white dinner jacket underneath, and adds a red carnation to his boutonniere. This is an iconic moment, used for forty years to typify what James Bond is all about; a moment that contains espionage, panache, and humor with the opening of a single zipper. In 2002, *Die Another Day* would pay homage to this moment when Pierce Brosnan removes his wetsuit to find a suit of clothes underneath in that film's pre-titles sequence.

Now, Bond goes to a nearby nightclub, where a whispered conversation gives us the gist of Bond's mission; to destroy a heroin operation. He will leave the country once he completes "unfinished business" with Bonita, the beautiful club dancer. In Bonita's room, we see her in her bath and enjoy a sexy bit of dialogue and a kiss, until Bond sees the reflection of an assassin in Bonita's eye. After a fierce struggle, Bond electrocutes his opponent in the tub, and delivers the immortal line "Shocking, positively shocking."

About the #1 choice, there is little argument. It is the defining Bond pre-titles sequence. *From Russia with Love* introduced the idea of a pre-titles sequence, but *Goldfinger* perfected it, and while later pre-titles sequences have more spectacular stunts, and more sophisticated filming, none are more successful at epitomizing what 007 is all about. How many summaries of Bond history are there that *don't* include the wet suit removal, the "shocking" quip, or both? The *Goldfinger* pre-titles sequence *is* James Bond.

The Spy Who Loved Me

After a British and Soviet submarine each disappears, General Gogol calls in Agent XXX, and M calls in James Bond. Cut to Bond in a log cabin in the Austrian Alps, in bed with a lovely blonde (credited as "Log Cabin Girl"). Bond receives a message via his watch and gets up to leave, prompting the blonde to exclaim "But, James, I need you!" Bond's reply, "So does England!" is a classic.

Bond skis off and Log Cabin Girl, a Soviet agent, immediately radios a group of agents on skis (one of whom is Sergei, XXX's lover). An exciting ski chase ensues, including Bond flipping over backwards on skis, and while skiing backwards, shooting Sergei with a gun concealed in his ski pole.

Next, Bond skis right off the edge of a cliff, an awe-inspiring freefall in perfect silence, until he opens his parachute, which turns out to be an enormous Union Jack.

The Spy Who Loved Me is a perfect pre-titles sequence, and the first to introduce the mega-stunt as a part of the form. Everything about it works smoothly; the quick set up of the situation, the paralleling of General Gogol and M, which will continue throughout the movie; the segue to Bond in flagrante delicto, the excellent dialogue, the exquisite ski action, and finally, that amazing jump. In 1977 audiences cheered when they saw the Union Jack, and who can blame them?

The Living Daylights

In one of his most unusual temporary headquarters (see MI6 AROUND THE WORLD), M is at his desk in a plane, briefing a group of 00 agents on training exercises that are about to commence. The three agents parachute onto Gibraltar.

The first agent is immediately shot with a paint gun in the mock combat, but the second agent is killed in earnest. When the third agent turns his head, we see the new James Bond, Timothy Dalton. Bond pursues the assassin, and jumps on top of the Jeep he's escaping in. Gunfire ignites the explosives in the back of the Jeep, while Bond and the killer fight through its roof. The Jeep goes off a cliff and crashes, while Bond uses his reserve parachute to escape just in time. He lands on a yacht, where a beautiful but bored woman in a bikini invites him to stay for a drink.

The Living Daylights uses misdirection to introduce the new Bond, giving us two actors as 00 agents who bear a strong resemblance to George Lazenby and

Roger Moore. These little misdirections, like the one that means to fool us that Agent XXX is a man in *The Spy Who Loved Me*, are always a bit silly, as pre-publicity will by now have let us know who the stars of the picture are! More interestingly, the war games give us an inside peek into Secret Service operations that is rare and enjoyable. There's a certain flesh on the bones of Bond's organization when we know how much M values the political face gained by success at this mission.

What follows is a hot action sequence with a clear storyline. The pre-titles sequence has mystery, violence, action, behind-the-scenes espionage, and sex, in addition to explosives and the all-important jump off a cliff. *The Living Daylights'* pre-titles sequence doesn't have a mega-stunt or a startlingly witty one-liner, but it also has no weaknesses at all, carrying the viewer through from the exciting beginning to the sly segue into the titles.

GoldenEye

A lone man, seen only from behind, runs along the edge of a dam, and bungee jumps nearly to the bottom, firing a piton to bring himself the rest of the way down. He breaks into a Soviet chemical weapons facility, and we see the face of our new James Bond; Pierce Brosnan. Inside, he meets up with agent 006, and together, they set the bombs to blow the facility.

When the two men are caught, and 006 apparently shot in the head, Bond uses the chemicals as a shield to escape. Once outside, with soldiers in hot pursuit, Bond steals a motorcycle and chases a small plane, trying to leap aboard and steal it. Struggling with the pilot, both men fall out. Undaunted, Bond gets back on the motorcycle and chases the plane off the edge of a cliff. With the pilotless plane falling, Bond leaps from the motorcycle mid-air and catches the plane in freefall, pulling himself aboard and pulling the plane up from a near-certain crash in the nick of time.

This pre-titles sequence serves as an outrageous and thrilling re-introduction of James Bond to the world after a six-year absence. It illustrates a great deal of what is right, and what is wrong, about the Brosnan-era Bond. It is, first and foremost, an interesting story, with the right mix of action and humor. It is, along with the entire movie, intelligently written, forming a bridge between the Bond of prior movies, and the post-Cold War reality of 1995. It introduces the first 00 agent besides 007 who has had so much as a speaking role, and of course, it opens with one of the most glorious stunts ever seen on the silver screen.

On the other hand, *GoldenEye* is the first Bond movie to give us an apparently impossible stunt tricked up with CGI. I can't say whether catching a plane in freefall is really impossible, because more science-minded fans than I have been arguing both sides since 1995. But the point is, no one actually did it, and that's the first time in Bond history that statement can be made about a stunt. This has horrified and offended fans who feel that part of what distinguishes Bond from lesser action heroes is the authenticity of the stunts.

A second flaw in this pre-titles sequence is a matter of height. Bond jumps down 700 feet to get into the facility, which is at the base of a dam. How then can the facility be at the top of a cliff during his escape? Finally, at nearly ten minutes, we see the Brosnan-era trend towards long, over-burdened pre-titles sequences.

With such an outstanding opening stunt, this pre-titles sequence could have ended with a shorter escape and been at least as thrilling.

You may be asking yourself, since this sequence is so flawed, why include it in the Top Five? In my opinion, the flaws are greatly outweighed by this teaser's assets. Two of the Top Five pre-titles sequences—*GoldenEye* and *The World is Not Enough*—would have been improved by cutting them short; both suffer from their era's peculiar need for over-the-top at every turn. Of the two, I prefer *GoldenEye*; *The World is Not Enough*'s excess is more egregious, and *GoldenEye*'s beginning more auspicious. I love the bungee jump, the break-in, the quick sketch of a relationship between the two men, the escape from the chemical warehouse. All perfect until that last moment, so I am inclined to be forgiving. Besides which, as we go down the list of pre-titles sequences, we'll find an increase in logical holes and odd decisions; the final arbiter is how much enjoyment we derive, and on that scale, *GoldenEye* has a top-notch teaser sequence.

TIE: *Licence to Kill* and *The World is Not Enough*

It was impossible to choose between these two. One is a sentimental favorite, the other, an action favorite. One is a flight of Bond action fantasy, the other contains a large dose of gritty realism. One draws directly from Ian Fleming, the other is a thoroughly modern trip around the world. Finally, one is a huge favorite of the fans and the general public, while the other is a personal favorite.

Licence to Kill opens with an incident borrowed from Fleming's short story "The Hildebrand Rarity." Later, the movie will introduce Milton Krest and his boat, the Wavekrest, also from that story, and will also use an incident from the novel **Live and Let Die** that was never used in the movie of that name.

In the pre-titles sequence, the DEA spots Franz Sanchez leaving Cuban air space and heading towards the Florida Keys. They send a helicopter to catch up with the Rolls Royce taking Felix Leiter, James Bond, and Sharkey to Felix's wedding, and Felix and James go after Sanchez. Meanwhile, Sanchez has caught his lover, Lupe, with another man, and while Dario cuts the man's heart out, Sanchez whips Lupe with a stingray's tail, something Krest did to his wife in Fleming's story.

When Felix and James arrive in the Florida Keys, a cat-and-mouse chase ensues, and Sanchez at first gets away. Bond then realizes the helicopter can hook Sanchez's plane, and with "Let's go fishing!" he engineers this clever capture. With Sanchez's plane in tow, the helicopter heads to the church, where Felix and James parachute to the wedding. As the Wedding March plays, our heroes enter the church with 'chutes trailing like bridal trains.

Remember that at this point, we have seen seven different Felix Leiters. Most fans have great affection for the character, despite the lack of continuity. So to see the return of David Hedison, with James Bond as his best man, is a joyful moment indeed!

To contrast this joy we have the earthy horror of Franz Sanchez and his brutal response to infidelity. In the short pre-titles sequence, much of his character is established; he risks capture just to "discipline" his girlfriend, and he outsmarts the DEA by leaving a decoy plane to be staked out. When he is captured, it is through a very clever and enjoyable stunt.

Finally, we close the pre-titles sequence with the immensely sentimental and satisfying jump into Felix's wedding. This is a crowd-pleaser, and a personal favorite, despite its similarity to the end of the comedy classic *The In-Laws*.

The pre-titles sequence to *The World is Not Enough* is the opposite of *Licence to Kill*'s in almost every way. The part that most people recall and adore is the boat chase, which is perhaps why a similar chase, done with hovercraft, was used in the pre-titles sequence for *Die Another Day*. The chase is undeniably fun, although rather similar to the original Bond boat chase in *Live and Let Die*; including a brief foray onto land.

In Bilbao, Spain, Bond meets with a Swiss banker. The banker's goal is to pay Bond off, but 007 is there for information and a fight ensues. The banker is about to talk when he is killed by his female assistant (credited as "Cigar Girl"). Bond pulls off a dazzling escape out the window by using the body of one of the banker's staff as an anchor, and then walks nonchalantly away.

Back at MI6, Bond meets Sir Robert King and turns over the money. A moment later, he notices an unusual chemical reaction on his fingers. Realizing in a flash that the money has been tampered with, 007 chases Sir Robert through the MI6 offices, seconds too late to prevent a bomb from taking his life.

Bond sees Cigar Girl outside of MI6 headquarters, in a powerboat on the Thames. Taking a boat from Q's lab, he gives chase in an extended sequence, which ends in Cigar Girl escaping in a hot air balloon and killing herself, and Bond falling onto the Millennium Dome and injuring his shoulder.

Where *Licence to Kill*'s pre-titles sequence is real-world, *The World is Not Enough*'s is fantastic. Where the former is built around relationships (between James and Felix, between Sanchez and Lupe, between Felix and Della), the latter is built around spectacle and action. Although the boat chase is a fan favorite, I think the pre-titles sequence goes on too long. To me, a perfect pre-titles sequence would have ended with Bond's daring leap out of the window in Spain, and his smooth walk away. After that, I'm ready for a title sequence and the movie itself to begin; a movie that could have included the death of Sir Robert King and the ensuing chase.

Casino Royale

Dryden arrives in Prague and finds Bond in his office. In taut dialogue, we learn Dryden is a section chief turned traitor, and that Bond is not yet a 00 agent. Cut to Bond in a brutal fight, then cut to Dryden pulling a gun on Bond. Their discussion continues; we learn the fight is with Dryden's contact (credited as Fisher). Cut back to the fight; Bond drowns Fisher in sink. Back to Dryden, and Bond shoots him midsentence. Finally, back to the bathroom where the fight occurred; as Bond picks up his gun, we see Fisher is not really dead, and Bond shoots him directly into the gun-barrel.

An instant classic, the first black and white Bond pre-titles sequence is pointed and brutal. It economically establishes essential information about what this movie will be. Here, Bond earns his 00 but is still a "blunt instrument" (as M later says). The cinematography is wonderful, almost film noir, using heavy shadows in Dryden's office and bright, blown-out light in the fight. The fight itself is a masterpiece of brutality, and shows us a Bond who is inelegant and relentless. Simply a great introduction of Daniel Craig and of what the Craig films will be.

Spectre

Bond, masked and in costume, attends a Day of the Dead festival in Mexico City. Spotting Sciarra, he starts moving in a different direction, taking Estrella to a hotel. She gets in bed, but he walks out the window, onto the roof, where he takes a rifle to a vantage point where he can spy on and shoot Sciarra.

Eavesdropping electronically, Bond learns Sciarra intends to blow up a stadium. He shoots Sciarra's contact, is shot at, and misses Sciarra. His shot hits the bombs intended for the stadium; the building Sciarra is in blows up and collapses on Bond, who slides down the collapsing roof onto a waiting couch.

Sciarra calls for a helicopter, but Bond pursues; in an aerial fight over Mexico City, Bond grabs Sciarra's ring off his finger, then throws him and the pilot from the helicopter. Zoom in, and we see the familiar SPECTRE ring.

The action in this sequence is top-notch, but it rates mention because of the bravura filming. A 4 minute 10 second continuous tracking shot, taking us from a massive parade, into a hotel, and out onto the roof, without a single cut. This is showy filmmaking, but also creates immediacy and a point of view. Add to that the truly magnificent Day of the Dead festivities, as good a crowd scene as we've experienced since *Thunderball*'s Junkanoo.

The Worst Pre-titles Sequences

The Man with the Golden Gun

We see Scaramanga and Andrea Anders sunbathing; Nick Nack arrives with champagne. On the other side of the island, a gangster arrives, and is greeted by Nick Nack. He is given partial payment and soon both the gangster and Scaramanga are fighting for their lives in a funhouse. We see James Bond, but it is only a mannequin.

Scaramanga kills the gangster and then shoots the fingers off of the 007 mannequin.

This pre-titles sequence doesn't work on a number of levels. First, it creates sympathy for the villain, by placing him in contrast to the fumbling and obnoxious gangster, and by dressing him in a cuddly sweatsuit. Second, it doesn't feature James Bond at all—and this is the second movie in a row with that lack! In fact, given the criticisms of Roger Moore's acting when he first stepped into Sean Connery's Oxfords, a lifeless mannequin is perhaps too ironic an appearance.

Finally, Rodney is too much a buffoon, too readily defeated, to impress us. We are very clear that Scaramanga is never in any danger from this man who talks to Al Capone's likeness. Without danger, there is no excitement; this is fake action, not the real thing.

Diamonds Are Forever

The *Diamonds Are Forever* pre-titles sequence begins promisingly. A peaceful Japanese room is seen, and the camera holds still for a quiet moment, until a body comes flying violently in. We hear Bond demanding to know where Blofeld is, and the answer "Cairo." Instantly, we are at a Cairo casino, where "Hit me" brings the inevitable result. Next, a beautiful woman on a beach is greeted by "Bond, James Bond," and in a deft move, Bond removes her bikini top and strangles her with it until she tells him where Blofeld can be found.

All of this is wonderful stuff, and I admire it immensely, but all of it is meant as a lead-in to the main action of the pre-titles sequence, and therein lies the problem.

Bond breaks into a clinic of some kind, and inside, we see Blofeld arranging for a plastic surgery procedure (we see models of his face at various stages). A man buried fully in a mud bath tries to shoot Bond, who defeats him by burying him in more mud. Bond is briefly caught, but frees himself and ties Blofeld to a gurney, which he pushes into another mud bath. He turns up the heat and says "Welcome to hell, Blofeld."

None of this makes any sense. A man in mud is fully clothed and carrying a gun? A man in mud can be defeated by mud? If so, why didn't the mud hurt him while he was in it? Blofeld lies stock still while being tied to the gurney, like a Laurel and Hardy character waiting to be punched. And again, Bond simply assumes that being in mud will kill Blofeld, although we have to assume that the reason all that mud is around is for people to bathe in it! If the mud was just stupid, or if the action was just weak, this wouldn't be a Bottom Five pre-titles sequence, but with both on its side, I'm afraid I have no choice.

For Your Eyes Only

Bond is visiting his wife's grave when a helicopter arrives to pick him up. As he leaves, seated in the back, the priest at the cemetery blesses Bond, insinuating to the audience that perhaps the priest knows what 007 has in store.

Soon we learn that Bond is not in an MI6 helicopter, and the villain's voice is heard through audio speakers. Seeing a white cat, we are meant to know this villain is Blofeld, although for legal reasons he was never named; he will be referred to as such here. Blofeld electrocutes the pilot, and takes over control of the helicopter remotely, intending to terrorize Bond before killing him.

Bond manages to get outside the helicopter and open the front door, where he throws out the body of the pilot and attempts to take control. Meanwhile, Blofeld steers the 'copter inside a glassworks. Bond finds and cuts the remote controller connection, flies out of the glassworks, and scoops up Blofeld's wheelchair. Blofeld begins screaming and begging for release, while Bond pats him on the head. 007 deposits Blofeld, still trying to negotiate his release, down a smokestack, presumably killing him.

A lot of people forgive the hideous action scene in this pre-titles sequence because the opening visit to Tracy's grave is so touching. And it is touching, but I'm not inclined to forgive. I have ranted about this scene sufficiently in the VILLAINS section. Suffice it to say, not only is the portrayal of Blofeld an embarrassment to the entire franchise, but the action itself is inadequate.

On Her Majesty's Secret Service

In the first pre-titles sequence designed to introduce a new Bond (George Lazenby), he is shown first by association. We start at MI6, where Q's ridiculous idea is dismissed brusquely by M. This tiny scene is all we'll see of Q in this movie until the very end. Once M mentions 007, we cut to him, again by association—a gunmetal cigarette case, an Aston Martin, and fast driving. Bond is passed by a red Mercury Cougar, and when he later comes across the same car parked, he sees a beautiful woman walking into the surf wearing evening clothes. Quickly he runs to her and pulls her out of the water. She faints in his arms.

Out of nowhere, three men appear, and one pulls a gun on Bond, while another grabs the woman (Tracy) and takes her away. When Bond frees himself from the gunman and a fight begins, Tracy's captor leaves her on the sand to join the fray. Bond defeats the three men, but Tracy jumps into Bond's car and drives quickly to her own car, and then makes her escape. Bond picks up her discarded shoes, looks into the camera and says "This never happened to the other fellow."

Where to begin? Some fans like this one, citing a convincing, pull-no-punches fight in the water, but that is little enough for which to praise a teaser sequence. Everything about this, with that one possible exception, is wrong, starting with a cold dismissal of Q from the movie. Many fans are happy when Bond eschews gadgets for guts, but none that I've ever met want such a beloved character sent out to pasture.

The next thing that bothers me is what Bond thinks he's rescuing Tracy from, as discussed in the *On Her Majesty's Secret Service* section. Are all women who walk into the water suicidal? My child's theory is that the spangly evening gown was very heavy, and Bond knew it would drag her into the water. (I've worn sequins; they have a point.) Then there's her strange fit of fainting, followed by a really bizarre fight. One thug abandons his kidnapping of Tracy mid-nap. Peter Hunt undercranks the whole thing so that it is jerky and surreal.

Finally, we have the one and only incident of a Bond film breaking the fourth wall. Bond fans love humor, but they don't want the joke to be on them, and few if any of us want to hear about "the other fellow," thank you very much.

TIE: Thunderball and Live and Let Die

Here are two pre-titles sequences that are partly successful, but don't quite make the grade. *Live and Let Die*'s pre-titles sequence is considerably less popular with fans because of Bond's absence from it, but it is a better film exercise than *Thunderball*'s pre-titles sequence. My personal Bottom Five is fairly representative of fan opinion, except that *Live and Let Die* usually appears somewhere. This fan or that will leave off *On Her Majesty's Secret Service* or *For Your Eyes Only* or what have you, and *Live and Let Die* will show up more often than not. So, I'm again declaring a tie, a neck-and-neck race between the one I personally think is lesser and the one that fans tend to vote for, with which I cannot entirely disagree. Some fans also include *A View to a Kill* on their Worst list, but only because of one stupid musical joke; the sequence is a little pale, but there's nothing particularly wrong with it that a lack of Beach Boys wouldn't cure.

Thunderball opens with a quick hint at Bond's mortality; the third movie in a row to do so. The gunbarrel zooms into the initials JB on a coffin, but the misdirection is short-lived. In a whispered conversation between Bond and a beautiful French agent, we learn that Bond was in France to kill Jacques Botier, and was foiled by Botier's natural death. When 007 sees the widow open the car door for herself, he is suspicious, and hurries back to Botier's home, where he learns that his enemy is alive. A terrific fight starts, in which Bond receives one of the few injuries that last past the scene in which it occurs.

Bond kills Botier and throws lilies on the body, just as men run in to defend him. Rushing to the roof, Bond escapes using his jet pack (pausing first to put on a helmet), and flies a short distance to his Aston Martin, where the French agent awaits him. The bad guys have given chase, but Bond foils them with water jets shooting from his stationary car.

Now, this isn't a bad sequence exactly, but it's weak. The jet pack is, in retrospect, a disappointment. Sure, it was the coolest thing since the cucumber in 1965, but it took a very short ride indeed, and required an awkward helmet-donning insert. Having the Aston Martin come back, but remain parked, was another let down. The DB5 also is covered with dirt or rust or something, and looks ugly. The DB5 should never look ugly!

At the opening of *Live and Let Die*, we see the United Nations Building against a New York skyline, and move into a meeting of the General Assembly, where the United Kingdom representative is killed by some sort of sound in his translation earphone.

Next we move to New Orleans. A man observes a solemn funeral procession. The man is stabbed, the trick coffin opens from below to take him in, and the procession becomes joyful—a true New Orleans funeral.

Finally, we are in an unnamed Caribbean location (which we will learn is the fictional island of San Monique). A Voodoo ceremony is taking place, and a man is killed by a snake as part of the ceremony.

Where some later pre-titles sequences are too long, this one is too short, or at least short in the wrong way. What we see is stylish and interesting; each murder is unique and the middle one is especially clever. However, this is the sort of thing that, in most pre-titles sequences, leads to M or the Prime Minister asking "Where's Bond?" Instead, it is the audience who asks. *Live and Let Die* has the only pre-titles sequence that lacks even an image of Bond. The pre-titles sequence also lacks any central action—there are no fights, no stunts; no spectacle at all. It is the opening of a mystery, not a Bond film, and although it is better than it is often given credit for, it simply fails to do its job.

Quantum of Solace

A short, intense car chase through winding Italian roads. Bond crashes into a truck but keeps going, losing his driver-side door in the process. Eventually he forces his pursuer off the road and down a steep incline, and arrives at an MI6 safe house in Siena, Italy. Opening the trunk, we see he has Mr. White tied up, and says softly to him, "It's time to get out."

This chase is simply impossible to follow, and far too dismal. In that way, it predicts the rest of the movie. The filming here zooms in, cuts constantly, uses lots of close-ups (a wheel, a bumper, Bond's eyes) but never shows us the action in a mid-range shot where we can actually follow what's going on. A cop radios that a gray Aston Martin is being followed by a black Alfa Romeo, but to me both cars appear black no matter how many times I view the scene. With all the close-shots and rapid cuts, there's no way to tell them apart.

After all this meaningless action, Bond steps out of a totaled car—a perfect opportunity for a quick quip. The quip does not arrive. The quip, indeed, never arrives, right through to the end of the film.

The post-titles film begins exactly where the pre-titles sequence ends, making one wonder why there is a pre-titles sequence at all.

THIS NEVER HAPPENED TO THE OTHER FELLOW

Th'ere are two questions with which Bond fans tend to break the ice: What's your favorite (Bond) movie, and who's your favorite Bond. The choice of a favorite Bond actor is an area of hot contention, an expression of loyalty, and a badge of devotion. No one lacks a favorite Bond, even those of us who love two or three or more.

I should pause for a moment to delineate the line between "favorite" and "best." The word favorite is inherently subjective, your favorite is the one that you have the most personal affection for; that is nearest to your heart. The word best, on the other hand, implies objectivity; measurable superiority. So the best actor is the one who best performed each of the various tasks required of playing James Bond, whereas your favorite is the one who has touched you in some way; the one who is Bond to you. My favorite Bond actor has long been Timothy Dalton, for a host of reasons; that he brought me back to Bond fandom after an absence of two decades, that he had a delicious romance with Kara Milovy that makes me melt, that he restored the hard edge to Bond that had departed the series with Sean Connery. But in forcing myself to look objectively at each of the actor's strengths and weaknesses, I have had to conclude that Dalton is not the best 007.

Each actor has his strengths and weaknesses, and a passion for each one says something different about the fans who love him. Let's run down their qualities in order.

Sean Connery

Strengths:

- Sex appeal, physical grace and magnetism.
- Convincing in a fight.
- A sense of brutality.
- An insouciant, flippant, lightness of performance.
- Excellent delivery of one-liners.
- The best acting career outside of the Bond role.

Weaknesses:

- A tendency towards emotionlessness; only Connery and Moore never had a real romance in the role, and Moore was seen to mourn Tracy.
- Some fans cite an occasionally problematic toupee (I never notice).
- In later films, a tendency to lisp (in *Never Say Never Again*, he can be distinctly heard to ask about the "United Shtates").

He's the One Who...

- Created the role.
- Is Scottish.
- Won an Oscar.
- Is Indiana Jones's father.

Fans Who Love Him...

- Have been Bond fans for a very long time (they're often Boomers), or...
- Appreciate the original in all things.
- Love Bond's sense of cool.

George Lazenby

Strengths:

- Physically imposing; good in a fight.
- An expressive face that sometimes speaks volumes.

Weaknesses:

- No acting experience.
- Stiff spoken delivery.
- Loud broadcasting of one-liners.
- A tendency to pose like a model.
- Too square-jawed; looks more like a traditional American hero than James Bond.

He's the One Who...

- Only played the part once.
- Is Australian.
- Got married (as Bond).
- No one remembers.

Fans Who Love Him...

- Are iconoclasts.
- Are fiercely loyal.
- Love the movie (*On Her Majesty's Secret Service*) more than the man.

Roger Moore

Strengths:

- Youthful good looks (until that last film!).
- Easy, laid-back delivery.
- A light touch with one-liners.
- An affection for his co-stars that was often apparent on screen.

Weaknesses:

- Unconvincing in action sequences and fights.

- Too tongue-in-cheek; emphasized his character's humor more than his strength.
- A sometimes schoolboy eagerness towards sex and a tendency to leer.

He's the One Who...

- Played a "gentleman spy."
- Was the first English Bond.
- Wore safari suits.
- Was "The Saint."
- Was a UNICEF ambassador.

Fans Who Love Him...

- Love Bond for his humor and one-liners.
- Are Gen Xers.
- Place *For Your Eyes Only* in their Top Five.

Timothy Dalton

Strengths:

- Talented actor with a dramatic flair.
- Eagerness to do as much of his own stunts as possible.
- Smoldering intensity.
- Terrific love scenes.
- Studied Fleming's writing to prepare for the role.

Weaknesses:

- Some fans find him humorless.
- Vampiric hairstyle in *Licence to Kill*.
- A sloppy dresser who didn't wish to be as dapper as Bond is known to be.

He's the One Who...

- Is controversial (see below).
- Always seemed on the verge of losing control.
- Is Welsh.
- Was in *Flash Gordon*.
- Was offered the part before George Lazenby.

Fans Who Love Him...

- Are fans of Ian Fleming's writing.
- Disdain the "funny" Bond movies.
- Love Bond when he's dangerous.

Pierce Brosnan

Strengths:

- Great emotional depth; equally at ease with anger, loss, and tenderness.
- Excellent at action; runs like the wind.

- Wonderful deadpan delivery of one-liners.
- Laughs more readily than any other Bond.
- Combines the strengths of his predecessors; cool, strong, intense, and humorous.

Weaknesses:

- Has often lacked chemistry with his co-stars.
- Has sometimes been too stiff in the role, especially in *Tomorrow Never Dies*.
- Some fans have remarked on his strange accent, which can shift alarmingly from British to Irish to American and back again.

He's the One Who...

- Was Remington Steele.
- Straightens his tie.
- Is Irish.
- Complained bitterly about Eon firing him.

Fans Who Love Him...

- Embrace the "new age" of high-tech Bond.
- Love the part of Bond that really *feels*.
- Often like him better than they like his movies.

Daniel Craig

Strengths:

- The most physically fit Bond—he trains intensely for each movie.
- Does many of his own stunts, and is masterful in a fight scene.
- Talented actor with a wide range.
- Handled a complex romance and subsequent grief with conviction.
- Those blue eyes.

Weaknesses:

- Sometimes humorless.
- The sex scenes are good, but not his forte.
- At 5'10", some fans deem him too short to play Bond.
- Not classically handsome.

He's the One Who...

- Was called the "Blond Bond"
- Curses like a sailor in interviews.
- Has sustained multiple injuries making Bond films.
- Is an "English bulldog."
- Is married to Rachel Weisz.

Fans Who Love Him...

- Love "back to basics" Flemingesque Bond.
- Might never have enjoyed Bond before him.

- Rate *Casino Royale* in their top five.

So Who's The Best?

Surveys have little variation to the answer. Once again, I combined hardcore fan surveys, casual fan surveys, and mainstream media surveys to derive a broad-based answer that satisfies all factions. Almost invariably, the order from best to worst comes out:

1. Connery
2. Craig
3. Brosnan
4. Moore
5. Dalton
6. Lazenby

Once in a while, a survey will result with Dalton and Moore's position switched (Dalton #4, Moore #5) but otherwise, no matter who you ask, given a sufficient sampling, this will be your answer. You'll find articles, of course, where Brosnan or Moore or Craig is listed as #1, but those are by single authors: I'm talking about aggregate data.

What is interesting is *why* this is the answer. First of all, Sean Connery gains the votes of a sizeable number of older fans who consider him the only James Bond, some whom have never seen Brosnan's or Craig's portrayal.

Many Connery purists are like me; they were turned off by Moore's tongue-in-cheek approach and dropped the franchise, never to look back. (I guess that makes me a reformed Connery purist.)

Among fans who are still watching Bond movies, have seen all of them, and eagerly anticipate new releases, Craig and Connery run neck-and-neck. Brosnan had that position before *Casino Royale*, but has lost esteem in the ensuing years. Sometimes fans prefer a newer actor but will vote for Connery out of loyalty, or because he is due extra props for creating the role. (None of this is conjecture, by the way. In addition to compiling a lot of survey data, I have also spoken to a lot of fans. A lot.)

My thoughts about my own favorite have changed a lot in the 14-plus years since I first wrote this book. I don't automatically place Dalton as a favorite anymore, although my affection for his portrayal hasn't waned. I place Dalton and Craig side-by-side: They both dug into Ian Fleming as source material. This gloomier portrayal wasn't suitable to a 1980s sensibility—Dalton was arguably ahead of his time. For the 21st century, it's exactly what audiences want.

Dalton's tenure has been outstripped by his successors, and I don't think he quite came up to Sir Sean. Prior to Craig, Dalton was the most romantic and emotionally moving of the group, as well as the edgiest. Clearly, he's been outstripped in the "edgy" department; I still love his romantic flair. These two men are Fleming's Bond, a Bond who sometimes hates his job.

For me, that leaves only two others to consider—Brosnan and Connery. Lazenby is no actor, and never mastered the role. Sir Roger Moore was accomplished in his own right, but he was too much the clown, and winked and smirked his way through too much of his career as agent 007.

My opinion of Pierce Brosnan was pushed forward by *Die Another Day*. His command of the character in that film was masterful, nuanced, and richly embodied. As Roger Ebert so succinctly put it in his review of that film: "I realized with a smile, 15 minutes into the new James Bond movie, that I had unconsciously accepted Pierce Brosnan as Bond without thinking about Sean Connery, Roger Moore or anyone else. He has become the landlord, not the tenant."

After seeing *GoldenEye* through *The World is Not Enough*, I could readily acknowledge Brosnan's excellence in the role, and still have no doubt that Sir Sean Connery was the best. But as Brosnan stepped forward, edging his performance up a notch, I began to notice small things about Connery's Bond that I liked less.

Comparing the two, we see that Connery is the more virile; he is almost animalistic and has the most powerful screen presence of any Bond actor. Brosnan is the more complex, the one who combines the most disparate elements of Bond. He can be cold-blooded, he can be emotional, and he has an excellent comic touch. (Craig is a great actor, but cannot approach Brosnan when it comes to comedy.)

Both Sean Connery and Pierce Brosnan are terrific physically. Connery had the edge in a fistfight, but I have never seen any action hero run the way Brosnan runs, like a gust of wind. Both are incredibly persuasive as the strong, rugged hero who can do it all.

Of the six actors, it is Connery whose non-Bond acting career is the most impressive, even given that he has had more time. Besides Connery, only Dalton has starred in a true all-time, classic, will-be-remembered-forever movie. For Dalton, that movie is *The Lion in Winter*, made when he was a very young man. For Connery, his greatest film is probably *The Man Who Would Be King*, but he has made so many films, and many of them great. One could easily cite *The Last Great Train Robbery*, *Highlander*, or *Murder on the Orient Express* (1974) as well. Connery is the only one of the crew to win an Oscar (for *The Untouchables*, which many would list as a great film, although I think it merely good).

But in Connery's tenure as Bond, there are several scenes where he backed off and avoided emotion, and lately, that bothers me. Think of *Thunderball*, in the scene on the beach with Domino. In the **Thunderball** novel, Bond tells Domino that he loves her, that he knew it was wrong to make love to her when he was going to tell her such terrible things, but his feelings were so deep that his passion overcame him. It is arguably the single most affective scene Fleming ever wrote, rivaling the ending of **On Her Majesty's Secret Service** . Claudine Auger plays the scene perfectly, with delicacy, bitterness, and loss. Connery, inexplicably, dons sunglasses, utterly backing away. He plays it coldly. True, coldness is a legitimate acting choice— but sunglasses? Imagine what Brosnan would have done with that scene!

Also troublesome is Aki's death in *You Only Live Twice*. It is Tiger Tanaka who pronounces her dead, and Bond doesn't even pause to look at her body before he proceeds to outline their plan of attack. Again, compare that to Brosnan's discovery of Paris Carver's body, or Dalton's discovery of Della Leiter.

Brosnan won over numerous "reformed purists," and proved himself worthy to fill Connery's shoes. Finally, when Craig stepped in, he so utterly rewrote the character (with Eon's help, of course), that he stands in a class by himself.

Timothy Dalton: Rumors, Controversy, and the Six-Year Gap

This is a good place to discuss the strange rumors, misapprehensions, controversies, and outright hostility that dogged Dalton's brief tenure with MI6.

If you discuss Dalton's career as James Bond on the Internet, here is what you'll "learn:" Dalton was always a second choice, the fans hated and still hate Dalton, it was fan hostility towards Dalton that caused *Licence to Kill* to fail in the box office, Dalton did such damage to the series that after *Licence to Kill*, a Bond movie wasn't made for six years, and Eon didn't want Dalton to return to the role in 1995 for *GoldenEye*.

Now here's the truth:

Timothy Dalton was Eon's first choice to play James Bond in *The Living Daylights*. When Dalton wasn't available, due to the filming schedule of *Brenda Starr*, they offered the role to Pierce Brosnan. Brosnan had to wait to find out if NBC was going to exercise their option to renew his *Remington Steele* contract for one more year. They did—on the very last day of the contract. So, Brosnan famously lost the role, and by then, Dalton was available.

I decided to survey Bond fans and movie fans, specifically seeking people who hated Dalton. In fact, I went out of my way to ask Dalton haters to participate, thinking they might otherwise blow off a survey that seemed to favor him. Even with that slant towards the most negative possible reaction, I found that only twenty percent of those surveyed were unhappy with Dalton's portrayal of James Bond. Of that twenty percent, several voters indicated that they liked *The Living Daylights* very much, and were only turned off by *Licence to Kill*, indicating, to me anyway, that the movie had more to do with their feelings than the man. Granted, twenty percent is too high from a movie producer's point of view, but it also isn't a groundswell, it isn't "everybody hates him," as common wisdom would have it.

What is notable is that the people who hate Dalton do so with extraordinary vitriol. Their hostility far outstrips anything that I feel towards George Lazenby, for example. They make enough noise that if you listen, you'll think it must be fifty or eighty percent of the fans. I did a second survey, to divide those who didn't hate Dalton between fans and those who thought he was just okay. Those who called themselves "enthusiastic" or "fans" outnumbered those who described themselves as lukewarm, and represented nearly half of the total number of voters (that's half of the 100%, not half of the 80% who didn't hate him).

Licence to Kill nosedived in the box office for a number of reasons, including a badly botched marketing campaign and release at the same time as *Indiana Jones and the Last Crusade*. It was the first and only Bond film to receive a "15" rating in England because of its excessive violence. Its dark theme had little appeal to the many Bond fans who were used to Roger Moore's reign. In short, I have never seen a legitimate industry analyst pin the blame for *Licence to Kill*'s relative lack of success on Timothy Dalton, whose previous Bond film was quite popular.

After *Licence to Kill*, Eon was ready to go ahead and create a third Dalton film. There had been problems with MGM, which was why *Licence to Kill* was so poorly marketed, but Eon had the next script in development. Lawsuits related to the ownership of MGM and of Bond licensing rights caused the majority of the delay.

Finally we must ask, did Eon fire Dalton? Well, I wasn't a fly on the wall, and neither were you. The rumors that Dalton was asked to resign are well-supported and credible. However, there are also rumors that there was conflict between MGM and Eon—the Broccoli family wanted Dalton to stay, MGM wanted him to go. Because the behind-the-scenes details have never been revealed, all we know is that Dalton resigned with good grace, and was not officially fired.

Who's Next?

As of this writing, *No Time to Die* is slated to be Daniel Craig's last Bond film. This seems definitive—he'll be 52 on its release, he's suffered numerous injuries during filming that get harder to recover from with age, and his film career outside of Bond is taking off (*Knives Out*, in particular, was a huge success).

I was one of those anti-Craig people when his casting was announced, and I was proven wrong. There aren't even rumors, right now, of who might be next. But I've learned my lesson and I won't jump on an anti-next-guy bandwagon. I think Eon will get it right.

THE LIVING DAYLIGHTS (1987)

Survey Says!

> Percent Favorite: 5.5%
> Top 5 Cumulative: 5/25
> Numeric Rating: 6.6/10
> Ranking: 9.26 (7th/25)

My Rating and Ranking

> Rated: 10/10
> Ranked: 4 out of 25

Summary

When General Georgi Koskov of the KGB defects, he reveals that his superior, General Pushkin, has a plot to kill Western spies called Smiert Spionam: Death to spies. Bond is assigned to kill Pushkin, but he is suspicious of Koskov and finds that Koskov's girlfriend, Kara Milovy, helped fake his defection. Bond and Pushkin fake Pushkin's death to flush out Koskov's plot, and learn he has teamed up with arms dealer Brad Whitaker in a scheme to defraud the Soviet government of millions and use the money in opium dealing. With the help of Kamran Shah of the Mujahadeen, Bond sabotages Koskov's opium. Felix Leiter is back to help Bond break into Whitaker's compound, where Bond kills Whitaker and Pushkin captures Koskov. Kara Milovy, a gifted cellist, is granted an immigration visa by General Gogol (now with the Foreign Service) so that she can play in both Western and Soviet orchestras.

> **James Bond:** Timothy Dalton
> **Kara Milovy:** Maryam d'Abo
> **General Georgi Koskov:** Jeroen Krabbe
> **Brad Whitaker:** Joe Don Baker
> **Kamran Shah:** Art Malik
> **Necros:** Andreas Wisniewski
> **Saunders:** Thomas Wheatley
> **Felix Leiter:** John Terry
> **General Gogol:** Walter Gotell
> **M:** Robert Brown
> **Moneypenny:** Caroline Bliss
> **Q:** Desmond Llewelyn
> **Directed by** John Glen

Discussion

Can I be objective about *The Living Daylights*? Oh, hell, I can critique anything, and be as fair as humanly possible. But can any of us be objective about Bond? When someone says a scene is boring, or a woman is beautiful, or a fight is exciting, those are all subjective terms. So, sure, I'm biased about *The Living Daylights* (see A BOND STORY (CONTINUED)), but I'd contend that we're all biased when it comes to our favorite secret agent. Nonetheless, if I'm going to write about the movie, it's only fair that I notice both its good side and its bad, and as ever, I'll try to be fair to the point of view of those fans who disagree with me.

First off, we have to acknowledge that this is the debut of a new Bond, and a controversial one at that (see THIS NEVER HAPPENED TO THE OTHER FELLOW). Many fans who hate Dalton don't want to hear it about Dalton's movies, but then again, Dalton can act circles around George Lazenby. Even Lazenby's fans say he's good in some scenes, or that he's good considering he'd never acted, or that they're sure he'd have improved. The apologists adore *On Her Majesty's Secret Service*, and even some people who aren't Lazenby fans love his one Bond movie. Why not, then, set Dalton aside for the moment, and look at his Bond film debut as a *movie*? *The Living Daylights* opens with a terrific punch, giving us an exciting and unique pre-titles sequence that gracefully introduces the new star. With Dalton himself gripping the top of the Jeep in much of the sequence, we know that 00 action is back.

The entire opening post-credits is outstanding. Ian Fleming's short story "Living Daylights, The" tells of Bond's wait at an East Berlin window for a KGB sniper he must kill. Instead of a defector, it's an escaping MI6 agent that both Bond and the KGB want. Knowing only that the escape will occur between 6 and 7 pm on one of three days, he watches an orchestra enter and exit their rehearsals while waiting, and develops a fascination for the beautiful cellist. Of course, she is the sniper, and he shoots to wound instead of to kill. The agent escapes, and the story ends with Bond speaking the title phrase, as in the movie.

The film adaptation of this portion of the tale is fine, straight-ahead stuff; as good in its way as *From Russia with Love*. Saunders is a great character who moves through a genuine arc, shifting bit by bit from bureaucratic prig to one of the good guys. Later, we believe Bond's rage when Saunders is killed, because (in part) we believe that Bond has come to like the guy. The reaction shot in that scene remains a classic, one of the standout "moments" of the series. Dalton haters will point to it as overacting, but those who accept Dalton without being big fans of Dalton or *The Living Daylights* will tend to include that reaction shot on "Favorite Dramatic Moments" lists (that's right, more fan lists!).

The relationship between Bond and Saunders starts out tense, desk jockey versus hero, and we, like Bond, sense the grit and unpleasantness of this particular job. This isn't an adventure, after all, it's an assassination, and to quote *The World is Not Enough* "cold-blooded murder is a filthy business." That filth is illustrated by the dusky Bratislava streets as Bond watches from behind the curve of a hammer and sickle. The segue into the pipeline escape is clever, breaking the tension but not the intelligence. We appreciate the wit of the escape, and of Bond outfoxing Saunders; Rosika's distraction in the control room is a good laugh.

The attack on the safe house is fantastic. One gets an awful "oh no" feeling of screwing up that is reminiscent of *Goldfinger*. Necros is a classic Aryan henchman in the "I miss Red Grant" mold. His accents, his step-by-step entry into a supposedly impenetrable location, and his use of headphones as a garrote are all terrific. The headphones in particular are a great device. One could object to the fact that he only listens to one song, but using "Where Has Everybody Gone?" as Necros's theme, and having the melody in the soundtrack to introduce his murders, is effective. Don't forget that this is the Bond film with a kitchen fight, including a burning grill, an electric carver, and boiling water; it's good to remember from time to time that your kitchen is a very dangerous place!

At this point in the film, we don't know that Koskov is the villain, although don't we all hope he is so that Bond can kill him after all that obsequious hugging and kissing and posturing? (Alas, Pushkin has that honor.) The scene with M is based on the belief that Koskov is the good guy, and shades of *Goldfinger* again! M threatens Bond with 008. Good ol' 008 must be a real button-down guy, always following orders whenever Bond is a naughty boy.

When we finally meet Pushkin, he has the strength of character that we expect from the charismatic John Rhys-Davies, and he is a worthy replacement for General Gogol. The confrontation in Pushkin's hotel room is another memorable dramatic "moment," one that shows off the assets Dalton brings to the production. The scene was originally written, with Roger Moore in mind, as a polite conversation over drinks. How much more memorable and interesting is the final result! This nicely moves into a faked assassination set piece that is just dynamite (no pun intended).

Some fans have complained that the character being discredited by Koskov should have been General Gogol, and indeed that's what the script originally called for. When Walter Gotell wasn't available for a key supporting role, he was "moved to Foreign Service" and given a cameo in the final scene. Of course, the movie would have benefitted if the audience had been as familiar with the character as Bond was, but the Bond films aren't designed for the hardcore fans, and the filmmakers in any case could not have assumed the viewer would know who Gogol was. With a quick bit of dialogue, Bond and M persuade us that General Pushkin is known to them, and so we can readily accept that Pushkin is the equivalent of the man we've known all these years. Getting a superb character actor to play Pushkin didn't hurt.

Kara Milovy is a real person, complex and fleshed-out, with goals, hopes, naivety and strength. Fans often complain about this as "the monogamous Bond movie." First of all, it isn't. Bond has a tryst with Linda, the woman on the yacht, at the end of the pre-titles sequence. The only monogamous Bond movie up to this point was *Diamonds Are Forever*, where Bond sleeps with no one other than Tiffany Case. (Both *Casino Royale* and *Quantum of Solace* are monogamous, and *Skyfall* may be, depending on whether you think Bond slept with Eve.)

Secondly, you can easily write off a "woman's point of view" if you like, but damn, I like that Bond and Kara have a relationship that develops romantically, as opposed to just sexually (Bond's normal M.O.). For my money, it's the best romance in the series (sorry, Tracy). Like Tracy, Kara is a "bird with a wing down" (Fleming's phrase), and Bond is attracted to her need. But he's also attracted to her talent, and, I think, to the way she represents an entirely different world than Bond's. She is a musician, she creates beauty; Bond, especially the literary Bond, often hates the ugly but necessary life of a spy. To touch someone innocent of violence, and gifted in a world that Bond admires but cannot enter, must be incredibly attractive. Kara acts the fool in the escape from the Afghan jail, standing like a mannequin while Bond fights for their lives, but it's her first experience with real danger, and she learns quickly. The next day she's spurring Kamran Shah's men to action and she decks a soldier tidily.

(*Note*: The above was written before Craig's movies, which have brought romance back to the series in a big way.)

I love the locations in *The Living Daylights*, a real step up from the last two films. John Glen worked on *The Third Man* when he was a young man, and Vienna's Prater Wheel scene is an homage to that Orson Welles classic. Perhaps his *Third Man* experience is why Vienna looks so lovely, so romantic, so magical. The contrast between gray Czechoslovakia (as it was then known—the city of Bratislava is now in Slovakia) and Vienna, followed by an exquisitely sunny Tangier, is remarkable. The Morocco locations used to stand in for Afghanistan are also excellent; wide spaces, stark deserts, sparse oases.

Also notable is the excellent action and stunts. The pre-titles sequence's parachute work and desperate Jeep ride, the fight off the back of the Hercules jet, the raid on horseback against the Afghan air base, the aforementioned kitchen fight—*The Living Daylights* puts the action back into action-adventure.

Unfortunately, the movie lacks villainy. Georgi Koskov is annoying, not evil, and his smug, self-satisfied routine gets old. I actually like that greed and amorality are his scheme, instead of Soviet glory or world domination, but it turns out that "slimy" just doesn't equal "Bond villain." The main thrust of his scheme threatens no one except Pushkin, Kara, and the handful of agents he must assassinate to convince MI6 that Pushkin is a threat. "Misuse of government funds," especially Soviet government funds, is hardly a cause for Bond to leap into the fray. As far as I can see, the U.S.S.R. really is buying weapons from Whitaker, who really will provide them. He's just using some float time to invest the money and make an even bigger profit. Other than the fact that opium is involved, my bank does the same thing, which is why it takes my checks so damn long to clear.

Brad Whitaker has a neurotic crazy-guy obsessive failure personality; kicked out of West Point, a roomful of statues with his own face; cool stuff, but it isn't really used. He could have been the centerpiece of the film, instead he throws off the pacing. His presence kind of causes the viewer to ask, "Wait, is *he* the villain?" As with *Octopussy*, another movie with near-equal accomplices as villains, the plot can become overwrought.

As far as Dalton is concerned, you, dear reader, must already know I adore him. He is romantic, smoldering, tough, and focused. He is the Bond I always wanted Bond to be, the Bond I longed for fruitlessly when Roger Moore had the role. Called humorless by his detractors, I like how he lets the humor happen around him, and how he holds back with the one liners, making them seem almost as stern as his dramatic moments. When he throws back his head and laughs with Kara at Kamran Shah's headquarters, it is a delightful moment made more enjoyable by the sense that this man's laughter is rare.

Speaking of Kamran Shah, he is a sterling example of why the Bond films have been wise to mostly avoid world politics. In 1987, our hero fighting alongside the Mujahadeen made sense to those who followed the headlines. In 2001 and 2002, *The Living Daylights* was a movie I avoided watching for a while, because the headlines after 9/11 made it too painful. I comfort myself with the knowledge that, since they didn't immediately drape Kara in a burqa, it is likely that Shah's group did not become the Taliban. Still.

At some point I made a conscious choice to set aside politics and enjoy one of my favorite Bond movies as entertainment. And I do.

High Points

- Timothy Dalton as James Bond.
- Exciting pre-titles sequence, good action from beginning to end, great way of introducing Dalton.
- Gritty adaptation of Fleming's short story.
- Top-notch aerial stunt sequence off the cargo net.
- Romantic relationship with the Bond girl, and a heart-stopping kiss on the Ferris wheel.
- Excellent locations in Vienna, Tangier, and the desert.
- Thrilling raid on the Afghan air base with action on multiple fronts and a clear narrative flow.
- John Rhys-Davies as General Pushkin.
- A lush John Barry score with multiple themes (the title song, "Where Has Everybody Gone?" and "If There Was a Man").
- The safe house break-in and the kitchen fight.
- The menacing and chameleon-like Necros.
- The death of Saunders.
- The first gadget-laden car chase in ten years.
- The cello-case sledding.

Low Points

- Koskov, the evil hugger.
- Under-use of the more interesting Whitaker.
- Confusing and meaningless scheme.
- In retrospect, Afghans as allies to the West (at the time it made sense).
- Kara's wimpy response during the Afghan jail fight, and her twisting her neck around and pulling random levers while flying the Hercules.
- Dull title sequence.

Quotable Quotes

Bond: "Exercise control, 007 here. I'll report in an hour."
Linda: "Won't you join me?"
Bond: "Better make that two."

Koskov: "If they close the border, how will I get out?"
Bond: "We have a pipeline to the West."

Bond: "I've had a few optional extras installed."

Bond: "Glad I insisted you brought that cello."

Koskov: "I'm sorry James. For you I have great affection. But we have an old saying: 'Duty has no sweethearts.'"
Bond: "We have an old saying too, and you're full of it."

Bond: "He got the boot."

Bond: "I know a great restaurant in Karachi! We can just make dinner."

Bond: "He met his Waterloo."

(Last lines:)
Bond: "You didn't think I'd miss this performance, did you?"
Kara: "Oh, James!"

Facts and Figures

SEXUAL ENCOUNTERS

<u>Two</u>: Linda and Kara Milovy.

BOND'S CARS

> 1986 Aston Martin Volante convertible (black)
> 1986 Aston Martin V8 Vantage (black)

DEATHS

<u>Twenty-one</u>:

- The SAS guy who says "Game's up, mate, you're dead," 004, the assassin who killed the previous two, the milkman, two at the safe house, Saunders, nine during the air base raid, one when the bridge is bombed, Necros, Whitaker, Whitaker's sergeant,
- Koskov (off-screen) (Pushkin says that Koskov is to be taken back to Moscow "in the diplomatic bag." Fans I have discussed this with cannot agree as to the phrase's meaning. Is he being returned to Moscow as a prisoner, or is he to be killed? Might Pushkin be making a pun on "body bag?" If you are convinced that Koskov is going to jail, the death toll is twenty).

Bond Kills:

- <u>Two</u> directly (Necros and Whitaker)
- <u>Two</u> indirectly (the pre-titles sequence assassin and the victim of the bridge bombing)

EXPLOSIONS

<u>Twelve</u>: In the pre-titles sequence, a very small one when the box of explosives falls off the Jeep, followed by the Jeep itself; three separate grenades thrown by Necros

at the safe house; blowing the road block with missiles (good one!); the shack on the lake; the self-destruct of the Volante; a long series at the air base (counting the series as one) that includes two big ones and plenty of small ones; the plane hitting Koskov's Jeep (wow!); another big one when the bridge collapses; and the Hercules crashing.

BOND'S FOOD AND DRINKS

Vodka Martinis

<u>Three</u>: At the hotel in Vienna, spiked with chloral hydrate in Tangier, and a pair waiting for Kara as a surprise in her dressing room as the movie ends.

Other Drinks

- Champagne given to Bond in the pre-titles sequence by Linda.
- Bollinger RD champagne brought by Bond for Koskov from Harrod's, but not opened.
- Felix gives Bond Jim Beam on his yacht in Tangier.
- In their room at Shah's headquarters, Bond and Kara have a bottle of vodka, but Kara knocks it out of Bond's hands when she hits him with the pillow.

Food

- Bond brings foie gras and caviar from Harrod's, and tells Koskov the foie gras is excellent.

GAMBLING AND SPORTS

- Target shooting at the Prater amusement park (Bond wins a big elephant for Kara).

Amaze Your Friends!

- This is the last appearance of General Gogol in the series. Walter Gotell played the character in six consecutive Eon Productions Bond films; in *The Spy Who Loved Me* through *A View to a Kill*, he was the head of the KGB. Here, that job has gone to General Pushkin and Gogol is with the Foreign Service. Walter Gotell died in 1997 at the age of 73.
- This is also John Barry's last Bond film. Barry orchestrated a total of eleven Bond films, beginning with *Dr. No*. Barry passed away in 2011, with five Oscars to his credit, although none for a Bond movie.
- Ironically, both Walter Gotell and John Barry have cameos in the final scene. Gotell, of course, plays Gogol and is introduced to Kara Milovy after the concert. John Barry is the orchestra conductor.
- Smiert Spionam is a phrase well-known to fans of Ian Fleming. Its abbreviated form is SMERSH, the Soviet assassination bureau that was Bond's enemy in many of the Fleming novels. SMERSH was a real organization, as Pushkin accurately said, created under Stalin.

Most Interesting Goofs

Concentric Circles: Bond cuts a small circle in the ice with the wheel hub of his Aston Martin. But the police car following him falls through a much larger hole.

Plane Crash: When Kara and Bond escape from the crashing Hercules jet, it is very low to the ground; low enough for their Jeep escape to work. Then they watch it crash from a noticeably greater height.

Fake Defection? This is a plot hole rather than a goof, and to be fair, I saw the movie five or so times before I even noticed, so it's not much of a hole. Nonetheless, what's up with Kara helping Koskov fake his defection? She poses as a sniper because the whole thing is a ploy, right? But it isn't a ploy, the KGB really are there at the concert, and really are searching for him later. So as far as I can tell, he really did defect (despite his plans to return to Moscow and deny it later).

What Was the Name Again? The end credits say that Walter Gotell play Anatol Gogol. The character's name is Alexis; M called him by name in his debut in *The Spy Who Loved Me*.

A BOND STORY (CONTINUED)

In the INTRODUCTION I began my personal Bond story, which culminated in seeing *Diamonds Are Forever* in 1971. At that time, I was still a little kid, and wouldn't see a movie without my parents for several more years. My father, as I said earlier, didn't like Lazenby. He didn't like Roger Moore either, and I never saw *Live and Let Die* or *The Man with the Golden Gun* in original release. By that time, Dad's health had improved, and he wasn't dragging us to movies just for the sake of sitting down.

Having skipped two movies, I no longer had the Bond habit. To me Bond was Sean Connery; Roger Moore was faking it as far as I was concerned.

When I saw *The Spy Who Loved Me* I was smitten. It's a glorious movie and I was entirely ready to re-embrace Agent 007. But then they made *Moonraker*. Like Dad, I'm a fan of Bond's serious side (see KILLER OR CLOWN?), and this movie was like being shown to the nearest exit for me. My Bond had been betrayed, and I turned my back on the franchise entirely.

After that, I watched Bond films from time to time, but my passion was gone. In 1983, I saw both Bond films released that year in the theaters, because I was dating a Bond fan. Having been waiting for Connery for a dozen years, I was heartbroken by *Never Say Never Again*. I enjoyed *Octopussy* a good deal more, but it didn't light my fire.

Actually, *Octopussy* was an amusing night. In my teens and twenties, I used to faint from time to time. Low blood pressure runs in the family. With age, blood pressure rises. When other people might begin having problems, we normalize. In '83, though, I was still inclined to land on the floor like a damsel in distress, especially if overheated. *Octopussy* did well in the theaters, and there was a line for tickets. It was August. You guessed it—I keeled over.

The theater (in Paramus, New Jersey) was next to a Red Lobster. My boyfriend played knight in shining armor to my distressed damsel. He saw the need to get me inside, to an air-conditioned spot with plenty of cold water. And lobster. After dinner, we saw a later showing of the movie.

Despite enjoying *Octopussy*, I wasn't thrilled. I had the same experience when my then-husband rented *Tomorrow Never Dies* for us one evening; we thoroughly enjoyed it, but it didn't rekindle my romance with Bond, James Bond.

I came back to Bond because of a movie discussion. Since my early teens, I have been a fan of movies in general; everything from film noir to Westerns to musicals. To that end, when the Internet Movie Database put up message boards in May of 1999, I became an active participant. In December of that year, someone posted a "favorite actor to play Bond" discussion, and I realized I'd never seen Timothy Dalton in the role. Well, my curiosity was aroused, so I rented *The Living Daylights*.

It was during *The Living Daylights* that I fell madly in love—with Dalton, with his performance, and with James Bond. This was the Bond I had always loved, the

Bond I had missed. I will always love *The Living Daylights* madly, and forgive its minor flaws, because it was *The Living Daylights* that clicked for me, and that brought me back to James Bond.

My kid, nine years old at the time, was out with their father that afternoon. I didn't think Ursula would like a Bond movie, and had decided to watch it alone. They came home unexpectedly early—during the Afghan airbase raid, to be exact. Ursula got instantly caught up in the movie. After it was over, I explained who James Bond was, and we decided to undertake a little family project—watch all 21 James Bond movies (including *Casino Royale* (1967 movie) and *Never Say Never Again*; it was before *Die Another Day*'s 2002 release) in chronological order. It wasn't long into this project that we were utterly hooked. Soon we were listening to Bond music in the car, and I was participating on James Bond message boards and researching Bond trivia.

During the course of that first run-through, I caught up on a few movies I'd never seen before, and came to appreciate and love even the worst movies. The bad movies, paradoxically, give me faith in the future of Bond. People complain about this movie or that—many fans intensely dislike *Die Another Day*, for instance—but I am fairly confident that the series will never again sink to the level of *A View to a Kill*, and even if it does, it has bounced back before. We (Ursula and I) have seen all the movies numerous times since then, and somewhere in there I decided to write a book. The past seven years (I am writing in 2006) have been all about James Bond. I owe that to *The Living Daylights*, and to my kid, to whom this book is dedicated.

A FEW OPTIONAL EXTRAS

O07 is famous for his gadget-laden cars. My goodness, but eyes did pop when the Aston Martin DB5 first showed up in *Goldfinger*. Along with Bond, everyone in the audience said "Ejector seat? You're joking!" And as we all learned, it was no joke.

As it turns out, only a handful of Bond movies have featured a chase with a gadget-laden car, it's just that they stand out as such a signature piece.

Gadget-Based Chases

Bond had fully-loaded car chases in the following films:

- *Goldfinger*
- *The Spy Who Loved Me*
- *The Living Daylights*
- *Tomorrow Never Dies*
- *Die Another Day*
- *Spectre*
- *No Time to Die* (based on the trailer)

In addition, gadget cars were seen (but not chased) in:

- *Thunderball*
- *For Your Eyes Only*
- *GoldenEye*
- *The World is Not Enough*
- *Casino Royale*
- *Skyfall*

So, What's In Those Cars, Anyway?

The 1964 Aston Martin DB5

Appeared in: *Goldfinger, Thunderball, GoldenEye, Tomorrow Never Dies, Skyfall, Spectre, No Time to Die*

License number: BMT-216A (In *GoldenEye*, the BMT-216A had to be changed for legal reasons. The plate for *GoldenEye* and *Tomorrow Never Dies* was BMT-214A; the original number was restored as of *Skyfall*)

Features:

- Bulletproof windshield, side, and rear window.
- Revolving license plate (BMT-216A, 471-EA-62, LU-6789)
- Audio-visual transmitter with mapping (GPS) in car, range 150 miles, used with homer.

- Armament controls in arm rest. (The *GoldenEye* arm rest had a champagne cooler)
- Smoke screen.
- Oil slick.
- Rear bulletproof screen that can be raised and lowered. Side and front (in headlights) wing machine guns.
- Ejector seat.
- Rotating "tire scythe" in hubcap, capable of shredding steel.
- High-pressure water jets (seen in *Thunderball* only).
- Color printer CD player (*GoldenEye* only)
- Audio link to MI6 in radio (*GoldenEye* only)

The 1964 Aston Martin DB5 (no gadgets)

The classic car, without gadgets, appears in *Casino Royale* (we assume it has no gadgets because it was obtained from Dimitrios, not from Q)

Note: Other gadget-free cars are not listed in this section, but in the sections on each individual movie. This one is listed just to avoid confusion with the gadget-laden DB5.

License number: 56526 (Nassau)

The 1977 Lotus Esprit S1 (Codename "Wet Nellie")

Appeared in: *The Spy Who Loved Me*

License number: PPW 306R

Features:

- Mud (or perhaps oil) shooter hidden in rear license plate (This has been called a "cement-sprayer," but I am hard put to figure out how cement can be stored in the back of the car without drying).
- Submarine conversion capability.
- Top and front missile launchers with targeting system.
- Underwater rear smoke screen. Dispenses limpet mines.

The 1981 Lotus Esprit Turbo

(A white Esprit Turbo with a red stripe self-destructs. Bond has a copper Esprit Turbo later in the film, license number OPW 678W. We don't see any gadgets in this car.)

Appeared in: *For Your Eyes Only*

License number: OPW 654W

Features:

- Automatic self-destruct on unauthorized entry attempt (thereby preventing us from seeing the rest of the features).

The 1986 Aston Martin V8 Vantage

(In *The Living Daylights,* James Bond drove two different Aston Martins. The Vantage was fully-loaded and customized for winter driving. The Volante was a convertible.)

Appeared in: *The Living Daylights*

License number: B549 WUU

Features:

- Police band radio.
- Laser in hubcap.
- Bulletproof windshield, side, and rear window.
- Front missile launcher with targeting display on windshield.
- Rear rocket motor.
- Retractable ski runners.
- Retractable tire spikes for ice traction.
- Timed self-destruct set from inside.

The 1995 BMW Z3

Appeared in: *GoldenEye*

License number: 8XB 608

Features:

- Parachute braking system.
- All points radar with pop-up display and warning sound.
- Self-destruct system.
- Stinger missiles behind headlights.

The 1997 BMW 750IL

Appeared in: *Tomorrow Never Dies*

License number: B MT2144

Features:

- Voice warnings in regard to hazards and safety.
- Remote-control operation using touch pad/video controller in cell phone.
- Machine guns.
- Front and rear rocket launchers.
- GPS tracking system.
- Bulletproof windshield, side, and rear window.
- Impact-resistant body.
- Fingerprint ID scan on glove box; retractable security tray in glove box.
- Variable-level security system.
- Electric shock on unauthorized entry attempt.
- Some sort of gas (perhaps teargas) emitted from underneath.
- Tire-puncturing spikes dropped from rear tray.

- Re-inflating tires.
- Cable-slicer in hood ornament.

The 1999 BMW Z8

Appeared in: *The World is Not Enough*

License number: V354 FMP

Features:

- Titanium armor.
- "Multi-tasking heads-up display."
- Remote control now in key ring, without video.
- Side missiles, targeting in steering wheel.
- Six beverage cup holders.

The 2002 Aston Martin V12 Vanquish (Codename "the Vanish")

Appeared in: *Die Another Day*

License number: BKE02 EWW

Features:

- Adaptive camouflage that renders the car invisible to casual observation.
- Voice warnings.
- Target seeking, motion-sensing shotguns.
- Computer-guided, armor-piercing missiles behind retracting front grille.
- High-powered machine guns behind retracting front grille.
- Crash cage with titanium plating, protecting body during rollover and weapons fire.
- Passenger ejector seat.
- Rapid-extension road-grip tire spikes.
- Thermal monitor with pop-up display screen.

The 2008 Aston Martin DBS V12

Appeared in: *Casino Royale*, *Quantum of Solace*

License number: TT 378 20 (*Casino Royale*), 72 GH3LD (*Quantum of Solace*)

Features:

- Hidden gun compartment.
- Hidden medical kit, which includes a defibrillator, a link to MI6 medical "hot room," and antidotes

The 2015 Aston Martin DB10

Appeared in: *Spectre*

License number: DB10 AGB

Features:

- Rear-facing double-barreled gun, with targeting (switch labeled "Backfire").
- Personally-programmed music (switch labeled "Atmosphere").
- Rear-facing flamethrower (switch labeled "Exhaust").
- Driver ejector seat with parachute. (switch labeled "Air").

LICENCE TO KILL (1989)

Survey Says!

> Percent Favorite: 5%
> Top 5 Cumulative: 6/25
> Numeric Rating: 6.7/10
> Ranking: 11.3 (11th/25)

My Rating and Ranking

> Rated: 7/10
> Ranked: 13 out of 25

Summary

On the way to Felix Leiter's wedding, for which Bond is the best man, Felix's "partners in the DEA" bring him in on a major coup—the arrest of notorious drug lord Franz Sanchez. Unfortunately, Sanchez bribes an agent to help him escape, and retribution is swift. Leiter is partially fed to a shark while his new bride, Della, is raped and murdered. Bond sets out for revenge, but neither the U.S. nor the British government will back him up. Resigning his license to kill, Bond travels to Isthmus with the help of Pam Bouvier, and infiltrates Sanchez's organization. Bond sets fire to Sanchez's enormous cocaine-processing facility, and then does the same to Sanchez himself.

> **James Bond:** Timothy Dalton
> **Pam Bouvier:** Carey Lowell
> **Franz Sanchez:** Robert Davi
> **Lupe Lamora:** Talisa Soto
> **Felix Leiter:** David Hedison
> **Dario:** Benicio Del Toro
> **Milton Krest:** Anthony Zerbe
> **Professor Joe Butcher:** Wayne Newton
> **Della Leiter:** Priscilla Barnes
> **M:** Robert Brown
> **Q:** Desmond Llewelyn
> **Moneypenny:** Caroline Bliss
> **Directed by** John Glen

Discussion

In 1979, *Moonraker* had a budget that exceeded that of the ten previous Bond movies combined. Then, from 1981's *For Your Eyes Only*, the budget was held to the same level. This got more and more challenging as the cost of everything went up, and by 1989, it took its toll. The biggest problem with *Licence to Kill* is that it looks cheap. It is the most unlovely of Bond films; with bland locations (except for the magnificent Olimpatec Meditation Institute) and flat, utilitarian set design. Krest's warehouse, the Leiters' suburban home, the brief glimpse of MI6 offices, all are minimalist and filmed in a flat, made-for-TV-movie light.

A second problem can be seen in the movie itself; *Licence to Kill* is too dark, too grim, too relentless. As discussed under KILLER OR CLOWN?, director Glen felt that Dalton's serious approach to the character demanded a serious movie. But man, wouldn't a laugh have felt good from time to time? The movie has two of the most gruesome deaths of the series; Milton Krest's exploding head and Dario's chopped suey.

Don't get me wrong, I like *Licence to Kill* and I think it has a lot to offer. But the fans who hate it because it is so dark have a point. It has a dark theme, some very dark villains, a dreary atmosphere, and nearly all of the jokes are delivered in the blackest of veins.

If you're a fan of Timothy Dalton, there's a sort of 'beggars can't be choosers' affection for this movie, despite its problems. Dalton's performance is superb. He is angry and driven, but also tender and affectionate. He is warm and playful at the wedding, amused by Pam, and compassionate towards Lupe. He has a razor's edge of cleverness with Sanchez, planting the right seeds at the right time, and allowing Sanchez to do the large part of bringing down his empire himself.

There is more to commend *Licence to Kill* than simply its lead performer. The pre-titles sequence, for one, is terrific. It's not just that parachuting into the wedding is a lovely coda, but that this is the culmination of a friendship and camaraderie which has lasted the life of the franchise; Leiter was there in *Dr. No*, and seventeen movies later, it feels damn good to see Bond as his best man, and it is especially nice for David Hedison to play Leiter—the first time an actor returned to that role.

Licence to Kill also has a fine group of villains. Robert Davi is an accomplished actor who immersed himself into the character of Sanchez, and managed to make bad skin seem like an Ian Fleming-style villainous deformity. The character is both charming and depraved; sadistic, vain, generous, paranoid, and filthy rich. His opening scene has the kind of over-the-top evil behavior that we've missed with the past several movies.

But more than that, the assemblage of henchmen is remarkable; a group of unique individuals, each manifesting a different face of evil. In fact, Sanchez and his crew form a social commentary on society's evils that was timely in 1989 and is still meaningful; a drug lord, a corrupt televangelist/seducer, a yuppie number-cruncher who cares only for the bottom line, and a military officer selling his services without compunction. The switchblade-wielding Dario gives a sense of street violence, and just for icing on the cake, Sanchez provides a roomful of prostitutes for his clients.

The standout henchmen, to my mind, are Dario and Professor Joe Butcher. As Dario, Benicio Del Toro glows in his second movie role; at age 22, he was the youngest ever Bond henchman, and you can see stardom in his future. In fact, there are times when his screen charisma is too much for the film that surrounds him. In a flat, unadorned picture with television-quality production values, del Toro is almost too good.

As for Wayne Newton's role, I love it! First of all, it is perfect casting, and secondly, sharp social satire. It is also damn clever; how can you fail to be impressed by the way donations and goals are used as code for drug buys. Sending this information out over the public airways, and using the meditation center to make a profit, is delightfully audacious.

Licence to Kill's plot is a love-it-or-hate-it affair. Many fans are unhappy with the rogue agent motif, and find Bond fighting a drug lord to be more typical of an American action hero than of agent 007. Other fans like the whole 'this time it's personal' thing. Certainly Bond's personal involvement leads him to make some very bad decisions. At the point where he's gotten Sharkey killed, or at the point where he has destroyed a Hong Kong Narcotics operation, you would think he'd realize that going rogue was a mistake that was causing more harm than good. The end result is to make Bond appear thoughtless. I like the revenge angle, but I think it would have played better if done as it was in *Die Another Day*, where Bond starts out as a rogue but is brought back into the fold as his mission begins to produce results. Still, I like the grit and the anger of this movie.

The revocation of Bond's license to kill is introduced with a neat bit of foreshadowing. M, at the Hemingway House, is at first faceless, and seen petting a cat—shades of Blofeld! This clues us in that M is an "enemy" this time around. The rest of that scene is less convincing, Bond fighting his way out rather than turn over his gun—why? Are guns that hard to come by? And then M saying "too many people" when there's clearly no one around. Too many cats, I'd say.

MI6 is better represented by Q, who has boyish fun in the field and gets to cuddle with Pam Bouvier. Many fans cite *Licence to Kill* as their favorite Q appearance. Too bad about Moneypenny, though, whimpering instead of showing the verve and competency that made Lois Maxwell such a favorite.

The stunts might be the best part of *Licence to Kill*. In the pre-titles sequence there's the terrific bit of hooking the plane; later there's waterskiing on bare feet, and at the end is that amazing burning car flying over the small plane—not a camera trick, by the way. The movie is certainly thrill-packed, although the scene that is most people's favorite in the film, the tanker chase, impresses me less than most fans. I can't quite buy it. From the first time I saw it, it screamed out to me that these were modified vehicles and the stunts were simply impossible. This sort of "no way" reaction is not what you want—movie magic should make you believe. The tanker chase also features some exceptionally cheap-looking back projection; it seems twenty years out of date. Again, this is because of the budget problem.

Carey Lowell and Talisa Soto are both weak, although some fans are very fond of Lowell's performance as Pam. Soto's two best roles have been in films where most of her part consisted of walking silently on the beach—in *Don Juan DeMarco* and *The Mambo Kings*. Here she has to speak, which stretches her acting talents to the breaking point.

Lowell just rubs me the wrong way. She opens with more-macho-than- thou sarcasm, then goes straight for strident feminism. In fact, I'd say she substitutes stridence for real feminism; she is forced and artificial. *Licence to Kill* was made more than a decade after *The Spy Who Loved Me*; by now we all know that Bond can accept and work successfully with a strong woman. At this late date, having a bossy American woman shout "Why can't you be *my* executive secretary?" is thick-headed. Later, she takes a distinctly whiny tone when explaining her deal with Heller. She may have had the big gun at the Barrelhead, but when push comes to shove, all she can do is whimper while Bond holds her own gun on her.

The woman who does best in *Licence to Kill* is Priscilla Barnes as Della, who is warm, open-hearted, and sweet; everything a joyful bride should be. Her acting is wonderful and her loss is really felt.

Overall, *Licence to Kill* is an unattractive Bond film, and not a fun one. But it has a lot to offer, some terrific action and stunts, some great villains, and Timothy Dalton's swan song as James Bond.

High Points

- Timothy Dalton's intense, emotional performance.
- The return of David Hedison.
- Powerful, witty, sadistic villain: Franz Sanchez.
- Good group of henchmen.
- Excellent teaser sequence.
- The wedding of Felix Leiter.
- The gentle, melancholy reference to Bond's tragic marriage.
- The hooking of Sanchez's plane.
- Waterskiing without skis.
- Everything about Wayne Newton, from the TV spot to the meditation center to "Bless your heart."
- Nice love scenes, especially the repeated "Why don't you ask me?"
- Exciting, fast-paced, with some really scary moments.
- Q's playful exuberance in the field.
- The death of Sanchez.

Low Points

- Talisa Soto's lifeless line readings.
- Cheap, uninteresting set design and flat filming.
- An excess of television stars (Anthony Zerbe, Everett McGill, Carey Lowell) accentuating the low-budget feeling of the film.
- "Dirty Love" at the Barrelhead Bar.
- The death of Milton Krest. Eeeew.
- Carey Lowell's uneven performance.
- Another lackluster Moneypenny courtesy of Caroline Bliss.
- Bond's increasing stubbornness and obsession as the folly of his actions gets clearer and clearer.
- Tanker chase is too far-fetched.

Quotable Quotes

Sanchez: "What did he promise you? His heart? Give her his heart."

Bond (before hooking the plane): "Let's go fishing."

Bond (to Della): "I'll do anything for a woman with a knife."

Bond: "Then I guess it's a farewell to arms."

Bond: "Let's make this a proper family reunion. Give me a gun."

Sanchez: "Remember, you're only president...for life."

Bond: "Watch the birdie, you bastard."

Sanchez: "Launder it."

Facts and Figures

SEXUAL ENCOUNTERS

Two: Pam Bouvier and Lupe Lamora

BOND'S CAR

None of his own.

DEATHS

Twenty-one:

- Lupe's boyfriend, Della Leiter, Sharkey, Ed Killifer, the driver of the armored truck transporting Sanchez, one of the men who killed Sharkey, two in the plane that Bond waterskis behind, one at the Barrelhead Bar, three Hong Kong agents, the MI6 agent sent to retrieve Bond, one of Sanchez's men killed by the female Hong Kong agent, Milton Krest, Dario, Colonel Heller, Truman-Lodge, two in the car that goes up in flames, Sanchez.

Bond Kills:

- Five directly (Killifer, two in the plane, one in the Barrelhead, Sanchez).
- Two indirectly (in the burning car; although you could hold him responsible for several of the deaths caused by Sanchez, such as the Hong Kong agents).

EXPLOSIONS

Seven: Bond shoots Sanchez's office (small), Sanchez retaliates, the cocaine facility goes up, first tanker (awesome!), tankers #2 and 3 hitting each other, tanker #4, flaming car (if you count fireballs), Sanchez himself.

BOND'S FOOD AND DRINKS

Vodka Martinis

<u>One</u> (or zero): Bond asks Pam to order him one at the casino, which she does, but then he leaves before it arrives. Pam drinks it.

Other Drinks

- Champagne at the wedding.
- Budweiser with lime ordered at the Barrelhead Bar, but the fight knocks it over before he drinks.
- Bond orders a case of Bollinger RD champagne sent to his room in Isthmus, but we never see him drink any.
- Drinks champagne with the President of Banco de Isthmus while opening an account.
- Drinks champagne while playing blackjack at the casino.
- Another champagne at the casino bar the next night.
- At the end, while on the phone with Felix, an indeterminate drink in a high-ball glass.

Food

- None, only black coffee.

GAMBLING AND SPORTS

- Maybe because of the Hemingway connection (see AMAZE YOUR FRIENDS) this movie has a fishing theme. Sharkey gives Felix and Della fishing lures as a wedding present; later, Felix and Bond say they will go fishing, and of course "fishing" is how Bond describes hooking the plane. In the Barrelhead, Bond is attacked with a trophy fish.
- Bond plays blackjack (like a real jerk-off) in the casino.

Amaze Your Friends!

- M has set up temporary quarters at the Hemingway House in Key West, Florida, the former home of novelist Ernest Hemingway. Hemingway had nearly fifty cats, including a "polydactyl" (six-toed) cat. That cat bred with the local population, and now, about half of the cats on Key West are polydactyls. Polydactyl cats are sometimes called "Hemingway cats" because of this. When Bond makes reference to "a farewell to arms" when asked to turn in his gun, he is referring to the novel of that name written by Hemingway.
- In addition to a farewell to arms, this movie was also a farewell to many significant people in the Bond series. Of course, it is Timothy Dalton's last Bond film, as well as Robert Brown's and Caroline Bliss's. It is John Glen's last time directing Bond, Maurice Binder's last title design (fourteen Bond titles before his death in 1991), and Richard Maibaum's last script (fourteen Bond scripts before his death in 1991.)
- By strange coincidence, both Bond girls in this film married well- known Hollywood stars in the same year. Talisa Soto married Benjamin Bratt in April of 2002, and in November of 2002, Carey Lowell married Richard Gere. Lowell

and Gere had one child together, and divorced in 2016. Bratt and Soto are still married, and have two children, as of 2020. By further coincidence, both couples are related to the show *Law & Order*, on which Carey Lowell and Benjamin Bratt have starred.

- Because of the film's violence, it was the first Bond movie to receive a PG-13 rating in the U.S. and a "15" in Britain.
- The road on which the tanker chase was filmed was rumored to be haunted. Numerous problems plagued that portion of filming, and many of the crew were horrified by what appeared to be a demonic apparition in the smoke (visible in still photos) following one of the tanker explosions.
- The President of Isthmus is played by Pedro Armandariz, Jr.—son of the actor who played Kerim Bey in *From Russia with Love*.
- The movie was originally titled *Licence Revoked*. The rumor is that the title was changed because Americans are too stupid to know what the word "revoked" means. The true story appears to be that most Americans associate the phrase with revocation of one's driver's license.

Most Interesting Goofs

Didn't get the invitation: A friend of Leiter's phones him the day after his wedding and says "Where ya been?" Either this is a goof or the guy isn't as good a friend as he thought he was.

Up and Down, or Side to Side? Sanchez whips Lupe with vertical strokes, but when Bond sees and remarks on her scars, they are horizontal.

Running on empty: The waitress delivers Bond and Pam's beers, and then they get knocked over in the scuffle. But the brand new, uncapped beers don't spill any liquid.

RATHER ODD MIXTURE OF STYLES

Whe James Bond meets Dikko Henderson in *You Only Live Twice*, Henderson immediately apologizes for his apartment by saying "You must excuse this rather odd mixture of styles." In fact, the odd mixture is very expressive of Henderson's character, helping us learn to know the expatriate agent in his brief time on screen. It is a typically outrageous and idiosyncratic Bond set.

The set design in Bond films both underscores and sets the tone. Like the best of Bond adventures themselves, the best set design is outrageous but not quite ridiculous, skating just at the edge of believable, and seems to come from a better, more luxurious, more sinister, and classier world than the one in which we live.

Bad set design is harder to define. Most set design in most films is serviceable; the characters are in a home or an office or a park; they have the furniture they need to sit in and objects they need to pick up; if the scene calls for a computer there's one on the desk. One rarely notices such things. In fact, if it wasn't in a Bond film, it wouldn't be called bad at all, merely unremarkable. Ordinary suburban homes wouldn't be bad if they didn't belong to prominent characters in a Bond film. Likewise, if set design looks cheap on an old *Star Trek* episode, or in a small indie film, we don't expect otherwise, but in a Bond film, it's a disaster.

When praising excellent set design, I am omitting sets which are primarily real world locations, such as Piz Gloria (*On Her Majesty's Secret Service*), Drax's mansion in *Moonraker* (Vaux-Le-Vicomte, in France) or Sanchez's home in *Licence to Kill* (Villa Arabesque, Acapulco). These wonderful places weren't designed so much as discovered.

Some excellent sets aren't all that noticeable. Syd Cain's painstaking recreation of the Orient Express in *From Russia with Love* doesn't raise eyebrows because it looks like...the Orient Express. Similarly, Peter Lamont personally visited and photographed the Casino de Monte Carlo in Monaco in order to recreate the interior for *GoldenEye*. The accuracy and beauty may not even be noticed by the casual viewer, but it fleshes out the sense of location. Bond sets are more famous for the opposite—sets that are larger than life, that strive to reach beyond accuracy into a really satisfying fantasy. For example, in *Goldfinger*, Ken Adam created Fort Knox as we'd wish it to look, with stacks of gold visible everywhere. The real thing is doubtless more prosaic.

A lot of movies can't really nail down that fantastic element. They go too far when they try, they look merely loud. This is especially true of movie sets in the 1960s and early 70s. The profusion of brightly-colored plastic furnishings makes everything look like it's taking place on the set of *Rowan and Martin's Laugh-In*. The deftness of the best Bond set design is that it hovers very close to the top without going over.

Among great sets, villain's lairs tend to be the most noticeable, but upon examination, we find that MI6 and private homes look pretty darn good, and some public locations are eye-poppers as well.

Top Five/Bottom Five

The Best Sets

1. *The Man with the Golden Gun*: Sunken MI6 headquarters
2. *Dr. No* Skylit interrogation room
3. *The Spy Who Loved Me*: Atlantis
4. *You Only Live Twice*: Hollowed-out volcano
5. *Diamonds Are Forever*: Willard Whyte's penthouse suite

The Worst Sets

1. *Licence to Kill*: Felix Leiter's home
2. *Live and Let Die*: James Bond's apartment
3. *Never Say Never Again*: Palmyra
4. *The World is Not Enough*: Caviar factory
5. *GoldenEye*: Alec Trevelyan's underwater control room

The Best Sets

The Man with the Golden Gun: Sunken MI6 Headquarters

Given the fame of Ken Adam, and the preconception that it is villains who always get the very best headquarters, it is remarkable indeed that this magnificent set is neither Adam's work nor a villain's lair. It is the mostly wildly conceived and nonchalantly executed set I have ever seen. The idea is ingenious, if a bit manic. Peter Murton laid patterned floors straight over the crooked reality, and placed stolidly ordinary desks and chairs atop the whole mad thing. Having the staff walk about as if nothing was more commonplace adds the cherry to this delightful design sundae.

Dr. No: Skylit Interrogation Room

Eon Productions made the first James Bond film for one million dollars—more in real dollars in 1961 than it is today, but still low-budget. Ken Adam made penny-pinching a virtue with our first sight of the evil Doctor's headquarters—the nearly empty interrogation room. When Professor Dent sees that he has to cross to a bare chair under a round skylight that casts an ominous cell-like shadow, he gulps in nervousness, and we know why. The room tells us a lot about our villain; his omnipresence, his subtlety, his power over people. Its simplicity and expressiveness make this set one of the greatest.

The Spy Who Loved Me: Atlantis

It's big, it's curvy, and it rises from the sea. The design includes both form and func-tion—the model of the Atlantis exterior was created with the purpose of the structure in mind—it's also amazing to look at.

Then there's the interior. A classically elegant dining room, a weird futuristic chair, big aquarium windows, highly functional shark-delivery elevator—truly a de-sign that meets all a villain's needs. Both the beauty and the complexity of this set make it a winner.

You Only Live Twice: Hollowed-out Volcano

This is probably the most famous set in Bond history, the one that pretty much de-fines bold Bond set design. Many fans would list it as number one, but let's face it, it isn't really attractive. It's awe-inspiring, it's innovative, it's startling, but it's also utili-tarian. I prefer the elegance of Atlantis, but the volcano set is groundbreaking in its ambition and scope, and remains one of the most memorable interiors in film (let alone Bond) history.

Diamonds Are Forever: Willard Whyte's Penthouse Suite

Just in case you were thinking that only villains live in really cool apartments, there's Willard Whyte's gorgeous suite atop the Whyte House. Oh sure, a villain lived there for a while, but he was just a squatter. This suite is the home of an eccentric inven-tor, a filthy rich recluse.

And really, if I were a filthy rich recluse, that's how I'd want to live. Sunken living room, shiny art objects, a three-dimensional model of my business posses-sions, and spycams in the bathroom. Why the hell not?

Honorable Mention

It goes without saying that the Bond films have more than five great sets, in fact, set design is almost as important to a great Bond movie as exciting action sequences, cool gadgets, and vodka martinis. The following chronological list may seem long, but it's just a sample of the best of the visual delights in Bond movies.

Dr. No

Decontamination

An elegant set-up, very formal and scientific looking, with the conveyer belts and op-portunity for a nearly-nude Ursula Andress. I like this one better than the *Dr. No* con-trol room.

Doctor No's Personal Apartment

Not just the stolen painting and the magnified aquarium, but indoor trees, and a conical fireplace.

From Russia with Love

Chess Tournament Room

...with its dizzying checkerboard floor and focal dais.

SPECTRE Island

Our first glimpse of an expansive villainous operation of this type. Dr. No had under-lings but he was basically a one-man show. This is different, with assassins in deadly training amidst formal English (presumably) gardens.

Goldfinger

Goldfinger's "Rumpus Room"

Every villain should have a rocking horse to entertain his guests until he can come and personally revolve and open the pool table.

Fort Knox

A close contender for the top five; nearly as famous as the volcano.

Thunderball

SPECTRE Headquarters

A secret passage, a cavernous meeting room, a panel behind which Blofeld can hide, and of course, rotating, sinking electrified chairs. Cool!

MI6 Meeting Room

A perfect counterpoint to SPECTRE's.

You Only Live Twice

Summit Domes

The U.S., Soviet, and British representatives have their summit inside geodesic domes that would have made Buckminster Fuller proud.

Dikko Henderson's Flat

A "rather odd mixture of styles."

Osato Chemicals

Large, open offices, discreet spyware, glamorous decor, attractive sculpture suitable for beating up bad guys, and a convenient wet bar.

Tiger's Subway Hideout

A real favorite of mine is the "down the rabbit hole" underground offices of Japa-nese Secret Service head Tiger Tanaka. The shiny passage with its undignified yet comfortable landing, the round cameras showing Bond his embarrassment, and fi-nally, the private train car waiting to whisk Tiger and his guest away in style.

Tiger's Home

Gorgeous Japanese gardens surround a lovely home with elaborate baths and a handy surgical theater.

Diamonds Are Forever

The Bridal Suite at the Whyte House

Almost as good as Willard Whyte's private suite is this extravaganza of white marble, soft fabrics, and an aquarium waterbed.

The Spy Who Loved Me

MI6 Egyptian Headquarters

Under the pyramids with a distinctly Middle Eastern feel.

The Liparus

Giant sub-swallowing tankers are cool if you like that sort of thing.

Octopussy

The Kremlin

A classic Ken Adam set; huge portrait of Lenin, moving seating arrangements, interactive map.

The Living Daylights

Bratislava

The best "ugly" set created for the series is Bratislava; dark streets, gray buildings, and Bond's window peeks from behind a gigantic hammer and sickle.

Die Another Day

The ice palace

Of course!

Skyfall

Macau Hotel Suite

Bond's hotel suite in Macau is a world unto itself, a labyrinth of wooden screens, archways, and enticing shapes and design.

Special Blue Ribbon Film Design Award

...and the winner is

You Only Live Twice for six sets appearing in the top five or honorable mention. *You Only Live Twice* is a masterpiece of design through and through.

Bottom Five

Licence to Kill: Felix Leiter's Home

Almost everything in this movie showed the creaks and groans of budget constraint, nothing more so than its set design. Everything looks flat and uninteresting, but how disappointing to finally see Felix Leiter off-duty and discover he lives in a bland suburban tract house.

Live and Let Die: James Bond's Apartment

The last time we were here was in *Dr. No*, and apparently he redecorated. I hope he fired the decorator when he came home and saw the big black dots. Ah, the seventies!

Never Say Never Again: Palmyra

Almost every set in this film looks flimsy and uninspired; Palmyra isn't worse, but as with Leiter's home, we expect more.

The World is Not Enough: Caviar Factory

Factory? Caviar? It's a creaky shed with a vat of axle grease.

GoldenEye: Alec Trevelyan's Underwater Control Room

How disappointing that the villain in this great film can only imitate Blofeld in *You Only Live Twice* (maybe he read the file). The hidden satellite dish in the lake should easily have been detected by Bond because he should have remembered it from his Japanese adventure. Alec even borrow's Tiger Tanaka's train car.

HOW EXPLICIT?

O ne of the periodic discussions in Bond fandom is the question of whether Bond should go for an R rating, which would allow some nudity, stronger language, and more explicit violence. It seems strange to some fans to have a hero who excels at killing and making love, without really showing either.

One of the things that I think is essential to Bond's appeal and longevity—and something that I've never seen mentioned—is that the Bond films are essentially innocent (bear with me).

Bond movies show sex without explicit nudity, violence without significant bloodshed or gore, and toughness without excessive foul language. By doing so, they allow us to experience the titillation of sex, violence and adventure without facing the reality. Bond films appeal to older children as much as to adults because they represent a fantasy of what we wish sex and violence could be like. The films feature innocent violence and innocent sex. One reason that many fans dislike *Licence to Kill* is that it is too violent. Yet it is no more violent than other Bond films—it merely shows more. In fact, the body count is lower in *Licence to Kill* than in many of the films, but there is more blood.

Bond films are fantasies. They allow us to explore our sex-and-violence-and-adventure-and-heroism fantasies without risk. The reason they are "without risk" is because they aren't real. As many movies strive for more realism, Bond maintains a firm grasp on the importance of the imaginary. Again, the most realistic Bond, *Licence to Kill*, is often one of the most unpopular. And what do people say about it? That it is too ordinary, that a drug lord is too real for a villain, etc. (The same complaints later target *Quantum of Solace*.)

Bond films are appropriate for older children because children have these fantasies. They want to see these things, but they also want to be shielded from them. In truth, so do adults. We want to imagine we are Bond, or the Bond girl, but in real life, we wouldn't be. This is the difference between a fantasy and a realistic movie—realism is about the characters, but fantasy is partly about us, about what we wish we could be.

Nudity is appropriate in a film when it establishes something real. But we don't want Bond sex to be real sex. Real sex is awkward and sloppy and involves condoms and consequences and emotion. Bond sex involves none of the above. Nudity doesn't belong in Bond's version of sex, because realism doesn't belong.

In the years since 1962, we moviegoers have come to expect more from our movies in a lot of ways—everything from more plausibility to better special effects. So Bond's sex has to get a little racier just as his explosions have to get bigger. But I hope Eon always stays on the side of fantasy.

I've been watching Bond with my kid—now an adult—since they were ten years old. As a child, they were more sensitive than average to things like movie violence. For that reason, and because I wish to be a good mother, I did not allowed them to see most action movies, with their strong language, toplessness, and bloody deaths and dismemberments. My kid loves Bond because they—like everyone else—are excited by, and interested in, sex, violence, voyeurism, and adventure, but when they were younger, didn't wish to face its reality. Bond satisfied that interest without being overwhelming. I think my kid is a model of what is right about Bond.

A survey of Bond fans that I conducted on CommanderBond.net (see RESOURCES) heavily supports my position. Although the sample was small, 85% wanted Bond movies to remain PG-13 (or the UK equivalent). Some of those suggested that exceptions could sometimes be made; fans were particularly concerned that the famous "carpet beater" scene be included in *Casino Royale* (it was), and suspected it would require an R rating to do it justice (it did not).

Most interestingly, 100% of the teen respondents wanted the movies to remain PG-13.

Several respondents mentioned that Bond is a film experience that can be shared with the family, and adults talked about taking their own kids to see Bond. This was my kid's response when I asked them again, at age fifteen. Families see these films together; it would be a shame, they said, to end that. Since I first saw James Bond with my father, I can't help but agree. Several teen and adult respondents also mentioned that raunchy sex and violence "just isn't Bond." There are plenty of movies, I was told, that can show us nudity and exploding heads; Bond is unique and apart from that.

Explicit sex, even full frontal nudity, would take away from the mystique of James Bond's perfect world, just as realistic violence would. Keep them clean, Eon!

GOLDENEYE (1995)

Survey Says!

> Percent Favorite: 6%
> Top 5 Cumulative: 11/25
> Numeric Rating: 7.2/10
> Ranking: 10.3 (9th/25)

My Rating and Ranking

> Rated: 10/10
> Ranked: 3 out of 25

Summary

Following the trail of a stolen stealth helicopter and a destroyed Russian research station, Bond rescues Natalya Simonova, a computer programmer who survived the destruction of the Severnaya station. From her, he learns of the GoldenEye device, a satellite which can create a powerful electromagnetic pulse in space, destroying computers and electronic systems in an entire city. With the help of Valentin Zukovsky, a former opponent, Bond discovers that the mastermind behind the GoldenEye theft is none other than former friend and colleague Alec Trevelyan, Agent 006, believed killed nine years earlier. After Natalya traces Trevelyan's computer system to Cuba, she and Bond travel there, where they disable the satellite and Bond kills Trevelyan.

> **James Bond:** Pierce Brosnan
> **Natalya Simonova:** Izabella Scorupco
> **Alec Trevelyan:** Sean Bean
> **Xenia Onatopp:** Famke Janssen
> **General Ourumov:** Gottfried John
> **Valentin Zukovsky:** Robbie Coltraine
> **Jack Wade:** Joe Don Baker
> **Boris Grishenko:** Alan Cummings
> **M:** Judi Dench
> **Moneypenny:** Samantha Bond
> **Q:** Desmond Llewelyn
> **Directed by** Martin Campbell

Discussion

(Note: This discussion was written before the release of Casino Royale, *the sixth movie to introduce a new Bond.* Casino Royale *formalized the "new beginning" motif by making it a reboot, and brought in the same director—Martin Campbell—to do it.)*

Each of the five Bond movies that introduce us to a new actor as James Bond has a special quality, but *GoldenEye* stands alone, nearly rivaling *Dr. No* with its sense of a new beginning. Not just a new Bond, but a new M and Moneypenny, a new director, and a brand spanking new budget, all after a six year hiatus that had many pundits, fans, and industry insiders proclaiming the death of 007.

Each of the five films has lingered on Bond's surroundings, teasing the audience before showing us his face, and each of the introductions, when we finally see our hero, has in some way typified that Bond's reign. Connery is first seen at the casino, casually and insolently winning at chemin-de-fer while bantering with a beautiful, sophisticated woman. George Lazenby begins by showing us the accouterments of his predecessor—the Aston Martin, gun, and cigarette case—and while driving very fast. Roger Moore begins in bed with a beautiful but unimportant woman. Timothy Dalton is introduced in the midst of a game that turns unexpectedly deadly. Each of these can in some way describe the actor's tenure; Connery, sophisticated and cool, Lazenby, trying hard to fill very big shoes and doing best in straight-out action, Moore, casually playful, and Dalton, deadly earnest. How then do we first see Pierce Brosnan's face? Upside-down.

(We could extend this to Craig, who is first seen in the shadows, and not yet a 00.)

That's what Brosnan, and *GoldenEye*, are going to do—turn James Bond upside-down. On the one hand, as the advertising proclaimed, Bond is Back, complete with vodka martinis, a hand of chemin-de-fer, and the Aston Martin DB5, to let us know that our hero is still the same man he always was. On the other hand, the Soviet Union is no more, M is a woman, and a double-0 has gone bad.

GoldenEye serves as a deconstruction of the Bond mythos, but unlike most deconstructionism, it is respectful, and stays inside the myth even while examining it. *GoldenEye* obliquely addresses the fact that it has been six years since the last Bond film, and that in the meantime the Iron Curtain has fallen. From the sometimes sarcastic but often incisive psychological examination of Bond, to M's snide remarks about "misogynist dinosaurs" and Xenia's view of Russia as "a land of opportunity," to the core plot involving a traitorous MI6 agent who was himself betrayed by Cold War policy, this is the movie that walks into the post-Soviet world and finds a place for Bond there. I think it does a great job, as you can see by the ranking I give it.

This first post-Cold War Bond examines what espionage and villainy might now constitute, as all of the characters struggle to find their place in a redefined world. Each character has a different point of view: M sees a world where statistical analysis has replaced the need for adventure. Xenia and Zukovsky see an open field for crime. Alec Trevelyan sees the place of revenge for crimes of the past era. Boris Grishenko sees an amoral world where technological skills matter more than how they are applied. One telling scene takes place in what amounts to a Soviet graveyard—a junkyard of old statues of Lenin and other Soviet icons. None of this is heavy-handed, primarily because it tells a compelling and exciting story, with interesting characters and exciting situations, so if there's some symbolism mixed in, hey, so what?

GoldenEye is quite popular among fans, but a vocal minority disparage it. I am still trying to figure out why. The arguments against it never make sense to me and I don't think I can fairly replicate them here. I think the movie has everything that's terrific about the franchise—Bond functions as a spy, finding out information instead of having it handed to him, the plot hangs together with no dangling set pieces (except for one amusing but unnecessary chase), it's great to look at, it has some dynamite explosions, some really sinister villains, an amusing ally, and the first really sexy villainess since *Never Say Never Again*'s Fatima Blush a dozen years earlier.

The superb cast sets the bar wonderfully high for Brosnan Bond movies. Judi Dench, Joe Don Baker, Sean Bean, Alan Cummings, and Robbie Coltraine, among others, are all respected actors who had already established themselves by 1995.

A completely new staff at MI6 gave Eon a chance to reimagine how the British Secret Service would be portrayed. This didn't happen, for instance, when Robert Brown replaced Bernard Lee, or when Caroline Bliss replaced Lois Maxwell. With the rest of the staff in place, the outfit continued business as usual without blinking. But with everyone replaced (except Q), MI6 itself feels new, more modern, and more in tune with this new Bond. This is in keeping with the theme of the movie; Bond finding his place in a new world, because a female M and a Moneypenny who jokes about sexual harassment are very new indeed.

Much of *GoldenEye* is built on contrasts and opposites. Alec Trevelyan is James Bond's opposite. The good girl is contrasted by one of the best bad girls. Xenia Onatopp has already been given enough wordage in the BOND GIRLS section; here I'll just note that she's fantastic, she helps bring a real edge to the action. A deadly villain from Bond's past, Ourumov, is contrasted with a deadly ally from Bond's past; Zukovsky. Jack Wade and Boris Grishenko also serve as opposites; both somewhat comical, with very amusing final scenes. Both are helpful (to 007 and 006, respectively) and intelligent—not merely comic relief.

Alec is well-conceived and well-played. He can anticipate Bond's moves because he's come as close as possible to being in Bond's head. I like how he turns off the bomb because he knows where the switch is on Bond's watch. That's the sort of little touch that makes the character work. With Alec's scarred face and insider knowledge, Xenia's strange way of exciting herself, and Boris's obsessive amoral vanity, we have a really quirky and interesting villainous ensemble to keep things moving. Each has a fitting and satisfying death, the lack of which is often a weakness in Bond films.

The scheme is also clever—we learned in *Goldfinger* that you don't have to conquer the world if you screw up the world's money, and Alec here substitutes the Bank of England for Fort Knox.

Opening with one of the greatest stunts you'll ever see, *GoldenEye* keeps the pace high. It is one of the most explosive Bond films (see THINGS THAT GO BOOM), and also features some terrific fistfights: Bond dispatches an attacker on the Manticore in a very *Goldfinger*-esque fashion. Bond battles Xenia and a thug in a steam room. Xenia kicks the daylights out of both Bond and Natalya, and finally, Bond and Alec go all out on top of the satellite dish. The only questionable action sequence is the tank chase. I waver between thinking it is fun and thinking it is dumb, and fan opinion is similarly divided. I gained greater respect for the scene when I learned that the chase was real—those tanks weren't tricked out like the tankers in *Licence to Kill*, Vic Armstrong's driving team did those brakes and skids with the real thing. And hey, it *is* funny.

The film features two fairly insightful conversations—Natalya and Bond in a pensive moment on the beach, and 007 and 006 facing off, with Alec's snide commentary about girls and martinis hitting a little too close to home. Some fans have complained about modernizing Bond with psychobabble, but I thought these moments were effective and not overplayed. They too, bring Bond into the 90s without dropping the past.

High Points

- Magnificent opening bungee jump.
- Wonderful Tina Turner song.
- Gorgeous title sequence with powerful imagery.
- Great debut by Brosnan.
- Human, complex Bond girl.
- Great villain, and great concept—the 00 turncoat.
- Great femme fatale in Xenia Onatopp; moody, outrageous, cigar-smoking, and perverse.
- Outstanding fight sequences, especially the finale between Bond and Trevelyan.
- The return of the Aston Martin DB5 (can you hear the cheering?).
- Intelligent, witty script that looks thoughtfully at Bond while keeping up the action.
- One of the best M scenes in the series.
- An equally great Moneypenny scene, and indeed she looks fantastic in eveningwear.
- Two terrific allies: Jack Wade and Valentin Zukovsky; both popular enough to return in later movies.
- Nice turn by Tcheky Karyo as the doomed Russian Defense Minister.
- The human popsicle death of Boris Grishenko; forever invincible.

Low Points

- The faked plane-catch in the pre-titles sequence, paving the ugly way for more CGI stunts while fans cry out for the real thing.
- A dreadful, empty-sounding score by Eric Serra, and an abysmal end-credit song by the same culprit.
- Plot exposition too rapid-fire, just a little confusing, with a few dangling plot holes.
- Natalya's shift from screaming at Bond to cuddling with him was a little jarring and sudden.
- St. Petersburg, mostly a studio set, is drab and unattractive.
- No romantic coda to the movie; Bond and Natalya never have the traditional sweet moment together, except for a brief kiss.

Quotable Quotes

Bond (first line): "Beg your pardon, forgot to knock."

Moneypenny: "You know this sort of behavior could qualify as sexual harassment."

Bond: "Really? What's the penalty for that?"

Moneypenny: "Some day you have to make good on your innuendos."

M: "If I want sarcasm, Mr. Tanner, I'll talk to my children, thank you very much."

M: "Unlike the American government, we prefer not to get our bad news from CNN."

M: "I think you're a sexist, misogynist dinosaur; a relic of the Cold War."

Bond: "That depends on your definition of safe sex."

Bond: "No, no, no! No more foreplay."

Bond (after escaping the helicopter with Natalya): "The things we do for frequent flyer miles."

Alec Trevelyan: "Why can't you just be a good boy and die?"

Bond: "You first."

Alec Trevelyan: "James. What an unpleasant surprise."

Alec Trevelyan: "For England, James?"

Bond: "No. For me."

Facts and Figures

SEXUAL ENCOUNTERS

<u>Two</u>: Caroline (the psychologist) and Natalya.

BOND'S CARS

1964 Aston Martin DB5 (silver)
1995 BMW Z3 (metallic blue)

DEATHS

<u>Approximately seventy-two</u>:

- Sixteen at the Arkangel facility (possibly more when the place blows up, but since we know that at least Ourumov and Trevelyan survived, we cannot be sure that anyone else was killed. It's also possible that the deaths of the people Alec shot during the Arkangel break-in were faked as part of his ruse, but I doubt it).

- Admiral Chuck Farrell and two Tiger helicopter pilots killed by Xenia.

- At Severnaya, about twenty working there, plus three MIG pilots.
- Russian Defense Minister Mishkin, his guard, twelve when Bond and Natalya escape the Defense Ministry.
- In Cuba, Xenia Onatopp, the pilot of the helicopter that Bond shot to kill Xenia, three when Bond enters the satellite base, nine when the pen bomb blows up, Alec Trevelyan, Boris Grishenko.

Bond Kills:

- <u>Twenty-five</u> directly (seven at Arkangel, twelve at the Russian Defense Ministry, Xenia, Xenia's pilot, three when he enters the satellite base, and 006).
- <u>Ten</u> indirectly (Bond doesn't know about the chemical spill in the satellite base, he throws the pen bomb as a diversion, so all of the deaths as a result of that bomb are indirectly attributable to Bond. There are nine plus Boris).

EXPLOSIONS

<u>Fourteen</u>: A small one to blow the door at Arkangel; the Arkangel facility; the Severnaya facility (massive); two MIGs that blow up, and one that crashes into Severnaya; a Jeep during the tank chase, then several cars in the same chase; 006's train—twice; first when hit by the tank, and then again when 006 sets a 3-minute bomb. Xenia's copter when she dies; the Cuban satellite base; Mischa when it blows up in space, and the satellite transmitter.

BOND'S FOOD AND DRINKS

Vodka Martinis

<u>One</u>: In the casino, with Xenia, Bond orders one, but doesn't wait for it to arrive, as he is intent on following her (perhaps he goes back in for it?).

Other Drinks

- Bollinger '88 champagne, in the armrest of the Aston Martin DB5, shared with Caroline.
- Bourbon on ice, with M.

Food

- None.

GAMBLING AND SPORTS

- Chemin-de-fer with Xenia.
- Swimming at the Grand Hotel in St. Petersburg

Amaze Your Friends!

- The name of this movie is derived from the name of Ian Fleming's Jamaican retreat. GoldenEye was where Fleming wrote all the Bond novels.
- Ferrari would loan Eon Productions the car Xenia drives only on condition that it not be seen losing a race. Hence, the scene was written so that Bond pulls over and lets Xenia go ahead.

- During the filming of the Ferrari vs. Aston Martin race, the two cars collided, and Eon paid approximately $80,000 to have the Ferrari repaired in time for the next day's shooting.
- The satellite dish used in this film was used two years later in the Jodie Foster movie *Contact*.
- For his first Bond film, title designer Danny Kleinman updated the gunbarrel, adding an animated motion effect to the shot.

Most Interesting Goofs

No Ice in the Ice: M offers Bond ice in his drink, but as he drinks, we see there isn't any. This wouldn't be a big deal except she makes such a fuss about drinking what she wants, not what her predecessor drank.

Strange Geography: The Arkangel Chemical Weapons Facility is at the bottom of a 700 foot dam. Amazingly, it is also at the top of a cliff so tall that a plane can dive down for almost a minute without reaching the ground. Rather impressive, but also impossible.

Complex Geography: Numerous goof-collecting websites have stated that Severnaya's position, as shown on the computer maps at various points, is not the same as where "the real Severnaya" is located. But the goof collectors spoke too soon! It turns out that Severnaya is a common part of Russian place-names. The one most fans come across is Severnaya Zemlya, a small group of islands in the Arctic Circle. But a bit of research also brings up Severnaya Osetiya-Alaniya, Severnaya Dvina at Zvoz, Severnaya Dvina at Abramkovo, and Askava Severnaya. So, the "goof" is in jumping to conclusions! Eon is off the hook this time.

Your Accent is Georgian? Bond identifies Xenia's accent as Georgian. She then asks if he's been to Russia. In the U.S and the West generally, people often say "Russia" when they mean the Soviet Union—even now, when it's the former Soviet Union. But a Georgian would never do so. Russia and Georgia are different countries and a Georgian would not equate them.

DANCING IN THE SHADOWS

Title sequences in James Bond movie are almost as iconic as the gunbarrel shot. They are beautiful abstractions, filled with silhouetted women dancing in shadows, yet suggesting plot elements. They're an extra pleasure, like an animated short before a Pixar feature.

Top Five Countdown

5. *Thunderball* by Maurice Binder: The first Bond title sequence that fits the image of what we now expect. The first one replete with sensual swimming women, bubbles, and water/light effects.

4. *From Russia with Love* by Robert Brownjohn: It is the simplicity of this one that is so startling. Everyone old enough to remember projectors has probably seen someone accidentally walk in front of one, and seen an image momentarily distorted and shaped by a body. Brownjohn used this effect to create an erotic dance of credits.

3. *GoldenEye* by Danny Kleinman: Borrowing heavily from *The Spy Who Loved Me*, Kleinman brings the title sequence into the computer age. Like *The Spy Who Loved Me*, it is phallic, humorous, and laced with political imagery significant to the movie's plot. Maurice Binder loved using any resource available to him, and would have happily embraced computer graphics. In this, the first computer-generated title sequence, Kleinman honors his predecessor.

2. *The Spy Who Loved Me* by Maurice Binder: One of the most exciting and startling of the title sequences. What Kleinman did digitally, Binder did first, the hard way. The imagery is erotic, phallic, political, humorous, suits the movie, and segues beautifully from the parachute jump. The first title sequence to use Bond himself heavily, interacting with the dancing girls.

1. *Die Another Day* by Danny Kleinman: When the (widely hated) title song, by Madonna, was released some weeks before the movie, many longtime fans wondered how Kleinman would be able to create a title sequence using something so staccato and hard. He succeeded brilliantly. The first Bond title sequence (other than *Never Say Never Again*'s non-sequence) to advance the plot. The sequence is new, innovative, visually gripping, and achieves the near-impossible. Bravo, Mr. Kleinman!

AND: *Skyfall* by Danny Kleinman: *Skyfall* is hands-down the most complex and intricate title sequence of the series. It's a movie unto itself.

It's beautiful to look at, but it's also just *packed*. It has the water Bond is falling into at the end of the teaser sequence, Skyfall itself, target practice, graves, ruins, a house of mirrors, plus the traditional dancing nude women. And then the whole thing repeats, except this time as a black-and-white kaleidoscope, so that everything becomes a kind of Rorschach inkblot, It's staggering, and I'm in love with it.

Bottom Five

Never Say Never Again has been omitted from contention, since it doesn't really have a title sequence. From the remaining twenty-four movies, these are the bottom five. Four are bland, unmemorable, and uninteresting copies of earlier, more exciting work, hardly worthy of individual descriptions. One, *Live and Let Die*, is not derivative, merely strange. The apparently African woman featured stares straight ahead in a ghastly fashion, and in this "blaxploitation Bond," it seems there are no ideas once that of having a black woman has been used.

> **5.** *Moonraker*
> **4.** *The Man with the Golden Gun*
> **3.** *The Living Daylights*
> **2.** *Live and Let Die*
> **1.** *Licence to Kill*: The worst because the imagery is senseless and static, and seen in conjunction with a poor title song.

The Complete List

Dr. No

> **Designed by:** Maurice Binder
> **Features:** Flashing dots, followed by overlaid silhouettes of clothed dancers, followed by the "Three Blind Mice" in silhouette, fading into the three men in Jamaica.

From Russia with Love

> **Designed by:** Robert Brownjohn
> **Features:** Titles projected on the undulating body, especially the belly and hands, of a belly dancer.

Goldfinger

> **Designed by:** Robert Brownjohn
> **Features:** Images from the movie shown inside the gold-painted body of a beautiful woman.

Thunderball

> **Designed by:** Maurice Binder
> **Features:** Watery images of nude silhouetted women swimming.

You Only Live Twice

> **Designed by:** Maurice Binder
> **Features:** The head and hands of a traditionally-garbed Japanese woman overlaid with images of volcanic activity.

On Her Majesty's Secret Service

> **Designed by:** Maurice Binder
> **Features:** Bond running from the pre-titles sequence into the titles and towards a martini glass. Images from the previous movie pour through the top as if it is an hourglass, while Bond hangs from a clock.

Diamonds Are Forever

> **Designed by:** Maurice Binder
> **Features:** Flashing diamonds, sometimes dangling from the neck of a white Persian cat, sometimes held or worn by a beautiful woman. Silhouettes within silhouettes create multiple illusions.

Live and Let Die

> **Designed by:** Maurice Binder
> **Features:** Images of skulls, flames, a Black woman with a distinct native island look staring straight ahead, and (oddly), a fiber-optic lamp.

The Man with the Golden Gun

> **Designed by:** Maurice Binder
> **Features:** An undulating woman, reflections on water, and a golden gun.

The Spy Who Loved Me

> **Designed by:** Maurice Binder
> **Features:** James Bond parachuting into the title sequence and into the hands of a beautiful woman. Images of female Russian soldiers marching and interacting with Bond in various ways—tiny women riding his gun, giant women shooting the gun, and a good bit of trampoline.

Moonraker

> **Designed by:** Maurice Binder
> **Features:** Segue from Jaws's pre-titles circus crash into circus imagery, then girls on trampolines in front of space imagery.

For Your Eyes Only

> **Designed by:** Maurice Binder
> **Features:** Sheena Easton, sometimes in extreme closeup, singing her title song (to date, the only singer to appear in the titles sequence), overlaid by water and bubbles, and silhouettes of Bond aiming his gun.

Octopussy

> **Designed by:** Maurice Binder
> **Features:** A small neon spotlight roves over the bodies of beautiful women. The light is variously in the shape of the titular octopus, or of a silhouette of 007.

Never Say Never Again

> **Designed by:** Micheline Roquebrune-Connery
> **Features:** There is no title sequence in the manner familiar to Bond fans. Opening credits appear over the beginning of the movie. This beginning, an adventure only loosely connected to the rest of the film, would have been the pre-titles sequence had *Never Say Never Again* been an Eon film.

A View To a Kill

> **Designed by:** Maurice Binder

Features: Women with neon-colored, glow-in-the-dark fingernails and lips, and sometimes glowing body paint, fire laser beams from glowing guns. Intercut are images of skiers and of Bond.

The Living Daylights

Designed by: Maurice Binder
Features: Watery images (oddly, as this has no tie-in to the film), a woman in sunglasses and a big hat, and some acrobatics. The sequence ends with a blond model inside a giant champagne glass.

Licence to Kill

Designed by: Maurice Binder
Features: The pre-titles sequence shrinks into the lens of a camera. Roulette tables, chips, James Bond with a beautiful woman, and more cameras predominate. The beginning of the film comes out of the same camera lens.

GoldenEye

Designed by: Danny Kleinman
Features: Women destroying Soviet symbols, a two-faced woman with a cigar in one mouth and a gun emerging from the other, gold background motif.

Tomorrow Never Dies

Designed by: Danny Kleinman
Features: A shatter of glass followed by a swoop into a series of digital images (circuitry, video static). Digitized women and transparent guns; women firing guns, dancing inside of and next to bullets.

The World is Not Enough

Designed by: Danny Kleinman
Features: Oil drops, oil slicks, and oil prisms. Women floating and sinking in oil, and then women made of oil. Oil drilling machinery moving in rhythm with the music. Globes ("the world") with oil or oil prisms on their surface.

Die Another Day

Designed by: Danny Kleinman
Features: Two women, "fire" and "ice," with those images inside their silhouettes, sending off sharp sparks as they strike their own bodies in dance. The entire sequence is overlaid on scenes of Bond in a North Korean prison, undergoing a tortuous ordeal. Scorpions are in both the film scenes of Bond and the abstract title sequence.

Casino Royale

Designed by: Danny Kleinman
Features: Card suits in various animated patterns. Bond shoots men who turn into explosions of card suits as they die. Vesper's face is briefly seen on the Queen of Spades. There are no other women.

Quantum of Solace

> **Designed by:** Mk12
> **Features:** Deserts and sand. Bond stands and shoots, and there are some nude women. Although the gunbarrel doesn't appear until the end of the film, cast names appear in dots suggestive of the gunbarrel sequence.

Skyfall

> **Designed by:** Danny Kleinman
> **Features:** Opens with Bond falling into the water from pre-titles sequence, Bond as a bloodied target, nude woman, guns and knives in the water turning into graves and then blood-red stags at Skyfall. Closeup on Bond's eye, and then he's shooting targets inside ruins. Silva appears, aiming at him. Water/kelp imagery turns into skulls. Fire burns Bond. Chinese dragons. Then a black and white kaleidoscope sequence, repeating every image in a Rorschach style, then back to the ruins which are a house of mirrors. In the end, we see Bond is shot, zoom into the wound which returns us to Skyfall and Bond's face.

Spectre

> **Designed by:** Danny Kleinman
> **Features:** From the pre-titles sequence's SPECTRE ring into dancing women. Bond (nude), the SPECTRE octopus and its tentacles, flame imagery, and love scenes with tentacles. Then shattered glass showing Silva, Vesper, Le Chiffre, M, a bunch of people standing solemnly, skull eyes opening, pictures burning, and Bond shooting. Then Bond and Madeline, Blofeld, and ending with a return to the ring.

LONDON CALLING

In movie jargon, to "establish" a location is to show the audience something that lets them know we are now at that location. If you see the outside of a building, and then see characters walking around inside, you know, as a viewer, that those characters are inside the building you just saw—the building has been "established."

John Glen, who directed a record five James Bond movies, has remarked that a red double-decker bus is a lovely and convenient way of establishing London. You see the bus, you know right away where you are. Well, sometimes idle curiosity grips me like a fever, and I had to know. I scanned through all five of Glen's Bond films, and sure enough, four of them establish London through use of the famous buses. The fifth visits only interior locations in London.

That got me started. How many different ways has London been established in the Bond movies? The first thing I found out was that London isn't established all the time. Often, M's familiar soundproof door, or Moneypenny at her desk, is sufficient to establish the location, and no exterior shots are used. So, following is a breakdown of London, or its absence, in the Bond films, and how London exteriors are established. Turns out, there is more than one way to get the job done.

London Isn't Visited: 2

You Only Live Twice

From burial at sea straight to Japan.

The Spy Who Loved Me

We don't know if Captain Benson—the submarine captain who meets with M, Bond, and others—is located in London or not. We never visit MI6 headquarters or any other location known to be in London.

Interiors Only: 8

From Russia with Love

We move from a park in Berkshire (about 50 miles outside of London) directly to MI6 interiors.

Thunderball

After the car chase, which is not in London, we move to MI6 interiors.

Diamonds Are Forever

Live and Let Die

Except for a very brief glimpse of the outside of Bond's front door.

The Man with the Golden Gun

Moonraker

For Your Eyes Only

Never Say Never Again

Spectre

> (First of two trips to London)

London Is Established: 11

Dr. No

> The camera gives us a close-up of a sign at "Le Cercle" that states "London" as its location.

Goldfinger

> An aerial shot gives us a view of a portion of the city that includes Big Ben.

On Her Majesty's Secret Service

> The shot cuts from M and Bond speaking at M's home (Quarterdeck) to London. A crane shot moves towards the College of Arms while Bond continues speaking to M, explaining that he's going to the College of Arms in London.

Octopussy

> John Glen's first double-decker bus.

A View to a Kill

> John Glen's second double-decker bus.

The Living Daylights

> John Glen's third double-decker bus.

Licence to Kill

> John Glen's final Bond film has another double-decker bus.

GoldenEye

> Martin Campbell also uses a double-decker bus.

Tomorrow Never Dies

> Oxford exteriors, MI6 interiors; on the phone, Moneypenny asks Bond where he is and he verbally establishes his location.

The World is Not Enough

> A caption reads "MI6 Headquarters, London" as we see an exterior shot of Vauxhall (the real MI6 headquarters).

Die Another Day

> The musical cue, "London Calling," establishes where the plane is landing, then we see Buckingham Palace.

Casino Royale

> A shot of the Parliament building and Big Ben, followed by M leaving a meeting.

Quantum of Solace

> A caption reads "London."

Skyfall

> First appearance: A caption reads "London, MI6," as we see an exterior shot of Vauxhall.
> Second appearance: We see a British flag flying and Big Ben in the background, as Eve joins Bond on the roof, indicating they're at MI6.

Spectre

> Second trip to London, a "London" title card.

So, we have five double-decker buses, two verbal cues, one musical cue, one sign, four captions, Buckingham Palace, and Big Ben three times.

Also note that, since it went up in 1998, the London Eye is often seen in shots of the London skyline.

TOMORROW NEVER DIES (1997)

Survey Says!

>Percent Favorite: 1%
>Top 5 Cumulative: 20/25 (tied)
>Numeric Rating: 5.8/10
>Ranking: 16 (18th/25)

My Rating and Ranking

>Rated: 9/10
>Ranked: 9 out of 25

Summary

When a Royal Navy frigate is sunk in the China Sea, MI6 suspects that media mogul Elliot Carver has sent a GPS signal that sent the ship off-course, in a plan to foment war in exchange for exclusive Chinese broadcasting rights. Investigating Carver's organization, Bond meets up with Wai Lin, a Chinese agent, and Paris Carver, Elliot's wife and Bond's former flame. After Paris is murdered by Carver, Bond and Wai Lin join forces, alerting their respective governments to Carver's involvement just in time. Bond kills Carver and "stays under cover" with Wai Lin.

>**James Bond:** Pierce Brosnan
>**Wai Lin:** Michelle Yeoh
>**Elliot Carver:** Jonathan Pryce
>**Paris Carver:** Teri Hatcher
>**Dr. Kaufman:** Vincent Schiavelli
>**Stamper:** Gotz Otto
>**Jack Wade:** Joe Don Baker
>**Henry Gupta:** Ricky Jay
>**Charles Robinson:** Colin Salmon
>**M:** Judi Dench
>**Moneypenny:** Samantha Bond
>**Q:** Desmond Llewelyn
>**Directed by** Roger Spottiswoode

Discussion

Two years earlier, Bond fans were treated to a movie that might be described as deep. *GoldenEye* is definitely fun, funny, and playful, but it's also contemplative, and stares down Big Issues of post-Cold War politics. *Tomorrow Never Dies* brings us back to a Bond that doesn't mean a damn thing. 1997's Bond film is a fun, noisy, action-packed, and rather wonderfully made confection, without the higher aspirations or depth of its predecessor.

If the adventure is perhaps run of the mill, the execution often goes the extra mile. Roger Spottiswoode's direction creates more art and visual interest than we are used to in a Bond film. The use of a tiny bit of slow motion in key scenes, and the use of foreground profiles (for example, when we first see Carver) is moody and effective. Foreshadowing is used effectively, such as when Paris uses the word "murder" just before her own. The pre-titles sequence opens within a video, which ties in well with the media-based theme of the film, and it opens onto a shot of Henry Gupta, without letting us know that he will figure prominently later. Two scenes are particularly deft; the beating Bond receives at Carver's party, juxtaposing the silence of a soundproof room with violence, and the sunken frigate-as-haunted-house scene, which gives enough horror to the deaths of these sailors to dignify them, something often missing in a shoot-'em-up action film. These artistic strokes work to make *Tomorrow Never Dies* a stronger movie.

Some fans find the plot ridiculous, but I think it's terrific. They argue that starting a war for ratings is absurd, but isn't that addressed within the movie? First of all ratings equal money—seeking them is no more absurd than cornering the market in gold or silicon chips. Elliot Carver is doing what William Randolph Hearst is said to have done, creating a war for circulation (as Carver himself mentions). Secondly, high ratings (and exclusive broadcasting rights) equal power, as Carver emphasizes more than once. This is a villain who seeks nothing less than the ability to control what people think.

Media villainy is very 90s, and corporate media dominance remains an important issue in the 21st century. It's a sensible choice after *GoldenEye*. Now that the Cold War Bond has been deconstructed, *Tomorrow Never Dies* brings us an evil that has nothing to do with communism, post-communism, or any other -ism.

Jonathan Pryce plays the role with theatrical style reminiscent of Steven Berkoff's Orlov in *Octopussy*. He is diabolical and sadistic. From the moment Elliot Carver first speaks, we hear the mania, the odd breathing, the glint of madness. Pryce does what Christopher Walken tried to do in *A View to a Kill* but with more success. I like that he seems mad right from the beginning, but mad in a way that you can easily imagine equates with success in the business world. In fact, if you've worked in business over any length of time, you've probably seen corporate heads with a bit of Carver's...shall we say, heightened reality. It's a shame that Carver's death didn't really work. I hate when people stand still and scream as death approaches. Elliot had plenty of time to jump out of the way, and certainly wasn't the type to panic.

The supporting henchmen are pretty good. Vincent Schiavelli as Dr. Kaufman is terrific in his one scene. He has most of the best lines in the movie. Ricky Jay as Henry Gupta has a great, understated screen presence. Gotz Otto is less successful, simply because he's so much a type, and never provides a reason to think of him as other than Aryan Superman #6 (see HENCHMEN). The rest of the henchmen are corporate goon types, justified in the context, but uninteresting nonetheless.

Did I mention the action? The film boast two excellent chases. The motorcycle chase is refreshingly straightforward. It is one of those through-the- streets anything goes affairs. But it isn't jokey and it is a bit of relief after the tank and tractor-trailer chases in the prior two films. The other is a gimmick chase, but of the "optional extras" variety— the remote-controlled BMW. It's a superb sequence marred only by one really dumb gadget—the wire cutter that just happens to be built into the BMW at the coincidental 'just right spot' for cutting just that height and thickness of cable. It's especially stupid because the chase doesn't depend on that sort of stretch—a remote-controlled car is stretch enough, and yet it is made believable until that moment. Don't forget a very good foot chase in Hamburg; while Wai Lin escapes by walking down the wall, Bond uses ingenuity and a flare for creating chaos to get away from Carver's men.

Beyond the chases (including that stunning leap over the helicopter) we have the extra action provided by Michelle Yeoh; some fans resent her having her own fight scene and complain that it's not really a Bond film if our hero takes a back seat to his co-star. I disagree; I think Pierce Brosnan is very much a presence throughout, but it would be crazy to hire a martial arts star and not let her show her stuff.

All of the Brosnan Bond films attempted a little more emotional nuance than we got in the early days, not always successfully. Here, the writers give him a poignant look at the past, which is hamstrung somewhat by Teri Hatcher's wooden performance. Hatcher fills out her evening gown admirably, but is not a strong enough actress for the rather sophisticated role she was given. Her line readings are flat, which is too bad, because the lines themselves are well-written. I like the concept of Paris Carver very much, but the execution leaves much to be desired. Fans tend to divide along these basic lines: They like Paris because she's sexy and looks hot in her stockings, and/or because of the touching way 007 reacts to her death, or they dislike her because of bad acting; personally, I see both points of view, and try to appreciate Paris's scenes for what they are meant to be.

But Paris is the sacrificial lamb; the main Bond girl is Michelle Yeoh as Wai Lin. Yeoh is fantastic in the action scenes and is a fine actress with a delicately expressive face. Unfortunately, there is minimal heat or sensuality between Bond and Wai Lin. I like how they get to respect each other and enjoy working together, but the sexuality is never there until the very last shot, which makes it feel obligatory rather than satisfying.

The supporting cast does well. *Tomorrow Never Dies* introduces Colin Salmon as Charles Robinson; Deputy Chief of Staff for M. Robinson was popular among the fans, and rightly so—he is unassumingly handsome with a good screen presence. Judi Dench returns as M, this time her antipathy has shifted away from Bond, who is doing, in her estimation, "his job," and towards an admiral who, she implies, thinks with his balls. Q has one of his best exchanges with Bond, but someone should have told him that red is not his color.

In many ways, *Tomorrow Never Dies* functions as a Roger Moore movie; it has a lot of gadgets, including at least one made-to-order for the very unlikely circumstance that arises. The film is pun-laden, the main Bond girl shows no attraction to 007 until she ends up in his arms, and the over the top villains provide a certain comic relief. On the other hand, the action is believable (in the sense that we believe our heroes are doing the work). There is a macabre undercurrent to the comedy, and none of the animals do double-takes. Roger Moore would never have had that scene in the hotel with the bottle of vodka—a fan favorite, with no small justification! This is definitely a Brosnan movie, and a good one.

High Points

- Remote-control car chase through the parking garage.
- A visit with The Doctor.
- Wonderful score that introduces David Arnold to the Bond films.
- Thrilling motorcycle chase through "Saigon," featuring excellent stunts and good use of location.
- A villain who restores the word "mad" to "mad genius."
- That dazzling fall down the side of Carver's building while holding onto the banner of his face.
- Bond, a hotel room, his thoughts, and a bottle of vodka.
- Another gorgeous and unique Danny Kleinman title sequence.
- Colonel Wai Lin's "Q lab."
- The introduction of Charles Robinson.
- Sharp confrontation between M and Admiral Roebuck throughout the pre-titles sequence.

Low Points

- Wooden performance by Teri Hatcher
- Lack of chemistry between Bond and Wai Lin.
- Too-convenient cable-cutting gadget in the otherwise nifty BMW.
- Using "Surrender" as the end-titles song! While I like Sheryl Crow's title song, k.d. lang's is superior and should have been up front.
- Yet another Aryan henchman.
- Unsatisfying deaths for Carver, Stamper, and Gupta.
- Desmond Llewelyn's hideous Avis jacket.

Quotable Quotes

Admiral Roebuck: "What the hell is he doing?"
M: "His job!"

Bond (his opening line; lights guard's cigarette...): "Filthy habit."

Admiral Roebuck: "With all due respect, M, sometimes I don't think you have the balls for this job."
M: "Perhaps. But the advantage is I don't have to think with them all the time."

Bond: "I always wondered how I'd feel if I ever saw you again."
Paris (slaps him)
Bond: "Now I know. Was it something I said?"
Paris: "How about the words 'I'll be right back'?"

Bond (as he cuts Carver's power): "Time for a station break."

Dr. Kaufman: "Believe me Mr. Bond, I could shoot you from Stutgart and still create the proper effect."

Dr. Kaufman: "I am especially good at the celebrity overdose."

Dr. Kaufman: "I am to torture you if you don't do it."
Bond: "Do you have a doctorate in that, too?"
Dr. Kaufman: "No, no, no. This is more like a hobby. But I'm very gifted."

Dr. Kaufman (as Bond is about to shoot him): "Wait! I'm just a professional doing a job."
Bond: "Me too."

Bond: "If I didn't know better, I'd say he'd developed an edifice complex."

Carver: "The distance between insanity and genius is measured only by success."

Wai Lin: "Trapped."
Bond: "Never."

Carver: "Mr. Stamper, would you please kill those bastards!"

Bond (last line): "Let's stay undercover."

Facts and Figures

SEXUAL ENCOUNTERS

Three: Prof. Inga Bergstrom (Danish instructor), Paris Carver, and Wai Lin.

BOND'S CARS

1964 Aston Martin DB5 (silver) (Blink and you'll miss it. It's parked outside Oxford while Bond is having his "Danish lesson.")
1995 BMW 750iL (silver)

DEATHS

Approximately one-hundred fifty-six:
- At the arms bazaar, seven plus two pilots.
- The entire crew of the Devonshire, estimated at 120.
- One Chinese MIG pilot.
- At the printing press, Bond shoots three and one dies by falling.
- Paris, Dr. Kaufman, Wai Lin's boatman, two during the parking lot chase are hit by their own bazooka.

- On the stealth boat, Bond stabs two, shoots one sneaking up on him, kills an additional eight, and six more die in the battle.

Bond Kills:

- <u>Twenty-three</u> directly (seven plus one pilot at the arms bazaar, three at the printing press, Dr. Kaufman, eleven on the stealth boat)
- <u>Four</u> indirectly (the pilot above Bond's plane killed by the ejector seat below, the one who falls at the printing press, and the two who die by their own weapon while chasing Bond)

EXPLOSIONS

<u>Ten</u>: In the pre-titles sequence, one from the cigarette lighter bomb, a big one and a smaller one from grenades, a barrage of explosions from the plane's guns, and a huge one when the Chester's missiles hit, plus two in the air battle. In Saigon, crates of fireworks are set off, and a helicopter explodes (that's a good one!). Bond's homemade grenade sets off an explosion on the stealth boat.

BOND'S FOOD AND DRINKS

Vodka Martinis

<u>One</u>: Ordered by Paris for Bond at the Hamburg party.

Other Drinks

- Champagne visible in an ice bucket with Professor Bergstrom.
- Bourbon with M in the limo (we see highball glasses, and we know from *GoldenEye* that bourbon is her preferred drink).
- After the Hamburg party, Bond drinks about a half bottle of straight vodka (Smirnoff Red). We see him drink three shots, but we can tell he's had more by the level in the bottle.
- When Bond returns to his hotel after stealing the GPS, we see champagne waiting for him in the hall, but he never drinks it (or even brings it into his room).

Food

- None.

GAMBLING AND SPORTS

- None, but Carver jokes about playing poker.

Amaze Your Friends!

- When Paris says "Tell me James, do you still sleep with a gun under your pillow?" she is obliquely making reference to *Thunderball*, where we see Bond sleep in exactly that fashion.
- *Tomorrow Never Dies* is the first James Bond movie with no direct or indirect reference to Ian Fleming's material. *Licence to Kill* was the first movie to lack an Ian Fleming novel or short story title, but it used scenes and quotes

from the novel **Live and Let Die** . The only Fleming reference in *GoldenEye* is the title.

- When the Chester is ordered to launch missiles, a switch is turned from "Peace" to "War."
- From the time the Chester reports "4 minutes 8 seconds to impact," until impact, 4 minutes 25 seconds pass. I consider this trivia rather than an error, because the movie doesn't tell us it is happening in real time—things we see Bond doing could naturally overlap with what we see happening with M and Admiral Roebuck.
- This is the movie where Bond gives up his Walther PPK for good (until *Casino Royale*, that is). Having been disarmed by Carver, he arrives at Wai Lin's headquarters in Saigon, where he picks up the Walther P99 and says "I must have Q get me one of these." The P99 replaces the PPK, which is considered an obsolete model. Brosnan's Bond carries the P99 in the remainder of his movies.
- Look familiar? If the scenes near Wai Lin's boat (when her boatman is killed) remind you of something, it's because they were filmed in Phuket, by the now-famous "James Bond Island" used in *The Man with the Golden Gun*.
- This movie was originally named *Tomorrow Never Lies*, but a typo in some early promotional material led to the change. It was easier at that point to change the name of the movie than go through the expense of replacing the material.

Most Interesting Goofs

Battle Stations? A red alert is called on the Devonshire, and we see everyone run to their posts. Later, when the drill penetrates the mess, we see crewmen sitting around eating, although the ship is still on alert.

Flying Fingers: When Carver uses his mini-keyboard to create headlines, his fingers fly without even the pretense of hitting appropriate keys. This is a very theatrical goof, as such an error would not be noticeable on stage, and Pryce is a theater actor.

Variable Windshield: A bazooka blows a hole in the windshield of Bond's BMW during the remote-controlled chase. The size of the hole varies widely from shot to shot. This is, of course, because several different cars were used.

I LOVE A MAN IN UNIFORM

James Bond holds the rank of Commander in the Royal Navy. The first M (and the second, if you hold with the theory outlined in ENCORE! ENCORE!) held the rank of Admiral. 007 is, from time to time, referred to as Commander, and his two obituaries—the fake one in *You Only Live Twice* and the premature one written by Elliot Carver in *Tomorrow Never Dies*—refer to him as a British Naval Officer.

(His third obituary, written by M in Skyfall, *refers to 007 as "Commander Bond, C.M.G., R.N.,"meaning that he is a Companion in the Order of St. Michael and St. George in the Royal Navy.)*

Bond in Uniform

You Only Live Twice: When Bond's death was faked, he was buried at sea in dress uniform.

The Spy Who Loved Me: When Bond arrives on the unnamed naval vessel for his briefing, he is in uniform. Note the appearance of the General Service Medal (GSM).

Tomorrow Never Dies: When Bond meets Jack Wade in preparation for his HALO (High Altitude Low Opening) jump, he is in uniform. Bond's medals are the GSM, the Rhodesia Medal, the Distinguished Service Cross, and the Order of the British Empire (OBE) ribbon.

M in Uniform

You Only Live Twice: When Bond meets with him after his funeral, M is in uniform.

The Living Daylights: In the pre-titles sequence, when briefing the 00 section on the training exercise, M is in uniform.

Moneypenny in Uniform

You Only Live Twice: Outside of M's office after Bond's funeral.

Diamonds Are Forever: Dressed as a customs officer at the hovercraft station.

ENCORE! ENCORE!

So you're watching a Bond movie, and you're thinking, "Hey! He looks familiar." "Wasn't he a good guy?" "Wasn't he a bad guy?" "Don't I know that face?" You're right, he is, he was, he was, and you do.

The Bond movies have reused numerous actors over the years, ranging from major allies who have become villains (Charles Gray) and vice-versa (Joe Don Baker) to stuntmen who have long been a part of the Bond team, and who are used in this or that stunt role in various films (Bob Simmons, Simon Crane). Spot the Encore Actor is something of a game among Bond fans, and here is a list that will allow you to win that game, along with some added tidbits.

The Complete List

Actor	Appeared as...	In...
Maud Adams	Andrea Anders Octopussy Extra on streetcar	*The Man with the Golden Gun* *Octopussy* *A View to a Kill*
Irvin Allen	Che Che Stromberg crewmen	*On Her Majesty's Secret Service* *The Spy Who Loved Me*
Carole Ashby	Octopussy Girl Whistling Girl (credited as Whistling Girl, but introduced as Dominique)	*Octopussy* *A View To a Kill*
George Baker	Sir Hilary Bray Captain Benson	*On Her Majesty's Secret Service* *The Spy Who Loved Me*
Joe Don Baker	Brad Whitaker Jack Wade	*The Living Daylights* *GoldenEye* and *Tomorrow Never Dies*
David Bauer	U.S. Diplomat Morton Slumber	*You Only Live Twice* *Diamonds Are Forever*
Martine Beswick	Zora (Gypsy girl) Paula Caplan	*From Russia with Love* *Thunderball*
Ed Bishop	Control Technician Klaus Hergersheimer	*You Only Live Twice* *Diamonds Are Forever*
Andy Bradford	Guard 009	*For Your Eyes Only* *Octopussy*
Robert Brown (See THE M CONTROVERSY)	Admiral Hargreaves M	*The Spy Who Loved Me* Eon Productions: *Octopussy* through *Licence to Kill*
Jeremy Bulloch	HMS Ranger Crewman Smithers	*The Spy Who Loved Me* *For Your Eyes Only* and *Octopussy*

Actor	Appeared as...	In...
Anthony Chin	Decontamination Tech. Goldfinger's waiter SPECTRE guard shot by Bond's cigarette Taiwanese Tycoon who"drops out"	*Dr. No* *Goldfinger* *You Only Live Twice* *A View To a Kill*
Tsai Chin	Ling Madame Wu	*You Only Live Twice* *Casino Royale*
Simon Crane	Gibraltar soldier #1 French helicopter pilot	*The Living Daylights* *GoldenEye*
Anthony Dawson	Professor Dent Ernst Stavro Blofeld (body)	*Dr. No* *From Russia with Love* and *Thunderball*
David de Keyser	Draco (voice) Dr. Tynan	*On Her Majesty's Secret Service* *Diamonds Are Forever*
Peter Ensor	Stromberg crewman Tycoon	*The Spy Who Loved Me* *A View to a Kill*
Kim Fortune	HMS Ranger crewman RAF officer	*The Spy Who Loved Me* *Moonraker*
Walter Gotell (see below)	Morzeny General Alexis Gogol	*From Russia with Love* Eon Productions: *The Spy Who Loved Me* through *The Living Daylights*.
Richard Graydon (see STUNTMEN)	Russian astronaut Draco's driver Francisco the Fearless	*You Only Live Twice* *On Her Majesty's Secret Service* *Octopussy*
Charles Gray	Dikko Henderson Ernst Stavro Blofeld	*You Only Live Twice* *Diamonds Are Forever*
Diane Hartford	Dancing Woman at Kiss-Kiss Club Card Player	*Thunderball* *Casino Royale*
David Healy	Houston Radar Operator Vandenburg Launch Director	*You Only Live Twice* *Diamonds Are Forever*
Burt Kwouk	Mister Ling SPECTRE #3	*Goldfinger* *You Only Live Twice*
Marc Lawrence	Gangster Rodney	*Diamonds Are Forever* *The Man with the Golden Gun*
Derek Lea	Stunt performer Stunt performer Guy Haines's bodyguard	*The World is Not Enough* *Die Another Day* *Quantum of Solace*

Actor	Appeared as...	In...
George Leech	Crewman Strangled SPECTRE skier Kristatos's Man	*Thunderball* *On Her Majesty's Secret Service* *For Your Eyes Only*
Valerie Leon	Hotel Receptionist Fishing Boat Woman	*The Spy Who Loved Me* *Never Say Never Again*
Mai Ling	Mei-Lei 2nd Bath Girl	*Goldfinger* *You Only Live Twice*
Billy J. Mitchell	Commander Pederson Admiral Chuck Farrell	*Never Say Never Again* *GoldenEye*
Michael Moor	Thug Kamran Shah's man	*Octopussy* *The Living Daylights*
Albert Moses	Bartender Saruddin	*The Spy Who Loved Me* *Octopussy*
Terrance Mountain	Raphael Uncredited henchman	*On Her Majesty's Secret Service* *Diamonds Are Forever*
Bill Nagy	Mr. Midnight Pentagon Official	*Goldfinger* *You Only Live Twice*
Peter Porteous	Lenkin Gasworks Supervisor	*Octopussy* *The Living Daylights*
Manning Redwood	General Miller Bob Conley	*Never Say Never Again* *A View to a Kill*
Nadja Regin	Kerim Bey's girlfriend Bonita	*From Russia with Love* *Goldfinger*
Milton Reid	Guard Sandor	*Dr. No* *The Spy Who Loved Me*
Robert Rietty	Emilio Largo (voice) Chef de Jeu Italian Minister	*Thunderball* *On Her Majesty's Secret Service* *Never Say Never Again*
Shane Rimmer	Hawaii control room operator "Tom," control room operator Voice of helicopter attack leader Captain Carter of the USS Wayne	*You Only Live Twice* *Diamonds Are Forever* *Diamonds Are Forever* *The Spy Who Loved Me*
George Roubicek	U.S. Astronaut (2nd capsule) Stromberg Crewman	*You Only Live Twice* *The Spy Who Loved Me*
Nadim Sawalha	Fekkesh Tangiers Security Chief	*The Spy Who Loved Me* *The Living Daylights*
Bob Simmons (see STUNTMEN)	Colonel Jacques Botier Would-be Car Thief	*Thunderball* *For Your Eyes Only*

Actor	Appeared as...	In...
Clem So	Casino guest SPECTRE Crime Boss	*Skyfall* *Spectre*
Mary Stavin	Octopussy Girl Kimberly Jones	*Octopussy* *A View to a Kill*
Victor Tourjansky (*see below*)	Man with Bottle Man with Bottle Man with Wine Glass	*The Spy Who Loved Me* *Moonraker* *For Your Eyes Only*
Gabor Vernon	Hungarian diplomat Borchoi	*Live and Let Die* *Octopussy*
Lizzie Warville	Gonzales' pool girl Russian Girl	*For Your Eyes Only* *Moonraker*
Michael Wilson	see below	see below

By the Numbers

If you're wondering how many actors from other Bond films appear in any given film, I'm here to help. Following is a list of movies showing the number of names from the above list that appear in that movie. It doesn't matter if it was the actor's first appearance (like Charles Gray in *You Only Live Twice*) or if the actor was coming back for more (Milton Reid in *The Spy Who Loved Me*); either kind of appearance is counted. The list is in descending order of "encores" featured.

> **14 actors:** *The Spy Who Loved Me*
> **12:** *Octopussy* and *You Only Live Twice*
> **9:** *Diamonds Are Forever*
> **8:** *A View to a Kill*
> **7:** *For Your Eyes Only*, *The Living Daylights*, and *On Her Majesty's Secret Service*
> **6:** *Thunderball*
> **5:** *Goldfinger*
> **4:** *From Russia with Love*, *Moonraker*, and *Never Say Never Again*
> **3:** *Dr. No* and *GoldenEye*
> **2:** *The Man with the Golden Gun* and *Casino Royale*
> **1:** *Licence to Kill*, *Live and Let Die*, *Tomorrow Never Dies*, *Quantum of Solace*, *Skyfall*, and *Spectre*

Trivia Bonus

Casino Royale features two record-setting encore appearances.

Diane Hartford had an uncredited appearance in *Thunderball*, as the woman in a red dress who briefly dances with Bond before Fiona Volpe cuts in. In *Casino Royale*, she is credited on a list of "Card Players," and is seen at the table with Dimitrios wearing a green evening gown. At 41 years between appearances, Diane Hartford holds a piece of Bond history.

Tsai Chin, who appeared in 1967's *You Only Live Twice* as Ling, the woman with Bond in Hong Kong in the pre-titles sequence, is poker-player Madame Wu in *Casino Royale* in 2006. Although not quite Hartford's record, this is the longest between credited appearances of characters with names (39 years).

Stuntmen

Keep in mind that stuntmen appear far more often than listed here; they are Bond, the villain, the girl, and anyone else who needs coverage. They might also appear in more small roles and walk-throughs than are listed here, simply because they are so often available on set when such a role needs filling.

The M Controversy

How do I explain this, except to say that this is one of those things that fans do? Anyone looking at the above list can easily see that the Bond films are happy to cast people who have played different roles in previous movies. It is not an impediment, because Eon doesn't really care about that level of continuity (or continuity much at all, but that's another chapter). Clearly, the good guy with the wooden leg who was killed in *You Only Live Twice* did not rise from the grave to become Blofeld in *Diamonds Are Forever*. Still, fans will from time to time wonder if That Guy (or Gal) is actually the same person, who happens to have appeared in a second Bond movie. After all, if Sheriff J.W. Pepper can appear inexplicably in Bangkok after meeting Bond in Louisiana, why can't that Las Vegas gangster in *Diamonds Are Forever* have been killed by Scaramanga a few movies later?

No dual role has generated as much interest, though, as that of Robert Brown. He first appeared in the Bond world as Admiral Hargreaves in *The Spy Who Loved Me*, where he was part of the briefing about the submarine tracking system. He reappeared as M in *Octopussy*, and remained in that role for four films. Many fans speculate that Brown actually played Hargreaves in all five films, and that Admiral Hargreaves succeeded Admiral Sir Miles Messervey as M, head of MI6. Some fans go beyond speculation about this and are downright adamant.

There is no direct evidence in favor of this theory, and just a bit of evidence against it. The favorable evidence that exists is indirect; it doesn't appear in the movies themselves. In 1995, Danjaq (Eon's affiliate) released the Ultimate James Bond Interactive Dossier on CD-ROM. (I'm grateful to Bond fan Alex Zamudio for bringing this to my attention.) These CDs clearly refer to Brown's M as a new character; his biographical data is listed under "M2," and he is referred to as being "like his predecessor." They do not mention Hargreaves, leaving open a third possibility: That Brown's M is neither Admiral Hargreaves nor Admiral Sir Miles Messervey, but a third person. Since the Dossier is an "official" release, and seems to have the blessing of the powers that be, some fans consider it canon. I wonder, though. Did Danjaq comb carefully over the contents? Or is it one fan's version (admittedly a very authoritative fan; the estimable John Cork)?

Evidence against the M-is-Hargreaves possibility is slight but real, and has the virtue of appearing directly in the films. First, by the time of Brown's tenure, it was very clear, not only that one actor could play multiple characters, but that multiple actors could play one character—namely, James Bond. If Bond can be Sean Connery, and then George Lazenby, and so on, then there's no reason to believe that Miles Messervey cannot first be Bernard Lee and then be Robert Brown.

In the Brosnan era, points against the Hargreaves theory accumulated, because we saw two significant characters depart the series. When Judi Dench took the role of M, and when John Cleese took the role of Q, each made clear reference to a predecessor. Thus, we can believe that this is how Eon treats the departure of a *character*, whereas we know that Eon ignores the departure of an *actor* (with the exception of Lazenby's breaking the fourth wall, no new Bond or new Moneypenny has ever been noticed as any different).

Further, we see that the M played by Dench redecorated her office somewhat, which is the normal behavior for the new head of any organization. The same pictures are on Brown's and Lee's walls.

The strongest evidence against Hargreaves being M comes to my attention from Bond fan Evan Willnow, who points out that Brown's M was of a lower rank than Brown's Hargreaves:

Take a look at M in the pre-titles of *The Living Daylights* on his shoulder is his Royal Navy rank—one thick gold bar and one thin bar with a loop. M is a Rear Admiral.

Now take a look at Admiral Hargreaves sleeve in *The Spy Who Loved Me*: One thick bar, a thin bar, and another thin bar with a loop. Hargreaves is a Vice Admiral.

So now unless Hargreaves was demoted—highly unlikely given that he is now trusted to run the Secret Intelligence Service—Hargreaves cannot be the same man.

I think Willnow's argument is decisive (though some proponents of the Hargreaves theory cling to the notion of Hargreaves being demoted). Neither side has a lock, but I have to say that the arguments in favor persist in sounding silly to me.

Victor Tourjansky's Drinking Problem

In *The Spy Who Loved Me*, James Bond drives his Lotus out of the water, to the astonishment of the beach-lovers present. One man, played by Victor Tourjansky, looks at the bottle of wine he is drinking, as if to ask if what he is seeing came from a bottle. I'm guessing anyone who would wonder such a thing has spent too much time with bottles!

Next up, *Moonraker*. While in the previous movie Bond had driven a land-based vehicle out of the water, in this one, he drives a water-based vehicle up onto the land. A man in the streets of Venice sees Bond's tricked-out gondola drive through town, and drops his glass to give his bottle the ol' double-take. Once again, it's Victor Tourjansky.

In the next movie, *For Your Eyes Only*, Bond avoids any water/land disparity. Instead, he skis across an outdoor restaurant table, pursued by bad guys on motorcycles. Holding his wine glass, our man Tourjansky stares after them in astonishment. Presumably, it is because he doesn't have the bottle that he doesn't stare at his drink—I think the label must be what he finds informative.

Is it three different characters with a similar reaction to booze, or is it one character who takes a lot of vacations at exotic spots? We'll never know.

The Michael Wilson Cameos

Michael Wilson, step-son of Cubby Broccoli, has been working on the Bond films for most of his life, beginning as a gofer and general assistant, and moving into script-writing and production. He and his half-sister Barbara Broccoli are the current producers of the Bond films.

Wilson has had a cameo in every Eon Bond movie since *The Spy Who Loved Me* (with one exception), and spotting him has become a bit of a fan hobby, not unlike spotting Hitchcock. Of course, Wilson hasn't Hitchcock's famous girth, so he takes up less room on-screen. In the DVD extras for *Die Another Day*, it was revealed that Michael Wilson is referred to by the crew as "Governor," and was so listed on the call sheet for that film's cameo.

Here, then, a complete list of how to spot Michael Wilson in the Bond movies, so that you can play along at home.

Goldfinger:

Wilson is one of Goldfinger's guards in the Fort Knox sequence, seen standing next to the truck that will crash through the gate.

The Spy Who Loved Me:

Seated behind Anya and Fekkesh at the pyramid show.

Moonraker:

Three brief appearances: Walking down the street with a child in front of the glassworks in Venice, then with Cubby and Dana Broccoli when Bond gets out of his gondola in Venice (the same scene as Victor Tourjansky's). Third, as a NASA controller who comments on the appearance of Drax's space station.

For You Eyes Only:

As a priest at the Greek Orthodox church where Bond meets Q.

Octopussy:

Two appearances: First, as a member of the Soviet security council (a role he will reprise in *GoldenEye*). Second, he is one of the tourists who helps pull Bond from the water when he escapes Khan's hunt.

A View to a Kill:

His voice can be heard in the background when Bond and Stacey use the elevator in City Hall when they are looking for files on Zorin's oil wells.

The Living Daylights:

> In the audience to Saunders's right when Bond and Kara attend the opera in Vienna.

Licence to Kill

> His voice is heard in the pre-titles sequence, saying "If they hurry, they might just be able to grab the bastard."

GoldenEye:

> Wilson's second appearance as a member of the Russian (no longer Soviet) security council.

Tomorrow Never Dies:

> He is seen in a video conference with Elliot Carver as Tom Wallace, Vice President of CMGN. They discuss blackmailing the President of the United States, and Wilson says "Consider him slimed."

The World is Not Enough:

> Standing at the door of the private gaming room at Zukovsky's casino. He hands Elektra King something to sign.

Die Another Day:

> Wilson's first credited role is as General Chandler, who appears in the situation room in South Korea and says "Get me the President." There is an earlier cameo in which he leans against a car in Cuba as Bond crosses the street.

Casino Royale

> Wilson plays the police chief whom Mathis has arrested.

Quantum of Solace

> He is seated in the lobby of the hotel in Haiti, reading a newspaper.

Skyfall

> For the first time in decades, Wilson does not appear. He was a pallbearer carrying one of the slain MI6 agents, but that scene ended up on the cutting room floor.

Spectre

> After the meeting at the Foreign Office, M walks up to C in the hall; we briefly see C talking with Wilson in the foreground.

General Alexis Gogol

No one supposes that Walter Gotell's earlier character, Morzeny, in *From Russia with Love*, is really General Gogol, for the simple reason that Morzeny was killed.

Gotell didn't appear again opposite Sean Connery, but returned as General Gogol, head of the KGB, in *The Spy Who Loved Me*. Gotell played that role in six consecutive Eon films: *The Spy Who Loved Me* through *The Living Daylights*. His presence gave a sense of continuity to the universe of espionage in which Bond lives.

The role of General Pushkin in *The Living Daylights* was originally written as General Gogol (hence Bond and M discussing how long they've known him). Walter Gotell wasn't available for such a lengthy role, and so the character was mentioned, given a new job in Foreign Service, and given a brief appearance at the end of the film; his final appearance in a Bond movie.

Walter Gotell died in 1997 at the age of 73.

THE WORLD IS NOT ENOUGH (1999)

Survey Says!

>Percent Favorite: 1%
>Top 5 Cumulative: 20/25 (tie)
>Numeric Rating: 5.8/10
>Ranking: 17 (21st/25)

My Rating and Ranking

>Rated: 6/10
>Ranked: 18 out of 25

Summary

Sir Robert King's stolen money, returned to him by Bond, is chemically treated to trigger a bomb that murders him at MI6 headquarters. The bomb's trigger required an insider. MI6 suspects international terrorist Renard, who years earlier had kidnapped King's daughter, Elektra. M, a friend of King and his daughter, sends Bond to protect Elektra and find the insider. After making love to Elektra, Bond follows her chief of security, Davidoff. When he finds a body in Davidoff's trunk, he kills and replaces Davidoff; impersonating a nuclear scientist inside a decommissioned power plant. There he meets Dr. Christmas Jones and confronts Renard, who steals a bomb. When Elektra reveals herself as her father's murderer, and kidnaps M, Bond and Dr. Jones team up with Valentin Zukovsky to prevent the villains from detonating a nuclear submarine off the coast of Istanbul. Zukovsky is killed saving Bond, who must kill Elektra in cold blood in order to stop her scheme.

>**James Bond:** Pierce Brosnan
>**Elektra King:** Sophie Marceau
>**Renard:** Robert Carlyle
>**Dr. Christmas Jones:** Denise Richards
>**Valentin Zukovsky:** Robbie Coltraine
>**Mr. Bullion (Bull):** Goldie
>**Charles Robinson:** Colin Salmon
>**M:** Judi Dench
>**Moneypenny:** Samantha Bond
>**Q:** Desmond Llewelyn
>**"R":** John Cleese
>**Directed by** Michael Apted

Discussion

Brosnan's third and fourth James Bond films have fans deeply divided. Both *The World is Not Enough* and *Die Another Day* are passionately loved, and passionately hated. For many, *The World is Not Enough* is the greatest Bond film in decades; an emotionally rich homage to *On Her Majesty's Secret Service* that will be remembered forever. For many others, *The World is Not Enough* is a mawkish soap opera, murky and muddled, with the worst Bond girl since Stacey Sutton.

(*Note:* Both *Die Another Day* and *The World is Not Enough* have experienced a sea change in fan feeling since 2006. This movie has dropped from a ranking of 11th to 21st, almost disappeared as a fan favorite, and crashed in Top Five Cumulative ranking from 10th to 20th. These two are the only Bond movies to change so dramatically since this book's first edition—suggesting that fan love is highest when a movie is newer, and repeated viewings have a high likelihood of changing fan affections. Earlier movies had probably already experienced that drop-off. It's also fair to say that Vesper Lynd has replaced Elektra King in fan affection. The discussion following is the original 2006 essay.

For discussion of changes in fan feeling on *Die Another Day,* see that chapter.)

The accusations of soap opera are certainly born out by the plot summary; a convoluted Who Did What To Whom that brings up family and emotional ties as central plot points. As you see above, My personal rating and ranking of *The World is Not Enough* are middle-low rating. It is, in my view, watchable and unremarkable. Thus, I am in neither *The World is Not Enough* camp, and can see both points of view.

The World is Not Enough has excellent production values, well put-together action sequences, and (with one notable exception) a very strong cast. The Bond films of the 1990s all have a polished and sophisticated feel to them that adds a bit of gloss to an already high-quality series. Even the worst of the Brosnan films (which, in my opinion, is this one) provides a quality film experience.

The movie starts well, with a smart and exciting action sequence at the office of a Swiss banker. Brosnan is edgy and in command in the scene, reminiscent of Sean Connery. But the pre-titles sequence goes on too long—over fourteen minutes—and becomes too much the movie proper. This high-pitched overkill is part of what older viewers object to when comparing early Bond films to the current batch. The pre-titles sequence might have easily ended with the witty use of a (temporarily) unconscious man as an anchor for a window escape, with the main movie beginning at MI6 headquarters. Or, the pre-titles sequence might have extended as far as King's murder (although no teasers except *Die Another Day*'s and *Skyfall's* have ended on a dark note) with the chase of "Cigar Girl" happening post-credits. As it stands, this movie had it seem nearly pointless to view the pre-titles sequences as separate, stand-alone affairs. If their boundaries stretch so far, how can we distinguish them from the movie itself? In all fairness, the boat chase is a huge favorite among fans, and is good fun, but I'd have liked it better if it had been placed after the titles.

From here we move into the territory that some fans find emotionally satisfying, and others mawkish. A funeral, a delicate, vulnerable woman, mistakes from M's past haunting her...is this a direction Bond should take? Fans disagree; for myself, I think it's fine as long as it's rare. If every movie is "this time it's personal," then "this time" loses its cachet.

Sophie Marceau is a favorite of many fans, particularly younger fans. She has an interesting, expressive face to match her complex performance—she is far more than the models-turned-actresses who so often populate a Bond film. Thirty-three years old when *The World is Not Enough* was released, and five years older than the other female lead, Denise Richards, Marceau is the first mature, sophisticated Bond girl since Maud Adams played Octopussy. She carries the emotional weight of her character fairly successfully, although I'd suggest that she is less persuasive at the end as a villain, when she lets histrionics do too much of her work. Prior to that, she is wonderful. Her love scenes with both Bond and Renard are excellent; sensual, seductive, and volatile. Her performance is the highlight of the movie for most fans, and many see her as a latter-day Tracy. Not least because of the homage mentioned earlier. In a ski sequence designed to be reminiscent of *On Her Majesty's Secret Service*, and with Elektra dressed in an outfit equally reminiscent of Tracy's ski-wear, Elektra is, like Tracy, caught in an avalanche.

Given the excellence of Sophie Marceau as a main villain (who at first appears to be a damsel in distress—Brosnan's Bond is always getting betrayed by insiders!) it is a shame that the rest of the villains disappoint. Robert Carlyle is a wonderful actor. In *Trainspotting*, he was genuinely creepy and menacing as an out-of-control addict, and in *The Full Monty*, he was a sympathetic and loveable ne'er-do-well father. Here, the acting works but the writing fails; the unique nature of a man without feelings is is under-explored; how can he walk, touch, eat, with no sensation? He could have been truly monstrous, instead his difference is largely nominal. He is almost tragic, and in the end there is a certain sympathy for him; like Bond he loved Elektra. Hence, Bond's coldness and hatred towards him feels out of place. The henchmen: Gabor, Bull, and Davidoff, are bland and essentially interchangeable—not an Oddjob in the bunch.

Fans are sharply divided on bringing M into the mainstream of action, with many saying that, with so great an actress as Dame Judi Dench, it is crazy not to use her to the fullest. Others, including me, feel that not only is it a breach of Bond tradition, but more importantly, it makes no sense for the character. M is too cool-headed, family ties or no, to break protocol and place herself in the midst of danger. Is it interesting to have M be personally connected to the villain? Sure. But in a film that references the most emotional of prior chapters, it seems like overkill.

The World is Not Enough's greatest weakness is visual; it is the ugliest Bond film, rivaled only by *Licence to Kill*. Kazakhstan and Azerbaijan are both bleak. The caviar factory and the decommissioned nuclear plant are dark and murky. The submarine's distorted angles make the climactic scene almost impossible to follow. While not every adventure can take place in Nassau, this one is overloaded with unpleasant locations filmed in grays and browns. The only color in the movie is provided by Elektra King's wardrobe.

Not merely visually murky, *The World is Not Enough*'s plot is a series of shadows and darknesses. Why is the money being returned? When did Elektra become a villain (before, during, or after her kidnapping)? What did Bond mean that Elektra "turned" Renard—wasn't he already a kidnapper and terrorist? What exactly is the deal with the pipelines? In a dark story of dark betrayals, at least something should have a little light shed on it!

In addition, *The World is Not Enough* panders to supposed audience preferences by giving us a bimbo nuclear physicist with a navel piercing; the much-despised Dr. Christmas Jones. In an overall dark, even gloomy movie, the action set pieces have a nonsensical, madcap quality. This, too, feels like pandering. Boat chase? Ski chase? Attack on the caviar factory? There's a disjointed quality to these scenes that reminds one that Bond movies give "Ooh, this would be cool" pride of place over making the plot work.

In this film, audiences were happy to see the return of two beloved allies: Charles Robinson of MI6 and Valentin Zukovsky. Zukovsky's character has been noticeably softened since *GoldenEye*. He is both less criminal and more polite. Nonetheless, he has great presence as played by Robbie Coltraine, and fans are still hoping that Elektra's shot didn't really kill him (it did).

Speaking of MI6, Moneypenny evidences jealousy towards one of Bond's paramours—the lovely Dr. Molly Warmflash. This is slightly out of character for Moneypenny—Lois Maxwell's version was downright helpful towards Bond's assignations, as we saw at the beginnings of both *You Only Live Twice* and *Live and Let Die*. Samantha Bond pulls it off without seeming too nasty, although whoever wrote the scene perhaps forgot that the essence of Moneypenny is either to pursue or be pursued, but never seem to have any real stake in the outcome. I like Dr. Warmflash, who is a little bit unmade-up and unglamourous, as I think is appropriate for someone in her position, but is still lovely.

Finally, note must be made of Desmond Llewelyn's final appearance and John Cleese's introduction. Although the ground was here laid for Llewelyn's eventual retirement, no one dreamed he would be killed in a car accident just as the movie was released. With hindsight, Q's "Always have an escape route" seems like a farewell, but Cleese insists that Llewelyn had intended to continue working for Eon for years to come. Llewelyn's departure is much-beloved, a fitting farewell after seventeen films (remember that Peter Burton played Q in *Dr. No*, and Q did not appear in *Live and Let Die*).

Cleese's introduction in the same scene is less successful. Fan discussion in the months following *The World is Not Enough*'s release tended towards the opinion that John Cleese would be great in the role, but that this particular scene was poorly scripted, and indeed, with *Die Another Day*'s release, this proved to be the case. Cleese's first appearance made him a fool, which is not what we want of Q. Furthermore, although an inventor might be socially inept, it defies reason that he wouldn't be at least functional around his own inventions. One suspects that screenwriters Purvis and Wade simply didn't know what to do with a comedian of Cleese's renown and they overplayed their hand.

High Points

- Desmond Llewelyn's poignant farewell scene.
- A sophisticated, complex Bond girl/villainess.
- The chilling torture-chair scene.
- Excellent, retro title song performed by Garbage.
- Boat chase.
- A vulnerable Bond, sustaining his first injury since *Thunderball*.

- Speaking of injuries, a cool fall onto the Millennium Dome, and a very nice segue into the titles, reminiscent of *The Spy Who Loved Me*.
- The return of Valentin Zukovsky.
- Beautiful ski cinematography, and the parahawks in that scene are interesting.

Low Points

- Murky, ugly cinematography in many scenes.
- Unappealing locations.
- Denise Richards as Dr. Christmas Jones, belly-baring physicist.
- Crowded, over-complicated plot with too little exposition.
- M in a helpless and despondent condition.
- Visual confusion aboard the submarine that probably seemed like a good idea in storyboards but made the sequence hard to follow.
- No interesting henchmen, and an uninteresting secondary villain (Renard) who should have been outstanding.
- John Cleese's idiotic portrayal of "R" as a man who doesn't know how to open a car door.

Quotable Quotes

Cigar Girl: "Would you like to check my figures?"
Bond: "I'm sure they're perfectly well rounded."

Bond (while undressing Dr. Warmflash): "Let's skirt the issue, shall we?"

Bond: "Elektra, this is a game I can't afford to play."

(Repeated by **Elektra, Renard, Bond**): "There's no point in living if you can't feel alive."

Guard: "What happened to Davidoff? I was told to expect him."
Bond: "Eh, he was buried with work."

Dr. Christmas Jones: "Dr. Jones. Christmas Jones. And don't make any jokes, I've heard 'em all."
Bond: "I don't know any doctor jokes."

Bond: "Cold-blooded murder is a filthy business."

Dr. Christmas Jones: "Do you want to put that in English for those of us who don't speak spy?"

Dr. Christmas Jones: "Someone's going to have my ass."
Bond: "First things first."

Dr. Christmas Jones: "What's the story with you and Elektra?"
Bond: "Strictly plutonic."

Bond (seeing his car cut in half): "Q's not going to like this!"

Bond: "The world is not enough."
Elektra: "Foolish sentiment."
Bond: "Family motto."

Bond (being tortured): "One last screw..."

Elektra: "You wouldn't kill me. You'd miss me."
Renard (on radio): "Yes?"
Elektra: "Dive!"
Bond (shoots Elektra): "I never miss."

Facts and Figures

SEXUAL ENCOUNTERS

Three: Dr. Molly Warmflash, Elektra King, Dr. Christmas Jones.

BOND'S CARS

1964 Aston Martin DB5 (silver) (Another barely-there appearance for the Aston Martin. It is seen in infrared, on the MI6 scanner, parked outside Bond's hotel, and it is how "R" manages to find Bond and Dr. Jones in flagrante delicto.)
1999 BMW Z8 (silver)

DEATHS

Approximately fifty-five:

- The Swiss banker and two of his assistants, Sir Robert King, Cigar Girl, four parahawk pilots, Arkoff, Davidoff, at least eight during Renard's theft of the nuclear bomb, three when Elektra reveals herself to M.
- In the attack on the caviar factory, two at the pier, one or two in each of two helicopters.
- The "skeleton crew" on the submarine seems to be about ten. Three when Zukovsky enters Maiden's Tower, Mr. Bullion (Bull), Zukovsky (fans speculate that perhaps Zukovsky didn't die, but let's count him), Gabor, Elektra King, one on the submarine whom Bond uses for a shield and Renard shoots, Renard, whoever of Renard's men were trapped on the sub when it exploded—presumably about eight (making Renard's crew and the originally skeleton crew equal in number).

Bond Kills:

- <u>Ten</u> or <u>twelve</u> directly (one of the bank assistants, Davidoff, three of Renard's men when Renard steals the bomb, either two or four in the helicopters at the Beluga factory, Gabor, Elektra, Renard).
- <u>Five</u> indirectly (the parahawks are all indirect; crashing while chasing Bond, the human shield was killed directly by Renard, but indirectly Bond knows that a human shield is a dangerous occupation).

EXPLOSIONS

<u>Nineteen</u>: King's money blows a thrilling hole through the side of Vauxhall, two small ones in the boat chase, the hot air balloon. One series (a total of six) from grenades dropped by the parahawks, two better ones when the first two parahawks crash, and a big one when the next two crash together and cause an avalanche.

In Kazakhstan on the ground a random explosion unconnected to the plot, a huge fireball at the nuclear plant that Bond escapes by swinging on chains. Subsequently, the entire plant goes up but it is still part of the first explosion; a nice one when the pipeline blows up (supposedly taking Bond and Jones with it). At the caviar factory, a helicopter shoots two fireballs at Bond, saw damage causes another, and then a helicopter explodes impressively, taking half the pier with it, another explosion on the pier and finally the last 'copter.

Bull's bomb and the underwater explosion of the submarine.

BOND'S FOOD AND DRINKS

Vodka Martinis

<u>One</u>: At Zukovsky's casino.

Other Drinks

- M offers Bond some sort of whiskey (probably her preferred bourbon), to which he significantly adds ice.
- With Zukovsky, Bond has two straight vodkas (Smirnoff).
- In bed with Elektra, the two finish a bottle of Bollinger champagne.
- Bond and Christmas Jones toast with champagne in the final scene.

Food

- No scenes of Bond eating. The meal that kills the submarine crew is fruit (a banana) and submarine (ha ha) sandwiches with brandy.

GAMBLING AND SPORTS

- We see roulette played in the background at the casino.
- Zukovsky offers Elektra blackjack or vingt et un; instead, she chooses a simple cut of cards, high card wins.
- Skiing

Amaze Your Friends!

- The title of the movie, and the statement that it is the Bond family motto, both come from *On Her Majesty's Secret Service*. In the novel, this is the motto of a family of Bonds to whom 007 is definitely not related. But in the film, Sir Hilary Bray asserts that this is definitely 007's family crest with the motto "orbo no sufficit" (the world is not enough).
- When MI6 moves to temporary headquarters in Scotland, we see that M has a portrait of the original M (Bernard Lee) behind her desk.
- When Bond says "Q isn't going to like this," it is the first (and only) time in the series that he has made reference to Q's reaction to the destruction of equipment.
- *The World is Not Enough* is the only movie in which Bond makes love to two doctors.
- Some fans have referred *to Die Another Day* as the first movie in which we see Bond actually having sex (as opposed to just before or just after), however, the infrared sight of Dr. Jones's leg moving underneath Bond's body surely is actual sex.
- The BMW Z8 was a brand new car, and wasn't ready in time for filming, despite much scrambling at the factory. The car used is actually a Dax Cobra with BMW body panels bolted on. So, being sawed in half was the only thing that Beemer could really do!

Most Interesting Goofs

A little formal: Elektra King has known M all her life—but calls her "M" instead of by name.

GPS mystery: Why was a boat that wasn't finished yet, and was meant for fishing (presumably in some out-of-town spot) equipped with a GPS system that tracked an enemy and had maps of the Thames and surrounding area?

That's a wrap: When M is imprisoned, first she has a large scarf, then she does not.

Sticky or not? When Zukovsky falls into the caviar vat, he is thrashing around in something thick, black, and muddy—a reasonable replication of caviar. When the camera cuts away and cuts back, he is in a thin, oily liquid that is more a dark gray, and looks nothing like caviar.

Feeling or not: Renard does many things that a man without sensation could not do, such as walk with a normal amount of grace, touch someone delicately, and so on.

I HAVEN'T SEEN YOU IN SIX MONTHS!

Continuity in the Bond Movies

There isn't much.

Sorry, I guess that doesn't constitute a satisfying chapter, does it? First, let me say that by continuity, I mean specifically from movie to movie. I don't mean continuity between movies and books, and I don't mean referring to past adventures that weren't shown in the movies. For instance, in *Goldfinger* Bond jokes with Felix about how close the enemy got to him in Jamaica. That sounds like continuity, but it isn't—Bond and Felix were together in Jamaica in *Dr. No*, but Felix was never injured, in fact, was never close to the enemy at all. This is nothing more than a neat bit of scriptwriting to make it appear that Bond and Felix have had more adventures together than we know about.

From Eon's point of view, continuity would be a headache, and ultimately, an impossibility. Their focus has always been on a timeless hero. To really pay attention to the history of the series, they would first have to acknowledge that 007 is at least seventy years old (prior to the reboot); he had his first film adventure in 1962, and M made reference to a previous mission—he was surely at least thirty at the time! Instead, they made the decision—wisely, I think—for Bond to be a mythic hero who exists in the eternal Now. When Caroline Bliss was hired, it became clear that Moneypenny, too, lives in the eternal present, infinitely flirting with Bond, infinitely his match, aging only with him.

Continuity of Character

Unlike James Bond and Miss Moneypenny, both M and Q seem to exist in time. We know this because in the Brosnan films, both characters have referred to predecessors. When the new M and James Bond meet in *GoldenEye*, Bond accurately notes that her predecessor liked brandy. When Bond meets "R" in *The World is Not Enough*, he is made aware of Q's advancing age, and hopes that Q won't be retiring soon. When Major Boothroyd, the character played by Desmond Llewelyn, departed the series (while Mr. Llewelyn passed away, it is not made explicit if Major Boothroyd retired or died), the character snidely called R in *The World is Not Enough* became Q, and referred to his predecessor with respect. (Other continuing characters at MI6 are discussed in the section HER MAJESTY'S SECRET SERVICE.)

Sylvia Trench, from whom this chapter derives its title, was intended as a long-term continuing character but made only two appearances. It is very clear that the Sylvia in *From Russia with Love* is the same character as in *Dr. No* (we have to make sure of this sort of thing, given Eon's propensity to reuse actors in different roles). In both movies, she mentions her passion for golf. When Bond is about to rush off and she complains, "I haven't seen you in six months!" We can assume that is the period of time that is meant to have passed since *Dr. No*.

Felix Leiter of the CIA was another continuing character; recognized by Bond each time, although not, apparently, missed in the years since his terrible injuries in *Licence to Kill*.

Jack Wade of the CIA only appeared twice, in *GoldenEye* and *Tomorrow Never Dies*, but was clearly known to Bond in his second appearance. It is amusing that in *Tomorrow Never Dies*, Bond says "Yo, Wade." This is a style of speech entirely unlike Bond, but suited to Wade, and so it reinforces the idea that Bond knows this man's style.

Sir Frederick (Freddy) Gray was the Minister of Defence in six Bond films, starting with *The Spy Who Loved Me* and last appearing in *The Living Daylights*. M acknowledged that he and Bond knew each other, but little character was established for Sir Frederick, and Bond's level of formality with him was inconsistent.

General Alexis Gogol appeared in the same six Bond films as Freddy Gray, five times as head of the KGB, and finally, as a senior official of the Foreign Service.

The one recurring villain of the series (prior to the Craig movies) has been Blofeld, adequately discussed in the VILLAINS chapter. There has been minimal continuity between his appearances. Not only have the actors differed, so have the accents and the hair (or lack thereof). Blofeld and Bond met in *You Only Live Twice* and then failed to recognize each other in the next film, *On Her Majesty's Secret Service*. Blofeld was a scientist in *On Her Majesty's Secret Service*, and then said "Science was never my strong suit," in the next film, *Diamonds Are Forever*. John Glen has said that he placed Blofeld in a wheelchair in *For Your Eyes Only* because of his neck injury in *On Her Majesty's Secret Service*—apparently forgetting that in *Diamonds Are Forever*, Blofeld was perfectly able-bodied.

Other characters who have returned, with some acknowledgment of continuity, are Sheriff J.W. Pepper (*Live and Let Die* and *The Man with the Golden Gun*), Jaws (*The Spy Who Loved Me* and *Moonraker*), and Valentin Zukovsky (*GoldenEye* and *The World is Not Enough*).

Continuity of Time

Usually in a Bond film, we aren't told what year it is, although fashions and technology pretty much tip us off. Once in a while, though, we're clued into current events or politicians.

- *The Man with the Golden Gun* references "the energy crisis."
- In *For Your Eyes Only*, Freddy Gray indicates that the Prime Minister is female, when he says "she'll have our guts for garters." Later, we see a couple imitating Margaret Thatcher and her husband.
- In *Octopussy*, the Soviet Premier is clearly meant to be Leonid Brezhnev.
- In *GoldenEye*, we learn that Russia is now a "new world, a land of opportunity," referencing the breakup of the Soviet Union.

Some references were never meant to be timely, as when we see Checkpoint Charlie in *Octopussy*—no one could have guessed that soon, it would no longer exist.

Fans have mixed feelings about current events references, as they violate the idea that Bond lives in the eternal present, and they can quickly make a movie seem dated.

In only one instance was a year specifically referenced—on Tracy's gravestone in *For Your Eyes Only* (see below). This is a clear example of why years shouldn't be referenced—as time passes, it becomes more and more ridiculous to think that Bond was married in 1969. Pierce Brosnan was a mere lad of sixteen in that year.

Continuity Between Movies

These are specific references within a movie to a previous movie. I believe this is a comprehensive list. Don't look for the *Die Another Day* references here—they get their own chapter. Most of the *Die Another Day* references aren't really continuity at all, they're homages. However, there are several notable instances of continuity, as you'll see. For now, though, let's stick with the previous twenty movies. Eighteen actually—*Dr. No* obviously couldn't reference its nonexistent predecessors, and *Never Say Never Again* exists outside the universe of Eon continuity.

From Russia with Love

- The return of Sylvia Trench, her golf fanaticism, and "I haven't seen you in six months!"
- Kronsteen discusses "our operative, Dr. No" with Blofeld.

Goldfinger

- Bond asks Mei-Lei for his attache case, which she says was damaged on examination. This is a reference to the attache case from *From Russia with Love*, which emits teargas when opened improperly.
- Bond asks Q "Where's my Bentley?" Bond's Bentley, well-known to fans of the Fleming novels, appeared parked near Bond and Sylvia in *From Russia with Love*.

On Her Majesty's Secret Service

- George Lazenby as Bond says "This never happened to the other fellow," breaking the fourth wall and referencing Connery's entire tenure as James Bond.
- After Bond resigns he packs his desk; we see Honey Ryder's knife and belt from *Dr. No*, Red Grant's garrotte/watch from *From Russia with Love*, and the rebreather from *Thunderball*, each with appropriate theme music playing.
- M and Marc Ange Draco have a conversation at Bond's wedding that seems to be a reference to their mutual involvement in Operation Grand Slam from *Goldfinger*.

The Spy Who Loved Me

- Anya Amasova begins to discuss Bond's marriage and Tracy's death; he cuts her off. Obviously the reference is to *On Her Majesty's Secret Service*.

For Your Eyes Only

- Bond visits Tracy's grave, which gives both the year of 1969 (the year that *On Her Majesty's Secret Service* was released) and the saying "We Have All the Time in the World;" Bond and Tracy's love theme from that movie.

The Living Daylights

- M mentions that Pushkin has replaced Gogol, referencing General Gogol's five previous appearances as head of the KGB.

Licence to Kill

- Felix Leiter tells Della that Bond was married once, "a long time ago," as Bond walks sadly away.

Tomorrow Never Dies.

- Paris Carver asks Bond if he still sleeps with a gun under pillow, a habit we first saw in *Thunderball*.

The World is Not Enough

- The title of this film, and Bond's calling the phrase a "family motto" are both derived *from On Her Majesty's Secret Service*.
- Elektra asks Bond if he's ever lost someone; Bond avoids answering. Some fans interpret this as another reference to Tracy, but if anything, it is a nod to knowledgeable fans, not a direct reference.

It's interesting, isn't it, that Tracy and *On Her Majesty's Secret Service* are the most referenced things in Bond movies, even though George Lazenby is all but forgotten?

The Daniel Craig Reboot Continuity

In 2006, *Casino Royale* was the first "reboot" of the James Bond series and its characters. In it, Bond earns his "00" (license to kill) status. He meets Felix Leiter for the first time, and Leiter doesn't have the injuries incurred during *Licence to Kill*. In the course of the movie, Bond acquires the Aston Martin DB5 he had in *Goldfinger*, and does not yet insist on a vodka martini, shaken, not stirred.

There is plenty of fan argument about the character of M. *Casino Royale's* director, Martin Campbell, acknowledged that it made no sense to cast Judi Dench as M when everything else was a total reboot—he just loved her in the part and wanted her in his movie. Is Dame Judi playing the same person in the Brosnan and Craig movies, or is the same actor playing two different people with the same job title? It does seem that the woman who was a "bean counter" who considers Bond a "relic of the Cold War" in *GoldenEye* and the one who 'misses the Cold War' in *Casino Royale* might not have a past in common. Still, it's an argument that can never be resolved.

All Daniel Craig movies are built on a tight sense of continuity—even when it makes no real sense. The effort to tie all the films together comes with plenty of plot holes, as shall be discussed in each movie's individual chapter. Despite its flaws, we can see that characters, time, and movies are all written to interconnect tightly:

- *Quantum of Solace* is fundamentally a sequel to *Casino Royale*, in which Bond grieves and seeks revenge for the death of Vesper Lynd, and the final scene, in which Yusef has given an Algerian love knot to his next victim, is a direct call-back to events of the prior movie.

- René Mathis (Giancarlo Giannini) appears in *Casino Royale* and *Quantum of Solace,* and in the latter movie, explicitly discusses characters and plot occurrences from the former movie.
- Jesper Christensen as Mr. White is only the second recurring villain in the series (unless you count Jaws). He appeared in *Casino Royale, Quantum of Solace*, and *Spectre*.
- Madeline Swann (Léa Seydoux) is directly tied to another character—she is Mr. White's daughter—and appears in both *Spectre* and *No Time to Die*.
- Christoph Waltz returns as Blofeld *in No Time to Die*, having been introduced in *Spectre*. He is the first actor to play Blofeld more than once (where Blofeld is seen).
- In *Spectre*, Blofeld explicitly ties the plots and villains of all three preceding movies together, much to the chagrin of Bond fans.
- Jeffrey Wright is the first actor to play Felix Leiter in consecutive movies (*Casino Royale* and *Quantum of Solace*) and returns in *No Time to Die*.
- MI6 characters all have continuity in these movies, building on facts introduced about them in previous films, including M, Mallory, Eve Moneypenny, and Tanner.

No Time to Die has not yet been released at the time of this writing, so this section could potentially be incomplete.

I'M A LITTLE CONFUSED

Le Chiffre: *"Welcome Mr. Beech. Or is that Bond? I'm, I'm a little confused."*
Bond: *Well, we wouldn't want that, would we?*

It is a trope of the spy genre that spies use false names. In the novels, Ian Fleming treats James Bond as a name so generic that no code name is needed (Tiffany Case, in the novel **Diamonds Are Forever** , ridicules the name: ""Why not choose Joe Doe?"). Although the name is bland, it is known to criminals and spies (as noted in Voyeurism in You Only Live Twice).

We understand that code names are routine in MI6, as both René Mathis in *Quantum of Solace* and Raoul Silva in *Skyfall* identify these names as code names. One might conclude that James Bond is one as well, but in *Skyfall* we see Bond visit his childhood home. He is recognized as James by Kincade, and the gravestone of his parents confirms his last name.

Following are all the false names that James Bond has used in the movies. In the course of twenty-five films, James Bond has used two types of names that are not "James Bond," first, false names used to create a persona—an actual fake identity. Second, Bond has impersonated other real people. I'll present these lists separately.

Fake Identities

From Russia with Love

> **David Somerset:** Bond's tickets on the Orient Express are under the names David and Caroline Somerset, Caroline being the false identity of Tatiana Romanova. The Somersets are from Derbyshire and have no children.

You Only Live Twice

> **Mr. Fisher:** In order to meet with Mr. Osato of Osato Chemical & Engineering Co., Bond posed as Mr. Fisher of Empire Chemicals.

Diamonds Are Forever

> **Mr. Jones:** Bond and Tiffany Case in the bridal suite at The Whyte House in Las Vegas under the names Mr. and Mrs. Jones.

The Spy Who Loved Me

> **Robert Sterling:** Bond posed as a marine biologist, accompanied by his wife, Mrs. Sterling (Anya Amasova) in order to meet with Karl Stromberg.

Octopussy

> **Charles Morton:** In order to allow him to visit East Berlin, Bond is given the identity of Charles Morton, a manufacturer's representative from Leeds who is visiting furniture factories in East Germany.

A View To a Kill

> **James St. John Smythe:** Bond uses this identity to gain access to Max Zorin's horse auction and estate. St. John Smyth is a wealthy Englishman who has inherited horse stables from his aunt.

> **James Stock:** To investigate Zorin in San Francisco, Bond poses as James Stock, a journalist from the London Financial Times.

The Living Daylights

> **Jerzy Bondov:** Bond is unconscious and transported by his kidnapper, General Koskov, who is disguised as his doctor. Bondov is the ID of the "patient" provided as he boards his flight.

Casino Royale

> **Arlington Beech:** MI6 provides Bond and Vesper Lynd with the identities of Arlington Beech and Stephanie Broadchest. Bond declines to use this fake ID, which is how the exchange quoted at the beginning of this section comes about.

Quantum of Solace

> **R. Sterling:** Bond's business card from Universal Exports says he is R. Sterling, possibly the same R. Sterling as in *The Spy Who Loved Me*.

Stolen/Borrowed Identities

On Her Majesty's Secret Service

> **Sir Hilary Bray:** Bond borrows the identity of the Sable Basilik of the London College of Arms in order to infiltrate Piz Gloria. Bray is there to investigate Blofeld's claim to the title Comte de Bleauchamp.

Diamonds Are Forever

> **Peter Franks:** Bond is provided with the identity of a diamond smuggler in order to infiltrate a diamond smuggling operation. On his way to meet his connection (Tiffany Case) the real Franks shows up, and a brutal fight ensues. Bond kills Franks and switches identities.

> **Klaus Hergersheimer:** Bond takes the real Hergersheimer's identity in order to spy on the operations of Whyte Industries.

> **Bert Saxby:** Bond uses a voice imitation device provided by Q in order to speak as Bert Saxby, Willard Whyte's employee.

The Man with the Golden Gun

> **Francisco Scaramanga:** Bond pretends to be Scaramanga, through the use of a fake third nipple, in order to meet with the businessman Hai Fat.

Octopussy

Colonel Luis Toro: Bond imitates a colonel in an unnamed South American country in order to sabotage an aircraft. As with Peter Franks, things go wrong when the real Toro appears.

The World is Not Enough

Dr Mikhail Arkov: Bond poses as a scientist from the Russian Atomic Energy Commission in order to find out Renard's scheme, leading him to a decommissioned nuclear power plant.

Die Another Day

Mr. Van Bierk: Bond knocks out the real Van Bierk, a diamond smuggler, to infiltrates Colonel Moon's Korean headquarters.

Quantum of Solace

Unnamed guest: Bond knocks out an unnamed guest and uses his identity to get the Quantum gift bag at the Tosca performance.

DIE ANOTHER DAY (2002)

Survey Says!

>Percent Favorite: 0%
>Top 5 Cumulative: 23/25
>Numeric Rating: 5.8/10
>Ranking: 20.7 (25th/25)

My Rating and Ranking

>Rated: 7/10
>Ranked: 14 out of 25

Summary

When Bond is betrayed on a mission to assassinate Colonel Moon of North Korea, he is captured. Released fourteen months later in a prisoner exchange for Moon's associate Zao, Bond, assumed to be a traitor, is deactivated and confined by MI6. He escapes MI6 and goes after Zao on his own, knowing the real traitor is still out there, and still associated with Zao. His quest leads him first to a genetics clinic in Cuba, where he meets JinxJohnson. Zao escapes, but not before Bond is able to connect him to diamond miner and philanthropist Gustav Graves. Reactivated, he is sent to a Graves event in Iceland, during which Graves announces his Icarus satellite, and Bond again encounters Jinx. Also on the mission is Miranda Frost, an MI6 operative posing as Graves's assistant. Bond discovers that Graves is really Colonel Moon, genetically altered at the clinic, and Icarus is really a super-weapon. Before he can kill Graves/Moon, Miranda reveals herself to be the traitor. Bond escapes with Jinx, who is with the National Security Agency. Together, they follow Graves and Frost to North Korea and stow away on his Antonov jet. Graves kills his father, the moderate General Moon, Bond kills Graves, Jinx kills Frost, and Bond, Jinx, and a whole lot of diamonds escape to a remote location.

>**James Bond:** Pierce Brosnan
>**Giacinta (Jinx) Johnson:** Halle Berry
>**Gustav Graves:** Toby Stephens
>**Miranda Frost:** Rosamund Pike
>**Zao:** Rick Yune
>**Colonel Tan-Sun Moon:** Will Yun Lee
>**Vladimir Popov:** Michael Gorevoy
>**Damien Falco:** Michael Madsen
>**Raoul:** Emilio Echevarria
>**General Moon:** Kenneth Tsang
>**Verity:** Madonna
>**Charles Robinson:** Colin Salmon
>**M:** Judi Dench

Moneypenny: Samantha Bond
Q: John Cleese
Directed by Lee Tamahori

Discussion

Whenever I watch *Die Another Day*, I think I'm watching a much better movie than it turns out I am. A funny contradiction, I know—how do I explain it? In a nutshell, I enjoy the daylights (the living daylights) out of *Die Another Day*, but a day or two later, I start thinking about some of the flaws. Problems that were swept away by the adrenalin-fueled joyride come to light in retrospect. For all its flaws, I rate the film considerably higher than most fans, because I'm one of those people who believes films are experiential affairs. Some people see a movie, analyze its qualities and what it all meant, and then decide whether or not to like it. Not me. I think a movie is meant to entertain, and if I was hugely entertained (which I always am when watching *Die Another Day*) then that makes up for a lot. Repeated rewatch has certainly lowered my opinion of the film in some ways, but it's a movie I always enjoy.

That said, *Die Another Day* has some serious flaws, flaws of a type that has made many fans angry, and these flaws deserve examination. The many fans who hate it have some strength to their arguments. So, let's look at both the good and the bad in *Die Another Day*.

The movie opens strong. The surfing sequence, filmed at the famous Jaws beach in Maui, was much ballyhooed in the press while it was being filmed (not unlike the Thames River boat chase in *The World is Not Enough*). Among fans, there was some backlash about this. Bond surfing? What next, Bond gets a tribal tattoo? In reality, it worked very well and was beautiful to watch, especially the way the surfers emerged, one by one, until the spectacle of three together was revealed.

What is so great about Bond? He thinks of the next thing and he does it; "mixes things up" as M so aptly says. He thinks, then acts, and never gives up. In forty years, most of the best Bond moments come out of this simple formula, and *Die Another Day* is full of those moments. In the pre-titles sequence, Bond, caught, sets off the bomb in the diamond case. He doesn't know what it will do, he just knows it will create an opportunity so he can do something. Once the opportunity comes, he does something. Then the next thing. Think, then act, and never give up.

Die Another Day is a movie in three acts; the first hour is hard-edged espionage that reminds me, in its focus and grit, of *Dr. No*. This hour takes us from North Korea, to Cuba, and finally back to London where Bond is brought back into the fold. His restoration is this section's denouement. Next we have a half-hour of fantasy action reminiscent of *You Only Live Twice*. This section starts when we arrive in Iceland, includes the unveiling of Icarus, the laser-beam fight, and the revelation of Miranda's betrayal, and ends with Bond's escape out the top of the diamond mine dome. The final forty minutes, the last act, is thoroughly modern, sharing more with *The Matrix* than with any Bond movie.

Most fans love *Die Another Day*'s first act, and most hate Act Three, while the jury is mixed on the middle section.

We can begin by praising the best overall acting in a Bond film since *From Russia with Love*. This, as I've said previously (see THIS NEVER HAPPENED TO THE OTHER

FELLOW), is Pierce Brosnan's acting masterpiece. Brosnan's centered, supreme confidence is richly illustrated when he strolls into the Hong Kong Yacht Club. It had such panache, such self-possession. What do you do if you don't have the clothes and the haircut? Act like you do. The audience loved it, and it said everything that needs to be said about both the character of Bond and Pierce Brosnan as an actor. Here we see he doesn't need the Brioni suits and the Walther to be Bond, he needs nothing more than himself.

Brosnan's cool gave the science fiction room to breath. As I said in KILLER OR CLOWN?, the movies can be outrageous, even silly, as long as Bond himself takes it seriously. If Brosnan had played the role like Roger Moore, it would have been *Moonraker*; too over the top, too goofy. Instead, his serious demeanor allowed the audience to accept the silliness. When he gets the invisible car, he behaves exactly as a serious person would upon "seeing" an invisible car. We maintain sympathy with our hero and suspend disbelief. Some fans have been outraged by that car, but Bond films have always been about staying one step ahead of current technology. Watching *On Her Majesty's Secret Service* today, we forget that in 1969 a portable copier was unheard of. Stealth technology is emerging now, and will probably never look anything like it does in *Die Another Day*, but its extension is well within the Bond tradition.

Brosnan smiled far less than usual. In his previous films, I have enjoyed that he was a Bond who could throw back his head and laugh. But here we see a man who had just gotten out of prison, who had been tortured extensively, and even in his love scenes his face is somber. His resuscitation of Jinx may be the strongest single moment of his entire career (not just in Bond movies). Brosnan's chemistry with Berry was hot, and this has been a weakness of his in the past. They were exciting together, both in the outrageous flirtation at the Cuban beach resort, and in their two love scenes. (The flirtation was marred by cheesy dialogue, but the interaction works for me anyway.)

Notice, too, that there wasn't a quip after every single death—not after Mr. Kil (whose bizarre end seemed to beg for one), or after Zao, or after Graves (although Graves got a quip just before he died). So, although there were plenty of laughs, the person of James Bond was never a tongue-in-cheek person. In fact, the dialogue was often minimalist. There were long scenes— the pre-titles sequence, the swordfight—where very few words were spoken. I like this for its own sake, although I'd add it was fortunate, given the weakness of so much of the dialogue. Most of the repartee was stilted and clichéd, and many of the one-liners were abysmal. ("Now there's a name to die for"? Puh-leez! Purvis and Wade need someone else scripting the quips.) (Apparently exactly what Phoebe Waller-Bridge was brought in for on *No Time to Die*.)

For all the intensity of Brosnan's performance, Eon answers the complaint of some fans that Bond had gotten too psychological. They've griped that our old school tough guy shouldn't be subject to the psychobabble of *GoldenEye* or *The World is Not Enough*. When Bond says *"This* is my defense mechanism." it functions as the answer to that gripe.

All the acting was top-notch, without a weak link to be seen (although some fans hate Halle Berry, as covered in the BOND GIRLS section). John Cleese, who wobbled in his Bond debut, was note-perfect in his sophomore appearance. Judi Dench, who waxed a bit too poetic in *The World is Not Enough*, is here back to her usual excellence. Toby Stephens had every sneer in place.

The visual production values were outstanding (excepting the computer effects) and this was a relief after *The World is Not Enough*'s ugliness. Iceland is dazzling. Cuba is amazing. London is vivid. Only Korea is too gloomy. The set design is also excellent; almost as good as Ken Adam's, if not quite hitting the *You Only Live Twice* mark. The exteriors were among the finest in the franchise. Tamahori really understands a sense of place. Cuba felt like Cuba (even though it wasn't), islands, jungles, ice lakes—each had its own sensibility. He even took a nod from Steven Soderbergh (*Traffic*) and gave different places slightly different tints.

Many fans have complained about bad back projection. This appears to be an effect of the DVD/Blu-ray release, and the changing digital technology. Back projection in the pre-titles sequence is bad on TV, but was seamless in the theater. Both Jinx's ridiculous dive in Los Organos and the wind-surfing scene are *terrible* computer effects, but filming was otherwise beautiful prior to digital remastering.

In many ways, *Die Another Day* showed an excellent mix of looking back towards its legacy, on the fortieth anniversary of the Bond films (see YOUR TWENTIETH, I BELIEVE), and looking forward, showing a willingness to take chances with the Bond formula. The most startling example of this is Bond's capture, and imprisonment for fourteen months. The capture itself is not unheard of; Bond was held prisoner for a significant portion of *Goldfinger* (and is imprisoned at least briefly in every movie but *Quantum of Solace*), but the length of time and level of deprivation was alarming. Most fans appreciated how daring this was, but there was a certain amount of backlash, some fans find the movie too dark, and others are simply convinced that Bond could not be held for that length of time without finding a way to escape.

Die Another Day also gives us the first instance of plot exposition during the title sequence, a startling and effective series of images that allow us a taste of what those hellish fourteen months were like. We also hear what, to many listeners, is a very un-Bond (and hated) title song by Madonna, but one that works well with the staccato imagery of the titles. The combination—an unusual title song over a one-of-a-kind (so far) title sequence, utterly violated the Bond formula and yet felt right, to me and to the majority of the audience at the time.

Other innovations include a bullet coming through the gunbarrel, thanks to some neat computer animation, and the very rare re-use of a gadget. Maurice Binder would have been happy to have a bullet zooming at the audience in1962 had the technology existed. As for the gadget, Bond shatters glass with his ring first to escape Graves and Frost, and then to rescue Jinx. Silly convention anyway, to have each gadget be single-use only.

Many of the modern Bond films, including the previous two, have lacked strong secondary characters. *Die Another Day* has nerdy Vlad and drooling Mr. Kil, not exactly Oddjob level (to say the least), but at least not bland and interchangeable. We also get an excellent ally in Raoul. Awakening a sleeper agent is old school espionage and was a joy to watch. Emilio Echevarria played the role well; first surprised at being reactivated after thirty years, then worried about what would be asked of him, and finally expansive in his help. Echevarria is well known in Mexico. He was pivotal in *Amores Perros* and had a supporting role in *Y tu Mama Tambien*—

the two most important movies out of Mexico in the years immediately preceding *Die Another Day*.

Having now praised this movie effusively, you're wondering when I'm going to start complaining, and I won't disappoint you. The movie has a long sequence that is egregiously bad, and potentially ruinous to the Bond franchise.

I am speaking primarily, of course, of the CGI, as discussed at length in THE MEGA-STUNTS. Here it seems to me like Eon had made a conscious choice to lower their standards, using the same phony action as imitators like *xXx*, instead of sticking to the real thing, as befits the leader of the pack. It's not just the poor and obvious computer effects, though, that bring down a heretofore excellent film. The action becomes over the top, overblown, and overwhelming. We shift into a gear so high that our senses are saturated. Seeing it in the theater is numbing at this point (it is more tolerable on home video or DVD). The laser-battle against Mr. Kil is exciting, and the betrayal scene with Frost and Graves is very good, but from the shattering of the glass floor, which I like, it is all too much. A ridiculous race car chase (Bond outruns a beam of light? Man, he *is* fast!) is followed by the ridiculous para-surfing sequence, another race, back to the ice palace, another chase, this one against Zao, with not one but two gadget-laden cars in a barrage of exploding missiles and zippity-doo-dah features, along with the rescue of Jinx. What might have been the calm of a briefing scene is made high voltage by Michael Madsen's intense and snarling presence, and only then do we reach the climax, involving a burning, crashing jet, the murder of a father by his son, and two hand-to-hand battles to the death. It is hard to catch my breath just writing about it!

If only Lee Tamahori had trusted his material enough to let it breathe, this could have been one of the greatest of Bond movies. True excitement needs that pause between action moments, or the audience stops caring. Fans gripe about the Antonov jet scene, but there's nothing wrong with its high-test action except that it comes on the top of too much action of too low a quality. Make the one section less intense, and replace digital stunts with real ones, and you have a five-star Bond film.

Suppose, for example, that Bond had entered Graves's dome after his interlude with Miranda in a different (dry) way; maybe with Miranda's help (she still playing the ally). Then, when Graves catches Bond, Bond falls into the steam pool and appears to drown. Then he uses the rebreather and the laser to cut out of the ice from below. This eliminates the race car chase, the ridiculous cliff fall, and the embarrassing para-surfing. Bond's rescue of Jinx stands alone on its very dramatic feet, and by the time they go back for Graves and the jet scene comes around, we're ready for more whiz-bang action, having had a breather and some dialogue to refresh us.

This super-amped pace isn't there for the quality of the movie, in my opinion, but to appeal to a younger generation, weaned on *The Matrix* and other action movies where the non-stop "action" is largely generated by special effects. Another example of this attempt at trendiness is the use of odd instances of slow-motion and the technique called "speed ramping," which is that slow-ZOOM-slow thing. In a few short years, this trickery will seem as dated as the polka dots in Bond's flat in *Live and Let Die*. A particularly laughable moment is when the camera gives us a slo-mo effect as Zao's long coat flaps behind him. If anything can be said to taste-lessly imitate the Wachowskis, it's this.

There is also a reliance in some action scenes on medium shots and a rap-idly moving camera, making it hard to see who is doing what to whom. The camera doesn't back away for us to get the full field of vision, making, e.g. the pre-titles hov-ercraft chase hard to follow—who is shooting what at whom, and where is it landing?

One steady complaint has been about product placement—the movie set a new record with $120 million worth of deals; well before release it was mocked as "Buy Another Day." The newspapers and Internet would have one believe there was no movie at all, just one long advertisement. In fact, most of the placements were neither obvious nor intrusive. The only one that really stuck in your face was British Airways. Other than that, there was no vodka bottle, and it made sense to have a scene with Bond shaving, although the electric razor is decidedly out of place. There was nothing as obvious as *GoldenEye*'s Perrier truck. Car placements are a bit of an exception—long before product placement was a big thing, car deals had to be made for movies that wrecked a lot of them. The cars were all appropriately Bondian, and the Jaguar, the only logo shot in the film, fit the mood.

How Times Have Changed: Many people reading the new edition must be thinking I'm off my rocker. When this book was first published in 2006, *Die Another Day* had a strong middle-of-the-pack fan ranking (12th out of 21 movies, and an av-erage star-rating (scale of 1–10) of 6.8. (Remember that star ratings in the first edi-tions were largely from fans and viewers, while in this edition they are from movie-ranking sites.) These are respectable if not stellar positions, and they were not from fans giving the movie a mid-level rating. Rather, fans were divided, as described above. Many adored the film and placed it among their favorites. I don't know what's become of those fans! Today, surveys place this movie dead last. I've heard many fans say it's the one and only Bond movie they don't enjoy re-watching (some reserve that "honor" for *Quantum of Solace*). Admittedly, most fans always hated the CGI, the invisible car, and Madonna's song, but the swordfight, Bond's return from imprisonment, and most of the first hour of the movie were lavishly praised. I stand by my original review, although my dislike of the dialogue has increased, and Berry's performance has lost some of its shine.

High Points

- Extraordinary title sequence that marries fire and ice imagery with dramatic torture scenes and staccato music.
- Bond's shocking capture and imprisonment.
- Lush, almost old-fashioned soundtrack with motifs suggestive of previous films.
- Bond's nonchalant stroll into the Hong Kong Yacht Club.
- Immensely satisfying Q scene; funny, poignant, full of those delightful refer-ences and a nod to Desmond Llewelyn, and Q momentarily getting the best of Bond.
- A return to real espionage, with an exchange of code words, a sleeper agent, a security breach, and concern for cover.
- Thrilling hand-to-hand fight scenes with no reliance on gadgetry.

- Bond's resuscitation of Jinx; one of the dramatic and emotional highlights of the series.
- The death of Graves, a worthy end to a vicious foe.
- Gorgeous locations and fantastic sets.
- Moneypenny's virtual reality fantasy; a sexy lead-in to a great crowd- pleasing laugh.
- The invisible car—a low point for many, but a jaw-dropper for me, and it allowed Bond to actually be impressed by something of Q's.
- The fire and ice motif; a rare use of a thematic element that runs from the title sequence, through the characterization and costuming of Jinx and Miranda, to the locations, and even to the villain's plot; "ice" (diamonds) creating fire in Korea.
- The fun homages (see YOUR TWENTIETH, I BELIEVE).

Low Points

- Fake cartoon race car hitting the side of the cliff; probably even worse CGI than...
- CGI para-surfing "stunt" sequence.
- Over-amped, over-loud third act.
- The frequent use of speed ramping and the sometimes silly use of slow motion.
- Jinx's clichéd dialogue.
- Very bad one-liners; some of the unfunniest in the series.
- Madonna's obnoxious cameo.
- Graves's stupid Terminator body suit.
- A beam of light that supposedly locks onto a heat signature cannot catch up with a race car going a bit over three hundred miles per hour. This is so stupid, and we are forced to watch it for so long, that it is a low point rather than merely a goof.

Quotable Quotes

Colonel Moon: "You will not live to see the day all Korea is ruled by the North."
Bond: "Then you and I have something in common."

Bond: "Saved by the bell."

General Moon: "I do not condone what they do here."
Bond: "Tell it to the concierge."

Bond: "I know the rules. And Number One is, no deals."

Chang: "Hong Kong's our turf now, Bond."
Bond: "Yeah, well, don't worry about it. I'm not here to take it back."

Raoul: "I love my country, Mr. Bond."

Bond: "I'd never ask you to betray your people."

Jinx: "So what do predators do when the sun goes down?"
Bond: "They feast...like there's no tomorrow."

Bond: "You know, you're cleverer than you look."
Q: "Hmm. Still better than looking cleverer than you are."

Bond: "You look like a man on the edge of losing control."
Graves: "It's only by being on the edge that we know who we really are, under the skin."

Miranda: "This is crazy—you're a double-0!"
Bond: "It's only a number."

Miranda: "I take it Mr. Bond's been explaining his Big Bang theory."
Jinx: "Oh, yeah, I think I got the thrust of it."

Vlad: "Hey, boss! He beat your time."

Facts and Figures

SEXUAL ENCOUNTERS

<u>Two</u>: Jinx Johnson and Miranda Frost.

BOND'S CAR

2002 Aston Martin Vanquish (silver)

DEATHS

<u>Twenty-two</u>:
- During the pre-titles, the jeweler who inspects the diamonds and six during the hovercraft chase.
- At the clinic, Jinx kills Dr. Alvarez and Zao's two men at the helicopter.
- In Iceland, Mr. Kil, two guys on jetskis who chase Bond, Zao.
- On the Antonov, General Moon, Vlad, four North Korean officials, Miranda Frost, Gustav Graves.

Bond Kills:
- <u>Eleven</u> directly (seven during the pre-titles, two guys on jetskis, Zao, Graves).
- <u>Five</u> indirectly (Vlad and four others who go out the window after Bond's gunshot depressurizes the Antonov).

EXPLOSIONS

Nineteen: In the pre-titles sequence, Bond's helicopter, Colonel Moon's Aston Martin, which sets off the fuel barrels and cascades into his entire facility (so count as two, the initial boom and then the big one), one hovercraft, three land mines.

In Cuba, the one that Jinx sets off and the one Bond sets off with oxygen. In the car vs. car fight, a total of five missile explosions, all small. The nuclear missile sent against Icarus explodes when defeated. Icarus alone doesn't count; it is lots of heat and flame but no boom, however, it sets off huge explosions in the DMZ in two waves (count as two); first when Graves shows his father how the land mines are being cleared, second when it hits M and Falco's location.

Small pair (together, count as one) when the Antonov jet is hit by Icarus, another when the jet finally goes (while Bond and Jinx are in the helicopter).

BOND'S FOOD AND DRINKS

Vodka Martinis

Two: One "shaken" on the flight, one with "plenty of ice" at the ice palace.

Other Drinks

- Bollinger '61 champagne at the hotel in Hong Kong
- Two glasses of rum with Raoul
- A mojito with Jinx (
- Bollinger champagne with Jinx while making love
- Bond is seen with a decanter of scotch whiskey in the virtual reality sequence. Since the scene isn't "real" he doesn't "really" have a drink.

Food

- At the Hong Kong Yacht Club, Mr. Chang recommends lobster with quail's eggs and sliced seaweed. A fruit bowl with grapes, banana, and apples is also in his suite there.
- At their hotel in Cuba, Bond and Jinx have a fruit bowl with pineapple, pear, and star fruit. In bed, Jinx slices a fig and shares it with Bond.
- Bond steals a grape from a fruit bowl in the clinic on Los Organos (see YOUR TWENTIETH, I BELIEVE).

GAMBLING AND SPORTS

- Jinx is swimming, apparently for recreation, although she could be in training for her swim away from Los Organos.
- Fencing at Blades (Miranda vs. Graves, Bond vs. Graves). Bond and Graves wager on their match. They then switch to swords but it is still, supposedly, in sport.
- Graves indulges in race car driving.

Amaze Your Friends!

- Cameos in this movie include Justin Llewelyn (son of Desmond), a witness to the Blades Club swordfight; Deborah Moore (daughter of Roger), the flight attendant who serves Bond a vodka martini, Gregg Wilson (son of Michael), whose name appears as the author of the article about Gustav Graves that Bond reads on his flight, and Oliver Skeete, a well-known show jumper in Britain, who plays the dreadlocked concierge at Blades who remarks that the place needed redecorating.

- Miranda Frost supposedly won the gold at the 2000 Olympics in Sydney, although the event was not specified (there are four events; individual and team epee and foil). The actual gold medal winning countries in women's fencing that year were Hungary, Italy, and Russia. In no case did Britain or the U.S. place in the top three. (Since she fenced at Harvard, we do not know if she was at Sydney representing the U.S. or Britain.)
- This is Michael Wilson's first credited role in a Bond film (see ENCORE! ENCORE!).
- Bond's file number, when it is sent to Zao, is 2747.
- Graves's dome in Iceland, which houses a greenhouse, a phony diamond mine, and Graves's living quarters, was filmed at the Eden Project in Cornwall, U.K.
- In Moneypenny's virtual reality scene, we see her finishing up the paperwork on the *Die Another Day* adventure. She has three windows open; the backmost one is Bond's, it says "Reclassified." Next is Miranda's, which is labeled "Missing." In front is the following press release:

  For immediate release through world press agencies:

  Freak electrical storm ravages North Korean minefield. Observation plane missing, crew unaccounted for. Fiery graves feared.

  The Democratic People's Republic of North Korea reported the loss of an observation plane in the freak electrical storm which swept the 38th Parallel on Sunday night, setting off landmines and exploding munitions, source close to the Demilitarized Zone...

Most Interesting Goofs

Flawed Determination: Graves holds a diamond to his eye, squints, and deems it "completely flawless." Anyone who knows the least bit about diamonds knows that this cannot be determined with the naked eye, and would not pretend to. Only the largest and ugliest flaws can be seen without a jeweler's loupe.

Her Healing Factor: During their swordfight, Miranda slices Jinx across the tummy; the camera gives us a close-up of the cut. When Bond and Jinx are playing with the diamonds in the final scene, which is a few minutes to a few hours later, her belly is unmarred. Perhaps she acquired a "healing factor" from her *X-Men* co-star, Wolverine?

No Internet Access? M complains that Falco withheld information from her, and should have informed her that Miranda Frost and Colonel Moon had been on the Harvard Fencing Team together. The membership of the Harvard Fencing Team is not secret, it is easily accessible on-line, and MI6's security check could easily have uncovered it.

Ouch! Outdoors in Iceland, grabbing a frozen metal wheel with your bare hands would surely rip the flesh off. This is probably a minor and unimportant goof, except that whenever I see it I wince in pain!

How's That Again? At his greenhouse headquarters in Iceland, Graves shouts something at Zao in Korean, and the subtitle reads "Kill him quietly"

YOUR TWENTIETH, I BELIEVE

A delight or a can of worms?

When the producers noticed that *Die Another Day* was the twentieth official James Bond movie and its release fell on the fortieth anniversary of *Dr. No*, they decided to pepper the film with homages, both subtle and overt, to the history (both literary and cinematic) of James Bond. This got out on the fan rumor mill well before the film was released. The production shots of Halle Berry in her bikini (see *Dr. No*, below) confirmed what had already been on the grapevine when the book **Birds of the West Indies** (see GENERAL REFERENCES) was spotted in an earlier still.

The "Q lab" scene of *Die Another Day* is chock-full of such references. It is set in an abandoned metro station and is crammed with props from earlier pictures. These are all overt references, quite on purpose, and is one of the amusing highlights of the movie.

Watching the film and playing 'find the homage' is entertaining. It also became a bit of a feeding frenzy. Rumors began that there was a homage for every previous Bond film, and when some didn't appear, obsessed fans stretched the definition of 'homage' past the breaking point. Ultimately, ridiculously far-fetched "references" began to appear on the Internet (Bond straightens his tie—an "obvious" homage to *The World is Not Enough*). More skeptical fans began replying sardonically, saying that "Bond, James Bond" is an homage, or "Bond kills the villain—that happened in previous films!" And while those are meant sarcastically, the over-enthusiastic offerings of more sincere fans were sometimes equally as nonsensical. Some were just plain wrong, like the fan who offered that the '61 Bollinger ordered by Bond in Hong Kong is a reference to *Dr. No*, even though that movie was released in '62, or the listing on the Internet Movie Database that indicates that "the cars Zao owns are all updated models of former Bond cars" which is not even a little bit true. Bond never drove a Jaguar, for one. It appears to me that Eon never intended a systematic reference to each Bond film; rather, they were just having a good time. The excessive homage-hunting kind of misses the point.

Some fans have gone all the way in the other direction, complaining that *Die Another Day* is nothing but derivative, and that the effort to place homages ruined the film. For myself, I find them great fun, but admit to rolling my eyes at the excesses of some of the reference-spotters.

The compilation below breaks the homages down into categories of likelihood, from Definitely down to I Think Not. For my Probably category, I have great confidence, but am purposely offering a grain of doubt as a counter-balance to the immense fan enthusiasm for thinking everything and anything is an homage. I have gone over every authoritative source and trashy rumor mill, and everything in between, for a list of possible homages. From those, I offer here only the ones that have a glimmer of possibility, or those that seem particularly tenacious in the face of disproof.

General References

DEFINITELY

- Q hands Bond his watch, saying "Your twentieth, I believe," referencing *Die Another Day* as the twentieth (official) James Bond film.
- In Cuba, Bond finds the book **Birds of the West Indies** by James Bond in Raoul's office, and thus decides to make "ornithologist" his cover. Ian Fleming owned the book **Birds of the West Indies** by James Bond, and it is from there that he got his character's name.

Dr. No

DEFINITELY

- When Bond escapes from the medical ship and emerges on the Hong Kong docks an electronic sound is heard. This is the same sound that accompanies the gunbarrel sequence of *Dr. No*, before the James Bond Theme begins.
- Jinx emerges from the sea wearing a bikini with a knife belt, just as Ursula Andress did in *Dr. No*, one of the movie's most overt homages.

I THINK NOT

- Several people have suggested that the car Bond drives in Cuba is the same as the one he drives in *Dr. No*, but this is not true. In the earlier movie, he drives a Sunbeam Alpine, and in *Die Another Day* he is behind the wheel of a Ford Fairlane.

From Russia with Love

DEFINITELY

- The Q lab has the briefcase from *From Russia with Love*.
- The Q lab has Rosa Klebb's knife-wielding shoe, and Bond checks its point.
- Jinx introduces herself by her full name, and then says "My friends call me Jinx." Bond responds "Mine call me James Bond." This is an echo of *From Russia with Love*, in which Tatiana says "My friends call me Tanya" and Bond responds "Mine call me James Bond."

PROBABLY

- Bond and a woman are watched and filmed in Bond's hotel room from behind mirrored glass.
- M says to Bond: "You had your cyanide" and Bond responds "I threw that away years ago." In the novel **From Russia with Love**, Bond is issued cyanide and throws it away in disgust.

Goldfinger

DEFINITELY

- Bond is introduced in the pre-titles sequence by stripping off his wetsuit to reveal a suit underneath (in *Goldfinger* a dinner jacket, in *Die Another Day* a casual outfit).
- In the Q lab scene, Bond and Q have the following exchange:
    Bond: "You must be joking."
    Q: "As I learned from my predecessor, Bond, I never joke about my work."
    The similar exchange in *Goldfinger* is:
    Bond: "Ejector seat? You're joking!"
    Q: "I never joke about my work, 007."

    This dialogue serves as both an homage to *Goldfinger* and a tribute to the late Desmond Llewelyn, who is absent from the Bond movies for the first time since *Live and Let Die*.
- Jinx is bound to a table in a laboratory while a laser moves closer and closer to cutting off a part of her body.

MAYBE

- Henchmen (Vlad, the generals) are blown out of a depressurized plane much as Goldfinger was, while Jinx struggles in the pilot's seat to regain control of the plane, much as Pussy Galore did.
- The wagering motif from *Goldfinger* was carried into *Octopussy* and then into *Die Another Day*. Bond plays a sporting game with a villain who cheats; he wagers something of special and particular value to the villain, and then wins. Because this motif has already been used in *Octopussy*, it is hard to view it as an homage rather than a standard plot device.

I THINK NOT

- The gadget-laden Aston Martin, and the use of the ejector seat, have been noted, but Bond has had gadget cars many times (see A FEW OPTIONAL EXTRAS). Although he hasn't used the ejector seat since *Goldfinger*, it's been there.

Thunderball

DEFINITELY

- Bond sneaks through a patient's room at the clinic, and eats a grape before departing.
- In the Q lab, Bond plays with the jet pack from the *Thunderball* pre-titles sequence.
- After leaving the lab, Bond and Q go to the subway platform where Bond will "see" his new car. On the wall is a vintage Player's Cigarette poster. In the

novel **Thunderball**, Domino Vitali delivers a long, wistful monologue about how, as a girl, she was in love with the character on that poster.

- To break into Graves's headquarters in Iceland, Bond uses the rebreather.

PROBABLY

- Bond sleeps with a gun under his pillow. Is this a reference to *Thunderball*, or a reference to *Tomorrow Never Dies*, which references *Thunderball*?

You Only Live Twice

DEFINITELY

- Miranda Frost tells M that Bond is a "blunt instrument." This quote was a favorite description of Fleming's for Bond; he used it in interviews and it is featured in the novel **You Only Live Twice** in the chapter titled "Blood and Thunder," where Blofeld tells Bond "You are a common thug, a blunt instrument wielded by dolts in high places."

MAYBE

- The music in the final scene, between Jinx and Bond, is very reminiscent of the "You Only Live Twice" theme; especially as the camera approaches the building.
- Using a subway (metro) station as secret base—possible but the resemblance is vague.
- Agent rappelling from high domed ceiling into the villain's base—visually Jinx certainly looks like the *You Only Live Twice* ninjas, but the context is different and the connection is again vague.

I THINK NOT

- The use of Japanese swords in both films has been cited, but I am unimpressed.

On Her Majesty's Secret Service

DEFINITELY

- When they are kissing, Miranda says to Bond, "Remember, I know all about you, 007. Sex for dinner, death for breakfast. Well it's not going to work with me." This refers to the novel **On Her Majesty's Secret Service** , which has consecutive chapters named "Love for Dinner" and "Death for Breakfast."

MAYBE

- The scene where Bond wakes up after sleeping with Jinx in Cuba is reminiscent of the scene where he wakes up after sleeping with Tracy for the first time. In both, he realizes he's alone, wonders where the woman is, and looks out the window; in the first movie seeing a pool, in the second a beach.

- Patients in the Los Organos clinic are being programmed with recorded messages, not unlike the "Angels of Death" in Blofeld's clinic.

I THINK NOT

- We see Bond in his office for the first time since this movie (albeit in virtual reality). Is visiting a location that we know has been there all along really an homage?
- Rumor had it that "OHMSS" is written on a CD on Moneypenny's desk when she is typing up the press release (quoted in the *Die Another Day* trivia). However, I zoomed into that screen large enough to read the press release and the rumor is wrong.

Diamonds Are Forever

DEFINITELY

- Although it is obscured, the magazine article about Gustav Graves that Bond reads on the plane has the subtitle "Diamonds Are Forever."
- In the Blades Club, Graves says to Bond "After all, diamonds are for everyone."

PROBABLY

- The use of diamond smuggling, and a satellite-weapon that uses a concentrated laser beam, is controversial. Some fans see it as an homage, and others see it as an uncreative rip-off of a previous plot.
- 007 and the Bond girl end the movie by discussing the villain's diamonds; she is frustrated that they cannot have them.

I THINK NOT

- Some fans think that the glass floor of Graves's office (which Bond shatters) is reminiscent of Willard Whyte's penthouse.
- One fan pointed out that Bond looks through a jeweler's loupe, which he learned to do in the novel **Diamonds Are Forever** . I think that's really stretching it.
- A villain gets a new face. Hmmm...the fans who suggest this forget that Blofeld supposedly kept his original face (disregarding the change in actors), it was merely henchmen whose faces were changed.

Live and Let Die

Because there aren't any definite, obvious references to *Live and Let Die* in *Die Another Day*, fans have been grasping at straws to find anything that could be construed as *Live and Let Die*-ish; one hates an incomplete list. A situation like this is what makes it apparent to me that there wasn't any Eon wonk with a checklist of references saying "Hey! We haven't done *Live and Let Die* yet!" There are only two possible references, and I think they are both pretty slim, but I place them under Maybe rather than I Think Not out of deference to the fannish urge to have something listed under each movie.

MAYBE

- Icarus blows up the minefields in the DMZ, which looks similar to the explosions that destroy Kananga's poppy fields.
- A magnetized gadget helps resolve a fight (magnetized watch in *Live and Let Die*, magnetized medical device in Cuba *in Die Another Day*).

The Man with the Golden Gun

PROBABLY

- The ring that breaks glass is called a "Sonic Agitator," very similar to the Macguffin from *The Man with the Golden Gun*, a "Solex Agitator."
- Bond is taken to a British ship in the waters off of Hong Kong, where MI6 has a field location.

MAYBE

- The rotating mirrors in the Los Organos clinic are reminiscent of Scaramanga's funhouse.
- The novel **The Man with the Golden Gun** has a scene between M and Bond where there is a sheet of protective glass between them.
- Colonel Moon demonstrates a weapon to Bond by destroying the aircraft that was 007's escape route, just as Scaramanga did after Bond arrived on his island.

I THINK NOT

- Some fans point to the diamond in Jinx's navel as similar to the golden bullet in Saida's navel.
- Several fans focus on a laser weapon that uses solar power. However, I don't see how this can be both a reference to *Diamonds Are Forever* and a reference to *The Man with the Golden Gun*.

The Spy Who Loved Me

DEFINITELY

- Graves arrives at Buckingham Palace via a Union Jack parachute, such as Bond used in *The Spy Who Loved Me*'s pre-titles sequence.

I THINK NOT

- In *The Spy Who Loved Me*, a car falls from above and lands upended in a rural shack. In *Die Another Day*, several cars fall from above and land up-ended in a rural field.
- The design of the ice palace, with its external curving "legs," is somewhat reminiscent of Atlantis.

Moonraker

DEFINITELY

- The movie *Die Another Day* is an adaptation of the novel **Moonraker**; something which was obvious to me when I first saw it, and was later acknowledged in an interview with screenwriters Purvis and Wade (yes, I'm giving myself credit, here). The story of that novel was never used in a Bond film—the movie of the same name used nothing except for the villain's name, a space- launch theme, and an escape from the rocket's exhaust.

   In the novel, Hugo Drax is a foreign industrialist who appears from nowhere (he is an amnesiac found among a group of refugees). He adopts England as his home and offers a space-based invention to help his beloved homeland. In actuality, though, he is an enemy agent (a Nazi) and the invention is a weapon that will destroy London.

   Bond first meets Drax in a cutthroat competition—playing cards—at the Blades Club (M's gentlemen's club). Later, he is assigned to help an MI5 agent named Gala Brand who is working for Drax undercover. Rosamund Pike's character was originally announced as Gala Brand. Purvis and Wade have explained that, as the character changed, they decided to give her a unique name, since she was no longer the character from the book. Presumably this is because Gala Brand was never a traitor, and remained a loyal agent.

PROBABLY

- Bond stays in the Presidential Suite.
- The swordfight has strong visual parallels to the swordfight in *Moonraker*, although how different do swordfights look? Still, the breaking glass, and especially knocking over a suit of armor, are very similar.

MAYBE

- A villain throws Bond's parachute out of plane—the scene is reminiscent of *Moonraker*, but I wonder how else a villain might keep Bond from escaping a crashing plane—it is probably just a confluence of plot points.
- Both movies have characters named Chang; in *Moonraker* an assassin, in *Die Another Day* a Chinese agent. Of course, *Tomorrow Never Dies* also has a character named Chang, so maybe this is just some sort of default Chinese name that Eon likes to use.

I THINK NOT

- A villain's vehicle goes over a large waterfall.

For Your Eyes Only

MAYBE

- The presence of a blonde Olympian/Olympian hopeful. Bibi Dahl whines that she wants a gold medal, Miranda cheated for hers.
- In both movies, Bond hangs from a cliff, and the rope slips, dropping him further down before the rope catches again.

I THINK NOT

- A fan spotted a yellow diving helmet in the Q lab scene, but I have not caught it in my many viewings.

Octopussy

DEFINITELY

- The crocodile boat, used by Bond to sneak onto Octopussy's island, is seen in the Q lab.
- The Acrostar jet used in the pre-titles sequence is seen in the Q lab.
- The coiled rope that Q 'was having trouble getting up' is seen in the Q lab.

MAYBE

- Wagering—see GOLDFINGER.

I THINK NOT

- Jinx's escape by diving off a cliff has been compared to Magda's leaving Bond's hotel via his balcony. (It has also been compared to the bungee jump in *GoldenEye*, proving that it's not a very definitive reference.)
- The plots have been found to be similar, inasmuch as a hardline Communist covertly plots against the West, and against the objections of more moderate colleagues; he plans the use of a destructive weapon on a border with the West in order to pave the way for a large ground invasion. Unfortunately, this is not an unusual or unique plot, so it hardly says "homage" to me. The plot of *The Fourth Protocol* (co-starring Pierce Brosnan) had more similarity to *Octopussy* than did *Die Another Day*.

Never Say Never Again

I THINK NOT

- Many fans have noted the similarity between Bond's first meeting of Fatima Blush and Jinx; both at a beachside bar while Bond is drinking and the woman is returning from participating in water sports, and both replete with flirtation and double entendre. As similar as this is, the idea that Eon would include a purposeful homage to a rival production strikes me as highly unlikely.

A View To a Kill

DEFINITELY

- The surveillance puppy (the "snooper") is seen in the Q lab.

MAYBE

- There's a strong similarity between using a piece of a crashed snowmobile to make a snowboard and using a piece of a crashed race car to make a surfboard.

The Living Daylights

DEFINITELY

- A cello is seen in the Q lab. Many fans refer to this as "Kara's cello," but I doubt very much that Kara would have given her beloved Stradivarius to MI6.
- Bond and the Bond girl escape a crashing plane by getting into a vehicle in the cargo hold and opening the cargo door.

MAYBE

- Peephole effect of the gunbarrel opens onto beach defenses in North Korea that look similar to the peephole shot of Gibraltar in *The Living Daylights*,

I THINK NOT

- The retractable spikes that were first seen in *The Living Daylights*'s Aston Martin reappear, with the same "traction" label in the car. See GOLDFINGER. Fans who think that a repeated car gadget is an homage haven't been paying attention to how much of the contents of the car is the same from film to film (even though the car itself often changes).
- Bond is chased across ice in his Aston Martin and uses gadgets in the chase. This one is a bit better, but falls just short of "Bond gets in a fight" for the vagueness factor.

Licence to Kill

DEFINITELY

- Bond encounters a female agent with a small gun holstered to her thigh.

I THINK NOT

- Many fans believe that the theme of a rogue agent, especially one on a mission of revenge, is an homage to *Licence to Kill*. I think those fans haven't seen enough spy and cop dramas to realize how common this theme really is.

GoldenEye

DEFINITELY

- Bond uses a laser-cutter in his watch to cut a hole (in *GoldenEye* the hole was in the floor of the train, in *Die Another Day* it was in the ice).

MAYBE

- In *Die Another Day*, when Bond is resuscitating Jinx, he says "The cold kept you alive." In *GoldenEye*, Bond and Natalya have the following exchange:

    Natalya: "How can you be so cold?"

    Bond: "It's what keeps me alive."

    Natalya: "No, it's what keeps you alone."

    The problem, of course, is determining if this connection is on purpose. It's hard to catch...so maybe the screenwriters didn't catch it either.

- Zao's appearance and death bear strong echoes of Trevelyan's. Both are villains whose faces were half-disfigured by an explosion set off by Bond. Both battled Bond and were left somewhat helpless, at which point something huge fell on them while they screamed.
- In Dr. Alvarez's office, Jinx sets a bomb's timer for three minutes—a significant timing in *GoldenEye*.

I THINK NOT

- Jinx's dive—see Octopussy.
- Bond believes the main villain was killed in the pre-titles sequence. He spends the movie pursuing someone else, with a different name, until he realizes the truth. This could as easily apply *to Diamonds Are Forever* and is, in my opinion, simply an espionage theme.

Tomorrow Never Dies

DEFINITELY

- The shot of a missile being fired at the Icarus satellite is a re-use of footage from *Tomorrow Never Dies*, where the missile was being fired at the terrorist arms bazaar.

MAYBE

- Bond attends a gala party at the invitation of the villain.

- Jinx wears a leather outfit with an attached rappelling cable. It is likely that this is standard-issue female spywear, but maybe it's a reference to Wai Lin.
- A character named Chang—see MOONRAKER.

I THINK NOT

- Once again, a car gadget is cited by fans who think the Vanquish's remote control constitutes a reference.

The World is Not Enough

PROBABLY

- Bond's virtual reality training program is almost identical to Level Two of the The World is Not Enough video game.

MAYBE

- Jinx has a similar boat, positioned for escape in a similar way, as Cigar Girl.

I THINK NOT

- Each movie has a geodesic dome: The Millennium Dome in *The World is Not Enough* and the Eden Project dome in *Die Another Day*.

Miscellaneous

PROBABLY

- In the conversation with Q after the virtual reality training session, Bond says that M's injury was "just a flesh wound." This appears to be a reference to *Monty Python and the Holy Grail*, in which John Cleese famously (and hilariously) refers to having his arms and legs cut off using the same phrase.
- When John Cleese as Q walks behind the invisible car, his legs are distorted by the mirror projection. This appears to be a visual reference to Cleese's famous Monty Python skit, "The Ministry of Silly Walks."

MAYBE

- It is possible that the character name "Colonel Moon" is a reference to the James Bond novel by Kingsley Amis titled **Colonel Sun** .

I NEVER JOKE ABOUT MY WORK

Q Branch is just about everybody's favorite department of Her Majesty's Secret Service. There, Bond is issued his various gadgets and, often, his car. There Q and Bond exchange banter that is sometimes hostile, sometimes aggrieved, and occasionally playful.

The Gadgets

These are the gadgets issued to Bond by Q Branch. Sometimes we see Q give these to Bond, and sometimes he simply has them. (Cars are covered under A FEW OPTIONAL EXTRAS and their features aren't detailed here.)

Dr. No

- A large Geiger counter

From Russia with Love

- A briefcase containing a throwing knife, a teargas canister that is released if the case isn't opened properly, a collapsible rifle with infrared sight, and fifty gold sovereigns.
- A device to test if a phone is being tapped.
- A tape recorder disguised as a camera.

Goldfinger

- Aston Martin DB5.
- Two homing devices; one that is magnetized to fit in someone else's car, one that is miniaturized to fit in the heel of Bond's shoe.

Thunderball

- Aston Martin DB5.
- Bell Textron jet pack.
- Tape recorder in a hollow book.
- Geiger counter miniaturized into a wristwatch.
- Underwater camera that takes eight pictures in rapid succession using infrared film.
- Mini-rebreather with four minutes' air.
- Flare pistol.
- Homing pill (radioactive pill; swallowed, then traced).
- Extra-large, rocket-powered scuba tank.

You Only Live Twice

- Safe-cracking device.

- Little Nellie, an auto-gyro that fires flare guns, has heat-seeking missiles and machine guns, and drops mines.

On Her Majesty's Secret Service

- Combination safe-cracker/copy machine. (In 1969, copy machines weren't common devices, so this was more impressive then.)

Diamonds Are Forever

- "Mousetrap" in holster to keep gun from being taken.
- Fake fingerprints.
- Combination piton-shooter rappel-rope.
- Voice imitator (same as Blofeld's).

Live and Let Die

- Magnetic watch with buzz-saw blade.
- A device to find bugs (listening devices).
- Code transmitter in toiletry kit, concealed in a brush.

The Man with the Golden Gun

- Goodnight has a Q-issued homer in her dress.
- Goodnight has a second, magnetized homer, similar to the larger homer in *Goldfinger*.

The Spy Who Loved Me

- Lotus Esprit S1.
- Wristwatch with plastic tape readout.
- Ski pole gun.
- Miniature microfilm reader.
- "Wet bike" packed in a suitcase.

Moonraker

- X-ray safe-cracking device.
- Dart-shooting wristwatch with five cyanide-tipped darts and five explosive darts.
- Wristwatch also has explosive with about a meter of fuse.
- "007" mini-camera.

For Your Eyes Only

- Lotus Esprit Turbo.
- "Identograph" face-identifying "3-D visual" (Q says it's 3-D, but it's simple line drawings—very 2-D) graphic database keyed into the databases of "Surety, Interpol, the CIA, the Mossad, and the West German police."
- Wristwatch with digital message display.

Octopussy

- Miniature microphone inside Faberge egg, with homer, keyed to (next item)
- Acid-emitting fountain pen with earpiece for egg microphone.
- "Standard-issue radio-directional finder" in wristwatch.

- Crocodile boat.

Never Say Never Again

- Laser watch.
- Exploding pen.
- Rocket-powered motorcycle.

A View to a Kill

- Super-polarized sunglasses.
- Camera ring.
- Bug detector hidden in electric razor.
- Check-impression maker.
- "Microcomparitor" (comparing the microchips).
- Surveillance robot.
- Conventional lock pick (at Zorin's estate).
- Sharper Image credit card/lock pick (at Stacey Sutton's home).

The Living Daylights

- Aston Martin V8 Vantage.
- Key-ring finder with stun gas and explosive set to whistled signals.
- Keys that "open 90% of the world's locks."
- Binocular glasses.
- Photo-database.

Licence to Kill

- Rappelling equipment in cummerbund.
- "Dentonite toothpaste" plastic explosive with cigarette detonator and re-mote controller.
- X-ray camera with laser-fire.
- Exploding alarm clock.
- Signature gun.
- Camera that conceals bullets.
- Broom that conceals a microphone/transmitter.

GoldenEye

- Zoom monocular with digital readout.
- Laser-cutter in wristwatch.
- 75 foot rappel cord with piton end in belt buckle.
- Magnetic (?) bombs set and reset in watch.
- Click-pen Class 4 grenade with 4 second fuse (3-click toggle).

Tomorrow Never Dies

- BMW 750il.
- Ericsson JB988 phone with fingerprint scanner, 20,000 volt security system, and remote control for car.
- Cigarette lighter bomb.
- Rappelling belt buckle

The World is Not Enough

- BMW Z8.
- Glasses with button-activated explosive.
- X-ray sunglasses.
- Survival tent/globe ski jacket.
- Light-up watch (used to light inside of survival tent).
- Rappelling watch (appears to be the same as the rappelling belt buckle in *Tomorrow Never Dies*).
- Universal lock-pick Visa card, card number 000 1234 5678 9010. (The first digit is never seen, but a leading zero seems likely given the rest of the number).

Die Another Day

- Aston Martin V12 Vanquish.
- Sonic Agitator ring that shatters glass.
- Laser-cutter in wristwatch (see *GoldenEye*).
- Rebreather (see *Thunderball*).

Casino Royale

- Implanted tracking device in Bond's arm.
- Medical kit with a defibrillator, antidotes, and a hot link to MI6.

Quantum of Solace

- "Tagged bills" given to Le Chiffre and used to trace connections to Mitchell.

Skyfall

- Walther PPK/S 9mm short with a micro-dermal sensor in the grip, coded to Bond's palm print
- Distress signal radio

Spectre

- Aston Martin DB10
- Exploding watch
- Smart blood that tracks vital signs and traces movements globally

The Experiments

These are the gadgets and (most often) weapons we see being worked on in the background of Q Branch. Poor old Smithers seems to do the most testing of these. When Q is at a special location (see MI6 AROUND THE WORLD), these are often related to that place.

Goldfinger

- Gas-emitting parking meter.
- Bulletproof vest that can take machine gun fire at close range.

Diamonds Are Forever

- Electro-magnetic RPM controller, used to trick slot machines.

On Her Majesty's Secret Service

- Radioactive lint.

The Man with the Golden Gun

- An area is carefully marked on a brick wall and then neatly blown up—could be working on a targeting system.

The Spy Who Loved Me

- Floating killer tea tray.
- Spring-loaded ejector chair.
- Bullet-firing hookah.
- Mud- (perhaps oil?)-firing canisters.
- Auto-triggered blade stabbing upwards from a table.

Moonraker

- Exploding bolos.
- Laser gun (later used in the climactic battle).
- Machine gun under siesta disguise.

For Your Eyes Only

- False arm-cast that can be triggered as a powerful bludgeon.
- Umbrella that closes with spikes, stabbing neck.

Octopussy

- Climbing rope.
- Door that, when handle is lifted, crushes the person at the door.
- Liquid crystal television with zoom camera.

The Living Daylights

- "Ghetto blaster" hiding a targeting bazooka.
- Person-eating couch.

GoldenEye

- Flame-launching leg-cast.
- Phone booth that fills with huge air bag.
- X-ray document scanner disguised as tea tray.

The World is Not Enough

- Bagpipe with machine gun and flame-thrower.

Spectre

- Some kind of very fancy assault rifle

Q Isn't the Only Gadget Master

Devices provided to people other than Bond, and/or by people other than Q, include...

- Wristwatch with hidden garrotte (Red Grant, SPECTRE, *From Russia with Love*).
- Rocket gun (Tiger Tanaka's "Q lab," *You Only Live Twice*).
- Cigarette that shoots exploding dart (Tiger Tanaka's "Q lab," *You Only Live Twice*).
- Fingerprint scanner/matcher (Tiffany Case, *Diamonds Are Forever*).
- Cigarette lighter in car that is actually a radio microphone (CIA, *Live and Let Die*).
- • "Golden gun" of unique caliber that fires one bullet, constructed from lighter, cufflinks, pen, and cigarette case (Scaramanga, *The Man with the Golden Gun*).
- Music box message center (XXX, KGB, *The Spy Who Loved Me*).
- Cigarette that emits sleeping gas (XXX, KGB, *The Spy Who Loved Me*).
- Motorcycle sidecar that is actually a missile (Stromberg, *The Spy Who Loved Me*).
- Poison needle pen (Holly Goodhead, standard CIA issue, *Moonraker*).
- Dart-shooting daily diary (Holly Goodhead, standard CIA issue, *Moonraker*).
- Flame-throwing perfume (Holly Goodhead, standard CIA issue, *Moonraker*).
- Radio in handbag (Holly Goodhead, standard CIA issue, *Moonraker*).
- Dream-inducing face mask (Gustav Graves, *Die Another Day*).
- Body armor that controls Icarus satellite and has 100,000 volt security (Gustav Graves, *Die Another Day*).
- Dragster adapted for ice driving (Gustav Graves, *Die Another Day*).
- Jaguar with missiles, machine guns, and thermal sensors (Zao, *Die Another Day*).

Wai Lin's "Q lab"

In Tomorrow Never Dies, we stop at Colonel Wai Lin's base in Saigon, where we see devices that would do Q proud. They are...

- Hidden control panel that moves multiple false walls, revealing the entire lab.
- Walls contain multiple video monitors and display cases, including numerous weapons displays.
- Display of gadget-watches.
- Computer message center/database.
- Flame-throwing dragon head.
- Chinese fan that shoots a webbing—multiple darts anchor cords to create a snare.
- Button that shoots some kind of large bludgeon.
- Rickshaw that we presume has some sort of gadgetry.

The Repartee

A sampling of Q's finest quotes.

Oft-repeated

Q: "Now pay attention."

Goldfinger

Bond: "Ejector seat? You're joking!"
Q: "I never joke about my work, 007."

Thunderball

Bond: "Everything you give me..."
Q: "Is treated with equal contempt. Yes, I know."

For Your Eyes Only

Bond (sees the deadly umbrella): "Stinging in the rain?"
Q: "That's not funny, 007!"

Bond: "Forgive me, Father, for I have sinned."
Q: "That's putting it mildly, 007."

Octopussy

Bond: "Someone seems to have stuck a knife in my wallet."
Q: "Ah, they missed. What a pity."

Never Say Never Again

Q ("Algernon"): "Now you're on this I hope we're going to have some gratuitous sex and violence."

Licence to Kill

Q: "Remember, if it hadn't been for Q Branch, you'd have been dead long ago."

GoldenEye

Q: "Need I remind you, 007, that you have a license to kill, not to break traffic laws."

Bond (seeing pen grenade): "They always said the pen was mightier than the sword."
Q: "Thanks to me, they were right."

GoldenEye and *Tomorrow Never Dies*

Q: "Grow up, 007!"

Tomorrow Never Dies

Q: "If you'd just sign here, Mr. Bond."
Bond: (clears throat)
Q: "It's the insurance damage waiver for your beautiful new car. Will you need collision coverage?"
Bond: "Yes."
Q: "Fire?"
Bond: "Probably."
Q: "Property destruction?"
Bond: "Definitely."

Q: "Personal injury?"
Bond: "I hope not, but accidents do happen."
Q: "They frequently do with you!"
Bond: "Well, that takes care of the usual wear and tear. Will I need any other protection?"
Q: "Only from me, 007, if you don't bring that car back in pristine order."

The World is Not Enough

Bond (to Q, upon meeting his new assistant): "If you're Q, does that make him R?"
New Assistant: "Ah, the legendary 007 wit. Or at least half of it."
(Based upon this dialogue, and the fact that John Cleese was listed as "R" in the end credits, some fans insist that R was the assistant's real title/name, despite the fact that Bond is being insulting and that the assistant takes umbrage.)

Q: "I've always tried to teach you two things. First, never let them see you bleed."
Bond: "And the second?"
Q: "Always have an escape plan." (Ironically, this is the last line Desmond Llewelyn ever spoke as Q.)

Die Another Day

Bond: "You know, you're cleverer than you look."
Q: "Hmm. Still better than looking cleverer than you are."

Bond: "You must be joking."
Q: "As I learned from my predecessor, Bond, I never joke about my work."

Skyfall

Q: "007. I'm your new Quartermaster."
James Bond: "You must be joking."
Q: "Why? Because I'm not wearing a lab coat?"
James Bond: "Because you still have spots."

James Bond: "A gun. And a radio. Not exactly Christmas, is it?"
Q: "Were you expecting an exploding pen? We don't really go in for that anymore."

CASINO ROYALE (2006)

Survey Says!

> Percent Favorite: 12%
> Top 5 Cumulative: 3/25
> Numeric Rating: 8.5/10
> Ranking: 7.15 (3rd/25)

My Rating and Ranking

> Rated: 10/10
> Ranked: 2 out of 25

Summary

In this "reboot," James Bond earns his double-0 status. He must defeat Le Chiffre, financier to international terrorists, in a game of high stakes poker. If Bond is successful, Le Chiffre will turn himself over to MI6 rather than be killed by the clients he has cheated, and he has invaluable intelligence. If Bond fails, the money he loses will directly finance terrorism.

Accompanying Bond to Casino Royale in Montenegro is Vesper Lynd, British treasury agent. Bond defeats Le Chiffre but is betrayed and kidnapped. He is tortured by Le Chiffre, but freed by the mysterious Mr. White, who kills Le Chiffre for his betrayal.

Recovering from torture, Bond finds himself falling in love with Vesper, when released from the hospital, he resigns from MI6 and goes away with her. But Vesper is the traitor, and drowns herself after turning over Bond's winnings to White's men. She's left clues for Bond, though, and as the credits roll, Bond has shot White in the leg and introduced himself as "Bond, James Bond."

James Bond: Daniel Craig
Vesper Lynd: Eva Green
Felix Leiter: Jeffrey Wright
Le Chiffre: Mads Mikkelsen
René Mathis: Giancarlo Giannini
Dimitrios: Simon Abkarian
Solange: Caterina Murino
Villiers: Tobias Menzies
Steven Obanno: Isaach De Bankolé
Valenka: Ivana Milicevic
Mollaka: Sébastien Foucan
Mr. White: Jesper Christensen
M: Judi Dench
Directed by Martin Campbell

Discussion

Eon co-producer Michael Wilson had spoken honestly about the need to reconsider Bond's direction. He and his half-sister and co-producer, Barbara Broccoli, were quoted in the New York Times as saying they were "desperately afraid, we would go downhill...We are running out of energy, mental energy. We need to generate something new, for ourselves." It is, perhaps, no coincidence that Wilson and Broccoli entered this period of paralysis after their mother, Dana Broccoli, passed away in February of 2004, leaving Eon's second generation on their own for the first time. I have often wondered if Dana's guiding vision had previously been underestimated. Many fans assumed that when Cubby Broccoli died in 1996, the second generation took over, but there was no floundering at that time, and in fact, the series was at a new peak. Broccoli and Wilson wanted a back-to-basics Bond, and indeed, the use of Fleming's first novel seemed to demand it.

Figure 16: Playing cards came as a premium with the initial DVD release of Casino Royale

Having heard that the new movie would be Bond's first mission after earning his double-0, fans quickly dubbed it "Bond Begins" (after the movie *Batman Begins*). Most fans welcomed the back-to-basics concept. In fact, many of us expected it. The hugest, most over-the-top films have historically been followed by a return to dark-edged espionage. *You Only Live Twice*, with its hollowed-out volcano and its plot to kidnap space shuttles, gave way to *On Her Majesty's Secret Service*, with virtually no gadgets, the briefest of Q scenes, and a tragic ending. Similarly, *Moonraker* was so big, so out there (literally), that *For Your Eyes Only* was the inevitable step back. In fact, since *Die Another Day* has a satellite shot into space, one could almost say that space themes are the *coup de grace* for "bigger is better" in the Bond world, and inevitably lead to a scaled back follow-up.

Entertainment columns suggested that Bond needed to compete with Jason Bourne. Which drove me crazy, frankly, because there'd be no *Bourne Identity* or its sequels in the first place if Bond hadn't made spying cool. But there is a point; that we live in dark times and film audiences want darker heroes. Many fans compared casting Daniel Craig to casting Timothy Dalton—the *other* back-to-basics, "Fleming's Bond" actor. The difference is, the 1980s were not the time for such a brooding hero, but the 21st century is.

The "origin" aspects of *Casino Royale* were done with grace and style. Yes, we see Bond change his clothing, driving, and drinking habits to become the secret agent we know and love, but it had none of the heavy-handedness of, say, *Indiana*

Jones and the Last Crusade, where *here* is why he's called Indiana and *here* is why he's afraid of snakes and *here* is why he uses a whip. That sort of thing is unnecessary; there are no such simple "whys" in life. But we're given something more here; we're given a character arc. A cocky, sure of himself, yet vulnerable Bond becomes, over the course of betrayal and torture and more betrayal, colder, more calculating, and less susceptible to the stirrings of his heart. As he dons a cool veneer, the Bond theme finally plays and the credits roll. And when that happens, ladies and gentlemen, sold out theaters all over the world thundered with applause.

I'm a convert to enthusiasm for Daniel Craig and for this film. When Craig was cast, I didn't like his looks or his style, and I didn't like the idea of a reboot. But now that I've seen the goods (many times) I'm glad I kept an open mind. *Casino Royale* is a masterful movie. Not so much "Bond is back," but a fantasy of Bond coming back that the movies have never truly fulfilled. Not since, oh, say, 1967 has there been so much power behind Bond's punch, and never has the punch been delivered with such brutality as Daniel Craig's.

It's a dark movie, and this has displeased the minority of fans pining for a return to Roger Moore's style. Bond seems to have given up the death quip; "That last hand, nearly killed me" was the only Bondish wordplay, and it was uttered at his own expense. When Bond "nails" one of Gettler's men in Venice, it seems to cry out for a death quip, yet Bond is resolutely silent. I'm not sure that all quips should be forever abandoned, but for this one movie, I have to say I'm pleased.

This is truly James Bond as fans want him, as Fleming saw him; blunt, hard, yet vulnerable. Capable of love, capable of killing, and feeling the effects of both. That director Martin Campbell and the producers have managed to package that Bond in a way that the general movie-going public loves is sheer genius.

Craig has an unlovely face that manages to be appealing, and a naked body that has made audiences forget his face, both when he rises from the sea *a la* Honey Ryder, and when he is stripped bare and tortured in a shockingly real scene.

Casino Royale is close to flawless. Yes I have things to put into the Low Points section, but I'm just nitpicking. I could say that some plot-points were confusing. The first time I saw it, I didn't realize that ELLIPSIS was the keypad code for access to the secure area of the airport. I didn't realize that the pivotal poker game took place over two days, and so the time sequence had me baffled. I didn't realize that it was Bond's earpiece that gave him away to Obanno; just didn't see it the first time, and I think it was the third time that I saw Le Chiffre go back for his inhaler before going upstairs to his hotel room where Obanno is waiting in ambush. (This is a crucial point because it's the inhaler that has the hidden bug.) The truth, though, is that the complex plot makes the movie more fun to watch with each viewing; I've had no sense of fall-off, as you sometimes do when revisiting beloved films.

One big complaint is the egregious product placement. Bond wasn't served by having Sony buy MGM, and apparently the right to have every MGM character use lots and lots of Sony cell phones and laptops. Lots. And lots. Not only do we see a careful close-up of every Sony logo, but the use of cell phones drives too much of the plot. Yes, it's clever to figure out who someone is in a crowd by calling the number and seeing who picks up, but when it's done repeatedly, it becomes the James Bond Cell Phone Movie. The Ford product placement is also hard to love. Yes, two gorgeous Aston Martins. But the Mondeo? Was a car ever less appropriate?

Other flaws include a strange sort of animation in the gunbarrel, which is minor but so iconic that it's worth mentioning. Chris Cornell's title song is the very definition of bland. My kid and I agreed that if you can watch a video with that much cutting, at that hyper-rapid a pace, and it's still dull, well there's no saving it.

Two great actors play allies Felix Leiter and René Mathis. One wonders why the producers would bother hiring an acclaimed actor like Jeffrey Wright to play Leiter and have him do so little. My guess is in order to establish the character and bring him back for the next movie; and isn't *that* great news? Giancarlo Giannini is another class act and gives Mathis the kind of depth that many such allies have had; think Pedro Armendariz in *From Russia with Love* or Topol in *For Your Eyes Only*.

I love the cast of characters. Bond films need to be colorful and diverse, they need to travel, and they need to show us the world. The motley crew around the poker table in Casino Royale's Salon Privé has the right kind of feeling. Mr. Fukutu with his ponytail, Madame Wu, the enormous Infante with his imposing presence (Fleming would have loved him) and maroon jacket, and Le Chiffre, weeping blood. Ian Fleming loved the bizarre (see DEFORMITIES AND DIFFERENCES), and he would have appreciated the care given to creating a Le Chiffre who was scarred and strange. Speaking of traveling the world, let's give both cheers and boos to *Casino Royale*'s location footage. On the plus side, the Bahamas are suffused in sunlight, and Venice is run-down and interesting rather than touristy-pretty. Montenegro looks gorgeous, but unfortunately it's not Montenegro at all, but Karlovy Vary, in the Czech Republic. (The Czech Republic takes a bow as itself in the beautifully filmed black and white opening in Prague.) Despite the film's breathtaking beauty and excellent cinematography, I am never happy when Bond "visits" a country he doesn't actually step foot in. There is no shooting in Madagascar, Uganda, or Montenegro, although the movie purportedly takes us to all three countries. This, I think, is a shame.

Speaking of not-Madagascar (actually the Bahamas), let's give a big hurrah to Sébastien Foucan, whose freerunning stunts gave us one of the best chase scenes in Bond history. When I talk to people who aren't necessarily Bond fans, but who've seen the movie, this sequence is invariably the one they comment on.

But perhaps the true highlight of the movie is not the action (not even the freerunning), or the gorgeous Aston Martins, or the acting, but the real, honest-to-God espionage, like fans have been begging for. Bond follows one clue to the next and learns from *spying*, rather than having the villain just give it away. With MI6 pulling through for Bond when he needs it, he doesn't seem like a superman. Clues, records, information, bribery, and ingenuity are what continually save the day in this film.

Although completely snubbed by the 2006 Oscars, *Casino Royale* was richly acknowledged by the BAFTAs (the British Academy of Film and Television Arts awards; a.k.a. the British Oscars). The movie received nine nominations for these prestigious awards, and Eva Green received a tenth nomination, for the "Orange Rising Star Award," a Best Newcomer award voted on by the public. Eva Green won this award, and *Casino Royale* won Best Sound, losing in the major categories. In this case, it really *is* an honor just to be nominated, because Best British Film, Best Actor, and Best Adapted Screenplay are the most prestigious nominations a Bond film had ever received up to this point. As a matter of fact, Daniel Craig did win Best Actor awards—from the British Evening Standard, and from the Saturn Awards.

The High Points

- Daniel Craig's jaw-dropping performance
- Return to a more serious, more Fleming-style Bond
- True-to-the-novel script; superb adaptation both of the book and of the book's sensibilities
- Creepy villains with scars and weeping blood and weird glasses
- David Arnold's old-school score
- Mind-blowing freerunning sequence
- Real espionage, following clues from point A to point B
- Eva Green's complex and vulnerable performance
- The shower scene
- Lush Bahamian cinematography
- Caterina Murino's brief but memorable role
- Brutal fight sequences
- Colorful characters, especially at the Casino Royale

The Low Points

- Ubiquitous Sony product placement
- "You Know My Name," a mediocre title song
- Use of fake locations
- Strange animation inside the gunbarrel
- Bond driving the ugly Ford Mondeo
- Overlong and somewhat confusing
- Jeffrey Wright is woefully underused
- Too-frequent mentions of arrogance and ego—we get it already!

Quotable Quotes

Dryden: "Shame. We barely got to know each other."
Bond: "I know where you keep your gun. S'pose that's something."
Dryden: "True. How did he die?"
Bond: "Your contact? Not well."
Dryden: "Made you feel it, did he? Well, you needn't worry. The second is..."
(Bond shoots)
Bond: "Yes. Considerably."

Obanno: "Do you believe in God, Mr. Le Chiffre?"
Le Chiffre: "No. I believe in a reasonable rate of return."

M: "In the old days if an agent did something that embarrassing, he'd have the good sense to defect. Christ, I miss the Cold War."

Villiers: "He's logged into our secure website using your name and password."
M: "How the hell does he know these things?"

Vesper: "I'm the money."
Bond: "Every penny of it."

Vesper: "How was your lamb?"
Bond: "Skewered. One sympathizes."

Bond: "Vodka martini."
Barman: "Shaken or stirred?"
Bond: "Do I look like I give a damn?"

Bond: "I'm sorry. That last hand...nearly killed me."

Bond: "I've got a little itch. Down there. Would you mind?"

Bond: "Now the whole world is going to know that you died scratching my balls."

Bond: "I have no armor left. You've stripped it from me. Whatever is left of me...whatever is left of me, whatever I am, I'm yours."

M: "If you do need more time..."
Bond: "Why should I need more time? The job's done. The bitch is dead."

Facts and Figures

SEXUAL ENCOUNTERS

<u>One</u>: Vesper Lynd. Bond *almost* makes love to Solange, but when he learns Dimitrios is going to the airport, he leaves her alone to go after him, and when he gets back, she is dead.

BOND'S CARS

> 1964 Aston Martin DB5, silver
> 2008 Aston Martin DBS, pewter (Aston Martin created the color especially for the film and called it "Casino Ice.")
> 2007 Ford Mondeo

DEATHS

<u>Approximately Seventy-four</u>:

- Dryden, Fisher (Dryden's contact), two shot by Mollaka, a burn victim at the construction site, Mollaka, Dimitrios, tanker driver killed by Carlos (the Skyfleet bomber), two cops in the car that was sucked up by the plane's wake, the passengers of the extension bus (estimated at fifty), Carlos, Solange, Obanno and his assistant, Gettler and four of his men.

- Mr. White and his men kill Le Chiffre and "everyone else" at the warehouse; assume "everyone else" means Kratt, Leo, and Valenka.
- Vesper.

Bond Kills

- <u>Nine</u> directly (Dryden, Fisher, Mollaka, Dimitrios, Obanno and his assistant, two of Gettler's men, Gettler.).
- <u>Four</u> indirectly (A burn victim at the construction site while chasing Mollaka; Bond set the fire, Carlos; he blows himself up but it was Bond who set him up to do so, two of Gettler's men; one falls into the water and doesn't come up; one is crushed by the elevator shaft when it falls on him, and then falls into the water.).

EXPLOSIONS

<u>Three</u>: The explosive fire on the construction site in Madagascar, the fuel tank explosion at the Nambutu Embassy, an extension bus that gets cut in two and then blows up during the airport chase.

BOND'S FOOD AND DRINKS

Vodka Martinis

<u>Five</u>: During the first round of play in the Casino Royale, Bond orders his first Vesper (a vodka martini with gin, vodka, Kina Lillet, and lemon peel). Then Mathis gets him a second. Then a vodka martini about which he does not give a damn, then a poisoned vodka martini that appears colorless (not a Vesper), then the Vesper that makes him decide its name.

Other Drinks

- Mount Gay with Soda: at the Ocean Club (basically rum and coke).
- Champagne: A bottle with Solange (they appear to have finished an entire bottle together. Bond then orders chilled Bollinger for Solange and leaves before it arrives). A flute of champagne snatched from a waiter's tray when meeting Mathis (he snatches two and Vesper gets the other).
- An indeterminate drink on the train before dinner, either whiskey or another rum and coke. There is also bottled water visible.
- Château Angélus claret shared with Vesper after dinner on the train.
- Whiskey after killing Obanno and his man.
- Saltwater to induce vomiting.
- A medicinal drink given to him by Mathis; Bond doesn't partake.
- Orange juice visible in the background when Mathis tries to get Bond to drink.

Food

- Bond orders "Beluga with everything" for Solange but doesn't have any himself.

- "Skewered" lamb on the train.
- There is a bowls of mixed olives and a bowl of nuts (seem to be macadamia) on the table when he first meets Mathis.
- Caviar with toast tips with Vesper after winning.

GAMBLING AND SPORTS

- Obanno plays pinball
- A cobra-versus-mongoose fight in Madagascar (with lively betting)
- A total of three poker games; Dimitrios versus Bond, Le Chiffre versus Madame Wu and the General, and the Casino Royale game. (Four if you count the "dead" one at the Body Works exhibit.)

Amaze Your Friends! (Best Trivia)

- *Casino Royale* has a strange history; the first Bond novel, but the 21st official film, its rights had passed from hand to hand. Ian Fleming sold his first novel twice, first to CBS for the one-hour *Climax!* production starring Barry Nelson, then to Michael Garrison and Gregory Ratoff. Then it was sold to Charles K. Feldman, who, with Columbia Pictures, made the 1967 spoof starring David Niven. Via Columbia, Sony Entertainment acquired the rights in the early 1990s, and Eon Productions sued to prevent them from making their own version of the novel. MGM and Eon won this lawsuit in 1999. Ironically, Sony ended up making the film after all, because Sony acquired MGM in 2004, and thus became co-owners of the James Bond franchise.
- Sébastien Foucan, who plays Mollaka, is an early developer of Parkour and the founder of freerunning—the chase we see in *Casino Royale* is freerunning, which allows more freedom of movement and incorporates more flips and spins, than Parkour.
- The name Solange is taken from the Ian Fleming short story, "007 in New York."
- A Bond girl and a Bond girl "extra" from the Sean Connery era appear in *Casino Royale* (see ENCORE! ENCORE!).
- Virgin founder Sir Richard Branson has a cameo in the Miami Airport scene. He can be seen setting off the security sensor and being gone over with a security wand.
- Eva Green appeared nude in Bernardo Bertolucci's *The Dreamers* and didn't want to do so again. She was asked to do the shower scene in just her panties, but she fought against it, and Daniel Craig supported her, arguing that it made more sense for her to be too upset to strip. (This is my favorite scene in the movie, and is so effective, I think, precisely because she is fully clothed, and he joins her clothed.)
- On March 13, 2007, the day that the *Casino Royale* DVD went on sale, it became the first DVD in high-definition format to ever reach top ten sales status. Amazon.com reported that the Sony Blu-ray HD format of the film debuted at #8 (the standard-definition DVD, in both widescreen and full-screen formats, also made the top ten).
- The final hand of the Casino Royale poker game was as follows:

- Board: Ace of Hearts, Eight of Spades, Six of Spades, Four of Spades, Ace of Spades
- Fukutu (the gentleman with the ponytail) had the King and Queen of Spades, giving him a flush (Ace, King, Queen, 8, 6 of spades)
- Infante (the overweight gentleman) had the Eight of Clubs and the Eight of Hearts, giving him a full house, eights over aces. He beats Fukutu.
- Le Chiffre had the Ace of Clubs and the Six of Hearts, giving him a higher full house, aces over sixes. He beats Infante.
- Bond had the Five and Seven of Spades, giving him a straight flush (4, 5, 6, 7, 8 of spades). Bond wins.

Most Interesting Goofs

Digitalis and Defibrilation: The drug Valenka gave Bond was digitalis, and he used an automatic external defibrillator (AED) to shock his heart (with Vesper's help). Here's the low-down: It takes **6 hours** for digitalis toxicity to kick in after a large dose. Defibrillation is not routinely recommended for digitalis toxicity because it can cause nasty heart rhythms (such as ventricular fibrillation) or it can cause the heart to stop beating (asystole). Bond was defibrillated while in asystole. This is not a good idea. Finally, many modern AEDs can set off the shock themselves once turned on; there's no need to manually trigger the shock. Additionally, nearly every model has a fault detector to make sure the circuit to the pads is working. (This information was provided by a doctor named Scott, whose interesting blog on medicine in pop culture, Polite Dissent, has sadly vanished.)

What Kind of Status Is That? The title sequence shows Bond's "007 status confirmed" in an official-looking form. But Bond doesn't have "007 status." He has 00 status, and he is agent 007.

Gettler's Bald Men: Gettler arrives at the meeting with Vesper with a man at his side, and three hiding in buildings nearby. The man at his side and one other man have facial hair. The two snipers with machine guns are clean-shaven; one has hair on his head and one has a shaved head. Bond shoots the mustachioed man in the building right away; that leaves the side-man and the two snipers. We see the bald sniper fall through a floor and into the water, and not come up. Then the side-man is crushed by the falling elevator shaft, and he, too, falls into the water. Then Bond electrocutes...the bald sniper. The sniper with hair is never seen again. Apparently, the bald guy died twice to spare his friend's life.

What's That Password Again? We see Bond smile to himself when he enters the password, it's 836547. But VESPER would be 837737.

YOU LIKE CLOSE SHAVES, DON'T YOU?

Agent 007 has been in some pretty tight situations over the years. Left in a crashing plane without a parachute (three times—in *You Only Live Twice*, *Moonraker*, and *Die Another Day*, so I guess he developed some expertise), about to be shot when the villain gets a phone call (*Tomorrow Never Dies*), discovering a poisonous tarantula in his bed (*Dr. No*)—it's not easy getting through the day when you're James Bond, and yet he's always managed to live to die another day.

So without further adieu, the Top Five Near Death Experiences of James Bond:

5. *Licence to Kill*

Wrists tied together, Bond is thrown onto a conveyer belt heading towards a chopper used to pulverize bricks of cocaine. For a moment, Bond uses the wristlets to hook himself to the end of the conveyer and avoid falling. But the evil Dario starts slicing his bonds. The whole thing is seriously scary, and when Dario falls victim to the fate meant for 007, we see how gruesome such a fate really is.

4. *Live and Let Die*

Left on a tiny bit of rock in a lake full of crocodiles, and just in case that wasn't scary enough, surrounded by hunks of raw meat. A nice false start when you think Bond's gadget—the magnetized watch—will save him. It fails. Moments before his escape, you see what Bond sees—the crocodiles in perfect alignment. Before that, you have no idea how he'll make it, and to the last second his escape is narrow, as the crocodiles snap at his shoes.

3. *GoldenEye*

Left unconscious and bound in a helicopter, with its own missiles targeted to hit it, with Bond and Natalya inside. Natalya screaming him into wakefulness doesn't seem very helpful at first, and he manages to escape without even getting himself untied—he literally used his head that time!

2. *Goldfinger*

Strapped to a golden table with an industrial laser working its way towards the family jewels. A classic close shave in a classic film.

And the number one close shave...

1. *Diamonds Are Forever*

Locked in a coffin inside a cremation oven, while flames lick around it. This one has it all: Claustrophobia, fire, helplessness...how can he possibly escape? He can't, of course. This as close to death as Bond has ever been, and there was nothing he could do about it; no tantalizing information he could drop, no last minute question to ask, no tricks to pull, no one to hit, shoot, or throw himself at. When the coffin lid opens, Bond is as surprised as everyone else.

FLASHBACK

T he Bond movies are, in many ways, filmed quite conservatively. They are linear and conventionally filmed. Slow-motion, for example, is rarely used (except in *Die Another Day*) and the black and white pre-titles sequence in *Casino Royale* was the first experiment with film color in 44 years. Bond films also rarely play with time sequence.

There are either three or four uses of flashback in all of James Bond history (as you'll see). This may win you something in a trivia game someday.

On Her Majesty's Secret Service

Blofeld's men kidnap Tracy from the avalanche's aftermath. As Bond unburies himself, he sees her being dragged off. Cut to Bond looking pensively out the window of M's office, seeing Tracy being dragged away. Is it a flashback? Or is it an artistic dissolve, scene into scene? It seems like a flashback but it isn't 100% clear.

Moonraker

The first unambiguous flashback is fully ten years later. In the very exciting centrifuge sequence; Bond begins to lose consciousness and recalls in snippets the scene where Q gave him the dart-shooting wristwatch, which he then uses.

Die Another Day

Having been released from North Korean imprisonment, Bond is unwillingly held in a medical facility by MI6. He recalls in flashback his time in the North Korean cell, where he learned to meditate and control his heartrate. He uses this ability to stop his heart in the present, causing doctors to rush in and giving him opportunity to escape.

Casino Royale

The pre-titles sequence has Bond confronting Dryden. Dryden says Bond can't be a 00 because his "file shows no kills." Immediately we cut to a flashback of the fight between Bond and Fisher. This lasts about 12 seconds, and we flash forward again, to Dryden pulling a gun on Bond, but the gun isn't loaded. Dryden asks how Fisher died, we flash back again, to what appears to be the rest of the fight. Then back to the conversation with Dryden. Bond kills Dryden and then we're back with Fisher; Bond finally killing him takes us straight into the gunbarrel.

QUANTUM OF SOLACE (2008)

Survey Says!

Percent Favorite: 0%
Top 5 Cumulative: 22/25
Numeric Rating: 6.3/10
Ranking: 15.8 (17th/25)

My Rating and Ranking

Rated: 6
Ranked: 19/25

Summary

Picking up immediately from the end of *Casino Royale*, Bond brings Mr. White to M, but White escapes, having revealed the existence of a widespread criminal organization.

Forensics connects White's organization to Port au Prince, Haiti. There Bond encounters Camille Montes and Dominic Greene, head of Greene Planet. Greene is working with Bolivian General Medrano. Bond follows Greene to Austria, where he eavesdrops on a meeting of White's organization: Quantum.

Bond seeks the help of René Mathis, and together they follow Greene to Bolivia. Greene plans to help depose the current Bolivian government and support Medrano's military coupe, in exchange for a seemingly worthless piece of land, actually the water source for all of Bolivia. Camille, meanwhile, seeks revenge on Medrano for the murder of her family. Together, Bond and Camille find the villains; Camille kills Medrano while Bond gets all the information he can from Greene before leaving him for Quantum to find and kill him.

In a coda, Bond confronts and captures Yusef Kabira, Vesper's traitorous lover, finding some closure on Vesper's betrayal and death.

James Bond: Daniel Craig
Camille Montes: Olga Kurlyenko
Dominic Greene: Mathieu Amalric
René Mathis: Giancarlo Giannini
Strawberry Fields: Gemma Arterton
Felix Leiter: Jeffrey Wright
Gregg Beam: David Harbour
Mr. White: Jesper Christensen
Elvis: Anatole Taubman
General Medrano: Joaquin Cosio
Yusef Kabira: Simon Kassianides
M: Judi Dench
Tanner: Rory Kinnear

Directed by Marc Foster

Discussion

Bond movies suffer when they try to ride the wave of current movie trends. Bond trying to be a blaxploitation movie gave us the horror that is *Live and Let Die*, trying to be *Star Wars* gave us the slogfest that is *Moonraker*, and trying to be *The Matrix* gave us the special effects nightmares found in *Die Another Day*. Predictably, trying to be a Jason Bourne movie did not work out for 007, giving us the widely-hated *Quantum of Solace*.

I'm so unfair, faulting several Bond films for being too jokey and ridiculous, and now turning my guns onto *Quantum of Solace* for being too dark. But it cannot be helped, this movie is *waaay* too dark. It's miserable. It's gray and cloudy and angry, full of revenge and tragedy and rape and dumpsters.

My brother suggested to me that I watch *Casino Royale* and *Quantum of Solace* back to back, as a double-feature. It's true that the latter movie improves considerably with the emotional context of Vesper's death fresh in one's mind. It's still a misery of a movie, badly filmed, convoluted and senseless in plot, imitative of Bourne, and unlike James Bond in fundamental ways. It has a few redeeming features, and some very good scenes, but it is overall an unpleasant experience.

Figure 17: As with Casino Royale, *there were playing cards with the Blu-ray release.*

The whole "sequel" business is underlined as problem when we see the closing gunbarrel sequence. Are we back to "Bond becomes Bond" again? *Again?* When *Casino Royale* (which had an opening gunbarrel) ended with the first playing of the James Bond Theme, this was supposed to tie it up as Bond becoming Bond. How does he become Bond twice?

The action is almost uniformly impossible to follow, featuring rapid cuts which prioritize adrenaline over the ability to follow what's going on. The pre-titles sequence deserves recognition as perhaps the very worst—it is two similar cars of similar color, filmed in such a way as to make it impossible to figure out who's doing what, who shoots whom, and what the hell is going on. There are extreme close-ups, then rapid shots of cars without a clear view of the driver. We're told that a black Alfa Romeo is chasing a gray Aston Martin, but no matter how often I watch, I see two black cars. By contrast, the major car chase in *Die Another Day,* problematic though it is, is smart enough to put the villain in a bright green car.

The fight with Mr. Slate in Haiti is no better, and seems lifted directly from a Bourne movie.

Quantum of Solace is a humorless movie—all the best lines belong to M, while Bond is largely stoic. And it's a sexless movie. There is one charming scene with the delightful Fields, but, for the first time in Bond history, no romance of any kind with the female lead. Olga Kurlyenko plays the "Bond girl," but she is, if anything, more miserable than Bond.

The film balances exposition with action quite poorly. It's *Go! Go! Go!* and then talk, talk, talk, so that both action and dialogue become tedious. Marc Forster is a stylish director who had never before done an action film. This obviously worked out so well with Lee Tamahori and *Die Another Day* that Eon was eager to repeat the experiment. (This is sarcasm).

The plot is convoluted and hard to follow. The Medrano/Camille plot is only superficially related to the Greene/Quantum plot, and neither is directly related to Vesper's death (Yusef was part of Quantum? I guess?), which is supposed to be what's driving Bond. It's also full of holes and inconsistencies. Producer Michael Wilson said in interviews that this movie starts about two hours after *Casino Royale* ends. How is that enough time for Mathis to be freed from having been "sweated," be given an Italian villa, and establish his retirement with a beautiful girlfriend? Why is there a luxury hotel in the middle of a barren desert? Why is it so lacking in anything luxurious? How does Medrano not know that his country has a drought? Who decided that chit-chatting during an opera was discreet?

There are some bright spots in the film. Strawberry Fields is a terrific character. She's got a bit of old-school Fleming about her, efficient, dedicated to the job, a little shocked at herself for sleeping with Bond. Tripping Elvis at the fundraiser party was a delightful surprise. She didn't deserve her dark ending.

The entire Tosca sequence is the highlight of the movie. Everything about it—the setting, the use of music and costumes, the view from backstage, and Bond's trick to expose Quantum, is fantastic. Yes, a meeting at the opera is implausible. It's also audacious, and I enjoyed the hell out of it. We have Bond in a tux, an elaborate setup, the use of music over the sounds of violence—it all works. It's real espionage, which you've read far enough to know I appreciate, in full Bond style. Definitely the most 007 moment in the film. Even the next small sequence at the airport is good—understanding why his credit cards are cut off and figuring out how to adapt. Alas for the movie that might have been, because all of this is true James Bond, but doesn't last long enough to get us through the rest of this dreary mess.

My friend points to the giant eye in Tosca as perhaps symbolic of Quantum seeing all, knowing everything, and while that is clever and kind of gorgeous, it's also evidence that Marc Forster imagined he was making an art film, not an adventure.

I absolutely adore René Mathis in both his Bond movies. Giancarlo Giannini is the perfect ally in the Pedro Armendariz mode. He brings warmth and wisdom to the character, and he is a genuine comfort to Bond. His final scene, dying in Bond's arms, is magnificent. Yes, the forgiveness speech is overdone, but an actor of Giannini's caliber has the power to sell it. The overhead shot of the camera backing away from Mathis's body in a dumpster is devastating.

I've seen fans complain about that—Bond would never do that. Well first of all, there's very little in the film that says "Bond" to me. Other than drinking Vespers, how is this the James Bond we know from 21 previous movies? Secondly, I think it's fair to see Mathis like that—we can say "Bond would never," but do we know that? For the most part, we never see the consequences of the deaths that surround Bond. Take Aki—one of my favorite Bond girls. In *You Only Live Twice*, we see Bond have barely a moment to mourn her; quickly the adventure sweeps him away, and her body is left behind. It's not in a dumpster, but is it honoring the dead? No, it's taking action, and that's what Bond does. That emotional moment, truly feeling the consequences of the deaths that fall by the wayside, is not something most Bond movies go for.

Yes, it worked. Yes, it was earned. The problem is, the movie is confused about what it is. A Bourne movie? An arthouse drama? A meditation on revenge and forgiveness? Or is it a Bond movie? If the writers and director aren't sure, the rest of us are lost.

The villains in this movie are dreadful. Mr. White is an exception, his presence in three consecutive movies is one of the best uses of continuity in the Craig films. But Dominic Greene is simply disgusting without being creepy or frightening or imposing, or anything else one might characterize as villainous. He defeats himself by cutting open his own foot with an axe, demonstrating incompetence more than villainy. General Medrano is worse—the first Bond villain whose primary characteristic is that he's a violent rapist. This is nauseating, and a line the Bond films were wrong to cross.

Camille, seeking revenge for the murder of her family, could bring *For Your Eyes Only* lead Melina Havelock to mind. But Camille has internalized her quest, as symbolized by the burn scars she bears all over her back. They are not disfiguring—the male gaze is not disrupted, because her face and figure are perfect—but they remind the audience that she is concerned with *her* pain and *her* injury; she has nothing left over for Bond. Thus, she works as an ally, but not as a traditional Bond co-star.

Quantum of Solace is a steep fall for the Craig films, and a huge fan disappointment. *Casino Royale* is consistently in the top ten in Bond film rankings, and makes frequent appearances in the number one slot. *Quantum of Solace* is almost always found in the bottom five. The tumble is dizzying.

The High Points
- The Tosca opera sequence
- The return of René Mathis
- ...and his tragic death
- Jeffrey Wright as Felix Leiter
- Mr. White cackling at M
- The many charms of Fields, "Just Fields"

- Beautiful location footage in Siena, Italy, including the Palio di Siena horse race
- Excellent, if controversial, title song, "Another Way to Die," by Jack White and Alicia Keys.

The Low Points

- The pre-titles sequence and its incomprehensible car chase
- Bourne-like action throughout
- Dark, gloomy action, characterizations, and dialogue
- Convoluted plot
- Unpleasant villains we do not "love to hate," but merely find repulsive
- Insufficient sex, romance, humor, and glamour
- Terrible pacing

Quotable Quotes

Bond: "I promised them Le Chiffre and they got Le Chiffre."
M: "They got his body."
Bond: "If they wanted his soul, they should have made a deal with a priest."

Bond: (at a cheap hotel) "What are we doing?"
Strawberry Fields: "We're teachers on sabbatical. This fits our cover."
Bond: "No it doesn't. I'd rather stay at a morgue. Come on."
James Bond: (in Spanish, to the desk clerk at a luxury hotel) "Hello. We're teachers on sabbatical and we've just won the lottery."

M: "Bond, if you could avoid killing every possible lead, it would be deeply appreciated."
Bond: "Yes, Ma'am. I'll do my best."
M: "I've heard that before."

M: "When someone says 'We've got people everywhere,' you expect it to be hyperbole. Lots of people say that. Florists use that expression. It doesn't mean that they've got somebody working for them inside the bloody room!"

Facts and Figures

SEXUAL ENCOUNTERS

<u>One</u>: Fields.

BOND'S CARS

2008 Aston Martin DBS, pewter
2008 Ford Edge SEL

DEATHS

Twenty-four:

- In the pre-titles sequence, White's men kill two cops, then two of White's men in a car crash.
- Mitchell (M's bodyguard) kills two – one we see, and the guard off-screen. Mitchell. Mr. Slate.
- The geologist hired by Greene, Guy Hayes's bodyguard, Mathis, the two Bolivian cops who (presumably) killed Mathis. Fields. The jet pilot.
- At the hotel, the Bolivian Chief of Police and three of his men, two of Medrano's guards. Medrano. Elvis. Greene.

Bond Kills

- Eight directly: Mitchell, Slate, the two cops in Bolivia, the Bolivian Chief of Police and three of his men.
- Five indirectly: White's men die in a car crash chasing Bond. The jet pilot crashes. Bond starts the fire in the hotel, which kills Elvis, Bond leaves Greene in the desert to be killed by Quantum.

EXPLOSIONS

Three: The Colonel's truck goes up with a nice boom. The hotel fire explosion is massive and quite spectacular. Then a third, small explosion when Bond blasts the hole in the hotel that saves Camille and himself.

BOND'S FOOD AND DRINKS

Vodka Martinis

Six Vespers on the flight to Bolivia

Other Drinks

- Whiskey after delivering White
- White wine ("cheap wine") with Mathis in Italy
- Champagne in the room with Fields before the party
- Champagne at Greene's party
- Beer when meeting Felix

FOOD

- None

GAMBLING AND SPORTS

- None

Amaze Your Friends!

- The shortest Bond movie (up to and including *No Time to Die*) at 106 minutes. I could put this under "High Points," but that would be mean!
- This movie features quite a number of homages to past Bond movies:

- o M asks Bond, "When was the last time you slept?" In *Dr. No*, M asks "When do you sleep?" to which Bond replies, "Never on the firm's time, sir."
- o Fields's death is an obvious reference to Jill Masterson's death in *Goldfinger*.
- o Bond and Camille walking out of the desert in eveningwear bears a strong visual similarity to the same event in *The Spy Who Loved Me*.
- o Bond and Camille have a conversation outside of the Bolivia hotel, with Bond helping to prepare Camille to kill Medrano; the entire thing is very much a riff on the short story "For Your Eyes Only."
- o Bond ringing the church bell is a reference to the bell room fight scene in *On Her Majesty's Secret Service*. This scene was also referenced in *Die Another Day*'s pre-titles sequence, when Bond says "Saved by the bell."
- o Bond's says to give Camille his business card. It is for Universal Exports and shows the name *R. Sterling*. 007 used the cover name Robert Sterling in *The Spy Who Loved Me* (see I'M A LITTLE CONFUSED).
- Fields's first name is never mentioned in the film, and in fact, she avoids telling it to Bond. The credits tell us she is Strawberry Fields.
- During filming, On April 19, 2008, Fraser Dunn, an engineer driving James Bond's Aston Martin DBS to the set, lost control of the car and ended up in Northern Italy's Lago di Garda (Lake Garda). Dunn was not seriously injured, but the car, worth more than $150,000, was totaled.
- The Palio di Siena is a horserace held twice a year, on July 2nd and August 16th, in Siena, Italy. The race is a huge tourist attraction, spectacle, and no-holds-barred battle, featuring ten horses and bareback riders. A pageant, the Corteo Storico, precedes the race.
- The Tosca scene was filmed at Philipp Himmelmann's 2007 production of Giacomo Puccini's "Tosca" at the Bregenz floating opera stage on Lake Constance in Austria. The part of the opera seen in the movie is the Te Deum scene and parts of Act 2.

Most Interesting Goofs

How is that spelled? Bond spells "G-R-E-E-N-E" for Tanner, but he's only heard the name, he's never seen it spelled.

Some drive: The car chase begins where *Casino Royale* ended: At Lake Como in Italy. Bond drives his car along the Via Gardesana Centro on the eastern shore. He then drives through the famous marble quarry of Carrara, which is about 180 miles south. He then arrives at the safe house in Siena, another 130 miles south.

Taxi? The CIA, Greene and Bond are seen arriving by plane in Bregenz, Austria. However, Bregenz does not have an airport.

WHAT DOES JAMES BOND DRINK?

To answer this world-shattering question, I've gone through every movie and analyzed every glass, bottle, and table setting. The individual movie chapters tell the tale in detail. But gathering it here, in one place, lets us look at overall trends.

What "Counts"?

These are drinks that Bond has, is seen to have recently had (empty glasses on the table, for example), pours, orders, offers, or is offered, whether or not we see him drink. Bond pours champagne for himself and Lucia Sciarra, then breaks the glasses before drinking—this counts as a drink of champagne.

The quantities noted below are not about what's happening to Bond's liver— I'm not his doctor or his psychiatrist. If Bond has champagne at a dinner, it is counted as one whether it's a glass or the whole bottle. As we often join a scene to the sight of an empty glass, it's impossible to be more detailed.

What is Bond's Favorite Drink?

You'd think it's a vodka martini, but it's not. It's champagne.

Over the course of 25 movies, Bond has had champagne 51 times, and vodka martinis 37 times (of which nine—three in *Casino Royale* and six in *Quantum of Solace*, were Vespers).

Roger Moore and Vodka Martinis

Roger Moore didn't want to be seen as imitating Sean Connery in any way. He never ordered a vodka martini for himself—every time he had one, it was ordered for him by someone else, beginning with Anya Amasova doing so in *The Spy Who Loved Me*.

Bond did not have a martini at all in *Live and Let Die*, *The Man with the Golden Gun*, *For Your Eyes Only*, or *A View to a Kill*. Roger Moore is the only actor to have played Bond without ordering a vodka martini, or to have acted in Bond movies that didn't feature one.

Drinks by Type

Type of Drink	Quantity
Champagne	51
Vodka martinis	37
Red wine	12
Unknown drink	8

Type of Drink	Quantity
Scotch whiskey neat	7
Vodka neat	7
Beer	6
White wine/sparkling white wine	3
Bourbon neat	3
Bourbon and ice	2
Cognac	2
Ouzo	2
Rum and Coke	2
Sake	2
Vodka rocks	2
Bourbon and water	1
Glüwein	1
Malt whiskey and branch water	1
Metaxa	1
Mimosa	1
Mint julep	1
Mojito	1
Port wine	1
Raki	1
Rum	1
Rum collins	1
Sazerac	1
Solera sherry	1
Unknown tropical drink	1

Champagne

The only movie in which Bond does not drink champagne is *Diamonds Are Forever.*

In a number of movies, Bond is picky about exactly what champagne he wants. These choices are noted below:

Movie	Champagne
Dr. No	Dom Perignon 1955
From Russia with Love	Blanc de Blanc
Goldfinger	Dom Perignon 1953
Thunderball	Dom Perignon 1955
You Only Live Twice	Dom Perignon 1959
On Her Majesty's Secret Service	Dom Perignon 1957
Live and Let Die	Bollinger (no year specified)
The Man with the Golden Gun	Dom Perignon 1964

Movie	Champagne
The Spy Who Loved Me	Dom Perignon 1952
Moonraker	Bollinger 1969
A View to a Kill	Bollinger 1975
The Living Daylights	Bollinger RD (no year specified)
Licence to Kill	Bollinger RD (no year specified)
GoldenEye	Bollinger 1988
The World is Not Enough	Bollinger (no year specified)
Die Another Day	Bollinger 1961
	Bollinger (no year specified)
Casino Royale	Bollinger (no year specified)

Dom Perignon 1955 is the only vintage ordered in two different Bond movies (*Dr. No* and *Thunderball.*)

Mixed Drinks

James Bond almost never has a mixed drink. Martinis mix booze with more booze, but 007 is almost completely uninterested in adding anything to his alcohol except more alcohol, water, ice, or a garnish. The exceptions are:

Movie	Drink
From Russia with Love	Bond and Tanya appear to have mimosas with breakfast
Goldfinger	Bond has a mint julep while in Kentucky (this also falls under NATIVE DRINKS, below).
Thunderball	Largo serves Bond a rum Collins (the rum, at least, is native)
Live and Let Die	Felix orders a Sazerac for Bond in New Orleans (a native drink)
For Your Eyes Only	Bond has glüwein—a hot, spiced wine
Never Say Never Again	Domino brings Bond an indeterminate tropical cocktail
Die Another Day	A mojito in Cuba with Jinx (another native drink)

Native Drinks

In the novels, Bond always drank whatever the local specialty was. In the movies, his drinking becomes much more habit-driven, resorting more and more to the vodka martini, but native drinks are often spotted.

Movie	Drink	Native to
From Russia with Love	Raki	Turkey
Goldfinger	Mint julep	Kentucky
Thunderball	Rum Collins	Caribbean (rum)
You Only Live Twice	Sake	Japan
Live and Let Die	Sazerac	New Orleans
	Glüwein	Austria
	Metaxa (perhaps)	Greece
For Your Eyes Only	Ouzo	Greece

What Does James Bond Drink?

Movie	Drink	Native to
Never Say Never Again	Tropical drink	Caribbean
	Mojito (a rum drink)	Cuba
Die Another Day	Rum	Cuba

UNIVERSAL EXPORTS, LTD.

T he frequent cover of both James Bond and MI6 as a whole is the import/export company Universal Exports, Ltd. (sometimes called Universal Export, without the "s", in the novels). It is a cover identity introduced by Ian Fleming in the Bond novels, and continued into the movies, most recently seen in *Quantum of Solace*. Here is a list of all Universal Exports references (hat tip to the James Bond Wiki for invaluable help; see RESOURCES).

In the Novels

Universal Exports made its first appearance in the second Ian Fleming novel, **Live and Let Die**, under the name "Universal Export." In **Moonraker**, "Universal Export Co." again appear as the cover for the Secret Service's London offices.

In **On Her Majesty's Secret Service** , Bond knows that Universal Export is over: "As cover, solid cover, Universal was 'Brûlé' with the pros. It had been in use too long. All the secret services in the world had penetrated it by now." In **The Man with the Golden Gun** we learn that the Universal Export has been replaced with "Transworld Consortium."

In The Movies

Here's a full list of Universal Exports film appearances.

Dr. No

Universal Exports is seen on a sign as Bond enters MI6 headquarters for a briefing.

On Her Majesty's Secret Service

Again, a sign outside MI6 headquarters.

The Living Daylights

Another sign outside MI6 headquarters.

For Your Eyes Only

The helicopter that arrives for Bond in the pre-titles sequence bears the Universal Exports logo on the side. Interestingly, this helicopter is actually sent by Blofeld, meaning that the cover has been blown—Blofeld knows that MI6 is Universal Exports.

Licence to Kill

Bond introduces himself as a Universal Exports representative when approaching Milton Krest's warehouse.

The World is Not Enough

Bond uses an employee ID card with a Universal Exports logo when he first meets Elektra King in Azerbaijan.

Die Another Day

When Bond arrives at the Cuban cigar factory, he says he's from Univesal Exports (see CODE WORDS).

Quantum of Solace

Bond gives Elvis a Universal Exports business card for R. Sterling (see I'M A LITTLE CONFUSED).

SKYFALL (2012)

Survey Says!

Percent Favorite: 2%
Top 5 Cumulative: 9/25
Numeric Rating: 8.3/10
Ranking: 11.5 (12th/25)

My Rating and Ranking

Rated: 9
Ranked: 10/25

Summary

While pursuing a stolen hard drive with the names of undercover agents, Bond is shot. When the MI6 offices are blown up by a computer hacker, Bond, missing and presumed dead, returns to active duty. The hacker is in possession of the stolen names, so Bond's first mission is to go after the man who shot him. This leads him Raoul Silva, a former MI6 agent who is the hacker targeting M with a personal vendetta. Silva is taken into MI6 custody, but this was part of his plan. He escapes and attempts to kill M. Bond takes M to his childhood home, Skyfall, for a showdown with Silva. Bond kills Silva but M is also killed in the battle.

James Bond: Daniel Craig
M: Judi Dench
Raoul Silva (a.k.a. Tiago Rodriguez): Javier Bardem
Gareth Mallory: Ralph Fiennes
Eve Moneypenny: Naomie Harris
Severine: Bérénice Lim Marlohe
Kincade: Albert Finney
Q: Ben Whishaw
Tanner: Rory Kinnear
Patrice: Ola Rapace
Bond's Lover: Tonia Sotiropoulou

Discussion

The last time I watched *Skyfall*, I waited for the first scene that legitimately bothered me, the first moment I disliked, then paused the film and checked the time: It was at the 1 hour 20 minutes mark. *Skyfall* has 80 minutes of sheer perfection. Then a scene that bothers me. Then some more really good stuff. Then a plot hole big enough to drive a train through. Then some *more* really good stuff. Then we get to Scotland, about which fandom has, shall we say, mixed feelings. Then there's an absolutely exquisite coda. And for all of that excellence, fans rain down on *Skyfall* like fury for its flaws.

Alfred Hitchcock referred to certain kinds of plot holes as "icebox scenes;" an implausibility that "hits you after you've gone home and start pulling cold chicken out of the icebox." Bond fans watch our movies over and over. We've seen each Bond film many times, and often we discuss them with one another. Thus, flaws that do not disrupt a movie under normal viewing circumstances become enlarged.

Skyfall is a movie that suffers from the way fandom watches, because the flaws it has are huge once observed, yet, in the theater, on first viewing—which is how movies are designed to be seen—it is inarguably a fantastic film.

Visually, *Skyfall* is absolutely a stunner. Cinematographer Roger Deakins received his ninth Oscar nomination for this film, and deservedly so (he would go on to receive a total of twelve nominations before winning in 2018 and 2020—see 007 AT THE OSCARS). The pre-titles filming of Istanbul, and post-titles of Calis Beach in Turkey are both gorgeous, and the approach to Glencoe, Scotland at the end is gasp-worthy. But the visual showstopper is surely Shanghai.

I love everything about the Shanghai sequence. I love the long stretch of silence, from Bond's arrival in China to the very end of the fight with Patrice, no words are spoken. It takes a smart filmmaker to make it clear to the audience what's happening (director Sam Mendes is another Oscar winner). I love the character work and plot exposition on display—Bond's struggle to hold onto the elevator, playing the theme of his injuries and potential unfitness—at the same time showing Patrice's ruthlessness and Bond's determination. I love the short, brutal fight in silhouette, and I love Bond trying to save Patrice long enough to get him to talk, whereas in *Quantum of Solace* he just kept killing his leads.

But what takes the whole thing from smart to stunning is the exquisite light show, the interplay of shadows, glass, and neon, making Shanghai itself a player on the stage. (Amazingly, Daniel Craig was never in Shanghai for filming—the city scenes and neon lights were captured and inserted into the studio shots of the fight.)

Skyfall opens with a (literal) killer of a pre-titles sequence in Istanbul—a return to one of my all-time favorite Bond locations. It's action-packed, with a tense, downbeat start, then a car chase, then a motorcycle chase, then a fight on top of a train, then that stunning fall, which takes us into what may very well be the best title sequence of them all (see DANCING IN THE SHADOWS). From there to Bond living on the beach, the attack on MI6, Bond's return, the meeting with Q, the hunt for Patrice, the hotel room with Eve, the Macau casino, and then meeting Severine on her yacht, the Chimera. What is wrong with *any* of that? Nothing I can think of.

The Q scene is an absolute delight. First of all, there's a Q! Yay! Second, Ben Whishaw is a fine actor, full of surprises; he takes the "inventor kid" trope and turns it into something special. The interplay between Q and Bond tickles me to death.

In many ways, this is Daniel Craig's first "Bond movie," in the sense of returning to who and what James Bond is. He opens the film as an established agent, neither newbie nor rogue. He is capable of a quip. "Last rat standing" isn't punny or particularly funny, but it *is* a quip, and this is the first Craig movie of which quips are a part. He shoots his cuffs when he jumps into the train during the teaser, and this is exactly what James Bond should do (and what Craig has never done before). Q is back, and by the end, Moneypenny is at a desk outside of M's bulletproof door. (There are no hats, but notice that Moneypenny's office has a hat rack. Just in case.) It gives a sense that all is right with the world.

I was vicious in my assessment of *Quantum of Solace*'s attempts at artistry, but here I think Sam Mendes got it right. The several thematic moments aren't over-played, because they're spread out among many characters. We can say that the theme here is age, and being put out to pasture. Obviously Bond, with his injury, his struggle with his marksmanship, and the failing test scores M keeps from him, is embodying this theme. But so is M, in both her meeting with Mallory where he asks her to resign, and in her testimony to Parliament. And so is Q, embodying youth, which Bond remarks upon, and meditating on age and time in the form of a paint-ing. And indeed, so is Silva, who explicitly draws parallels between himself and Bond, both "betrayed" by M when she traded Silva to the Chinese, and told Eve to "take the bloody shot." Not all of these scenes worked equally well, but the interwo-ven threads of the theme *do* work.

The "British bulldog" is introduced as a desk ornament—and as a metaphor for Bond himself, a symbol of British tenacity and courage, echoed in M's obituary for Bond, where she calls him "an exemplar of British fortitude"—exactly like the bulldog. The bulldog is the opposite of being put out to pasture—it hangs on regard-less, and shows its spirit in its refusal to let go.

Compare it to the notion of forgiveness in *Quantum of Solace*, which takes the form of Mathis and M each lecturing Bond about it. Or even arrogance and ego in *Casino Royale*, again, Vesper and M lecturing Bond. Here the idea of having a theme at all is done with much more subtlety and grace.

There are other fairly nice cinematic flourishes, like the fall into water at the beginning being echoed by the fall into Skyfall's lake at the end, or Eve saying "Sometimes the old ways are the best," only to have Kincade repeat those exact words much later in the film, in a very different context. Bond had a strong reaction when Eve said it, which makes me wonder if this wasn't something Kincade said of-ten when Bond was young. Finally, notice that when Kincade says this important line, he says it about a knife—the knife Bond will subsequently use to kill Silva.

And, Silva says he will give M a "goodbye kiss," which is what, eventually, and tragically, Bond gives her.

But let's get to the hour-and-twenty mark and turn a more critical eye onto *Skyfall*. The abandoned island is a terrific location (supposedly off the coast of Ma-cau, actually Hashima Island in Japan), and Silva's creepy introduction is startling and effective. The speech about rats, the homoeroticism, all of this works for me. But when Silva shoots Severine, that is absolutely the *wrong* place for a quip. Frankly, Bond's face registers more anger when Silva later shoots up the DB5. Sev-erine deserved better.

I enjoy Silva's capture, and M's first confrontation with him, but then it's one big icebox. The first thing I noticed was that Silva had a large metal implant in his mouth—a dramatic reveal to be sure, but in such a secure facility, surely that would be taken from him! It's not *quite* a goof, and it has no real plot relevance; apparently it was just an irresistible visual.

Q's attempt to break Silva's computer security is the digital key that triggers the next hack—opening the cell and other doors so that Silva can escape. Q then re-alizes this was "years" in the planning. But this is one of those omnipotent villain plots that cannot withstand scrutiny. (To make matters worse, it is used two films in a row.) Silva did not know exactly when he'd allow himself to be captured. He could not have known that M would be questioned by Parliament, or when or where that would occur. None of those components could have been planned years in advance. And the train? I cannot make sense of the train.

I recognize that hacking and loss of privacy are very of-the-moment anxieties, and so hacking plots consecutively in *Skyfall* and *Spectre* make a kind of sense. I also recognize that that super-genius computer hackers make plotting easy. Whatever you want the villain to do, he can do; it's like all the new superpowers suddenly appearing in *Superman II*, any plot point that needs to be resolved, you just give the villain the next magic hack trick. It's lazy.

Next, Bond takes M to Scotland to draw Silva out, but with neither the weaponry nor manpower to truly stand against him. The scheme is ill-conceived, and since Q and Mallory are in on it, unjustified—either could have provided needed help without alerting Silva. Think about how inconsistent this is. The very mention of Skyfall got Bond to get up and walk out of a test he knew was critical, yet now he wants to go there, of every place on earth he might think to go? In addition, he knows his flat in London had been sold because he was "dead," surely he might have some uncertainty about the status of his childhood home?

If he *must* go to Skyfall, a better plan would be to drive there, scope it out, figure out defenses and weaponry, and only thereafter "leave breadcrumbs" on a call into MI6 from M, meanwhile getting reinforcements.

The Skyfall sequence is something many, many fans refer to as *Bond Home Alone*. Without weapons or allies, Bond, M, and Kincade boobytrap the house, which is, yes, what Macaulay Culkin did in *Home Alone*. It's surprisingly effective when watching, but in retrospect, it's bizarrely un-Bond.

I can live with the house fight, but what is *very* wrong here is giving Bond a childhood, and embellishing it with so much detail.

Bond movies jump on trends. *Quantum of Solace* jumped on Bourne and hyper-action. *Skyfall* jumped on the postmodern need to give everyone and everything a back story. We now know the "origin" of Peter Pan, Willy Wonka, J.R.R. Tolkien, and Christopher Robin, to name but a few. It's an appalling trend that takes the magic out of storytelling and makes it all a set of blocks that have to be fit together just so.

Of course, this started with *Casino Royale*, the "reboot" trend giving a certain amount of "origin," but *Casino Royale* didn't feel compelled to fill in the blanks, wisely understanding that blanks are mysteries, and that audiences can handle reading between the lines.

Up until this moment, *Skyfall* was an excellent movie with a few plot holes. But taking a mythic character and demythologizing him is a consequential error. Continuity has always been handled with the lightest of touches in the Bond universe (see I HAVEN'T SEEN YOU IN SIX MONTHS!), and this allows the series to continue indefinitely. Repeating a character like Mathis is not unlike bringing back Zukovsky, or Leiter. Avenging Vesper is not unlike avenging Tracy. But turning Bond into a character locked into time is a mistake on a larger scale than this one movie (and this mistake will drastically worsen with the next movie). Indeed, *Skyfall* remains an excellent movie—but one with dire implications for the future of James Bond.

The dénouement of *Skyfall* is also controversial. Silva's madness and M's death are either a beautiful scene or weirdly out-of-place. It depends on your tolerance for drama in a Bond film. I thought it was powerful. My complaint is that M was wounded by some random thug during battle, and then hid her wound for no real reason, so that her death was unconnected to the main thrust of events. She wasn't killed by Silva—indeed, we have no idea who killed her.

Overall, *Skyfall* is an immensely satisfying film, as a Bond movie and as cinema, and its flaws cannot outweigh that. Its strangeness is, in some ways, a part of its charm. However, if we continue to give this much backstory to Bond, he will cease to be the James Bond we know, and become merely one more movie character.

High Points

- Action-packed pre-titles sequence
- One of the greatest title sequences
- Fantastic score by Thomas Newman which utilizes the terrific, Oscar-winning song by Adele
- The entire Shanghai sequence, culminating in a thrilling lightshow/ fight with Patrice
- Naomie Harris as Eve
- Return of Bond-ish behavior; wry comments, sharp dressing, and a vodka martini
- Silva's chill-inducing rat speech
- Revealing the Aston Martin DB5 in storage brings me joy every time.

Low Points

- Those komodo dragons are 100% CGI—and it shows
- Macau was never visited—the skyline and exteriors were constructed entirely from CGI and do not resemble the real Macau
- Bond's cold-hearted response to Severine's death
- Implausible super-hacking train plot
- Giving Bond a childhood with this much detail
- The *Home Alone* combat
- M's testimony feels very implausible—are we really discussing the "meaning" of spying?
- M's meaningless death from an anonymous assailant.

Quotable Quotes

M: "Where the hell have you been?"
James Bond: "Enjoying death. 007 reporting for duty."

Doctor Hall: "Gun"
James Bond: "Shot"
Doctor Hall: "Agent"
James Bond: "Provacateur"

Doctor Hall: "Woman"
James Bond: "Provacatrix"
Doctor Hall: "Heart"
James Bond: "Target"
Doctor Hall: "Bird"
James Bond: "Sky"
Doctor Hall: "M"
James Bond: "Bitch"
Doctor Hall: "Sunlight"
James Bond: "Swim"
Doctor Hall: "Moonlight"
James Bond: "Dance"
Doctor Hall: "Murder"
James Bond: "Employment"
Doctor Hall: "Country"
James Bond: "England"
Doctor Hall: "Skyfall...Skyfall"
James Bond: "Done"

James Bond: "For her eyes only."

James Bond: "Hire me or fire me, it's entirely up to you."

Q: "007. I'm your new Quartermaster."
James Bond: "You must be joking."
Q: "Why? Because I'm not wearing a lab coat?"
James Bond: "Because you still have spots."

James Bond: "A gun. And a radio. Not exactly Christmas, is it?"
Q: "Were you expecting an exploding pen? We don't really go in for that anymore."

Eve: "Sometimes the old ways are the best."

Silva: "Ooh, see what she's done to you."
James Bond: "Well, she never tied me to a chair."
Silva: "Her loss."
James Bond: "You sure this is about M?"
Silva: "It's about her. And you. And me. You see, we are the last two rats. We can either eat each other, hmmm? Or eat everyone else. How you're trying to remember your training now! What's the regulation to cover *this*? Well, first time for everything, yes?"
James Bond: "What makes you think this is my first time?"
Silva: "Oh, Mr. Bond!"

Q: "Oh Shit. Shit shit shit."

M: "How old where you when they died?"
James Bond: "You know the answer to that. You know the whole story."

M: "Orphans always make the best recruits."
James Bond: "Storm's coming."

Kincade: "Sometimes the old ways are the best."

James Bond: "What was it you said? 'Take the bloody shot.'"
M: "I made a judgment call."
James Bond: "You should have trusted me to finish the job."
M: "It was a possibility of losing you or the certainty of losing all those other agents. I made the only decision I could and you know it."
James Bond: "I think you lost your nerve."
M: "What are you expecting, a bloody apology? You know the rules of the game. You've been playing it long enough. We both have."
James Bond: "Maybe too long."
M: "Speak for yourself."

M: "I fucked this up, didn't I?"

(Last lines)
Mallory: "So, 007, lots to be done. Are you ready to get back to work?"
Bond: "With pleasure, M. With pleasure."

Facts and Figures

SEXUAL ENCOUNTERS

<u>Three</u>: In Turkey, the woman listed only as "Bond's lover," Eve, and Severine (regarding Eve, see *Did They or Didn't They?* under Bond Girls)

BOND'S CARS

1964 Aston Martin DB5 (silver)

DEATHS

<u>Approximately fifty-seven:</u>

- 2 already down plus Ronson in the pre-titles
- CNN reports six dead at MI6 but M is with 8 coffins, so count 8
- Patrice kills two (a guard and his target). Patrice. Severine's bodyguard. Hussein assassinated on TV. M says three agents are dead (assume Hussein is one of them).
- 3 of Silva's men on the island. Silva kills 2 guards while escaping, 3 guards at the hearing. There's a lot of gunfire and confusion at the hearing but it seems like 5.
- At Skyfall, Bond gets 4 right away with the DB5, then Kincade gets 2, 3 down from booby traps, then Bond shoots 2, Kincade gets 1, then Bond gets 2 more, 2 in the helicopter, plus 5 when Skyfall blows (we saw 7 plus Silva get off the helicopter and there are now 2 left), Bond kills 1 in the water, Silva, M.

Bond Kills

- <u>Thirteen</u> directly: 3 of Silva's guards on the island, 9 of Silva's men at Skyfall, Silva
- <u>Nine</u> indirectly: Patrice (he falls), Severine's bodyguard (the dragon gets him), 2 in the helicopter when Bond blows Skyfall, plus 5 of Silva's men in the blast

EXPLOSIONS

<u>Ten</u>: Vauxhall goes up in a boom. There's a small one in the tube station, another small one to blow Skyfall's door, and 2 sparkly ones when M blows the light fixtures, then 2 more. A big one when the Aston Martin DB5 is blown up, which makes you think that's the big one and so when Skyfall itself blows, you think *that's* it, and wow, and then the helicopter crashes into Skyfall, and WOW that's impressive.

BOND'S FOOD AND DRINKS

Vodka Martinis

<u>One</u>: With Severine in the casino (she has champagne)

Other Drinks

- A Heineken in Turkey with his lover
- In the bar in Turkey, a whiskey while betting on the scorpion
- In the bar the next morning, there's an empty glass beside him. He then buys a whiskey and takes the bottle and a glass from behind the bar
- He has a bottle of bourbon and a glass when M comes home to find him there
- On the Chimera (Severine's yacht) she has a bottle of champagne and two glasses waiting for him
- 1962 Macallan whisky with Silva (he drinks his when Silva puts the other on Severine's head)

Food

None.

GAMBLING AND SPORTS

- I'm not sure if there's a name for betting on whether or not a scorpion will bite you—but they did that.
- Bond swims at his hotel in Shanghai.
- At the Macau casino, Bond bets at a roulette table and then tells Eve to put the suitcase full of money on red.

Amaze Your Friends!

- The scenes of Bond living in a beach town after being "killed" were filmed in Calis Beach, Fethiye, Turkey. Assuming we're meant to believe Bond is living more or less where he washed ashore, it's definitely not Calis Beach, which is almost 500 miles from Istanbul, and on a different body of water entirely (the Aegean Sea, whereas Istanbul is on the Sea of Marmara).

- The painting Q and Bond discuss in the National Gallery is The Fighting Temeraire (1838) by Turner.
- Silva's base is inspired by Hashima Island, off the coast of Nagasaki. The real island was used for reference footage and a CGI-enhanced establishing shot. In the film, it is nowhere near Nagasaki, but is a short yacht trip from Macau.
- In defending herself before the board of enquiry, M quotes from Tennyson's "Ulysses."
- The box M leaves to Bond gives her name as "Olivia Mansfield." This was seen in a 2013 prop exhibition.
- Director Sam Mendes intended the gunbarrel to be at the opening of the film, "If you see the film, the film starts with Bond walking down a corridor towards camera and lifting a gun. The gunbarrel is him walking, stopping and lifting a gun. When I put the two together it looked ridiculous - shoot the gun already! We tried and couldn't make it work."
- The obituary reads "A senior officer of the Ministry of Defence, Commander Bond, C.M.G., R.N., is missing, believed killed, while on an official mission to Turkey.
    Commander Bond..."
- Bond's parents' gravestone reads
    "In memory of/Andrew Bond/and/Monique Delacroix Bond"
- This is the first use of the word "fuck" (fucked) in a Bond movie.
- A deleted scene explains the scheme that Patrice and Severine were involved with. Stolen paintings were sold to art collectors; when the collectors arrived to pay, they were murdered, allowing Silva to keep both the money and the painting.

Most Interesting Goofs

Who Are You? Bond says to Eve, "We've never been formally introduced." Really? They were on a mission together!

Instant Will: The conversation about British fortitude, and indeed the conversation about the bulldog ornament, both took place well after M might have had an opportunity to update her will.

How Many Home Invaders? Silva's first group spreads out and 12 can easily be counted. But 14 are killed before the helicopter arrives– either a goof or 2 were wounded and got back up.

Underground Slide: (From MI6-HQ.com) All London Underground escalators have safety signs placed on the medians between stairs to prevent anyone from sliding down them.

FIFTY YEARS OF BOND

Ten years after the fortieth anniversary homages embedded in *Die Another Day* (see YOUR TWENTIETH, I BELIEVE), Eon decided to repeat the trick with a host of references and homages in *Skyfall*, to honor Bond's fiftieth anniversary.

Predictably, fans behaved the same way, finding references under every rock. In an effort not to be repetitive, I'll skip the unlikely and ridiculous, and just list the clearly visible references as well as some maybes that are fun to contemplate. Even greatly reducing the list of "references" that fans have cited, to those I find at least somewhat plausible, I still think the final list is significantly longer than what Eon intended. Still, enough of these are real that they remain fun to examine.

References that I think are 100% certainly intentional are highlighted in **bold**.

Dr. No

The *Dr. No* "homages" don't reference the film at all. Rather, they mark the release date of the first movie, referencing the whole idea of "fifty years of Bond."

- **Silva offers Bond 50 year-old Macallan whiskey, with its year, 1962, clearly visible. 1962 is the year *Dr. No* was released, and *Skyfall* in 2002 was its 50ᵗʰ anniversary.**
- **On October 5, 2012, 50 years to the day after Bond's film debut, at 00:07 a.m. GMT, Adele's "Skyfall" theme song was released.**

From Russia with Love

- In the pre-titles sequence of *Skyfall*, Bond runs through the Istanbul Grand Bazaar, where Kerim Bey had his secret offices.
- In *Skyfall*, Tanner remarks about rats in the MI6 tunnel; Kerim Bey and Bond walk through rat-infested tunnels in Istanbul.
- In *From Russia with Love,* Bond garrotes a villain with his own garrote. Similarly, Bond garrotes Patrice with his stolen hard drive necklace.

Goldfinger

- Bond says to Q, "You must be joking," (the same line is used as a tribute in *Die Another Day*).
- The small radio homer Q provides is quite similar to the one in *Goldfinger*.

Live and Let Die

- The komodo dragon sequence could be seen as a callback to *Live and Let Die*, which had an alligator that had taken a bite out of the villain's henchman, and had Bond escaping a similar fate by walking across alligators' backs. In *Skyfall*, a henchman meets a worse fate, and Bond's escape is similar.
- Both movies have flaming skulls in the title sequence.

The Man with the Golden Gun

- In each movie, a bullet is analyzed after it is removed from Bond's body.
- In each movie, Bond visits a floating casino in Macau; the Macau Palace in *The Man with the Golden Gun,* and the Floating Dragon Casino in *Skyfall*.

For Your Eyes Only

- Bond provides analysis of the bullet taken from his chest, saying it's "for her eyes only."
- The line "That's putting it mildly," is spoken in both films.

Octopussy

- A car chase comes to a climax atop a train before Bond wrestles a henchman through a train tunnel. (It's hard to know if this is a conscious nod to *Octopussy* or a film cliché.

Licence to Kill

- In *Licence to Kill,* Pam wears a backless black dress with a Beretta 950 strapped to her thigh, at the villain's casino. In *Skyfall*, Severine wears a backless black dress, a Beretta 70 strapped to her thigh, at the villain's casino. The thigh-holster was also noted as a reference in *Die Another Day,* when Peaceful Fountains of Desire wore one to Bond's room.
- Bond is given a signature gun that reads his prints and locks for any other user.

GoldenEye

- Q says to Bond, "What did you expect, an exploding pen?" In *GoldenEye*, this is exactly what Q does give to Bond.
- In *GoldenEye*, M says, "Unlike the American government we prefer not to get our bad news from CNN." In *Skyfall*, we see Bond getting bad news from CNN (Wolf Blitzer specifically).
- Both *GoldenEye* and *Skyfall* make reference to Bond being an orphan, and MI6 recruiting orphans. It is unlikely to me that this is a specific *GoldenEye* reference, and more likely that both are callbacks to Ian Fleming's writing. The novel **You Only Live Twice** reveals that Bond is an orphan. A recent book about Maxwell Knight, the real-life inspiration for M, states that, yes,

MI5 and MI6 recruit orphans because they are loyal and see their spymaster as a "father figure." Ian Fleming, of course, would know this. In *GoldenEye*, 006 says, "We're both orphans, James...MI6 knew my background when they recruited me." In *Skyfall*, M says, "Orphans always make the best recruits."

Die Another Day

- Both movies refer to the 1997 transition of power in Hong Kong. This is probably a coincidence, and not a reference, but it is interesting nonetheless.
- In *Die Another Day*, Bond is tortured in Asia, and doesn't break. He mentions he threw away the cyanide capsule meant for such a situation. He is then traded in a prisoner exchange. In *Skyfall*, MI6 agent Silva is traded in a prisoner exchange, and then tortured in Asia without breaking. He takes his cyanide capsule and does not die. Refusal to break and the cyanide capsule can both be seen as direct Fleming references.
- A villain shoots depleted uranium bullets at Bond in both movies.

Casino Royale

- Both movies have Bond saying "Don't touch your ear" to someone undercover. (One could see this as a character trait or a particular caution of Bond's, rather than a homage through the fourth wall.)
- In both movies, Bond uses construction equipment in a chase (a frontloader in *Casino Royale,* an excavator in *Skyfall*).
- In both movies, MI6 implants a tracker into Bond's body. (This is likely an ongoing concern of MI6's rather than a homage.)
- Bond examines himself in a mirror, bleeding, before he rinses the blood under the sink's tap.
- In *Casino Royale*, M says, "Bond, don't ever break into my house again." In *Skyfall*, he does so.

Quantum of Solace

- Bond pursues a villain across tiled city rooftops. Normally I'd consider this a weak statement—like "Bond gets into a fight"—but the visual similarity is striking.

THE AGE OF BOND GIRLS

This originally appeared as an essay on The Film Experience *(http://thefilmexperi-ence.net/) prior to the release* of Spectre. *It has been edited and updated.*

W hen Monica Bellucci was announced as part of the cast of *Spectre*, the media was replete with headlines like "James Bond finally falls for a woman his own age." It was the oft-repeated "finally" that put me in an analytic mood. Was this really the first time ("finally") that Bond has been with a woman his own age? How often has there been a really large age disparity?

I analyzed each movie to derive some statistics. James Bond is almost al-ways with two or more women per film, but we can generally identify the "main" and "secondary" woman. I decided, for the sake of my own sanity, to disregard however many other women there might be, with the following exceptions: *You Only Live Twice* has three women of almost equal importance. Meanwhile, *On Her Majesty's Secret Service, The Spy Who Loved Me*, and *The Living Daylights* give us only one im-portant woman each. Sure, Bond made love to other women in each film, but they had little screen time and were strictly fly-by-night. Let's not trouble ourselves.

No Firsts for Bellucci

Spectre is not the first time that Bond has been with a woman his own age, alt-hough Bellucci is definitely the oldest woman who has had a primary or secondary love interest role in a Bond movie—she was 51 in 2015, when *Spectre* was re-leased. In four previous films, Bond has been with a woman older than himself. Syl-via Trench (Eunice Gayson), appearing in both *Dr. No* and *From Russia with Love*, was 2 years older than her costar. Pussy Galore (Honor Blackman), in *Goldfin-ger*, was five years older. Tracy di Vicenzo, the woman Bond married in *On Her Maj-esty's Secret Service*, was played by Diana Rigg who was a year older than George Lazenby's Bond. It's interesting that Tracy, the most important woman in Bond his-tory was not a younger woman. And then in *Spectre*, Monica Bellucci is four years older than current Bond actor Daniel Craig.

The Younger Women

How many years younger is too young? It's kind of random; any number could be ar-gued. As my own spouse is seven years younger than me, I chose seven years as a reasonable cut-off. That gives us only three additional instances of Bond being within an appropriate distance of his costar; in all cases, these were Sean Connery films (Honey Ryder, Jill Masterson, and Fiona Volpe make the cut-off). Upping the range to 8 years adds Eve Moneypenny to the list, and upping it to 9 means that Paris Carver and Solange are included (costars of Pierce Brosnan and Daniel Craig, respectively). There is no reasonable range, though, that includes any Roger Moore or Timothy Dalton movie.

Paris Carver (Teri Hatcher) is an interesting case. In *Tomorrow Never Dies*, she's a woman from Bond's past; you'd think a little age would work for the role. Teri Hatcher was 33 when she played the part; Sela Ward, who was 41, was considered but rejected specifically because of her age.

007 Ages. Bond Girls Do Not.

One of the obvious causes of age disparity is that the "right" age for a beautiful woman is frozen in these films. Bond's age range is vast, from 30 in *On Her Majesty's Secret Service*, to 58 in *A View to a Kill*. Yet every woman in the Bond movies prior to *Spectre* is between 21 and 39. While each actor (except Lazenby, who played 007 but once) ages in the role, the women he plays opposite do not. This means that the age disparity increases per film per actor, and in the case of Moore, who was the oldest Bond by far (he made 4 films past the age where every other Bond actor had hung up his license to kill), it's really dramatic... even uncomfortable.

The thing about Roger Moore is he was incredibly young-looking, even though he was actually older than Connery. At the point where Connery was looking long in the tooth (42, gray, and a little paunchy in *Diamonds Are Forever*) Moore came along with a perfect, unlined baby face. Moore was 46 in *Live and Let Die*, making him 22 years older than costar Jane Seymour. But because he looked no more than 35, it didn't seem egregious. Unfortunately, when time caught up with Moore, it did so all at once; suddenly he was a dirty old man, still sleeping with women in their 20s when he was 58.

Age difference was actually addressed in *For Your Eyes Only*, wherein Bond finally met a woman he deemed too young. Bibi Dahl (Lynn-Holly Johnson), attempts to seduce Bond. He turns her down with, "You get your clothes on, and I'll buy you an ice cream." Bibi Dahl ("baby doll"—get it?) is dressed and treated as a teenager, and Bond has no interest in sleeping with her.

In real life, though, the actress was 23 at the time, just a year younger than Carole Bouquet, who played the main Bond girl, and was fully 30 years younger than Moore.

Daniel Craig, the Loner

Let's take a moment to acknowledge that Daniel Craig's movies have all been outliers where romance is concerned. *Casino Royale* gives us the most conventional "Bond girl" relationship, but even then, Bond is alone at the end for the first time in 007 film history. It is common for a secondary Bond girl to be killed in the course of a film, but only in *Casino Royale* did both women die. In *Quantum of Solace*, Bond never sleeps with the primary Bond girl; he again ends up alone. In *Skyfall*, the only woman who can be seen as a primary love interest is Eve Moneypenny (although we don't know that's who she is until the end). The movie gives us a "did they or didn't they" scene to keep the long history of flirtation between 007 and M's assistant alive. *Skyfall* is the third of three Daniel Craig Bond movies in which 007 ends up alone—Eve Moneypenny now behind her iconic desk, and the secondary Bond girl (Bérénice Marlohe, 33 at the time) dead at about the film's halfway point.

So, this brings us to *Spectre*: The presence of Lucia (Bellucci) is unusual, but for a Daniel Craig movie...that's not unusual.

Some Numbers

- Sean Connery averaged just eight years older than his costars.
- George Lazenby was a year younger than his only important costar.
- Roger Moore averaged an appalling 22 years older than the women he was involved with as Bond.
- Timothy Dalton averaged 19 years older.
- Pierce Brosnan averaged 14.5 years older.
- Daniel Craig is 10 years older on average (including Monica Bellucci).
- Overall average is 14.5.

Adding in *No Time to Die*

As of this writing, *No Time to Die* remains unreleased.

- Madeline Swann returns—only the second Bond girl (after Sylvia Trench) to make a repeat appearance, and the first primary Bond girl to do so. Obviously, the age difference between Léa Seydoux and Daniel Craig remains the same.
- Paloma (Ana de Armas) appears destined to be the main Bond girl (I'm guessing). She is three years younger than Léa Seydoux.
- Lashana Lynch plays Nomi. She is a year older than Ana de Armas. As I am mostly not counting a third woman per film, I'm leaving her age out.
- Craig's average increases to almost 12 years, and the overall average goes up to almost 15.

SPECTRE (2015)

Survey Says!

> Percent Favorite: 1.5%
> Top 5 Cumulative: 18/25
> Numeric Rating: 6.4/10
> Ranking: 16.1 (19th/25)

My Rating and Ranking

> Rated: 7/10
> Ranked: 17 out of 25

Summary

James Bond, without the authority or knowledge of MI6, pursues a lead left to him by M after her death. The trail takes him to Mr. White, who sends Bond to his daughter, Madeline Swann. Bond discovers a conspiracy involving terrorist attacks around the world, connected to a man named Franz Oberhauser, whom he knows from childhood. Meanwhile C, head of the Joint Security Service, wants to dismantle the 00 program and bring all the world's security services under a single all-seeing umbrella. Bond and Swann find Oberhauser, who is now named Ernst Stavro Blofeld. Blofeld reveals that C is working for him, and that all the tragic events of Bond's past were orchestrated by Blofeld. Bond and Swann escape and get to London in time to stop C's Joint Security Service from controlling all world intelligence. C is killed but Bond declines to kill Blofeld, instead leaving MI6 to ride off with Madeline Swann.

> **James Bond:** Daniel Craig
> **Madeline Swann:** Léa Seydoux
> **Oberhauser/Ernst Stavro Blofeld:** Christoph Waltz
> **Lucia Sciarra:** Monica Bellucci
> **Hinx:** Dave Bautista
> **Mr. White:** Jesper Christensen
> **C:** Andrew Scott
> **Marco Sciarra:** Alessandro Cremona
> **Estrella:** Stephanie Sigman
> **M:** Ralph Fiennes
> **Eve Moneypenny:** Naomie Harris
> **Q:** Ben Whishaw
> **Tanner:** Rory Kinnear
> **Directed by** Sam Mendes

Discussion

Spectre is a movie with good points and bad points. It is, no doubt, bloated and over-long, with ill-conceived villains and a meandering plot. It's also lush and beautiful, with praiseworthy locations, interesting characters, and fabulous cars. With points on both sides of the scale (points we'll discuss shortly), why is this movie not a mid-pack one, but instead, so reviled? It all comes down to "retconning."

According to Merriam-Webster, which traces the earliest use to 1973, "*Retcon* is a shortened form of *retroactive continuity*, and refers to a literary device in which the form or content of a previously established narrative is changed." To retcon is to rewrite history in order to make it fit with the current plot. Often, a retcon corrects an error, such as when an entire early issue of "The Hulk" referred to the hero as "Robert Banner" instead of "Bruce Banner." This was retconned by later saying that the character's full name is Robert Bruce Banner.

Spectre is retconning on a massive scale, and the thing is, it is done for no real reason. Blofeld didn't *need* to be the 'author of all Bond's pain.' There was no past inconsistency or error being cleaned up by this grand unification of all of Bond's adventures. Rather, screenwriters John Logan, Neal Purvis, and Robert Wade simply...felt like it? It must have seemed, in the writing, magnificent. It was not.

Tying all of the Daniel Craig movies together doesn't make sense. It isn't "grand." Instead, it feels petty and small. Set aside—for now—the thousand ways that it makes no sense at all, that it doesn't fit the facts as laid out in the previous movies. It takes James Bond, unbreakable spy, strong, resolute, loyal, standing for what he believes is right, and it takes his enemies and their complex and implacable evil, and turns the whole thing into an unresolved squabble between two young boys. Ernst Stavro Blofeld, feared mastermind in a total of five Eon movies (plus *Never Say Never Again*), faceless evil in two of them, is now reduced to a jealous child.

His schemes, as laid out when we first meet him—the masterful conference room scene in Italy—are wide-ranging, genuinely evil, and worthy in scope of a complex international crime organization, which is what SPECTRE is. But when we get to his Moroccan compound and see yet another room full of computers that know all—already a cliché in *Skyfall*, and now a repetitive one—the power of that organization is reduced in our eyes. This is just another hacker. Bond was tied to a chair in that room full of computers by Silva, now he's bound to a chair *near* it by Blofeld. Much of it is incredibly well done, but that's not the point. The point is, this film takes away the magic, and replaces it with the banal, and that is unforgivable. As beautiful as the film is, as excellent as several of its sequences are, retconning Blofeld just pissed fans off.

As I said, most retcons are created to fix errors. Sometimes they tie up loose ends to move a story forward. But this one, because it was sloppily done, *creates* errors and loose ends. How did Blofeld know that Vesper and Bond would be assigned together? If he didn't, then her betrayal had nothing to do with 'authoring Bond's pain.' If he did, well, how could he? How could he know that Le Chiffre would lose all his money and try to win it back at poker, and that MI6 would send Bond to that game, as well as a Treasury agent? How could Blofeld have known that Bond would pursue Patrice, and through him, find Silva? How is that a chess board to arrange?

And why bring in Bond's childhood anyway? The Craig movies have spent too much time "inventing" Bond. *Casino Royale* was supposed to do that, the film in which he earns his 00, and gets the rough edges knocked off. It's a legitimate, if controversial, choice to "reboot" the series, but at this point, it's well and truly re-booted. Then, *Quantum of Solace* decided to keep up with the invention aspect, directly following *Casino Royale* and ending with the gunbarrel, as if to say, *now* he's Bond. Next, *Skyfall* is a meditation on the meaning of Bond, the 00 section, and British fortitude. It's also a journey to Bond's childhood, showing his parents' grave-stone as he loses his surrogate mother. Why, then, does Craig's fourth movie *also* have to be an origin story? James Bond doesn't need more origin, he just needs his next adventure.

All of the above is rather darkly critical, but there is much to commend *Spectre*. The pre-titles sequence is nothing short of magnificent (see HEROIN-FLAVORED BA-NANAS). It's not just the stunning tracking shot—although it really is stunning. (*Spectre* director Sam Mendes was nominated for an Oscar in 2020 for *1917*, a movie in which virtually the entire thing is a single tracking shot.) It's that everything we love about Bond is packed into the sequence. There's the exquisite use of location, the gorgeous Dios de la Muerte celebration (reminiscent of *Thunderball*'s Junkanoo), Bond smoothly following the villain while taking time to seduce (or be seduced by) a beautiful woman. Then seamlessly moving to his mission, and when it goes awry, rolling with the punches, for a terrific chase, yet another ill-fated helicopter (they all do seem to explode in Bond movies, don't they?), fantastic mid-air stunt work, and even a bit of humor.

Bond's return to London is great as well. All the bureaucracy nonsense is a slog, but then we get to Bond's apartment, M's mysterious video, some good fun with Q, and then Italy.

Everything in Italy is genuinely magnificent. It's not merely that the filming is gorgeous, which it is, but that the location gets a top-notch Bond treatment. Rome is my favorite kind of Bond location, very rooted, not a 'tourism highlights' reel, but a real look around. The funeral, the Sciarra mansion, the secret meeting, and the car chase all showcase Rome beautifully.

The funeral and Bond's ensuing tryst with Lucia Sciarra are terrific scenes. Chilling, mysterious, then a melancholy mix of tragic and sexy. I love that Bond left Felix's contact information with Lucia—this is the man who left Solange and Fields to die, and he's not making the same mistake this time.

The SPECTRE conference is another scene reminiscent of *Thunderball*. It begins well, but then we get the needle scratch of Blofeld recognizing Bond. Of course, this could have gone any number of ways, so the first time I saw the movie, it intrigued me. Now? Now I know how it all ends, so I despise it. But it leads to a great car chase, with a combination of action and humor that Craig's movies have completely lacked hitherto. Sorry about 009's taste in music, James.

And then Austria. Once again, well-deployed locations, the remote cabin and the clinic are both worthy of the Ken Adam era. This is production designer Dennis Gassner's third consecutive Bond film, and he's done great work each time, but this movie is his best—every design element feels lush and classic. I haven't yet mentioned Morocco, or the train, or Blofeld's lair—they're all perfection.

The scene with a broken and dying Mr. White is a highlight of this film, atmospheric and compelling. You can hardly call White's death tragic—he was a villain through and through—but he created sympathy at the end. It leads into the next scene, Bond's first meeting with Madeline, which is also excellent, and also classic Bond. The contrast in these two scenes is stark; the shadowy, gloomy, dirty cabin of the father, the bright, airy, angular, clean clinic of the daughter.

Bam, bam, bam, good scene follows good scene. Q's escape on the ski lift, the car chase and Hinx's rising from apparent death, L'Americain. It's easy to look at each of these pieces and think you're watching a very good movie. But alas.

By the way, since Hinx rose from apparent death in Austria, are we meant to be sure he won't do so again? He was pulled from a moving train, but we never saw him die.

When I think of *Spectre*, I think of Mexico City first. I love that scene so much that it becomes hard to remember how much I dislike the retconning, or Christoph Waltz as Blofeld. Waltz is terribly miscast. His manic style of gleeful villainy worked in *Inglourious Basterds* but doesn't suit the character. We've had, over the years, Blofeld who is cool and removed, Blofeld who is thuggish and mean, and Blofeld who is just a bit gay, but we've never before had a "cuckoo" Blofeld, wild-eyed and grinning.

The movie is long, and meandering, with many good scenes, but on the other hand *so many* scenes. Plot holes begin to force themselves into one's field of vision. Why were three different killers (Sciarra, Guerra, and Hinx) sent to kill White when he'd already been poisoned? Why send *six* guys to pick up one non-violent doctor at her clinic? Irritation creeps in—has a "secretly the villain" character ever been more obvious than C? Eon got it right with Elektra in *The World is Not Enough*—we were fooled. This time he might as well be twirling his moustache. Why is Bond rogue and grounded again? Didn't we *just* do that?

Finally, we arrive at Blofeld's compound, magnificently designed and presented. Bond's arrival is note-by-note a repeat of *Dr. No*—the obsequious welcome, the change of clothes in locked rooms. An auspicious beginning, yet now we well and truly tank, with the long and drawn out story about poor Franz's poor childhood. Again, the torture is a powerful scene, except that Waltz gets on my nerves, but the container ruins the contents.

And now, *now*, we still have to get back to London, have an endless, *endless* denouement about Bond's past (with helpful pictures), blow up a building, kill C, crash *another* helicopter, break up with Madeline, reunite with Madeline, and steal another Aston Martin from Q. I'm exhausted just typing it all up.

I feel like, in the future, this will be a movie I will greatly enjoy watching in half-hour segments from time to time, but right now, I'm too mad at it.

The High Points
- The return of the opening gunbarrel
- The opening tracking shot through Mexico City
- A mid-air helicopter roll *are you kidding me*
- Great locations and great production design throughout
- Lush cinematography with an interesting play of light and shadow
- Beautiful Thomas Newman score
- Monica Bellucci as Lucia

- A complex and interesting main Bond girl, Madeline Swann, who lets us believe Bond would ride off with her at the end
- A scary, nearly unbeatable henchman in Hinx, who brings back the Oddjob vibe to the henchman role
- A terrific chase with a gadget-laden Aston Martin through the streets of Rome
- The re-introduction of humor (but not camp) into Bond action sequences
- Respectful, not kitsch, nods to past Bond films (*Thunderball* conference room, *From Russia with Love* train fight, *For Your Eyes Only* helicopter fight, *Dr. No* villain's lair)
- Ralph Fiennes's first full-film performance as M, bringing together, at last, the traditional MI6 team of M, Q, Moneypenny, and Bond (and Tanner).

The Low Points

- The retconning of Bond's past to insert Blofeld's influence into every earlier Craig movie
- Christoph Waltz's weird Blofeld portrayal
- The fairly ridiculous house of horrors, with pictures from Bond's past, constructed in the derelict MI6 building
- Obvious CGI when the roof Bond is on collapses in the pre-titles sequence
- Andrew Scott's over-obvious villainy as C
- The insanely long run-time and the bloat it allows.

Quotable Quotes

Sciarra: "A la muerte."
Buyer: "A la muerte."
Bond: "Bottom's up."

James Bond: "I'm sorry for your loss."
Lucia Sciarra "You knew my husband?"
James Bond: "All too briefly."
Lucia Sciarra: "What do you do?"
James Bond: "Life insurance."
Lucia Sciarra: "A little late for that."
James Bond: "For your husband, yes. What about you?"
Lucia Sciarra: "Me?"
James Bond: "I hear the life expectancy of some widows can be very short."
Lucia Sciarra: "How can you talk like this? Can't you see I'm grieving?"
James Bond: "No."

Blofeld: "You're a kite dancing in a hurricane Mr. Bond. So long."

Madeline Swann: "Don't think for one moment this is where I fall into your arms seeking solace for my dead Daddy."

M: "You're a cocky little bastard, aren't you?"
C: "I'll take that as a compliment."
M: "I wouldn't."

Facts and Figures

SEXUAL ENCOUNTERS

Three: Estrella (in the pre-titles sequence), Lucia Sciarra, and Madeline Swann

BOND'S CARS

> 2015 Aston Martin DB10
> 1964 Aston Martin DB5

DEATHS

Twenty-eight (not counting the mass terrorist attacks)

- Three men with Sciarra, Sciarra, the helicopter pilot, two men who come for Lucia, Hinx kills Guerra, White is poisoned.
- Six of Hinx's men at the clinic and ensuing chase
- Hinx is pulled off the train but we don't get confirmation that he's dead
- Ten guards escaping Blofeld's compound, C, two pilots in Blofeld's helicopter.

Bond Kills

- Seventeen directly: Two of the men with Sciarra, Sciarra, the helicopter pilot, two men who come for Lucia, one of Hinx's men at the clinic, Hinx (if we assume he's dead), ten of Blofeld's guards
- Eight indirectly: One of the men with Sciarra dies in the explosion, five of Hinx's men in crashes during the chase, two pilots in Blofeld's helicopter.

EXPLOSIONS

Seven: The pre-titles bomb explosion that topples a building. In the chase leaving the clinic, one of the cars explodes crashing into a building. A bigger one when the small plane crashes. In the Morocco compound, Bond's watch, then it blows the compound, then BOOM the whole compound goes. Vauxhall.

BOND'S FOOD AND DRINKS

Vodka Martinis

Two (or one): On the train, Bond and Madeline have vodka martinis dirty. At the Hoffler Klinik, Bond orders a vodka martini, but they don't serve alcohol (see below).

Other Drinks

- A bottle Macallan whisky is visible when Moneypenny goes to Bond's apartment. He offers her a drink but neither has one.
- Bond leaves a bottle of champagne for Q when he steals the DB10.

- Bond pours two glasses of champagne—for himself and Lucia—but then breaks them.
- Bond orders a vodka martini at the clinic. It is replaced with a "prolytic digestive enzyme shake," which he refuses.
- Bond finds and drinks an unidentified bottle at L'Americain—as it is a clear bottle and Belvedere has a promotional relationship with the film, it could be Belvedere vodka; Madeline declines to share it, and drinks red wine.
- When the mouse wakes him at L'Americain, Bond seems to have a beer.
- He is offered champagne at Blofeld's compound and declines.

Food

None.

GAMBLING AND SPORTS

None

Amaze Your Friends!

- The safe house is called "Hildebrand." This is a reference to an Ian Fleming short story, "The Hildebrand Rarity." Elements of that story appear in the movie *Licence to Kill*.
- In the Bond novels and earlier films, SPECTRE is an acronym for Special Executive for Counter-intelligence, Terrorism, Revenge, and Extortion, and is properly spelled in all-caps. The movie *Spectre* doesn't say what, if anything, the word stands for, and the title is styled "Spectre." For consistency, I'm continuing to capitalize the name of the organization (but not the film)—perhaps in *No Time to Die* we'll find out if this is right or wrong.
- The building for the "Hoffler Klinik" is actually a restaurant, the Ice Q, in the ski resort town of Sölden, Austria. The location now also houses an exhibit called "007 Elements."
- At 148 minutes, *Spectre* is the longest Bond movie to date. It will be surpassed by *No Time to Die,* at 163 minutes.

Most Interesting Goofs

Bloodless DNA: Bond takes a bloody ring from Sciarra's finger. By the time he hands it to Q it is completely clean. Yet, despite the fact that Bond has handled it and it has been wiped clean, Q is able to detect DNA traces. Goof or ridiculous pseudo-science? You decide.

Carry on, nothing to see here: No police react to the massive explosion and building toppling in Mexico City, and no crowds are dispersed as a helicopter comes *that* close to crashing into them.

Not that dirty: Bond and Madeline order "dirty" vodka martinis on the train, but the drinks arrive clear. Dirty martinis have olive juice and are not clear.

Doomed? Thallium poisoning is treatable, even after several weeks.

The guests in the next room must have hated him: Mr. White returned to L'Americain every year, often with Madeline. Yet she didn't know he had a secret room there. Additionally, the only way into that secret room was to build and tear down a wall each visit, yet she never noticed. This seems...unlikely.

THE RATINGS AND RANKINGS

Because these surveys always generate such interest, I am putting them all in one place here. "Fan" favorites are survey results, I am contrasting them with my personal votes.

One of the things that changed dramatically in the years between the first edition of this book and the latest has been how survey results have been obtained. There are fewer discussion boards in the world, meaning data from general movie fans have been harder to find (the IMDb, for example, once had lively discussion boards). Social media tends to be harder to poll.

It's also pretty fascinating to look at how opinions have shifted over the years, so I am here presenting the 2006 data side-by-side with 2020's updates.

Favorite Film

2006 Fans: *Goldfinger* by an untouchable margin of over 25%.
2020 Fans: *On Her Majesty's Secret Service*, at a passionate 17%
Mine: *From Russia with Love*

Top Five Cumulative

Obviously, the top five of any one person matches the first five movies on their ranking (below). But a large number of number 2 or 3 votes, e.g. will push a movie up on a top five cumulative list, so that the top five of fans surveyed differs slightly from the full rankings.

Fans in 2006	Fans in 2020	Mine
1. *Goldfinger*	1. *On Her Majesty's Secret Service*	1. *From Russia with Love*
2. *From Russia with Love*	2. *From Russia with Love*	2. *Casino Royale*
3. *The Spy Who Loved Me*	3. *Casino Royale*	2. *GoldenEye*
4. *GoldenEye*	4. *Goldfinger*	4. *The Living Daylights*
5. *The Living Daylights*	5. *The Living Daylights*	3. *The Spy Who Loved Me*

Ranking (Films in Order of Preference)

Fans in 2006	Fans in 2020	Mine
1. *Goldfinger*	1. *On Her Majesty's Secret Service* (+3)	1. *From Russia with Love*
2. *From Russia with Love*	2. *From Russia with Love*	2. *Casino Royale*
3. *The Spy Who Loved Me*	3. *Casino Royale*	3. *GoldenEye*
4. *On Her Majesty's Secret Service*	4. *Goldfinger* (-3)	4. *The Living Daylights*

Fans in 2006	Fans in 2020	Mine
5. *GoldenEye*	5. *Dr. No* (+3)	5. *The Spy Who Loved Me*
6. *For Your Eyes Only*	6. *The Spy Who Loved Me* (-3)	6. *Diamonds Are Forever*
7. *The Living Daylights*	7. *The Living Daylights*	7. *Goldfinger*
8. *Dr. No*	8. *Thunderball* (+1)	8. *Dr. No*
9. *Thunderball*	9. *GoldenEye*	9. *Tomorrow Never Dies*
10. *You Only Live Twice*	10. *For Your Eyes Only* (-4)	10. *Skyfall*
11. *The World is Not Enough*	11. *Licence to Kill* (+5)	11. *You Only Live Twice*
12. *Die Another Day*	12. *Skyfall*	12. *Thunderball*
13. *Tomorrow Never Dies*	13. *Live and Let Die* (+2)	13. *Licence to Kill*
14. *Octopussy*	14. *You Only Live Twice* (-4)	14. *Die Another Day*
15. *Live and Let Die*	15. *Octopussy* (-1)	15. *Octopussy*
16. *Licence to Kill*	16. *Moonraker* (+2)	16. *For Your Eyes Only*
17. *Diamonds Are Forever*	17. *Quantum of Solace*	17. *Spectre*
18. *Moonraker*	18. *Tomorrow Never Dies* (-5)	18. *The World is Not Enough*
19. *The Man with the Golden Gun*	19. *Spectre*	19. *Quantum of Solace*
20. *A View To a Kill*	20. *The Man with the Golden Gun* (-1)	20. *The Man with the Golden Gun*
21. *Never Say Never Again*	21. *The World is Not Enough* (-10)	21. *Never Say Never Again*
	22. *Diamonds Are Forever* (-5)	22. *Moonraker*
	23. *A View To a Kill* (-3)	23. *On Her Majesty's Secret Service*
	24. *Never Say Never Again* (-3)	24. *Live and Let Die*
	25. *Die Another Day* (-13)	25. *A View to a Kill*

Numeric Ratings

There was simply not enough data from fans this time around—ratings in 2020 combine the data found on three sites: Metacritic, Rotten Tomatoes, and IMDb.

Movie	Fans 2006	Critics 2020	Mine
Dr. No	8.9	8.2	9
From Russia with Love	9.25	8.47	10
Goldfinger	8.8	8.73	9
Thunderball	8.05	7.4	9
You Only Live Twice	5.57	6.77	8
On Her Majesty's Secret Service	9.27	6.93	4

Movie	Fans 2006	Critics 2020	Mine
Diamonds Are Forever	5.75	6.37	8
Live and Let Die	5.42	6.30	2
The Man with the Golden Gun	4.35	5.17	6
The Spy Who Loved Me	7.37	6.83	10
Moonraker	3.27	6.33	5
For Your Eyes Only	8.38	6.43	7
Never Say Never Again	6.97	5.67	5
Octopussy	4.0	6.57	7
A View To a Kill	2.58	4.67	2
The Living Daylights	7.57	6.63	10
Licence to Kill	8.02	6.70	7
GoldenEye	7.72	7.17	10
Tomorrow Never Dies	7.1	5.80	9
The World is Not Enough	7.6	5.77	6
Die Another Day	6.8	5.8	7
Casino Royale		85.0	10
Quantum of Solace		63.0	6
Skyfall		83.3	9
Spectre		63.7	7

RESOURCES

O ver the course of a relatively short period of time, I discovered first that I was mad for James Bond, next that I enjoyed absorbing information, opinions, and trivia about 007, and finally, that I had acquired sufficient knowledge and ideas to write a book. In this process, I have found numerous resources of great value. Many I had at hand well before I began to write, but more were acquired by research as part of putting a book together. The web pages have all been checked for accuracy quite recently.

The single best way to find information about the James Bond movies is to watch the movies. Investing in the complete Blu-ray collection is invaluable; not just because the movies are always at your fingertips, but because the bonus features are interesting, informative, and expansive. Likewise, the single best way to learn about the James Bond novels is by reading them.

Books

Fiction

The Ian Fleming Material

If you're not familiar with the Fleming novels, it may surprise you to discover that they were written in a very different order than the movies were made. Reading the books in order is eye-opening. For instance, there's a famous scene at the beginning of the movie *Dr. No* in which M takes Bond's Beretta away and replaces it with the Walther PPK. M points out that the Beretta was in part responsible for an injury on Bond's last mission that hospitalized him for six months. This entire scene is taken straight from the book, but the "last mission" referred to is the mission of **From Russia with Love** —the previous book, but the next movie.

Here's the order and years in which Fleming wrote his Bond books:

- **Casino Royale** (1953)
- **Live and Let Die** (1954)
- **Moonraker** (1955)
- **Diamonds Are Forever** (1956)
- **From Russia with Love** (1957)
- **Doctor No** (1958)
- **Goldfinger** (1959)
- **For Your Eyes Only** (1960) (A collection of four short stories: "For Your Eyes Only," "Risico," "From a View to a Kill" and "The Hildebrand Rarity")
- **Thunderball** (1961)
- **The Spy Who Loved Me** (1962)
- **On Her Majesty's Secret Service** (1963)
- **You Only Live Twice** (1964)

- "007 In New York" (1964) (This short story originally appeared in U.S. editions of Fleming's non-fiction travel book, Thrilling Cities; it is included in current editions *of* **Octopussy and the Living Daylights**)
- **The Man with the Golden Gun** (1965) (Published posthumously.)
- **Octopussy and the Living Daylights** (1966) (A short story collection that originally included "Octopussy," "The Property of a Lady," and "The Living Daylights." Current editions include "007 in New York" as well. Collected posthumously.)

Figure 18: This stamp set was issued by the Royal Mail (UK) in 2008. Won by the author in a contest.

Post-Fleming Fiction

Personally, I have little interest in the post-Fleming novels (I've read a few), but that's my own quirk—I don't usually read fan fiction either. I just have an irrational passion for original sources. Many fans really enjoy the James Bond novels listed below. (I am omitting novelizations of movies, which are a different animal altogether.)

- **Colonel Sun** , by Kingsley Amis (writing as Robert Markham) (1968)
- **James Bond: The Authorized Biography of 007** , by John Pearson (1973) Ian Fleming biographer Pearson writes Bond's biography as if he is a real person, and maintains that conceit throughout this entertaining fiction disguised as fact.
- **Licence Renewed** , by John Gardner (1981)
- **For Special Services** , by John Gardner (1982)
- **Icebreaker**, by John Gardner (1983)
- **Role of Honour,** by John Gardner (1984)
- **Nobody Lives Forever**, by John Gardner (1986)
- **No Deals, Mr. Bond** , by John Gardner (1987)

- Scorpius, by John Gardner (1988)
- Win, Lose or Die , by John Gardner (1989)
- Brokenclaw, by John Gardner (1990)
- The Man from Barbarossa , by John Gardner (1991)
- Death is Forever , by John Gardner (1992)
- Never Send Flowers , by John Gardner (1993)
- Seafire, by John Gardner (1994)
- Cold (a.k.a. Coldfall), by John Gardner (1996)
- "Blast From The Past" (short story), by Raymond Benson (1997)
- "Midsummer Night's Doom" (short story), by Raymond Benson (1997)
- Zero Minus Ten , by Raymond Benson (1997)
- The Facts of Death , by Raymond Benson (1998)
- High Time to Kill , by Raymond Benson (1999)
- "Live at Five" (short story), by Raymond Benson (1999)
- Doubleshot, by Raymond Benson (2000)
- Never Dream of Dying , by Raymond Benson (2001)
- The Man With the Red Tattoo , by Raymond Benson (2002)
- Devil May Care , by Sebastian Faulks (2008)
- Carte Blanche , by Jeffery Deaver (2011)
- Solo, by William Boyd (2013)
- Trigger Mortis , by Anthony Horowitz (2015)
- Forever and a Day , by Anthony Horowitz (2018   )

The **Young Bond** books are a new series of adventures in which Bond is 13 years old. The series is marketed towards children in Harry Potter fashion. Adult fans speak highly of them.

- Young Bond: Silverfin , by Charlie Higson (2005)
- Young Bond: Blood Fever , by Charlie Higson (2006)
- Young Bond: Double or Die , by Charlie Higson (2007)
- Young Bond: Hurricane Gold , by Charlie Higson (2007)
- Young Bond: By Royal Command , by Charlie Higson (2008)
- The Young Bond Rough Guide to Lond on, by Charlie Higson Puffin Books/Rough Guides (2007) (A 64-page booklet featuring London locations from **Double or Die** .)
- Danger Society: The Young Bond Dossier , by Charlie Higson (2009) (A complete guide to Young Bond. Includes the Young Bond short story "A Hard Man to Kill")

The **Moneypenny Diaries** are official spin-off adventures of M's secretary, Miss Moneypenny (given the first name of Jane).

- The Moneypenny Diaries: Guardian Angel , by Kate Westbrook (a.k.a. Samantha Weinberg) (2006)
- "For Your Eyes Only, James," by Kate Westbrook (a.k.a. Samantha Weinberg) (2006 short story)

- **Secret Servant: The Moneypenny Diaries** , by Kate Westbrook (a.k.a. Samantha Weinberg) (2006)
- "Moneypenny's First Date With Bond," by Kate Westbrook (a.k.a. Samantha Weinberg) (2006 short story)
- **The Moneypenny Diaries: Final Fling** , by Kate Westbrook (a.k.a. Samantha Weinberg) (2008)

Non-Fiction

Behind the Scenes

- <u>Must read</u>: **The Battle for Bond: The Genesis of Cinema's Greatest Hero** , by Robert Sellers (2007)
  The definitive history of the fraught collaboration Ian Fleming, Jack Whittingham, and Kevin McClory that shaped Bond's future.

If I'm going to be completely honest, I have to say I don't love any of the "insider" books I've read by actors and crew. They're interesting for the obsessive fan like me, but often they're shoddily edited and rather pedestrian. I think what I dislike most about these autobiographical books is that they operate entirely from the author's memory—I haven't seen one yet in which the author fact-checked to make sure that what he remembers from twenty or thirty years ago is correct.

One that you might check out, which many fans are fond of, is **For My Eyes Only** by five-time Bond director John Glen. I found several errors of fact in it, but it's a wry look at the goings-on during eight of the Bond films (three for which Glen was editor/second unit director, and five which he directed).

Another good one is **My Word is My Bond** by Roger Moore. I was lucky enough to get an autographed copy from Sir Roger himself, which I naturally treasure.

Encyclopedic Books

A number of books approach the Bond films in an encyclopedic fashion, either alphabetically or chronologically (film-by-film). Some are pretty lightweight. The following are my favorites (alphabetically).

- **Adrian Turner on Goldfinger** : Bloomsbury Movie Guide No. 2, by Adrian Turner (1998).
  This is a lovely, quirky book that stands out from the crowd. Unlike other books, its focus is a single film, but more than that, it includes a little of every- thing: Trivia, interviews, even fan fiction by Mr. Turner.
- **The James Bond Encyclopedia: Updated Edition,** by John Cork and Collin Stutz (2014)
  Keep in mind that any "official" book like this one will soft-pedal criticism. This is still essential because John Cork is the keeper of encyclopedic Bond knowledge.
- **Some Kind of Hero: The Remarkable Story of the James Bond Films,** by Matthew Field and Ajay Chowdhury, (2015)

Comprehensive, with everything but the kitchen sink, by authors well-known in Bond fandom.

- **The James Bond Movie Encyclopedia**, by Steven Jay Rubin (2020, revised edition)

  An earlier edition was one of my very favorites. This new edition, reorganized, with new movies fully integrated, promises to be even better. Mr. Rubin writes well and has a huge range of material, including the Eon films, *Never Say Never Again* and both the 1954 and 1967 versions of *Casino Royale*, bless him.

- **The Essential Bond: The Authorized Guide to the World of 007**, by Lee Pfeiffer and Dave Worrall (2002, revised edition)

  Very thorough, witty, opinionated, and lavishly illustrated. This one has some of the best photos I've seen, and is incredibly comprehensive. A must-have for the Bond enthusiast. The book focuses on Eon films, and treats *Never Say Never Again* and 1967's *Casino Royale* only in a brief appendix. An updated edition includes *Die Another Day*.

- **Ian Fleming's James Bond: Annotations and Chronologies** for Ian Fleming's Bond Stories, by John Griswold (2005)

  Strictly literary, dealing with Ian Fleming's 007 novels and short stories, and not addressing the films at all, this is a delight for the obsessive fan. Truly a life's work, Griswold includes a glossary of obscure references and slang used in each tale, details the chronology of each story and its relation to the others, and provides exhaustive detail on such trivia as locations and play-by-play in the golf match between Bond and Goldfinger.

- **James Bond: The Man and His World—The Official Companion to Ian Fleming's Creation**, by Henry Chancellor (2005)

  Historian Henry Chancellor is the first Bond author granted access to Fleming's notes, drafts, and correspondence; in fact, the full Fleming archives. For Fleming literary enthusiasts, this has an enormous amount of exciting new material, but there's little about the movies.

Picture Books

- **The Essential Bond**

  Mentioned above, you just must get this one if you love pictures.

- **James Bond: 50 Years of Movie Posters**, by DK
- **James Bond: The Secret World of 007**, Updated (2008)
- **Ken Adam Designs the Movies, James Bond and Beyond**, by Ken Adam and Christopher Frayling (2008)

Social Commentary

Rather a heady category to be putting James Bond in, but some writers have noted that Bond has a social, political, and sexual content. What was going on in the real world of spying and espionage while each of the Bond films were made? How did feminism affect Bond? What was Bondmania as a social phenomenon? How has

Bond changed with the changing times? Here are three excellent books to explore if these questions intrigue you as much as they do me.

- **Ian Fleming and James Bond: The Cultural Politics of 007**, edited by Edward Comantale (2005)

   This lovely book, is a collection of scholarly essays presented at a university conference on Ian Fleming and James Bond. Some of it is terribly dry; at least one essay is virtually unreadable, and some of it is fascinating. This is of course expected in a book where each essay has a different author. An absolutely unique collection of viewpoints.

- **Licence to Thrill: A Cultural History of the James Bond Films**, by James Chapman (2001)

   Dr. Chapman, holder of a Ph.D. in British Film Propaganda, is a professor of media and culture. The book is occasionally dry, but the information is excit- ing.

- **The Politics of James Bond: From Fleming's Novels to the Big Screen**, by Jeremy Black (2000)

   Black is a prolific author of books about political history.

The Internet

Since I wrote this book in 2006, many Bond websites have disappeared. Most discussion boards have been replaced by Facebook or other social media, and some of the best fan sites have folded. All sites listed have been verified as live as of 2020.

Official Sites

The Ian Fleming Estate: www.ianfleming.com

James Bond Films: www.jamesbond.com *and* 007.om

   The official MGM site, heavily graphical. Features official news and promos.

   Follow on Twitter @007

The James Bond International Fan Club: http://www.007.info

   The only official fan club and a spiffy general website as well.

General-Topic Websites

MI6: The Home of James Bond https://www.mi6-hq.com/

   The largest Bond site in active existence, with a podcast, an encyclopedia, and an active news stream. Jam-packed. Also has a message board.

James Bond Wiki: https://jamesbond.fandom.com/

James Bond Radio: http://jamesbondradio.com/

   News, reviews, interviews, a podcast, a Twitter feed, and a blog. Kind of all-in-one!

The James Bond Dossier https://www.thejamesbonddossier.com/

BondMovies: http://www.bondmovies.com

When the internet was full of fan sites of all kinds, a trove like this was still better than most. Now it's exceptional! Films, girls, gadgets, plus bloopers, behind the scenes, sound clips; even guitar tabs—really loaded! Frequently updated, too.

Bond Supplement: www.007bs.spyw.com

Digs deep into books, games, movies, and more.

Commander Bond: http://commanderbond.net

A James Bond news blog, attached to extensive forums and old forum archives.

Universal Exports: http://www.universalexports.net/ and https://www.facebook.com/007UniversalExports/

Universal Exports, a.k.a Univex007, is amazing. Greg has kept this thing going since 1996, and as it's been upgraded, he's kept the archives, so pretty much everything you ever wanted to read or look up about 007, and many things you never imagined, is there. Current as of this writing with forthcoming news on *No Time to Die*.

The Spy Command https://hmssweblog.wordpress.com/

Originally a blog affiliated with Her Majesty's Secret Servant, when that site shut down in 2015, it changed its name. It covers Bond and other spies, and some general entertainment news.

Specialized Sites

Being James Bond: http://www.beingjamesbond.com/

Emphasizes James Bond as a lifestyle and way of being, from sports and recreation, to mixology, to mental health. The site includes videos, podcasts, news, and there's a tie-in book.

Bondian: http://www.bondian.com

A literary concordance, this website provides information on everything written about James Bond. Search by author, title, subject, and more. Find obscure articles, such as the Connect Bible Studies "James Bond 007" booklet. Very current.

The Bond Experience: http://thebondexperience.com/

Collector David Zaritsky lets you inside the world of Bond with videos and blogs. Collection and styling are the two main focuses, but there's a lot here and David is a delight.

Bond Lifestyle: https://www.jamesbondlifestyle.com/

This site focuses on how to live like James Bond, it emphasizes products (clothes, watches), collectibles, and instruction (Texas Hold'em).

On the Tracks of 007: http://www.onthetracksof007.com, https://www.facebook.com/groups/onthetracksof007/

The website devoted entirely to James Bond locations; much free information, plus books available for purchase. They also have a travel club which from time to time promotes trips to exotic locations seen in Bond films. Celebrated their 25th anniversary in 2020.

James Bond location hunters also post pictures of their "finds" on the site's Facebook group or Twitter.

Hunting Bond: https://huntingbond.com/

Another location-hunter site, this one is more graphical, more personal, and less complete. It focuses more on exploring, rather than listing, each location. I love both approaches.

James Bond Locations: https://jamesbondlocations.blogspot.com/

Fewer locations than other location-hunter sites, but each site is more lavishly and thoroughly photographed. Plus sites from other movies, such as *The Thomas Crown Affair (1999)*.

The Thunderball Obsessional: http://obsessional.uk/new.htm

You've got to admire such a single-minded fan. This is a thorough and thoroughly obsessed site.

Message Boards

When I first wrote *The Ultimate James Bond Fan Book*, message boards were a newish phenomenon that required explanation. Now they're practically obsolete. Most people participate in Facebook groups or other social media instead. A couple of excellent James Bond message boards still exist, and they're worth checking out if you enjoy dedicated conversation on 007. Message boards have an organizational structure that Facebook lacks, and allow you to look up old discussions and even search for keywords.

Boards also develop personalities of their own, and it can be quite special to be a part of a community of like-minded fans.

Absolutely James Bond http://www.ajb007.co.uk/

CommanderBond.net: https://quarterdeck.commanderbond.net/

MI6 Community: https://www.mi6community.com/

Conventions

Bond Fan Events: BondFanEvents.com

Bond Fan Events has been "Bonding fans together for over 20 years." Each is unique, usually tours to different Bond-related locations, often with special guests, parties, etc. I've attended two, one in New York City, and one a Bahamas cruise.The limited attendance (fifty is usually the maximum) and specialized atmosphere makes these events friendly, focused, and thrilling.

Chiller Theater: http://chillertheatre.com/

A wide-open genre collector's event held twice a year (spring and Halloween) in New Jersey. This is mostly shopping and autographs, plus a costume party, with little in the way of speaker programming. Very crowded and kind of exciting and weird, the one I attended had a lot of Bond stars, but other years, there are none.

Collectormania: http://www.filmandcomicconbirmingham.com/

A British collector's event for memorabilia and autograph enthusiasts. No admission fee, but no events either; strictly for the collector, but lots of Bond toys and accouterments available.

INDEX

Lightning Source UK Ltd.
Milton Keynes UK
UKHW051118191121
394250UK00006B/517